Three Genres

The Writing of Fiction/Literary Nonfiction, Poetry, and Drama

———— *Eighth Edition* ————

Three Genres
The Writing of Fiction/Literary Nonfiction, Poetry, and Drama

STEPHEN MINOT
University of California, Riverside

UPPER SADDLE RIVER, NEW JERSEY 07458

Library of Congress Cataloging-in-Publication Data

Minot, Stephen.
   Three genres : the writing of fiction/literacy nonfiction, poetry, and drama / Stephen
Minot. — 8th ed.
      p. cm.
   Includes index.
   ISBN 0-13-171977-7
   1. Authorship.   2. Creative writing.   I. Title.
PN145.M5 2007
808'.02 — dc22   2006019405

Editorial Director: *Leah Jewell*
Acquisitions Editor: *Vivian Garcia*
Editorial Assistant: *Christina Volpe*
Director of Marketing: *Brandy Dawson*
Production Liaison: *Fran Russello*
Permissions Researcher: *Mary Dalton-Hoffman*
Manufacturing Buyer: *Christina Amato*
Cover Art Director: *Jayne Conte*
Cover Design: *Kiwi Design*
Cover Illustration: *Watercolor by Virginia S. Minot*
Director, Image Resource Center: *Melinda Patelli*
Manager, Rights and Permissions: *Zina Arabia*
Manager, Visual Research: *Beth Brenzel*
Manager, Cover Visual Research & Permissions: *Karen Sanatar*
Composition/Full-Service Project Management: *Vijay Kataria/Techbooks*
Printer/Binder: *Courier Companies, Inc.*

Credits and acknowledgments borrowed from other sources and reproduced, with permission,
in this textbook appear on page 454).

Pearson Education LTD. London   Pearson Education North Asia Ltd
Pearson Education Singapore, Pte. Ltd   Pearson Educación de Mexico, S.A. de C.V.
Pearson Education, Canada, Ltd   Pearson Education Malaysia, Pte. Ltd
Pearson Education — Japan   Pearson Education, Upper Saddle River, New Jersey
Pearson Education Australia PTY, Limited

10 9 8 7 6 5 4 3 2 1
ISBN: 0-13-219738-3

To Ginny
Special thanks for editorial assistance through eight editions
and now for the artwork that graces the cover.
   All this with cheerful patience.
Love abounds!

CONTENTS

PREFACE

FOR STUDENTS

What Are Your Goals?

Most readers skip prefaces. They want to plunge right in. That chance will come. If you want to make the most of this text, read this preface.

Let's begin with an important question that only you can answer: Why are you interested in creative writing?

There are many possible motives. Only you know which apply to you. It's worth some careful thought because your answer will determine how you use this text. Here are three of the most common reasons people become involved in creative writing:

1. For many, learning more about literature is the goal. There's no better way to increase your understanding of poetry, fiction, or drama than to write them. Learning by doing is effective in all the arts. And in sports, too. Those who have spent time learning to play the violin have a special understanding of classical music. And what better way is there to appreciate soccer or baseball than to play it? If you have actually spent the time it takes to write a sonnet, a short story, or a play, you will understand what each literary form has to offer.

2. Others hope that creative writing will become a long-term avocation. A great majority of those in creative writing classes or adult workshops don't plan to make writing their primary vocation. They're like those who play a musical instrument seriously but without any intention of joining the Boston Symphony. They devote time to improving their skills, they join workshop groups, and they may even publish from time to time, but writing remains an avocation, not a vocation.

3. For a much smaller group, writing will become a central commitment. It's not an easy route. College students may have to slight other courses. When they graduate, they will probably have to find work in another field

to earn enough to eat and pay the rent. In spite of these challenges, they identify themselves as *writers*, *poets*, or *dramatists*. To support this notion, they must allot a portion of each day to reading published work in a close, professional way. They attend readings and conferences and talk to other writers. Most important, they write regularly. In short, they are immersed in a particular genre — not only creating their own work, but also drawing from the best of what has been published.

Which group do you fall into? If you are just beginning as a writer, you may well be in a fourth category — those who are curious but unsure about what will develop. All they know for sure is that they're not going to find out simply by wondering. They're determined not to become one of those wistfully passive adults who keep saying, "I've always wanted to write."

It may be that you will begin with high expectations and will discover after graduation that you are really a reader rather than a writer. But you won't have lost anything because you will have become a far more perceptive reader than you were before. The pleasure you take in reading will be greater.

Or perhaps you will begin with a commitment to one genre and find that your real talent and interest lies in another. Writers, unlike ballet dancers and atomic physicists, don't have to start early in their lives and stay on a single track. In writing, anything is possible at any stage and at any age. No aptitude test or teacher can predict how much talent and commitment will develop and whether you will eventually produce a significant body of work.

What This Textbook Can't Do

Never mind speed reading. Skimming this textbook won't help you at all. It's essential that you take extra time to study the stories, poems, and plays. The analytical chapters will show you what to look for, but they won't be helpful if you haven't examined the literary examples first.

And no textbook on writing can be a substitute for time spent actually writing. A book on how to swim isn't going to do much for you until you jump in. Creative achievement rarely comes in a triumphant burst as so many Hollywood films suggest. Writing and revising can be absorbing, but they take time and conscientious effort.

There is an important difference between what is called a *content text* such as those you are used to in literature, history, philosophy, and the like, and a *process text* such as this. Content texts can be read at a steady pace. They provide facts and concepts. Process texts such as those in the creative and performing arts guide your creative efforts. You learn by doing. *Doing* in this case means writing.

Finally, this textbook will not try to persuade you that every step will be fun and games. There are no cartoons or photos of writers hard at work. *You* are the writer here. This text has been written by someone who really enjoys the act of writing, and my goal is to share that enjoyment.

If you are taking a course or participating in a writing group, those discussions can be valuable and a real pleasure. This text will help keep the analysis in focus. It will provide the concepts and terminology to make the discussion specific and helpful.

Ultimately, however, the creative process requires spending time alone. This text can make that effort more rewarding. And it certainly will speed the process of development.

How to Get the Most from This Text

You bought this book. It wasn't cheap. But there are five ways to make it a good investment:

• Part I includes eight highly varied nonfiction and fiction works. Read each for pleasure first; then reread it carefully to analyze the structure and the tone. Do this before you go on to the analytical chapters that follow. Take a few informal notes about the material and your reactions. Don't wait for the following chapters or a class discussion to form your opinions for you. Be an active reader. Trust your own insights.

• In Part II, spend extra time on the collection of poems in Chapter 26. This chapter is called "Plunging In" for good reason. Most of these works will be new to you, but not for long. Almost every one will be used later to illustrate different poetic techniques, so you will be returning to them repeatedly. As with Part I, however, don't wait for the text to do the analysis. Do your best to draw as much as you can from each poem initially. The special effort you devote to these poems will make this part more meaningful.

The same applies to the plays in Part III. In short, exercise your critical abilities before turning to other sources.

• Try to use the terms introduced in this text accurately and often. Some will be new to you, but when you start to use them in discussions, they will become familiar and valuable. They'll help you be precise in discussing literary works.

Remember that any word in **boldface** is in the Glossary-Index at the end of the book. You can use it to refresh your memory.

• If any specific point seems unclear or puzzling, get help. Talk it over with your instructor or someone else using the text. Or e-mail me at s.minot@juno.com. I don't have the time to read manuscripts, and there may be a delay in my response, but I will be happy to answer brief questions.

• Mark up your book with legible, helpful marginal notes. Link the concepts and approaches with works you have read both here and in handouts or supplemental anthologies. Underline passages that are important. Tests have shown that those who take reading notes or make marginal comments improve their comprehension. Doing so converts passive reading into active involvement.

All this is a longer process than simply reading a textbook from beginning to end. Creative writing is not a skill that can be mastered in 10 easy steps. There are no shortcuts. It is a slow process of growth — growth both in your understanding of what literature has to offer and in your ability to create new work with your own individual stamp.

Student Supplement

The creative café (www.prenhall.com/creative cafe) is prentice Hall's online creative writing forum. Learn new writing techniques and insider tips from established writers and editors. Site users can view videoclips, participate in workshops, and much more.

PREFACE

FOR TEACHERS

Why a New Edition?

An eighth edition? Isn't it about time you got it right?

Wrong question. A textbook on creative writing isn't like a manual on mixing concrete. Everything about the creative process is malleable.

First, students' needs and expectations change. A work that draws students into the world of literature one decade will strike those in the next educational "generation" as naive or pedestrian. Consciously or unconsciously, we who value literature do proselytize. We want to use works that will attract today's students while giving them enough complexity and variety to stretch their abilities.

Second, analysis and advice that seem highly effective in manuscript don't always fare as well as expected when tested in many classrooms. *Three Genres* has been adopted in all 50 states and in a great variety of institutions. Meeting the needs of such a range calls for repeated fine-tuning. There are good reasons for every change in each edition, and most of them are rooted in a multitude of classrooms. I rely heavily on the responses of both instructors and students through e-mail (address listed at the end of this preface).

Third, although the text is new for each succeeding class of students, it becomes more than familiar for those who use it regularly. Instructors need fresh examples, fresh approaches to the art of writing.

Finally, just as any teacher should be open to trying new approaches in the classroom, a revision of a textbook should reflect a willingness to take a few chances. This eighth edition incorporates changes in both the order of the material and its breadth without, I hope, losing the original vision.

The Mechanics of a New Edition

Revised editions are sometimes greeted with skepticism, but I can assure you that they are far from a simple matter of shuffling chapters. It is at least a 2-year process. The first step is to elicit feedback. Four formal critiques from teachers are commissioned by the publisher. These are anonymous and represent different types of schools in various regions of the United States. In addition, I maintain a file of comments I have received. Opinions vary, of course, and sometimes contradict each other directly.

Tough questions have to be answered. The list of the "seven deadly sins" of fiction, for example, has just as many enthusiasts as detractors. Is the list intimidating or a blessing? This is a judgment call. Will the political overtones in Patricia Montley's hilarious but opinionated *Valley Forgery* in this edition offend some? Stay tuned. Ultimately, I have to make a series of decisions.

Then there is the matter of permissions. In many cases, even works that are retained have to be renegotiated. Some agents and certain publishers are unrealistic about what is a fair permission fee. Even with the help of a good permissions editor, bargaining is a slow and frustrating process. It takes four months at best.

Then comes the actual writing. By revising about one-third of the text and replacing one-third of the examples, I try to strike a balance between change and continuity. At best, this process takes another six months.

It then takes another full year from the time the completed manuscript is delivered to the publisher to the date on which the book is available. My wife and I proofread the original manuscript, the edited manuscript, and the page proofs as do the professional proofreaders — two of them this time. (Even after these nine professional proofreadings, every new edition contains a few elusive typos!) This is all a long, time-consuming process, but we hope that it results in a text that meets the needs of both teachers and students.

What's New This Time?

1. *The addition of literary nonfiction.* The most pronounced new feature is the addition of *literary nonfiction.* It has been incorporated into Part I under the new title of "Nonfiction/Fiction." Many instructors will find it effective to begin the course with literary (or *creative*) nonfiction in order to encourage students to explore their own lives. In Chapter 6, they are introduced to the inventive aspect of fiction. This approach should help clarify the distinction between the two types of writing, a distinction often muddied even at writers' conferences.

Instructors who would prefer to have their students move directly into fiction, however, will find starting the course with Chapter 6 logical and smooth. The text is entirely flexible in this regard.

2. *Nonfiction/Fiction now placed first.* To facilitate the inclusion of nonfiction, I have revised the order of the three sections. "Part I: Telling a Story: Literary Nonfiction/Fiction" now comes first, poetry is next, and finally drama as before. This reflects the order a majority of instructors already use, which is justification enough. In addition, it should assist students who have no writing experience to begin with the least technical and perhaps the least intimidating genre.

3. *A new chapter has been added: Chapter 35, "Poems for Self-Study."* In past editions, almost every poem included in its entirety was used to illustrate an aspect of the genre, some in considerable detail. Those instructors not assigning a supplementary anthology found it difficult to encourage the study of poems entirely on their own. The poems in Chapter 35 have not been analyzed and so can be used for class discussion. A wide variety of styles and approaches, both formal and free verse, is included.

4. *The "Troubleshooting Guide" chapters have been moved from the Appendices to the ends of each part.* These troubleshooting guides were added in the previous edition to help students look up areas that are giving them trouble and also to allow instructors to augment their written comments by allowing them to recommend certain parts for review. Because the guides were relegated to the Appendices at the end of the book, they were often forgotten. Moving them to the ends of the three parts should make them far more convenient.

5. *New works have been added to all three parts.* Three examples of literary nonfiction and two new stories have been added to Part I. Fifteen new poems have been added to Part II — these in addition to the collection intended for self-study. And Part III has been expanded from three to four plays, including the winner of a national search for new dramas. The infusion of new work provides a rich variety of literary techniques for analysis.

6. *The outlines at the beginning of each chapter have been redesigned.* In response to reader requests, the headers are now separated by bullets and provided with page references. In this way, the outlines become a handy index to the topics in each chapter.

7. *The Instructor's Manual will now be available online.* Those adopting the text can access it at www.prenhall.com select "search our catalog by ISBN" and enter 0132197383. Select instructor Resources on the left hand side. A link to download the instructor's manual will be available.

Making Full Use of *Three Genres*

A number of instructors have assigned *Three Genres* as an optional or supplemental text. This may be a helpful with advanced classes, but the text has not been designed for casual browsing. The most effective way to justify its adoption is to assign certain chapters on specific days and ask students to discuss some of the techniques covered in that part. If supplemental anthologies are used, they will help students apply the approaches described here to additional works. This encourages students to use this text actively rather than merely as a resource.

For poetry, the new Chapter 35, "Poems for Self-Study," can serve in the same way. Assign specific poems to individual students in advance with the request that they come to the next class ready to discuss them. This will also help them apply the concepts they have learned.

Special Thanks

I owe special thanks to Vivian Garcia, my editor, who has continued the good working relations I have had with Prentice Hall over the years. I am also grateful to Mary Dalton-Hoffman who once again handled the thorny matter of permissions with skill and patience.

Thanks also to the teachers and students who have made comments and suggestions about the last edition. I'm also grateful to a number of anonymous critics for their thoughtful suggestions: Stacey V. Santoro-Murphy, Joliet Junior College; Janis Donaldson, Fayetteville Technical Community College; Mary Troy, University of Missouri-St. Louis; William J. Cobb, Penn State University; Eileen Donvan-Kranz, Boston College; Jo Angela Edwins, University of Tennessee at Knoxville.

Finally, it is hard to express what I owe to my wife, Virginia Minot. Her unfailing support over the years and, specifically, her late-night proofreading sessions and her editorial suggestions both for these editions and my novels and story collections have been invaluable. I am particularly proud of the fact that her art was selected by the publisher for both the seventh and this eighth edition. Ours has been a remarkable collaboration enlivened with love.

Stephen Minot
s.minot@juno.com

PART I

Telling a Story: Literary Nonfiction/Fiction

1 Literary Nonfiction

- *Three Ways of Telling a Story in Prose: The Factual Report, Literary Nonfiction, and Fiction (1)* • *Common Forms of Literary Nonfiction* • *Personal Experiences (2)* • *The Biographical Sketch (2)* • *Opinions (3)* • *Reflection (3)* • *A sense of Place (3)* • *A Slice of History (4).*

We start telling stories almost as soon as we can put sentences together. As kids, we may make no sharp distinction between reality and make-believe. Most of the time, we get away with it. But as we get older, most of us learn that mixing the two can get us into trouble. Worse, adults who choose to ignore this distinction can even end up in jail.

When we write a **narrative**[1] (a series of events), we have a choice of three approaches. The first is **factual writing**. This includes essays on historical events, cultural and scientific developments, and newspaper reporting. Most of the writing we do in school and college is factual. Even when the topic deals with characters and a plot, as in historical accounts and biography, such writing sticks to the facts and the events as they occurred. Factual writing can contain opinions and even present an argument (as in an editorial, for example), but it doesn't invent facts or alter events. The style in such works tends to be straightforward and the tone impersonal.

The second approach is **literary nonfiction**. It is also called creative nonfiction. I use "literary" so as to avoid tedious arguments over what is "creative," but the phrases are identical in meaning. They describe essentially factual writing in which there is an emphasis on the writer's personal feelings and experiences. The style is frequently more informal, even conversational. Such writing is "literary" because there is often a heightened concern for language such as the use of evocative word choice, metaphors (see **image**), or **symbolic** details.

The third approach is **fiction**. When you write fiction, you are free to invent without being called a liar. Fiction writers often make use of details from their own lives, but these aspects are altered, combined, and reshaped to meet the needs of a literary work. I'll return to fiction in Chapter 6.

---

[1]Words in **boldface** are defined in the Glossary-Index.

One way to differentiate these three types of writing is to remember that for each there is a primary obligation. When you work on a factual essay, you must stick with the facts or events being described. Literary nonfiction also requires you to honor the facts or events as they occurred even though your approach may be more personal and phrased in more evocative language. When you write fiction, however, your sole concern is to create an effective artistic work.

The following table gives you an overview of these three types of prose writing:

FACTUAL WRITING	LITERARY NONFICTION	FICTION
(First priority: factual accuracy and objectivity)	(First priority: factual accuracy presented with personal feeling and evocative language)	(First priority: the literary merit of the story or novel)
News reports Research papers Historical analysis Literary criticism	Personal experience Biographical sketches Opinion pieces, Reflection A sense of place, A slice of history	Short stories Novels

PERSONAL EXPERIENCE

By far the most common form of literary nonfiction is an essay based primarily on personal experience. Sometimes the work deals with events that are dramatic and unusual: struggling with a life-threatening disease, playing professional football, being raised by a single blind parent. But most personal experience essays provide insights into less dramatic life experiences.

For example, the death of a close relative may not interest readers who don't know the family, whereas an essay focusing on how unnerving random chance can be would have much more potential. Or arguing with a parent about what actually occurred on a particular day years ago is not in itself unusual or interesting compared with an essay that explores how our emotional needs distort our memories. Such minor incidents will interest readers if you make an effort to probe your feelings honestly, examine the implications, and present your material with a vivid style.

The word **memoir** is occasionally used to describe all personal experience pieces, but more often it is limited to those works in which an older writer recalls events from the past, frequently from his or her childhood.

THE BIOGRAPHICAL SKETCH

Biography is a broad category that covers a variety of approaches. Generally speaking, a book-length study of an individual's life comes under the heading of factual writing, not literary nonfiction. The style in such work tends to be straightforward and relatively objective. The author remains invisible.

Short biographical pieces, however, tend to be more personal and more concerned with the literary use of language. We call them biographical *sketches* because they usually focus on a specific aspect of the subject's life or character.

If you are writing about someone who is accessible, consider conducting an interview. It will help if you can select in advance a particular aspect on which to focus. More about that in Chapter 5. If you plan to work on a historical subject, you will have to rely on research. Be sure to draw on more than one source to maintain originality.

OPINIONS

Most editorials and political articles are forms of factual writing. But if you decide to write subjectively, entering the work personally by using "I," the treatment naturally becomes less formal, the tone more relaxed, and the style less utilitarian. These aspects make the work literary nonfiction.

For example, a newspaper editorial opposing the use of drugs by young people may be impassioned, but the language will probably be as straightforward as a driver education textbook. If the same theme, however, is presented through the author's actual and truthful memory of recovering from a heroin addiction, the tone will naturally become personal. The shift in style, tone, and personal involvement makes the work literary nonfiction.

REFLECTION

Many writers keep a literary **journal**. It is an informal notebook for recording reactions to whatever they have been reading, ideas for future work, fragments, and reflections on the pleasures and frustrations of daily life. It differs from a diary in that it does not limit itself to the events of each day.

Some reflective essays read like journal entries. There is, however, one fundamental difference between the two. Journal entries tend to be random thoughts and experimental fragments. A reflective essay may seem to meander at first, but eventually its focus and direction are made clear. As a literary work, it has a structure that is artfully disguised. You will see an example of this in "Unwired" by Hilary Masters in Chapter 3.

A SENSE OF PLACE

The fifth of these six types of literary nonfiction presents a verbal picture of a specific place. Any place can be made interesting if you select an aspect that is unusual or significant.

As we will see in Chapter 4, success depends on selecting vivid and memorable visual details. It is also important to reveal a variety of emotional response to avoid the bland approval so often adopted by journalistic travel pieces.

A SLICE OF HISTORY

History provides a good source for literary nonfiction, but it is chosen less often than other approaches. This is partly due to the fact that it's often a challenge to limit the topic to something that is manageable. In addition, many historical sources are primarily factual, making it difficult for you to provide a personal connection and subjective responses we expect in literary nonfiction.

There is nothing rigid about these six approaches to literary nonfiction. They are simply the most common. Remember, too, that they can be used in combination. A personal experience essay about a camping trip, for example, may include a lot of biographical material about the leader of the group. But at some point in the revision process, it will be important to determine what your emphasis will be. Is your primary concern about your own development or a series of fresh insights about the leader of the group?

2 True Experience

Killing Chickens

Literary Nonfiction

by Meredith Hall

I tucked her wings tight against her heaving body, crouched over her, and covered her flailing head with my gloved hand. Holding her neck hard against the floor of the coop, I took a breath, set something deep and hard inside my heart, and twisted her head. I heard her neck break with a crackle. Still she fought me, struggling to be free of my weight, my gloved hands, my need to kill her. Her shiny black beak opened and closed, opened and closed silently, as she gasped for air. I didn't know this would happen. I was undone by the flapping, the dust rising and choking me, the disbelieving little eye turned up to mine. I held her beak closed, covering that eye. Still she pushed, her reptile legs bracing against mine, her warmth, her heart beating fast with mine. I turned her head on her floppy neck again, and again, corkscrewing her breathing tube, struggling to end the gasping. The eye, turned around and around, blinked and studied me. The early spring sun flowed onto us through a silver stream of dust, like a stage light, while we fought each other. I lifted my head and saw that the other birds were eating still, pecking their way around us for stray bits of corn. This one, this twisted and broken lump of gleaming black feathers, clawed hard at the floor, like a big stretch, and then deflated like a pierced ball. I waited, holding her tiny beak and broken neck with all my might.

I was killing chickens. It was my 38th birthday. My brother had chosen that morning to tell me that he had caught his wife — my best friend, Ashley — in bed with my husband a year before. I had absorbed the rumors and suspicions about other women for 10 years, but this one, I knew, was going to break us. When I roared upstairs and confronted John, he told me to go fuck myself, ran downstairs and jumped into the truck. Our sons, Sam and Ben, were making a surprise for me at the table; they stood behind me silently in the kitchen door while John gunned the truck out of the yard. "It's okay, guys," I said. "Mum and Dad just had a fight. You better go finish my surprise before I come peeking."

I carried Bertie's warm, limp body outside and laid her on the grass. Back inside the coop, I stalked my hens and came up with Tippy-Toes. I gathered her frantic wings and crouched over her. John was supposed to kill off our beautiful but tired old hens, no longer laying, last month to make way for the new chicks that were arriving tomorrow. But he was never around, and the job had not been done. I didn't know how to do this. But I was going to do it myself. This was just a little thing in all the things I was going to have to learn to do alone.

I had five more to go. Tippy-Toes tried to shriek behind my glove. I clamped my hand over her beak and gave her head a hard twist. I felt her body break deep inside my own chest.

Two down. I felt powerful, capable. I could handle whatever came to me.

But I needed a rest. I was tired, exhausted, with a heavy, muffled weight settling inside. "I'm coming in," I called in a false, singsong voice from the kitchen door. "Better hide my surprise." Ten and 7, the boys knew something was up, something bigger than the moody, dark days John brought home, bigger than the hushed, hissing fights we had behind our bedroom door, bigger than the days-long silent treatment John imposed on me if I asked too many questions about where he had been and why. Sam and Ben were working quietly in the kitchen, not giggling and jostling the way they usually did. Their downy blond heads touched as they leaned over their projects. I felt a crush of sadness, of defeat. We were exploding into smithereens on this pretty March day, and we all knew it.

"I have to make a cake!" I sang from the doorway. "When are you guys going to be done in there?"

"Wait! Wait!" they squealed. It was an empty protest, their cheer as hollow as mine.

Our old house smelled good, of wood and the pancakes the three of us had eaten this morning, in that other world of hope and tight determination before my brother's phone call. We lived on a ridge high over the mouth of the Damariscotta River on the coast of Maine. From our beds, we could all see out over Pemaquid Point, over Monhegan Island, over the ocean to the edge of the Old World. The rising sun burst into our sleep each morning. At night, before bed, we lay on my bed together — three of us — naming Orion and Leo and the Pleiades in whispers. Monhegan's distant light swept the walls of our rooms all night at 36-second intervals. Our little house creaked in the wind during February storms. Now spring had come, and the world had shifted.

"Help me make my cake," I said to the boys. They dragged their chairs to the counter.

"Mum, will Dad be home for your birthday tonight?" Sam asked. Both boys were so contained, so taut, so helpless. They leaned against me, quiet.

Guilt and fear tugged me like an undertow. I started to cry.

"I don't know, my loves. I think this is a really big one."

Bertie and Tippy-Toes lay side by side on the brown grass, their eyes open, necks bent. I closed the coop door behind me and lunged for the next hen.

"It's all right," I said softly. "It's all right. Everything's going to be all right. Shhh, Silly, shh." I crouched over her. Silly was the boys' favorite because she let them carry her around the yard. I hoped they would forget her when the box of peeping balls of fluff arrived tomorrow.

"It's okay, Silly," I said quietly, wrapping my gloved fingers around her hard little head. She was panting, her eyes wild, frantic, betrayed. I covered them with my fingers and twisted her neck hard. Her black wings, iridescent in the dusty sunlight, beat against my legs. I held her close to me while she scrabbled against my strong hands. I started to cry again.

When I went back up to the house, Bertie and Tippy-Toes and Silly and Mother Mabel lay on the grass outside the coop.

Benjamin came into the kitchen and leaned against my legs. "What are we going to do?" he asked.

"About what, Sweetheart?" I hoped he was not asking me about tomorrow. Or the next day.

"Nothing," he said, drifting off to play with Sam upstairs.

We frosted the cake blue, Ben's favorite color, and put it on the table next to their presents for me, wrapped in wallpaper. I wanted to call someone, to call my mother or my sister. Yesterday I would have called Ashley, my best friend, who had listened to me cry and rail about John again and again. Instead, I brought in three loads of wood and put them in the box John had left empty.

"Sam, will you lay up a fire for tonight? And Ben, go down to the cellar and get a bunch of kindling wood."

Like serious little men, my children did what I asked.

"What are we going to make for my birthday supper?"

"I thought we were going to Uncle Stephen's and Aunt Ashley's," Sam said.

"Know what?" I said. "Know what I want to do? Let's just stay here and have our own private little party. Just us."

I felt marooned with my children. I sat at the table, watching while they did their chores, then headed back out to finish mine.

Minnie Hen was next. She let me catch her and kill her without much fight. I laid her next to the others in the cold grass.

Itty-Bit was last. She was my favorite. The others had chewed off her toes, one by one, when she was a chick. I had made a separate box for her, a separate feeder, separate roost, and smeared antibiotic ointment four times a day on the weeping stubs. She survived, and ate from my hand after that. She had grown to be fierce with the other hens, never letting them too close to her, able to slip in, grab the best morsels and flee before they could peck her. I had come to admire her very much, my tough little biddie.

She cowered in the corner, alone. I sat next to her, and she let me pull her up into my lap. I stroked her feathers smooth, stroke after stroke. Her comb was pale and shriveled, a sign of her age. I knew she hadn't laid an egg for months. She was shaking. I held her warmth against me, cooing to her, "It's all right, Itty-Bit. Everything's going to be all right. Don't be scared." My anger at John centered like a tornado on having to kill this hen. "You stupid, selfish son of a bitch," I said. I got up, crying again, holding Itty-Bit tight to me. I laid her gently on the floor and crouched over her. The sun filled the coop with thick light.

That night, after eating spaghetti and making a wish and blowing out 38 candles and opening presents made by Sam and Benjamin—a mail holder made from wood slats, a sculpture of 2-by-4s and shells; after baths and reading stories in bed and our sweet, in-the-dark, whispered good nights; after saying "I don't know what is going to happen" to my scared children; after banking the fire and turning off the lights, I sat on the porch in the cold, trying to imagine what had to happen next. I could see the outline of the coop against the dark, milky sky. I touched my fingers, my hands, so familiar to me. Tonight they felt like someone else's. I wrapped my arms around myself — thin, tired — and wished it were yesterday.

Tomorrow morning, I thought, I have to turn over the garden and go to the dump. Tomorrow morning, I have to call a lawyer. I have to figure out what to say to Sam and Benjamin. I have to put Ben's sculpture on the mantel and put some mail in Sam's holder on the desk. I have to clean out the coop and spread fresh shavings.

THE IMPORTANCE OF A SECOND READING

Why a second reading? Because this is how one goes beyond the surface facts and examines how the writer has presented his or her work. It is in the second or third reading that one learns about literary techniques.

Actually, the word *reading* can describe two quite different activities. Passive or recreational reading is the sort we do when we want to turn off and be entertained. It is a relatively inexpensive, legal pastime that has no dangerous side effects. We all need to do it from time to time, but we do so more for pleasure than for growth.

Active reading, on the other hand, is what writers do. It is an analytical activity. When we read actively, we go beyond personal reactions ("I liked that character," "I'd hate to live that way") and examine literary aspects ("the theme is hidden until the end," "the character is revealed through action, not dialogue"). As writers we are examining the work for unusual techniques ("a flashback within a flashback — does it work?" "that house is being treated like a character"). When we read this way, every work becomes a learning process.

Active reading may require finishing works you don't enjoy. There is no way to evaluate them accurately until you do. In such cases, the pleasure you derive is analytical. If you find the work unsuccessful, figure out why. Sometimes you can learn as much from fiction you dislike as from works you enjoy.

For some, active reading means keeping a pencil and paper handy for notes — not only on plot development and names of characters but also on interesting techniques. If you keep a literary journal (strongly recommended), it's worth jotting down your reactions there. Make your comments full enough and legible enough so that later they will bring the work back into focus the way a photo album helps you recall past experiences.

WHAT TO LOOK FOR IN "KILLING CHICKENS"

The first time you read this nonfiction work you probably winced at the act of killing chickens and felt compassion for the narrator. If you describe the work to a friend, those are the aspects you're likely to mention first.

On your second reading, however, you should take a close look at the literary choices the author made in relating this true story. Why, for example, did she devote so much space in this short essay to describe the act of killing each beloved pet? True, the events were, we assume, what she actually went through, but this is *literary* nonfiction, remember, not a journal entry. The author not only has the right but also the obligation to stress certain scenes and downplay others. Her goal is not just to record the episode like a reporter; she is concerned with shaping and highlighting the literary aspects.

Her husband, remember, has not only been unfaithful over the course of 10 years, but he has also slept with her best friend. And she was told this on her birthday. And the man has taken off abruptly. In a diary she might have been directly analytical — "I've never been so furious." A journalist might describe the killing in a single factual paragraph, but as a *literary* writer she has separated the gruesome details into five separate scenes. Her rage is dramatized in these brutal actions. Only once it is reflected in her dialogue when she says to one of the chickens she loved: "You stupid, selfish son of a bitch."

Notice too the phrasing she uses to calm the chicken who is "the boys' favorite": "It's all right. . . . Everything's going to be all right." It is sadly close to the assurances she has given to her two sons, an assurance she can't herself feel.

On your second (or third) reading, it's well worth taking a close look at the **tone** of this work. The situation is grim enough to have justified self-pity. But she has chosen not to do so. There is also plenty of evidence that she has from time to time generated courage and determination. But she has chosen to reveal an equal number of moments when she faces bewilderment and doubt. The tone she uses shifts just as it may have in the experience: shock, pity, a brief moment of feeling "powerful, capable" followed by "guilt and fear." In the end, she doesn't analyze her feelings but focuses instead on the list of practical tasks that she will face the next day.

Notice that when we shift from a passive reading to an active and analytical reading, we move from our emotional responses — what we like and dislike — and focus instead on the literary aspects of the work itself.

3 Nonfiction in a Reflective Mood

Unwired

Literary Nonfiction

by Hilary Masters

This guy rings our doorbell and offers me $100 for one of the insulators that sit like glass bells on the top sills of our front windows. He wants the blue one, what I would call a Chagall blue with "No. 19" embossed on its skirt, along with the name of its maker — the Hemingray Company. The same company also made the other ones, and our assortment caught his collector's eye as he passed by on the street.

A couple of them are clear glass; two more in shades of blue, and another one is amber. They seem to be made of poured glass, and their acorn shape is ringed by ridges and grooves designed to separate and hold the different transmission lines that once pulled across their glass surfaces. I don't remember how we came by them; most likely they were found objects in this old house we have restored. They still conduct energy, but of a different sort, a refracted light that ornaments the front room to ignite the eye and signal the senses.

As a boy I spied insulators like these on the cross arms of utility poles that stood sentry along the route of visits to relatives in Kansas. From the back seat of my grandfather's Buick, they appeared to be currants or raisins my grandmother had forgotten to put into the breakfast muffins, for they had become black against the prairie sky. Their different colors could not be appreciated from the ground. Sometimes a crow or a few meadowlarks would land to perch between them and make their dressed file irregular and perhaps lend a different pulse to the humming lines.

Their different colors described the kind of lines that they suspended above and across the country, whether power lines or telephone cables, and I would guess these colors were coded to tell linemen what sort of voltages they repaired and carefully lifted into place. Some carried electricity, and others carried the homely language of family history. "Mother died this morning. Come home."

But that wasn't always the case. Originally these different hues of blue and amber, the clear glass, were irrelevant to their use. The same companies that made the glass jars that mid-19th-century home-makers used to put up fruit and vegetables for winter meals were enlisted to make insulators for Mr. Morse's crackling telegraph lines. Initially these wires were buried underground, but their messages became short-circuited and diminished by leakage, so it was decided to lift them overhead and onto poles. But as any of us who went to Scarritt School could have told them, the wooden poles would draw the messages into the ground with the same corruption. So some kind of object had to be found that would come between the wood and the current carried on the wire. At first ceramic doorknobs were used, but they were impractical because the wires would easily slip off their smooth round-ness and short out. Then someone invented this glass acorn with ridges that held the wires in place, and a whole industry was created — out of scrap.

The glass left over from the primary product — canning jars — was remelted and poured into the molds, so they could be of any color. If the Hemingray Company made its famous Globe jars in azure in the morning, then azure insulators would be turned out that afternoon. If clear glass was used for fruit jars, then the insulators produced next would be clear. And so on. It was one of those fortuitous happenstances of human endeavor that no longer seems possible. Today the waste of our ingenuity must be buried out of sight, almost guiltily, and useless.

The colors of the different insulators became relevant when electrical lines joined those that carried telegraph messages and later the human voice, and it became important to tell one line from another on the poles that began to staple the countryside. The insulators themselves became more sophisti-cated. A hollow space about the size of a broomstick was cast within each and threaded so the unit could be screwed down over a corresponding thread in the wooden peg fixed on the pole's crossarm. The first insulators had no such design and were merely fitted down over a smooth peg, but experience showed that a storm could blow them off their perch to interrupt the transmission. The Hemingray Company also added its own innovation, duly patented, of a serrated edge around the bottom of the insulators, and these little points were meant to drain rainwater quickly and therefore min-imize the interference caused by a natural phenomenon — always a threat to human invention.

I knew of such challenges first hand because of my Saturday afternoons spent at the Chief Theater, where Jimmy Cagney and Pat O'Brien would regularly meet disasters with heroic insouciance. They were fast-talking linemen vying for the gentle goodness of a Wendy Barrie, but then the lines go down. "It's the tower on Brown's Ridge," O'Brien shouts through the onslaught. Water runs in rivulets from the hood of his lineman's slicker.

"I'll hook it up," Cagney says, with that lopsided grin that lets you know that he knows he will die in the process. Kindly Dr. Christian, remarkably au courant with the latest info from the Mayo brothers, was about to save the little Cranshaw girl, when the lights went out. But Jimmy lifts the right cable back onto the No. 19 blue insulator made by the Hemingray Company — someday to be collected and worth $100 — and the lights go back on. At the same time, a pip, like the flare of a match, occurs at the top of the tower on Brown's Ridge.

Such melodramas are quaint and amusing today when put beside the internal storms of personality that absorb us; the mannered cruelties between children and parents, the psychic wounds we have been educated to look for as we dress for the day. All of it energy gone awry. Moreover, the new communication, handheld and wireless, requires no insulators from the Hemingray Company, which in fact stopped making them in 1967. So what is to protect us standing on the ground from this promiscuous energy and raw immediacy? No longer confined to cables, our humdrum pollutes waiting rooms and restaurants and even innocent street corners. We are swamped by our own accessibility and even threatened on the highway by this wanton facility, as some state legislatures have recently determined. "I don't want to know all this," my grandmother often complained in response to some report in the Kansas City Star of an overnight brutality. What she meant was, did she need to know this information to keep house for my grandfather, pack my school lunch, change the bed linen, and bread the fish for supper? But the item became an inert particle within her soft sensibility, and today the continual fallout of the commonplace buries us — our bins overflow. Plains storms no longer threaten the hookup, because the current onslaught is self-generated trivia, and nothing can insulate us from the force of its insignificance. It is an irony, foreign to those old movies, that the genius of our invention has only exposed how really boring and paltry we are.

Maybe we have reached that stage in our history on earth when we have nothing more to say that is interesting, that after five million years or so, it's all been talked out. The limitations on travel to other worlds have become discouragingly obvious, and perhaps we are similarly bound to subject matter. The trajectory of our chatter follows the earth's curvature; our words do not fly up so much as they go round and round faster.

In the horror of the last century, the risks of intelligence have so shocked us that we reach for the banal, not just with a cell phone but in our politics, our literature — our quotidian. Jimmy Cagney is dead, and no one seems willing to handle fresh ideas. A residual meditation plays in the depth of this azure glass on my windowsill, and I have learned its value. No meaning is conveyed beyond its pleasing shape and its color, and there is nothing more to be said.

HIDDEN STRUCTURE IN REFLECTIVE WORK

On first reading, "Unwired" seems strangely uneven in style and disorganized in content. We're used to essays that announce their themes at the outset and move logically, point by point, toward a conclusion. "Unwired," however, starts almost conversationally with "This guy rings our doorbell and offers me $100 . . ." No thematic statement there. This is clearly not going to be a formal essay. It seems as if it will be some kind of personal experience. We assume that something will happen with this stranger at the door.

But that's the last we hear of the man. The focus shifts to the insulators themselves. The author describes what they look like as if that is his primary concern. The description and historical development are factual, but the style is far from the objective approach of a manual. He recalls seeing them when he was a kid driving with his grandfather. They looked like "currants or raisins my grandmother had forgotten to put into the breakfast muffins . . ."

The surprises don't end there. After devoting a good portion of the piece to the history and development of insulators, he veers off to his memory of seeing old Jimmy Cagney films, particularly those in which the actor played a lineman keeping the electric lines up during terrible storms. No, the author hasn't forgotten the insulators, but he is into a related topic.

Only after all this meandering does the piece come around to the primary theme: "No longer confined to cables . . . We are swamped by our own accessibility . . ." Cell phones, radio, and television have thrust the horror of disasters right in our face. He recalls his grandmother's response to the news report of a violent crime: "I don't want to know all this." Anyone who has watched the local news on television will know what she (and the author) are getting at.

What does this have to do with glass insulators or melodramatic films about keeping the lines of communication open? He ties it together this way:

> Plains storms no longer threaten the hookup, because the current onslaught is self-generated trivia, and nothing can insulate us from the force of its insignificance.

A formal, straightforward essay might have started off with a thematic statement like this: "Radio, television, and other wireless media have flooded us with trivia. It's time to rediscover the value of objects that have no meaning beyond their beauty of shape and color."

If this is his point, why didn't he put it that way? Why creep up on his subject so indirectly and pepper his work with memories from his own life? He could have been more direct, and that approach wouldn't be better or worse. Just different.

What he chose to do was to create a literary work in the form of rambling monologue that, in addition to presenting a particular theme, gives pleasure in its literary shape. If you look at the essay this way, it becomes a work of art that resembles his collection of insulators: both reward us with, as he puts it in his summary, "... its pleasing shape and its color ..."

VITALITY IN DETAILS

As we saw in the case of "Killing Chickens," literary nonfiction can be organized around a story line just as fiction usually is. Narratives provide a clear sequence of events and have the potential to hold the reader's interest. A reflective essay, however, may move idea by idea the way a conversation does. Such essays will have to hold a reader's attention in some other way. It helps to present detailed information that will probably be new for most readers. Although most of us are familiar with glass insulators that can still be seen on rural electric lines, few have seen one up close. And fewer still know about their history.

The author of "Unwired" gives all this information in an entertaining way. Rather than the dry and factual style of an encyclopedia article, his tone reflects the personal feelings of someone who finds them beautiful.

In describing them initially, he writes, "They still conduct energy, but of a different sort, a refracted light that ornaments the front room to ignite the eye and signal the senses."

He then gives us a capsule history of insulators from the unsatisfactory attempt to use ceramic door knobs to those the Hemingray Company developed, using the various colors of glass left over from their preserve jars.

Providing fresh information involves some research, but more often it is a body of knowledge you have already acquired, such as playing a guitar, rock climbing, or teaching disabled children. As a basic guideline, remember that generalities numb readers; specifics stimulate.

PRESENTING OPINIONS: STATED AND IMPLIED

A reflective essay that doesn't at least imply some opinion held by the author is probably too diffuse to hold interest. It's apt to bore the reader like a lecturer who isn't interested in his or her subject.

As we have seen, "Unwired" finally makes some clear assertions about how we are buffeted by information and would do well to appreciate objects that simply give pleasure through their beauty. This view is not just implied; it is stated directly toward the end. The pace of the essay is leisurely, but remember that the author is criticizing how addicted we have become to blunt, brief bursts of banal communication.

Opinions are also embedded in "Killing Chickens," but they are implied rather than stated. We sense the rage of the narrator through the way she kills those birds, and behind that emotional response is implied the author's view of unfaithful husbands. The end of the essay reflects the author's opinion about the best way to respond to having one's life shattered by a selfish dishonest man. A direct statement might have been something like this: "I realized that wallowing in anger and self-pity would get me nowhere; I'd better concentrate on all the little things that have to be done." Put bluntly, however, this statement might make the piece sound like a moral lesson, so instead she simply lists the tasks she would face the next day.

What, then, is the difference between what we have been calling a personal experience piece or a meditative piece and a true opinion essay? It is simply a matter of degree. When you finish reading a work, ask yourself "What is the author's *primary* emphasis?" More important, when you look over the first draft of your own work, take a close look at what you want to emphasize. Sometimes what you had planned as an opinion piece has become cluttered with personal experiences, or what you had intended to be the study of a historical figure has been overshadowed by your opinions. Decide which approach will be the most effective.

4 Impressions of a Real Place

On Leaving Florida

Literary Nonfiction

by Marjorie Sandor

In early June, Newnans Lake is a glossy mud-green, the color of secrets. I take another step deeper in and cast my dry fly, a 12 Yellow Humpy made in Montana, toward a faint dimpling twenty feet out, though any rise around here is as likely to be an alligator as a fish. They say there are a couple thousand gators in this lake, and as I cast, one of them groans hoarsely in the mangroves behind me. My fishing companion, a colleague from the nearby University of Florida who takes pleasure in testing an outsider's mettle — especially a *girl's* — explains that two big people standing in the water will send any self-respecting gator the other way. But I'm not big, and not convinced. Only my torso is currently above water; choice bits are below, and my companion chooses this moment to realize *all of a sudden* that he's left his grass shrimp on the tailgate of his truck. He thrashes off through the water toward the mangroves, and that, as the nursery rhyme goes, "leaves only one."

I'm beginning to doubt the wisdom of my quest to gain Florida *machisma,* but after six years here, my husband and I will be moving to the West, and this looks like my last chance to get a glimpse of the real Florida. Ever since we decided to move to Oregon, I've felt twinges of regret in advance, a disturbing mix of relief and shame over my failure to acclimatize. So when my colleague, a native Floridian, agreed to take me fishing one last time, it seemed like a requisite ceremony, the divestiture of a failed initiate.

In fact, the conditions he set bore all the marks of a ceremonial dressing-down. "Take off those damn hip waders," he said. "And that fishing vest, too — we'll have none of that fancy shit." And so on: I would have to wade in my shorts. I could tote my fly rod and a couple of flies if I must, but I'd better be prepared to put grass shrimp on the end of my tippet if I really wanted to catch fish. I submitted, and now here I stand, perfectly alone, my legs numb, as if they've been anesthetized prior to amputation. Still, this guy seems to know the region's secret places, its guarded heart, lushly complex and easily maddened; like it or not, he's my last-minute guide to a paradise faintly familiar and more than faintly inimical.

The familiar is simply this: at first, the city of Gainesville, in the north central region of the state, reminded me of my hometown in southern California, a place I hadn't lived — or known I had missed — for over fifteen years.

Even the weekend of the job interview, I felt keenly a sense that any minute I might round a corner and happen onto a street I knew. Maybe it was the palms and live oaks, the historic Thomas Hotel with its red-tiled roof and fountains and borders of azaleas, or the orange groves and horse pastures outside the city limits, which reminded me dimly of pictures I'd seen of the San Gabriel Valley before development, with its great ranchos and groves of orange trees. But my nostalgia was rimmed with suspense, for here there were coral snakes and alligators, sticky vines curling under window frames, and cockroaches the size of baby mice. In the rainy season, chairs and books were lightly veiled in green. Even the produce looked different to me: okra, in particular, shocked me a little with its velvety fuzz, its fantastic pearls-and-slime within. Here was the sensuality of the deeply native — inviting, then rejecting, the stranger.

My husband and I were living in Boston at the time, and apart from the fact that it was winter and our teaching jobs were temporary, I believe I applied for the Florida position out of curiosity. I went to the campus interview blindly, cheerfully, without even consulting a map, the way you might go to a movie without seeing the preview. All I had to go on was a brief burst of enthusiasm from the university's creative writing program director (himself a Yankee) when he telephoned to arrange the visit.

"We've got great bird life," he cried. "And you don't need a sweater."

So the seduction began. When I stepped off the plane in Gainesville, it was mid-January and seventy degrees, the air itself some rare form of bliss. The director ushered me swiftly into his ancient sage-gray Pontiac the color of Spanish moss, and announced that we were going straight to "the Devil's Millhopper." I thought he was making a joke about the interview process, but no, he was in fact referring to a natural phenomenon — a 120-foot-deep sinkhole where the limestone substrata had caved in. As I stepped carefully down the dappled trail in my interview shoes, I couldn't fight the pleasurable incongruity of those fancy black pumps moving down and down into a green funnel of magnolia, dogwood, violets, and ferns, with little springs running out of its steep sides to form a small pool below. As we stood at the bottom, remote from sunlight, an iridescent blue lizard hesitated, oracular, on my shoe.

That night, after the interview, I called my husband and told him what I'd seen that day: a huge flock of sandhill cranes; egret and ibis and great blue heron; a big shimmery blue-black bird called the anhinga, perched on a cypress stump with its wings spread wide to dry. Alligators, armadillos, little country stores, and huge trees right in town. "It smells good here," I said. "And you don't need a sweater."

And he: "If they offer, take it."

*

Back in Boston, we prepared for our new life as if we were going on an exotic adventure-vacation, buying new cameras, maps and guidebooks, and flimsy tropical-theme shirts. We were, I see now, simply an updated version of the naive American settler, the kind who not all that long before us headed into the unknown with parakeet and piano and joyous misconception, only to pitch the whole lot out the back of the wagon months later.

But not yet: even as the close heat of our first summer descended, the seductive nostalgia I'd felt on my first visit held me fast. The birdsong of my California childhood pierced the neighborhood quiet at dawn and dusk: raucous jays, the manic repertoire of mockingbirds, the cool triplicate sighs of mourning doves. The Spanish had come to the west coast of North America as they'd come here, in search of fabled golden cities and unfathomable wealth, and who could blame them? It seemed appropriate, and a little spooky, that Ponce de Leon named Florida before he actually landed. "Isle of Flowers," he apparently said as he sighted land from the deck of his fragile caravel in 1513. Back home in Spain, they were celebrating the Feast of Flowers, and he believed the place to be an island, so ultimately the name is built entirely out of wish, mistake, and the memory of home — for what else do we have at times of discovery? Once landed, how shocked he must have been by the mysteries of the actual.

Someone urged us to buy a canoe: this was the best way to explore the wilderness. This statement is not untrue. It's just more precise to say that the canoe gives Florida a chance to explore *you*. On our first trip down the Suwanee River, I recall, we were leaning back in the silky air, taking in the hypnotic buzz of insects and the still lifes of turtles on logs, and saying to each other, *I'll bet this is what Eden was like* — when that primitive fish, the alligator gar with its long snout and studded spine, leaped up into the air and slapped itself down in our boat like a curse. It took us about twenty minutes to get it out of the canoe, with Sisyphean hoists of the paddle, until at last we tumbled it, thrashing, over the side. Our nerves were shot, but the day wasn't over: a few minutes later I went off into the woods to take a pee and discovered, at my feet, a cottonmouth moccasin — dead, as it turned out, but who can escape that first impression?

Whenever we canoed on a spring creek with our daughter, we held her tight against our own desire to leap into that water, so limpid and full of light, a dazzling turquoise wherever the springs bubbled up through the limestone. A simple, perfectly safe outing, you'd think, if it weren't for the little white signs posted at intervals: BEWARE! ALLIGATORS. BEWARE! RABID OTTERS.

Still, we saw great blue heron lifting heavily out of reeds, the sudden launch and twist of a red mullet three feet into the air, the long springcreek runs with their water hyacinths and freshwater grasses rippling out under the surface — a Monet run amok. For a while we lived eleven miles south of Gainesville in the town of Micanopy, a village of rutted sand roads and persimmons hanging low enough to pluck without stretching at all. Our neighbor George, a rangy and generous woodworker, kept his studio's backdoor open so anybody could wander on up anytime. His tables and lampstands were curved and sinuous, not unlike the snakes he said were "on the move" in the spring, looking for mates. He warned us pleasantly to stay alert: one of them might, at any moment, drop right out of a tree. It was George who told us the history of the place: how it had been inhabited longer than anyone knew, starting with the Timuacuans, a sun-worshiping people here long before the Spanish conquest. The town itself was named for the Seminole chief Micanope, who refused, along with Osceola and four other chiefs, to sign the treaty of Payne's Landing. Osceola himself had once made a bold attack on the fort here. George told us also about the two gods of the Florida Seminole: Ishtoholo, the Great Spirit, and Yo-He-Wah, the one who commands devils and brings catastrophe — and whose name cannot be spoken in daily life, only chanted during ceremonies at which he is appeased with dances and sacrifices.

"Have you noticed yet?" George asked. "You dream pretty strange when you sleep on so many Indian graves."

Driving back and forth between Gainesville and Micanopy, on old Highway 44 that cuts across Payne's Prairie, I once saw a sunset that made me think of that split Seminole spirit. The sunset was one that only Florida can produce: half of it a row of delicate shell-pink wisps, the other half all fire and flame, like the first Technicolor documentary of a volcano. Two skies in one place, like the two sides of a human face in an old tintype, where one half is full of benign light and the other is brooding and sinister.

*

Maybe the end was inevitable. Within a year or two it was the violent sky that we began to see, a god grown too big in our minds. We had no rituals and nothing to sacrifice — only the futile modern lyric of complaint. On our explorations out of town, we awoke to more ugliness than beauty: the paper mills and huge tracts of quick-growing slash pine; the long, high fences surrounding the corrections facilities outside of town. Someone told us there were seventeen such institutions within a thirty-two-mile radius of Gainesville, and we repeated this statistic to ourselves with grim satisfaction. One year, a serial murderer made his nightly camp in the woods just outside of town, coming in to take the lives of five university students in shockingly theatrical displays. The Florida forest, filled with beauty and danger . . . took on another atmosphere in our imagination. It was a place to fear, a place that drew in solitary nature lovers who never came back — for reasons having nothing to do with wilderness.

There is, in the air over Newnans Lake this June day, the faint hush of a test being administered. I glance toward the mangroves to see if my colleague is ever coming back, and as I do, something long and silver vaults into the air like a knife thrown by a performing chef. Alligator gar, I'm pretty sure, but at the moment it hardly matters. I'm tingling all over, glad to be alive in this place that never stops surprising.

At last my companion emerges from the woods and joins me in the water. He looks a trifle disappointed that I'm still in one piece. We try the grass shrimp for an hour, but there's no action.

"It's not going to happen today — not here," he says in a way that chills me. "Let's get out of here."

It's his own property we retreat to, where he has a little sinkhole of his own, a pond he's stocked with bream and catfish and a couple of snapping turtles — along with a big old mudfish he swears got in there all by itself.

Watching me cast my Yellow Humpy, he sighs. I've got too much slack in my line and I don't know how to set the hook, but I catch bream after bream. "I can see you have the luck," he says, master of the derogatory compliment. "Let me see that thing." He takes the fly rod, lifts it high, and slams the Humpy down on the water, laying the line out perfectly straight, the fly perfectly placed at the edge of the duckweed. Then he yanks it back up so hard the water appears to boil, a tempest in a sinkhole. No fish.

I take the rod back, offering my hesitant beginner's casts — the equivalent of the lob in tennis, all height and no distance. This doesn't seem to matter to the catfish that comes blasting up from God-knows-where to take the fly.

As I leave my colleague's house, I hand him the ruined Humpy.

"Thanks," I say. "I'm going."

"Goodbye," he replies. "Good luck out there."

I wave a shaky goodbye and head for my car, keeping an eye on the sandy trail for the cottonmouth, the bejeweled and deadly coral snake. It's June, after all, and the snakes are once again on the move. There's a symphony of smells in the air: harmony and cacophony, everything at once. I can't describe it.

Could I, if I'd lasted longer? Years from now, out in Oregon, I'll still be trying to compose the scene: the nose-prickling fust of marsh, the dank rich of forest floor and the clean sharp lift of pine, the sweet weight of magnolia. I'll swear I smell the delicate orange, though I might be dreaming of that other grove I lost. There's no separating the smells of our remembered places, their skies, their dreams benign and sinister. This Florida, the Florida I'm leaving, won't leave me. It is the lush green vine of memory that grows in my nomad sleep, finding a way into the next wilderness I hope to call home.

THE IMPACT OF SIGHTS, SOUNDS, AND SMELLS

Creating a sense of place depends, above all else, on vivid visual details. In addition, sounds and smells are effective.

Watch out for modifiers. Routine adjectives like "beautiful," "impressive," "awe-inspiring," or "bleak" and "desolate" don't in themselves create pictures. You can't see a "beautiful" or photograph a "desolate." Only things create pictures.

To make an impression, sights, sounds, and smells have to be fresh and precise. One of the characteristics of routine travel pieces and brochures is the habitual use of overused words and outright clichés such as "a tropical paradise," "a winter wonderland," "a land of contrasts," and "a Mecca for tourists." These trite phrases are the junk food of hack writers.

"On Leaving Florida" is packed with a vast array of precise and vivid visual details. When Sandor adds a modifier, she selects an adjective that adds to the distinctiveness of the object described. In the opening sentence, we are told that the lake is "a glossy mud-green." It's not just green. It is a particular shade and quality of green. When the author first arrived in Florida, she thought perhaps it would look like California, but she soon discovered that here there were

> . . . coral snakes and alligators, sticky vines curling under window frames, and cockroaches the size of baby mice. In the rainy season, chairs and books were lightly veiled in green.

In this short passage there are five different visual details. Notice that the cockroaches are not described as "big" or "enormous." It's hard to make cockroaches more revolting than they are by nature, but comparing them with baby mice does so vividly.

In her first visit to a deep sinkhole she sees more pleasing sights:

> . . . a green funnel of magnolia, dogwood, violets, and ferns, with little springs running out of its steep sides to form a small pool below. As we stood at the bottom, remote from sunlight, an iridescent blue lizard hesitated, oracular, on my shoe.

The phrase "a green funnel" helps us imagine descending into that 120-foot sinkhole. And the lizard is first individualized by being "iridescent blue" and then, perhaps because of its big eyes and solemn stare, made mysterious and wise like an oracle. How often have you seen a lizard described as "oracular"? That's a truly distinctive description.

Sight, of course, is only one of five senses. This essay is unusual in the degree to which it also uses smells, sounds, and even the sense of touch. Take another look at this passage describing one of their canoe trips:

> . . . we were leaning back in the silky air, taking in the hypnotic buzz of insects and the still lifes of turtles on logs . . .

The feel of the air is "silky," a feeling like silk, a tactile image. "Hypnotic buzz" is for the ears. And the arrangement of turtles is like an artist's still-life painting. Three different senses in one sentence!

At the end of the essay she writes that even miles from Florida she will be trying to recapture the best that the state had to offer. In this case she intensifies visual images with a highly original reference to smell:

> . . . I'll still be trying to compose the scene: the nose-prickling fust of marsh, the dank rich of forest floor and the clean sharp lift of pine, the sweet weight of magnolia.

You may not be familiar with "fust" — it's not in most dictionaries — but "fusty" is in common usage as the stale, musty smell that often comes from rotting trees. She gives you a hint with "dank rich of forest floor," combining it with the "sharp lift of pine," the scent rising. The writing here is as dense as it is in many poems; but if you read it carefully, all these lush odors create a vivid sense of being there.

USING HISTORY

Distinctive places have distinctive histories. This is true of every geographic region in the United States or abroad. Even a city block or an acre of farmland has a past. It's not always necessary to include the history of a place you are describing, but often it adds depth.

In "On Leaving Florida" the author is careful to remind you that the area she is describing has a history that goes back far before the arrival of Europeans. Her neighbor George tells her

> . . . how it had been inhabited longer than anyone knew, starting with the Timuacuans, a sun-worshiping people here long before the Spanish conquest. The town itself was named for the Seminole chief Micanope, who refused, along with Osceola and four other chiefs, to sign the treaty of Payne's Landing. Osceola himself had once made a bold attack on the fort here.

If you read the book, *The Night Gardener* (Lyons Press), from which this piece was excerpted, you will discover that the author has drawn on many such historical references.

Historical background requires research, and research takes time. But the Internet has made searches less arduous, sometimes even fun. For local places, regional historical societies can be helpful. And don't forget the contribution of long-time residents who may turn out to be living research centers.

One word of warning, however: extended quotations can stop the forward movement of your essay. As long as they illustrate a point you have made, they can serve.

MIXED FEELINGS: THE IMPORTANCE OF AMBIVALENCE

Many travel pieces written for newspapers or magazines are primarily advertisements. They select all the good features and ignore the rest. A few reverse that, entertaining the reader with the author's complaints.

Although "On Leaving Florida" is focused on a particular place, it is also a good example of an extended personal experience. The author describes her emotions in detail, and those emotions are highly mixed.

Having diametrically opposing emotions about a person or place at the same time is called **ambivalence**. Often it consists of love and hate, but it can also take other forms such as fascination and fear, reverence and hostility. When we think about friends or relatives, we don't like to admit to such feelings, so they are carefully avoided in greeting card verse and sentimental fiction. But when we are writing on a literary level, honesty is essential. This often requires describing our ambivalent feelings.

Essays or stories that focus exclusively on the good qualities of a person or place quickly become unconvincing. Some degree of ambivalence assures the reader that you are being honest. It's what gives a work the ring of authenticity.

For Sandor, the ambivalence is embedded in her reactions to the state of Florida. The essay repeatedly veers from her genuine feeling of respect and even awe on the one hand and her recognition of its harsh, ugly, and occasionally dangerous aspects on the other. Her memory dwells on each aspect alternately.

5 Creating Your Own Literary Nonfiction

EXAMINE YOUR OWN EXPERIENCES

As you turn to writing your own literary nonfiction, a good place to start looking for a topic is your own life. As we have seen, precise details drawn from your own experiences lend a sense of authenticity. Even the most conventional life is a storehouse of interesting incidents waiting to be developed.

Don't be intimidated by professional writers who have invested months or even years immersing themselves in some foreign culture, profession, or sport for the sake of an article or book. The fact is that there is no such thing as an uneventful life.

You won't discover such episodes, however, by staring at a blank sheet of paper or a computer screen. Inspiration is vastly overrated. You need to review your life experiences with some sense of direction.

If you have had an unusual childhood or adolescence, you're in luck. Even if it was unpleasant at the time, it can provide the basis for highly effective nonfiction.

Oddly, some people are reluctant to share the more dramatic aspects of their lives. Often this comes from a desire to blend in. Remind yourself, however, that ours is a country that thrives on multiculturalism. Readers are curious about the great variety of our ethnic, religious, and social differences. If you have a unique background, share it with pride.

If, for example, you came to this country as a refugee, your experiences will be vivid for most readers and will hold their interest even if the details are disturbing. If you were raised by parents of the same gender or have deviant sexual preferences, you may hesitate to reveal such details in an autobiographical manner, but if you overcome your hesitation, your readers will be both sympathetic and concerned.

Even if your life has been more conventional, look closely at those experiences that remain in your memory. Chances are that they have stayed with you because they're vivid. Here are four areas to consider:

1. *Ceremonies.* Recall weddings you may have attended as well as funerals, graduations, birthday celebrations, and family gatherings at holidays. Don't get sidetracked by films you have seen. Hollywood is drawn to these areas like flies at a picnic. Stick to what you know, to what really happened. Ignore the part that went according to plan. That's of little interest to you as a writer. Look for moments of awkwardness, uncertainty, even anger. What you want are the details everyone else wants to forget: your sister tripping on her way to the altar, your uncle getting drunk at Thanksgiving, your best friend's refusal to attend his own graduation. It's the rough edges of formal occasions that you're looking for.

2. *Role Reversals.* You may not enjoy recalling those times when you as a child had to had to act as the parent to your father or mother, but such moments are apt to reveal hidden strengths or weaknesses. In a similar way, a younger sibling sometimes has to act as an adviser to an older brother or sister. These situations are apt to evoke **ambivalent** feelings, the illogical fusing of disparate emotions such as distaste and pleasure or compassion and resentment. Incongruous emotional reactions are often what differentiate a bland account from one that provides honest insights.

3. *Moments of Sudden Growth.* With luck, we all progress from childhood to adolescence to adulthood to senior status, but the process is not smooth. We acquire new abilities and new insights in spurts. Occasionally, there are setbacks. Transitions can be joyful or painful. Feel-good films recount the endless ways that falling in love can convert mean-spirited and selfish individuals into models of perfection, but leave that to Hollywood. Even though something similar may have happened to you, readers will associate your account with countless scripts.

That doesn't mean that you have to be negative, however. Abject fear (a boating accident, a medical crisis, a near-fatal fire) can push an individual to a new level of maturity. If something like that has occurred in your life, try to capture what it actually felt like. Don't glamorize it. Insincerity shows through.

Sudden growth often springs from contact with someone else — a parent, a brother, a sister, a teacher, a cop, or a coach. And don't neglect negative role models — those who shape your development by revealing through their actions what you don't ever want to become.

4. *Moments of High Emotion.* Great joy, abject terror, and deep depression have one thing in common: intensity. Intensity makes them possible subjects for literary nonfiction. However, you need more than a peak of emotion. The reader wants to know what came before. How did it occur? And how did it affect you? A news item of how you were mugged is only a news item. Don't fall back on that clichéd summary, "It's an experience I'll never forget." It shaped you in some way, and you may have to probe a bit before you discover just how it did.

5. *Reversals of Expectation.* Many reversals have become too familiar to be convincing. We all know that when amateurs attempt to put on a theatrical show, they will eventually succeed, or when a lovable but lame race horse goes through training, he will finally win the big race. For a reversal to be effective, it must be original and truly unexpected.

If, for example, you are stutterer and you discovered that when you played a demanding role on the stage you were able speak without hesitation for the first time is your life, this would make an excellent base for a personal experience piece.

Reversals take many forms. Everyone knows how an unusually bright student is praised by teachers. But perhaps only you know from personal experience what it is to be taunted by classmates as "teacher's pet" or "nerd," isolated from your peers. This might lead you to detest the very teacher who admired you. These are circumstances in which assumptions about a situation are reversed, and that reversal is worth developing.

As popular as personal experience is as a base for literary nonfiction, it shares with all nonfiction writing one serious temptation: tinkering with the facts. The temptation is greater with autobiographical pieces than with any other type. When the material is personal, it is less likely that readers will detect deceptions. Remember, though, that in choosing literary nonfiction as a genre, you have established a moral contract with your readers: they assume that you have been loyal to the facts.

You may, of course, decide that the experience would have greater potential as fiction. Often this alternative is well worth considering. But if you plan to do that, start from scratch by transforming places, events, and characters. More about that in the next chapter. But if you decide to stay with nonfiction, stick with the facts as they occurred. Let your memory, not invention, provide the details that will give your work vitality.

CONSIDER THE LIVES OF OTHERS

Enough about you! Some of the best samples of literary nonfiction are focused on someone other than the author. If you are not used to this type of writing, start off with someone you know. Conducting an informal interview is a good way to start.

Occasionally you will know in advance what you want to concentrate on — a musical or literary ability, for example, or a sports achievement. If you don't have a focus, ask about the respondent's childhood, school experiences, or preferences.

Try to avoid aimless conversation. An interview is not chit-chat. The best way to stay on track is to compose a list of questions in advance. Use the list, but be flexible. If your respondent reveals something that sparks your interest, follow up on it. Be careful, also, not to comment on his or her answers. Keep looking for a dominant characteristic of that individual that will give the reader a sense of having actually met him or her.

Interviewing older people about their childhood can be rewarding, but there are special considerations you should keep in mind. When dealing with individuals who are very old, be careful not to sound patronizing. If your respondent is not sure of English or was raised in a culture far removed from yours, it is all too easy to adopt the tone we sometimes use when asking questions of a child. You can show genuine interest without using saccharine phrases such as "that's *fascinating*," "that's a-*mazing*," or "you're ter-*rific*."

In addition, let your respondent's mind wander and let him or her repeat material. It may take a little more time, but remember that it often takes an older person a while to dredge up details from decades ago. If there are contradictions, don't comment on them directly. Instead, return to this area later for clarification.

Interviewers vary on whether to use a tape recorder. A recording may help you clarify details and reproduce actual phrasing when you write up the interview, but the machine may intimidate some respondents. Ask them in advance.

No matter who you are interviewing, keep these three principles in mind: (1) Prepare your questions, but don't be a slave to them. (2) Show interest, but don't introduce your own views. (3) Unify your essay by focusing on a particular aspect of your respondent.

REVIEW YOUR PREFERENCES AND OPINIONS

Most newspapers have an **Op-Ed** section. The term is an abbreviation for "opposite the editorial page." The longer, signed articles and letters to the editor are often informative, but they tend to be more concerned with argumentation than style and personal feelings.

A better source of literary nonfiction is in journals such as *Creative Nonfiction* and *The Georgia Review* (see Appendix B for additional titles). Most of the work in such these publications meet our criteria for literary nonfiction by making use of personal feelings and experiences as well as by employing literary techniques such as evocative language, **metaphors**, **irony**, implication, and sometimes techniques of **prose rhythms** (described in Chapter 23).

A factual essay arguing for an increase in the minimum wage, for example, may offer statistics and background information, but the style is apt to be no more creative than a lawn-mower instruction manual. There is nothing wrong with this since both the argumentative essay and the manual have a specific and utilitarian purpose. But it's unlikely that readers will return to either just for pleasure.

A literary nonfiction piece, on the other hand, will usually humanize such a topic. The author might, for example, interview three garment factory workers. The use of case histories won't automatically transform such essays into literary nonfiction, but the technique provides an opportunity to dramatize the topic and provide greater depth. If written with a sense of compassion and attention to style, the essay will go beyond the level of a straightforward argument to become literary nonfiction.

This distinction is also seen in art. Some painters have expressed social and political views in their paintings. But we value their work for its artistic quality just as much as for its social or political message. In contrast, political and patriotic posters emphasize the message more than artistic expression. Once that cause is over, the posters are torn down. They have served their purpose. Fully developed works of art are like literary nonfiction in that their value continues even after the political or social issues have faded.

LET YOUR MIND WANDER

Daydreaming is rarely encouraged in secondary school, but if you want to plunge into writing, this may be one way to do it.

If this approach interests you and you have been keeping a **journal,** look over the entries and see if one might be reshaped to develop a subtle sense of order.

If you don't have a journal as a starting point, jot down the titles of two literary works you enjoyed and two you disliked. Analyze what you liked in the first pair and what put you off in the other two. If you recalled where you were when you read these, see if you can reconstruct your subjective mood. Did that affect your final judgment? And just how do we make decisions about that we read?

If you do keep a journal, you will have collected many samples of mental grazing. It's a good idea to review the entries from time to time the way you might browse through an old photo album. As I pointed out previously, the entries themselves are not likely to be even first drafts of literary nonfiction, but they may suggest a topic or at least a direction for exploration.

Even if you have not been keeping a journal, you can cast about for topics in a random manner. Write down the names of four people you admire and four you dislike. Can you detect what it is that you look for in friends? Is there a reflective essay there?

Now select and describe briefly four periods of time in which you were really happy. Some may be social occasions, but don't forget times when you were alone. It will help if you focus on different types of pleasure.

Next, do the same for four periods of time that you hope you will never have to repeat. Then look over your material and see if there are patterns you hadn't expected to find. What exactly is pleasure for you? This may result in some self-discovery, and describing what you have discovered may well be the beginning of a reflective essay.

A reflective essay may end up being an opinion piece or even an argument. Or it may take the form of a biographical sketch. But don't force it into a shape that doesn't seem appropriate or true to your own feelings. An observation about the way people interact or seek contentment can be in itself rewarding if the view is fresh and original.

REVISIT A PARTICULAR PLACE

Take a close look at places that made an impression on you — either pleasant or unpleasant. Consider not only your hometown or city but places you have visited. The advantage of focusing on a familiar setting is that you can make use of very specific visual details, as well as smells and sounds the way Marjorie Sandor did in "On Leaving Florida."

To activate your memory, make a list of the various places you have lived, leaving a space between each heading. Then fill in specific visual details you associate with each place. As you look over your notes, linger with each place and imagine someone asking you, "What was it like?" This is your reader speaking to you. Your answer may launch a nonfiction article.

Sometimes it may seem that there is nothing in these scenes that will strike your readers as truly new. Remember, though, that a good deal of nonfiction writing is learning how to see with fresh vision what you simply took for granted before you started writing.

Once you have selected a place, make a long list of details — not only the visual aspects but also the smells and sounds. Then write a paragraph or so describing your honest feelings about the place. Pay special attention to mixed feelings. At that point, see if you can identify an aspect no one else has considered. Once you have identified these elements, you will be ready to share your view and your feelings with readers who have never been there.

No matter what the subject, **tone** is important. The same place can be treated with affection, wonder, bitter resentment, or even rage. Or the tone may be a mix of feelings. When we look back on our childhood neighborhood, for example, our sense of pleasure may be equally mixed with discontent.

Be sure to keep an eye out for contrasts. Again, be careful to avoid clichés. The best way to do this is to find the details that will *show* the contrasts. Visual details, for example, will dramatize the contrast between the rundown commercial district of a city and a nearby affluent suburban neighborhood. Minor incidents will contrast the hostile nature of life on a particular city street as opposed to the sense of shelter experienced once one arrives safely home. The smells and sounds recalled from a summer job in a slaughterhouse might provide a sharp contrast to a weekend hike in the woods when the job was over.

FOCUS ON AN INCIDENT IN HISTORY

Using historical material requires a ruthless process of reduction. No one (I hope) has to be told that "the Roman Empire" is not a subject for a single essay. Cutting it down to "Julius Caesar" reduces it to those seventh-grade papers lifted so deftly from encyclopedias. If, however, you track down one of Julius Caesar's financial supporters who built a fortune by providing fire protection to wealthy homeowners and letting the homes of others burn to the ground, you might be on to something.

There are a number of questions you should ask yourself before deciding on a particular historical topic. First, is the incident narrow enough in scope to be described in a few pages? As the Julius Caesar example shows, finding a workable topic is like activating a zoom lens, continually moving closer to very specific fragments of history.

Second, is it something that is not already known to the reading public? Shakespeare beat you to it in describing the rise and fall of Julius Caesar, and even he took five acts to do so. Hunt for overlooked scraps of history.

Third, does the topic suggest some parallel with our own times or a connection with larger historical events? This isn't essential, but it adds another dimension. Significantly, our example of campaign financing in Caesar's time has a certain familiar ring.

In the search for historical topics, don't ignore fairly recent events. Something that occurred 20 years ago may have a significant impact on our lives today. Frequently you will find yourself dealing with social issues.

The closer the material is to the present, the more likely it is that you can develop a personal connection. If, for example, you are considering the subject of drug use, consider giving your treatment a human dimension by including your own experiences or those of people you have interviewed. If you are able to contrast shifts in attitude, your essay enters the area of historical nonfiction.

As a general rule, the farther back you go the more difficult it is to find a well-documented incident that is manageable. Perhaps because of this, short historical essays tend to focus on fairly recent events. Often they are blended with personal experience. In such cases, there may be no sharp line between a memoir and a historical piece. When an older writer recalls being let out of school to see the German dirigible *Hindenburg* pass overhead with its distinctive swastika on the tail, the recollection of a personal experience is blended almost equally with a historical event.

6 Fiction

The Freedom to Invent

When you turn from literary nonfiction to fiction you cut the tether with the truth. You may (and often will) use facts, places, or events taken from your own life, but you will be altering and reshaping them to fit the literary needs of the story.

When you write fiction you are telling an untrue story in prose. It is "untrue" in the sense that it is partly or wholly made up. It is an artistic creation in that it stands on its own, regardless of how much it may make use of characters, events, and settings from life. Like playwrights and poets, writers of fiction are free to assume the existence of ghosts, unicorns, or Hobbits. We can use material close to us — parents or friends, for example — without being accurate. As writers of fiction, we are free to present our material through the eyes of a **persona**, someone who may be quite unlike us. A story or novel cannot be criticized for being "untrue"; it is judged on whether it *seems* true. This is known as *verisimilitude* (see **realism**).

One of the best ways to achieve this sense of authenticity is to draw heavily on the world you know best — your own life. Some beginning writers feel that their lives have been too ordinary, but everyone has had complex relationships with parents or foster parents, all have had to deal with people their own age, everyone has had defeats, successes, and learning experiences. And every experience is unique.

Although literary nonfiction gains impact from the fact that it is based on actual events and facts, the strength of fiction lies in its quality as a literary creation. If a story uses bits and pieces of the writer's experience, those fragments are simply miscellaneous building blocks used the way a carpenter might salvage scrap lumber.

Our lives are that scrap heap: a jumble of unconnected events and repetitious activities. But you have to be selective. There is nothing as dull as a step-by-step account of what has happened to you over the length of an average day. No one wants to know how long you brushed your teeth or what you had for breakfast. A fiction writer's goal, remember, is to select only the details that will contribute to a story. Some will be borrowed from life, and some will be created from imagination.

Even a lengthy and dramatic episode from your life that might make an entertaining **anecdote** in conversation almost always needs to be revised extensively before it can be transformed into a successful story. This is why we call the fiction process "creative."

These revisions of personal experience take many forms. Unrelated details have to be cut, and new material has to be added. Some of these changes will be minor; others will involve creating a wholly new character or new scenes. In fact, if you find yourself using a personal experience without alteration it really is literary nonfiction. If you plan to use the freedom that fiction allows, start revising and reshaping your material.

If you are still undecided whether to approach a new work as literary nonfiction or as fiction, here are three situations that call for a fictional approach. First, there are many personal experiences that are simply too mild to hold readers. They may have the potential for insights, but not the power. They have to be reshaped — in some cases, fundamentally — to have the impact you want.

Second, sometimes things happen to us that are too **melodramatic** to be handled in a short work. Violent events may take over a short literary work so that there is no room for characterization or subtlety of theme. A fictional treatment can tone down the actual suicide of a friend by focusing on the reaction of a sister or brother.

Third, the personal experience may be so close to you that you find yourself unable to revise anything. One way to overcome this is to write a story from the point of view (see **means of perception**) of someone else.

Pure invention also has its risks. The most serious problem is imitation. You have to make sure that you are not sliding into the ruts of some well-known **convention**. More about that in the next chapter.

We also have to be on guard against **therapy writing**, the unconscious (or occasionally deliberate) distortion in which anger and resentment about people we know and detest blots out subtle characterization. Revenge fiction sometimes sells well, but only if you are a celebrity.

With careful revision we can achieve the **tone** we want to achieve. Keep reminding yourself that fiction is not a diary entry even if it is written to resemble one; fiction is an artistic creation with its own sense of unity and significance.

Editing our experiences is something we all do in daily conversation without much thought. If you and your parents have spent a weekend in, say, Chicago for the first time, what you report as memorable may be quite different from their versions. In telling others about the event, all three of you will stick to the facts but will focus on different aspects depending on your interests.

For fiction writers, however, this editing process becomes a much more radical and deliberate process. The events may only serve as a jumping off point. Our only obligation, remember, is to make a good story, one with unity, an identifiable **theme**, and credible **characterization**. The resulting work only *seems* like life itself.

Suppose, for example, you want to base a story on an intense argument between a man and a woman you overheard in a restaurant. You may decide to use much of their exact phrasing (pure fact) but make them brother and sister (invention) and put them in your uncle's house (factual memory), telling the story from the point of view of a six-year-old daughter listening to them (invention) during a terrible rainstorm (factual memory from another occasion). If you do this right, no one will be able to separate what was drawn from life and what was created from your imagination. The two have become fused into a single, credible story.

SIMPLE VERSUS SOPHISTICATED FICTION

As soon as we talk about the merit or worth of an artistic work, we enter the slippery area of what is good and what is bad. It is so difficult to defend the worth of a story that some people duck the issue entirely by saying, "I only know what I like."

Personal preference, of course, is everyone's privilege. Some like gentle stories, some want heavy drama; some prefer stories about women, others like to read about men. Arguing seriously about our preferences is as pointless as debating whether dogs are better than cats.

There is, however, one distinction about which we can reach agreement: some stories, like some poems and plays, are relatively **simple**, while others are significantly more **sophisticated**. These terms are enormously helpful for writers and underlie all of the analysis in this book.

Essentially, sophisticated works "do" more in the sense that they explore the themes and the characters with greater insight than do simple works. They also make more intricate and subtle use of plot and setting. This text is concerned with sophisticated writing, but that focus does not imply that such work is "better." It is simply "other" in the sense that the biologically simple crayfish is different from the far more sophisticated dolphin.

The span between the simplest fiction and relatively sophisticated fiction is enormous. Compare a comic strip about adolescents such as *Luann* or *Zits* with a novel about adolescents such as John Knowles' *A Separate Peace* or J.D. Salinger's *The Catcher in the Rye*. These cartoons and the novels are similar in that they are all samples of fiction. That is, they all tell untrue stories in prose. Furthermore, they all have plots, characters, settings, and themes. Also they share certain basic fictional techniques: dialogue, thoughts, and action. They even draw on the same age bracket — that highly charged transition period between childhood and adulthood. Before we brand comics as "childish," remember that many intelligent adults read them with pleasure each morning. Conversely, while almost all readers agree that *The Catcher in the Rye* is an excellent example of literary fiction, a few find it immoral and therefore "bad."

How, then, can we describe the difference between these two works objectively? To start with, the portrayal of the fictional protagonist in *Zits* is relatively uncomplicated. The plots in that strip tend to be brief and limited in scope. Comic strip characters rarely deal with such issues as teen pregnancy or drugs. The portrayal of Holden Caulfield, the protagonist of *The Catcher in the Rye*, on the other hand, is sophisticated in that he deals with fairly complex moral issues and inner doubts. He struggles with the complexities that most teenagers have to face.

The enjoyment many take in reading a comic strip is an escape from the challenges of everyday life. We all need that from time to time. In general, we read such episodes once and then forget them. In contrast, the pleasure derived from reading *The Catcher in the Rye* comes from a greater understanding of the world around us. We can return to it and draw more from it in another reading. In short, each type of fiction serves a different need.

Be careful not to confuse this literary use of *sophisticated* and its popular use, which describes a person who is socially suave and urbane. The *portrayal* of a character (**characterization**) can be sophisticated even if the character is not. Literary sophistication refers to the degree to which the work develops characters (and themes too) with complexity, depth, and range of insight. Mark Twain's Huck Finn, for example, and Carson McCullers' Frankie in *Member of the Wedding* are certainly presented as unsophisticated individuals, but the subtlety and insightfulness with which these authors present their characters and the novels as a whole are literarily sophisticated.

There are an infinite number of gradations between the simplest forms of fiction and the most sophisticated. Juveniles — stories and novels written for adolescents (now called young adults) — are far more intricate in characterization and theme than comic strips. Gothic novels, for all their repetition of plot and setting, have a certain sophistication of vocabulary, but they are not intended to be as subtle or insightful as literary novels. In fact, a standard, mass market gothic novel manuscript may well be turned down by a publisher if it departs too far from the familiar and relatively simple pattern. In the case of murder mysteries, most of the sophistication takes the form of ingenious plots, but thematically they tend to be fairly simple. The fact that murderers often make a simple but crucial error is not exactly a fresh insight. Such novels are "a quick read" for most enthusiasts.

There are only two large-circulation magazines that still publish sophisticated short stories today, *The New Yorker* and *Harpers*, but there are literally hundreds of literary journals and quarterlies such as *Glimmer Train, Story*

Quarterly (both all-fiction), *The North American Review,* and *The Virginia Quarterly Review.* (A longer list appears in Appendix B.) These publications usually vary their offerings from relatively accessible pieces to works that, like sophisticated poetry, may require some effort on the part of the reader. Those who are seriously interested in writing sophisticated fiction should spend as much time reading as they do writing.

As a writer, how high should you aim? It would be a mistake to start out by attempting an extremely complex plot and an intricate theme. If you have one or two interesting characters and a single, insightful event, you can write a story that is fresh and rewarding.

As you gain experience and get in the habit of reading new work regularly, you will want to examine what makes some works more sophisticated than others. Take a close look at the four basic elements of the story: plot, characters, setting, and theme.

Plot, whether simple or sophisticated, consists of a sequence of actions. Simple fiction usually limits itself to a single, straightforward plot. Simple plots such as those recurring on television tend to be based on well-used **conventions** known as **formulas**. Plots like the-good-cop-with-good-wife-is-tempted-by-drug-money are, for all the noise and profanity, tranquilizers derived from familiarity and repetition.

Sophistication of plot does not necessarily mean complexity. What one aims for is a sequence of events that provide new insights. The determining factor is not how many twists and turns the plot may take but how successfully it contributes to characterization and aspects of the theme.

Characterization, the portrayal of fictitious characters, is also significantly different in simple and sophisticated works. In simple fiction, the **protagonist** or primary character may be extremely active (the restlessness of a James Bond or Batman), but you never get to know him or her the way you might come to understand someone in life. What you see is a repetition of the same traits and attitudes. The good stay good, and the bad stay bad. It's not likely that you'll see James Bond renounce society and join a monastery or Tarzan become addicted to cocaine and sell the rain forest to finance his habit.

Fully developed characters in sophisticated fiction often reveal mixed emotions. Sharply contrasted feelings take the form of **ambivalence,** a simultaneous blending of opposite feelings such as love and hate for another person or a mix of courage and panic. Motivation may include both honorable and selfish elements. Behavior may reveal both maturity and childishness on different occasions, contrasts similar to those you may have seen in a close friend.

Setting in simple fiction often relies on geographic clichés that are repeated over and over. Students in New York are described as living in Greenwich Village even though that area has not been a low-rent bargain for more than 50 years; businessmen have their offices on Madison Avenue; San Francisco lawyers work "in the shadow of the Golden Gate"; artists in Paris have studios looking out on the Eiffel Tower. "Originality" often takes the form of the exotic — a ski resort high in the Andes, a spy headquarters 400 feet below the Houses of Parliament, or a royal palace constructed entirely in glowing Lucite on the planet Octo. Bizarre settings often serve no purpose other than visual appeal. They tend to dominate rather than contribute to characterization and theme.

The setting in sophisticated fiction, on the other hand, generally avoids both the old clichés and the bizarre. It may be based on a place known to the author or largely invented, but the details are fresh, not borrowed, and unobtrusive. Ideally, the setting helps to develop the theme.

Theme is another aspect of fiction that varies with the degree of sophistication. The theme of a work of fiction is the portion that comments on the human condition. Simple themes repeat what we already know. Many of these are borrowed from television. So-called action thrillers on television (successors to the once-popular detective stories in magazines) endlessly repeat the theme, "Crime doesn't pay, but it's exciting to watch someone try." Situation comedies repeat the notion that misunderstandings regularly lead to absurd confusions all of which are finally resolved without causing harm to anyone. Injustices are terrible but corrected in the end. These thematic patterns are so simple and are repeated so often that they become **hackneyed**. It takes both skill and practice to produce such work, but the goal is quick entertainment, not memorable or insightful themes.

Sophisticated fiction, in contrast, tends to develop themes that have depth and insight. Dishonest acts usually have a variety of consequences, some of them surprising. Misunderstandings frequently result in lasting damage. Outrageous injustice may endure or take another form. We learn something from such thematic suggestions. Our view of the world is altered, even if only slightly.

If, as I assume, your goal is to write fiction that will linger in the mind of the reader and provide new insights, guard against the easy and the glib. Strive for freshness and insight. All this is too much to keep in mind as you write your first draft of a story. To some degree, let the work unfold on its own. But when you have a chance to read what will probably be the first of several drafts, shift from your writing mode to that of critic. Judge the degree of sophistication by examining what is called the five **narrative modes** of fiction: dialogue, thought, action, description, and exposition. These are the basic tools of the genre.

- **Dialogue** and *thought* are two effective ways of suggesting character. In simple fiction they fit a familiar mold and reveal familiar types known as **stock characters**. Heroes speak heroically and cowards snivel. In sophisticated fiction dialogue and thoughts reveal the subtle nuances of character — the variations that we detect only in those we know well. Often dialogue and thoughts are played against each other so as to reveal a contrast between the inner and the outer person.

- *Action* is the dominant mode for simple fiction, particularly in adventure stories. As we will see in the examples in this text, sophisticated fiction also makes use of action because it provides a sense of urgency. But action is never employed for its own sake. Instead, it serves as a way to develop both characterization and theme.
- *Description* can be important even though it tends to slow the forward motion of a story. Descriptive details are justified when they are relevant. That is, they should have some purpose and a sense of authenticity.
- **Exposition** is perhaps the most dangerous of the five narrative modes. It refers to those explanatory passages that give background information or commentary directly. Exposition is risky because in simple (and inept) fiction it is often used to explain character and, worse, present the theme directly. "Old Mack looked tough, but he had a heart of gold" labels an aspect of character that in fiction would be better revealed through action and dialogue. It also uses a cliché.

  You're on safe ground if you limit exposition to peripheral or incidental information: "He had just turned 40" or "She had never been in Chicago." Sophisticated fiction reveals the rest through action and dialogue.

  The reason for limiting the use of exposition is that literarily sophisticated fiction depends in part on giving readers the feeling that they themselves have come to know the characters on their own. The process is similar to the way we make judgments about people in daily life. We listen to what people say and watch what they do, and then we come to conclusions. In fiction, of course, the dialogue and action are carefully selected by the author, but when we read, we like the illusion of discovering significance on our own.

THE FORMS OF FICTION

Fiction is commonly classified as falling into four categories: the short-short story, the story, the novella, and the novel. These terms are handy, but they are far from precise. There is no sharp line between one length and the next.

- **Short-short stories** are usually defined as being between 500 and 2,000 words long. Since a typed, double-spaced manuscript (see Appendix B for details) comes to about 250 words a page, a short-short is from two to six pages. Contests for short-shorts are normally limited to 1,500 words, or about six pages. For contests, be sure to determine your word count accurately.

  Because of their brevity, most short-shorts have no more than two characters presented in one or two scenes in a brief time span. There is a temptation to indulge in trick endings, but with restraint you can generate real insight into character, feeling, and human relations.
- **Short stories** generally run from 2,000 words (8 pages) to 6,000 words (24 pages). Some are longer, but these become increasingly difficult to place because the greater length will force a magazine editor to reduce the total number of works in an issue. The great advantage of this length over the short-short is that it allows one to deal with more characters, have a more intricate plot, and make greater use of setting. But the short story is still a relatively tight art form.

- **Novellas** generally run between 50 and 150 typed pages, halfway between a story and a novel. Occasionally magazines will include one novella or will devote a special issue to several, but novellas are more often seen in published collections along with short stories by the same author.

- **Novels** are more than just stories that have been expanded beyond 250 pages—or at least they should be. The length allows an author to do interesting things with the plot and to develop subplots. One can introduce more characters than in a story or novella, and some of them can change and develop over the course of time. The theme or themes of such a work can be broader and more intricate than in the shorter forms.

When you start writing, the short-short story is a good form to work with. In developing your creative abilities, it is important to try a number of different approaches — first person, third person, light tone, serious tone, close to experience, far removed from experience. You can achieve new skills and find your own voice better through a series of short-short stories than by locking yourself into a longer work too soon.

THREE MOTIVES FOR WRITING FICTION

Whenever you become involved in creative work, it is worth asking yourself just what aspect of the activity is motivating you. Doing this may help you to determine in what direction you want to move right from the start.

There are many reasons for writing fiction, but they tend to fall into three broad groups. Since each involves a different approach and different goals, it is important to examine them separately.

- First, there is the *private motive*. This describes writing that is mainly for our personal pleasure. It is intended for an audience of one — ourselves. Often it takes the form of journal entries. Spontaneous and usually unrevised, journal writing requires no special training. Entries may be valuable for recording or clarifying our own feelings or as a way of sketching out possible scenes in fiction, or they may be just good fun as a release. But in either case they shouldn't be passed off as finished work.

- The second is the *commercial motive*. In its pure form, **commercial fiction** is the opposite of private writing because it is motivated largely by outer rather than inner demands. It is writing for others. Commercial writers usually define their work as a craft rather than an art, and their primary goal is monetary reward. They produce entertainment. Many spend more of their time writing nonfiction than they do fiction since the demand is greater.

  The fiction produced by commercial writers tends to follow certain familiar **conventions** — the love story, high adventure, war, crime — because there is a large market for that kind of writing. As with businesspeople, their goal is to supply what the market wants. Although there is a tendency for literarily minded individuals to look down on commercial writing, it is an honest profession that fills a need.

- The third is the *literary motive*. Although it is a primary factor in the creation of most literature, it is perhaps the least understood. Writers in this area are like painters, sculptors, and composers who value the quality of the work they produce. Having an audience is obviously important, and being paid for one's efforts seems only fair; but making money is not the principal drive. Because of this, they do not generally tailor their work to meet the whims of the public, nor do they cater to commercial markets. They measure their efforts against what they consider to be the best fiction they have read.

  Because literary writers require readers who have relatively sophisticated taste and experience, they must often (although not always) be content with a relatively small audience. Their novels may not be bestsellers, and their short stories frequently appear in "little magazines" that have small circulations and cannot pay their contributors lavishly — if at all. Writers in this area usually have to supplement their income — often by teaching. Many continue writing even when they receive nothing for their work. But when they publish they have a special satisfaction in knowing that they are reaching readers who will spend time with their work and will react to it with some sensitivity. In addition, they are working in one of the few areas where they do not have to compromise. For many, this is very important.

  The literary motive is sometimes difficult for nonwriters to understand, especially in a society that tends to judge worth on the basis of economic reward. It helps, though, to compare the literary writer with the opera singer who knows that rock singers earn ten times as much. Opera continues not because its performers like being paid less but because this is what they do best and enjoy most.

The emphasis in most creative writing courses is on sophisticated rather than simple work. The same is true of this text. This does not mean that personal entries in a journal are without value. Nor does it mean that commercial writing, which by definition is aimed at a wide audience, is to be scorned. What it does mean is that because sophisticated or literary writing requires careful study and a lot of practice, many people find writing courses and a text like this helpful. Selecting the kind of writing you want to do depends entirely on what motivates you.

These motives for writing are not exclusive. Every writer, like every artist in the broadest sense, is driven by a combination of all three. Those who are concerned primarily with sophisticated writing, however, share a respect for literature as something of value in itself. With this as a base, there is no end of possibilities for fresh creativity.

7 Finding and Shaping Fresh Material

A majority of successful stories give readers the sense that they are getting to know real people, real places, and credible events. This is why writers so often turn to their own lives for material. What could be more authentic than the people, the places, and the experiences one knows firsthand?

But as I pointed out in Chapter 6, creative writing is almost always a blend of what we know well and what we invent. Where does this new material come from? Ideally, it springs from our imagination, stimulated by what we have read, seen, and heard about.

All of us like to think of our creative imagination as pure and uncontaminated, but remember that it also contains a clutter of stolen goods. These are those old plots, characters, and settings picked up from movies and television. If we are not careful, we are apt to use bits and pieces from these shopworn sources unintentionally. When facing a writing deadline, you may even be tempted to use one intentionally. But if you do, you will probably damage the rest of the piece.

Familiar **plot** patterns and **stock characters** are **clichés** on a big scale. When commercial writers of fiction and scriptwriters adopt these **conventions** purposely, it is politely called **formula writing**. Like fast food, formula writing serves a wide market and often earns top dollar, but it usually lacks subtlety and insight. When these conventions show up in sophisticated fiction, they contaminate an otherwise successful work. They are the tattered remains of material that often wasn't fresh even in the hands of professionals.

For instance, how many movies and television dramas have you seen in which the charming, lovable stranger comes to town, makes friends everywhere, wins the heart of a sweet and beautiful girl, only to be revealed as a huckster and a fraud? As soon as readers recognize even a fragment of such a familiar pattern, they are apt to slip into the glazed half-attention with which they frequently watch a standard television drama or listen to background music at a restaurant. Imagination is essential in creative writing, but be careful to check the source of what you think is creative invention.

THE "SEVEN DEADLY SINS" OF FICTION

How can you spot and reject stolen material? Essentially by reading a lot. Here are seven danger areas to watch out for. They are not deadly in a literal sense, but they can do lethal damage to any work of fiction. They are literary sins because of the way they undermine the best intentions.

The popularity of particular stock plots and character types shifts from year to year, but these seven are especially prevalent today. I list them not to discourage invention but to save you from spending valuable time on a story idea that may well be doomed from the start.

• **The High-Tech Melodrama.** A **melodrama** is any piece of fiction or drama that is overloaded with dramatic suspense. Unlike true drama, it is excessive. Television's relentless drive for more viewers tempts many scriptwriters to step over the line between drama and melodrama. What can be more entertaining than a disturbed adolescent with the power to destroy Washington, D.C., at dawn next Thursday?

Terrorists are merely the most recent form of melodramatic sociopaths. Whether the protagonist is cast as a seedy detective, a rogue cop, or a vice squad chief with an addiction problem, the props usually include both guns and fast cars. The plot turns out to be search-and-kill. The high-speed chase is repeated as regularly as was the shootout in Westerns of the 1950s. Replacing the magnum with a laser and moving the chase to another galaxy may be a challenge for the special-effects department, but the plot is remarkably similar, and the characters seem to speak the same lines.

It is not guns and uniforms by themselves that present the problem. If you have gone hunting, served on a police force, or been in the military, you could draw on those experiences and find ways of sharing them with your readers. But serious problems arise when you start to borrow material from scriptwriters who themselves are borrowing from earlier scripts. Watch out for characters — male or female — who always maintain their cool in times of stress and reveal nothing of themselves. Guard against that too-easy dichotomy between the good and the bad. Keep asking yourself: Where did I get this stuff? Is it secondhand property?

• **The Adolescent Tragedy.** The adolescent period is an excellent one for sophisticated fiction as long as you keep your material genuine and fresh in detail. But there are three pitfalls: lack of perspective, sentimentality, and, once again, melodrama.

Lack of perspective occurs when the experience is too recent and the author is more concerned with his or her feelings than the work as fiction. The result may end up like an extended diary entry. There are two warning signs: when you find yourself calling your fictional characters by the names of their nonfictional counterparts and when you feel you shouldn't change the plot because "that's not the way it really happened."

To avoid this lack of objectivity, make sure that enough time has elapsed between the event and your attempt to convert it into fiction. The more emotional the experience, the more time will be required to gain some measure of detachment.

Sentimentality is a fictional virus often caught while watching television. The first symptom is the distant sound of violins. The difference between the sentimental story and one that is genuinely moving is a matter of sophistication. Sentimental stories sacrifice in-depth characterization and subtle themes in order to evoke tears.

Watch out for that miserable but blameless little boy and his totally evil father, the blind girl whose only friend is a blind puppy, or the terminally ill patient with four days to live who falls in love with a gorgeous nurse. You don't have to be a cynic to spot these as tricks to trigger the emotions.

But what if you really were brutalized by a vicious father or found love in a hospital? Your job would be to develop characters with depth and find ambivalences that will break the mold and convince the reader that this is a genuine experience. In some cases you may have to alter the situation radically to avoid even the appearance of sentimentality. "That's the way it happened" is never an excuse for bad writing.

Melodrama is tonally the opposite. In musical terms, sentimentality is played with plaintive violins while melodrama pounds on the drums. Here is one sample in essence: good kid is drawn into gang membership, is soon forced to test his manhood by shooting his brother, and is then knifed by a rival gang. How can this be melodramatic when events this violent occur every day on the street? Because it has been worked over too often; because it would take a full novel to develop; because we can spot the ending from reading the first paragraph; because it sounds like another high school instructional film on the evil of gangs. Those telltale signs will kill the story faster than a magnum.

Again, what if it almost happened to you? Find some corner of the experience that only you know about. Avoid the big, familiar pattern. Focus on an aspect the rest of us never thought about before.

• **The Twilight Zone Rerun.** Like the fiction of Edgar Allan Poe, the scripts of the television program *The Twilight Zone* are characterized by the strange and the bizarre. They are entertaining even as reruns, but most episodes depended heavily on a gimmick. A **gimmick** is a tricky idea worked into fiction or a script, one that surprises. Or is supposed to.

In one program, for example, a nearsighted book-lover who is the sole survivor of World War III discovers an undamaged library for his private use. As he reaches for a treasured book, he — you guessed it — drops and breaks his glasses. Dramatic, yes, but it is **simple** entertainment. The trick becomes more important than the development of character or subtlety of theme. Like the anecdote or well-told joke, it depends on a punch line. Once read, there is little reason for going back to it.

• **Vampires Resurrected.** Count (and Countess) Dracula have, in their golden years, managed to upstage werewolves, though just barely. The resurrection seems to have originated not in Transylvania but in Hollywood. It was once good dream stuff, but the convention has been repeated so often that it has sunk to the level of comic strips and Halloween masks. Even professional scriptwriters, experts in recycling previously recycled works, are reduced to treating it as self-satire. There is little likelihood that a beginning writer — even one who is well-read — can in eight pages breathe life into either the once-proud count or his recently liberated countess.

• **The Baby-Boomer Gone Wrong.** This is one of the most common patterns in college writing courses. The protagonist is a young, upwardly mobile individual who has put career and the acquisition of material objects ahead of personal relationships and spiritual values. He drives a Porsche, has a Jacuzzi, and lives in Silicon Valley or some mythical place with the same climate. In the end, he pays for his sins and succumbs to drink, drugs, or a bullet — sometimes all three.

These plots have their roots in the Faust legend — medieval tales portraying a hero who sells his soul to the devil in exchange for knowledge and possessions. It has been redone in opera and countless films. The devil usually gets the best lines.

It would be nice to think that such plots were inspired by Goethe's play, the operas of Berlioz and Gounod, Theodore Dreiser's novel, *An American Tragedy*, or stories such as F. Scott Fitzgerald's "Winter Dreams," all of which build convincing characters who echo the Faust myth. But it seems more likely that the source is movies and television dramas, many of which do no more than dress the characters in different costumes.

In keeping with the times, the Faust plot is occasionally refashioned with a young woman as unhappy protagonist. But gender reversal alone does not create insight into character and theme. True, such individuals exist in significant numbers, especially in so-called developed nations, but it takes real skill to avoid the timeworn ruts of imitations that are based on imitation.

Suppose, however, you knew a hard-driving individual who really did own a Porsche and tragically did commit suicide? It would still be a risky incident for short fiction. Suicide is generally too complex a subject to handle convincingly in a short-short story. You may have to substitute some subtler indication of a character's sense of defeat and despair. Even then, it would be a challenge to keep the story from resembling a poorly disguised sermon.

- **The Temptations of Ernest Goodwriter.** The protagonist walks up and down the beach, planning a great novel. He is tempted by invitations of fun-loving but superficial friends and an offer to join a major advertising firm. After a tedious period of agonizing indecision, he returns to his typewriter or computer and his high literary principles.

Or perhaps he is in New York and will not change a word of a novel he has already written. Or he is in Los Angeles and is torn between trying to write a great novel that may or may not find a publisher and being paid a fortune to write formula scripts.

Hack writers have recycled this plot by giving the lead to a woman, shifting the setting, and trying other art forms (jazz musicians and painters mostly), but the plot and theme fit the same mold.

The sad fact is that morality tales make poor fiction. They are unconvincing because the characters have been upstaged by abstract ideas: good pitted against evil with no complexity or insight into the way people really live. In some cases the hero is so wooden you can't help hoping he or she will "go Hollywood," make a fortune, and live happily ever after.

- **My Weird Dream.** Recording your dreams can be interesting and valuable — for your analyst. But for the rest of us, the aimless plot and shifting scenes are tedious at best. Only a conscientious writing instructor will actually get to the end.

Dream stories do have a history of sorts. In the 1920s they were called **automatic writing**. Writers simply typed whatever came into their heads for three hours and called the final 15 pages a "story." Occasionally, segments were published (mostly in a magazine called *Broom*), but no one has republished them — for good reason.

There was another flurry of interest in the late 1960s, when this kind of writing was defended as "literary tripping," a hallucinogenic voyage on paper. Again, the writing was more fun than the reading.

The passing fad of aimless composition should not be confused with **stream-of-consciousness** writing. This technique, made famous by James Joyce, is designed to give the illusion of entering the mind of a fictional character. It is used as a part of story, usually as the thoughts of a character we have already come to know through more conventional writing. As such, it is a literary device with a purpose. A dream without a context belongs in your journal.

Discouraged? Don't be. These are worst-case scenarios. If you avoid them, you will save yourself hours of time trying to create fiction with tainted material.

Remember that creativity is by nature a positive process and that your sources for fresh and convincing material are infinite. As soon as you begin to examine your friends, your relatives, your hometown, and the experiences that contributed to your growth, you will have no need for shoddy, overused material. In addition, you will find that the planning and the writing itself generate insights about yourself and your world.

THE AUTHENTICITY OF PERSONAL EXPERIENCE

Using personal experience selectively and honestly is almost a guarantee that your fiction will be fresh and convincing. This is particularly true for those who are just beginning to write fiction. As you gain experience, you will learn how to keep one foot in the circle of familiarity while stepping out with the other. Memories of a summer job on a construction crew, for example, might allow you to explore what it would be like to be foreman or, pushed further, a civil engineer in conflict with the foreman. Some of the more demanding moments of baby-sitting might serve as the basis for a story dealing with the life of a single parent. At the outset, it is wise to stay relatively close to the original experience.

Finding a good incident with which to work may come easily, but often it will not. Even experienced writers have dry periods. Because "waiting for inspiration" is just a romantic way of describing procrastination, it is important to learn how to look for material in a constructive way. Here are some areas that are worth exploring.

Family relationships are natural subjects for fiction. Remember, though, that your feelings about those who have been close to you are rarely simple. Many are charged with **ambivalence**, mixed feelings of love and resentment. You may resist the notion that you have such contradictory feelings, but they are surprisingly common. They are also fruitful material for fiction.

The relationship one has with parents not only shifts day by day, it changes in more general ways over the years. Often it progress from idealization through disillusionment to a new acceptance, usually based on a fairly realistic evaluation. But every family is different. Your job as fiction writer is to find one or two incidents that will reveal these shifting attitudes without resorting to direct analysis.

Such shifts in relationships don't have to be highly dramatic. A major or traumatic change in a relationship may prove too large in scope to be handled in a short-short story. Subtle shifts that surprised you at the time often serve as manageable material for fiction.

In addition to child–parent relationships, there are a variety of other family connections that also keep changing: brother and sister, two sisters and a maiden aunt, two brothers and their cousin, a daughter dealing with a stepfather, or the reactions of three brothers to their uncle. Relationships like these fluctuate in real life, and the shifts are remembered because something was done (action) or said (dialogue) in such a way as to reveal and dramatize the change.

If such shifts in attitude seem difficult to reveal in the relatively short span of a short story, study the poem entitled "The Paradise of Wings" by Theodore Deppe on page 218. In this poem, the warm affection the narrator and his sister felt for their grandfather is radically and dramatically altered. Not only that, their view of what was once a special place becomes hateful. All that in four stanzas!

To some degree you can use such relationships directly, but often you will have to transform experience into something related but different — a process of **transformation** I will explain shortly.

Love relationships have been used a great deal in fiction, so certain patterns have become **hackneyed** from overuse. But don't let this put you off. Genuine emotions are always fresh. You can avoid the conventions of commercial fiction by asking these two related questions: What were my *real* feelings? Were there any **ambivalent** emotions?

On very rare occasions you may find that even the most honest development of an experience will seem on paper to resemble a scene from a second-rate movie. It's most unlikely, but perhaps you really did patch up a relationship while standing on the shore of Lake Concord under a full moon in June as violin music wafted from a distant cottage. As a writer of fiction you will simply have to break the mold. Douse the moon, change the name of the lake, squelch the music, and give the characters some uneasiness about that reconciliation. The truth is no excuse for bad fiction.

Some of the best relationships to examine are those with individuals who are much younger or older. Your first impulse will be to present the material through the eyes of the character who is closest to your own age. But try writing a page or two from the point of view of the other character. Even if you don't use that version, it may help you to see more aspects of the relationship.

For an overview of your resources, the following chart may help you to explore the complex relationships you have with those around you. At the top are people who are older than you and at the bottom those who are younger. As the author, you are at the center.

Diagrams, of course, don't write fiction. The function of this chart is merely to stimulate your memory and to suggest where to look for good material. To make full use of it, jot down the names of individuals you know whose relationship with you has the potential for fiction.

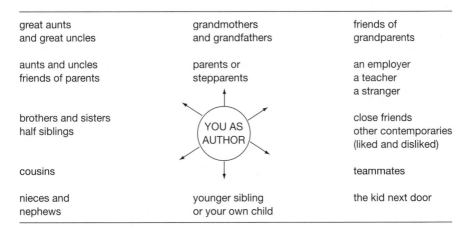

After you have selected two or three individuals from your own life, ask yourself how your relationship with them had an impact on you or on them. Did you learn anything from them, or they from you? Did the friendship itself improve in some interesting or dramatic way? Or was it shattered by events? Did the relationship lead to a surprising discovery about yourself, the other person, or a third person? Did any of these individuals change your attitude in a positive and growing way or, conversely, a negative way that created bitterness or resentment? Did it affect your development for the better or worse?

While examining these possibilities, take notes and use the actual names of people and places. Since you are exploring aspects of your own life, the notes you take are private. Keep them in your journal.

In addition to personal relationships, consider places that have stayed in your memory. Someone else's home, perhaps, or a shopping plaza, or a vacant lot where you used to play. A view from a car window or a kitchen seen only once may have lingered in your memory with extraordinary sharpness. If so, they have remained for a reason. If you have studied the poem by Deppe on page 218, notice the highly significant use of the landscape at the opening and closing of that poem.

Once you have characters, a situation, and a setting to work with, you are like a carpenter who has gathered the materials needed for construction. It may be that the outline of a story will come to you at this point. If so, you're in luck. But creative writing tends to be much sloppier than building a house. Don't worry if you don't have a clear plot plan and theme in mind. All you need is more material than you can ever use and the faith that somehow your story will begin to take shape. With these you are finally ready to start writing fiction.

TRANSFORMATION: THE TRIGGER THAT TURNS FACTS INTO FICTION

Recalling the people, places, and experiences of your life is a natural first step in the creative process, but this material is a collection of facts, not fiction. Although some published stories may seem like camcorder re-creations from the author's life, they almost never are. All that raw material has to go through a process of transformation.

Transformation refers to basic alterations of events, characters, viewpoints, or settings — occasionally all four. It is so fundamental and so primary that it is sometimes referred to as a process of **metamorphosis**, a basic change in plot, setting, or characterization.

Unconscious transformation often alters our memories even before we begin to plan a story. Without being aware of doing so, we block certain events and highlight others. We alter chronological sequences, forget that certain characters were present, shift scenes. For evidence of this phenomenon, listen to two people describe the same vacation trip. In a more serious vein, read the sworn testimony of different witnesses to the same crime.

In casual conversation we often restructure memory to protect our own egos, maintain modesty, get a laugh, clarify or dramatize an incident. Indeed, we are often *expected* to alter events. "Come on," someone says when we take too long telling a story, "get to the point."

Unconscious transformation of memory can occasionally work against us. We may be censoring an experience by making a fictional character kinder, wiser, or more moral than the model on which she or he is based. That kind of unconscious transformation can sanitize an experience or a character, making the story too bland or too vague.

We all tend to be shy when we contemplate writing about our friends and relatives. We are apt to have feelings about them that we don't want to advertise. Even if we feel very close to a parent, friend, or lover, we also see aspects in him or her that are less than perfect. Occasionally, we may even spot aspects of ourselves that are less than perfect. Most of us can recall a number of incidents we would never reveal to a friend, much less to total strangers. How can we put these on paper for everyone to read?

More serious, unconscious censorship may prevent us from getting started at all. What is described as *writer's block* is frequently a reluctance to deal with material that is still too close and personal.

The solution to these problems is *conscious transformation*. Don't confuse this with *revision*, a more subtle process that doesn't start until you have completed the first draft. Transformation is the first step in converting those bits and pieces of factual data floating around in your memory into a coherent narrative known as fiction. It involves restructuring, reordering, and a good deal of fabrication.

Conscious transformation should come early in the creative process because it is what frees you from the actual events, the people, and the setting in your memory. Until you start willfully reshaping those details, you will remain loyal to your memory. Transformation changes how you view your work. No longer will you see it as a journal entry about you and your life; it is now an artistic creation with a life of its own. It is fiction.

To begin, change the names of your characters. This is essential if you are going to give them fictional identities of their own. Fictional names will also help free you from the events as they occurred. As a general rule, fictional names are more memorable if they are slightly unusual and varied in length. Leave Dick, Jane, and their dog Spot for the younger generation. My apologies to those with popular names, but we are talking about fiction here.

If you still feel overly influenced by the people you have selected as models, change the physical appearance of their fictional counterparts. If the person you have in mind is fat in reality, consider making the fictional version thin; if his wife is actually tall, you might make her short. More radical, consider changing the gender of a character. This may seem impossible at first, but sometimes it is easier than you might think — especially with children. One note of caution: when refashioning characters, be careful not to picture them as flawlessly beautiful or handsome. Such absolutes are what gave Hollywood a bad name.

Often the events may have to be transformed as well. Highly personal episodes may have to be refashioned to release you from an understandable reticence. Consider presenting the story through the eyes of a character not based on yourself. Painful childhood memories, for example, can be made manageable by telling the story through the eyes of a parent or a sibling.

Changing the setting is another possibility. Moving the story to another locale is a basic transformation that in some cases creates a fresh vision.

How much transformation is necessary? Sometimes very little. But there are two warning signs that are clear indications that more alterations are needed. First, if you find yourself referring to your **protagonist** as "I" and to your other characters by the names of their actual models, you are still thinking of the piece as factual writing. Second, if you catch yourself saying, "I can't have them do that; it just didn't happen that way," you're in trouble. There is no clearer indication that you still feel limited to the events as they occurred. Keep changing the factual details until you feel in control. That's when your creative imagination takes over. That's when your loyalty shifts to the literary work itself. You are now writing fiction.

LITERARY SHAPING

Essentially, transformation of people, events, and setting is a psychological necessity. It's a first step. The next step is shaping the material so that it will make the best possible short story.

Even though you have transformed the events as they occurred and re-created them into a fictional plot, they may still be cluttered by details left over from the original experience. Fragments of personal experience left in a story for no good literary reason are essentially junk details. At best, such details are mere clutter; at worst, they can mislead the reader by appearing to give importance to something that actually contributes nothing to the story. What you leave in should have a purpose even if it is subtle.

To achieve this clarity of purpose, you may have to shift or consolidate scenes and invent action and dialogue not because that's the way the event occurred but because that's what the story needs.

The same is true of characters. You have already transformed them from their original appearance and given them their own fictional names, but you may find that further changes will be necessary so they will contribute to the literary work. For example, a character may have to be toned down to keep him or her from dominating a story. Or another may have to be developed and dramatized. The more you write fiction, the more you will be able to fuse two people you know into a single fictional character. There may be times when you come to know one of your fictional characters so well you forget who the original model was.

Initially, the **theme** or central concern of a story may take shape without much thought. But after completing the first draft, ask yourself just what the story is suggesting about our lives or our society. See if you can phrase this in a complete sentence. You may want to shape your material — expanding one section, cutting others — to clarify what you want the story to suggest.

Suppose, for example, you are writing about a couple and their two adolescent children driving to a distant beach on a hot August day. The car breaks down on a city street miles from home. Such an incident (perhaps originally suggested by personal experience) has the feel of a short story because it is vivid and has the potential for both conflict and the resolution of conflict. But what aspect will serve as the best thematic center? It's up to you as a writer to determine what will make the best story. Here are some alternatives:

1. Focus on the father. Develop him as a husband who over the years has taken his wife for granted but discovers to his chagrin that she handles a crisis like this better than he. He loses his temper, but his rage, the story suggests, is less directed against the car than it is against her for being so competent.

2. Focus on the mother and highlight her relationship with their normally rebellious adolescent daughter. In this version, the father is all but eliminated by having him go in search of a garage, and the son is simply deleted on the grounds that the story is too short to handle all four characters. Mother and daughter start to bicker, but the shared heat and boredom actually bring them together in a new though slightly grudging acceptance of the other.

3. Focus on the son by satirizing a totally incompetent father and a domineering mother. The son understandably leaves the family and hitchhikes back on his own. He makes it home late that night but only after being mugged. Broke and humiliated, he expects punishment, but instead is greeted with tears of concern. Astonished, he realizes his parents aren't quite as awful as he used to think.

4. A more radical reshaping might focus on the girl and drop the rest of the family. Make her 18 and the driver a self-assured 24-year-old boyfriend. The car breaks down, and he tries unsuccessfully to determine the trouble. She discovers a burned-out fuse and replaces it. He appears to be impressed, but then sulks all the way home. She does her best to cheer him up by flattering his abilities. She appears to succeed, but as he drops her off at her house she is disgusted at his childishness and the compliant role she has played and tells him that she doesn't want to see him again.

These four stories could have sprung from the same experience. Each went through a process of basic transformation so the author could see them as fiction, and then each was reviewed to see which could be shaped into the best possible story. These decisions will be partly based on personal preferences but also on literary judgments. Those who have read a lot of fiction have an advantage in making literary decisions like these.

There may be times when such basic restructuring will make you feel that the entire story is crumbling before your very eyes. Too much choice can be a problem. In that case, try to reestablish what it was that drew you to the incident in the first place. That is, rediscover the personal connection.

As these examples show, good fiction almost never starts with an abstract idea. It is launched with a situation involving characters interacting with each other. It is energized with some type of conflict. Once the transformations break the connection with experience, you are free to work on the story as a literary creation.

8 Escapes

A Story

by Ann Hood

What I do with my niece Jennifer is this. I ride the cable cars again and again, paying four dollars each time. She is fourteen and gets a thrill hanging off the side of the car as it plunges down San Francisco's steep hills. She says it is like flying, and indeed the wind does pick up her Esprit scarf, the one decorated with purple and yellow palm trees, and tosses it stiffly backward in the same way that Charles Lindbergh's scarves appear in old flying photos of him.

I take her to Candlestick Park for the Giants' last game of the season and sit shivering under an old blanket I bought in Mexico long ago. Jennifer does not understand baseball, but I try to explain it to her. Three outs to an inning, nine innings to a game, the importance of a good shortstop. But she does not get it. When Chris Sabo of the Reds strikes out she says, "Caryn, why is it still their turn? You said three outs to an inning."

"But three strikes," I tell her, "is just one out." Jennifer shakes her head and closes her eyes for the rest of the game. Even when I shake her and say, "Look! A home run!" she keeps her eyes closed, does not move.

We spend an entire day at the Esprit factory outlet. Jennifer fills a shopping cart with bargains. She is tall, like her father, my brother, was. She is fourteen and already almost six feet, and so thin that her hip bones poke out from her faded blue jeans. She does not have to wear a bra. She keeps her hair long, so that it flies around her head like a golden cloud. One of the saleswomen asks Jennifer if she is a model. "Me?" Jennifer says, confused, embarrassed. She slouches even more than usual and shakes her yellow hair. Then she walks away. But when we go into the dressing room and she sees that there is no privacy, no curtains or doors, that everyone is standing half-naked in front of mirrors, Jennifer leaves her shopping cart and walks out of the store without trying on a thing.

What I do not do is mention Jennifer's arms. Tiny uneven scars creep up her wrists like a child's sloppy cross-stitch. She wears long-sleeved blouses, and dozens of tiny bracelets, but still the scars peek through. I pretend that Jennifer's wrists are as smooth as the rest of her. That the scars are not even there. I don't ask her any questions about it. Instead, I take her to the Top of the Mark at sunset. I bring her to Seal Rock where we stare through telescopes at the sea lions sunning themselves.

Right before Jennifer came to stay with me, my boyfriend, Luke, left. He said he needed to try his luck in New York. Maybe, he said, he'd become really famous there. Like Laurence Olivier. That was in August and I haven't heard from him since.

Sherry, Jennifer's mother, called me on a Saturday morning in late September and said, "You've got to take her. She's been kicked out of school. Sell her. Adopt her. I don't care. Just take her. I'm going nuts." I looked out my window at the California sky, a bluer, higher sky than anywhere else in the world. Since Luke left, I hadn't done much of anything except swim two miles a day, go to work at the tiny magazine office on Polk Street where I'm a copy editor and dream of where to escape to next. Sometimes, I rented old movies, ones with Barbara Stanwyk and Joan Crawford in them. Ones that forced me to cry.

While I looked at the sky I thought about my life as a flat straight line like a dead person's heart on a monitor. Sherry told me that Jennifer was really out of hand now. "And I have my studies to worry about," Sherry added. She was in travel-agent school. On weekends, she got to take junkets to Puerto Vallarta and New Orleans.

I had not seen Jennifer in almost two years when Sherry called me that day. My brother Daniel had been dead for almost ten years. So I'm still not sure what made me say yes, I'll take her for a while. Except for maybe the thought of sharing that ultrablue sky with someone seemed so appealing, and the thought of a few bleeps and peaks in my life seemed like a good idea.

Before she hung up, Sherry said, "Don't feel compelled to talk about her cutting her wrists or anything. She wants to put that behind her."

"What?" I said. Had I missed something here? I thought. Jennifer had cut her wrists? They say suicide is contagious and Daniel had done it, hung himself in his jail cell where he was serving time for dealing drugs. "I thought you weren't going to tell her," I told Sherry. We had invented a story when it happened to Daniel. He was in a car accident, we'd decided. He fell asleep at the wheel.

"I didn't," she said. "It must run in your family or something."

"It does not," I said, wishing I had not agreed to take Jennifer. What did I know about teenagers? Or suicide? Or anything at all?

On Fisherman's Wharf, Jennifer buys more bracelets. They are copper or gold, with tiny beads in the center or chunks of stones, turquoise and amethyst. I wait, bored, gazing at the Golden Gate Bridge while she chooses them from the street vendors that line the sidewalks. She has been with me for two weeks and shows no signs of leaving. Yesterday, she got a postcard from Sherry in Acapulco, written entirely in Spanish. She read it, her face a blank, then tossed it in the trash. "I didn't know you could read Spanish," I told her.

"I can't," Jennifer said.

Jennifer loves all the tourist trap things around the wharf. She spends hours in the souvenir shops and pushing her way through the crowds. She does not smile much, but here her face softens and I almost expect her to break into a grin. Daniel was a great smiler. And so was Sherry. But their daughter's face is set and hard. A mask.

"What's that?" she asks me as we eat our crab cocktails at the crowded food stall. We are crushed against a family of tourists wearing identical pink-and-blue striped sweatshirts, all fresh-faced and blond.

I look at where she is pointing, across the bay.

"Alcatraz," I tell her.

She frowns. "Alcatraz."

"It was a maximum-security prison."

"Can we go there?" she asks me. Her eyes are topaz. They remind me of a tiger's.

"Maybe next week," I sigh, tired of sight-seeing.

"Okay," Jennifer says, fixing her eyes on the hunk of rock in the water. Around her neck, a charm on a chain catches in the sun. A cable car.

"That's pretty," I say. "When did you buy it?"

She looks at me now. "You can have it if you want," she says. She slips the chain over her head and holds it out to me.

"No, that's okay," I tell her.

But she is putting it on me even as I protest. The little gold cable car settles against my collarbone. I feel guilty for not wanting to take her to see Alcatraz and I promise myself we'll definitely go next week. If she hasn't gone home to Miami by then.

I get a letter from Luke in New York. It is written on paper with his initials on the top, and sounds like it is from a stranger. He tells me about the weather there, and how difficult it is to figure out the subway system. He signs the letter "Sincerely, Luke."

"Who's Luke?" Jennifer asks me.

I did not show her the letter, so I figure she has been looking through my things. Somehow, this does not even make me angry. My tiny apartment on Fourth Avenue has been so lonely that the idea of sharing it and everything in it makes me almost happy. For a while, Luke's shirts were crammed into my one closet, his deodorant and toothbrush and comb cluttered my bathroom. Now, Jennifer's things are mingling with mine. When I turn off the bathroom light, her toothbrush glows orange. Her multitude of bracelets are everywhere I look, as if they are actually reproducing.

So I tell her who Luke is without mentioning that she really shouldn't be reading my letters.

"Did you love him?" she asks me.

I only shrug. "Who knows?" I say.

"Did my mother love my father?" she asks then, suddenly.

I answer, "Yes," immediately, but then I wonder about my answer. To me, Sherry and Daniel were like Bonnie and Clyde. They were always doing something illegal. Their apartment was filled with an air of danger. Once, in a kitchen drawer, I saw dozens of stolen credit cards. Their cars disappeared mysteriously. They kept scales and spoons and plastic bags where other people kept pots and pans. How do I know that they loved each other? But Jennifer seems satisfied with my easy answer.

Jennifer says, "Some things don't make sense to me. Like why was my father in a car in Pennsylvania when we lived in Miami? And why aren't there any pictures of us all together?"

"I don't know," I tell her. "I was away at the time." I don't fill in the details, that I was living in St. Thomas, serving tropical drinks and soaking up the sun until my skin turned very brown.

She studies my face for a long time, searching for something that I can't give her.

When Sherry calls I ask her when she will take Jennifer back. "She should go to school," I tell her.

"She'll be expelled again anyway. She steals from kids' lockers, takes whatever she wants. Can you believe it?"

I feel like both Jennifer and Sherry are hiding things from me, giving me little bits and pieces but keeping the big parts to themselves. I try to imagine Sherry in the small pink house she and Jennifer live in. Jennifer has told me that they have orange trees in their backyard, and a plastic pink flamingo on their lawn. I can see Sherry there, in her high-heeled sandals and platinum hair. I used to think she looked exactly like my old Barbie doll, all pointy breasts and tiny waist. Her hair is blond like Jennifer's, but bleached and molded into a tight bubble. That is how I imagine her as she talks to me now, a Barbie doll in her Florida toy house, surrounded by bougainvillea and orange blossoms, staring blankly at a plastic lawn ornament.

"She is nothing but trouble," Sherry is telling me. "Stealing and cheating on tests. She actually copied a *Time* magazine article about Houdini and handed it in as her report on a famous person. Like the teacher wouldn't know someone else wrote it."

Jennifer is stretched out on my couch, lazily flipping through a magazine. She does not seem to be listening to the conversation.

"Well," I ask Sherry, "what's the problem?"

"Who knows? I'm trying to make a better life for us. Travel agents get discount tickets and hotels. We could see the whole world if we wanted to."

Over the years, Sherry has learned many skills. She was a licensed electrologist, removing women's mustaches and shaping their eyebrows. She booked bands for a nightclub and tried her hand at calligraphy. None of it worked as well as her days with Daniel breaking the law.

"I would think she'd want to travel," I say. It was all that I used to want, my way of getting out of tough spots, of leaving men and looking for new ones.

Sherry laughs. "All she wants is to make trouble. But you say she's being good there, so let her stay for a bit more."

I want to explain that I am tired of Jennifer being here. That she is not really helping me decide what to do next. That I have an urge, once more, to pick up and go. To L.A., maybe. Or even Hawaii. Luke signed his letter "Sincerely" and I want to run.

But I say none of these things. I just stare at Jennifer and wonder how she could have actually done it to herself. How she felt when it didn't work. From Miami, Sherry makes excuses for having to hang up. She doesn't ask to speak to her daughter, and I don't offer.

"Wow," Jennifer says when I take her to my tiny, cramped office. "Look at all of these places." She touches the photographs that line my desk and walls and shelves. Pictures of Peru and British Columbia, of people climbing a frozen waterfall and of seals in the Galápagos Islands.

From my window, I can see hookers on the corner, a man drinking something from a paper bag. They call this area of the city the Tenderloin. That sounds gentle to me. Tender loins. This is not a gentle place.

"Have you been to all these places?" Jennifer asks me. She holds out a picture of a dense jungle. She has on a new ring, a thin gold one with two hearts dangling from it.

"No," I tell her. "I just put them in the magazine."

"If I could," she says, still clutching at the jungle photograph, "I would go everywhere. Around the world. I'd even volunteer to go on the space shuttle."

I frown, thinking about Sherry. "When your mother finishes travel-agent school—"

Jennifer laughs. "She'll never finish. She never finishes anything."

"She told me you were expelled from school," I say softly.

Now Jennifer sighs. "I was. I'd rather stow away on a ship than go to school every day. There's nothing there."

"She told me—"

"Whatever she told you is true," Jennifer says firmly.

"Oh."

My eyes drift to her wrists, to her bracelets and beneath them, to her scars.

"Caryn," Jennifer says, "what was he doing in Pennsylvania? What was his job?"

I hesitate. His job was dealing drugs, I say in my mind.

Jennifer laughs again. "My mother says I'm a wild thing. She says I'm like my father." She leans out the open window, too far out. My heart seems to slow down, to freeze. I think, she is jumping from this fifth-floor window but I can't reach out in time to grab her. Then she pulls herself back in, and looks at me as if she didn't just dangle five stories.

"I like looking out," she says. And then she smiles. A smile that makes her face look like it hurts.

Somewhere, I have a map of Hawaii. I will find it, I decide, and study it. I will make plans for a new life in the shadow of a volcano. I've served drinks before at seaside resorts. I can do it again. The names of the islands are magical. Maui and Kauai. For days, the fog here in San Francisco has been thick as mashed potatoes and it is starting to depress me. Every morning, Jennifer is staring at me, waiting for answers. It's time, I think, to move.

I search my drawers but the map is gone. What I find instead are handfuls of jewelry: the bracelets Jennifer likes to wear, and thick ropes of rose quartz and yellow jade, and earrings made of dangling crystals and rings in all sizes. There is no way that Jennifer could have bought all of this jewelry. Where would she get the money? I lay everything out across my bed, and it sparkles and winks at me in the late-afternoon light. Then I put it all away.

The fog is still thick on the day we go to Alcatraz. We wait in line, then crowd onto the ferry. I have paid an extra dollar for us to get the recorded tour, which comes from a bright-yellow Walkman and clunky headphones that make us look like Martians. Jennifer is wearing a Cal Berkeley sweatshirt and a boy asks her if she goes there.

"I'm in ninth grade," she tells him.

The boy walks away.

On the island, we walk through the steps that the tour instructs us to take. Stop at the sign that says DINING HALL, we are told. Take a right on Michigan Avenue. Stand under the clock. Look at the pictures on the wall. We do whatever the voice tells us, like robots. Jennifer's tape is two steps ahead of mine, and every time I approach her it seems she has to walk on to somewhere else.

The recorded voice tells us how on New Year's Eve, the prisoners could hear music and laughter from a yacht club across the bay.

We step inside a cell and pretend we are in solitary confinement. All around us, families snap pictures of each other behind bars. I stand in my cell in the dark and close my eyes. The voice tells me about the cold, damp air here. About all the tricks inmates used to help them get through solitary. Throw a button on the floor and try to find it in the dark. Imagine entire movies.

I can feel Jennifer come and stand beside me, I can smell the perfume she wears all the time. She takes my hand in hers.

"Imagine being locked in here and knowing that San Francisco is right across the bay," she says. "Hearing people at a party."

I open my eyes. "But we can walk out," I tell her. "We're not in solitary."

"I know," she says. "But imagine."

We are way behind on our tapes now. And we have to fast forward to catch up. Quickly, Jennifer and I go through the prison, poking our heads into cells and rooms, until we find the rest of the tour. We are at the end, listening to a description of escapes from Alcatraz.

There were many that failed, the voice croons in my ears, and only one that perhaps was successful. I listen to the details of that escape, of how the men collected hair from the barber shop floor to use on papier-mâché masks of their faces. How they dug for months to get through the prison walls to an air shaft. They were never found, the tape tells me.

Jennifer and I stand on the top of Alcatraz, looking out. Her hair is blowing wildly in the cold breeze, but she does not try to control it, to hold it down.
"I know you took all that jewelry," I tell her. "I know you stole it."
She doesn't answer me. I cannot see her face under her blowing hair.
Finally, she says, "I like to think they made it."
"Who?"
"Those three men who tried to escape. Maybe one of them didn't drown. Maybe at least one of them is free."
I gaze down the rock to the water pounding the shore. I don't agree with her. I think they must have all died down there.
"About that jewelry," I say.
She turns to me. "Here," she says. "Take it." She unclasps each bracelet, letting them drop into my hands.
"I don't want them," I tell her. "That's not the point."
But she keeps taking them off, until finally she has bare arms, and all of her crooked scars are revealed. She is standing before me, arms turned upward, naked of all the turquoise and amethyst and copper.
I take her wrists in my hands, lightly. There are so many questions I could ask her. So many things I want to know. But what I realize, standing there, feeling the bumps of her skin under my hands, is that there really is no escaping. Not for Sherry, not for Jennifer, not for me. The only thing left to do is to stick it out.
Jennifer's eyes are set right on me. She says, "If I really wanted to do it, I would have made the cuts deeper. And up and down instead of across. No one understands that I knew the real way. The right way. But I just wanted to see what would happen, to faint or go away for a little while."
"It's not worth it," I say. "Sooner or later you have to come back."
She nods. There are tears in her eyes, but they could be from the stinging salty air, like mine. The ferry is chugging toward us, and still holding on to each other we slowly make our way down that rock.
We stand in the line, waiting for the ferry to take us back.
Suddenly I turn to Jennifer. "Your father did it," I say. "He hung himself."
Her expression doesn't change at all.
"He was in prison," I continue. "For drugs. And he killed himself."
"I know," she says. "I found the death certificate last year when we moved. I wanted my mother to tell me the truth."
I say, "That's the truth."
The ferry arrives, and we move forward, toward it. Its steps are steep, and we have to link arms for the climb.

9 Viewpoint

Who's Seeing This?

• *Viewpoint (means of perception): the character through whose eyes we see the action (60)* • *The advantages of a single means of perception (61)* • *The technique of withholding information in "Escapes" (61)* • *Multiple viewpoints (62)* • *Testing alternative viewpoints (63)* • *First or third person? (64)* • *The focus of the story (65)* • *Reviewing your options (66)*

Fiction, unlike drama or film, is presented through the eyes of a specific character. What we see and hear are what that character sees and hears. We enter his or her mind, but we can only guess what the other characters are thinking.

When we choose to write a story in the first person, the viewpoint is necessarily the **narrator**, the character who appears to be speaking or recalling the events. The narrator refers to him- or herself as "I." For example, "I looked at my grandfather, wondering if the old man had understood." The reader knows only as much as the narrator does.

When we use the third person, the narrator is referred to as "he" or "she," but generally the viewpoint is also limited to a single character: "The boy looked at his grandfather, wondering if the old man had understood." The **viewpoint** is that of the boy. We know what he is wondering and so we are "in his head." We don't know what the grandfather is thinking, and if the story continues with a single point of view, as most do, we readers, like the boy, will not find out what went on in the grandfather's head until the old man reveals his thoughts through what he says or through his actions.

The terms **viewpoint**, **point of view**, and **means of perception** are synonymous, so I will use them interchangeably. But don't confuse the literary use of *point of view* with its other use referring to *attitude*, as in "from the British point of view." Remember that when applied to fiction *point of view* is a precise literary concept — and an important one.

THE ADVANTAGES OF A SINGLE MEANS OF PERCEPTION

A great majority of short stories and many novels limit the means of perception to a single character. It's possible, of course, to use more than one viewpoint. To go back to our example, one could have the next sentence read, "Actually the old man was thinking about supper and hadn't heard a word the boy had said." Possible, but few stories take that route. The single means of perception has been the dominant approach in short stories since the 19th century. There are exceptions — especially in novels — which I will describe shortly, but they are rare.

This apparent restriction bothers some beginning writers because it seems limiting. There are, however, three distinct advantages to limiting the means of perception to a single character:

- First, the limited means of perception tends to increase the reader's sense of identification with the story's central character. One of the pleasures of reading fiction is being drawn into the situation. This capacity to enter a story, known as "the willing suspension of disbelief," is not necessarily generated by feelings of sympathy or respect for the central character. As readers we can easily imagine ourselves as a reprehensible individual. How else can we experience what it's like to be a criminal, a monk, or a member of the opposite sex? We simply imagine ourselves as someone else. This is why we sometimes describe reading as being "under the spell" of a compelling story.

  When the viewpoint shifts from one character to another, the reader has to shift gears with each transition. Those shifts "break the spell" briefly. This is particularly true of the short-short story.
- Second, a limited means of perception makes it easier to arouse the reader's curiosity. Suppose in our fictional example the grandfather was pretending not to understand because he was planning to steal the boy's winning lottery ticket. Revealing this too early by entering his mind exposes his true character too soon and may well wipe out the reader's question about his true motives and character. While essays often announce the theme right at the start, stories are more likely to reveal the truth in bits like luring pigeons one grain at a time. In fiction, what we as authors withhold from the reader is as important as what we reveal.
- Finally, a single viewpoint often helps to prepare for a climax. Not all stories end on a dramatic note, but most reveal some important insight that has been held back. Withholding information in the writing of a story is like keeping secrets, and we all know how difficult it is to do that if you have told more than one person.

THE TECHNIQUE OF WITHHOLDING INFORMATION IN "ESCAPES"

"Escapes" is an excellent example of how a single means of perception helps the author to withhold information until she is ready to reveal it. Early in the story we are as baffled as the protagonist, Caryn, as to why Jennifer, who obviously loves shopping, abruptly leaves her heaping shopping cart in the dressing room and "walks out of the store without trying on a thing." Had the author decided to reveal Jennifer's feelings, she might have felt obliged to add, "Jennifer knew that there was no way she was going to reveal the scars on her wrist in a room with no privacy." Instead, the story reveals the facts about Jennifer's wrist cutting in stages, maintaining the reader's curiosity.

Notice that when the cutting is revealed, it is through dialogue. Jennifer's mother says on the phone, " 'Don't feel compelled to talk about her cutting her wrists or anything. She wants to put that behind her.' " We learn this just as Caryn does, and we are jolted just as she is.

In the same way, the fact that Jennifer has been shoplifting regularly is not revealed until Caryn discovers it toward the end of the story. By that time we can see the parallel with Jennifer's parents who seemed to Caryn "like Bonnie and Clyde . . . always doing something illegal."

The entire process of learning the facts in small stages is expressed directly through Caryn's thoughts: "I feel like both Jennifer and Sherry are hiding things from me, giving me little bits and pieces but keeping the big parts to themselves." This also applies to how the author keeps hiding things to maintain the reader's curiosity. It's an approach that is made easier by having the story presented through the mind of a single character.

MULTIPLE VIEWPOINTS

Although most fiction is presented through a single means of perception, some use multiple viewpoints. Most examples are in novels that are presented in the third person. Because of a novel's length, the psychological jolt that occurs when the means of perception shifts from one character to another is less obtrusive. Even in a novel, however, that break has some of the same effect as a shift of scenes in a play. For this reason, most novelists select only two or three characters to serve as the alternating means of perception. Often entire chapters are presented through the eyes of one character rather than shifting frequently. Only occasionally is the same technique used in short stories.

Another form of a divided means of perception is when the author in a third-person work steps in and presents information or opinions. This is called **author's intrusion**. The term doesn't refer to those minor bits of exposition that simply fill in background or provide a transition to a new scene. "He had served in the Infantry for three years before returning to college . . ." for example, provides factual information without being intrusive.

True author's intrusion presents the author's views or provides information not known by the protagonist. In the 18th and 19th centuries it was not at all unusual to have detailed commentary on a character ("He was a dour gentleman with a military man's high regard for order") or generalized observations ("Such outrageous behavior is rarely condoned these days").

This approach has become less popular today because the trend has been away from the impression of listening to a narrated story, replaced by the illusion of entering a story directly as you do when watching a film.

When one starts writing fiction there is sometimes a temptation to use author's intrusion at the opening and closing of stories. This is a natural inclination due to the years of training we have all had writing essays in which we state the theme at the opening and rephrase it at the end. But fiction, as you know, is not factual writing. The reader of fiction comes to know characters and see thematic patterns indirectly through the action and dialogue.

Remember too that when we write the first draft of a story we are still thinking about what the theme of the story will be. The introductory paragraph may well be a note to yourself. Quite often that analytical first paragraph and the summarizing last paragraph can be chopped off, allowing the reader to draw conclusions from the plot and the dialogue.

Because author's intrusion has been out of fashion for so long, it now seems fresh and innovative when employed skillfully. You will see an unusual and effective example in the opening paragraph of "Obst Vw," the story that appears in Chapter 16. Look for it.

As we write, we as authors are **omniscient** because we are (or ought to be) all-knowing. We know everything about our characters and what will become of them. Because we choose what we will reveal at each stage of the story, the approach is often referred to as *limited omniscience*. Remember, though, that the choice of what to reveal is up to you.

TESTING ALTERNATIVE VIEWPOINTS

When you start a new story, there is a tendency to stay with the viewpoint that first occurred to you. Nine times out of ten, this will be the right route. Still, you can't be sure whether you're missing an even more effective approach unless you visualize your material with alternative viewpoints. Even if you stay with your original conception, the very act of imagining the material through different viewpoints often generates new insights.

What, for example, would happen if we shifted the point of view in "Escapes"? Set aside the question of whether a transformation might be less effective. Simply consider how a particular change would affect the story.

If you review the opening of the story, you will see how easily those first two paragraphs could be converted to Jennifer's point of view. It might start out like this:

> I ride the cable cars again and again. My aunt seems willing to pay the four dollars each time. Like any fourteen-year-old kid, I get a thrill hanging off the side of the car . . .

If you shift the means of perception to Jennifer, however, you would lose the opportunity of arousing the reader's curiosity early in the story. You would have to reveal her feelings when she refuses to try on the clothes in the dressing room for fear of showing the scars on her wrist. This would not be disastrous, but it would be a missed opportunity.

In the same way, you would miss the jolt that comes when her mother, Sherry, says to Caryn on the telephone, " 'Don't feel compelled to talk about her cutting her wrists . . .' " Again, by itself this would not be a problem, but it is another missed opportunity.

Like any such fundamental shift in the means of perception, there are assets and liabilities. There might be an advantage in giving the reader more insights about Jennifer's relationship with her mother and her rebellious behavior in school. But you would miss the opportunity to reveal her background and emotions in stages like peeling an onion.

Once you have completed the first draft of a story, it will probably seem as if it couldn't possibly be presented through the eyes of another character. The time to test different alternatives in point of view is in the early stages of planning.

FIRST OR THIRD PERSON?

It does make a difference whether you cast a story in the first **person**, using "I," or in the third person, referring to your protagonist as "he" or "she." But the difference is more subtle than you might imagine. Oddly, it is sometimes difficult to remember whether a story you read the day before used the first or third person.

Here is the opening of "Escapes" converted to the third person:

> What she does with her niece Jennifer is this. She rides the cable cars again and again, paying the four dollars each time. Jennifer is fourteen and gets a thrill hanging off the side of the car as it plunges down San Francisco's steep hills.

The only change in wording other than "I" to "she" is the second use of "Jennifer" since there might be confusion there by using "she."

Clearly this story could have been written either way. Converting it would be easy. You might find yourself using the names of the two characters more often since "she" in some cases might be confusing (such as in the opening). The reader would hardly notice. Shifting from first to third person is far less radical than changing the means of perception.

Still, it is worth reading the first page of a new story in both ways. Your initial choice may be the right one, but there are advantages to each that are worth considering.

One good reason for using the first person is that you may want to maintain the naiveté or innocence of a protagonist. In the case of "Escapes," Caryn is getting into a situation that is far more complicated and demanding than she had thought. The stages she goes through getting to know Jennifer are the same stages the reader goes through. Even more subtle, she gradually learns more about her own needs. These are also revealed to the reader in steps, right up to the ending when she and the reader realize that each of them will need each other as they ". . . move forward . . ." and have to ". . . link arms for the climb."

Another advantage of using the first person is that you can adopt the tone of a story being narrated out loud. Such stories occasionally identify a listener, but more often they do not. The illusion is usually created by word choice and phrasing. Very few authors indulge in phonetic spellings like "goin' " for "going" and " 'em" for "them" because spelling changes easily become obtrusive. But you can suggest a regional or foreign accent through phrasing without altering the spelling of a single word.

The first person is also useful when the primary point of the story is to ridicule or satirize the narrator. You can achieve an effective **irony** when characters try to justify or defend themselves in ways that actually damn them in the reader's eyes.

Oddly, the first person may not be the right choice for a story based on an event that is recent and is recalled with highly charged feelings. To put this more positively, using the third person is an excellent way of holding material at arm's length. If you have just broken up with someone who was important to you or are trying to deal with a recent death, try transforming the event by selecting the third person. And if doing that doesn't work, shift the means of perception.

The greatest advantage of the third person is flexibility. The writer can withhold information just as easily as with the first person but in addition can occasionally insert background information.

The popular notion that the first person provides a sense of immediacy or realism that cannot be achieved in the third person is not justified. Readers enter a story using "he" or "she" just as easily as they do one that begins with "I." But the decision of which to use should not be made carelessly. Although your first inclination may be entirely justified, consider the alternative. If in doubt, convert a sample paragraph from first person to third or the reverse fairly early in the writing.

THE FOCUS OF THE STORY

The **focus** of a story is the character who is the central concern. It is the answer to the question, "Who is this story really about?" Don't confuse focus with **viewpoint**. In many cases, the character through whose eyes you are seeing the events is also the focus of the story, but not always.

It is possible, for example, to write a story essentially about a father as seen through the eyes of his son. Or a story that focuses on the marriage of a young couple could be written from the point of view of the mother-in-law.

"Escapes" is an interesting example of a story with a double focus. You might assume on your first reading that Caryn is the focus since the story is told through her eyes. But look at the title. "Escapes" is plural. There are two people involved. Then look at the ending again. It does not say "I move forward" as it might if this was a story about Caryn alone. The wording is ". . . we move forward . . ." and just so you won't miss the significance of that, the last sentence ends with ". . . we have to link arms for the climb." The climb to what? The climb toward putting their lives together. The focus of this story is on two people who are about to escape the past. This is no Hollywood ending, however; those prisoners who tried to escape Alcatraz remind us that the task will be challenging.

Focus is also closely tied to **theme**, an aspect I'll return to in Chapter 21. The thematic focus of "Escapes" might be described as the need to reach out to others. Our concern here, however, is the means of perception and the fact that it may or may not be the most important character.

REVIEWING YOUR OPTIONS

When a story idea first comes to you, it will probably be a mix of personal experience and invention. Let it run through your head like a daydream. Don't concern yourself at this early stage about the means of perception, person, and focus. If you analyze too much too soon, you may lose the feel of the story.

There will come a point, however, when it seems as if you have enough to work with. This is when some writers like to make a few notes about plot and characters so they won't lose the original concept. This is also when you should consider alternative strategies of presentation. Transforming a story by altering the point of view or the focus is a lot easier when it is still in your head than it is when a draft is down on paper or on your computer screen.

Shifting a story from third person to first or the reverse is not as radical a transformation as changing the means of perception. But as we have seen, it involves more than changing "I" to "he" or "she." If you have any doubts about which approach is most appropriate for a particular story, take the time to write a paragraph each way. To a large degree, this is an intuitive choice.

Focus, on the other hand, is fundamental. It requires that you know which character (or pair of characters) is your primary concern. It also requires that you examine the theme or central concern of the story. Make every effort to get these aspects right. Have you turned the spotlight on the right character? Do you really know what the story is suggesting?

Sometimes you may be inclined to forge ahead with the first draft without being sure, and there are writers who recommend doing this. But hiking without a map or compass has its risks. Whatever you do, develop a clear focus before you ask others to spend valuable time reading the draft. Claiming that it should mean whatever readers want it to mean is simply asking them to do your work.

One final note of reassurance: there will be times when in spite of your most careful efforts you will discover late in the development of a story that the means of perception really should be changed. Or, worse, you may realize that the character you had thought was the focus of a developing story is not the true subject. All your efforts may seem to crumble. It's panic time!

If this happens to you, here are four first-aid steps that may make the difference between life and death for the story:

1. Don't tear up the draft. Hollywood movies show frustrated writers ripping pages from the typewriter and crumpling them. Don't. The draft may look better in the morning. Besides, hitting the delete key doesn't have the dramatic impact of crumpling sheets of paper.

2. With regard to the means of perception, simply rewrite the first page with the viewpoint changed. You can tell far better from writing an actual sample than you can by trying to analyze the situation in the abstract. See if your sample page *feels* better. Trust your instinct.

3. If changing from first to third person is what is bothering you, write a sample page each way. Again, trust your instinct. This is a nonproblem.

4. Selecting the right focus should be a primary concern. If you have doubts in this area, look carefully at your first and last pages. Try setting the manuscript aside and writing the first and last pages from memory. A new opening and closing may be just the transformation you need.

If you still feel uncertain, ask a trusted friend or, better yet, members of a class to read over a close-to-final draft. Ask them specifically to describe the focus of your story in a complete sentence. Their responses may help you make some final revisions.

10 Rwanda

A Story

by Stephen Minot

"This pathetic little goat," Francine says at dinner, "a beautiful black thing, all tied up, of course, lying on his side, looking up at me, the whites of his eyes showing, terrified."

"You can't buy them all," her husband says gently.

Max and Katy nod. "Or convert the country to vegetarianism," Max says.

Dumb, Francine thinks, bringing it up. The image has clung to her — those desperate eyes. But trying to describe it makes her sound naive. Every market in Africa has live animals ready for slaughter, and the quick slice of the knife is surely no worse than the claws and teeth of a predator. She knows that. Still she can't shake the picture — like some kid with a nightmare that won't fade.

Because her husband, Frank, is an economic adviser to the new government in Rwanda, they have a relatively nice house with a guest room. They enjoy being hosts for a number of fellow expats working in the area. Max and Katy are in wildlife management, working to the north in Uganda. This is a reunion of sorts for the four of them, the first time they have had a real visit since graduate school at Michigan State.

No matter how she feels, Francine is not naive. In her Peace Corps days she put two years into Cameroon, living in the field, seeing much of her work undermined by tribal conflicts and hatred. After graduate school she married Frank and worked for a year with Save the Children in Ethiopia, the warfare in the north no less brutal than the combat in nature, meat-eaters against grazers.

By comparison, life here in Rwanda is surprisingly benign. Being married to Frank is a part of it. What problems there are can be faced together, surmounted. Being assigned to a house that turned out to have no furniture, for example, was an irritation that soon became laughable. In a week they found craftsmen who made tables, chairs, and a bed from scratch. Running water and electricity are intermittent, but she has lived in areas without either.

The house itself is a pleasure even by American standards — one story with a large patio out front looking down on the tarred road that winds its way to Kigali. It's a lush, hilly country, so high in altitude as to be cool most of the time. True, they have lost the key to the patio and have to be content to see the view through the locked French doors, but other than that the place is almost embarrassingly agreeable.

Still, they are unmistakably not in the States. What passes for a supermarket sells terrible food; Francine prefers to spend an hour or two each morning at the public market, bargaining for meat and produce. The U.S. agency for which Frank works had vaguely promised a position for her too, but it never materialized. As foreign aid workers, they are used to uncertainty and disappointment.

"But I know what you mean," Max says. "Dumb animals have a way of getting to you. We had a hell of a time with our very first topi."

"Oh God," Katy says, laughing. "What a mess!"

She and Max have been in Uganda for two months conducting a study of topis, a type of antelope. Financed by a small foundation, they have pathetic funding compared with Francine and Frank. They managed to buy a battered four-wheel-drive Suzuki and set up camp two full days from the nearest road or habitation. Without a mailing address, they have arranged to have their meager allotment sent to Frank in Rwanda and plan to come once every other month to pick it up along with other mail. "Showers, money, and friends," Max said when they first arrived. "The essentials of life." In that sequence they drained the hot water supply with their showers and then made a trip to town to cash his wages for shopping the next day. Now it is their first evening together, the beginning of a three-day visit.

Francine is surprised at how little they have changed since graduate school: Katy with her frizzy Orphan-Annie hair and freckled face, Max with his untended black beard. The gentle giant, they used to call him.

"You'd think we'd know what we're doing," Max says, "but no one does. Remember those *National Geographic* specials? It's not like that at all. You have to figure things out as you go along, and half the time you're wrong."

"Half?" Katy says. "You're generous."

Frank laughs. "Sounds like economics."

"Much worse," Max says. "Numbers stay still. The trouble with animals is that they don't. They never do what they're supposed to."

"Particularly topis," Katy says.

"We had to tranquilize a bunch of them," Max says, "to get these radio transmitters attached so we could track their migration. They're like gazelles that way, always on the move. But no one knew what dosage to use."

"Like we were the first," Katy says. "I mean, that's how we got the job. Until us, no one even heard of topis."

"Well, no one with funding," Max says.

"Anyhow, the dosage goes by weight, but how do you weigh them without tranquilizing them first? Talk about Catch 22!"

"We're softies, so we guessed light."

"It's a drug, after all. You can kill them with an OD."

"So he starts staggering around like a drunk, but he won't fall."

"We try to tie his legs," Katy says, giggling. "We get the rope around one leg, but then he hooks it on one horn and gets all tangled up with it. Us too. The Three Stooges in the bush. And he bites! He's a grazer, right? He's not supposed to bite, but he does, squealing like a pig. We can't knock him out and we can't leave him staggering around, too tangled to run. He'd be a free meal for some lion and it would be our fault. I mean, we're there to *help* them, for chrissake. Uncle Sam's gift to the topis. Poor them! Anyhow, we spent two hours with him. We were black and blue with kicks. Max was bleeding. Hopeless!"

"A total disaster."

They are all laughing except for Francine. "But what happened?" she asks. "What happened to him?"

"Oh, he died," Max says, suddenly serious. "The poor bastard. Must have been his heart. And dehydration."

"We felt terrible. But what else could we do?"

The next day Frank is off at 7:00, punctual as usual. He feels he has to set an example for his Rwandan co-workers. After all, he's there to establish order.

He doesn't like the fact that so much of his work is administrative, keeping him in Kigali. He would prefer field work. Something like Max's. But Francine envies him. At least he has a position. He is using his expertise as an agricultural economist. He's helping them rebuild the economy. For all her degrees in nutrition, Francine is just hanging around and cooking breakfast and lunch like some missionary wife. Even housecleaning and the evening meal are taken care of by Victoria, a tall, young local girl with the high cheekbones and slim Arabian lips of many Tutsi women. Between Victoria's by-the-day help and the houseboy Thomas who lives in a hutch on the property, there is almost nothing left for Francine to do. Some wives, she reminds herself, might find this an ideal life — learning about the country without effort. But it leaves her restless and unfulfilled.

Katy has all the luck. No advanced degree, no special training, yet she is out in the field sharing in wildlife management. Too disorganized to finish her graduate work, she has ended up with a real job, helping Max. And she seems to thrive on adversity. It's all an adventure for her — like some kid on her first camping trip.

Max's task for the day is to get their ailing Suzuki to a garage. Designed as a recreational car, it was never intended for extensive off-road travel and fording rivers. It was even rammed by an irate water buffalo. Max drives to the unmarked garage Frank uses, a shabby, bullet-scarred building with a clutter of cars and trucks in the yard. Almost all the work is done outside, much of it by teenage boy apprentices, mostly dark-skinned, heavy-set Hutus who work for nothing with the hope of eventual employment. Max stays with the car, making sure they do what they're supposed to do, while Francine and Katy walk to the market.

"God, it's terrific being around crowds again," Katy says. "All these people-sounds and the horns and the smells — cooking meat, sweat, animal crap — Luscious!"

"I was kind of envying you — out in the bush and all. Just the two of you in your tent."

Katy laughs. "That's what we *thought* it would be, me Jane, swinging from vines. But it's just scrub country. And we're not exactly alone."

"Tribesmen?"

"No, carnivores. At night. Close enough to hear them grunt. They're not supposed to attack tents, but you wonder if they've read the same manuals. Anyhow, one night of being sniffed at was enough for us. We started sleeping in the Suzuki. A crimp in our sex life, I can tell you."

"No one warned you about that? — the lions, I mean."

"No one warned us about anything. I mean, we wrote up the proposal kind of blind. We had no idea how much it would cost or anything, so we guessed low. They must have figured they were getting a couple of sacrificial lambs on the cheap. That's what those critters were figuring too — a couple of lambs. But hell, how else could we spend six months in Uganda? It sure beats East Lansing. Besides, Max needed a thesis topic. Already he knows more about topis than anyone else. He'll be Mr. Topi by the time we get back."

"And you? Can you get an article out of it?"

"God, I'm no good at that. You know that. I bought a journal the day before we left, but I forgot to pack it. It's enough that I help Max."

They were passing the meat stalls — hunks of pig or goat turning on spits and smelling delicious. Vendors called to them in Kinyarwanda, grinning, pointing to their wares.

"Let's get a pig or something," Katy says. "I'm real meat starved."

"I thought you were a veggie."

"You get over that in the field. Our nearest market is two full days' drive away, so what we eat is either dried or in cans. A lot of beans. If we had a real gun instead of those dart things, I think I'd go after topi."

"In Uganda without a gun? Isn't that risky?"

"Hey, antelopes don't have guns and they get along fine. Right now I feel like a hungry carnivore. How about that one?" She points to a hunk of unidentifiable meat on a spit.

Francine shakes her head, wondering if perhaps it's monkey. "I'd rather stick to raw stuff. At least that way I know what I'm eating. Besides, we don't have room for a whole animal. We've only got one sack."

Katy stops dead and slaps her thighs like a kid. "Damn, damn, damn. I forgot my basket."

"No problem; I've got my filet. It stretches big enough for everything — except a pig."

"But my wallet's in the basket. In our bedroom. God, is it safe? Max cashed the checks yesterday. Two month's pay in cash."

Francine rolls her eyes, but she feels obliged to be reassuring. "Don't worry. It's safe."

Back in graduate school, Katy's inability to take proper lecture notes or keep up with the reading or even remember exam dates was a shared joke. Funny until she flunked out. Here it's no joke. "At least you didn't lose it on the street. It's O.K. at home."

"You sure? It's all we've got for supplies."

"The house is locked, and Victoria doesn't come until late afternoon. She doesn't have a key anyhow."

"But the houseboy — doesn't he live there?"

"Thomas has his own little cabin — the hutch, we call it. It's outside. He doesn't have a key either. Don't worry, I've got enough money for whatever we need."

She can feel a sharpness in her voice. She's forgotten how they all catered to Katy — lending her lecture notes, giving her alarm clocks (which she often forgot to set), tutoring her before exams. They weren't able to keep her from flunking, but that didn't seem to bother her. Incredibly, gentle Max never criticized her. How is it, Francine wonders, that some people go through life letting others solve their problems?

They end up with a heavy load of meat wrapped in newspaper and vegetables. They also have dried fruit and canned goods for Katy and Max to take back to Uganda. Francine, tired of carrying it all, buys a second filet while Katy is off on her own. Perhaps that way they can begin to keep their purchases separate, though without sales slips it's is going to be impossible to calculate what Katy owes her.

Francine is trying to redistribute their purchases in the two sacks when Katy returns with a whoop. "Look what I've got!" she cries, her voice shrill with delight.

Francine looks up. Katy is holding a crude little wicker cage with two bright yellow birds.

"Oh great," Francine says. "Just what you need in the bush. Max will be delighted."

"I knew you'd love them," Katy says. "I'm going to name them after you two — Francine and Frank."

It is late afternoon before the car is ready and they can return. Predictably, Max doesn't object to the birds. "You can teach them to sing," he says, noticing what Francine had missed — that the poor creatures are silent, sullen as prisoners.

"Sure, Francine says. "You can teach them Bach cantatas."

"Oh, but we don't have a tape player," Katy says.

Thomas, the houseboy, responds to the horn and opens the gate, smiling and nodding as he always does. At the house, he unloads the two filets, flashing his grin at Max and Katy as if they are old friends. Short, solid, and very dark, he is unmistakably a Hutu. His smiles are his only means of communication since he doesn't know a word of English or French either. A country boy with little or no education, he speaks only Kinyarwanda. But he's delighted at little things. He takes to the sad little birds, whistling softly to them, trying to stroke them.

As soon as everything is unpacked in the kitchen, piled without order on the table and chairs, Thomas goes back outside to wash the two cars. That is his ritual. Without being asked, he always washes whatever car had just returned from the dusty streets of Kigali, sweeping the floor mats and polishing the glass. He seems to have a penchant for order, humming or whistling as he mops floors, tends plants, and irons clothing. Francine has been told that he is, incredibly, the sole survivor of his entire village.

It is a relief for her when Victoria the house girl shows up. Each afternoon she walks several miles from her home to prepare the evening meal and wash up afterward. Although Victoria knows no English, she speaks French with a lovely, lilting accent.

Tall, slim, she has the perfect looks and grace of many Tutsi women. Straight-backed and copper-skinned with high cheekbones, she reminds Francine of Nefertiti. She might have made Francine uneasy but for the fact that she is a devout Seventh-Day Adventist. She is merry but never gives even a hint of flirting.

Calmly and efficiently Victoria rearranges the supplies, separating the food that Francine normally buys from the dried and canned goods bought by Katy. Somehow she is able to do this without help. Then she places a wine bottle and four glasses on a tray and hands it to Francine. "S'il vous plait," she says with a smile, gesturing to the four Americans to get out of her kitchen and let her start cooking.

Francine has always admired Victoria's competence and, equally, her lack of servility. It does not seem surprising to Francine that Victoria's tribe, the Tutsis, are, in spite of their minority status, back in control after all that bloodshed.

In the living room the Americans sip wine and recall graduate school life. It seems to Francine that there is less anxiety and anger now that they are involved in what they had planned to do. Even Frank loosens up a bit, offering a toast to reunions and old friendships. Then Max says he would like to work out what they owe before they forget.

"Not now," Katy says. "This is party time."

"While it's still fresh in our minds," Max says. "And before we finish this bottle." He gets up and goes into the guest room. "Where's the wallet?" he asks.

"Right in the basket. I meant to take it . . . ."

He calls for her to come in, his voice just a bit sharper than usual. Pouting, Katy gets up, muttering, "It's right there, for God's sake."

There is a moment of silence, and then Katy's wail fills the house: "*Oh shit!*"

Francine raises her eyes, smiling. "Just like the old days."

But it is worse than the old days. At the end of a half hour they realize that the wallet with all Max's pay has not simply been misplaced; it has disappeared. Gone. Vanished. Nothing else is missing. Just the wallet and the money.

Victoria and Thomas have helped in the search. With six of them at work, there isn't a square inch in the house that hasn't been examined and re-examined.

"Enough," Frank finally says. "Let's figure things out."

The four expats sit down in the living room while Thomas and Victoria go on searching in the kitchen, hopelessly looking on shelves and under chairs, places that have been covered countless times.

"I can't believe it," Frank says, his voice low in spite of the fact that neither servant can understand English. "I really can't. But one of the two of them took it."

"No way," Francine says.

"Outsiders would have ransacked the place. That's what they do. What they don't take, they smash. Someone right here saw Katy come in with that basket and the wallet. Someone got in without breaking a window or a door."

There is a moment of silence. Then Francine feels an electric jolt pass through her.

"Good Lord, the key."

"What key?" Katy asks.

Frank describes now the key to the patio has been missing for two weeks, how they searched for it endlessly and given up. "If anyone had the key they could climb over the patio wall from the outside and open the French doors. One of those two has been holding that key."

"Impossible," Francine says. Having no other suspect, her rage and indignation swings against Katy. It's Katy and her carelessness that's to blame.

"I'll start with Victoria," Frank says. He calls her in, his voice steely. Francine wants to stop him, to stop the humiliation. She wants to tell Victoria that this is only a formality, that Frank has to do it against his will, that this is what one does in inquests. Francine is not religious, but she can't believe that a Seventh-Day Adventist would steal. Francine listens to the interrogation, only half following their exchange in French. She keeps her eyes on the coffee table. Making eye contact, she feels, will somehow make her a part of this, will imply complicity. Somehow it's important for her to maintain her distance, her objectivity, as if watching some foreign trial on CNN.

Frank's French is fast, but she can catch phrases. He is asking Victoria when she left home, how long it took her to walk, what she was doing earlier in the day. He keeps circling back to the same questions, phrasing them slightly differently. Who did she see? With whom did she talk?

Victoria's answers are brief, straightforward. She does not mumble or hesitate. Incredibly, she doesn't seem to resent the grilling. It occurs to Francine that perhaps the girl had been expecting it. In this country, inquests and trials are a daily occurrence. Victoria isn't even offended at being asked to empty her pockets and the little leather sack that serves as purse. What a meager collection of possessions: tiny mirror, brush, nail file, identity card, a few folded bills, a leather-bound book no bigger than a pack of cards — a bible? —, three photos stapled together. Such a simple life! How, Francine wonders, did this girl manage to survive when entire Tutsi villages were being butchered with knives and machetes?

After an agonizingly long time Frank nods and tells her to move to a different chair. He does not smile or even thank her. Without raising his voice, he calls Thomas in. The poor boy has been listening at the door to the kitchen, though the only word he understands is his own name. Frank nods to the chair Victoria has vacated, the chair nearest to the light. The inquisitional chair. Frank turns to Victoria and asks her in French to ask Thomas what he was doing from the time he woke up until the family returned from town. While Victoria is translating from French into Kinyarwanda, Frank says to the rest of them in English, "Crazy, using one suspect to translate for the other." He doesn't have to add that they have no choice. Kinyarwanda is an astonishingly complex language with more cases than Latin. None of them have learned more than the simplest phrases.

Thomas' answer to Victoria's question is spoken so softly that they can hardly hear. His smile is gone. The poor kid, Francine realizes, may well be reliving interrogations from Tutsi tribesmen.

Victoria turns to Frank and translates the testimony into French. Frank takes a deep breath and begins what turns into another long series of routine questions, many of them repetitious. It is, Francine sees, a pointless ritual, but what else can they do? As outsiders, they are running a trial. They must. During one of Thomas' longer statements, Frank says in English: "Max, head for the bathroom but then sneak out back. Go through Thomas' hut. Search everywhere — under the floor mat, feel the mattress, you know, everything."

Max waits a minute, then stretches, excuses himself. The questioning goes on. The redundancy becomes increasingly absurd, but everyone in the room acts as if each query has some hidden significance.

When Max finally comes back, it is clear that he has found nothing. He slumps into his chair without speaking. Finally he yawns and speaks casually.

"I found the wallet in his shoe. All the money is there. And the patio key. I've buried the wallet in your sugar jar."

No one speaks or moves. It is as if they are playing a game of freeze. Then Frank goes on with another pointless question. When he is through with the French he says in English, "It's your turn, Francine. Go into the kitchen and call the police. And lock us in here. He may try to bolt, and I don't want him to see us locking doors."

Francine remembers to wait a moment and then leaves. Yes, she thinks, Thomas might well bolt. But wouldn't that be best? They have the money back. The poor boy is desperate. He has no future in this country, no chance of a fair trial with the Tutsis in control. But she knows exactly what Frank would say. He would point out that Thomas would work for other Americans and steal from them too. Frank has a high regard for the law. And so, she realizes, does she. Softly she locks the door behind her.

The phone call is an agony of confusion. Her French is stumbling, their French is provincial, the connection is bad, and she is trying to whisper. "Pardon," the officer keeps saying. "Questque vous dites?" His tone is polite, formal. She envisions some slim, educated Tutsi struggling to deal with this inarticulate foreigner.

Finally, he seems to grasp the situation. She feels a wave of relief. But incredibly he explains that their only jeep is out on patrol or broken down or out of gas, and would she be so kind as to come down to town and pick them up?

For a moment she is stunned into silence. A picture of Keystone cops flashes through her mind. But Frank's weary voice reaches her: The four of them are locked in that room with a man who may bolt, may get violent.

She returns to the living room and explains the situation in English. After a pause she yawns, stretches, tells Victoria in French that she is tired of all this and is going to bed.

In minutes she has opened the gate and driven slowly without lights beyond sight of the house. Then she steps on the accelerator with abandon. All she can think of is Frank going on with one stupid, meaningless question after another, stalling, watching Thomas' every move. An endless, dreamlike, pointless interrogation. How can it be, this transformation of dear, friendly Thomas into the enemy? He might even have a knife concealed on him. If desperate, wouldn't he use it?

She drives through town recklessly, her hand on the horn. There are no police to worry about and few cars. Still, the streets are unlit and she must swerve to avoid stray dogs and pigs. If hit, they could disable the car. And then what?

To her relief, the police are ready for her. Three of them, black-booted, armed with holster on one side and billy club on the other. These are Tutsis who have established law and order. She is desperate to hustle them into the car, but each must shake her hand in the French tradition, and each must introduce himself by name. She wants to tell them to shut up, to get moving, but she dares not offend them. She smiles, nods, shakes hands. "Bon soir monsieur . . . Bon soir monsieur."

When they return to the house, she is sure they will post a guard at a side window, but they continue to observe proprieties. All three wait in a line while she unlocks the kitchen door and then unlocks the door to the living room. Not breathing, she tries to avoid a quick fantasy — corpses sprawled, faces contorted, pools of blood.

None of that. She enters, followed by the three policemen. Everyone stands. The chief goes through the hand-shaking ritual — including the expressionless culprit.

The crisis has ended. Max gets the wallet, dusting off sugar, and the patio key. He shows them to the police. They nod. They see it all. No need for further evidence. They say a few words to Thomas in Kinyarwanda. He accepts the verdict, his face totally blank.

Suddenly he bolts. "The door!" someone shouts. Francine has left it open. Quick as a gazelle he dives for it. But a policeman, lean as a cat, trips him. Thomas is down. All three police are on top of him, slamming his head against the floor, producing lengths of rope from nowhere, binding him, hands behind his back, legs tethered. They kick him brutally.

Thomas looks up from the floor, a poor black creature lying on his side, the whites of his eyes showing terror for the first time.

"Stop!" Francine shouts. "For God's sake . . ."

For an instant, everyone looks at her. They wait for her to go on, to explain what she means. Surely she must know. But what *does* she mean? Stop what? Stop whom? Before she can wrestle with her thoughts, the police have hoisted the prisoner up, prodding him, half dragging him. They assume that she will drive them back to the station. As she must. With a sudden sense of weight, an appalling gravity, she realizes that she is no longer an observer. She is now a part of this country.

11 The Making of a Story

• Difficulty in tracing the development of published stories (78) • The factual skeleton of "Rwanda" (78) • Basic transformations: history, characters, and viewpoint (79) • Revisions while writing (80) • Learning from early drafts (81) • The melding of memory and invention (82)

One of the best ways to improve your fiction-writing ability is to read published work. In most cases, however, what we study is limited to the final, printed version. This is particularly true of work written since the advent of the computer. While in the past many authors had copies of early drafts that revealed how a manuscript developed, the computer leaves no such paper trail. We have to guess about where the material came from and what kinds of transformations and revisions might have gone into the shaping of that work.

To make matters more difficult, many writers are reluctant to discuss those long hours of effort because they like to maintain the illusion that each work is an inspired burst of talent. It is slightly embarrassing to admit that the creative process almost always involves periods of uncertainty, self-doubt, reappraisal, and rewriting.

The following case history of "Rwanda" is not conjecture. It's a record that only an author can provide about his or her own work. The stages this story went through are not unusual. If you are taking a workshop course in writing, you may not have time for this much reworking, but one of the ironies of fiction writing is that the more proficient you get, the less satisfied you become with early drafts. Though this chapter focuses on a single story, its primary purpose is to illustrate a process of development that applies to all fiction. If you find this approach helpful, you might want to track down a similar analysis of another story of mine, "Sausage and Beer," which appears in previous editions of this text. It may be available in your library or through the Internet.

THE FACTUAL SKELETON OF "RWANDA"

Much of "Rwanda" is based on an actual setting and on personal experience. I was lucky in that respect. Most stories require more invention. I was in fact a visitor in Rwanda and so could use both memory and journal entries in the description of the setting. These details were important, especially in the market scene. And the house with the patio and the French doors is in fact one that my son occupied several years ago.

As for the events, the basic sequence or skeleton of the story actually occurred. There was indeed a house boy who stole the patio key and after several weeks used it to steal a wallet. We were able to apprehend him and collectively made the decision to turn him in. The day after it occurred, I knew that this was an experience that might lend itself to fiction.

One of the factual elements that I found promising was how it resembled the basic patterns of the mystery story and the trial. It echoed the structure so frequently repeated in literature and on television. Unlike **melodramatic** TV scripts, the situation was relatively mild — no police chase, no shooting. But this was to my advantage, keeping me clear of hackneyed **conventions**. It gave me a structure in which I could focus on the characters and the thematic suggestions.

I was also intrigued by the complexity of characters struggling to deal with three languages. Such situations strike me as emblematic of global problems in communication.

The following day I was sure that I would try to use the experience as a short story at some point, but while journalists can work directly with experience and often write while traveling, most writers of fiction have to let an experience rest a bit. As I pointed out in Chapter 6, when you are too close to a personal experience, you are apt to let the events and characters dominate your writing. It takes time before you can transform the material into effective fiction.

In this case, many years intervened. By the time I began reshaping the episode as fiction, Rwanda had experienced one of the most horrifying cases of genocide the world has ever seen, and the minority Tutsi tribe had once again taken over from the Hutus. It was a historical cataclysm far greater than anything I could deal with in a short story. My first challenge was how to focus on what I had experienced without becoming entangled with the rebellion.

BASIC TRANSFORMATIONS: HISTORY, CHARACTERS, AND VIEWPOINT

My first transformation was to alter the historical period. I was afraid that if I placed the story as it occurred in prewar Rwanda, the reader might assume that I was primarily concerned with some aspect of that catastrophic event. In point of fact, we were surprisingly unaware of the degree to which tensions were rising. To avoid the historical aspect, I decided to move the story to the postwar period. I wasn't entirely sure yet what the theme would be, but I knew it would probably deal more with the characters than with history.

Next, I eliminated all extraneous characters — myself, my wife, and an unidentified Rwandian neighbor who hung about as if, perhaps, he knew what was going on. In early drafts, I tried working with just three Americans, leaving Frank unmarried. This seemed like a manageable cast of characters.

It's a slow process to provide enough background to present even one character in depth. (Remember how many details the author of "Escapes" had to
slip in to give you a sense of knowing Caryn and her niece Jennifer.) The story
form is tight, and there is no room for characters who are only observers. In
a short-short story — up to about six typed pages — two or three characters
are about all one can handle.

But I knew this story would have to be longer. It would take time simply to unfold the mystery. And I began to feel constricted having Frank unmarried as was my son at the time of the event. I needed another woman to
provide a contrast with the rather scatterbrained Katy.

As soon as I added Francine as Frank's wife, I could see that she should
be the one who would be the most sensitive to the plight of the house boy at
the end of the story. To do this, I had to start from the beginning again, shifting the means of perception from Frank to Francine. This, of course, required
a whole new draft. Not even a sophisticated computer can change the point
of view for you.

As I remember it, we all had uneasy feelings about sending such an apparently agreeable man to prison, but rather than state that in the form of
exposition, it seemed far more subtle to have Francine reveal those feelings
primarily through her dialogue. The opening of the story came rather late as
a way of preparing the reader for her sensitivity.

If you look over these early transformations of the original experience,
you will see one common denominator. The decision to change the historical
period, the invention of a new character, and the shifted viewpoint were
made on **literary** grounds. That is, they were not made with the hope of coming closer to what actually happened but, rather, with an eye to what would
make this a more effective work of **fiction**.

Those who have read a lot of fiction have an advantage here. One ac-
quires a sense of what will and will not be effective. But regardless of your
reading background, the creative process is similar. The more you, work on
shaping a particular story, the less concerned you will become about the
original experience and the more you will focus on literary aspects.

In "Rwanda," some but not all transformations were made early. It's best
to have the basic structure in place before beginning to write, but you have
to be willing to consider radically fresh approaches after completing a first
draft. In this case, I had hoped that the experience would, in a sense, write
itself. But I should have known that almost no experience becomes good fiction without structural changes.

REVISIONS WHILE WRITING

Those who are new to fiction writing sometimes think of "revision" as consisting of one-word changes. But it's not long before you find yourself
adding or deleting whole paragraphs — sometimes pages. Revising usually

takes far more time than writing the original draft. And these changes are not always a matter of careful thought.

Occasionally a scene will begin to take on a life itself. When that happens, let it roll. You can always cut sections later. In my case, the market scene blossomed on its own. Open markets are vibrant and, unlike supermarkets, alive with interaction between shoppers and merchants. Instead of canned music, the din is a mix of voices, laughter, shouting, and the bleating of animals. And the smells are of food and spices. Describing all that lured me for pages. The scene grew out of proportion. Later I had to trim it to fit the needs of the story.

The same was true in the development of Katy. With successive drafts she grew increasingly disorganized and impulsive. She seemed to do this on her own. It was her decision to buy those birds at the market, not mine. I'm not even sure whether Rwandan markets had birds for sale. If the competent woman on whom this fictional character was originally based ever reads this story, she will be dismayed. I will have to remind her that this is fiction and that fictional characters are creations on their own.

LEARNING FROM EARLY DRAFTS

Early drafts can suggest ways to develop fresh aspects of your story. They can even help you see a unifying theme. This was true in the writing of "Rwanda."

In early drafts, I was primarily concerned with the sequence of events. My efforts were what is called *plot driven*. If I had left it at that stage, it might have been an entertaining story but one that lacked **resonance** or depth. I hadn't put much thought into what thematic suggestion might develop.

After working on successive drafts, however, I recognized an uneasy ethical question that I and perhaps others have experienced. It is apt to arise when you have entered a new environment for a period of time — a different culture, say, or a different work environment. Without warning you find that some of your attitudes or beliefs have changed. Perhaps you realize that you have become tougher or more tolerant. Or you may find some of your ideals being compromised. Such shifts in your outlook may be positive, but others may leave you feeling uneasy.

This, it seemed to me, is what is happening to Francine. She is sensitive enough to understand why an apparently good and honest person can be driven to steal, and she is realistically aware of how brutal some judicial systems can be, but at the end she finds herself an accomplice. Here she is about to drive the police back to the station. She has become one of them.

Once I realized that this **theme** was becoming a unifying concern, I had to rewrite both the beginning and the end of the story. They were the last set of revisions. This is a good illustration of why most stories require successive drafts before they reach their potential. Early drafts can speak to you. They can suggest new aspects and new possibilities.

THE MELDING OF MEMORY AND INVENTION

Every story has a different ratio of memory to invention. Many, however, share the same stages of development. The process begins with a specific memory we can think of as the skeleton. Next, we begin to restructure the events and the characters with radical transformations that may be decided on even before the actual writing begins. When these transformations draw on memories unrelated to the original experience, they usually need invention to make them fit.

Once into the writing, the revisions begin. Some may consist of memories from other times in your life. Others may be pure invention. Face it, fiction writers are as unscrupulous as magpies, borrowing and stealing whatever suits their fancy. That's why we call it *creative* writing.

Here is a rough breakdown of the initial episode, thefts, borrowing, and total inventions that went into "Rwanda."

THE INITIAL MEMORY
   The sequence of events as they actually occurred
   The interior of the house and the outdoor market
   Three of the four American characters
   Both Rwandan characters and the police

BORROWED MEMORIES FROM OTHER SOURCES
   A friend who was disorganized and free spirited
   The memory of seeing goats tied up—in Greece, I believe
   A bird market in Paris

PURE INVENTION
   Frank's wife, Francine
   The opening conversation
   Francine's ride to the police station
   The house boy's struggle to escape
   The recapture by the police

As you can see from this outline, ascertaining whether a story or a novel was "based on personal experience" is about as futile as determining whether an automobile is "American made."

Before you declare a story finished, make sure that all those fragments of remembered and invented details have become melded into a single, unified work. Read it over with a cool, objective eye. Be particularly careful to check the following three areas for continuity and consistency:

Transitions: When two fictional scenes were originally based on two quite different experiences, make sure that there are no inconsistencies. If, for example, your characters live in a ranch-style house, make sure they don't go up the stairs in the next scene. If they have a dog in one scene, don't let it become a cat in the next. In my case, I had to invent a way of getting the two American wives to the market without their husbands.

Characters: On the simplest level, make sure bearded characters stay bearded and someone on crutches doesn't run to answer the phone. More subtle problems arise when you base a fictional character on two different acquaintances. Make sure that your fictional portrayal is a new creation, so consistent that he or she seems real. Katy's personality, for example, was based on someone entirely different. I had to be careful to make sure that the two portrayals blended into a single fictional character.

Scenes: Guard against contradictions and omissions. If you have three characters arguing, don't lose one of them. If he or she falls silent, say so. Characters not accounted for at least briefly may seem to disappear. Try to visualize who is "on stage" in each scene. And pay attention to the passage of time. Don't end a lunch scene with a character saying "good night." For me, it was a challenge to keep all six characters "on stage," especially since two of the six didn't speak English.

To achieve **verisimilitude** you have to keep going over your work from start to finish, seeing it as a whole. Imagine yourself as someone else reading it for the first time.

12 Structure

From Scenes to Plot

> • *Clock time distinguished from psychological time (84)* • *Scene construction in two stories (85)* • *Scene awareness (86)* • *Varieties of plot patterns: chronological, flashbacks, frame stories (86)* • *Crucial paragraphs: openings and closings (89)* • *Controlling the pace of plot (90)*

Clock time moves at a steady rate. And in one sense, so do our lives. Awake or asleep, our allotted time flows from birth to death minute by minute at an unvaried pace.

Psychological time, however, does not. Take a moment to review what you did yesterday from when you woke up until you went to sleep again. As soon as you begin putting the events into words, that smooth chronology turns into a list of separate segments: getting dressed, eating breakfast, and, for students, attending classes, taking a coffee break with friends, holding a conversation in the hall, and eating lunch.

For nonstudents, the activities will be different, but regardless of the content, the memory of the day has quite unconsciously become structured. Although the *clock* has been moving without a break, our *memory* as we look back records a sequence of distinct episodes.

In daily conversation we divide our activities in the same way with very little conscious thought. But the episodes we recall have certain recurring characteristics that every writer of fiction should consider. First, we often identify them by where they occurred — the **setting**. Second, we recall who was there — the *characters*. Third, such episodes remain clear long after we have forgotten what came just before and just afterward. The dull periods of time that merely link one episode with the next (driving, waiting, reading, watching television) tend to blend together and blur quickly. In conversation, we may fill in long blocks of time with a simple phrase such as "After waiting four hours for the rain to stop . . ."

Finally, we don't always remember these events in the order in which they occurred. Students complaining about bad teachers they have had are not going to start with kindergarten; football fans recounting dramatic games they have watched are not going to begin with the first one they attended. Fiction tends to imitate these patterns. What we call *episodes* in life become **scenes** in fiction. These are the basic units. And their arrangement is what we call **plot**.

SCENE CONSTRUCTION IN TWO STORIES

Scenes in fiction are not as clearly defined as they are in drama, but they are similar in their formation and their purpose. A new scene is signaled most clearly when the setting changes, but often all it takes is a character arriving or leaving. No double space is required to show these divisions; readers are used to fiction being segmented at least roughly into a series of scenes.

If you try to recall the scenes in "Escapes" without looking back, the ones that will come to mind will probably be those in San Francisco, in Caryn's apartment, and, most vividly, on the island of Alcatraz. They stand out because each has a distinctly different setting. But if you examine that story with a writer's analytical eye, you will see that there are actually 10 separate scenes. Not only that, eight of them are identified specifically in the first sentence of that scene. The other two are in Caryn's apartment and are clear from the context. Here is a list with the identifying phrase in quotation marks. You will find it helpful to mark these in your text starting with page 53.

1. "cable cars . . . San Francisco . . ."
2. "Candlestick Park" — the baseball game
3. "Esprit factory outlet" — shopping
4. "on a Saturday morning in September" — a **flashback** going back to when Jennifer's mother first called
5. "on Fisherman's Wharf" — more shopping
6. Caryn's apartment — a letter from Caryn's former boyfriend
7. "When Sherry calls" — her second phone call
8. "my tiny cramped office" — they talk about travel
9. Caryn's apartment
10. "the day we go to Alcatraz"

This may seem at first to be needlessly analytical, but remember that we are now examining how the story has been put together. We are studying the structure of the story from a writer's point view, not simply reading it for pleasure.

Each of these scenes has a specific setting, and the setting of each contributes to the theme. The cable-car theme reveals Jennifer's longing to be free and without cares. The shopping scenes show her compulsive nature, an ominous note; the scene in which they look at travel brochures amplifies her cable-car mood, and the prison of Alcatraz develops their feelings of being trapped and their determination to take control of their lives. Each scene has a function.

In Chapter 9, we examined how the author of that story withheld information by limiting the means of perception to Caryn. If you examine this list of scenes you can see how the scenes control the rate at which essential information is revealed.

"Rwanda" is a longer story, but it has fewer scenes. If you mark them in your text yourself, it will help you see fiction in structural terms. The story has more background information given as exposition, and this blurs the separation of scenes somewhat, but essentially there are seven of them. This includes one flashback to their graduate-school days.

Notice that both stories use the early scenes to fill in background (including one flashback scene in each story). The concluding scene in each story is long, unmistakably distinct, and the most dramatic.

SCENE AWARENESS

As a writer, should you concern yourself with scene construction from the start? It depends partly on how long the story will be. **Short-short stories** (six pages or fewer), often require no more than one or two scenes. But as we have seen, longer works usually require more.

Some writers find it helpful to begin with some kind of informal outline, recognizing that it may be revised as needed. Others prefer a more intuitive approach, starting with a situation and a few characters and letting the plot develop on its own. There is nothing wrong with this, though it may take several drafts before the story takes shape.

No matter what approach you prefer, as soon as your first draft is down on paper, take time to examine the scene construction. If the story seems fragmentary, it may be because there are too many brief and poorly developed scenes. See if you can combine some. If the story seems static and slow moving, consider breaking up your longest scene into two, using a different setting for each.

When the story as a whole seems too long, there is sometimes a tendency to nibble at it word by word. After an hour of such work, you may find that you've cut less than a paragraph. It is far more effective to look at the scenes and weigh the possibility of eliminating one entirely.

Think of scenes as the building blocks of fiction. They not only help with all aspects of revision, they are fundamental to our next concern, the varieties of plot patterns.

VARIETIES OF PLOT PATTERNS

The two stories you have read so far move **chronologically** from scene to scene. Each has one **flashback** to provide background information, but essentially they both move toward the climatic scene without skipping around. This is the pattern in most stories, particularly those that are relatively short.

The flashback, however, is a simple and fairly common variation in the chronological story. It is an unobtrusive method of introducing events that occurred at a previous time. The term, first used by film writers, describes more than a simple reference to the past seen through a character's thoughts or dialogue. A true flashback consists of a whole scene with action and, often, dialogue that occurred before the main action of the story known as **base time**.

A common way to enter a flashback in a past-tense story is to use the past perfect tense ("had") briefly like this:

> At 13 she had begged her father to give her a driving lesson. "I'll be real careful," she had said. "I'll drive like Aunt Susan." But she forgot about Aunt Susan once she was on the highway. Her father never gave her another chance.

The opening phrase, "At 13 she had begged . . ." establishes when the flashback took place, and "had" cues the reader to the fact that this occurred earlier than the primary time span or **base time** of the story. Even those who are entirely unfamiliar with grammatical terms like "past perfect" find using "had" quite natural, and readers know exactly what is going on. That use of "had" is often not extended beyond the first sentence, however.

Getting out of the flashback — that is, returning to base time — merely requires a phrase that identifies the time shift like this:

> "Even now after 30 years she drove like a wild teenager" or simply, "But that was years ago."

Similar cues are used when you are writing in the present tense. The only difference is that the shift in tense is from the present to the simple past tense.

There is a flashback in "Escapes" that is so seamless you may have missed the transition on first reading:

> Sherry . . . called me on a Saturday morning in September and said, "You've got to take her . . ."

You may not have noticed that the story is being presented in present tense, but the abrupt and brief shift to the past tense ("called") is a subtle cue that the phone call occurred before Jennifer came to visit.

The end of that flashback is just as simple. We know that we are back to the main section of the story partly because there is a new paragraph and a shift of scene but also because we are back to the present tense:

> On Fisherman Wharf Jennifer buys more bracelets. They are copper or gold. . . .

These are details that are easy to miss unless you are reading closely as a fellow writer.

Flash-forwards are rare, but they do have a particular use. There is an excellent example in Sharon Solwitz's story "Obst Vw," which appears in Chapter 16. In a daring stylistic tactic, she opens the story with an event that will not occur until a year after the story that follows:

> Next year, writing his personal experience essay to convince admissions at Penn he's Ivy League material despite uneven grades, he'll describe in amusing detail the one baseball game his father took him to, and get in on a scholarship despite his father's explicit pessimism.

Flash-forwards have an interesting effect on the **tone** of a story. They almost invariably increase the **distance** between the reader and the material. When we as readers are given information not yet known to the characters, we, in a way, rise above the story, looking down on the action.

Multiple flashbacks are sometimes used when the author wants to suggest a complicated set of clues leading to a symbolic or literal trial. Joseph Conrad's novel *Lord Jim* is in this form, as is William Faulkner's well-known story "A Rose for Emily." Such an approach tends to fragment the story line, of course, and it may be for this reason that it is usually found in longer works and those that have a type of mystery or trial to maintain the story's unity and the reader's interest.

The **frame story** traditionally refers to fiction in which a narrator relates events that occurred previously. In a sense, the entire work is one long flashback. Sometimes this is presented in the third person; but more often the narrator speaks in the first person, recalling one or more incidents that occurred some time in the past.

"Escapes," for example, could have begun like this:

> Over the years, Jennifer and I have become like mother and daughter — even now that she is married with three of her own children. But you'd never have guessed it from that rocky first month when she came to stay with me in my little apartment in San Francisco.

And if the story were to have a complete frame, the ending would have been rounded out with a return to the time period of the opening scene:

> So we did, each in our own way, escape the prison we had found ourselves in back then, but we needed each other to achieve it.

These alternatives would have wiped out much of the story's subtlety. They state the theme directly rather than having it unfold through action and dialogue.

Think twice before you consider the frame pattern for a **short-short story**. It tends to clutter a work of that length, and as you can see from the previous example, it's apt to present the theme too bluntly.

CRUCIAL PARAGRAPHS: OPENINGS AND CLOSINGS

When you have finished your first draft, take a close, critical look at your opening paragraph. If it is a long and rambling description of the setting or the characters, it may be that you were still uncertain about how to launch the new work. Sometimes it can be cut entirely. Leisurely starts don't engage readers. In addition, they can seem dated, echoes from the 19th century. Contemporary short stories frequently jump in quickly.

How quickly? Look closely at the point at which the reader enters the mind of the character who will be the means of perception. "Escapes" begins with a flurry of action on those cable-car rides and the narrator's irritation at paying four dollars for each one.

Establishing the point of view quickly is even more important with stories using the third person. In "Rwanda" the opening scene has four individuals all involved in an ongoing conversation. Which character is going to be the means of perception? We don't know until the fifth sentence when Francine chastises herself: "Dumb, Francine thinks, bringing it up." The fact that we have entered her mind and share her feelings establishes her as the means of perception. Psychologically, the story begins at this point.

When you look over the first draft of a new story you are writing, see how long it is before you establish just who will be the means of perception. If an entire paragraph is primarily an explanation of the situation or a description, ask yourself whether the reader will be impatiently waiting for the story to start. This is when your best solution may be to cut the whole first paragraph. The information it provided can be broken up and inserted at various points later.

One way to study openings intensively is to go through an anthology and read nothing but first paragraphs. Which ones draw you into the work and which do not? How quickly is the situation established? Take some notes and compare different approaches. Some will seem to violate everything I have recommended, but you can learn from them too.

Endings are equally crucial. The challenge is to reveal or expand the theme indirectly rather than stating it as one does in an essay. Once again, that familiar bit of advice applies: show, don't tell. Let the reader discover the aspects you consider important rather than laying them out in exposition.

Some stories prepare for the ending by providing what James Joyce called an **epiphany**. Although he used the term in a somewhat more limited sense, it has come to mean an important moment of recognition or discovery. It may be an insight that the reader and the protagonist discover at the same time, or it may be something only the reader perceives.

In "Escapes," there is such a moment when Caryn tells Jennifer the true facts about her father's suicide. But we don't fully understand how their attitudes changed until the very end:

> The ferry arrives, and we move forward, toward it. Its steps are steep, and we have to link arms for the climb.

The author doesn't have to state that they feel a new determination, that they have a long way to go but will help each other to take control of their lives.

In "Rwanda," the shift in Francine's attitude is also shown in terms of action. She finds herself getting ready to drive the police and their prisoner back to the police station. Here, however, I have added a final sentence describing her thoughts.

As you can see from these two stories, endings don't have to be highly dramatic. A sophisticated short story, after all, usually deals with character and attitudes. Such themes rarely require violence and death. Often they can be revealed by some small, apparently insignificant piece of action (as in "Escapes") or action and thoughts (as in "Rwanda") or a line of dialogue.

You can see the range of options if you take the time to compare 10 final paragraphs in an anthology just as you did with openings.

CONTROLLING THE PACE OF PLOT

Every reader can sense whether some sections in a story drag while others move quickly. A writer, however, has to know why this has occurred.

In part, the **pace** of fiction is controlled by the style — particularly the length and complexity of the sentence structure. Long sentences slow the pace. This is discussed further in Chapter 23. By far the greatest factor, however, is the **rate of revelation**. That is, a story seems to move rapidly when a great deal is being revealed to the reader; conversely, it slows down when the work turns to digression, speculation, description, or any type of exposition.

The pace is up to you as author. You can, if you want, maintain a high rate of revelation simply by developing what reviewers like to call an "action-packed plot." This is how many best-selling suspense novels and adventure stories maintain the pace.

When you write sophisticated fiction, you have to be on guard against both ends of the spectrum: an unrelentingly high rate of revelation may maintain interest for a while, but then may bore readers for lack of significance. The work will seem superficial. But if you dwell too long on descriptive passages or background information, the forward motion of the story will grind to a stop. The best way to avoid these two risks is to vary the pace throughout the work.

Openings are frequently given a high rate of revelation. It helps to plunge into an ongoing situation that will arouse the reader's interest. In "Escapes" it is the riding of the cable cars, a description charged with motion. "Rwanda" jumps right into the middle of a conversation.

Both of these stories launch a situation that arouses the curiosity of the reader. Once you have drawn your reader into the work, you can afford to fill in the setting and provide background. That's when the author of "Escapes" takes the time to give information about Jennifer's mother through the flashback. The forward motion slows a bit here in order to fill in background. "Rwanda" also fills in background just as soon as the opening dialogue is concluded.

As a story develops, it is a good idea to continue alternating between the vitality of fresh plot development and the richness of description and exposition. In this way the pace of fiction often resembles that of a skater: the forward thrust is followed by a glide. If the glide is too long, the story, like the skater, will lose momentum.

The best time to review the pacing is when you have completed the first draft. Read the work without stopping and notice where it seems to slow down. If your low-key sections are brief, you have no problem. But if even you find it slow, consider careful cutting or adding new developments.

On the other hand, if your story strikes you as "full of sound and fury" without serious significance, ask yourself just what theme you want to suggest and then consider moderating the dramatic action. The short-short story is a relatively delicate form, and it is all too easy to drown out thematic concerns with a thundering drumbeat of action. A story ending with a fatal shooting can be revised to seem less like a routine television scene if you replace the death with an injury; a story capped by a suicide (often a too-easy solution) may be more convincing if the protagonist shows his or her despair in a more subtle way.

Much depends on the length of the work. A short-short story of three to six manuscript pages may be based on a single scene and may move at essentially the same pace from beginning to end. The longer a story, the more natural it is to have multiple scenes. As soon as you do that the pacing becomes increasingly important.

"Escapes," for example, seems like a relatively short story when printed, but it would come to 15 double-spaced pages in manuscript. A story of this length can afford a few relatively slow-paced scenes such as the telephone call and the extended description of Jennifer's mother.

It is sometimes difficult to judge the pacing of a story you have just written because you are still so close to the material. If you don't have a deadline looming over you, set the manuscript aside for a day or two and then read it nonstop as if for the first time. Or try to find others to read it. Even if they are not writers, they will be able to discuss your pacing.

13 Minding the Store

A Story

by Jim Ray Daniels

Carl Jacks was the kind of guy who got drunk and beat up his own friends, so you can imagine he didn't have a lot of them. We were all afraid of him, and I think he figured that was just as good.

At a party in Mound Park, Carl had punched out two of his buddies who were trying to convince him not to drive home. Mound Park was off Eight Mile Road, the border between Detroit and Warren, and it took police from both cities to take care of Carl. He took a few clunks on the head. But Carl had an incredibly hard head and incredible luck — the police let him go. His friends wouldn't press charges.

I worked at the Jolly Giant Party Store, which was close enough to our high school to get a lot of kids trying to pass themselves off as eighteen, the drinking age in Michigan back then. I was only sixteen myself, but the owner — this crazy guy named Charles who had Little Richard's thin mustache and some of his flamboyance — liked me and gave me a job. I used to stop in every day after my paper route for an Orange Crush and some chips and listen to him bullshit about how to fix the world. Charles lived with his friend, Marcel, who was always formal and serious. He was a CPA and did the books for a lot of the local businesses. I never saw him without a suit on.

None of the customers knew about Marcel. Charles, for all his flamboyance, kept the whole sexual thing in check. He knew what kind of neighborhood his store was — a working-class area on the edge of Detroit — and he wanted to stay in business. The video store next door had a waiting list for those Real Death videos — spliced-together clips of people getting killed.

Marcel came in every night at closing time to help shut things down. He called me Mr. Cummings. He had the faintest wisp of a smile, and I usually saw it after Charles said something clever. Charles' other employee was Martha, an old Polish woman who was a carryover from the previous owner. "Those two," she'd say to me, and roll her eyes at Charles and Marcel. Her husband had lost an arm in an industrial accident and was home on disability. Her only son was an alcoholic in and out of trouble with the cops. A couple of guys shacking up? "Eh," she'd say, "They seem happy."

So, there I was, checking i.d.'s when I wasn't old enough to drink myself. I was never tempted to sell to my underage friends. Charles trusted me, and I didn't have much else going for me back then — I had bad acne, and I was scrawny as hell. I knew that I was never going to kick anybody's ass, so when Carl Jacks came in the store, I was probably more afraid than the time Charles and I got robbed.

Carl pushed his way in at around seven on a Friday night. It was still light outside, but judging from Carl's behavior at some of the parties I'd been to, he usually started pretty early.

He came straight for me, though I was at the candy counter selling Flying Saucers and Lucky Suckers to the Deveraux girls who lived around the corner.

"Hey man, I need some Mad Dog."

Mad Dog, Mister Death. I never heard anyone ask for it by its official name, Mogen David 20/20. Twenty percent alcohol. Wino wine for the new generation.

I swallowed hard, as if I was actually trying to eat one of those dry Flying Saucers. At that moment, I wanted to be flying away in one.

"Uh, yes, yes, we do — on the shelf there." I pointed behind me. It was against the law to chill the fortified wines. Charles didn't sell any cold wine period. He didn't want it to become a wino store. That was the kind of compromise he'd make — sell it, but not cold, so he wouldn't sell very much of it.

Carl swiveled, then turned back quickly. "I mean cold."

"We don't carry it cold. It's against the law."

He shook his head as if trying to comprehend that astounding bit of information. When Carl got crazy at a party, he'd shake his head like that, wandering in circles, deliberately crashing into people.

But there wasn't much room to wander in the Jolly Giant, and he was sober, so he grabbed two warm bottles and set them on the checkout counter. I stood frozen, the cute little Deveraux girls looking up at me. The younger one, Darlene, snot streaming into her mouth, waited expectantly for me to hand over the box of Lucky Suckers so she could pick one out. If it said, "It's a winner" inside, she would get a free one.

Charles stood behind the deli counter slicing some Polish ham. "Bobby, will you get that?"

"Shit," I said under my breath. "Listen girls, I've got to wait on that man over there. I'll be right back." The Deveraux girls nodded solemnly. Working the candy counter, now *that* was real power — everything desired under glass, and I stood behind it.

I was trying to get to the checkout counter fast enough to keep Carl from getting too pissed off but slow enough to figure out a strategy. He was only a junior, so I didn't think he was eighteen.

Charles was watching me, the meat slicer idly whickering the air. I looked over at the Deveraux girls. Little Darlene was licking off the snot and swallowing.

"Do you have any i.d.?" I nearly whispered.

Carl stood there laughing to himself. He could have made a good line-backer, but he was more on the bar bouncer career track, and that was only if he could get himself under control.

"Wait a minute," he said, and turned and went outside back to his car.

I turned to Charles. "Hey Charles, this guy's gonna come back in and kill me. You want to take over?" He kept on slicing as if he didn't hear me.

Before I knew it, Carl stomped back into the store and tossed his driver's license across the counter at me. Not only was he eighteen, he was nineteen. I should have known somebody like Carl had been held back a time or two. One more time, and he'd be in my class. I made a silent prayer he wouldn't fail again.

"Thank you," I said, and gently pushed the license back toward him.

After I'd bagged the bottles and given him his change, he leaned toward me. I was wrong — he'd already started drinking. "Next time, keep some cold ones for me, okay, buddy?"

"Sure," I said, just happy to keep my pimply face intact for another day.

He exploded out the door. I looked out the window and saw a couple of freshman girls sitting in the back seat of his rust-bucket Chevy.

"Oh Lord, save them," I said. Then I felt little sticky fingers on mine and I turned and waited on the Deveraux girls.

Flying Saucers were hollow, multi-colored saucers with little balls of hard candy rolling around inside. The saucers tasted like communion hosts. The balls tasted like small pebbles. Kids would bite a hole in the side and pour the aliens down their throats. For a penny, you could be a monster. Not such a bad deal, I suppose.

Stocking the candy counter was one of Charles' favorite things about owning the store. The liquor paid the bills, but the candy filled Charles' bulging, sick heart. At the time, we didn't know it was sick. Charles ended up being the third person in the state of Michigan to get a heart transplant, and he lived five years with it, which was pretty good back then. Mysterious Marcel was with him to the end, soberly holding his hand then and not caring who saw.

Charles used to stand in front of the candy counter on the spot where the tile floors had been worn through down to bare cement.

"You know how many kids have stood here and pressed their face against this, glass and looked at this candy and put their golden pennies on the counter top and pointed their stubby little fingers and took their tiny paper bags and were happy?"

Charles imagined himself a poet, though he read the worst crap imaginable. One book was called *Thoughts about Myself, and Other Deep Mysterious Things*. No kidding. He loved the hell out of that one. He used to sit on beer cases in the back and read it aloud to me and Martha on slow rainy days in this phony voice I imagined he thought was super sensitive. We used to howl with laughter, and I think Charles laid it on thick for us. Listening to him read, laughing with Martha in that warm little store, I felt like I had a family. When I walked in the store every day after school, dropped my books, and put on my clerk's apron, I felt like home. I've never had another job in my whole life where I felt like that.

Martha treated me like a grandson. I think she'd always wanted another shot at mothering, so she was working on me. She was one of those people who could look the same for twenty years, so I really had no idea how old she was — maybe around sixty. Her cheeks were full of sass and good humor, and I loved her back just a little bit.

Charles let me do my homework when business was slow, and Martha always made sure I got it done. Sometimes Martha'd fry up some pierogi and kielbasa on the hot plate in the back room, and we'd have a little Polish feast. "I need to fatten you up, Bobby," she'd always say, as if a little weight was all I needed.

Though Charles complained about the smell of frying onions, he and I always fought over the odd last pierogi. When I think of that store, I think of the three of us eating off our laps. No customers. Well, maybe the Deveraux girls or Squeaky Kowalski or some other neighborhood kids just hanging out, hoping somebody'd spill some change or toss them a pity nickel. But we'd just be sitting there smiling and nodding at each other, chewing openmouthed, our cheeks bulging.

I did have a family, of course. I don't want to say much about them — it would sound like typical teenage whining: my parents don't understand me, blah, blah, blah.

Okay, just a couple of things: my older brother and sister were one year apart, and my younger brother and sister were one year apart. I was in the middle, with four years between me and anyone else. My mother got me two department-store birds for my birthday one year, and they both died within a week. After the first one died, she got the other one a mirror for companionship. I think the second bird died from looking at himself so much, and I think that's what was killing me those years — too much looking in the mirror and not liking what I saw. "Boo hoo, that's enough whining," as Charles would say. He never talked about his own family, and I didn't ask.

When you're sixteen, your own family is usually not what you want, no matter what they're like, so you wander the world desperately looking for some other community to accept and love you. Sometimes you end up like Carl, with fear and hatred instead. I could never find my spot on the social map of our school. I was one of the dumbest kids in the classes for smart kids.

I did have a girlfriend though. Jeanette. She was kind of homely, like me, but she had beautiful breasts that I could cup in my hands some nights after her trusting parents went to bed and left us alone in the living room watching TV. When she'd come in the store, Charles always waited on her, elaborately bagging her purchases and putting the change in her hand, holding it till she turned red. He knew I was insanely jealous. But it was just Charles, so I could laugh it off.

"I love the sensuous," he said once. He had opened up a canned Polish ham and was scraping off the jelly it was packed in. "Oh, feel that meat. Oh, smell all that meat. It's so primal!"

"What's he going on about now?" Martha asked.

I burst out laughing. "Meat," I said.

"Oh, Lord," she said.

"Oh, yes!" Charles shouted. I didn't understand Charles, but I knew he had a good heart — well, maybe I mean "soul," the heart that counts, finally, in the end.

I started keeping a couple of cold Mad Dogs in the cooler, and Carl came in every Friday and Saturday night for them. When he entered the store, I hurried to the cooler and pulled out his Mad Dogs from where I'd hid them. Charles kept quiet about it. I think he'd heard the fear in my voice that first day. I doubt Charles'd had much success dealing with bullies himself.

Carl had been in my gym class the previous year, and I was a witness to one of the most famous Carl Jacks stories. We all had to box. You got paired off by weight, then went at it. I boxed Rich Dunn, and we each got a C+, two scrawny kids flailing at each other with those heavy gloves. Coach Bums laughed and smiled when we were done. "Well, wasn't that cute?" he said.

One day Coach Bums was showing us some boxing moves while we sat sprawled on the mats. Carl was yakking it up with some of the other goons when Coach stopped and slowly turned toward them, gave them his hard stare.

"Jacks, you think you know it all. Get up here, and I'll demonstrate on you."

Carl slowly stood, laughing that stupid laugh. He's the kind of guy who could kill somebody while smiling the whole time. He put on the gloves, and Coach said, "Okay, Jacks, now you try to hit me."

Carl laughed even harder. "Naw, this is a trick."

"No, come on," Coach said. "Try and hit me."

Carl's thick arms dangled at his sides, and he started to turn away from Coach, who relaxed just enough so that Carl could whirl around and deck him with a punch square on the nose.

Coach went after Carl, and they were duking it out when the athletic director came rushing out of his office to break it up. Coach had a busted nose. Carl looked okay as they hauled him away. "He told me to hit him," he kept saying, and laughing — he knew he had them. He was sent home for the rest of the day, then got permanently excused from gym class.

I'd never believed in pure evil. There had to be some good in everybody, right? I was beginning to think Carl had some good in him. He had punched out the worst tyrant of a teacher in the school and had gotten away with it — that gave him some hero points. Something besides fear made me try to please Carl — something I didn't like, but couldn't stop. I went out of my way to keep him happy. Maybe it was that I felt protected, though I should have known better.

The Deveraux girls were addicted to the two worst candies — "Flying Saucers" and "Lucky Suckers." Their father was a drunk. Working in a liquor store, you knew. You knew whose hands shook, whose eyes wandered over the rows of orderly bottles with sick lust.

Even Martha's son sometimes stumbled in to the Jolly Giant to make her pull a bottle down and put it in a bag and take his money. It must have given him a perverse pleasure, one of the few of his dismal days. "I told you to take your business someplace else," Martha would tell him in a monotone. I think he usually did go somewhere else, but from time to time, he'd show up near closing to get one more bottle and taunt his mother. I'd watch helplessly while her cheeks sagged, her eyes filled with tears, and her whole body seemed to take on another twenty years. Charles was gentle with her on those nights, draping her faded green sweater over her shoulders as he led her out the door, giving them a squeeze before she walked off alone toward home.

"What made you buy this place?" I asked Charles one day. It was a wonderfully cluttered store — a wide deli counter ran across the back wall, hard liquor lined the far wall, with the checkout in front of it alongside a bakery counter (fresh baked goods delivered daily from Oaza bakery in Hamtramck) and, of course, the candy counter, which was wedged into a corner near the door. The candy and baked goods were in tall slanted glass cases that Martha constantly cleaned in a losing battle against sticky fingerprints.

When the fresh bread arrived in the morning, it smelled like heaven. Because of school, I missed most mornings, so every Saturday, Charles would let me tear into a fresh warm loaf. He called it Communion Time — he loved to watch me devour it. I shook my head like a dog with a shoe, the whole loaf in my mouth. I couldn't get enough of what that store gave me.

"I always liked neighborhood stores, where you really get to know your customers," he said. He used to sell men's clothes at an exclusive store out at Somerset, the fancy mall twenty miles to the west, twenty miles further from the city. He inherited "a tidy sum," as he put it, when his mother died, and bought Gene's Jolly Giant. Newer customers called him Gene — or Mr. Jolly Giant, which Charles loved, puffing up dramatically. Charles even loved the old red neon sign out front, which flashed what was supposed to be a giant, though it looked more like a fat midget.

Charles' grandparents had owned a small corner grocery, where he had spent a lot of his childhood. Above his meat counter he hung an enlarged, blurry photo of them standing in that store. He railed against the large supermarkets. "Cow barns," he called them. "And we're the cows going to slaughter down the anonymous aisles while this country loses its soul. Loses its soul, I tell you."

"Amen," Martha'd say, rolling her eyes. Her eyes got a workout around Charles, but she needed a workout — every minute in that store was a minute away from her depressed husband and alcoholic son. "He lost an arm, and they took his heart with it," she was fond of saying about her husband Mike, and when he came by to walk her home some nights, and I saw his long gloomy, defeated face, I could not argue with her.

Charles had to sell booze to hang on to his nostalgic dream. He had to pay the devil. "I knew the liquor license was what made the business go," he said, "but I never thought about what it would do to me to see those same desperate people every single day.

"Look, you don't see the tile worn all the way through in front of the liquor. You know why? The men and women who stand there have a name on their lips when they arrive and it's the name on one of those bottles. Do you see hesitation? No. Do you see indecision? No. You see desperation and fear. And who gives them what they need? I do, Bobby. I am the Candy Man, see? The kids don't know what they want. There's a whole beautiful world of sweetness there before them. . . ."

I liked it when Charles talked to me like that, like an adult. He made himself vulnerable in ways that no adult I knew did. Everyone — parents, teachers — they all put on the front. They never admitted they were wrong.

After the Deveraux girls gave their suckers a few discouraged licks and wandered home, I asked Charles, "Are you mad at me about something?" I grabbed a penny pretzel and stuck it in my mouth.

"No, no," he said, then quickly, "Yes. I mean, I am concerned about your relationship with Mad Dog Man."

"Relationship?" I laughed. "What, are you jealous?" I instantly regretted saying those words, but they were out there, hanging in the air of the small, cluttered store, no getting them back.

After a long silence, Charles' voice turned hard. "I don't want you keeping any more cold Mad Dog for that boy." He said "boy" with a dismissive sneer.

"He'll kill me," I whined.

Jeanette and I had broken up two weeks earlier. I'd seen her kissing another boy at a party and had grabbed her arm — a little rough, I think now. "Why?" I'd asked her.

"I'm drunk," she said. I had gone to the party sober after the store closed at ten. She'd been out with her friends for hours.

"How'd you like it if I was out here kissing somebody else?" I looked around at the milling, swaying circles of teenagers — everybody seemed drunk.

"Oh, go ahead," she said, "kiss somebody else. Go ahead and kiss somebody," then she exploded with a shrill laugh that scared the hell out of me. I turned and walked away, and we hadn't spoken since.

"Robert," he said, "We have to stick up for ourselves in this world against the Mad Dog Monsters who will rub our faces in the dirt and then make us pay them for the privilege. I cannot stand here and watch this go on any longer."

"He'll kill me," I repeated hopelessly. He put his hand on my shoulder, and I flinched.

"I'll wait on him," Charles said, "Like I should have the first time."

Carl came in Friday night, right on schedule. Most of the evening, I'd been hiding in the walk-in cooler, but Carl sniffed me out. He saw the walk-in door ajar and swung it open. I was sitting on a half-dozen cases of Pabst Blue Ribbon twelve-ounce cans.

"Oh, hi," I said. "Just cooling off."

"Knock it off, smartass. Where's my cold Dogs?"

"We — the boss said we can't keep any — any more cold ones for you."

"Ah, shit, you pimple-faced pussy." He slammed the cooler shut, and I was locked in. I felt like I wouldn't mind freezing to death, but it wasn't to be that simple. He yanked the door open again and pulled me out by the collar.

"Can I help you with something?" It was not Charles, but Martha, who came out from behind the deli counter. What was Charles doing? He was visibly swaying, trying to steady himself against the checkout counter. Carl was still holding me.

"Let go of him," Charles pleaded, his voice cracking. "I'll call the police."

"And do what, tell them you got this underage punk selling booze?"

That stopped us. We were used to the routine — if someone we didn't know came in, Martha or Charles would sell the liquor. Carl wasn't as stupid as he appeared. He must have willfully failed. I could see him doing that — failing, to spite the world.

I turned back to the walk-in and pulled out the one bottle I'd hidden as insurance, in defiance of Charles, and handed it to Carl.

"Just one?"

It was the kind of compromise I imagined Charles making. "Yeh — it's all we got left," I said, shrugging my shoulders up around my neck.

He silently took it up to the counter, then he grabbed a warm one off the rack and set it beside the cold one.

My heart was flipping like a stuck record. Martha stood in the aisle, arms folded over her chest, directly in Charles' line of sight, behind and to the right of the pacing Carl Jacks.

"We don't want your business, warm or cold," Charles said.

"Okay . . . *faggot*," Carl said, smiling. He relaxed like he did right before he punched the coach. "Duck, Charles," I yelled, and he lowered his head.

Carl caught him above the right ear. "Shit," Carl said, "Shit, shit, shit," shaking his hand. He'd crunched it against Charles' skull. Carl reached for the bottles with his good hand, but Charles quickly snatched them off the counter and placed them on the shelves behind him. Blood trickled from behind his ear.

"I'm getting out of here," I said, "I quit!" I ran out the door and all the way home. It was early spring, and the cold March air buried itself in my chest. I'd left my jacket behind, and I was still wearing my work apron, but I didn't care. They couldn't do that to me — neither of them.

Maybe I should have rejoiced at Charles standing up to Jacks, or worried about his injury, but I only thought of the possibility of getting my own ass kicked. Quitting might save me. I wanted the simple life of that photograph above the meat and cheese, two old people in aprons surrounded by the clutter of their small store, satisfied and proud. Like I told Jeanette, I didn't want to kiss anybody else.

You wouldn't think it'd be that big a deal, whether you keep somebody's cheap wine cold or not. But I was beginning to learn that the big things were in the little things. Carl never did kick my ass, but it's not something I'm proud of. By the time his broken hand healed, he'd probably found another store to keep it cold for him. After all, he was old enough to get it anywhere. For all he knew, I quit in support of his need for cold Mad Dog.

I never asked about what happened after I left that night, but I do know that Carl never came in the store again. I know, because after a couple of sleepless weeks, I got up enough nerve and walked into the Jolly Giant early one Saturday morning to apologize, and, like the best families, they took me back.

14 Creating Tension

"Well, it's a pleasant little story." If you hear that about a piece you've just written, don't smile. It may sound like a compliment, but it isn't.

Creative writing classes and magazine editors receive too many "pleasant little stories," and often the authors remain oblivious to what is wrong with them. A dull story is like a dull meal at a restaurant; patrons don't complain, but they don't come back. The sad aspect is that the chef, hearing no specific complaints, never improves.

What those pleasant little stories lack is **tension**. Tension in fiction is what gives it energy and vitality. It's what keeps the reader reading. Without tension, a story goes limp. And unread.

There are many different ways of creating tension, but they all consist of pitting one element against another. These are the most common ways of producing tension:

- **Conflict.** This is the most easily identified. It can take the form of one against one, an individual against a group, or a struggle against nature.
- **Internal conflict.** Although often a subtle form of tension, it can become a dominant concern as we will see when we apply it to "Rwanda."
- **Mistrust.** Suspicion can be one-sided or mutual. It can damage friendships, family relationships, or even a marriage.
- **Foreboding.** The staple of horror flicks (often enhanced by ominous music), it can also be used subtly in sophisticated fiction.

Although we will be examining these as separate devices, they are often used in conjunction with each other. Each has the power to turn a slack story into one that is dynamic.

CONFLICT: STRUGGLING AGAINST ADVERSARIES

There is something elemental about pitting one individual against another. In its basic form, the **protagonist** or **hero** takes on an enemy. We're used to that in plays, narrative poetry (particularly ballads), and, most often, film.

In simple work, conflict can be emphasized to such a degree that it blots out subtlety of **characterization** and **theme**. Adventure stories from Edgar Rice Burroughs' *Tarzan* series to most television thrillers pit characters against enemies with great regularity. The conflict in such work is fairly straightforward: the good guys are good, and their opponents are unmistakably bad. Few if any are bothered by inner doubts. The pattern is essentially the same when an individual faces a group such as a gang, a mob, or enemy troops. Occasionally, the hero must outsmart not only the evil bunch, but also law enforcers, a good example of how complexity of plot doesn't necessarily create subtlety.

With associations like these, it's no wonder that beginning writers sometimes avoid all forms of conflict and keep their characters passive or isolated. But there is no need to avoid conflict in even the most sensitive fiction. It will add essential vitality to your work as long as you make sure that it doesn't take over and become the dominant concern.

"Minding the Store" is an excellent example of a subtle story based on an unmistakable conflict. The adversary is identified right from the start:

> Carl Jacks was the kind of guy who got drunk and beat up his own friends, so you can imagine he didn't have a lot of them. We were all afraid of him, and I think he figured that was just as good.

A classic villain! One might wonder from this opening blast whether this will turn out to be an action story with good pitted against evil. As if to confirm our doubts, the very next paragraph is a **flashback** showing us that Carl Jacks is fully as dangerous as described. If he turns out to be all this bad and the narrator equally good, what chance is there for subtlety?

But initial judgments when reading fiction are not to be trusted. As if to reassure us, the story moves on to describe the Jolly Giant Party Store and those who work there. We almost forget about Carl Jacks before he explodes on the scene once again.

If you mark the scenes that focus on Carl Jacks, you will see that there are four and that they are spaced out. Between them are scenes and background that contribute to the concerns of the story. It is clear from this that the conflict between the narrator and Carl Jacks is not in itself the **theme**.

Conflict is equally important in "Rwanda." If you isolate that aspect of the story, you can see that it resembles the murder mystery pattern of many television plots: a search for the culprit, his capture, his attempt to escape and recapture.

What keeps this simple **convention** from dominating the story? First is the fact that, as we saw in "Minding the Store," less than half of the plot is devoted to the conflict itself. In this case, a great deal goes on before they even discover that the wallet has been stolen.

Second, by muting the violence, the conflict is kept from dominating the story. As in "Minding the Store," the climax is kept at a level that can be handled in a short story. In a **hackneyed** film script, the last third of the plot might have been devoted to a wild chase scene culminating in the thief's bloody death.

Third, a slightly comic detail keeps the conflict from getting out of hand. In "Rwanda," the absurdity of a police force without available transportation and the officers' insistence on maintaining the European custom of shaking hands with everyone provides a lighter element. True, this detail was taken directly from the events as they happened but it was my choice to include them. My sense was that they would help keep that part of the story from becoming **melodramatic**.

Conflict, then, plays an important part in both stories, but it has been used with restraint and not allowed to become the central concern.

INNER CONFLICT

One of the characteristics of simple fiction is that characterization is rarely muddied by inner conflict. Superman never deals with the conflict between his macho lifestyle and his reluctance to enter into a serious relationship with a woman, Spider-Man is never tempted to enter a life of crime, and Batman never comes to terms with his enduring attachment to his young companion.

"Escapes" is a good example of a story that makes extensive use of inner conflict. It first appears in the telephone call with Jennifer's mother. In that flashback, we get the first hint of Caryn's mixed feelings about caring for Jennifer. "I'll take her for a while," Caryn says. Her resistance increases at the end of that conversation when she hears that the girl has apparently tried to commit suicide. She is unwilling to express this aloud, but her misgiving is shown through her thoughts:

> . . . wishing I had not agreed to take Jennifer. What did I know about teenagers? Or suicide? Or anything at all?

In the second phone call with her sister-in-law, Caryn asks when she can send Jennifer back. She gets no clear answer, but we learn about her inner anguish again through her thoughts:

> I want to explain that I am tired of Jennifer being here. That she is not really helping me decide what to do next. That I have an urge, once more, to pick up and go. To L.A., maybe. Or even Hawaii.

Notice that she wants to say this but can't. All these negative feelings are countered by the fact that she is by nature a caring person (note the play on her name) and that Jennifer is her niece.

This combination of resentment and attachment is a good example of **ambivalence**, a conflicting mix of emotions that occurs so frequently in sophisticated fiction — and more than we like to admit in life. It runs through the length of this story.

Are these mixed feelings resolved? Never fully. Certainly not with hugs, kisses, and tears. At the end Caryn and Jennifer are together though they realize that the future will not be easy.

If you read the story closely, you will see that there is another example of mixed feelings. It's a minor detail, but it helps reveal Caryn's present state. A part of her misses her former boyfriend Luke. We know this because she keeps his shirts "crammed into [her] one closet" and she doesn't throw out "his deodorant and toothbrush and comb." Yet she hardly seems devastated when he sends a brief and chilly letter signed "Sincerely, Luke." When Jennifer asks whether Caryn loves him, she only shrugs. She might have said, "I do and I don't."

In "Rwanda" Francine's inner conflict is the dominant emotion at the very beginning and again at the end. Her compassion for living creatures like the goat and, at the end, the thief, is countered by her realistic self who knows, as her husband might have put it, "you can't save them all."

Notice how these inner conflicts in both stories are presented. They are revealed primarily through dialogue. Each story uses thoughts briefly, but most of what we discover about their inner conflict is implied by what they say.

If you are just beginning to write fiction, you may be tempted to present inner conflicts directly through exposition ("He was being tugged in two opposite directions") or poorly disguised thoughts ("It's so frustrating, he thought, to be tugged in two opposite directions.") Resist! Let the reader discover the mixed feeling by what the character says and does. In some cases, characters reveal more about their feelings than they realize.

MISTRUST THAT CREATES TENSION

Mistrust tends to be more subtle than outright conflict. It can exist without even being recognized by those involved. But it has the power to keep characters on edge, apprehensive, or even fearful. Such feelings are passed on to readers, fueling a sense of anxiety that is a form of tension. All three stories are charged with different types of mistrust. It runs as an undercurrent in "Escapes." The two characters don't confront each other directly. Instead, they behave like two cats circling each other in edgy mistrust. In "Rwanda," suspicion grows dramatically toward the end.

FOREBODING

Stories arouse the reader's emotions through small details. If these details are dark, the reader has the sense that something ominous will happen. The tethered goat at the opening of "Rwanda" is followed by Max's tale of the topi capture, and both provide a forewarning.

"Minding the Store" opens with the description of a brute who will linger in our memories even though the scenes that follow are lighter. We are sure that some kind of violence will ultimately occur.

In the case of "Escapes," the opening scene is not ominous, but the more we learn about Jennifer's history the more we suspect that something may go terribly wrong. The sense of foreboding builds in increments. First, we hear about her apparent suicide attempt, then her history of stealing and cheating. It is truly ominous when Jennifer "leans out the open window, too far out." The scene at the Alcatraz prison is dark with implication. The sense of foreboding doesn't end until the last two sentences.

If you plan to create a sense of foreboding, be careful not to be obvious or repeat it too often. If readers get the feeling that you are manipulating their feelings, they may lose the sense of being in the story. The work will seem contrived.

DRAMATIC QUESTIONS

In Chapter 12, I pointed out how often stories begin with action that will arouse the reader's curiosity. This helps get a story started.

Not all stories follow this pattern, of course, but it is an approach that is frequently used for good reason. If you review the openings of the three fiction stories you have read so far, you will see that in spite of striking differences in content, each plunges the reader into a lively and ongoing situation. This is followed by background information.

The next step is to move the story forward once again. The best way to do this is to provide new questions about what will occur. Think of these as **dramatic questions**.

Suppose you have started with a child answering the door and confronting a strange, bearded man with two enormous suitcases. Who is he, and what does he want? There is a starter. But as soon as the stranger's identity is clarified (a notorious Uncle Harry from Australia, for example), we can raise another: Is he really an uncle? Can we trust him? Will he ask for money? This might be the point at which you could provide more background material, slowing the pace of the story.

The next question might be whether your protagonist will have to give up her bedroom for this man. As in the stories you have read, you can create a series of dramatic questions. As soon as one is answered, another is introduced.

Authors, of course, are not trying to frustrate their readers by creating dramatic questions. This is simply an effective way to maintain interest. One doles out information in "bits and pieces," keeping careful track of what I have described as the **rate of revelation**. Revealing too much too soon can make the story's outcome predictable. Avoid leaving questions unanswered at the end, however, since that will make the work as a whole seem obscure and unsatisfying.

Important as tension is, dramatic impact can be pushed too far. Make sure you don't turn your work into a **melodrama**. Jennifer in "Escapes" doesn't commit suicide; the narrator in "Minding the Store" is never beaten to a pulp by the town bully. Such endings would so dominate the stories that the reader would remember nothing but the plot. As a general rule, plot in a literary short story should be a means to develop themes and character, not an end in itself. Put another way, tension is necessary to keep your work energized and moving forward, but it shouldn't be pushed to the point where it becomes the most memorable aspect.

RECHARGING A SLACK STORY

Lack of vitality is apt to be more of a problem than too much of it. There may be occasions when even after all your efforts your story is still too mild. If this happens, don't give up. Even if you have completed a few drafts, you may well find aspects of the work that contain the seeds for greater tension. It helps, though, to know where to look.

The areas most likely to need revision are relationships between characters. Pick out minor differences of opinion or attitude and see if you can intensify them. Often such revisions will be enough to generate the tension you need.

If this doesn't work, you may have to subject the characters to a **transformation** as described in Chapter 7. You don't have to destroy the more harmonious aspects, but you can revitalize a character by providing him or her with a strong sense of **ambivalence**. This often helps to generate some inner tension.

Finally, make sure that you haven't explained too much of the theme or aspects of your characters, depriving your readers of the chance to draw conclusions on their own. If you have whole paragraphs of exposition, consider cutting them. Try to reveal these aspects more subtly through what your characters do and say.

Remember that the degree of tension is entirely up to you as author. In most cases, it is a mistake to blame the situation you have chosen as being inherently melodramatic on the one hand or without dramatic potential on the other. Use your creative imagination to adjust the degree of tension. Your goal is to hold interest without sacrificing characterization and thematic insight.

15 Setting

Where Am I?

"Where am I?" is the common cry of those regaining consciousness. It is also the instinctive question of a reader who has just begun a new story or novel. This is why most stories establish the setting along with the means of perception fairly early.

As we have seen, a dynamic opening may justify postponing the setting for a paragraph or two. But try not to postpone it for too long. There is a strangely abstract tone to stories that seem to float in space. Some authors delay orienting the reader intentionally, but if you try this it should be for a good reason.

Like a stage set, the surroundings help to place readers in the story. A particular house, a room in that house, a field, a beach, or a factory assembly line — these and countless other settings provide important visual details. Helping readers see where they are not only establishes **verisimilitude** — the illusion of reality — it may also contribute to characterization and theme.

Some stories, of course, make minimal use of setting, but even the most dreamlike fantasies, like dreams themselves, usually provide details that help readers imagine themselves in a specific place. As writers, we have to judge how much to emphasize the setting and which aspects to highlight.

How long can you wait before orienting the reader? In most full-length short stories of 10 or more manuscript pages, the setting is established within the first two pages. In a short-short story, you may want to establish the setting even sooner. Remember that additional details can be filled in later.

HOW MUCH DETAIL? MAJOR VERSUS MINOR EMPHASIS

In Chapter 19, you will be reading a story, "The Bank Robbery," in which there is almost no use of the setting. All you need to know is that the story is set in a bank. In contrast, the three stories you have read so far not only provide many details, but they also use them to amplify the theme.

"Escapes" is an interesting example. The setting is clearly identified as San Francisco, but for the first two thirds of the story the selection of that city does not seem essential to the theme. After all, other cities have roller coasters that would be similar to riding the cable cars, baseball parks that rival Candlestick Park, and clothing outlet stores. But Alcatraz is a unique setting. Where else can the author find a way to place these two women temporarily in a prison? The sense of being trapped without hope of escape is essential to the theme. The city of San Francisco may have been a natural choice for the author simply because she is familiar with it, but Alcatraz serves a special purpose.

I've already explained how the setting in "Rwanda" was determined by an actual experience, but the African setting was not inserted just for the sake of novelty. This is not a story that could easily be transformed to a U.S. city. It gave me a chance to develop a character who is caught between two cultures.

Don't assume, however, that writing fiction depends on being familiar with foreign countries. Of all three of these stories, "Minding the Store" makes the greatest use of the setting. The importance of the setting, however, is easy to miss on first reading because of the informal as-if-spoken style of the first-person narration. The narrator, Bobby, seems to ramble on without direction, providing flashbacks on occasion and even jumping into the future briefly. But this apparent lack of direction does allow the author to keep inserting significant details about both the Jolly Giant Party Store and those who work there.

The following quotations come from different parts of the story. If you read them as a group, you will see how what may seem at first to be a story about a 16-year-old and the school bully is actually focused on a different theme. Notice the closely related words, *family*, *home*, and *mothering* and the warm, affectionate tone in these scenes:

> Listening to him read, laughing with Martha in that warm little store, I felt like I had a family. When I walked in the store every day after school, dropped my books, and put on my clerk's apron, I felt like home.
>
> Martha treated me like a grandson. I think she'd always wanted another shot at mothering, so she was working on me.
>
> When I think of that store, I think of the three of us eating off our laps. No customers . . . we'd just be sitting there smiling and nodding at each other, chewing open-mouthed, our cheeks bulging.

And now the very end of the story:

> ... after a couple of sleepless weeks, I got up enough nerve and walked into the Jolly Giant early one Saturday morning to apologize, and, like the best families, they took me back.

The **plot** of this story is held together rather loosely by the demands of Jack the bully and the none-too-successful attempts of Bobby the kid to deal with him, but the **theme** has to do with what constitutes a truly supportive family.

I'll return to the subject of themes in Chapter 21, but for now focus on how a setting can contribute to a story's central concern. The setting here is the Jolly Giant Party Store. Except for a few flashbacks and one other brief scene, the setting remains right there almost as if this were a one-act play. In the course of the telling, the setting becomes a true home, and the nature of a true home becomes the central concern of the story.

Contrast these with the stage set used in so many sitcom television shows and even some plays, a layout known as "the sitcom living room." The details are mind-numbingly familiar: couch in the middle, coffee table centered, upholstered chairs on either side, front door to the left, and stairs to the right. It's a clichéd setting best described as "one size fits all."

Generally speaking, the settings in literary fiction have three basic qualities: they are *distinctive*, *specific*, and *relevant*.

- *Distinctive* settings are often adapted from places where the writer has lived, worked, or at least visited — a party store, for example, or a former prison. If you have a family photo album or have maintained a journal, review them. It helps if you select an environment you as writer know well, but also consider places you have seen briefly and can use as a point of departure. If it's a setting that will be unfamiliar for most readers, it will have a special intensity.

- *Specific details* may seem insignificant by themselves, but collectively they create a more vivid picture than vague adjectives do. In "Escapes," for example, we know what the area around Caryn's office is like not from adjectives like "rundown" but from what she can see from her window: "hookers on the corner, a man drinking something from a paper bag." In "Minding the Store," our sense of being there is sharpened by the fact that around the candy counter there is a "spot where the tile floors had been worn through down to bare cement." In "Rwanda" we are reminded that the treatment of servants is substandard by the word that describes where their houseboy lives as "a hutch."

  When you select details that will make a setting vivid, it is natural to think of the visual aspect first, but don't forget smells, sounds, and temperature. The open market in "Rwanda" strikes Katy with these details: "All these people-sounds and the horns and the smells — cooking meat, sweat, animal crap — Luscious!"

  The range of smells is limitless: musty cellars, kitchens in which liver and onions are being fried, oily-smelling filling stations, the trace of cigar smoke in a car. As for sounds, some houses are plagued by the roar of traffic while others are located near a jetport. Characters have to yell in an auto-body shop or a disco, reducing dialogue to short phrases. Desert winds can dominate one environment and pounding surf another. Any of these can increase the impact of your setting.

- *Relevance* is not an absolute requirement; sometimes it's enough to have a setting that simply establishes a mood. But there is an additional benefit if you can find a setting or even a minor detail that also contributes to the theme. As we have seen, the entire setting of Alcatraz in "Escapes" contributes to the sense of being trapped in lives with no future, so it helps to develop that theme by having the fog "still thick" on the day Caryn and Jennifer go there.

REAL PLACES VERSUS INVENTED SETTINGS

Some stories name an actual city or state as the setting, while others create one entirely from imagination. The majority take a midcourse, suggesting a geographic region without using known place-names. Each approach has its advantages and potential problems.

Of the three stories you have read, "Minding the Store" is the least specific in terms of geography. There is just one brief reference to the store being "in a working-class area on the edge of Detroit," but it could have been set in any American blue-collar neighborhood.

In contrast, "Escapes" is unmistakably rooted in the San Francisco area. It would take massive rewriting to set it anywhere else. The use of Alcatraz is the most prominent borrowing from an actual place and would be the most difficult to replace. Other locations such as Candlestick Park and Fisherman's Wharf lend themselves to the vivid sense of realism.

Keep in mind, however, that when we say "actual place" with reference to fiction, we are still dealing with illusion. Fictional settings are imaginary because they are always filtered through the mind's eye of a writer. If 10 stories make use of the same city, they will be significantly different. Each one will be shaped by a unique imagination. Your true choice, then, is not, "Should I set this story in a real city?" but "Should I use the name and certain details of an actual city in the exercise of my imagination?"

There are two advantages to drawing on a known city and naming it, as is done in "Escapes." First, it can serve as a geographic shorthand for the reader. There are features of our larger cities that are known even by those who have not been there. In addition, using a real city or countryside can be a convenience for you as a writer if you know the area well. It will save you the trouble of making up your own map.

But there are a few risks too. Unless you are really familiar with the city or countryside you are using, you may find yourself borrowing details you have unconsciously absorbed from other stories and from television. Students who have never been to New York City, for example, may fall back on such standard conventions as jazz clubs on 52nd Street (long since gone) or impoverished artists in Greenwich Village (driven out by rising rents) The same is true for Paris. If in blind ignorance the author spices a story with shots of the Eiffel Tower, cancan dancers, and prostitutes with hearts of gold, the fiction is bound to reflect the musical comedies from which this material was taken.

To avoid these weaknesses, make sure you know what you are writing about. Even when you are familiar with the city, avoid its most obvious aspects. Focus instead on districts and details that will seem fresh but authentic to your readers.

Another problem is psychological. You may find yourself too closely bound to a particular house or neighborhood. This can limit your imagination. The best solution is to break the mold by making a major **transformation** in that setting.

Many writers prefer to keep a little distance between themselves and the setting by inventing place-names even when they are using an actual area as a base. Doing this helps to liberate the imagination in the same way that inventing the names of characters does. It gives authors flexibility while still preserving the sense of authenticity that one can achieve by using details one knows well.

John Updike describes this relationship between a real place and fictional settings in his foreword to *Olinger Stories*:

> The name Olinger is audibly a shadow of "Shillington," the real name of my home town, yet the two towns, however similar, are not at all the same. Shillington is a place on the map and belongs to the world; Olinger is a state of mind, of my mind, and belongs entirely to me.

In this spirit, Updike used Olinger, Pennsylvania, in 11 short stories. The names and ages of the protagonists vary, but essentially they are the same boy. The approach is similar to that of Sherwood Anderson in *Winesburg, Ohio*. On a broader scale, William Faulkner blended historical and fictional elements in this way in his stories and novels set in his imaginary Yoknapatawpha County, Mississippi.

There is a long tradition of fiction that makes much more direct use of specific regions than any of these stories. Known as **regionalism**, or, formerly, **local color** writing, it became particularly popular toward the end of the 19th century. Mark Twain, Bret Harte, and Sarah Orne Jewett were the best-known practitioners. A number of lesser-known writers, however, gave the term a bad reputation by concentrating on regional dialects and customs in a patronizing manner.

Regionalism in the best sense is flourishing today. Successful examples depend on two elements: personal familiarity and respect. You really have to know what you are writing about if you are going to do justice to the people of a specific region or culture. It is important to write from the inside, not as an outside observer.

Make sure you know your limits. If, for example, you spend some time in New Mexico as a tourist, you may gather some excellent material for a story about tourists in New Mexico, and you certainly will be able to draw on the physical characteristics of the area, but that doesn't mean that you are equipped to depict the life of a Navajo on the reservation. Leave that to those who have lived there.

TIME AS SETTING: HOUR AND SEASON

The time of day or night is often important in a story. When a character is hurrying to catch a plane or get to a wedding, you can add to the suspense by identifying the time precisely, sometimes more than once. Whether it is a foggy morning as it is in the last scene of "Escapes" or nighttime as it is when Francine in "Rwanda" drives through the unlit streets to the police station, the hour can be an important part of the setting.

Watch out, however, for a pattern that has become so common that it has turned into a cliché: the wake-up opening. It takes many forms, such as a ringing alarm clock, the flicker of a fading dream, the smell of coffee, or a pounding headache. They are all too familiar and draw on the too-neat link between the start of the day and the start of a story.

Fewer stories, but still too many, conclude with a version of the old film ending: watching the sun go down and "looking forward to another day." Try something new.

Even if you are not making specific use of the time of day, keep track of it in your own mind. Doing this will help you to avoid careless errors such as having a character take a morning coffee break, engage in dialogue, and without a transition head home for supper. All it takes is a simple phrase: "At the end of the day, she . . ."

Carelessness in time sense can also lead to an error that is subtler but almost as damaging: a character goes to his friend's apartment to see if he can borrow her car for the weekend. She lets him in and they sit down. He says, "Hey, can I borrow your car?" and she says, "Sure." He gets up and leaves. The plot has advanced, but credibility is lost. People don't generally sit down as if for a conversation and then say one sentence. What's missing is some reference to the rest of what went on. It doesn't have to be in dialogue form; you can use exposition to allow for the requisite small talk and the passage of time, something like, "He explained in detail how his car had broken down again" or "She was reluctant but finally agreed."

The time of year is another aspect of time that may prove to be helpful. If the season has no real significance in a story, you can ignore it without the reader even noticing. Such is the case in the stories you have read here, but occasionally it can become a major focus in a work of fiction.

HISTORICAL PERIODS

Most short stories are set in the same historical period as the one in which they are written. This is partly because it takes time to establish the atmosphere of an earlier period, time that one can't easily spare in so short a form. In addition, if you move back to the 19th century, it is difficult to avoid having your stories resemble Westerns, historical romances, or so-called costume gothics with their standard plots and stereotyped characters.

There are, however, two ways of using an earlier historical period effectively without running the risk of echoing **formulaic** fiction. In both approaches the writer maintains some personal link with the earlier time. First, it is sometimes possible to develop good fiction from extensive conversations with elderly people such as grandparents. Thanks in part to lightweight audio cassette recorders and camcorders, there has been a growing interest in oral history of the immediate past. If your subject is willing to provide it, material gathered in this manner can become the basis of fiction (or literary nonfiction as well) that has the true ring of authenticity.

You do have to pick your subject carefully, of course. Some people are more articulate than others. Some enjoy recalling their past, but others do not — sometimes for understandable reasons. If your informant is agreeable, however, let him or her do plenty of talking. You may have to ask an occasional question in order to clarify certain facts, but try not to be too directive. Let your informant determine the direction of the conversation.

The other use of the past applies only to those writers who are themselves old enough to remember when life was different. The accumulation of memory is one of the compensating benefits of age, and that layering of experience is an excellent source for fiction just as it is for literary nonfiction.

One word of caution, however: be careful not to place undue emphasis on the differences between the period being described and the present day. If you draw too much attention to how inexpensive things were, for example, the reader may begin to view the material as quaint. Try instead to draw readers into that period. Help them share it.

REVISING THE DETAILS

Once you have decided on an appropriate setting, move ahead with the writing. If you have questions about the details, don't let them hold you up. Set them aside until you are finished with the first draft.

After you have completed the first draft, take a close look at all aspects of the setting. If you plan to draw on the setting in a significant way, as is the case of stories you have just read here, it's time to look closely at how you handled the details. There are three areas that deserve your special attention:

- First, look for aspects that could be highlighted. If, for example, the setting is primarily in a city in the summer, have you included sounds of traffic? Have your characters reacted to the heat? Or if your characters are climbing a mountain, have you included references to the view that would help the reader share the experience? Since long descriptive passages can slow the pace of a story, consider separating the visual glimpses like snapshots.
- Second, look for descriptive passages that should be trimmed. I mentioned earlier that in a preliminary draft of "Rwanda" I included more visual details about the open market than were appropriate. It was easy enough to trim them.
- Third, weed out aspects of the setting that run counter to your theme. Suppose, for example, the author of "Escapes" had actually visited Alcatraz on a sunny day, and she described it that way in an early draft. This would have been "true to life," but it would have undercut the sense of foreboding and uneasiness she was trying to establish. Merely hitting the delete key would let her roll the fog back in.

Should your setting have symbolic details? Not necessarily. Many stories use settings that merely provide a vivid sense of place. If you do see some aspect of the setting that has symbolic potential, however, be sure that it is subtle enough to blend in with the story.

I'll have more to say about using symbols in Chapter 21, but for now notice how aspects of the setting become symbolic in the three stories you have read. The prison in "Escapes," the tethered goat in "Rwanda," and the red neon sign depicting the Jolly Giant in "Minding the Store" all take on a broad and significant meaning.

When working with the setting in your own work, always remember that place and time are not mere adornments to a story. They are a part of what you see and feel as you write. Even more important, they are the primary means by which your readers are going to enter your story and experience it as if they were physically present. It is this sense of being there that makes fiction an "as-if-real" experience.

16 Obst Vw

A Story

by Sharon Solwitz

Next year, writing his personal experience essay to convince admissions at Penn he's Ivy League material despite uneven grades, he'll describe in amusing detail the one baseball game his father took him to, and get in on a scholarship despite his father's explicit pessimism. And he'll do well, though he's not as brilliant as his father, just a pretty smart kid who's used to working hard. But now on Rachel's bed, unraveling a hole in the knee of her jeans while her parents yell at each other downstairs, he cannot join in her raillery. "Let's go," he says.

"Wait. This is the part about who was the first unfaithful one!"

"Let's go!" he says. He has a curfew, a job to get up for tomorrow. Then there's the air outside the house, the smell of new grass mixing with the smell of Rachel when she lets him touch her under her T-shirt.

"Dame, please. It's funny, really. It's high comedy."

But she doesn't protest as he takes her hand and leads her down and outside.

Rachel is seventeen, a year older than Demian, though in the same grade. She lost a year when she went, as she says, loony, and spent several months in the bin getting her spirit broken to the point where she'd attend school and respond, numbly, to teacher and test questions. Still, her grades are better than his. Sometimes it seems to him he can't stand her, half an inch taller than he is, the way when she's not thinking about it she arcs down into herself like a long-necked bird, the way tall girls aren't supposed to. He used to love to play baseball, it was all he wanted to do — if not on the field then in a symbolic version with cards and dice in his room — and when this feeling of loathing comes over him, it brings on a desire for baseball, for playing shortstop, to be specific, standing between second and third with his knees bent, whispering in the direction of the batter — hit it to me, I dare you. He remembers his two best friends from then, brothers a year apart, Tom and John Frank, the clean, sharp edge of the way they bad-mouthed each other after the game. And then the queasiness comes, because something he has done with Rachel or is about to do has rendered him unfit for baseball.

He walks quickly now, a step ahead of her, over to the playground behind the local preschool, where they've gone the past months to talk and kiss and perform all but the final technical act of sexual intercourse. The ground is laid in gravel through which sharp, hard weeds poke up, but the chain-link fence is low enough to climb over, the large wooden sandbox lies half in the shadow of the building, the sand is cool and dry and molds after a while to one or the other's back.

Tonight, though, they do not embrace. Rachel sits down on the dark side of the sandbox. At first she seems to have disappeared. Then he sees in the dark the lesser darkness of her face, the pale stretch of her shoulders, too wide for a girl. She smells sour and sweet like strawberries. He is moved by something in Rachel, her craziness, her cynicism, facets of personality he dimly perceives he may have to own some day. He remembers a school assembly where she danced on center stage with the other dancers weaving around her, her turns and leaps bolder than theirs, more complete. "Rachel," he says, "I really like you."

She doesn't respond, but the prickle of the skin of his arms tells him he said the wrong thing. He tries again. "You're a really good dancer." He elaborates on the performance he saw, comparing her dancing to the way he used to feel about baseball. Still feels sometimes. She doesn't help him out. Her silence is a hole he walks around and around.

"Rachel," he says in despair, "I feel bad for you." He doesn't mention her parents. Really, he doesn't want to talk about them. Their dads by some fluke knew each other in college, and Rachel's sometimes asks him how his father's doing, a show of interest or courtesy his father doesn't return. Demian himself can barely manage to speak to her father, who makes more money than his father and calls him the Old Hippie. "Ask him about Woodstock," Mr. Geller once said, and Demian said, "Why don't you ask him yourself," knowing his father hadn't gone to Woodstock, as Mr. Geller also knew. Mr. Geller is soft-looking and bottom-heavy like an old pear. Demian can't stand Mr. Geller, has only broached the subject as a gift for Rachel.

She says, "They're not my real parents."

He laughs, though she has said that before.

"I'm going to divorce them," she says. "There's a new law, in Vermont."

"In Massachusetts, I think."

She shrugs, irritated with his quibble. He talks quickly to assuage her. "Then you can marry *my* parents."

"Who wants your parents?"

"What's wrong with my parents?"

"Your father has a mean streak."

"No he doesn't!"

His eyes have adjusted to the light. He can see the parts of her face that jut out, eyebrows, cheekbones, slope of nose. She seems too sharply constructed, a witch woman, though she's sitting cross-legged like a child, pouring handfuls of dry sand over her thighs. "He won't let you do stuff for no reason," she says. "For spite."

Demian knows that in similar words he has complained to her about his father, who gave him a curfew earlier than that of his friends' younger brothers, frequently refused him permission to attend parties, and who wasn't planning — he'd warned him — to let him get his driver's license till he was eighteen years old. Teenagers have glop for brains, he'd said. Though as a teenager himself — his mother had told him — he'd dropped out of college and done a lot of the drugs teenagers were supposed to say no to these days. Demian hasn't really spoken to this father since the day he refused to sign the learner's permit. But now Demian says, "He has his own ideas. He does what he thinks is right and not what everybody else does!"

She claps her hands.

"What is that supposed to mean?"

"You are so *canned.*"

He's about to stand up, leave, maybe. But she takes his arm. "Demian, I love you."

"So you can say anything you want to me?"

She puts her arms around him, thrusts her tongue into his mouth. He keeps up his end of the bargain. Soon he is urgent, panting. She is, too. His fingers are wet with her. As usual he tries to pull off her shorts. As usual she pushes away from him. Once he questioned her, learned that her non-compliance had to do with something apologetic she detected in his attitude toward sex. Since then, his efforts have been mild, ritualized. She is his first real girlfriend. He is pleased to be kissing and touching her even at the level of intimacy she has ordained. She hurls herself at his hand, trembling.

He has to be home by 10:30 and it's 11:35 by the oven clock as he tiptoes across the kitchen. He has never missed curfew before, but the evening is still warm on his skin, he fells invulnerable. And his father is surely asleep.

He takes his shoes off in the living room. His father is *inactive,* his mother says. The understatement of the year, Demian thinks. Tired from working in the bookstore, which doesn't bring in enough for him to hire a manager, his father often falls asleep on the couch in front of the ten o'clock news, and Demian and his mother have to prod him up to bed.

But he's up now, standing in his PJs at the top of the stairs. His long, thin, still young-looking face is blank; not even his lips seem to move as he says, "You're grounded." His lips are pressed close together, a tuck in the long swatch of his face, but the words linger in the air well after his lanky body has vanished behind the master bedroom door.

In bed Demian is stiff with fury. There is no recourse; the only question is how long. And even worse than not seeing Rachel is seeing her with the weight of his father's edict on his shoulders, making him smaller than he is, unworthy of her.

Four years from now Demian will fly home from school in time to watch his father breathe in comatose sleep, then cease breathing — feeling nothing, because from now on nothing he does for good or ill will have any impact on his father. Later he'll rage at his father for dying before he was ready for him to die, and later still he may decide that if his father wasn't ideal he did the best he could. But now Demian has hopes for what he can be to his father and what his father can be to him.

Demian is up early, hours before he has to leave for Bi-Rite's, rehearsing the speech he'll give his father at the breakfast table. He has it outlined in his head like a five-paragraph essay, and now with the sun turning the sky pink, then blue, he sits at the kitchen table while his mother, who has to leave soon to teach summer school, performs five or six brisk cleaning and cooking acts. His father sips coffee. His father butters a piece of rye toast, as slowly as an old man, though his hair is still thick, his face unlined; people sometimes think he's Demian's older brother. Demian says casually into the space between bites, "I want you to reconsider."

His father looks to the left, the right, all around the room. "Who's talking? Is somebody talking to me?"

Demian's ears feel hot. This is the first direct statement he's made to his father in several months. "Dad, I'm never late. I shouldn't be punished the first time I mess up. Give me a second chance."

"Look, you." His father's voice is quiet, but it takes up the room. "If some dude walks into my store with a gun, and I say hey now just wait a minute, do I get a second chance?"

Demian sees the illogic of his father's argument, but his father stands up, leaning forward as if about to fall on him. "If you get sick, kiddo. If your heart hurts, air sticks in your throat, you say with your last feeble breath, God, Jesus, Krishna, whoever — please, what did I do, could you please, please give me a second chance, what's He going to say to you? Tell me, Demian."

Demian wants to ask his father what makes him think he's God, but the air or something is stuck in his throat.

"Let's say you get your girlfriend pregnant, Demian. Let's say for the sake of argument you knock up your young lady. But you aren't ready to be Papa yet. You want to walk across Turkey in your stocking feet. You want to climb Mt. Tamalpais and keep on going."

His father has just said more, it seems, than he has ever said to Demian before. His hands are waving, his face is white, and Demian's mother pats his back, leads him back to the table. She gets him more coffee, hovers over him, though she's running late, till his face warms up. He kisses her good-bye a beat longer than he has to. Says nothing to Demian. Demian feels sick, choking on the words he can't speak to his father." Mom," he whispers after door is shut, "is he mean, or what?"

"Demian," she says, "you've got to give him some slack. The business isn't going well."

"Who cares?" Demian's voice rises. Every once in a while he's allowed to sneer in front of his mother. It's his one respite, acting like his father in front of his mother. "Mine isn't going well, either." He watches her face, prepared to shut down at the first sign of her disapproval.

"Demian," she says, "he may have to declare bankruptcy. Don't say anything to him, please. Eat your breakfast."

Her lips look blue, like the lips of little kids who have been in the water too long. Demian eats his cereal, a piece of toast, then, absentmindedly, the rest of his father's toast. It's not even eight o'clock, he has plenty of time. He eats while his mother says nice things about his father. How good he is to her. How well his friends like him, even the rich, much-respected ones. Demian is aware that people listen when his father speaks. Demian would like his own friends to treat him as his father's friends treat his father. Sometimes he quiets his voice, thins it out a little, to see if that's the trick.

"He's way too smart for what he does," His mother is saying. "He did well in college without studying. He could remember everything he'd ever read. He was a great talker, there was nothing he couldn't have done if he'd wanted to — do you know how high his IQ is?"

"Higher than mine," Demian says.

His mother doesn't protest, just shakes her head as if in wonder. "He never got time to sit and figure things out. He was too young to have a child."

"Mom," Demian says, "he was twenty-six when I was born. He's forty-two."

"He was too young," she says firmly, gathering up her books. "But he loves you like crazy, you ought to know that."

Pedaling to work Demian thinks about his father's IQ how many points it might be higher than this own, and tries to see him as the Disappointed Man in his mother's fiction. He says *bankrupt* under his breath, trying to diminish his father enough to forgive him. It doesn't work. He tries to feel his father's love for him, remembering a ballgame his father took him to on his tenth birthday — him and his best friend, John Frank, and John Frank's father. He remembers sitting next to John in the back of their old Rabbit with his baseball glove in his lap for catching foul balls. Remembers listening to his father up front talking with John's father, John's father laughing at his father's jokes, though John's father drove a Volvo and everyone called him Dr. Frank. Demian was proud of his father. It was clear even then that although his father talked less than his friend's father, it was his father's words that thickened in the air. His father had given him and John their own tickets to hold, and jouncing along on the back seat, they squinted at the blue and white cardboard oblongs, discussing the numbers and letters that stood for what they were about to experience. SAT AUG 1:20 PM. AISLE 518 ROW 5 SEAT 242. GAME #52 CHICAGO CUBS VS. NEW YORK METS. ADMIT ONE SUBJECT TO CONDITIONS ON BACK NO REFUND NO EXCHANGE. There was one set of letters he couldn't fathom: OBST VW. He showed the ticket to John. "Obstetrician?" John asks.

"Its a beer ad. Obst Blue Ribbon!"

"That's *Pabst* Blue Ribbon!"

"I know, fart head."

Only when they got to the park and sat down in seats behind a pillar that let him see half the field if he craned to the right, did he realize the letters stood for Obstructed View. At first he didn't mind. He'd never been to a major-leagued game before. The smell of hot dogs and popcorn filled his mouth and nose, the stands were cool and dim like a naptime bedroom, the playing field bright green under the sun. He put his glove on, waiting for his father to sit down next to him, not necessarily to talk to him, since of course he had more to say to Dr. Frank, but just to be there so Demian could ask him questions or maybe just sit quietly beside him, watching him watch the game. But when Demian had finished taking in the brightness and darkness, and located his favorite Cub, Shawon Dunston, who could hurl the ball like the end of a whip, his father was still standing in the aisle. "We'll get you guys after the game," he called to them, holding out a five-dollar bill. "Don't eat too much." Demian took the bill, folded and folded it again as his father and Dr. Frank descended the steep steps, vanishing toward seats Demian knew had an unencumbered view of the field. Still, he wasn't sure what to make of the turnaround. It wasn't exactly what he'd pictured when he'd asked on his tenth, his double-digit birthday, not for something to ride or look at or hold in his hand, but for an event to experience with his father. The man who took his father's seat told him stories about the ballplayers' personal lives. It was lots of fun sitting with John, leaning hard one way around the pillar to watch the ball come off the bat, then the other way to see where the ball ended up. Shawon Dunston threw the ball into the dugout, and the Cubs still won. But although he and John wore their gloves all nine innings, the foul balls went to seats below them in the sun. And although he and John kept good track of the game, marking the P.O.'s, F.O.'s, K's, H's on their scorecards with their short yellow ballpark pencils, some of the balls fell where neither of them could see. The man in his father's seat said Shawon Dunston would never learn to take a walk because he was mentally retarded. When Demian's father returned for them after the game, the skin of his arms looked dark gold in the sun, and it was clear to Demian that the game he'd seen was not as good a game.

Demian leans back in his chair at the Geller breakfast table, puts his feet on a second chair, takes the cup of coffee Rachel has poured him. He's never had coffee before, and he gulps it like milk, burns his throat, swallows his grimace. Rachel doesn't ask him why he isn't at Bi-Rite's this morning. She talks rapidly, of nothing he has to respond to. She's barefoot, in a long, wrinkled shirt she must have slept in. He imagines what's under the shirt; his face burns. Her brown hair looks white blond on the side where the sun hits.

She runs into the kitchen, returns with a plate of kiwi and nectarines, and two dark blue cloth napkins. But on the gray tile of the kitchen floor she has left patches of red. She is limping. He watches, frozen, as blood wells out of her foot. She sits down, crosses her leg over her knee, eats a nectarine, while her blood drip-drips onto the gray tile. He thinks, Why doesn't she wipe it up? Should he wipe it up? Someone should wipe it up. It gives him the creeps, these bright red splashes, but the cloth napkin she presents him seems too fine for this use. He's looking around for paper when she throws a piece of broken china onto the table in front of him. "Parental carnage," she says.

It's the source of her injury, picked up from the kitchen floor — a white shard, triangular in shape, a thin gold line around the part that had been rim. The broken edge is red. *"Carnage,"* she says, accenting and softening the last syllable like a French word. This morning her father had relieved some of his anger by throwing a cup at the refrigerator. Her mother relieved hers by refusing to sweep. "They need to *see* this," she says, placing the broken piece of china on the blue cloth napkin in the middle of the breakfast table. She seems thrilled almost, as if the bloody shard is the final piece of the puzzle of her life. She arranges a kiwi on the napkin, a bud vase alongside. "It's our new centerpiece! A still life! What'll we call it, *Terror at Teatime?*" She speaks with a British accent, biting off her words with her teeth. "No, something simple: *Daddy.* That's it — *Daddy!*"

He starts laughing. "That's terrific. It's really funny." He laughs more, in loud bursts. He has never laughed like this before. He tells her the story of the one baseball game his father took him to, exaggerating his hopes so that their obstruction by the pillar seems purely comic. She takes his hand, squeezing hard, and he elaborates, this time stressing his naïve reverence for his father, his father's indifference. What had his father called out, descending the stairs? Demian doesn't remember now, makes it up: "Try and have fun, kiddo!" "We'll be thinking of you, suckers!" "Look, you — you're lucky you weren't offed in utero!" It doesn't sound like his father but makes him laugh hysterically.

She starts laughing, too. "He slapped me this morning. I told him what I thought of people who can't control themselves, and he held me by the hair and slapped my face. Like this." She grabs a hunk of her hair, yanks her head to one side, giggles. "He said, 'I'll show you how I control myself.'"

He smooths her hair where she yanked. He has begun shaking a little, though he doesn't feel sad or scared. "Sometimes in the room with him I feel like I don't exist. I don't have a body. I don't know how to talk, even." He's shaking harder, down to the soles of his feet. He has never spoken like this. "He'd slap me, too, if he thought I was important enough. The truth is, I bore him. Poor Dad, bored by his son." He replays what he said, awed by what seems to be the utter truth of it. It seems reckless and marvelous saying these things about his father. He's an explorer, charting ground never before seen by mortal eyes. "I really don't need him. If he died tomorrow it wouldn't make the least difference in my life. It might improve things."

Later, with his father's blood leaking into his brain, he'll remember what he said, and even though over the years his father had grown no more interested in him, he'll think for a moment of all the things his father wanted to do that he couldn't do, couldn't ever do now, and he'll sit down in a chair by the bed, for a moment unable to breathe.

But now he's on his knees before Rachel's chair. She puts her arms around his shoulders, presses her face to the top of his head. He hears her heart beating through her T-shirt. His teeth are chattering, and to stop them he starts kissing her through her shirt — her shoulder, the two round bones at the top of her chest, the long swell of breast. In the past he has treated this part of her body reverently, but now he sucks as if he were drinking, wetting the cloth of her shirt till it feels to his lips like rough, wet skin. He has stopped trembling. "I hate him," he murmurs, almost lovingly.

"Has he ever knocked your mother down? Called her a slut? Said he could smell it on her? I'm in the same room, here at this very table eating my cantaloupe."

He can't tell if she likes what his mouth is doing, but she has made no objection. He raises her shirt, observes her body in the daylight; thinks, *There is so much of her.* He says, "He made me sit behind a pole. He traded in his ticket and sat with a buddy. The only baseball game he ever took me to."

It doesn't sound quite awful enough. He looks at her for confirmation, but she seems not to have heard him. "Has he ever come home drunk and gotten in bed with you? And when you screamed he put his hand over your mouth? And when you bit his hand he told lies to your mother? Who still thinks you're a slut though she doesn't say so?"

"Is that true, Rachel?"

She shakes her head no. "Another example of my sick imagination."

Her voice is light but he can't shake off the terrible picture. "If it were true I'd kill him."

"Me, too."

Her last comment comes without inflection. He tries to read her face, but it doesn't help. He hugs her hard. She returns it with a slight time lag, mechanically stroking the back of his head. She seems uncharacteristically passive. He feels sure that if he were to take off his pants, she'd sigh once, then let him have her. The thought terrifies him. "Rachel, where are you?"

She looks at him, smiling with the corners of her mouth only. He wants to be gone from here, to be riding back to Bi-Rite's, whose manager is a friend of his dad's and might not question the excuse he'll make up on the way. But Rachel is sitting so still in her chair, she seems to take up no space. He imagines that if he left her, he'd never find her again. When he called, her mother would say, *She's traveling in Europe.* Her mother would say, *There's no one here by that name.*

"Rachel," he whispers. He touches her face, the curves of her arm, side of her knee, arch of her wounded foot, softly so as not to miss her faintest whispered response. Her foot feels cold, and he warms it between his hand and his face. Then he put his lips to the injured spot, cleaning off the dried blood with his tongue, smoothing down the flap of the torn skin.

17 Dialogue

The Illusion of Speech

Dialogue is the illusion of speech in fiction. It may seem like a tape recording transcribed on paper, but it is, like all aspects of fiction, an artistic creation.

Almost all stories that deal with two or more characters use dialogue. There are good reasons for this. If you don't let your characters reveal themselves and unfold the plot through what they say, you will find yourself depending on **exposition**. This means explaining more and showing less. What you had intended to be fiction will begin to sound like an informal essay with a lot of commentary from the author.

Dialogue serves two important functions. It helps create convincing characters, the subject of Chapter 18, and it can advance the plot without the author explaining what is about to occur. This brief sample of dialogue, for example, reveals what will happen next:

"Tomorrow I'm driving to Cincinnati to find my sister and bring her back home."

The first step in learning how to write effective dialogue is to listen to how people talk. This requires listening analytically. It's hard to do this when you yourself are engaged in conversation. Far better to eavesdrop. Restaurants and cafeterias are good places for this. Listen for contemporary phrasing, incomplete sentences, frequency of interruptions, and patterns of dominance. Even the pauses are worth noting.

Having said that, I must reiterate the fact that successful dialogue in fiction is not a tape recording of what you hear in the cafeteria. The difference is that because casual talk is cheap, we squander it daily in chitchat that, though pleasurable, is largely uninformative and directionless. It is filled with empty phrasing and redundancies. *Phatic* is a little-used word that describes speech used for sociability rather than for exchanging information. Much of what we call "small talk" is phatic. Small samples may be appropriate in fiction, but if you pad a story with aimless chatter, the result will be boring.

Dialogue in fiction often creates the *illusion* of characters speaking casually, but a good writer can also use such passages to communicate attitudes and aspects of character to the reader. Take this apparently random exchange between Demian and Rachel in "Obst Vw." It begins with Rachel talking about her parents:

> She says, "They're not my real parents."
> He laughs, though she has said that before.
> "I'm going to divorce them," she says. "There's a new law, in Vermont."
> "In Massachusetts, I think,"
> She shrugs, irritated with his quibble. He talks quickly to assuage her. "Then you can marry *my* parents."
> "Who wants your parents?"
> "What's wrong with my parents?"
> "Your father has a mean streak."
> "No he doesn't!"

This exchange is half bitter, half joking, erratic, and fragmentary — all the earmarks of a tape recording capturing two teenagers talking. But if you look closely as a fellow writer, you will see how the author has communicated Rachel's hostility toward her parents and Demian's strongly **ambivalent** feelings about his father. It's a strong mix of rage (we later learn he hasn't spoken to his father "in several months") and a hidden streak of affection, as seen here by his denial that his father has "a mean streak." The passage also reveals the volatile relationship they have with each other — rapidly switching from sympathy to irritation to contradiction.

The same is true of the dialogue that opens "Rwanda." Francine's description of the tethered goat and Max's report on the attempt to tranquilize a topi are broken up the way casual conversation normally is, but the two passages place the reader in Africa and contrast two quite different attitudes toward animals — a contrast that will later test Francine's own deepest feelings.

Fictional dialogue, then, frequently mimics the random sequences of casual conversation while inserting subtle cues about the characters and some of the themes that are embedded in the story.

FOUR CONVENTIONS OF WRITING DIALOGUE AND THOUGHTS

Conventions are not rules, they are simply identifiable patterns that are widely used. The conventions of writing dialogue and thoughts in fiction are mechanical cues that are so familiar to readers that they are hardly noticed.

Most writers follow these conventions because they want the mechanics to be inconspicuous. The dialogue itself has to be fresh and true to character, but the arrangement on the page should be so familiar that it is not noticed. This is one of those cases in which art should conceal technique. That is, the creative aspect of your work should conceal the mechanical aspects.

- First, most (but not all) stories use quotation marks around words spoken out loud but not around thoughts. This is a helpful distinction that readers are used to. Single quotation marks (like apostrophes) are used to set off quotations within quotations. Here is an example that includes thoughts, quoted material, and a speaker quoting someone else:

> If only, she thought, the rest of the committee had heard how enthusiastic her client had been over her proposal.
> "He really liked the design," she said to her husband that evening. " 'It's the best we've seen so far,' he told me. Those were his exact words."
> Her husband shook his head in sympathy.

If one speaker's words continue for more than one paragraph without a **dialogue tag** ("he said" or "she said"), use quotation marks at the beginning of each paragraph but not at the ends until the close of the quoted material. This may seem odd, but it's a familiar convention.

- Second, most writers indent the first line of speech of each new speaker. Doing this may appear to waste paper, but readers are used to it. One advantage of regular indentation is that in lengthy exchanges between two characters, the reader doesn't have to be told each time who spoke. Use **dialogue tags** simply as reminders from time to time. The sample from "Obst Vw" quoted on page 124 is a good example.

- Third, don't hesitate to use "said" repeatedly. Readers respond to tags such as "she said," "he said," and "I said" the way they do to punctuation marks. Because of this, most writers since the 1930s repeat them freely. For years you have been told to avoid repetitions, and generally that's good advice, but dialogue tags are an exception. It sounds amateurish to keep using substitutions like "she retorted," "he sneered," "she questioned," "he hissed." Repeated alternatives like these become obtrusive.

    In this connection, guard against adding modifiers to "said." There is usually no reason to write "said angrily" or "said shyly," since the tone is almost always clear from the dialogue itself. If it's important to reverse the tone one might expect, it may be more effective to use a separate phrase as in "'You absolute idiot,' she said, her tone still loving."

- Fourth, contemporary writers rarely try to imitate spoken language by using phonetic spelling. You can find examples in 19th century writing (Mark Twain's *The Adventures of Huckleberry Finn*, for example, and the contemporary fiction of Susan Straight), but it tends to slow down the pace of reading, and unless it is done skillfully, it can draw attention to itself. Revising the spelling on the printed page is so noticeable that it exaggerates the effect one is trying to create. If used heavily, it also poses a risk of sounding patronizing.

For these reasons, most authors prefer to catch the flavor of a regional or foreign accent through word choice and characteristic phrasing rather than tinkering with conventional spelling.

PARAPHRASING: INDIRECT QUOTATIONS

When our friends talk, we have to listen to every sentence. Even when they repeat themselves. Even when they bore us. That's a mark of friendship. But your readers have no such contract. When they're bored, they will quit reading.

When dialogue stops advancing the plot or expanding our understanding of the speaker, it's time for a paraphrase. Grammatically it is known as an **indirect quotation**, but it's not really a quotation at all. It describes what was said in condensed form without quotation marks. Its simplest use is to avoid quoting routine or uninteresting conversation by substituting a summary:

> She told him that she had missed her flight, had decided to spend the night with her aunt, and asked him to meet her early the next morning.

Indirect quotations can also be used to paraphrase much lengthier and more general exchanges. Since it's not a good tactic to portray a long, dull conversation with a similarly long, dull block of dialogue, paraphrasing may be your best solution, as in these two samples:

1. The conversation at the funeral parlor touched on the weather (remarkably warm), the traffic on Elm Street (growing worse), and what auto mechanics are charging these days (shocking).
2. She thought he would be pleased to see her after all these years, but instead he spent the entire dinner telling her about his miserable dog's long succession of ailments and eventual demise.

In addition to summarizing dull dialogue, paraphrasing is sometimes used to dramatize events that, though lively, don't justify the space they would take to handle in dialogue. This often applies in scenes that are not central to the story:

> When she finally came home, he met her at the door and in a rush spelled out the domestic disasters of the day: kitchen sink plugged, the twins' refusal to nap, the computer meltdown, and the cat giving birth in the linen closet.

Often indirect quotations are used in conjunction with direct quotes. In "Escapes," for example, the author wisely does not bore the reader with an explanation of how baseball is played, but instead uses a direct quotation to highlight Jennifer's response:

Jennifer does not understand baseball, but I try to explain it to her. Three outs to an inning, nine innings to a game, the importance of a good short-stop. But . . . [w]hen Chris Sabo . . . strikes out she says, "Caryn, why is it still their turn? . . ."

THE ILLUSION OF THOUGHTS

As we have seen, effective dialogue in a story creates the illusion of echoing the sound of actual speech. What, then, do fictional thoughts echo? Nothing, really, but what we imagine thoughts might sound like if we could hear them. We write out thoughts as if they were spoken dialogue without using quotation marks, but in reality what goes on in our heads rarely uses sentences or even words.

True, we occasionally force order on our thoughts to generate something close to speech:

Wait a minute, he told himself. First, I should buy some flowers and then a bottle of wine. If I can't afford a cab, there's still time to walk.

The phrase "he told himself" shows how close the thought is to spoken dialogue. It is the kind of deliberate thinking that we may even mutter out loud.

There is a similar example in "Obst Vw" when Demian notices that Rachel has cut her foot and her blood is dropping onto the kitchen floor:

He thinks, Why doesn't she wipe it up? Should he wipe it up? Someone should wipe it up.

A great majority of what goes on in our heads, however, is far less structured. Many thoughts come in flashes, essentially without words. For this reason, thoughts are often described in ways that are less precise than dialogue. Going back to "Rwanda," there is an example at the beginning in which Francine chastises herself for talking about the tethered goat:

Dumb, Francine thinks, bringing it up. The image has clung to her — those desperate eyes. But trying to describe it makes her sound naive. Every market in Africa has live animals ready for slaughter, and the quick slice of the knife is surely no worse than the claws and teeth of a predator. She knows that.

The passage begins with a direct quotation of what went through her head. The next sentence gives us a visual picture of what she recalled. The remainder of the passage is technically exposition, though it reflects her feelings.

Stories written in the first person weave back and forth from thoughts to exposition even more easily than third-person stories. Because "Minding the Store" is written in a deceptively informal style in the first person, some of the narrator's thoughts come surprisingly close to the theme. In this passage, which I quoted earlier, Bobby is talking about those pleasant times when Charles read aloud from his journal:

> Listening to him read, laughing with Martha in that warm little store, I felt like I had a family.

"Escapes" is also written in the first person, but Caryn, the narrator, is an adult and more verbal, so her thoughts are closer to what she might say aloud. But they are brief passages woven into the story unobtrusively as in this case:

> So I am still not sure what made me say yes, I'll take her for a while. Except for maybe the thought of sharing that ultrablue sky with someone seemed so appealing, and the thought of a few bleeps and peaks in my life seemed like a good idea.

Notice how in that description of what is going on in her head there is a line that is a direct quotation of what she said to her sister-in-law, but because it is a part of her thoughts quotation marks are not used.

When composing the thoughts of a fictional character, be careful not to use thoughts unrealistically merely to present background facts to the reader. This is particularly unconvincing if the details are well known to the character as in: "I am 23 years old, tall, handsome, and from Omaha." Material such as this to be credible as thought would have to be motivated ("They wouldn't treat me like that back in Omaha, he thought"). Or it can be slid into dialogue, again in the context of what is going on ("Just because he's handsome doesn't mean that . . . "). Or as a last resort it can be stated as exposition ("He was 23 that spring, but he still missed Omaha").

One excellent way to explore the various ways that thoughts are revealed in fiction is to review stories you have already read and circle passages that give the reader a glimpse into the mind of a particular character. You will discover that these passages are significantly different from dialogue. The boundaries are less distinct. Sometimes it's hard to distinguish thoughts from description or from exposition. But this is how it should be. Thoughts, after all, are slippery and elusive.

THE ILLUSION OF A FOREIGN LANGUAGE

Creating the illusion of a character speaking in a foreign language has always been a challenge. And with the United States becoming an increasingly multicultural nation, it grows in importance.

There are several approaches. About the only agreement among writers is that the traditional Hollywood film solution of having characters speak English with a foreign accent is an almost comic failure.

The purest solution is simply to use the other language. This is entirely logical and effective if the fiction is intended for the small but growing number of periodicals that cater to a bilingual readership. If the fiction is intended for a general audience, however, long foreign language passages will confuse and irritate many readers.

For this reason, foreign language passages are usually kept brief. Occasionally the English translation is added either after a dash or in parentheses.

The most common approach, however, is to use English throughout, identifying the language being spoken in the tag: "'How well do you know him?' she asked in Spanish." Or, "Speaking French he asked, 'How well do you know her?'" You can avoid the direct quotation altogether if you use indirect speech: "She asked in Spanish how long he had known her."

If you are using this approach with longer passages, consider adopting some of the word order that is characteristic of that language. It is sometimes helpful to translate a few foreign idioms directly into English as Hemingway occasionally did with his Spanish-speaking characters. This can add the flavor of a foreign language without making the characters sound as if they were speaking English with an accent.

PACING: MAINTAINING FORWARD MOTION

Long blocks of dialogue tend to slow the forward motion of a story. It's not the dialogue itself that does this; it's the lack of action. There are stories written entirely as a **monologue**, one character talking. But if you look at these stories closely, you will see that they maintain interest in one of two ways: by reporting lively events or by revealing a lot about the narrator that he or she is not aware of. In general, though, dialogue is broken up with action and occasional exposition.

A series of short, fragmentary exchanges of dialogue can do wonders to enliven a scene that has become bogged down in description or low-key action. But if sustained for too long, an unrelieved exchange between two characters can become monotonous. If alternating lines of dialogue are about the same length, they will create a ping-pong effect.

The best way to study different ways of balancing dialogue and other modes is to thumb through several stories without actually reading them. Look for the indentations and the quotation marks. You can see how often dialogue is used and the length of quoted passages from the typography. You will see that in most cases the author has avoided entire pages without dialogue and, at the other extreme, entire pages made up of one long monologue. Again, this is not a rule; it is simply a pattern that most authors find effective.

Determining the frequency of passages in dialogue is not something that should concern you when writing the first draft. Let the story develop naturally. Then read the draft aloud and look closely at your pacing.

SPEECH PATTERNS: CHARACTER AND MOOD

If you listen analytically to people you know, you will discover that many have distinctive rhythms. Fast talkers sometimes trip over themselves, leaping from one idea to the next. In extreme cases, they will fail to use complete sentences in their cascade of speech. At the other extreme are the slow talkers. They may use long sentences.

Then there are those who use irritating little phrases like "You know?" or "Right?" as needless punctuation. They can be used to individualize a fictional character's speech.

Students have an advantage when it comes to analyzing speech patterns because they can listen to instructors without having to respond. If you take notes on the recurring speech characteristics, you may also get credit for appearing to be fascinated with the lecturer's subject.

A word of caution, however: remember that any identifiable speech pattern is twice as noticeable on the page as it is when listening to someone speak. Variations from the norm leap out at the reader. If you use such patterns, keep them subtle.

Speech patterns also define the mood of the speaker. This is as true in fiction as it is in life. Calm, reflective moods are often characterized by longer sentences and greater attention to grammatical conventions such as completing sentences with a subject and a verb. But with moments of crisis, dialogue often becomes fragmentary, abrupt, and frequently redundant. Take a close look at the dialogue in this climatic scene in "Minding the Store":

> "We don't want your business, warm or cold," Charles said.
> "Okay . . . *faggot*," Carl said, smiling. He relaxed like he did right before he punched the coach. "Duck, Charles," I yelled, and he lowered his head. Carl caught him above the right ear. "Shit," Carl said, "Shit, shit, shit," shaking his hand. He'd crunched it against Charles' skull.

Notice, first, that once Charles has made his statement, every utterance has been limited to one or two words. No one speaks in complete sentences. These fragmented utterances are close to the way people actually speak in a crisis, and as a result, they provide dramatic impact to the scene.

Notice also that the author has not used verbs like "shouted," "bellowed," or "roared." Nor has he used a single exclamation mark. The volume is quite clear from the context.

Finally, take a professional look at the brief burst of profanity. When profanities or obscenities are sprinkled through a story like an overload of pepper on a pizza, they lose effectiveness. The writer can't generate greater impact for a particular scene because the profanities or obscenities have become commonplace from overuse.

In contrast, this story has been narrated by a 16-year-old kid whose language is essentially clean. This allows the author to add a verbal punch to the confrontation scene to match the physical one.

We have focused on the techniques that help make the writing of dialogue and thoughts more convincing, but ultimately you will have to rely on your ear. For this reason, keep reading your work aloud. Consider asking a friend to read sections of your dialogue aloud. Listen to the opinion of others — even if they are not writers. They can help you spot unconvincing passages even if they can't suggest ways to correct them. Both dialogue and thoughts in fiction are illusions, but your job as a writer is to make them seem genuine.

18 Characterization

Creating Credible People

No, writers don't actually create people. They create fictional characters. Although the characters we meet in stories and novels are illusions, we often have the sense that we have come to know real people.

This is particularly true with characters that are drawn well enough to reveal different personal aspects. These are called **"round" characters**. Sometimes they remain in the memory of a reader as clearly as an old friend. Characters that are not well developed and serve primarily to advance the plot are called "flat." These terms were first suggested by the novelist E.M. Forster not as precise categories but as useful generalizations.

HOW WE LEARN ABOUT PEOPLE

Before we turn to the art of creating as-if-real characters in fiction, consider for a moment how we get to know people in daily life. We meet strangers frequently. Some we will never see again: friends of friends, store clerks, or the TV repair person. With others, however, we make an effort to find out what they are really like.

Rightly or wrongly, we often start with a quick visual assessment. We all know how risky, unreliable, and unfair this process usually is, but still we do it. We make unjustifiable judgments such as "assertive," "shy," "wimpy," "cool," "arrogant," or "nerdy" on the basis of physical characteristics, dress, use of language, and the like.

Next, we start the conversation ritual. Talking with strangers is a form of exploration: we ask what they do for a living, what films they have seen lately, or how long have they've lived in the neighborhood. With students, the questions tend to focus on courses taken, taste in music, and whether you have mutual friends. On the surface these seem like bland queries, but they're ways of finding out what the other person takes seriously and what he or she is like as an individual. Deeper questions such as political loyalties and religious beliefs are usually postponed until later, and the approach is apt to be more cautious and indirect. If we move too fast, we're considered nosy, so we tend to be evasive. This is why we spend so much time talking.

Talk, however, is not enough by itself. To get to know someone well, we need to see him or her in action. When we say, "But I don't really know him," we usually mean that you two have talked a lot but haven't done much together. Activities such as dancing, bicycling, hiking, or participating in a social club give us a chance to see whether someone's behavior matches what we thought we learned from conversation. No one likes being caught in a thunderstorm while on a long hike or staying up all night in rehearsals for an amateur dramatic performance, but we do learn more about people when we share stressful experiences.

These various stages in the process of getting to know someone well have one aspect in common: they provide a great clutter of specific details from which we draw certain conclusions. Many of these details are of no value, some are inaccurate, and others are highly informative. The process of getting to know someone well is inefficient and slow, but trying to bypass it through services such as Internet dating can lead to serious miscalculations.

HOW WE LEARN ABOUT FICTIONAL CHARACTERS

Learning about characters in fiction *seems* to be similar, but that's an illusion. Fiction, especially the short story, can't afford to be that leisurely. So while getting to know a character in fiction appears to use the same methods, the process we call **characterization** is enormously compressed and ingeniously hidden. What might take months in life can be compressed into 15 minutes of reading. To maintain the reader's sense of personal discovery, the writer of fiction has to supply a series of little hints, and they have to be slipped in stealthily.

The most effective techniques of revealing character without being obvious are dialogue, thoughts, and action. In addition, you can occasionally fall back on a direct statement, speaking as the author. Using **exposition** raises problems that I will explain shortly, so most writers use it only rarely.

CHARACTERIZATION THROUGH DIALOGUE AND THOUGHTS

Much of what you learn about a person in daily life is through dialogue. Even if people don't tell you exactly what is going on in their heads, they reveal themselves indirectly through what they say. The same is true in fiction.

"Obst Vw" is unusual in that even secondary characters are revealed in some detail through what they say. We learn a good deal about the father, for example, from an angry outburst that is so illogical it is sadly funny. Demian has been grounded and has asked his father for a second chance. The father scoffs, asking if God would give him "a second chance" if Demian were dying. Then, groping for still another wild analogy, Demian's father says:

> "Let's say you get your girlfriend pregnant. . . . But you aren't ready to be Papa yet. You want to walk across Turkey in your stocking feet. You want to climb Mt. Tamalpais and keep on going."

This is an absurd exaggeration, but it reveals more about the father than he realizes. At 42, he still has the longing for freedom and adventure that he himself apparently missed. Through this outburst we see in the father an unstable mix of authoritarian rigidity and childish longing. This is a fairly complex insight considering that he is only a secondary character.

Shortly after that, we get a glimpse into the inner feelings of Demian's mother as well. It becomes clear that she has an overriding sense of loyalty to her husband despite his dark moods and occasional irascibility. How do we learn this? Not by the author telling us but through this exchange:

> "He's way too smart for what he does," his mother is saying. "He did well in college without studying. . . . He never got time to sit and figure things out. He was too young to have a child." "Mom," Demian says, "he was twenty-six when I was born. He's forty-two. . . . "He was too young," she says firmly, gathering up her books.

This dialogue contributes to our understanding of her by revealing not only her unquestioning defense of her husband, but also a certain stubbornness even in the face of contrary evidence. In addition, it gives us further insight into Demian's anger. From his point of view it is grossly unfair to be blamed for his father's failures.

As you can see from these examples, dialogue is a particularly effective device for revealing not only outward characteristics but internal conflicts as well. We also see internal conflict and inconsistency in Rachel's dialogue. The most dramatic example is when she describes what seems to have been a sexual assault by her father. Horrified, Demian asks if that is really true:

> She shakes her head no. "Another example of my sick imagination."

This quick switch of attitude reflects a pattern of vacillations in Rachel. Sometimes she is stoic about her parents' violent hostilities, joking about their fights. But on other occasions she exaggerates the extent of their depravity, describing her father in melodramatic terms. Then, as in this case, she switches back, making a dark joke about herself. What we see in Rachel is someone desperately trying to cope with an impossible home life, veering from one approach to another.

CHARACTERIZATION THROUGH ACTION

In simple fiction like thrillers and mass-market historical novels, action often serves as the primary method of revealing character. Fighting an opponent or struggling against some aspect of nature is a fairly blunt literary tool. It clearly identifies who are the good guys and who is the enemy, and it frequently sells well. But the downside is that it tends to blot out subtle aspects of character. For this reason, action tends to be restrained in sophisticated fiction.

"Escapes" is a good example of this restraint. There is action, but it is not highlighted. Caryn and Jennifer ride the cable cars, go shopping, and visit a former prison; but Jennifer does not fling herself out the window, nor are they trapped overnight in a cold cell at Alcatraz. There isn't even a physical fight. True, a suicidal gesture and an earlier successful suicide are important, but they occur before the start of the story. They are, in dramatic terms, offstage. We learn about them through dialogue.

In "Minding the Store," action is used both at the beginning (through a flashback) and toward the end. Action, however, is not an end in itself. The story ends, you remember, not with violence or conflict but with reconciliation.

As we have seen, "Obst Vw" makes extensive use of dialogue and thoughts to develop the characters, but there are two major samples of action that also provide important insights. For Demian, it is the baseball game in which his father leaves him in the seat with an obstructed view rather than sitting with him. It's far from child abuse in the traditional sense, but we can see how deeply it affected him by the way Demian keeps returning to the event. Representing an accumulation of disappointments, it becomes a kind of emblem of his relationship with his father.

As for Rachel, she is revealed in significant ways by the incident in which she cuts her foot on a broken cup and refuses to bandage the injury. She lets the blood drip on the floor, trying to make a joke out of it. This revealing bit of action is supplemented by dialogue to reveal how her self-pity is mixed with her rage against her parents: "They need to *see* this," she says while letting her blood "drip-drip onto the gray tile."

The actual breaking of the mug earlier that morning is another sample of action that gives us a vista into the daily life of her parents: the father vents his anger by throwing the cup against the refrigerator, and the mother makes her statement by refusing to sweep it up. These two are minor characters, but this brief bit of action reported in just two sentences reveals a good deal about them and their relationship.

The ending of "Obst Vw" is in some ways similar to that of "Minding the Store." In contrast with the violent emotions and action at the dramatic climax of each story, they both end with a quiet and positive act: Demian kisses Rachel's injury, "smoothing down the flap of the torn skin" as if to heal her emotional injuries, and Bobby, after "a couple of sleepless weeks," returns to the Jolly Giant to apologize and is quietly accepted.

THE DRAWBACKS OF EXPOSITION

There will be times when you as a writer will tire of all this indirection and will be tempted to bypass it with a solid block of character description or analysis of the plot. As I pointed out in Chapter 9, such passages were popular in 18th- and 19th-century novels with thumbnail descriptions such as this:

> She had the appearance of a fresh and innocent young girl, but beneath that bashful smile there lay a willful obstinacy that was both an asset to the community and a grievous fault in the mind of her husband.

Such descriptions of character actually switch the means of perception to the author. They are generally avoided today because readers like the sense of getting to know characters on their own. Many (but not all) authors believe that for them to comment on character or plot in their own voice is like having a playwright step on stage and address the audience directly.

There is, however, an unusual and striking exception to this in the opening of "Obst Vw." It is an unmistakable example of **author's intrusion** that runs counter to the advice I have just given. Solwitz as the author provides information about a shift in Demian's attitude that won't occur until a year after this story ends. (Review page 115). This is a **flash-forward** in which the point of view is necessarily the author's.

Although unusual, its justification has to do with **tone**. Whenever an author steps in like that, the intrusion briefly establishes a sense of **distance**, a pulling back from the story. In this case, it assures the reader that while these two characters often speak **melodramatically**, their anguish will pass in time.

Descriptive passages are somewhat less obtrusive when the story is written in the first person. In "Minding the Store," for example, the narrator slips in brief descriptive details so unobtrusively that the reader is hardly aware of them. "I was only sixteen myself," for example. Later, he states that he was glad to keep "my pimply face intact for another day." And he describes Marcel as someone "who was always formal and serious." Because these details are coming through the voice of a narrator, they don't have the feel of an author's intrusion.

COMBINING TECHNIQUES: GETTING TO KNOW DEMIAN

We've been looking at the ways dialogue, thoughts, and action can reveal a fictional character as if the techniques are quite separate. In actual practice they are used together, sometimes even within a single sentence. If you look closely at the way we come to know Demian in "Obst Vw," you will see that the reader is responding to multiple cues throughout the entire story.

This in-depth examination of character and feelings is particularly important in this story because the theme deals in part with the ways people misunderstand each other. As you have probably noticed, the title refers not only to the obstructed view seat Demian was given at the baseball game, but also to the obstructed vision the two young adults have of their parents and, equally, the view the parents have of their offspring. In fact, almost all the relationships in this story are badly damaged by limited and distorted views of each other.

The reader's view, however, is in no way restricted. We get to know both characters better than do their own parents. We achieve this knowledge through what they say, do, and, in the case of Demian, think. When the author steps in, it is only to give us some perspective, not to analyze the characters directly. Here is a partial list of what we learn about Demian, along with the various ways the author has informed us:

1. *He loves Rachel deeply.* We learn this (a) *Through dialogue*: Awkwardly trying to avoid clichéd expressions of love, he tries, "I really like you" and "I feel bad for you." (b) *Through actions*: We see both his strong physical attraction for her and his concern for her as well. At the end of the story we see him symbolically trying to ease her psychological injuries by treating her physical wound, putting "his lips to the injured spot . . . smoothing down the flap of torn skin."

2. *He has mixed feelings about both Rachel and sex.* We see this (a) *Through thoughts*: As they sit in the sandbox she seems to him "too sharply constructed, a witch woman . . ." Toward the end of the story it seems to him that she would "let him have her," but "the thought terrifies him." (b) *Through past dialogue* referred to without quoting: Earlier she had told him that she found "something apologetic . . . in his attitude toward sex." He was, we gather, of two minds.

3. *A part of him hates his father.* We learn this (a) *Through action*: He doesn't speak to his father "for several months" after his father refused to sign his learner's permit for driving. (b) *Through thoughts*: When his father grounds him for returning home late, he feels "stiff with rage." He tries to feel sympathy when his mother tells him that his father is facing possible bankruptcy, but "it doesn't work." (c) *Through dialogue*: Later he is able to tell Rachel, "If he died tomorrow it wouldn't make the least difference in my life. It might improve things."

4. *Another part of him admires and even loves his father.* We come to see this (a) *Through thoughts*: When they are driving to the baseball game and Demian hears his father talking with Dr. Frank, he feels "proud of his father." At the game, Demian wishes his father would stay with him "just to be there so [he] could ask him questions or just sit there quietly beside him, watching him watch the game."

And years later when his father is dying, "he'll think for a moment of all the things his father wanted to do that he couldn't do . . . and he'll sit down in a chair for a moment unable to breathe." (b) *Through dialogue*: When Rachel says his father "has a mean streak," he denies it. And later, " 'I hate him' " he murmurs, almost lovingly."

5. *He is conscientious.* This is revealed (a) *Through action*: He conscientiously holds an after-school job. (b) *Through dialogue*: He argues calmly with his father about being grounded, yet finally accepts his father's strict curfew.

6. *He is also rebellious.* We see this (a) *Through action*: He visits with Rachel when he should be at work and considers "excuses he'll make up . . ." (b) *Through thoughts*: He feels like "an explorer" charting new ground when (c) *Through dialogue;* We hear him say to Rachel that his father's death would mean nothing to him.

7. *He is unconsciously competing with Rachel for the title of who has been the most damaged by their parents.* We learn this (a) *Through dialogue*: He tells her the story of his father taking him to the baseball game. (b) *Through thoughts*: "It doesn't sound quite awful enough" in comparison with her situation.

This is a relatively short story, yet we end up knowing Demian far better than we do a new friend even after hours of talk. All the author's exposition has done is to assure us that despite these tormented emotions he will eventually "do well." As readers we have the feeling we have made these discoveries on our own, but in fact we have responded to a variety of carefully inserted cues in the form of action, dialogue, and thoughts.

Don't, however, let this analysis intimidate you! We have been examining a final draft, the end point. It's important to do this just as it is valuable for a dancer or musician to examine and analyze the performance of a professional. The process of getting to that point, however, is usually messier, filled with indecision and uncertainty. Once that first draft is down on paper, keep going over it, looking for ways to revise the dialogue and the action so that each reveals more about your characters. If you stay flexible, you may also discover in them aspects you hadn't previously considered. Individually, these changes may be minuscule, but gradually they will contribute to full and complex characterization.

ONION SKIN DISCLOSURE: JENNIFER REVEALED

The onion is often used as a metaphor to describe stories that unfold their characters layer by layer. "Escapes" is an excellent example. Our first view of Jennifer, you remember, is of an apparently exuberant 14-year-old girl riding the cable cars of San Francisco. Like many kids, she "gets a thrill hanging off the side of the car," her scarf flying. There is no hint here of the resentment and anger that dominate her inner life.

Although many stories unfold this way, notice how different this opening is from "Obst Vw," which begins with a flash-forward that gives us a quick glimpse of how things will work out for Demian. And the initial view of Jennifer also differs from the opening scene in "Minding the Store" with its a description of a bully who clearly will at some point give the narrator a hard time.

In "Escapes" it is not until the third paragraph that we get a hint that something troubling is going on with Jennifer below the surface. Confused by the baseball game, she "closes her eyes for the rest of the game." The next hint comes at the clothing store where she fills her cart, selecting items with apparent enthusiasm but, when facing a dressing room with no privacy, "walks out of the store without trying on a thing."

The next layer of the onion comes in the following paragraph when we see Jennifer's arms. "Tiny uneven scars creep up her wrists like a child's sloppy cross-stitch." Already we've come a long way from that initial picture of the apparently joyful teenager, but we keep wanting to know more. These small revelations are what I described earlier as "dramatic questions" in the building of plot, though here plot and character development go hand in hand.

In quick succession we learn that Jennifer (a) has been "kicked out of school," (b) has apparently tried to commit suicide, and (c) that her father had successfully committed suicide "in his jail cell where he was serving time for dealing drugs."

The story weaves her state of mind in with that of Caryn's to form two interrelated themes. As they visit Alcatraz, the story reveals (a) that Jennifer has been a compulsive shoplifter specializing, significantly, in bracelets; (b) that she has a softer, dependent side we haven't seen before ("She takes my hand in hers"); and (c) that she is aware that stealing is wrong (she takes off her bracelets, revealing her scars). At last, (d) she is willing to face the reality of her self-destructive behavior ("'If I really wanted to do it, I could have made the cuts deeper'"). And (e) we learn that Jennifer has known about her father's suicide for some time, and, (f) most important, what she has longed for is honesty and trust ("I wanted my mother to tell me the truth"). The story ends with Jennifer and Caryn linking their arms.

The unfolding of the layers of Jennifer's character progresses from that defensive pose characteristic of those deeply disturbed to the beginnings of trust and honesty. But the author is careful not to be unrealistically optimistic at the end. A simple "feel-good" story written for a mass-market magazine might end with a hug, tears, and laughter, implying that their problems have all been solved. Ann Hood, however, guards against that with the final sentence about the steep steps and how they linked arms for the climb.

The onion approach to character revelation works particularly well with stories in which there is a narrator who is, like the reader, unaware of the full situation at the beginning.

Although we have focused on the unfolding of Jennifer's character, don't forget that to a slightly lesser degree Caryn, the narrator, is also being revealed. Although she is not presented in that step-by-step manner, we come to understand her needs through the fact that her boyfriend had left her "right before Jennifer came to stay with me." Later she reflects, "My tiny apartment on Fourth Avenue has been so lonely that the idea of sharing it and everything in it makes me almost happy."

In addition, her sister-in-law, Sherry, is revealed through her phone conversations as restless, impatient, unsympathetic, and selfish — all that without a bit of exposition. It is unusual to come to know three characters this well in a story of this length, but it is important that they all be included because the dominant theme applies to all of them: "What I realize . . . is that there really is no escaping. Not for Sherry, not for Jennifer, not for me. The only thing left to do is to stick it out." Notice, incidentally, that this bit of reflection is a bit too bluntly analytical to serve as an ending. Instead, it is placed earlier. The actual conclusion comes in the form of the significant action of linking arms as they leave.

I offer one word of warning about using the onion approach. Don't confuse this potentially subtle approach with the trick ending. This simple but entertaining type of story as seen in O. Henry's work and countless murder mysteries depends on cues that turn out to be false. Misleading information is carefully planted to intensify the surprise at the end. The onion approach, in contrast, is not a trick. It reveals aspects of the truth gradually and in stages.

THREE ESSENTIALS OF EFFECTIVE CHARACTERIZATION

Not all stories are based on fully developed, "round" characters. As you will see when you read the next story, "The Bank Robbery" in Chapter 19, some stories use "flat" characters to illustrate ideas in the tradition of the **fable** and **parable**. More about this in Chapter 20.

Our focus in this chapter has been on characters that are complex and convincing. If you review such characters in the stories and novels you have read, you will notice that most of them fulfill these three characteristics: they are consistent in what they say and do, they are complex, and they are highly individualized. These qualities are goals to aim for.

Consistency is the dominant characteristic of minor characters. Rachel's mother in "Obst Vw," Charles' lover Marcel in "Minding the Store," and the houseboy Thomas in "Rwanda" remain undeveloped even though they have important functions in each story. They are "flat" as opposed to "round" and as such are essentially consistent.

But even well-developed characters have a certain consistency. We may be puzzled by how Demian and Rachel treat each other with alternating affection and wariness, but we come to understand why as we learn more about their parents. We may wonder why Charles didn't come to aid Bobby sooner in "Minding the Store," but a close reader will recall that there is an explanation in Charles' heart a condition that eventually killed him. All the fully developed characters in the stories you have read so far reveal contrasting aspects in their attitudes, but not one of the characters acts in a way that is unexplained at the end of the story. That is the key to consistency.

Complexity is what differentiates fully developed or "round" characters from those that serve only one function. To achieve complex characterization, you have to reveal more than one aspect of a character. You can do this by establishing a pattern, countering it in some way, and showing how both elements are part of the whole character.

Caryn in "Escapes," for example, appears at first to be an independent type. She has a job and an apartment. But in subtle ways the author lets us know that she is lonely and without a sense of direction. It is not surprising at the end of the story when she reaches out for companionship.

In "Obst Vw," both characters try to laugh at what hurts them the most. Rachel insists that the sound of her parents shouting at each other is "funny, really. It's high comedy." And when she jokes about the cut on her foot, calling it " 'parental carnage,' " Demian starts laughing. " 'That's terrific,' " he says, " 'It's really funny.' " But in the end his sense of compassion for her is revealed in his actions. Rage, bitter humor, and love have alternated throughout the story.

To achieve complexity in characterization, provide some type of fresh insight, something not revealed early in the story. This may be an aspect that the reader shares with the character, as in "Escapes," and, finally, "Minding the Store," or it may be an insight only the reader fully appreciates, as in "Obst Vw."

If the change is too subtle or obscure, readers will feel that the story lacks **closure**, that sense of being fully completed. "I'm not sure what the point is," your readers are apt to say. If the change is too great or unconvincing, however, readers will feel that the character lacks consistency. "I just don't believe she would behave like that," they might say, and the story has failed. Shifts in attitude must be credible.

Individuality is what makes a character memorable. Characters have to be interesting in some way, and it helps if they are introduced through an original plot and vivid setting.

A story about Tom and Mary who attend a typical university and spend the afternoon in a typical student cafeteria complaining to each other about their typically awful parents is not going to hold the attention of even your most admiring reader.

What individualizes Demian and Rachel and makes them memorable is the sequence of shifts in mood I referred to previously. They are also made more memorable by the contrasting settings: the sexually charged scene in the preschool sandbox, the ballpark scene with its obscured view, and Rachel's family kitchen with shards of a broken cup on the floor.

Be careful, however, not to overdo the attempt to be different. There comes a point when distinctiveness turns artificial and unconvincing. An inconsequential tale about two bickering college roommates is not going to be improved by transforming it into an inconsequential tale about two bickering mutants living in a burned-out funhouse amid the rubble of World War III. Individuality for its own sake becomes a **gimmick,** a contrived and superficial attention getter.

As you can see from the stories you have read, well-developed characters should be consistent enough so that at least by the end of the story we understand why they said and did what they did; they must be complex enough to seem real, not just types; and they must have enough individuality to make them interesting and memorable. If this seems like a tall order, remember that these qualities do not snap into place in the first draft. They are the goals you keep in mind as you move through successive versions.

19 The Bank Robbery

A Story

by Steven Schutzman

The bank robber told his story in little notes to the bank teller. He held the pistol in one hand and gave her the notes with the other. The first note said:

> *This is a bank holdup because money is just like time and I need more to keep on going, so keep your hands where I can see them and don't go pressing any alarm buttons or I'll blow your head off.*

The teller, a young woman of about twenty-five, felt the lights that lined her streets go on for the first time in years. She kept her hands where he could see them and didn't press any alarm buttons. Ah danger, she said to herself, you are just like love. After she read the note, she gave it back to the gunman and said:

"This note is far too abstract. I really can't respond to it."

The robber, a young man of about twenty-five, felt the electricity of his thoughts in his hand as he wrote the next note. Ah money, he said to himself, you are just like love. His next note said:

> *This is a bank holdup because there is only one clear rule around here and that is WHEN YOU RUN OUT OF MONEY YOU SUFFER, so keep your hands where I can see them and don't go pressing any alarm buttons or I'll blow your head off.*

The young woman took the note, touching lightly the gunless hand that had written it. The touch of the gunman's hand went immediately to her memory, growing its own life there. It became a constant light toward which she could move when she was lost. She felt that she could see everything clearly as if an unknown veil had just been lifted.

"I think I understand better now," she said to the thief, looking first in his eyes and then at the gun. "But all this money will not get you what you want." She looked at him deeply, hoping that she was becoming rich before his eyes.

Ah danger, she said to herself, you are the gold that wants to spend my life.

The robber was becoming sleepy. In the gun was the weight of his dreams about this moment when it was yet to come. The gun was like the heavy eyelids of someone who wants to sleep but is not allowed.

Ah money, he said to himself, I find little bits of you leading to more of you in greater little bits. You are promising endless amounts of yourself but others are coming. They are threatening our treasure together. I cannot pick you up fast enough as you lead into the great, huge quiet that you are. Oh money, please save me, for you are desire, pure desire, that wants only itself.

The gunman could feel his intervals, the spaces in himself, piling up so that he could not be sure of what he would do next. He began to write. His next note said:

> Now is the film of my life, the film of my insomnia: an eerie bus ride, a trance in the night, from which I want to step down, whose light keeps me from sleeping. In the streets I will chase the wind-blown letter of love that will change my life. Give me the money, my Sister, so that I can run my hands through its hair. This is the un-fired gun of time, so keep your hands where I can see them and don't go pressing any alarm buttons or I'll blow your head off with it.

Reading, the young woman felt her inner hands grabbing and holding onto this moment of her life.

Ah danger, she said to herself, you are yourself with perfect clarity. Under your lens I know what I want.

The young man and woman stared into each other's eyes forming two paths between them. On one path his life, like little people, walked into her, and on the other hers walked into him.

"This money is love," she said to him. "I'll do what you want." She began to put money into the huge satchel he had provided.

As she emptied it of money, the bank filled with sleep. Everyone else in the bank slept the untroubled sleep of trees that would never be money. Finally she placed all the money in the bag.

The bank robber and the bank teller left together like hostages of each other. Though it was no longer necessary, he kept the gun on her, for it was becoming like a child between them.

20 | Liberating the Imagination

In Chapter 7, I stressed the fact that one of your best sources of fresh material is your own experience. If you have been writing stories, you have probably been transforming episodes from your own life by altering the **point of view**, rearranging events, and changing the **setting**. You are getting used to the process of creating fictional characters by using aspects of people you have known or briefly met. These are the steps most writers take when creating carefully developed, realistic stories.

But what about those flights of fancy that suddenly sweep in like a sudden squall? They may spring from some absurd and unrealistic notion. Like the tornado in *The Wizard of Oz*, they can have the power to propel you into a fantasy world. Some may be distortions of the world we know; others may be dreamlike. They may lack "essential" elements such as well-developed characters or a realistic setting. Or they may exaggerate some aspect of style, pushing language beyond the conventional range.

How can one stimulate such explosions of imagination? And if we manage to get them down on paper, how are we to judge whether they are merely journal entries — more fun to write than to read — or concepts worth developing into a story to be read by others? This chapter deals with innovative flights and what to do with them.

ACTIVATE YOUR IMAGINATION

You can't force yourself to be creatively innovative any more than you can will yourself to be funny. But you can explore fanciful plots and experiments in style to see what develops. If your imagination is quirky, fresh approaches may come easily. While most samples will remain as entries in your journal, there is always the chance that one of them will have promise and will warrant the time and effort it takes to develop a story.

The appeal of innovative fiction varies. Some writers find its emphasis on novelty too close to the tricky and too far removed from the richness of subtle characterization. Others are drawn to experimental work almost from the beginning. Although your preference will depend a lot on what you have read and enjoyed, every writer can benefit from an introduction to fiction that pushes beyond the conventional — work such as Steven Schutzman's "The Bank Robbery."

One of the best ways to explore new directions is to keep a literary **journal**. A journal can be handwritten, typed in a loose-leaf notebook, or recorded as a special file on a computer. Journal writing frees you from the sense of commitment you feel (or should feel) when writing what you hope will be a fully developed story. Because journal entries are private, you don't have to worry about how others will respond. Journal writing liberates your imagination.

Don't confuse a literary journal with a diary. Your journal is the place for dialogue fragments, reactions to fiction or poetry you have read, story ideas, and fantasies. Your journal is for you what a sketch book is for painters.

Past entries are well worth reviewing. If you find one that shows promise of being developed, set your journal aside and shift gears. Work intended for readers requires a different mind-set.

Whether you have been keeping a journal or not, here are four other possible directions to get you started. Consider them warm-up exercises.

1. **The "What-If" Game:** What if your sister developed the ability to fly? Would you be jealous or proud? How would you explain her to friends? Or what if all the dogs of the world rebelled against their masters on the same day? What if a blind man had the ability to hear the thoughts of those around him? What if an accomplished flutist found that she could not play without attracting swarms of monarch butterflies?

2. **Turning "Like" Into "Is":** We all use **similes** and **metaphors** in daily conversation almost without thinking. Turning these into literal situations often has bizarre results. If a good friend's laugh is *like* a sheep bleating, what if he *becomes* a sheep at awkward moments? Would others pretend not to notice? Could he maintain old friendships? Would his wife give up her love of lamb chops? Or if a sleepless night is *like* a video of all the day's problems, what if a character goes to the movies and finds the film *is* all his day's problems with himself playing the lead role? And what if his wife, sitting beside him, has apparently seen a film with herself as the lead? How does he find out what she has been watching? Will they go back the following night? Will they bring the children?

3. **The Undirected Fantasy:** Let yourself go. Write fast and without plan. Borrow from fairy tales, dreams, or daydreams. It might be boring for others to read, but it has its function in the privacy of your journal. The dreamlike plots and bizarre characters may surprise you. You can look at them as vistas into your unconscious or, if you dislike psychological analysis, as possible material for fiction. Entertain yourself. See where your imagination will lead you.

4. **Stylistic Games:** Describe an automobile accident entirely through the dialogue of three characters. Avoid all exposition and description. Use what they say to reveal what they are like as characters and how they differ from one another. Or write a short scene involving action using "you" rather than "he" or "she." If you need a starter, begin with "You're waiting in a restaurant for your best friend to join you when you see your brother cross the room with a policeman."

Write two versions of the same scene, one with the longest sentences you can construct without sounding absurd, and the other in the shortest possible sentences.

Experimentation has no limit in journal entries. As soon as you decide that you are working on something you hope to share with others, however, your goals and your approach should shift. Without losing your original vision, you should examine the nature of the piece and explore ways of shaping it.

BUILDING ON A PREMISE

Many innovative works of fiction are based on a **premise**, a single, identifiable distortion of the world as we know it.

The **fable**, for example, is one of the oldest forms of premise fiction. Although Aesop wrote his fables more than 2,500 years ago, they are still part of modern culture. Some contemporary writers adopt the same approach. The premise in most fables is simply that animals can talk, think, and behave like people. Quite often, fables also suggest a moral of some type — either serious or satiric.

When the fable form is extended so that each character is consistently a **symbol** for some abstraction, the result is an **allegory**. In John Bunyan's *Pilgrim's Progress* the premise is that abstractions like "glib" and "deceitful" can be seen as characters with names such as Mr. Worldly-Wiseman and the smooth-talking Mr. Legality. *Pilgrim's Progress* was written in the 17th century and for more than 100 years was almost as popular as the Bible. More recently George Orwell employed the allegory for his political satire, *Animal Farm*.

A premise can take many different forms. The as-if element may be that a king can be blessed (and cursed) with the ability to turn everything he touches to gold. King Midas has become part of our culture. In Lewis Carroll's *Through the Looking Glass* the reader accepts the notion that there is a parallel world that exists behind mirrors.

Many of Franz Kafka's stories and novels are based on an initial premise. Everyone knows that adolescents sometimes feel like an insect and are treated as such, but Kafka took this one step farther. In "The Metamorphosis" a young man actually becomes a six-foot cockroach. (If you haven't read it, take the time to look it up.) When we suffer from a sense of guilt and worthlessness, we may feel that life is like a trial, but in Kafka's novel *The Trial* the protagonist finds himself actually immersed in a dreamlike, unending court case. If you take this fictional route, be careful not to rewrite Kafka.

The single premise is also used in some science fiction works, especially short stories. In longer works the number of premises increases, often creating an entire civilization. Such work may become a **fantasy**.

The line between literary works based on a premise and science fiction is hotly debated, but one difference is the emphasis that literary works often place on character and feelings. This is true of Kafka's "The Metamorphosis" which focuses on what it is like to be an adolescent in a rather rigid and traditional family. There are many exceptions, but science fiction tends to deal more with social issues.

DEVELOPING FANTASY

While premise fiction deals with a single as-if exception to the world as we know it, **fantasy** creates an entirely new environment. This may be a futuristic society on Earth or one in a distant galaxy. The characters may be human or some other species. The highly popular Harry Potter series is a fantasy in which the protagonist and others are given unusual powers. The environment is like our world in some respects but quite different in others, in the tradition of some fairy tales. J.R.R. Tolkien created a land of Hobbits in his trilogy, *The Lord of the Rings*. The world he pictures is further from reality than that in the Harry Potter series. In *Watership Down*, Richard Adams deals with a society of rabbits.

Notice, however, that these examples are long works — either novels or even a series of related novels. This is partly because it takes time to create a new universe. Innovative short stories tend to draw on a single premise or on departures in style.

INNOVATIONS IN STYLE

Innovative use of style is limitless. I have suggested some in the list of warm-up exercises listed at the beginning of the chapter. Another is to create the illusion of uninterrupted thoughts by abandoning normal syntax and punctuation. In the famous **stream-of-consciousness** section toward the end of James Joyce's *Ulysses*, Molly Bloom's thoughts are presented without punctuation. The sequence of topics is not arranged logically but meanders by association.

A brief, contemporary example of innovative narration is seen in "Gotta Dance," by Jackson Jodie Daviss, a story that appears in Chapter 22. The protagonist is a young street dancer striking out on her own. Her narration is not unusual until she begins dancing. At that point, it explodes in a burst of enthusiasm. In this passage, she describes the climax of her performance:

> Then I did my knock-down, drag-out, could-you-just-die, great big Broadway-baby finish. Didn't they applaud, oh honey, didn't they yell, and didn't they throw money.

The phrasing here goes beyond the familiar impression of a character talking to the reader. Those questions without question marks are not questions at all; they are expressions of wonder and enthusiasm. The language has left the level of realism and echoes the spirit of the moment.

Another approach suggested in the warm-up exercises is to avoid "he," "she," and "I," replacing them with "you," as in this anonymous description of a bipolar "high":

> Buoyed with mindless joy and confidence, you dazzle your friends and confound your enemies. You are filled with generosity and love, leaving $100 tips and giving your wallet to a homeless man. You phone friends and strangers, giving them advice for hours at a time. It's not your fault that your speech comes too fast for others to understand. It's not your concern when they insist you can't buy two new beautiful cars with no money in the bank. You've left them all behind. You're spinning too fast for the world to catch up.

The defense of the "you" is that it thrusts the reader directly into the situation; the risk is that in longer stories it can become tiresome.

Some authors have created almost a new language, mixing English with jargon or, in other cases, **dialect**. In novels, the author has the time to teach the reader how to respond to a new vocabulary. This is what Anthony Burgess does in his novel *A Clockwork Orange*. Most readers find it confusing at first, but those with patience gradually learn how to respond to it. The same is true in *Far Tartuga*, by Peter Matthiessen, in which a Caribbean dialect is used so directly that the reader has to make some effort to master it. This particular approach lends itself to the novel more easily than the short story because of the time it takes to master it well enough to read it at a normal pace.

Another stylistic innovation is seen in **postmodern fiction**. This places such a strong emphasis on ingenuity of language itself that characterization and plot all but disappear. In some cases reader interest is maintained, if at all, with wit and verbal ingenuity.

Metafiction is a relatively recent approach in which characterization is also downplayed. Instead, the story is designed to illustrate or echo the craft of writing itself.

In John Barth's highly readable story "Lost in the Funhouse," for example, the boy in the fun house (as it is normally spelled) is also the author in the process of writing. Barth stops the action periodically to comment on how the story is or is not progressing. The fun house becomes fiction with all its tricks, special effects, and distortions. At the end, the protagonist is described as one who will go on to "construct funhouses for others . . . though he would rather be among the lovers for whom funhouses are designed."

Other experiments in style make extreme use of dialogue. In Virginia Woolf's novel *The Waves*, for example, each unnumbered chapter begins with a page or so of highly poetic prose describing the sun and the changing landscape. The remainder of each chapter is presented in the form of unbroken dialogue shifting among six characters. Because there are no references to action and no exposition, the reader comes to know these six characters from childhood to old age entirely through their reminiscences and their reactions to each other and the world about them. The novel has to be read at the deliberate pace we use for poetry.

As you can tell from these various examples of published work, stylistic innovations tend to be unique and difficult to describe in the abstract. If experimentation interests you, the best approach is to read some of the readily available examples I've mentioned and let them give you the courage to invent new approaches.

"THE BANK ROBBERY": MULTIPLE INNOVATIONS

Clearly, "The Bank Robbery" is not a conventional or realistic story. The characters are "flat" — without background or development, the plot is dreamlike, and the setting is little more than a bare stage. Our inclination is to look for a single innovative technique that, when identified, will snap the piece into focus. But it's not that simple. It takes several readings to see in this story at least three different experimental departures. They are as follows:

- A *premise story* that asks the question, What would happen if a bank robber and a teller fell in love?
- A *fantasy* that uses a comic, dreamlike plot and poetic language to satirize a whirlwind courtship.
- An *allegory* in which the characters are merely devices for presenting a little essay comparing money and love.

This is the kind of story that might well have begun with a simple premise, the sort that one jots down in one's journal. But like many promising premises, it presents the writer with a challenge: What can I do with it? Many television skits are based on a premise. The good ones can be funny even without canned laughter, but they are entertainment pieces that are soon forgotten. When you use a premise in literary fiction, the work must have some substance, something that will stay with the reader. The premise in "The Bank Robbery" is only a launching pad.

Once this story is in orbit, it quickly becomes a fantasy. The notes the bank robber writes and the inner reflections of both characters, go far beyond the initial premise.

Spinning into a fantasy mode gives the writer much greater freedom, but it presents a second challenge: How can a piece that has all the freedom of a dream be focused so that it has some structure, some direction? The basic form in this case is a courtship: two young people meet, they exchange comments about the need for money, the young woman feels danger in the air, but at the same time she feels "as if an unknown veil has just been lifted." Eventually she goes off with him, the two of them described as being "like hostages of each other."

Viewed this way, the work is essentially a love story. For "money," read "love." What gives it substance is the ways in which the two characters reveal feelings that are shared by most of us: the need for money (love) ("When you run out . . . you suffer . . . "), the alarm that accompanies falling in love ("Ah danger . . . you are the gold that wants to spend my life."), and the way in which a couple in love becomes indifferent to the rest of the world ("Everyone else in the bank slept . . . ").

The ending suggests a happy conclusion for this love story. The gun he has been holding from the beginning in a macho fashion fades away in the manner of dreams and becomes ". . . like a child . . ."

The story can also be read as an allegory. The difference is that when we discuss allegories our focus shifts from characters to ideas. Allegorical characters become mere vehicles for dramatizing abstractions. If we read the story this way, the two primary concepts are money and love. At first, money dominates. "Oh money, please save me," the robber says to himself. " . . . for you are desire, pure desire, that wants only itself." A counter view is presented by the woman who says, "But all this money will not get you what you want."

If this story were a **parable**, we would look for a moral message in that exchange, but if there is a moral in this story, it certainly is not central. An allegory doesn't necessarily preach. When we look at this story as an allegory, it reads like an illustrated essay about the nature of love and money. The two **abstractions** are joined toward the end with her statement "This money is love." To test her assertion, read the story again, replacing all the bank robber's references to "money" with the word "love."

It is a matter of choice whether you prefer to think of this story as a fantasy treatment of a courtship with the emphasis on the characters or as an allegory with the focus on two abstractions, money and love. The difference between the two is a matter of emphasis. In either case, a very short story has elevated a simple premise into a highly sophisticated example of innovative fiction.

THE LURE OF OBSCURITY

The greatest risk when writing innovative fiction is sliding into obscurity. While this problem is most common among beginning writers, it occasionally damages the work of established authors as well. There are several reasons obscurity is so tempting.

The first is the mistaken notion that what was fun to write must necessarily be fun to read. The sad fact is that reading an unintelligible story (or, worse, hearing it read) is as unrewarding as listening to someone else's child describe a wandering and apparently interminable dream. Leave pointless rambling where it belongs — in your journal.

Second, there is a misguided hope that an aimless work written from the heart must necessarily have some secret meaning that, though unknown to the author, can be ferreted out by a conscientious reader. Overworked and underpaid writing instructors and editors waste countless hours patiently trying to interpret stories that don't contain anything to interpret.

Such work is often submitted to writing classes not out of malice but because the student has heard teachers provide explanations of published works that seemed unintelligible on first reading. Some students conclude that if an instructor can draw meaning from difficult literary passages, he or she can do the same with carelessly composed student work. Not even a well-read and well-trained teacher, however, can draw meaning from random and thoughtless writing. It's a disservice to ask others to spend time on work you yourself don't understand.

The third and most serious misconception is the claim that a work of fiction should mean all things to all people. True, a group of readers will see and respond to different aspects of any work. But there is almost always a core of agreement. In "The Bank Robbery," for example, some readers may focus on the love story while others concentrate on the more abstract concerns about money and love, but the story obviously does not satirize politicians or support animal rights. Claiming that a work should mean whatever we want it to mean is admitting that it has no meaning.

The best way to guard against obscurity in your work is to keep the reader in mind. When you are ready to share a story with others, make sure you have worked long and hard to meet them halfway.

THE RISKS OF SIMPLICITY

Premise stories are the most at risk. We see so many single-premise television skits, we are apt to aim too low. The simple premises I suggested earlier in this chapter are good ways to prod your imagination, but unless they are developed, the result will have no more substance than the skits that are written simply for a quick laugh.

Directionless fantasies sometimes show promise if they are enlivened with wit from time to time, but a conscientious reader will soon tire of the futile search for some kind of structure, and conscientious readers are hard to find.

One of the most effective ways of giving substance to an innovative story is to use it to develop **satire**. Satire uses some degree of exaggeration to criticize or ridicule an institution, an attitude, a tradition, or even an individual. The **tone** can range from light and whimsical to bitter and vitriolic.

If you take this route, see if you can go beyond the simple effort to generate laughter. Leave that to the standup comics. Try to generate some insights that lie beneath the comedy. The eternal story of Humpty Dumpty, for example, is a good laugh for kids, but at the time it was written it was known to ridicule Richard II of England. Today it is used to describe leaders who topple from power in spite of efforts by "all the king's horses and all the king's men."

There is light satire in "The Bank Robbery" if you focus on the young man's mania for money and the young woman's fascination with danger, which she describes as being "just like love." These are the ingredients of countless stories. But when you look carefully at what the story is suggesting about our longing for money and love, you know that you are dealing with complex and important issues.

WHAT WORKS?

The more innovative a work, the more difficult it is for writers to evaluate their own work. Because the familiar elements of traditional fiction such as a logical plot and credible characters may have been altered or even abandoned, one loses the usual ways of determining what succeeds and what does not.

The first question to be faced is one I have touched on previously: the degree of obscurity. What may be clear to you as the writer may remain baffling to readers. With such stories, you will have to depend heavily on the reactions of readers.

If you are in a writing class, you are in luck. Innovative fiction is like poetry in that it has to be read more carefully than traditional fiction, so fellow students will be of more help than those who don't normally enjoy reading challenging work.

Writing seminars can be enormously valuable, but try not to sit through them passively. There are ways of getting the most out of even the best courses and, conversely, ways of wasting that opportunity. Don't, for example, start by explaining to the readers what you are trying to do in a story. You want to hear their reactions first.

In some classes, the students are hesitant to be open and honest when discussing a complex and experimental work. No one wants to appear dumb, so unsuccessful works are sometimes treated too gently. They are described as "interesting," which is a polite way of shrugging.

It may be that the readers' comments will continue to be evasive or too kind to be helpful. You learn nothing when a well-meaning student says, "Well, I don't really know what you're doing, but I kind of liked it." It's up to you to ask them exactly what they found puzzling.

If they start to describe your work in ways you believe are all wrong, don't stop them. You need to know how readers will interpret your story without you standing there to correct them.

The comments in advanced seminars tend to be blunter, so you may find it more tempting to defend your work. Resist! Remember that even the most critical comment or suggestion may turn out to be useful. Listen carefully and take notes. Later, you can sort out which comments are worth taking seriously and which can be ignored. Sometimes the suggestion you found the most unjustified during class turns out to have some merit after a day of cooling off. It won't be easy, but try to keep your own intent to yourself until after the general discussion is over.

If you are not taking a course, try to find two or three individuals who are familiar with experimental fiction. Ask them for their reactions. If they are friends, you may have to urge them to avoid chitchat and vague responses. As in a class, it will be important for them to be honest and specific in their comments.

The degree of obscurity is, of course, only one of many aspects you hope to learn from a class or a group of readers. It's important to find out whether they found the **tone** appropriate and consistent. If your work is satire, did it strike them as too mild or excessive? Did they find the innovation fresh and original, or did it echo the style of a published author? And did they find the work insightful? Did it probe the subject with enough depth?

Nonrealistic fiction provides many possibilities, but like **free verse** it is not formless. It is not literary anarchy. A piece may have begun spontaneously with little or no plan, but before it is ready for others to read, it has to be shaped and given purpose. There are many different traditions that you can draw on and learn from. Take the time to familiarize yourself with them so that you can distinguish an informal journal entry from a story with literary merit.

21 Heightened Meaning

Metaphor, Symbol, and Theme

Literary nonfiction tends to use **abstractions** freely. Words like "self-consciousness," "memory," "hostility," and "joy" can't be visualized, but they are both acceptable and useful in all types of essays. Nonfiction works like "Unwired" and "On Leaving Florida" are good examples.

Fiction, on the other hand, often translates words like these into **images** that we can see or feel. Compare, for example, the two versions of these three statements:

ABSTRACT STATEMENT	VISUAL VERSION
Sometimes she is self-conscious about her height.	She arcs down into herself like a long-necked bird.
It was a moment that would remain in her memory forever.	She felt her inner hands grabbing and holding onto this moment.
Hostilities between parents often do damage to their children.	She is limping . . . blood wells out of her foot.

The second choices taken from "Obst Vw" and "The Bank Robbery," provide visual impressions that are both more vivid and more memorable than the corresponding abstract statement. Similar as they are in this respect, each one represents a slightly different technique. The first of these three visual versions is a **simile**, the second is a **metaphor**, and the third is a **symbol**. These three terms will be discussed in this chapter.

Casual readers don't have to know how they differ. It's enough that such readers have a vivid sense of what is being described. But practicing writers who take their craft seriously have to know which approach will best suit their needs. And there is no effective way to discuss those choices with fellow writers unless we use basic analytical terms accurately.

HOW SIMILES AND METAPHORS WORK

First, some quick definitions. A **simile** is a comparison in which we state that one item (often an **abstraction**) is like something **concrete**. Frequently this is a visual image, but it may be anything we can respond to with one of the five senses. Thus, "She fought like a lion" implies strength and courage. Notice, however, that it is not a simple comparison as in "Lemons are like oranges." We are not suggesting that this woman used claws or bit her opponent. We are saying only that the way she fought brings to mind the ferocity of a lion. It's impossible to see abstractions such as ferocity, determination, or courage, but we can easily visualize a lion in action.

A **metaphor** serves the same function, but it makes the comparison without "like" or "as." This distinction is more significant than one might think because a metaphorical statement is literally untrue. It is only **figuratively** true. In this case we might have, "She is a lion when fighting for civil rights." *Is* a lion? Well, is *like* a lion. When we analyze metaphors, it is helpful to convert them into similes.

Similes and metaphors are both called **figurative language** or **figures of speech** because they use words in a nonliteral way. A **symbol**, incidentally, is not a figure of speech for reasons I will explain shortly.

Some authors use figurative language more than others. It is possible to write a highly effective story without using a single figure of speech or symbol. Most authors do use at least a few, however. In this collection, all the stories contain both figures of speech and symbols.

In some cases similes and metaphors are used together so naturally that one hardly notices the difference. In "Obst Vw," for example, Demian makes this statement about his relationship with his father:

> "Sometimes in the room with him I feel like I don't exist. I don't have a body."

This is such a familiar feeling that we hardly think of it as figurative language. But to feel "like I don't exist" is a simile since to feel *like* that is literally true. The next statement, "I don't have a body," is a metaphor because it is literally untrue. Notice how much more impact it has as a metaphor than it would have as a simile: "as if I don't have a body."

Figurative language is not mere decoration added to make one's style sound elegant. It is natural to common speech. Many of the examples we hear in daily life are so common that they have become **clichés** — similes and metaphors that have lost all impact from overuse.

Stockbrokers aren't visualizing an animal when they refer to a "bull market," parents have no picture in mind when they ask children to make their rooms "neat as a pin," and none of us is sure why a whip is "smart."

Similes and metaphors that heighten the meaning, make it vivid and intense, have to be fresh and original. If they are harmonious with the vocabulary and speech patterns of a character, they will blend with dialogue or narration just as naturally as with exposition.

In "Minding the Store," for example, it seems natural for the narrator to say "My heart was flipping like a stuck record." It's not a very sophisticated simile, but he's not a very sophisticated kid.

"The Bank Robbery," on the other hand, is written in language that in some ways resembles poetry. It has similes, metaphors, and symbolic suggestions that require several readings. At the moment when she apparently falls in love, for example, she feels as if "an unknown veil had just been lifted." This strikingly original simile brings to mind the marriage costume in some cultures in which the bride symbolically raises a veil.

As in many poems, this story contains more metaphors than similes. When the young woman first confronts the bank robber, she "felt the lights that lined her streets go on for the first time in years." We assume from this that she had been living an uneventful life and felt her life suddenly light up. The author could have used a simile by saying "it felt *as if* the lights came on," but without the "as if" the figure of speech adds to the dreamlike tone of the work.

In another passage, the author describes through a metaphor the sudden bonding between these two people. Notice, however, that within the metaphor there is a simile:

> The young man and woman stared into each other's eyes forming two paths between them. On one path his life, like little people, walked into her, and on the other hers walked into him.

The two paths are presented directly without "like" or "as," but the author adds to that a whimsical detail that pictures all the details two lovers share as "like little people."

VEHICLES AND TENORS

The terms **vehicle** and **tenor** were originally suggested by the critic I.A. Richards, and they are used frequently by writers and poets because there is no better way to analyze precisely why one figure of speech is effective and another fails. As in poetry, the terms are also essential for an understanding of how similes and metaphors differ fundamentally from symbols.

The **vehicle** of a simile or metaphor is the **image** itself — a concrete object, something we can see or at least hear or feel. The **tenor** is the implied subject. It is often but not always an abstraction. If these terms are new to you, think of the **vehicle** as the transporter delivering a picture to the reader. As for the **tenor**, think of in*ten*tion since it is the writer's intended meaning, usually an abstraction.

Here are some samples, the first of which I have already quoted in connection with characterization. They are all metaphors. I have added italics to the vehicle in each case.

From "Obst Vw":

It seems reckless and marvelous saying these things about his father. *He's an explorer charting ground never before seen by human eyes.*

The tenor here is his feeling reckless and marvelous — both abstractions.

From "Obst Vw":

She doesn't help him out. Her silence is *a hole he walks around and around.*

The tenor here is implied. It might be described as "something he can't deal with directly and so must keep avoiding as he talks."

From "The Bank Robber":

Reading, the young woman felt *her inner hands grabbing and holding onto this moment of her life.*

The tenor is also implied here. It might be described as: "She realized that this moment in her life would remain with her forever." Notice how vivid the author's metaphor is compared with the commonly used cliché, ". . . was etched in her memory."

THE IMPACT OF A SYMBOL

We are all familiar with **symbols** when they appear in political cartoons. The American flag, Uncle Sam, the cross, the Star of David, and the White House are all built into the culture as representing abstractions such as a country, a religion, or a branch of government.

Literarily simple novels — particularly historical romances and gothic tales — have their fairly obvious symbolic images: the drinking of a toast by two evil plotters in which the wine spills, assuring us that they will fail; howling dogs on the moors signaling once again that someone is in torment. These are sometimes referred to as **public symbols** because they are widely known. In fact, they are so common that most have become clichés.

Sophisticated fiction, in contrast, uses fresh images. The term *private symbol* is occasionally used but is rather misleading. *Original symbol* would be a far more accurate term. Such symbols are devised for a particular literary work rather than borrowed from the warehouse of well-known symbols. The meaning of an original or unique symbol is revealed through the context of the story or novel. As a result, those who have not read extensively sometimes have difficulty in identifying them.

Let's go back to our original example of a metaphor: "She was a lion in battle." The image of the lion, the vehicle, is introduced simply for the purpose of comparison. There is no actual lion in the story. That's why we call it a *figure of speech*. It is used figuratively, not literally, to describe the tenor, courage.

Contrast this, however, with a story set in Africa that deals with a real lion. If the story is intended to contrast the cowardice of a hunter with true courage, it might be possible to describe the lion in ways that suggest the quality of courage. If this is done carefully, the lion could be made into a symbol for those qualities. The lion actually exists, but it has been imbued with a meaning greater than itself.

There is a central symbol in "Escapes" that deserves special attention. It is a place rather than an object. Alcatraz is not just a vivid setting, it is a prison. And the author makes sure that you won't miss its symbolic importance. Caryn and Jennifer enter a cell and they pretend that they "are in solitary confinement." Jennifer says:

> "Imagine being locked in here and knowing that San Francisco is right across the bay. . . . Hearing people at a party."

This emphasizes the isolation of these two characters. They have no friends there other than each other. Like the prisoners, they can hear the sounds of San Francisco but are not a part of it.

Caryn points out that they can walk out of the prison, but later she reflects on this:

> I realize, standing there . . . that there is really no escaping. Not for Sherry, not for Jennifer, not for me. The only thing left to do is to stick it out.

That prison has become a symbol for their state. Physically they can leave, but in a deeper sense they — indeed all of us — will always be in solitary. Like the prisoners, we devise tricks to help us deal with this isolation, but the best we can do is "to stick it out." With this in mind, they "link arms for the climb."

Contrast this with a story in which the image of a prison is used as a vehicle in a simile. It might be as brief as this: "Being trapped in a monotonous, dead-end job was for her like being locked up in some prison." Or, converting that to a metaphor, "Her life had become a prison." These statements don't refer to a real prison. The word *prison* in these two cases is being used simply as a figure of speech.

Incidentally, many readers study "Escapes" without noticing that the narrator's name is also symbolic. Caryn is revealed as one who is *caring*. One note of warning, however: symbolic names are risky indeed. Chris is too often bearded and saintly; Victor is predictably one who wins or, ironically, loses; and Adam is a firstborn who eventually gets thrown out of his Edenic home. Only a few names, such as Willy Loman (low-man) in Arthur Miller's *Death of a Salesman*, are unobtrusive. If you are going to select a symbolic name, make it original and so subtle that many of your readers will miss it.

Symbols also play a major part in "Obst Vw." In fact, there are two of them. It is a highly symmetrical story dealing with two characters almost equally. Their problems are revealed through two separate symbols, each of which is given a prominent emphasis. These symbols become central to the story.

Before I go on, try to identify on your own the primary symbol for each character. Remember that occasionally titles serve to highlight a symbolic detail, as in "Escapes."

For Demian, that ticket with the abbreviation "obst vw" is a clear and tangible symbol. It suggests the obstructed vision Demian has of his father and his father's view of him. In addition, it comments on the relationships Rachel's parents have with each other and that Rachel has with them. In a minor but significant way, it also applies to the absurdly inaccurate view Rachel's father has of Demian's father, calling him "the Old Hippie" for no logical reason. In fact, every relationship in that story with the possible exception of Demian and Rachel themselves is damaged by an obscured or distorted view.

The central symbol characterizing Rachel's emotional state is appropriately more dramatic. As we saw at the beginning of this chapter, it is blood. The father has thrown a coffee cup against the refrigerator in his rage, and the mother has shown her disdain by refusing to sweep it up. It is the daughter who is bleeding — a vivid symbol reaffirming the well-known fact that children are injured when parents fight.

The real subtlety of that injury lies in Rachel's attitude toward it. Instead of bandaging the cut, she flaunts it, sitting there "while her blood drip-drips onto the gray tile." It's her statement to them. "They need to *see* this," she says. The gesture is partly a longing for sympathy and partly hostility. It may also be an unconscious appeal for Demian's sympathy. At the end of that story, you remember, Demian kisses the injured spot, "smoothing down the flap of torn skin," a sincere but possibly futile attempt to heal her wounds, both physical and emotional.

Notice that the vehicles of these two symbols — the ticket marked "OBST-VW" and the broken cup — have both been expanded into **scenes**, each with its own **setting**. The entire episode at the ballpark and the scene in the kitchen become symbolic. If you read those scenes over you will see how many details refer in different ways to the tenor. Notice, too, that these symbols are not just dropped into the story, like UFOs from outer space, they are planned for and used extensively. They are, to use a slightly shopworn metaphor, woven into the fabric of the story.

Symbols don't have to loom as large as these. Some, better described as symbolic details, are so brief that they are easy to miss on first reading. Here is a whimsical example from "Minding the Store":

> Newer customers called him Gene — or Mr. Jolly Giant, which Charles loved, puffing up dramatically. Charles even loved the old red neon sign out front, which flashed what was supposed to be a giant, though it looked more like a fat midget.

That red neon sign is a kindly symbol of Charles himself — both his slightly comic "puffed up" self and the gentle midget self.

For some readers, picking out figurative language and symbols seems like a literary game that detracts from the pleasure of a story. As a result, they may avoid any symbolic suggestion for fear of sounding artificial or self-consciously literary. Keep in mind, however, that reading as recreation is different from reading (as we have been here) analytically as a writer. The only way to create subtle symbolic suggestions in your own writing is to study how others have done it.

A few reassurances may help. First, symbols are not necessary ingredients in fiction. Excellent stories and novels — sophisticated in the best sense — are written without even the hint of a symbolic detail.

Second, neither figures of speech nor symbols are the invention of teachers. They are part of common speech. We use figurative language without much conscious thought. We dream in symbols. Fantasies tend to be symbolic. Symbols have been a special concern of writers in every age because the visual element often provides a far greater range of suggestion than can be achieved through straightforward, literal language.

Finally, very few stories are ruined for a reader if he or she does not recognize symbolic elements at first. This may have been true for you when you first read any of these stories. "Obst Vw" depends heavily on symbols, but the story can be enjoyed without knowing that.

If you are planning to introduce symbols in your own work, keep them subtle. Far better that some of your readers miss your symbolic suggestions than to find them absurdly obvious. A blatant symbol exposes your effort as author. As soon as that happens, the illusion of reality breaks and the story seems contrived.

In the interest of subtlety, think twice before you let a serious story depend utterly on a symbol. Schutzman's "The Bank Robbery" is filled with symbolic details from the title to the last line, but the light and fanciful **tone** keeps it from getting heavy. Picture what "Escapes" would be like if the entire story were set in that prison or if "Obst Vw" were limited to the kitchen, Rachel's foot dripping from start to finish. The best approach is to move cautiously and let the story suggest to you what might be made symbolic. The goal is to have symbolic details serve the story, not dominate it.

THE IMPORTANCE OF THEME

Journal entries don't usually have clear **themes**. They experiment with different styles or subject matter, record reactions to literary works, and muse on one's life. Sophisticated fiction, on the other hand, almost always implies an unstated central concern. Readers look for it. If you don't provide some kind of theme, they are apt to ask, "What's the point?" or "What are you getting at?"

There are many ways to define **theme**, but I have found that this is the simplest and most useful for writers: *theme is the portion of any narrative work that comments on the human condition.* This applies to fiction, literary nonfiction, narrative poetry, drama, and film. In most cases, the "comment on the human condition" is implied, not stated.

If you think of theme in this way, you will never confuse it with **plot**. Plot is what happens. When we talk about plot, we name characters and describe events. When we talk about theme, we discuss in abstract terms the underlying suggestion of the story.

To describe the theme of a story, use a full sentence, not just a word. "Isolation" is not the theme of "Escapes." It's a topic. Even "fear of isolation" is not yet a statement. You need a complete sentence, such as "Fear of isolation leads us to reach out and share our lives with another person."

Because the theme is almost always implied rather than stated, different readers will phrase it differently. Those variations reflect what aspect each person feels is most important. When discussing a story in a group, remember that total agreement in this area is not necessary. It is important, however, to reach a consensus as to what the story is suggesting thematically.

When the work being discussed is your own, make a real effort to remain silent — at least at first. This is the only way to find out what aspects reached your readers and which did not.

All thematic statements are necessarily simplifications. They are abstract distillations of meaning. As you can see, most sophisticated stories have a cluster of related themes. Often there is a dominant concern that provides thematic focus and then a cluster of related themes. For this reason, some critics and writers prefer the phrase **central concern** rather than *theme*. The two terms are used in the same way.

Turning to "Obst Vw," there are several different statements we could use to describe the central concern, but they all deal with the relationship between adolescents and their parents. Remember that *theme* doesn't describe the plot or even mention the characters by name. One statement might stress the harm done to young people this way: "Parental indifference can be as damaging to an adolescent as actual violence." Another might focus on how the effects differed: "Parents who act out their rage in front of their children do more serious and lasting damage than those who are merely distant and insensitive." Others might prefer to highlight a more positive aspect: "When young people feel cut off from parental affection, they sometimes find solace with someone their own age."

As you analyze the themes in published stories, it may seem as if authors somehow hold all those threads in their heads from the start. Not so. What you read in print is a final draft, and rarely do authors have all those intellectual concerns in mind when they begin a new story. Developing thematic concerns is an evolving process.

Here, then, is an important aspect of the creative process that can't be taught: a complex story speaks to its author through successive drafts. The story itself develops certain characters and highlights certain scenes. Most important, it often informs the writer about new thematic possibilities. Each suggestion, of course, requires more rewriting. The author who quits after the first draft will never hear the story suggest new implications that might be developed. Although the notion of a dialogue between the story and the author is a metaphor, it is often an important part of the creative process.

WHEN THEMES NEED REVISION

If you conclude that there is something wrong with the theme of your story, you may be tempted to abandon the work. The situation may well be serious, but it's not necessarily fatal. Here are some correctable problems.

A recurring weakness in student fiction is settling for a theme that is a **truism**. That is, the theme is nothing more than a widely accepted and obvious assertion. Who wants to read a story that does little but remind us that you should say "no" to drugs, that you shouldn't drink and drive, or that people who don't express their emotions get into trouble. These are all reasonable assertions, and they may serve as part of a theme, but if that is all a story suggests, it's going to seem as dull as one of those newspaper editorials you don't finish reading.

At the beginning of the fiction section, I warned against seven "deadly sins" — plot patterns that have become clichés. Thematic clichés are sometimes harder to identify, but they can be equally serious. If you take the time to compose a thematic statement that describes your story and all you can come up with is one of those trite slogans, you know you're in trouble.

But all is not lost. Often you can salvage such a story. One way is to look closer at the characters you are working with. A banal theme is usually a sign that you have started with an idea rather than a character or a situation. You may not have to scrap the whole story if you can develop greater subtlety in characterization. "Obst Vw," for example, could be described as having a simple theme, such as "Bad marriages produce unhappy children," but as we have seen from composing various thematic statements for that story, it has a far greater range of concerns.

A second weakness is excessive reiteration of a theme. Avoid having every scene bluntly repeat the macho quality of the protagonist, the dishonesty of a corrupt businessman, or a fundamental contrast in the political views of a husband and his wife. When the author's intent becomes blatantly obvious, the story loses credibility.

The solution, once again, is to look more closely at the characters. If a character was conceived as a **stereotype** such as a typical homeless man, a typical lawyer, or a typical firefighter, replace him or her with a disguised version of a person you know. Then explore that person's individuality. Look for ironic contrasts, mixed feelings, and strengths and weaknesses. Remember that materialists aren't always grasping, spiritual types aren't always motivated by pure thoughts, and dishonest people are occasionally capable of kindness and even love.

Demian's father, for example, is rigid and often insensitive to the feelings of others, but not unrelentingly so. Look at the pressure he is under at work and the frustrations left over from his own adolescence. Review what his wife says in his defense. There's more to him than a stereotype of a stern father, and even Demian occasionally recognizes this.

Don't be afraid to develop odd twists and apparent contradictions in human relationships. As you develop a credibly complex character, the story will no longer strike the same note repeatedly. And in the process, you may find that the theme becomes richer, more original.

Themes that are obscure present a third problem that warrants careful revision. I've already warned against a plot that is baffling (as indeed "The Bank Robbery" may have seemed on first reading). But a clear plot with an obscure theme can be just as dissatisfying. In some cases, you may find that you can't describe the theme of your own story in a single sentence. That should tell you something. Or the theme may be obvious to you but not to others. If three or more conscientious readers are puzzled, making comments such as "What are you getting at?", don't assume they are all dumb. Having this kind of input available is the advantage of working in a writing class or with a group of fellow writers.

If the theme needs clarification, resist the temptation to add a line of exposition at the end explaining the story. Instead, see if you can find ways of dramatizing the theme through action, dialogue, or thoughts earlier in the story. You might also consider a concluding action that will bring the story into focus. If you review the endings of a number of stories you have read, you will see how many ways there are to highlight a theme in the final paragraph without explaining everything to the reader in the form of an analytical statement.

"Escapes" is a good example. The theme is revealed in three stages. First, both characters imagine what it would be like to be held in solitary confinement. The dialogue reminds us how isolated each of them has been. Second, Caryn through thoughts expresses the idea that none of us can escape the sense of being in isolation. We can only "stick it out." Finally, in the form of action they "link arms for the climb." The theme of that story is unfolded throughout the work, but notice how these three key passages take the form of dialogue, thoughts, and finally action.

Theme is only one aspect of a story. The freshest and most insightful theme won't make a story succeed if the characters are not convincing and the action plausible. But without originality and complexity of theme, a story becomes nothing more than a simple piece of passing entertainment. A truly sophisticated work of fiction appeals to the mind as well as to the emotions.

22 Gotta Dance

A Story

by Jackson Jodie Daviss

Maybe I shouldn't have mentioned it to anyone. Before I knew it, it was all through the family, and they'd all made it their business to challenge me. I wouldn't tell them my plans, other than to say I was leaving, but that was enough to set them off. Uncle Mike called from Oregon to say, "Katie, don't do it," and I wouldn't have hung up on him except that he added, "Haven't you caused enough disappointment?" That did it. Nine people had already told me no, and Uncle Mike lit the fire under me when he made it ten. Nine-eight-seven-six-five-four-three-two-one. Kaboom.

On my way to the bus station, I stopped by the old house. I still had my key and I knew no one was home. After ducking my head into each room, including my old one, just to be sure I was alone, I went into my brother's room and set my duffel bag and myself on his bed.

The blinds were shut so the room was dim, but I looked around at all the things I knew by heart and welcomed the softening effect of the low light. I sat there a very long time in the silence until I began to think I might never rise from that bed or come out of that gray light, so I pushed myself to my feet. I eased off my sneakers and edged the rug aside so I could have some polished floor, then I pushed the door shut.

Anyone passing in the hall outside might've heard a soft sound, a gentle sweeping sound, maybe a creak of the floor, but not much more as I danced a very soft shoe in my stocking feet. Arms outstretched but loose and swaying, head laid back and to one side, like falling asleep, eyes very nearly closed in that room like twilight, I danced to the beat of my heart.

After a while, I straightened the rug, opened the blinds to the bright day and walked out of what was now just another room without him in it. He was the only one I said good-bye to, and the only one I asked to come with me, if he could.

At the bus station, I asked the guy for a ticket to the nearest city of some size. Most of them are far apart in the Midwest and I liked the idea of those long rides with time to think. I like buses — the long-haul kind, anyway — because they're so public that they're private. I also like the

166

pace, easing you out of one place before easing you into the next, no big jolts to your system.

My bus had very few people on it and the long ride was uneventful, except when the little boy threw his hat out the window. The mother got upset, but the kid was happy. He clearly hated that hat; I'd seen him come close to launching it twice before he finally let fly. The thing sailed in a beautiful arc, then settled on a fence post, a ringer, just the way you never can do it when you try. The woman asked the driver if he'd mind going back for the hat. He said he'd mind. So the woman stayed upset and the kid stayed happy. I liked her well enough, but the boy was maybe the most annoying kid I've come across, so I didn't offer him the money to buy a hat he and his mother could agree on. Money would have been no problem. Money has never been my problem.

There are some who say money is precisely my problem, in that I give it so little thought. I don't own much. I lose things all the time. I'm told I dress lousy. I'm told, too, that I have no appreciation of money because I've never had to do without it. That may be true. But even if it is, it's not all there is to say about a person.

There is one thing I do well, and money didn't buy it, couldn't have bought it for me. I am one fine dancer. I can dance like nobody you've ever seen. Heck, I can dance like everybody you've ever seen. I didn't take lessons, not the usual kind, because I'm a natural, but I've worn out a few sets of tapes and a VCR. I'd watch Gene Kelly and practice until I had his steps. Watch Fred Astaire, practice, get his steps. I practice all the time. Bill Robinson, Eleanor Powell, Donald O'Connor, Ginger Rogers. You know, movie dancers. I'm a movie dancer. I don't dance in the movies, though. Never have. Who does, anymore? I dance where and when I can.

My many and vocal relatives don't think much, have never thought much, of my dancing — largely, I believe, because they are not dancers themselves. To be honest, they don't think much of anything I do, not since I left the path they'd set for me, and that's been most of my twenty-three years. These people, critical of achievement they don't understand, without praise for talent or dreams or the elegant risk, are terrified of being left behind but haven't the grace to come along in spirit.

Mutts and I talked a lot about that. He was a family exception, as I am, and he thought whatever I did was more than fine. He was my brother, and I backed everything he did, too. He played blues harmonica. He told bad jokes. We did have plans. His name was Ronald, but everyone's called him Mutts since he was a baby. No one remembers why. He never got his chance to fly, and I figure if I don't do this now, I maybe never will. I need to do it for both of us.

The bus depot was crowded and crummy, like most city depots seem to be. I stored my bag in a locker, bought a paper and headed for where the bright lights would be. I carried my tap shoes and tape player.

When I reached the area I wanted it was still early, so I looked for a place to wait. I found a clean diner, with a big front window where I could read the paper and watch for the lines to form. I told the waitress I wanted a long cup of coffee before ordering. After a half hour or so, she brought another re-fill and asked if I was ready. She was kind and patient and I wondered what she was doing in the job. It seems like nothing takes it out of you like wait-ress work. She was young; maybe that was it. I asked her what was good and she recommended the baked chicken special, said it was what she'd had on her break. That's what I had, and she was right, but I only picked at it. I wanted something for energy, but I didn't want to court a side ache, so the only thing I really ate was the salad. She brought an extra dinner roll and stayed just as pleasant the whole time I was there, which was the better part of two hours, so I put down a good tip when I left.

While I was in the diner, a truly gaunt young man came in. He ordered only soup, but he ate it like he'd been hungry a long time. He asked politely for extra crackers and the waitress gave them to him. When he left, he was full of baked chicken special with an extra dinner roll. He wouldn't take a loan. Pride, maybe, or maybe he didn't believe I could spare it, and I didn't want to be sitting in a public place pushing the idea that I had plenty of money. Maybe I don't know the value of money, but I know what discretion is worth. The guy was reluctant even to take the chicken dinner, but I convinced him if he didn't eat it, nobody would. He reminded me of Mutts, except that Mutts had never been hungry like that.

When the lines were forming I started on over. While I waited, I watched the people. There were some kids on the street, dressed a lot like me in my worn jeans, faded turtleneck, and jersey warm-up jacket. They were work-ing the crowd like their hopes amounted to spare change. The theater pa-trons waiting in line were dressed to the nines, as they say. There is something that makes the well-dressed not look at the shabby. Maybe it's guilt. Maybe it's embarrassment because, relatively, they're overdressed. I don't know. I do know it makes it easy to study them in detail. Probably makes them easy marks for pickpockets, too. The smell of them was rich: warm wool, sweet spice and alcohol, leather, peppermint and shoe polish. I thought I saw Mutts at the other edge of the crowd, just for a moment, but I remembered he couldn't be.

I was wearing my sneakers, carrying my taps. They're slickery black shoes that answer me back. They're among the few things I've bought for myself and I keep them shiny. I sat on the curb and changed shoes. I tied the sneakers together by the laces and draped them around my shoulders.

I turned on my tape player and the first of my favorite show tunes be-gan as I got to my feet. I waited a few beats, but no one paid attention until I started to dance. My first taps rang off the concrete clear and clean, meas-ured, a telegraphed message: *Takka-takka-takka-tak! Takka-takka-takka-tak! Takka-takka-takka-tak-tak-tak!* I paused; everybody turned.

I tapped an oh-so-easy, wait-a-minute time-step while I lifted the sneakers from around my neck. I gripped the laces in my right hand and gave the shoes a couple of overhead, bola-style swings, tossing them to land beside the tape player, neat as you please. I didn't miss a beat. The audience liked it; I knew they would. Then I let the rhythm take me and I started to fly. Everything came together. I had no weight, no worries, just the sweet, solid beat. Feets, do your stuff.

Didn't I *dance*. And wasn't I *smooth*. Quick taps and slow rolling, jazz it, swing it, on the beat, off the beat, out of one tune right into the next and the next and I never took one break. It was a chill of a night, but didn't I sweat, didn't that jacket just have to come off. Didn't I feel the solid jar to the backbone from the heavy heel steps, and the pump of my heart on the beat on the beat on the beat.

Time passed. I danced. A sandy-haired man came out of the theater. He looked confused. He said, "Ladies and gentlemen, curtain in five minutes." I'm sure that's what he said. Didn't I dance, and didn't they all stay. The sandy-haired man, he was tall and slim and he looked like a dancer, and didn't he stay, too.

Every move I knew, I made, every step I'd learned, I took, until the tape had run on out, until they set my rhythm with the clap of their hands, until the sweet sound of the overture drifted out, until I knew for certain they had held the curtain for want of an audience. Then I did my knock-down, drag-out, could-you-just-die, great big Broadway-baby finish.

Didn't they applaud, oh honey, didn't they yell, and didn't they throw money. I dug coins from my own pockets and dropped them, too, leaving it all for the street kids. Wasn't the slender man with sandy hair saying, "See me after the show." I'm almost sure that's what he said as I gripped my tape player, grabbed my sneakers, my jacket, and ran away, ran with a plan and a purpose, farther with each step from my beginnings and into the world, truly heading home.

The blood that drummed in my ears set the rhythm as I ran, ran easy, taps ringing off the pavement, on the beat on the beat on the beat. Everything was pounding, but I had to make the next bus, that I knew, catch that bus and get on to the next town, and the next, and the next and the next. Funeral tomorrow, but Mutts will not be there, no, and neither will I. I'm on tour.

23 Style and Tone

Style is the manner in which a work is written. All fiction has style. You can't compose without it any more than you can write your name without revealing your handwriting.

Varieties of style run all the way from *inconspicuous* to *conspicuous*. Inconspicuous styles may have identifiable characteristics, but the average reader is not aware of them. The fact that such work does actually have a style becomes clear if you compare a contemporary story or novel with one written in 1900 or earlier. The style we use is shaped by the age in which we live, our unconscious inclinations, and our conscious choices as individual writers.

A majority of stories and novels employ what is essentially an inconspicuous style. This includes both those written in the third person like "Rwanda" and, to a somewhat less degree, those written in the first person like "Escapes." As readers we are aware of a narrator in "Escapes," but she tells her story in a fairly straightforward manner.

In contrast, *conspicuous style* is unmistakable. Usually it is devised for a particular work, but some authors use a distinctive style in all their work. In a few cases, you can identify the author from a sample page just as easily as you can recognize the voice of a friend on the telephone. The fiction of Ernest Hemingway, for example, tends to have short, relatively simple sentences, while that of Henry James is distinctive for its lengthy, complex sentences and an extensive vocabulary that frequently sends a conscientious reader to the dictionary.

In describing conspicuous styles, the term **voice** has come into prominence in the past few decades. In its broadest and least helpful sense, it is used as an unneeded synonym for **style**. The word is much more valuable if we limit it to styles that are highly distinctive such as the one in "The Bank Robbery."

Although "The Bank Robbery" is written in the third person, distinctive styles are more frequently found in first-person stories narrated by a **persona** as in "Gotta Dance" and "Minding the Store." Because these two stories have the unmistakable sound of spoken language, using the term *voice* is entirely appropriate.

In "Gotta Dance," for example, the voice is conspicuous and unique. Although we don't learn much about her background and her name is used only once, we gain a sense of what she is like from the way she speaks.

To see the contrast between an inconspicuous and conspicuous style, here are two passages that are similar in that they each describe a moment in which the narrator makes an important decision. The first is from "Escapes" and the second from "Gotta Dance":

> I had not seen Jennifer in almost two years when Sherry called me that day. . . . So I'm still not sure what made me say yes, I'll take her for a while. Except for maybe the thought of sharing that ultrablue sky with someone seemed so appealing.
>
> Uncle Mike called from Oregon to say, "Katie, don't do it," and I wouldn't have hung up on him except that he added, "Haven't you caused enough disappointment?" That did it. Nine people had already told me no, and Uncle Mike lit the fire under me when he made it ten. Nine-eight-seven-six-five-four-three-two-one. Kaboom.

With that comic echo from a rocket launching, the reader of "Gotta Dance" is sure from the start that this story will do lively things with style. And we are not disappointed. The innovations become more pronounced as soon as Katie begins to dance. That entire scene outside the theater is an excellent example of fiction with a distinctive **voice**.

Because there is no end to the number of stylistic effects you can achieve, the analysis of style can become confusing. Surprisingly, however, style is determined by just six factors:

1. **Diction**, the choice of words
2. **Syntax**, sentence structure (short, long; simple, complex)
3. **Density**, the presence or absence of figurative and symbolic language
4. **Narrative modes**, the relative emphasis on dialogue, thoughts, action, and exposition
5. **Tense** past or present
6. **Person**, first ("I"), third ("she/he"), and very occasionally "you" and "they"

Don't think of these as a checklist to be considered before you start a new story. Trust your inclinations and get that first draft down on paper. These basic elements of style, however, are enormously important when you begin revising. In addition, they have two other functions: they will help guide any discussion group by keeping the analysis precise and helpful. And, equally important, they will give you a way to analyze the style in a published work with precision.

DICTION

Those of us who write in English have one real advantage: we have far more words at our disposal than do those using any other European language. We have one set of words from our Norse-Germanic heritage and another from Greek and Latin sources filtered through French. In addition, we have borrowed from the Chinese ("gong," "tong"), Hindi and Tamil from India ("khaki," "curry"), Eskimo ("kayak," "igloo"), and a great many other languages. English, to the dismay of foreign students, has been a hospitable language for centuries, adopting whatever is useful as its own.

This makes for a great deal of duplication. Many of our words with an Anglo-Saxon or Old Norse origin have a corresponding word with a Greek or Latin source. Although they have essentially the same meaning, they almost always have different **overtones**. In general, Anglo-Saxon words (on the left in the following list) are considered more informal. Some, not listed here, are viewed as obscene. Those with Greek or Latin roots (on the right) strike us as elevated or formal:

sweating	perspiring
grabbed	embraced
boat	vessel
got in	entered
hate	detest
the sea	the ocean

Then there are words that have distinctly different overtones regardless of derivation. A *car* seems less expensive than *automobile*, but *motor car* is reserved for the truly luxurious. Real estate agents deal with *houses, homes, properties,* and *estates*. We unconsciously view the terms on a scale from modest to expensive.

How does all this affect us when we write fiction? Word choice is a major factor in characterization, and it can also reveal aspects of theme. The impact of diction is most evident in stories that are presented in the first person through a narrator. Works like "Minding the Store" and "Gotta Dance" create the illusion of spoken language largely, though not entirely, through the diction.

"Minding the Store" achieves this voice without blatant cues like dialect, heavy use of contractions, or conspicuous slang. In this passage, for example, he uses only two substandard phrases, yet clearly it has the sound of a 16-year-old kid:

> Charles trusted me, and I didn't have much else going for me back then —
> I had bad acne, and I was scrawny as hell. I knew that I was never going to
> kick anybody's ass . . .

The narrator in "Gotta Dance," on the other hand, is far more volatile. She uses slang as in "kaboom" and "Feets, do your stuff." She also uses one-syllable words that create a lively rhythm like ". . . and the pump of my heart on the beat on the beat on the beat."

While diction is particularly important when the story is told in the first person, it also has a major impact on third-person fiction. The words that characters use in dialogue also shape our view of them as well.

In reviewing the dialogue of your characters, consider age, education, and personality. Each will use a slightly different **level of usage**, ranging from formal to slang. Background may also be a factor. A city cab driver, for example, will have a different vocabulary from, say, a dairy farmer. Just a few words that seem "out of character" will spoil the sense of realism.

Fiction, of course, is not written word by word. When the writing is going well, let it flow. The time to take a close look at your diction is when you read over the completed first or second draft. Decide what effect you want to achieve, and revise accordingly.

SYNTAX

Syntax means sentence structure, and it can have as much to do with the stylistic effect as diction. There is a subtle but significant syntactical contrast in the dialogue in "Obst Vw." Both Demian and Rachel tend to use short, simple phrases as in this sample:

> "Who wants your parents?"
>
> "What's wrong with my parents?"
>
> "Your father has a mean streak."
>
> "No he doesn't."

Demian's parents, on the other hand, often use somewhat longer sentences. In a passage already quoted, Demion's mother speaks deliberately.

> "He's way too smart for what he does. . . . He did well in college without studying. He could remember everything he'd ever read. He was a great talker, there was nothing he couldn't have done if he'd wanted to — do you know how high his IQ is?"

Notice how the grammatical structure breaks down as she becomes more emotionally concerned. The fourth sentence runs on with a comma instead of a period (what was called a *comma splice* when grammar was taught) and then is continued after a dash which in formal English would have been a period. This is not careless writing. Grammatical rules are often bent in fiction to reveal the mood of the speaker.

The same lengthy and altered syntax is used by Demian's father. The content is an absurdly exaggerated response to Demian's simple request for a second chance. What concerns us here is how the fractured syntax underscores his simmering rage and frustration:

> "If you get sick, kiddo. If your heart hurts, the air sticks in your throat, you say with your last feeble breath, God, Jesus, Krishna, whoever — please, what did I do, could you please, please, give me a second chance, what's He going to say to you?"

This is a grammarian's nightmare, filled with incomplete and run-on sentences; its disjointed structure reflects not only his mood but also the depth of his own frustrations.

On a happier note, Katie's manic mood in "Gotta Dance" is echoed in her long and fragmented sentences:

> Quick taps and slow rolling, jazz it, swing it, on the beat, off the beat, out of one tune right into the next and I never took one break. It was a chill of a night, but didn't I sweat, didn't that jacket just have to come off. Didn't I feel the solid jar to the backbone from the heavy heel steps, and the pump of my heart on the beat on the beat on the beat.

In formal nonfiction, a passage like this would be criticized for having *run-on sentences*. But this is innovative fiction. The rhythm of those long sentences with their repetitions echo the unbroken rhythm of her dancing. You can almost hear her taps with "on the beat on the beat on the beat."

As you can see from these examples, long sentences don't necessarily slow the pace. It depends on the rhythm, the diction, and the context. If you have a computer program that will correct your syntax and grammar, you may want to use if for formal essays and reports, but turn it off when writing fiction. Rely instead on your ear. Read passages out loud and judge for yourself what creates the effect you want.

Most fiction, however, is written with relatively standard syntax. That means using sentences with subjects and verbs and varying the length for variety. It also means selecting diction that is appropriate and accessible. If you try to impress your readers with long, complex sentences and words you found in a synonym dictionary, you will be indulging in what is known as **overwriting** or, worse, **purple prose**. The writing will seem artificial or affected.

DENSITY

A **dense style** is achieved when a lot is implied about characterization and theme. With such work we often draw more from the second reading than we did the first time through.

Low density doesn't necessarily mean a story was badly written. We may refer to it as "fun," "entertaining," or "clever." With novels the phrase is "a quick read." The implication is that enjoyable as it may be, we are unlikely to read it twice.

Density is achieved when a story develops one or more characters in some detail, when the theme has complexity and insight, or when figurative language and symbolic suggestion are used heavily.

"Obst Vw" is a good example of dense style partly because of the way it explores the subtleties of not just one but two central characters. Even Demian's parents are revealed with more complexity than are most secondary characters. In addition, the story also presents several themes dealing with parents and their children as well as the relationship between adolescents. And as we have seen, both characterization and themes are presented through symbolic details such as the "obst vw" baseball ticket and Rachel's bleeding foot. In short, there is a lot going on in that story.

The density in "The Bank Robbery" does not come from detailed or realistic characterization. Instead, the complexity lies in the development of the theme and a dazzling array of symbolic language. In spite of its brevity, its density, like that of some poems, calls for several readings.

Returning now to your own writing, there may be times when you feel that the style of a story you are working on is too light, too insubstantial. In such cases you may want to develop a character's **ambivalent** feelings or reveal more about a second character. Sometimes a single theme can be expanded to become a cluster of themes.

A less frequent problem occurs when you find that you have taken on too many threads so that the story begins to seem confusing. This is not true density; it's clutter. In such cases, you may want to back off and focus on a single aspect. Or consider developing a humorous aspect. This is a matter of **tone,** which I will turn to shortly.

In short, lack of density makes fiction seem slight; excessive density can make it turgid or, worse, confusing. Determine the level of density that is appropriate for your material.

THE BALANCE OF NARRATIVE MODES

The third method of influencing your style in fiction is the balance of **narrative modes**. I am using *mode* in the special sense introduced at the beginning of the fiction section: dialogue, thoughts, action, description, and exposition.

Stories such as "Escapes" or "Gotta Dance" that appear to be presented through a first-person narrator are in a sense all dialogue. But the approach is only an echo of actual speech, so work like this is almost never placed in quotation marks.

In spite of sounding like narration, first-person stories make use of narrative modes in varying degrees just as third-person work does. "Escapes," for example, uses short samples of dialogue throughout the story, but "Gotta Dance" uses almost none. Of the stories written in the third person, "Rwanda" and "Obst Vw" use dialogue the most.

Another approach, not represented here, is to emphasize **dialogue** to the extent that almost the entire work becomes an exchange between two or more characters. This often has the effect of increasing the pace, but at a cost: it becomes much more difficult to present visual details such as the setting and the characters.

Description, one of our five modes, is important in some stories and not in others. In "Escapes," for example, Jennifer is described as "almost six feet, and so thin that her hip bones poke out from her faded blue jeans." Her neighborhood and the prison itself are both described in some detail. "Gotta Dance," in contrast, gives no details about Katie, the protagonist, except for her clothing. The emphasis in that story is on action, especially when she is dancing.

This does not mean that you should strive for an even balance of the five narrative modes in every story. It does suggest, however, that you should be aware of how that balance can affect the overall stylistic effect. If an early draft of a story seems heavy and slow, consider adding dialogue. Giving your characters a chance to talk often adds energy to an otherwise leaden story. On the other hand, if your story seems superficial or trivial, it may be that you have relied too much on insignificant dialogue and not enough on thoughts and description.

The two modes that give the most trouble are thoughts and **exposition**. Thoughts, like description, slow the pace. If that seems to be the trouble, get your protagonist moving and talking. Look at the way Katie's action in "Gotta Dance" keeps that story alive even though the motive for that action is a deep melancholy over the death of her brother. More dialogue may also help enliven a story that has become bogged down with introspection.

Too much **exposition** is even more dangerous. Not only does it slow the pace, it may also explain too much. As I have pointed out previously, fiction normally depends on action and dialogue to maintain the reader's sense of discovery. Exposition, even when filtered through a narrator, nudges a story in the direction of the essay.

While action can enliven your style, too much may make the story superficial. Action-packed plots can take over, reducing the development of characterization and thematic aspects.

The balance of modes shouldn't be a major concern when working on your first draft. Examine it when you start revising. There is no harm in favoring one mode over the others in a particular story, but try to judge how this approach has affected your work. A few revisions at this early stage may make a major difference in the work as a whole.

TENSE

The matter of **tense** has become a controversy of sorts over the past few decades. Traditionally, most short stories and novels were written in the past tense: "The rain continued, but on Thursday she decided to go to the gym anyway." Starting in the early 1980s, however, an increasing number of authors began using the present tense like this: "The rain continues, but on Thursday she decides to go to the gym anyway."

Some argue that it is illogical and therefore disruptive to imply that events are occurring at the time of the telling. But most readers lose themselves in the story after the first paragraph and forget what tense it is in. Can you, for example, recall which three of the six stories in this volume are written in the present tense?

Present-tense enthusiasts often claim that fiction is livelier and more immediate in that tense. If this were so, however, past-tense fiction would not have dominated fiction for more than a century.

There is one good technical reason for adopting the present tense. If a story in the past tense contains a number of **flashbacks**, the author normally cues the reader with the past perfect each time: "Ten years ago she had told her husband that gyms were a waste of money." If the flashback is developed, it then reverts to simple past tense: "Laughing, she told everyone the dues were driving them into bankruptcy." If the main part of the story is written in the present tense, however, the author can signal the start of those flashbacks simply by shifting to the past tense and staying there. "Obst Vw" for example, one of the three stories in this book written in the present tense, enters that lengthy flashback about going to the ball game simply by shifting from the present tense to the past. The past tense is used for the entire scene, ending with a return to the present tense: "Demian leans back in his chair . . ."

The choice of whether to use the past or present tense in a story may seem like a major one, but its effect on fiction is almost negligible. If you are uncertain as to which tense to use with a particular story, try an opening half-page first in past tense and then in present. One will seem better than the other, and you can invent a good explanation later.

VARIETIES OF TONE

Whereas **style** has to do with the manner in which a work is written, a distinctly literary element, **tone** deals with the emotional aspect. In general usage, it can refer either to the emotion generated by the work itself or to the author's attitude toward that work.

The **tone** of a work itself can be described with adjectives like "comic," "amusing," "dark," "exciting," "sad," "merry," "eerie," or "depressing." When

tone is applied to the author's attitude toward his or her material, it can be described as "close," as in works that seem autobiographical, or "distant," as in Schutzman's comic but rather detached style in "The Bank Robbery." The author's tone can also be critical or disapproving of characters or institutions. It is important when discussing tone to make it clear whether you are talking about the story itself or the author's attitude toward the material.

"Gotta Dance" is a particularly interesting example because the tone of the story is not the same as the author's tone toward the subject matter. As we begin reading the story, the tone appears to be lighthearted. Katie is about to do something that all her relatives urge her not to, and we assume that this will be a comic story of rebellion. The tone becomes slightly more serious in the scene when she returns to her home. That's when we learn by implication that her brother has died. Still, the story has a basically cheerful feel to it. When she arrives in a strange city and begins to dance, the tone turns truly manic. "Feets, do your stuff" she exclaims to herself and goes into a whirlwind performance. But at the very end it becomes clear that the attitude of the author toward her work is unmistakably serious:

> I had to make the next bus, that I knew, catch that bus and get on to the next town, and the next, and the next and the next. Funeral tomorrow, but Mutts will not be there, no, and neither will I. I'm on tour.

At that point we realize that the apparently lighthearted tone of Katie as narrator is a front. She is sustaining her own courage and determination to pay homage to her dead brother. To quote the author discussing this work, the subject of this story is grief:

> Some of us deny it, others wallow in it, and many simply limp along with it. . . . The people who seem to me to deal most successfully with grief are those who accept it and use the very intensity of it to transform the unbearable into something that can be borne with grace.

What tone should you adopt? Your first inclination may be the best, but not always. If you are writing a story that is at least partially based on personal experience, it will seem natural to present it with the tone you still feel. Remember, though, that what you are writing is fiction, not a diary entry. If the episode you are using might strike readers as a bit melodramatic or sentimental, it may be wise to lighten up a bit.

This is exactly what Solwitz does from time to time in "Obst Vw." Her protagonist is seriously alienated from his father, but the author is careful not to let the story sound like a soap opera in which the son is driven to suicide by an insensitive father. That flash forward at the very beginning in which we as readers learn that Demian will in a year's time look back on the trip to the baseball game with amusement assures us that the incident won't utterly destroy him. It provides a touch of objectivity, and objectivity is the best guard against melodrama.

Even in that agonizing scene when Rachel has cut herself on the broken cup, there is something wryly comic about her act of letting the blood drip on the floor, a sad, futile, but offbeat attempt to make contact with her parents.

These two stories provide an interesting contrast in tone. "Gotta Dance" sustains a lighthearted tone in spite of the fact that the author's approach to the subject is serious. In "Obst Vw," on the other hand, the characters are darkly depressed about their parents and adopt a somber, almost melodramatic tone, but the author reminds us in different ways that theirs is not a life-and-death situation. The author's tone is one of genuine concern tempered with gentle amusement.

IRONY AND SATIRE

There are several types of **irony**, but they all involve a reversal of either meaning or expectations.

Verbal irony is achieved when characters or authors say something that is intentionally different from what they really mean. In casual conversation we often call this **sarcasm**, although sarcasm is generally limited to statements that are hostile and critical. Irony is a broader term that can take the form of simple understatement, as when someone describes a hurricane as "quite a blow." Stronger irony can be a full reversal of meaning, as when the same character, while watching a house being washed away in the storm, says "Great day for a sail." We don't call him crazy because we know (or should know) that he or she is speaking ironically rather than literally.

Verbal irony in fiction occurs most often in dialogue. It suggests a character who is wry and given to understatement. As such, it is one more way that dialogue can help define character. We see it in Rachel's dialogue as the two teenagers are listening to her parents shout at each other at the beginning of "Obst Vw":

> "Wait. This is the part about who was the first unfaithful one! . . . It's funny, really. It's high comedy."

Dramatic irony is similar except that the character making the statement does not understand the true significance of what he or she is saying. It is called "dramatic" because it often is used in plays, especially those that make use of mistaken identities. It would be dramatic irony, for example, if in a play a swindler enthusiastically outlines his scheme to someone known to the audience as the very person he has already cheated.

Fiction written in the first person also lends itself to dramatic irony. The irony occurs when the narrators or minor characters inadvertently reveal more about themselves than they realize. In "Escapes," for example, Caryn's sister-in-law describes her daughter, Jennifer, as ". . . nothing but trouble. . . . Stealing and cheating," without realizing that this applies to the way she and her husband lived before he was arrested.

Cosmic irony, or *irony of fate*, also involves a reversal, but in this case the reversal is in events rather than words. It refers to any outcome that is the opposite of normal expectations. One often hears it used in a careless way to describe anything that is unexpected. True irony is stronger than that. It is ironic for a composer like Beethoven to lose his hearing or for an Olympic swimmer to drown in his or her own bathtub.

Historical events occasionally provide ironic twists that are too blatant for fiction. It is bad enough that America's first major toxic waste disaster should occur in a place called the Love Canal, but what story writer would have dared call the polluter the Hooker Chemical Corporation? Ironically, fiction can't always use true events and names if it is going to maintain credibility.

Satire is best defined as exaggeration for the purpose of ridicule. It is almost always rooted in irony, but as you can see from the previous examples, irony doesn't necessarily involve ridicule.

Most satire adopts a serious or even solemn **tone** while making fun of the topic through exaggeration. Occasionally the technique is reversed and a serious subject is treated as if it were high comedy. Either way, there is always a charged contrast between the apparent tone and the true intent.

Many readers are introduced to simple satire through magazines such as *Mad* and *National Lampoon* and films such as those produced by the Monty Python group and Woody Allen. Neither these nor the satiric sketches often seen on television are very subtle. In fiction there is usually a greater intricacy both in the humor and in the themes.

"The Bank Robbery," for example, starts out with a situation that might lend itself to a simple television skit: an unusually articulate bank robber hands over his note stating that "money is just like time" and he needs more. The teller doesn't panic; in fact, she is struck by the fact that danger is "just like love." With the admirable calm of a writing instructor, she tells the would-be thief that his note "is far too abstract."

To this point, the satire seems to poke fun at two rather sophisticated individuals going through the bank robbery ritual with some philosophical insights. There are also echoes here of a couple meeting at a singles bar — she feeling the thrill of meeting a lively young man, and he feeling "the electricity of his thoughts" as he moves on to the next stage of the conversation.

But there is another satiric theme going on. His attitude toward money and his method of getting some is an exaggeration of what some claim is a male fixation: "When you run out of money you suffer." In response, she points out that ". . . all this money will not get you what you want." That may seem too sensible to be satiric, but look at what is going through her mind as she speaks: ". . . hoping that she was becoming rich before his eyes."

In the end, what he demanded, money, becomes love and she gives it to him. That's when they become "like hostages of each other." The story as a whole has become a satire of what we perceive as a desperation for money and how that desperation is ultimately a longing for love.

Complicated? Definitely. Worth several readings? Absolutely. But remember that we're not dealing with the fast food of fiction. This is a work to be savored and enjoyed.

While the tone of this story is positive and softened with wit, satire can also serve as the voice of protest. As such, it often becomes bitter and hostile. Or it can become cynical. Tom Wolfe's highly readable and frequently comic *The Bonfire of the Vanities*, for example, is a novel in which every character is without a saving grace.

If writing satire interests you, keep in mind these two potential dangers. The first is lack of focus. Decide in advance just what kind of person, institution, or attitude you want to ridicule. Keep your satiric attack precise and detailed even if, like Schutzman's, it is complex.

The other danger is a matter of excess. If your exaggeration becomes extreme, you might find the piece turning into slapstick. Such work may, like cartoons, be very funny but, also like cartoons, be quickly forgotten.

If your taste turns to subtle social satire, read work of J.P. Marquand and Peter DeVries. For more biting satire, try George Orwell's *Animal Farm*, a comic but ultimately savage attack on Soviet communism of the 1930s, or Joseph Heller's *Catch-22*, a funny yet bitter view of war. In addition, consider the British novelist Evelyn Waugh and the short story writer Raoul Dahl.

Studying different approaches in style and tone in the abstract will help you learn about your options. And it should make your analysis of your own work and that of others more precise. But in the years to come your growth and development will come not from my analysis but from extensive reading of fiction itself.

24 Troubleshooting Guide: Fiction

Topics for Quick Review

This Troubleshooting Guide is designed primarily as a self-help listing of recurring problems in the writing of fiction. Use the page references when revising your work. In addition, some instructors may find it useful to use this list to supplement their written comments on your work. Rather than taking the time to explain some aspect of fiction, they can simply ask you to review certain pages.

The headings and subheadings are grouped alphabetically. Some topics are cross-listed under different headings for quick reference. There are similar guides immediately following the poetry and drama sections.

For a complete listing of all terms and concepts used in this text, refer to the Glossary-Index at the end of the book. It contains brief definitions and page references.

PART II

The Writing of Poetry

....

25 What Makes a Poem a Poem?

• *Five characteristics of poetry (187)* • *The poetic line (188)* • *The use of images (189)* • *The sound of words (190)* • *The rhythms of language (191)* • *Density (191)* • *Simple versus sophisticated poetry (192)* • *Using poetic conventions to achieve originality (196)*

Yes, but is it really a poem? This question is often asked when we discuss poetry — particularly contemporary work — but we rarely take the time to answer it. Defining poetry seems difficult because the **genre**[2] includes such an astonishing variety of forms. Types vary from lengthy Greek epics to three-line **haiku**, from complex **metrical** schemes to the apparent formlessness of some **free verse**.

In spite of this variation, however, there are certain basic characteristics shared in varying degrees by all poetry. These not only help to distinguish poetry from **prose**; they also suggest special qualities that have drawn men and women to this genre since before there were written languages.

As readers, we have come to expect these aspects. When one or more are missing, we may sense it without knowing exactly what is wrong. As writers, however, that vague sense is not enough. We have to identify just what aspect has been ignored.

There are five fundamental characteristics that distinguish **poetry** from **prose**:

• Using the poetic **line** rather than the sentence as the primary unit
• Relying more on **images** than on abstractions
• Cultivating the *sound* of words
• Developing **rhythms** of language
• Creating **density** by implying far more than is stated

Poems vary in the degree to which they make use of these five characteristics. Although all poems rely on the line as a basic unit of composition, the

---

[2] Words in **boldface** are listed in the Glossary-Index.

other four in our list may be pronounced or barely noticeable. Still, all five characteristics remain the core of what makes poetry fundamentally different from prose.

Because these distinctions are so important for both readers and writers of poetry, each deserves a close look, both here and in subsequent chapters.

THE POETIC LINE

When you write **prose**, the length of the line is determined simply by the size of the paper you are using. If your work is published, your editor or compositor, not you, will determine the length of those lines. The length will vary depending on whether the work is printed in magazine columns or book pages. Prose writers, then, have full control over the sentences they write, but they leave line length to others.

Not so with poetry. The poet determines where each line is to break. Line length is part of the art form. For a compositor to change the length of a line in poetry would be as outrageous as revising the wording itself. This first characteristic, then, is embedded in the very definition of the genre.

The importance of the line in poetry is more than just a matter of definition. It is for most poets the basic unit of composition. When we write prose, we naturally think in terms of sentences, but when we turn to poetry, we usually move line by line.

Most poets also use sentences and they usually punctuate them in the conventional manner, but the effect of the grammatical structure is muted by the use of lines. Only occasionally are lines complete sentences in themselves.

In fact, when too many lines end with a period, they tend to create the singsong effect we associate with nursery rhymes and comic verse. The best way to avoid this is to allow the sentence structure and the idea or feeling expressed to continue smoothly into the next line.

The importance of the line in poetry is fundamental; its use actually preceded the written word. **Epics** such as *The Iliad* and *The Odyssey* were apparently memorized and recited before they were written, and the rhythm of spoken lines was an essential aid to memorization. So was **rhyme**. Even today there are individuals who have memorized their native epics without being able to read or write.

As soon as poetry was recorded on the page, there was less need for memory aids. But poetry has never lost its roots in the spoken language or its reliance on the line. This is why most poets keep reading their work aloud as they compose so they can both hear and see the lines as they develop. It also accounts for the increasing popularity of poetry readings and recordings available at most libraries and on the Internet.

With metered verse, the length of the line is determined at the outset. **Meter** is based on a recurring pattern of stressed and unstressed syllables in each line, so the length of the line is set by the poet's choice of a metrical scheme. Writing a metered poem does not mean giving up control; it merely means that the choice is made at the beginning of the poem rather than line by line. Meter is a structuring of natural speech rhythms, just as formal dance steps are agreed-on patterns drawn from improvised dancing.

Free verse is like freestyle dancing in that it has no preset structure. The length and nature of each line are determined as the poem develops. But, again, as in freestyle dancing, those variations can be extremely important. They can be used to control the pace of reading, to emphasize a key image, to establish rhythms, and sometimes even to shape the printed poem in some significant way.

Maintaining control over the line is an invaluable asset of the poet, a privilege not shared by writers of prose. It is an absolute distinction that differentiates all verse from all prose.

The remaining four characteristics of poetry are not as absolute. One can find poems that do not make use of them all. But they are qualities that we associate with the genre. They help define poetry and distinguish it from prose.

THE USE OF IMAGES

The second characteristic of poetry is its heightened use of **imagery**. We think of images as objects we can see, but actually the term includes anything we can respond to with one of the five senses — sights, sounds, tastes, tactile sensations, and even smells. That may seem like a wide net, but think of all the **abstractions** it excludes — words like *love, hate, democracy, liberty, good, bad,* and *death*. Indeed, *life* itself is an abstraction.

Essays tend to be rooted in abstractions. Philosophical works, for example, often explore the nature of good, evil, or truth. They use abstractions to describe abstractions. Take this oft-quoted sentence: "The price of liberty is eternal vigilance." Three abstract nouns and one abstract adjective. Economic articles that analyze the gross national product, poverty, or profit margins do the same.

Many poems also deal with abstract themes such as love, loyalty, and honesty, but they usually translate those broad concepts into objects or actions we can see or respond to through one of the senses. The abstraction *desire*, for example, is too general to have an impact on a reader. We know what it means, but only intellectually. The poet Appleman helps us *feel* an aspect of desire by comparing it with the ocean's undertow. (The poem is on page 219.)

We all know what *rage* is when we are angry at someone. But when we try to describe it, we have trouble. It's hard to put into words. The problem is that we can't really see it. But the poet Dorothy Barresi can. She creates a dreamlike view of rage in which there is plenty to see. She shares that image for us in her poem "Mystery" (page 218).

Images can be used by themselves or to create **similes, metaphors,** and **symbols**. More about that later. The point here is that most poetry is rooted in objects we can see or respond to through the other senses. Poetry is by nature sensate — a genre of the senses.

THE SOUND OF WORDS

When we recall how poetry began by being spoken, chanted, or sung, it's clear why it frequently makes more use of the sound of language than does prose. It is no accident that the word *verse* applies not only to poetry but also to the sung portion of a song, that *ballad* describes both narrative poems and songs that tell stories, and that a *refrain* is a repeated line in either a poem or a song. Poetry is never far from voice.

For those who have not read much poetry, **rhyme** may seem to be the primary way of linking words by sound. This is natural enough since we have heard rhyme used in jingles, nursery rhymes, and simple ballads. Ending two or more lines with matching sounds is relatively easy to do. But when rhyme is too regular it becomes obtrusive. It can easily take over, sounding like a monotonous drum beat and dominating the more subtle aspects of a poem. Because of this, those poets who use rhyme almost always adopt various ways of muting it, techniques that will be described in Chapter 29.

In addition to rhyme, there are two other ways of linking words by sound: by matching the initial letter ("*g*reen as *g*rass") or by selecting words in which internal syllables echo each other ("tr*ee*s and l*ea*ves"). The paired words, of course, must appear close enough to each other so that the reader can hear the linkage.

"Winter Ocean" by John Updike is very short poem distinguished primarily for its exaggerated use of sound:

> Many-maned scud-thumper, tub
> of male whales, maker of worn wood, shrub-
> ruster, sky-mocker, rave!
> portly pusher of waves, wind-slave.

I will return to this poem in Chapter 29 on the sounds of language, but for now simply circle the pairs of words that are linked by initial sounds like "many-maned" and the middles of words such as "male whales." These outnumber and upstage the rhyme endings.

Occasionally these same techniques are also used in prose. We hear them mainly in oratory and in dramatic sermons where repetition of initial sounds and recurring phrases create effects similar to those in "Winter Ocean." Most prose, however, whether spoken or written, makes little use of auditory effects. It is poets who have maintained an awareness of how melodious the sound of language can be.

THE RHYTHMS OF LANGUAGE

Rhythm in language is like the beat in music. It can be as pronounced as the drum in a martial band or as subtle as a string quartet.

Because spoken language — especially English — stresses some words more than others, it is easy to create a thumping rhythm by creating a line that contains two stressed words, a pause, and two more stressed words. If we borrow the subject matter from the Updike poem, "Winter Ocean" (190), we might come up with something like this. The italics identify the stressed words:

> The *winter sea*   is *king* of *all*
> It *mocks* the *sky*   and *batters* the *land*,
> Yet *sailors know*   it's a *slave* to the *wind*.

A subtler way to create rhythm is to count syllables rather than words and to employ them in a recurring pattern. This is called **syllabics**. The **haiku** is about the shortest example of this approach. It has five syllables in the first line, seven in the second, and five in the third. Samples of Etheridge Knight's use of that form appear on page 204. Other poets create their own sequence, repeating it in successive **stanzas**.

While syllabics depend on the *number* of syllables in each line, **metered** poetry is based on patterns of stressed and unstressed syllables. Over time, certain recurring patterns became traditional and given names like **iamb** and *trochee*. Here are two lines taken from Richard Wilbur's "The Pardon" (page 213). Notice how each line is made up of five pairs of unstressed and stressed syllables.

> In my kind world the dead were out of range

> And I could not forgive the sad or strange

For purpose of analysis, read these lines aloud with an exaggerated emphasis on the stressed syllables marked with a stress mark ('). When you read the poem as a whole for pleasure, however, use a normal, conversational manner. The meter will become a subtle rhythmical background.

I will return to metrical techniques in greater detail in Chapter 30, but this overview will give you an idea of how many options you have.

Although **free verse** does not use either **syllabics** or **meter**, it develops rhythm in other ways. A common approach is to use both variation in line length and indentations to create rhythms. The poems by Janeya Hisle (page 313) and E. E. Cummings (page 210) are particularly striking examples.

DENSITY

The fifth and final characteristic of poetry is **density**. Poetry usually packs more meaning and suggestions into a passage than does a prose paragraph of the same length. One way poetry achieves this is to draw on the **connotative** meaning of words and phrases. Prose, in contrast, tends to limit itself to the **denotative** meanings — their literal definition.

Waking, for example, denotes literally the end of sleep, but it can also imply (or connote) awareness, as in "I suddenly woke to the idea that . . ." *Sleep* has, in addition to its literal meaning, the connotation of death. So when Theodore Roethke begins "The Waking" (page 209) with the statement, "I wake to sleep, and take my waking slow," we recognize, at least on second reading, that he is describing how he moves into life's experiences like someone beginning a new day. Yet, he savors each moment, knowing full well that he is mortal and will ultimately die. Notice, however, that it took me 30 words to explain rather clumsily in prose what he communicates in nine.

Density like this is often achieved through comparisons known as **similes** and **metaphors**, and through **symbols** — all of which will be discussed in Chapter 28. What is important here is the fact that these devices are not mere decoration; they are ways of making language suggest far more than its literal meaning.

The fact that poems are concentrated does not mean they necessarily have to be short. Long **epic** poems such as *The Iliad* and *Beowulf* deal with mythic and historical events that unify a culture. In our own age, epic tales are more frequently presented in the form of novels or films.

Contemporary poets have turned increasingly to their own experiences, feelings, and insights. Even when poets are exploring broad aspects of the human condition, they tend to draw on their own lives, implying the general through material that is personal and specific.

When you start writing poetry, the most fertile sources to consider will be your own experiences and your feelings about those experiences. But poetry isn't simply a collection of feelings spilled out on the page like journal entries. Useful as journals are, their entries are no more than sketches that some artists save to recall specific scenes. A poem explores the significance of an experience, or an insight, probing beneath the surface. To do this effectively requires density.

SIMPLE VERSUS SOPHISTICATED POETRY

What is a *good* poem? This question invites a second: good for what? If a poem is intended for a mass market — as greeting cards are — it should have a positive message and be phrased in unvaried metrical lines with a regular rhyme scheme. Both the sentiments and the phrasing should be familiar, not fresh or startling. To be "good," a mass-market poem should soothe, not probe.

Poems that are **literary**, however, are intended for readers who are looking for an entirely different experience. They want poetry that opens up and explores different aspects of the human experience. They enjoy word play and subtle use of sound and rhythm. They are willing to deal with disturbing insights. They expect the language to be fresh and don't mind if it is sometimes challenging. Some readers like poems that emphasize language itself, playing with words in complicated ways; others prefer work that focuses on what it is to be a human being.

There are problems, however, with calling this kind of poem *literary*. For one thing, the term seems a bit pretentious when applied to contemporary work. Besides, then we face the problem of defining *literary*. Our problems are compounded when we call it "good" poetry. This seems like a value judgment and implies that popular, mass-market verse is "bad." It is as subjective as calling classical music "good" and popular music "bad." There is no quicker way to plunge a group of two or more into an afternoon of fruitless bickering.

The best solution is to borrow two terms from the language of science. To a biologist, simple forms of life are *simple* and complex forms are *sophisticated*. Thus, the bird is not better in any objective sense than the jellyfish, but it is far more sophisticated in that its potential as a living creature is greater. The organism is more complex.

In writing — as in nature — **simple** and **sophisticated** are not absolutes. They represent a scale with an infinite number of points. The clever, comic verse of poets like Ogden Nash and Dorothy Parker are certainly more sophisticated than nursery rhymes but less sophisticated than the poems of, say, Richard Wilbur. The works of an individual poet will also vary. The fact that someone is able to write highly sophisticated work that is dense in meaning and complex in treatment does not mean that he or she can't also write comic verse or light, satiric pieces.

Should all poetry be sophisticated? Of course not. We still enjoy 14th- and 15th-century Scottish **ballads**, metrical tales of adventure and passion; and millions have been delighted with more recent ballads by poets like Rudyard Kipling and Robert Service. Today we have the highly popular work of Rod McKuen, and the verses of Hallmark cards have reached more readers than T.S. Eliot and Robert Frost combined. And we all enjoy **occasional verse** — poems written for special occasions such as weddings or birthdays. Writing popular but essentially forgettable verse is an honest craft that requires practice. There are "how-to" books that help those who want to succeed at it, but this textbook is not one of them.

Sophisticated writing — poetry, as well as literary nonfiction, fiction, and drama — is the subject of this text. Such work offers fresh insights and new ways of looking at our lives, but it is not necessarily cluttered or obscure. Sometimes a three-line haiku manages to convey more than a long and intricate work. Complexity of meaning is not always achieved by using little-used words, obscure literary references, or complex metrical schemes.

Verse, incidentally, is a broad term that includes simple work intended for mass readership as well as more sophisticated work. Although *verse* is often used as a synonym for **poetry**, many prefer to reserve the word *poetry* for sophisticated verse.

Joyce Kilmer's "Trees" has been used many times in battles over what is and what is not "good" poetry. Let's stay clear of that futile debate and instead take a cool, objective look at what makes it an excellent example of highly popular simple verse. Here are the first three of its six stanzas:

> I think I shall never see
> A poem lovely as a tree.
>
> A tree whose hungry mouth is pressed
> Against the earth's sweet flowing breast;
>
> A tree that looks at God all day
> And lifts her leafy arms to pray; . . .

What can we say objectively about these six lines? First, they are clearly not prose. They are written as verse. The length of the lines is an immediate give-away: the pattern has been set by the writer. Second, we can hear some kind of regular rhythm simply by reading it aloud. Third, the intentional use of sound is unmistakable: the lines are grouped in pairs that end with the same sounds to form rhyming **couplets**. Fourth, because trees don't literally have hungry mouths, we must conclude that a **metaphor** is being used. That's four of the five characteristics we associate with verse.

We can also identify the work as a sample of relatively simple verse. As in nursery rhymes, there is great regularity to the rhythm and to the rhyme. Without knowing anything about the meter, one can detect four distinct beats to each line, and every rhyme is an exact matching of sound landing on a stressed syllable. This regularity creates a singsong effect. Like the beat in a marching band, it dominates.

Conspicuously missing, however, is density. There is nothing new or insightful about the assertion that trees are beautiful. The poet is repeating a commonly held view, a **truism**. Seeing the tree as a praying figure is somewhat **hackneyed**. We can't say that the poem is "bad" since it has given pleasure to millions of readers. But we can say that both the poetic techniques and the assertion it makes are on a simple level.

By way of contrast, here in its entirety is a two-line poem by Ezra Pound:

In a Station of the Metro

> The apparition of these faces in the crowd;
> Petals on a wet, black bough.

If this were printed in a solid line like prose, we would probably assume that it was merely a fragment — perhaps from a journal — and skip over it quickly. But because it is presented with a title and in two lines, we are assured at the outset that this is a poem and that it is intended to be read with some care. As with "Trees," the very shape of the work on the page has influenced the way we will read it.

How seriously should we take it? After a single reading, it is clear that this is not a comic jingle, nor is it a conventional statement about the beauty of nature. No truism, it is a fresh and vivid picture. The wording is intriguing: how can a crowd in the Paris subway (or any subway) be seen like an "apparition," and in what way might the faces resemble "petals on a wet, black bough"?

Let's take a closer look. What are the overtones that come to mind? An "apparition" is a sudden, ghostlike appearance, dark and perhaps ominous. As for those petals, they have been torn loose in a rainstorm (the bough is wet) and plastered on a "black bough." It's a dark picture. We like to think of commuters in the subway as purposely traveling by their own choice and in control of their lives, but what choice do petals have when blown loose in a storm and plastered on a wet bough?

It would be a mistake to read more into the poem than this. The mood is dark, and the suggestion about the lives of commuters is bleak. Perhaps there are other occasions in which we are victims of forces beyond our control, but the poem doesn't say so. It is not making any grand statement about our lives. It is a quick glimpse in which our notion of what it is to be a commuter is nudged. If, after studying the poem, you find yourself waiting silently in a crowd, you may well view the scene in a different, more vivid way than you would have otherwise. Rather than being soothed with a truism, your outlook has been enhanced.

There is no rhyme in this poem, but like the lines from "Winter Storm" quoted previously, it has a number of linkages in sound. "Crowd" and "bough" echo the same sound in what is known as a **slant rhyme**. The second line has two linked pairs: the *e* sound in "p*e*tals and "w*e*t" and that heavy *b* in "*b*lack" and "*b*ough." Unlike most prose passages, these lines are linked together not only with meaning, but also with sound.

The essential difference between this poem and "Trees" is that Kilmer makes a conventional or commonplace assertion about trees in general, whereas Pound gives us a unique insight drawn from a very specific scene. In addition, the two poems represent a difference in technique that often distinguishes simple from sophisticated work: Kilmer employs rigid metrical and rhyme schemes, whereas Pound mutes both the rhymes and the sound linkages so that they do not become obtrusive. As we will see, there is a tendency in sophisticated poetry to mute the impact of both meter and rhyme even when the work is regularly rhymed and metered. "Trees," like much mass-market verse, actually stresses them.

Simple verse has various functions. In the case of **ballads**, it entertains by presenting a simple story, often a lament, in a rhythmical manner. Ballads can be and frequently are put to music. Greeting card verse soothes by rephrasing conventional beliefs and sentiments. **Occasional verse** can enliven or memorialize special occasions such as weddings or birthdays.

Sophisticated poetry, in contrast, provides more lasting rewards: it gives us pleasure through fresh insights, genuine feelings, and the subtle use of form. It may startle us into seeing the world and ourselves in a different light. When it speaks to us, we don't throw it away after the first reading. We savor it.

USING POETIC CONVENTIONS TO ACHIEVE ORIGINALITY

Are there poetic rules? No. But that doesn't mean that anything goes. There are **conventions** that poets make use of in an infinite number of ways.

An artistic convention is any pattern or device that is used in a large number of works. As we have seen, the poet's control over line length is one of the conventions that differentiates poetry from prose. Beginning each line with a capital letter is a convention that some poets use and others do not. Heightened use of images to create metaphors and symbols is a looser convention.

The use of **meter** — patterns of stressed and unstressed syllables discussed in Chapter 30 — is a more precise convention. It is highly regarded by some poets like Robert Frost and Richard Wilbur. Another convention unique to poetry is rhythmical patterns created by line length and vertical spacing. This device is one of the characteristics of **free verse**. It is preferred by poets like E.E. Cummings and Jayena Hisle. **Rhyme** is also a convention enjoyed by some and not by others. Traditional forms such as the **sonnet**, **haiku**, and **villanelle** — described later — are all conventions worth considering.

Every art form has its conventions. Popular music lovers, for example, distinguish blues from bluegrass and rock from jazz. Artists distinguish realists from impressionists, surrealists, and minimalists. Within each category there are usually subdivisions. Familiarity with basic terms makes conversation about music or art more precise and enjoyable even for the casual listener. Those who compose music or who paint use these conventions to shape their own work and to develop their own individuality.

Without being familiar with poetic conventions, the would-be poet runs the risk of merely writing prose in short lines. Such work may be deeply sincere, but so can the efforts of a violinist who refuses to practice. On the other hand, allowing poetic conventions to stifle individuality and genuine feeling can make the work sterile. As we have seen, heavy-handed use of rhythm and a blatant rhyme scheme help make Joyce Kilmer's "Trees" poetically simple. It is *conventional* in the precise sense that it adheres to a number of conventions in a rigid and wooden manner.

As with any creative art, the first step is to explore and then practice the conventions of the genre. There is no freedom in ignorance. Only if you have actually written a sonnet or a typographically innovative free-verse poem are you really free to decide which approach is best for you.

Practicing poets base their decisions partly on personal preference and partly on the needs of a particular poem. They can do this only when they are at home with various techniques.

The following 11 chapters deal with the conventions of the craft and, equally important, ways of muting those conventions so that they stay in the background. These chapters will also help you read poetry with greater insight.

Two of these chapters are made up of poems for study. The selections are highly varied, representing many techniques and approaches. It is essential that you read these poems carefully. Most of those printed in Chapter 26 will be used as illustrations of poetic techniques throughout the poetry section. But it is important for you to analyze them on your own first. Valuable as it is to read critical comments and study techniques, your development as a poet over the years will depend on your increasing ability to analyze work on your own. Long after you have read this text, poems themselves will be your teacher.

26 Plunging in

A Selection of Poems

• Why poets read poetry (198) • Why it is essential that you study these poems before reading the following eight chapters (198) • Active versus passive reading (198) • Index of poems in this chapter (223)

Musicians listen to music. Scriptwriters study films. Novelists and short story writers read fiction. Poets read poetry. It's as simple as that. One problem is that many of those who want to write poetry have listened to more music and seen more films than they have read or listened to poems.

The reason poets read, aside from the pleasure, is that like any art form poetry cannot be created by following a series of rules or instructions. Creativity is not a science or a computer program. The poet relies on having in memory a backlog of many works. These provide a sense of what is possible in the genre.

For some, there will be a real temptation to skip over this chapter and get to "the real stuff." Wrong! *This* is the real stuff, these poems and the second selection that comprises Chapter 35. The analytical chapters will suggest ways to read poetry with greater insight and how to draw on published work when creating your own work. If you skip over these chapters, you will be like the absent-minded gardener who waters and fertilizes the ground but has forgotten to plant the seed. This book will speed your development, but reading the poetry itself is an essential first step.

ACTIVE VERSUS PASSIVE READING

Much of our daily reading is passive. Our eyes glance over the newspaper like a grazing cow, pausing and moving on without much thought. During the day, words wash over us in the form of billboards, instructions, and recipes. Even in the evening when we have a chance to choose what we read, we often turn to a magazine article, story, or novel as entertainment.

This was true even before television, but the tube has influenced us all. TV dramas emphasize the visual over the verbal, and their scene changes are rapid. Like all dramas, they eliminate the chance to review poignant segments. With some exceptions, many lack subtlety or insight.

Poetry requires an entirely different approach. Because it tends to be **dense** in meaning and implication, a single casual reading often seems confusing. The subtleties of word choice, rhythms, and the sound of language slip by unnoticed. It's easy to blame the poem when the fault is more often the way one reads. You can't enjoy the scenery if you're driving at top speed.

Active or deliberate reading is important if we are going to enjoy a poem. And it is essential if we plan to write poetry. Every poem can teach us something, but only if we take the time to study it. Here are some tips on how to shift from passive to active reading:

- Slow down. The poem will remain a blur if you read it as fast as a newspaper article or a short story. There is no "speed reading" when it comes to poetry.
- Give it multiple readings. Three at least: one aloud for the sound and rhythm, one deliberately line by line for analysis, and a third time at a normal pace again.
- Return to puzzling lines or phrases. Use your dictionary when needed. (I prefer an electronic dictionary for speed and helpful word origins.)
- Use a pencil. If the book is your own, underline what you like and circle what puzzles you. If you have looked up a new word, pencil in a brief definition. If you are using a borrowed copy, consider photocopying the pages.

It will take you an hour or so to read the poems in this chapter. I strongly recommend that you break your time into two half-hour sessions. Taking brief but legible notes may seem time consuming, but it will benefit you in several ways. Those notes will provide you with a written record for you to review later. In addition, the very act of recording your impressions has been shown to improve your memory. Taking notes will guarantee that your reading has been active, not passive.

Almost every poem in this chapter will be discussed in some way later in this poetry section. You may want to review the poem when it is referred to in the analytical chapters. Page references will always be given. Even if you don't review the poem again later, your notes will give you, the tremendous advantage of recalling at least in general terms the poem as a whole.

I have provided brief comments or questions at the end of each poem to help you study the work effectively. They are intended only to get you thinking about the poem analytically.

Analysis, however, is only a part of the reading process. After you have examined the characteristics of the poem, read it again just for the pleasure of it. If you are by yourself, try reading it aloud. Another approach is to go over this chapter with one or two friends, taking turns reading aloud and discussing each poem in turn.

If you have not enjoyed much poetry in the past, relax. There is something here for everyone — some humor, some pathos, and plenty of insight to make you think about your own life and experience. Some are written by men, and about an equal number are by women. The poems include a wide range of types, both metered and free, and the poets represent a variety of ethnic backgrounds. Of course there will be poems you don't enjoy. Like people you meet at a party, they won't all be your type. But remember this: a poet can learn something from every carefully composed work.

Design

ROBERT FROST

I found a dimpled spider, fat and white,
On a white heal-all, holding up a moth
Like a white piece of rigid satin cloth —
Assorted characters of death and blight   5
Mixed ready to begin the morning right,
Like the ingredients of a witches' broth —
A snow-drop spider, a flower like froth,
And dead wings carried like a paper kite.

What had that flower to do with being white,
The wayside blue and innocent heal-all?   10
What brought the kindred spider to that height,
Then steered the white moth thither in the night?
What but design of darkness to appall? —
If design govern in a thing so small.

Because this is a **sonnet**, it has a regular **rhyme scheme**. Why is this less obtrusive than the rhyme in "Trees" (page 194)? How is the poet using "appall" in the next to last line?

Winter Ocean

JOHN UPDIKE

Many-maned scud-thumper, tub
of male whales, maker of worn wood, shrub-
ruster, sky-mocker, rave!
portly pusher of waves, wind-slave.

This poem is dominated by linkages in sound. There are only two **rhymed** pairs, but there are many more connections that link the beginning sounds of words and sounds within words. As for **theme**, how does "wind-slave" counter the suggestion in the rest of the poem?

As the Cold Deepens

ELIZABETH W. HOLDEN

She is eighty-six
and her friends are dying.
"They're dropping like flies," she grumbles
and I see black winged bodies crumbling
on window sills when we open our summer house.   5

Flies all over!
Brushing them onto the floor, sweeping
them up, we drop black mounds into the bag.
"What a mess!" my mother declares.

I think of flies   10
how they live in a weightless armor
tough, resistant like a finger nail.

My mother is almost weightless now,
her flesh shrinks back toward bone.
Braced in her metal walker   15
she haunts the halls, prowls
the margin of her day, indomitable
erect in this support
that fuses steel with self.

At noon the flies mass on the sills   20
flying up and down the pane
pressing for sun.
What buzzing agitates the air
as the swarm becomes a single drive
a scramble up, a dizzy spin.   25

It is hard to hold the light
which grows weaker every day.
The temperature is falling
The glass is cold.

In how many different ways is the speaker's mother compared with flies? What is being suggested by the two references to temperature at the end of the poem?

The Gift

CAROLE OLES

Thinking she was the gift
they began to package it early.
They waxed its smile
they lowered its eyes
they tuned its ears to the telephone   5
they curled its hair
they straightened its teeth
they taught it to bury its wishbone
they poured honey down its throat
they made it say yes yes and yes   10
they sat on its thumbs.

That box has my name on it,
said the man. It's for me.
And they were not surprised.
While they blew kisses and winked   15
he took it home. He put it on a table
where his friends could examine it
saying dance saying faster.
He plunged its tunnels
he burned his name deeper.   20
Later he put it on a platform
under the lights
saying push saying harder
saying just what I wanted
you've given me a son.   25

Describe the **tone** of this poem. (Review tone in the Glossary-Index.) What is
the poet implying when she uses "it" for the subject?

Anger Sweetened

MOLLY PEACOCK

What we don't forget is what we don't say.
I mourn the leaps of anger covered
by quizzical looks, grasshoppers covered
by coagulating chocolate. Each word,
like a leggy thing that would have sprung away,   5
we caught and candified so it would stay
spindly and alarmed, poised in our presence,

dead, but in the shape of its old essence.
We must eat them now. We must eat the words
we should have let go but preserved, thinking
to hide them. They were as small as insects blinking   10
in our hands, but now they are stiff and shirred
with sweet to twice their size, so what we gagged
will gag us now that we are so enraged.

"What we don't say" is vividly pictured in a series of **metaphors**. Circle
them. Now take a close look at the last two lines: How is the word "gag"
used in two different ways?

Sonnet 29

WILLIAM SHAKESPEARE

When in disgrace with fortune and men's eyes,
I all alone beweep my outcast state,
And trouble deaf heaven with my bootless[3] cries,
And look upon my self and curse my fate,
Wishing me like to one more rich in hope,   5
Featured like him, like him with friends possessed,
Desiring this man's art, and that man's scope,
With what I most enjoy contented least,
Yet in these thoughts my self almost despising,
Haply I think on thee, and then my state,   10
Like to the lark at break of day arising
From sullen earth, sings hymns at heaven's gate,
   For thy sweet love remembered such wealth brings,
   That then I scorn to change my state with kings.

Like many **sonnets** the **tone** shifts after the first eight lines, providing a vivid
contrast with that of the last six. Study the **rhyme** scheme here and compare
it with that in "Anger Sweetened," a contemporary sonnet.

What the Mirror Said

LUCILLE CLIFTON

listen,
you a wonder,
you a city

[3]bootless: useless.

of a woman.
you got a geography   5
of your own.
listen,
somebody need a map
to understand you.
somebody need directions   10
to move around you.
listen,
woman,
you not a noplace   15
anonymous
girl;
mister with his hands on you
he got his hands on
some
damn
body!   20

The **tone** of this poem echoes informal speech. Pick out phrases that are common in speech but avoided in formal writing. Although the poem appears to be formless on first reading, it actually has a **refrain** that gives it structure. What is it?

After Spring

CHORA

After spring sunset
Mist rises from the river
Spreading like a flood

Haiku

ETHERIDGE KNIGHT

1

Eastern guard tower
glints in sunset; convicts rest
like lizards on rocks.

4

To write a blues song
is to regiment riots
and pluck gems from graves.

5

A bare pecan tree
slips a pencil shadow down
a moonlit snow slope.

Haiku in English traditionally have five syllables in the first and third lines
and seven in the middle line. They also tend to draw on some aspect of nature and state or imply a particular season. Which of these conform to all
three **conventions**? Look closely.

Always the One Who Loves His Father Most

CLEMENT LONG

Always the one who loves his father most,
the one the father loves the most in turn,
will fight against his father as he must.
Neither knows what he will come to learn.

The one the father loves the most in turn
tells the father no and no and no,
but neither knows what he will come to learn
nor cares a lot what that could be, and so

tells his father no and no and no,
is ignorant of what the years will teach
nor cares a lot what that could be, and so
unties the knot that matters most, while each

is ignorant of what the years will teach,
they'll learn how pride — if each lives out his years —
unties the knot that matters most, while each
will feel a sadness, feel the midnight fears.

They'll learn how pride — if each lives out his years —
will lose the aging other as a friend,

will feel a sadness, feel the midnight fears.
The child and then the father, world without end,

will lose the aging other as a friend.
And then the child of that one, too, will grow —
the child and then the father, world without end —
in turn to fight his father, *comme il faut*,

will fight against his father, as he must,
always, the one who loves his father most.

This is a **pantoum**, a verse form explained in detail in Chapter 31. For now, focus on the way lines 2 and 4 in each **stanza** are repeated as lines 1 and 3 in the next stanza. Can you see a relationship between this series of repetitions and the **theme** of the poem?

The Narrow Mind

DICK ALLEN

It lives in a small backwater, and it doesn't know
Much more than dragonflies and darning needles.
The plash and galump of a frog. What it wonders
Is how do I get through another day.
It feeds on what's been whispered to it   5
In secret meetings at dusk, and what's proclaimed
By flights of crows. It likes
Lying on a sunlit log or wading
To shore with its fellows — where it seeks
Places it hasn't any trouble squeezing into.
What it demands, the few times it demands,   10
Is never to be shaken. But if that happens,
It wants the right to reassert itself.
And will die for that right. You can find it
By heading west at sunset, its spot   15
Marked by bubbles rising to the surface.
The brighter you are, the more likely it will greet you
With suspicion, so to get close to it
You must tell it stories that it wants to hear.
If you would expand it, if you would lift it out,   20
First consider its age and if it's strong enough
To live anywhere else. Elsewise.
You either must row around it or overwhelm it
With goodness and mercy and bribes.

Poets generally title their poems with an **image** — something that can be seen or perceived with one of the five senses. Robert Frost's "Design" (page 200) is an exception, and so is this poem. In each case, though, the theme of the poem is implied through visual details. To appreciate "The Narrow Mind" fully, describe in a paragraph of prose an imaginary person who illustrates Allen's description.

This Winter Day

MAYA ANGELOU

The kitchen in its readiness
white green and orange things
leak their blood selves in the soup.

Ritual sacrifice that snaps   5
an odor at my nose and starts
my tongue to march
slipping in the liquid of its drip.

The day, silver striped
in rain, is balked against
my window and the soup.   10

This poem draws on several of the five senses. Identify them. Notice also that the **theme** suggests a contrast. What is being contrasted with what?

The Bay at West Falmouth

BARBARA HOWES

Serenity of mind poises
Like a gull swinging in air,
At ease, sculptured, held there
For a moment so long-drawn-out all time pauses.

The heart's serenity is like the gold   5
Geometry of sunlight: motion shafting
Down through green dimensions, rung below rung
Of incandescence, out of which grace unfolds.

Watching that wind schooling the bay, the helter-skelter
Of trees juggling air, waves signalling the sun   10
To signal light, brings peace; as our being open
To love does, near this serenity of water.

This poem opens and closes with the **abstract** word "serenity." Find and circle the **concrete** nouns that are used to help us see and feel this serenity.

On a Maine Beach

ROBLEY WILSON

Look, in these pools, how rocks are like worn change
Keeping the ocean's mint-mark; barnacles
Miser on them; societies of snails
Hunch on their rims and think small thoughts whose strange
Salt logics rust like a mainspring, small dreams   5
Pinwheeling to a point and going dumb,
Small equations whose euphemistic sum
Stands for mortality. A thousand times
Tides swallow up such pools, shellfish and stone
Show green and yellow shade in groves of weed;   10
Rocks shrink, barnacles drink, snails think they bleed
In their trapped world. Here, when the sea is gone,
We find old coins glowing under the sky,
Barnacles counting them, snails spending slow
Round lifetimes half-awake. Beach rhythms flow   15
In circles. Perfections teach us to die.

Like Robert Frost's "Design" (page 200) this poem is rooted in a close examination of a specific scene from nature. Notice how references to money ("coins") and time ("mainspring") expand the **theme** to comment on our mortality.

Is It Well-Lighted, Papa?

JAMES BERTRAM

Is it well-lighted, Papa — this place
where you have gone to escape and erase
dreams gone dry and bare-teethed critics' remarks
that tormented you like the old man's sharks?
Do we dare term your suicide disgrace?   5

Clean, like your prose, the bell tolled and the chase
no longer, you knew, was "El Campion's" race.
A final shotgun sentence rings truly stark.
Is it well-lighted, Papa?

Weak man or strong man? Why can't we embrace   10
the truth: a fawn with a grizzly bear face.
For despite your indelible machismo mark,
you always told us how you feared the dark.
Is it well-lighted, Papa?

Notice how the question posed in the title is repeated as a **refrain** in each of
the three **stanzas**. The poem is a **rondeau**, and the use of refrains is one of its
elements. For further analysis of the form, see page 275. For now, however,
focus on the way the refrain highlights the key question the way a repeated
chorus does in some song lyrics. As for the subject, notice the many references to Ernest Hemingway and his work.

The Waking

THEODORE ROETHKE

I wake to sleep, and take my waking slow.
I feel my fate in what I cannot fear.
I learn by going where I have to go.

We think by feeling. What is there to know?
I hear my being dance from ear to ear.   5
I wake to sleep, and take my waking slow.

Of those so close beside me, which are you?
God bless the Ground! I shall walk softly there,
And learn by going where I have to go.

Light takes the Tree; but who can tell us how?   10
The lowly worm climbs up a winding stair;
I wake to sleep, and take my waking slow.

Great Nature has another thing to do
To you and me; so take the lively air,
And, lovely, learn by going where to go.   15

This shaking keeps me steady. I should know.
What falls away is always. And is near.
I wake to sleep, and take my waking slow.
I learn by going where I have to go.

Like Robley Wilson's "On a Maine Beach" (page 208), this poem deals with our mortality. But notice that neither poem relies on **abstract** words such as "life" or "death." Roethke uses "wake" to suggest birth and "sleep" for death. They are easier to comprehend. What is implied with the repeated phrase "learn by going where I have to go"?

Coast to Coast

PHILIP APPLEMAN

The bird that shook the earth at J.F.K.
goes blind to milkweed, riverbanks, the wrecks
of elm trees full of liquor and decay —
and jars the earth again at L.A.X.

Once, on two-lane roads, our crazy drives   5
across the country tallied every mile
in graves or gardens: glimpses in our lives
to make the busy continent worthwhile.

Friendly, then, the smell of woods and fields,   10
the flash of finches and the scud of crows,
the rub of asphalt underneath our wheels
as tangible as sand between the toes.

From orchards out to prairies, then to cactus,
the rock and mud and clay were in our bones: 15
as birches turned to oak, then eucalyptus,
we learned our lover's body stone by stone.

Now, going home we're blind again, seven
miles above the earth on chartered wings:
in a pressurized and air-conditioned heaven
the open road's a song nobody sings.   20

This poem is based on a contrast. His preference is unmistakable, but it is presented indirectly through the details he uses. If you circle the phrases that imply a strong preference for driving and a disdain for flying, you will see how opinions can be presented in poetry indirectly through **images** rather than stated analytically as they often are in essays.

"Buffalo Bill's"

E.E. CUMMINGS

Buffalo Bill's
defunct
      who used to
      ride a watersmooth-silver
                stallion   5
and break onetwothreefourfive pigeonsjustlikethat
                             Jesus
he was a handsome man
                and what i want to know is
how do you like your blueeyed boy   10
Mister Death

Here is an extreme version of **typography**, similar to "We" by Janeya
Hisle (page 313). What is being suggested by running words together in
line 6? ("Pigeons" refers to clay pigeons used for target practice.)

Morning Swim

MAXINE KUMIN

Into my empty head there come
a cotton beach, a dock wherefrom

I set out, oily and nude
through mist, in chilly solitude.

There was no line, no roof or floor   5
to tell the water from the air.

Night fog thick as terry cloth
closed me in its fuzzy growth.

I hung my bathrobe on two pegs.   10
I took the lake between my legs.

Invaded and invader, I
went overhand on that flat sky.

Fish twitched beneath me, quick and tame.
In their green zone they sang my name

and in the rhythm of the swim   15
I hummed a two-four-time slow hymn.
I hummed *Abide with Me.* The beat
rose in the fine thrash of my feet,

rose in the bubbles I put out
slantwise, trailing through my mouth.   20

My bones drank water; water fell
through all my doors. I was the well

that fed the lake that met my sea
in which I sang Abide with Me.

Rhyming couplets (see **Stanza**) are often avoided in serious verse because of
the risk of creating a singsong effect. Notice how Kumin mutes the **rhyme** by
having the sentences continue into the next line. Take a close look at "the
beat" on line 17. How many different types of **rhythm** does that describe?

Lizards and Snakes

ANTHONY HECHT

On the summer road that ran by our front porch
    Lizards and snakes came out to sun.
It was hot as a stove out there, enough to scorch
    A buzzard's foot. Still, it was fun
To lie in the dust and spy on them. Near but remote,   5
    They snoozed in the carriage ruts, a smile
In the set of the jaw, a fierce pulse in the throat
Working away like Jack Doyle's after he'd run the mile.

Aunt Martha had an unfair prejudice
    Against them (as well as being cold   10
Toward bats.) She was pretty inflexible in this,
Being a spinster and all, and old.
So we used to slip them into her knitting box.
    In the evening she'd bring in things to mend
And a nice surprise would slide out from under the socks.   15
It broadened her life, as Joe said. Joe was my friend.

But we never did it again after the day
    Of the big wind when you could hear the trees
Creak like rockingchairs. She was looking away
    Off, and kept saying, "Sweet Jesus, please   20

Don't let him hear me. He's as like as twins.
   He can crack us like lice with his fingernail.
I can see him plain as a pikestaff. Look how he grins
And swings the scaly horror of his folded tail."

This is a **narrative poem**. That is, it tells a story. It appears at first to be a simple, amusing tale, drawing on a childhood memory. But the light tone ends dramatically in the last stanza. What do the boys learn about Aunt Martha's beliefs and fears?

The Pardon

RICHARD WILBUR

My dog lay dead five days without a grave
In the thick of summer, hid in a clump of pine
And a jungle of grass and honeysuckle-vine.
I who had loved him while he kept alive

Went only close enough to where he was   5
To sniff the heavy honeysuckle-smell
Twined with another odour heavier still
And hear the flies' intolerable buzz.

Well, I was ten and very much afraid.
In my kind world the dead were out of range   10
And I could not forgive the sad or strange
In beast or man. My father took the spade

And buried him. Last night I saw the grass
Slowly divide (it was the same scene
But now it glowed a fierce and mortal green)   15
And saw the dog emerging. I confess

I felt afraid again, but still he came
In the carnal sun, clothed in a hymn of flies,
And death was breeding in his lively eyes.
I started in to cry and call his name,   20

Asking forgiveness of his tongueless head.
. . . I dreamt the past was never past redeeming:
But whether this was false or honest dreaming
I beg death's pardon now. And mourn the dead.

Like "Lizards and Snakes" (page 212), this is a narrative poem and appears to be taken from a childhood memory. But the dream described in the fourth stanza presents more complex themes. Why does the **narrator** feel guilty, and how does he or she seek redemption?

Balances

NIKKI GIOVANNI

in life
one is always
balancing

like we juggle our mothers   5
against our fathers

or one teacher
against another
(only to balance our grade average)

3 grains salt   10
to one ounce truth

our sweet black essence
or the funky honkies down the street

and lately i've begun wondering
if you're trying to tell me something

we used to talk all night   15
and do things alone together

and i've begun

(as a reaction to a feeling)
to balance
the pleasure of loneliness   20
against the pain
of loving you

Read this poem aloud, pausing at each double space. Notice that while Giovanni uses no punctuation, the spaces are used to cue the reader when to pause. The first half of the poem reads like an arbitrary list of examples illustrating the statement in the first three lines; but with "lately i've been wondering" we learn the **occasion** (the specific cause) for the narrator's interest in balances.

Rhymes for Old Age

CHASE TWICHELL

The wind's untiring saxophone
keens at the glass.
The lamp sheds a monochrome
of stainless steel and linens,
the nurse in her snowy dress
firm in her regimens.   5

The form in the bed
is a soul diminished
to a fledgling, fed
on the tentative balm of spring,
sketch for an angel, half-finished,
shoulder blades the stubs of wings.   10

Darkened with glaucoma,
the room floats on the retina.
The long vowel of *coma*
broods in the breath, part vapor.
What has become of the penetralia?
Eau de cologne sanctifies the diaper.   15

Flood and drag, the undertow.
One slips into it undressed,
as into first love, the vertigo
that shrinks to a keepsake of passion.
Sky's amethyst
lies with a sponge in the basin.   20

In **theme** this poem is similar to Elizabeth Holden's "As the Cold Deepens" (page 201), but the condition of the old woman is worse and the **metaphors** used are more demanding. Each **stanza** has a word you may want to look up in a good dictionary not just for the meaning but for the **overtones** that are suggested: in the first stanza, "keens"; in the second "fledgling"; in the third "penetralia"; and in the last "vertigo." Ask yourself two questions: In what ways is an old and dying woman like a fledgling? And how can descent into death be like descent into "first love"?

Names of Horses

DONALD HALL

All winter your brute shoulders strained against collars, padding
and steerhide over the ash hames, to haul
sledges of cordwood for drying through spring and summer,
for the Glenwood stove next winter, and for the simmering range.

In April you pulled cartloads of manure to spread on the fields,   5
dark manure of Holsteins, and knobs of your own clustered with oats.
All summer you mowed the grass in meadow and hayfield, the mowing
    machine
clacking beside you, while the sun walked high in the morning;

and after noon's heat, you pulled a clawed rake through the same acres,
gathering stacks, and dragged the wagon from stack to stack,   10
and the built hayrack back, uphill to the chaffy barn,
three loads of hay a day, hanging wide from the hayrack.

Sundays you trotted the two miles to church with the light load
of a leather quartertop buggy, and grazed in the sound of hymns.
Generation on generation, your neck rubbed the window sill   15
of the stall, smoothing the wood as the sea smooths glass.

When you were old and lame, when your shoulders hurt bending to graze,
one October the man who fed you and kept you, and harnessed you every
    morning,
led you through corn stubble to sandy ground above Eagle Pond,
and dug a hole beside you where you stood shuddering in your skin,   20

and lay the shotgun's muzzle in the boneless hollow behind your ear,
and fired the slug into your brain, and felled you into your grave,
shoveling sand to cover you, setting goldenrod upright above you,
where by next summer a dent in the ground made your monument.

For a hundred and fifty years, in the pasture of dead horses,   25
roots of pine trees pushed through the pale curves of your ribs,
yellow blossoms flourished above you in autumn, and in winter
frost heaved your bones in the ground — old toilers, soil makers:

O Roger, Mackerel, Riley, Ned, Nellie, Chester, Lady Ghost.

The subject of this poem is clearly farm horses, but the theme is broader
than that. Take a close look at the tone of this tribute and ask yourself

whether it might be applied to people. What kinds of people come to mind? Turning to the poem's organization, circle the words that suggest seasons. What period of time is covered? Finally, can you speculate why the poet may have purposely chosen long, slow-moving lines for this particular subject?

A Secret Life

STEPHEN DUNN

Why you need to have one
is not much more mysterious than
why you don't say what you think
at the birth of an ugly baby.
Or, you've just made love   5
and feel you'd rather have been
in a dark booth where your partner
was nodding, whispering yes, yes,
you're brilliant. The secret life
begins early, is kept alive   10
by all that's unpopular
in you, all that you know
a Baptist, say, or some other
accountant would object to.
It becomes what you'd most protect   15
if the government said you can protect
one thing, all else is ours.
When you write late at night
it's like a small fire
in a clearing, it's what   20
radiates and what can hurt
if you get too close to it.
It's why your silence is a kind of truth.
Even when you speak to your best friend,
the one who'll never betray you,   25
you always leave out one thing;
a secret life is that important.

Consider (but do not reveal) one or two opinions or feelings you would not tell anyone. Then take a close look at the **simile** on line 19 suggesting that these secrets are "like a small fire." List all the characteristics of a fire that might also apply to your private world.

Mystery

DOROTHY BARRESI

Their words harden in the turning air,
little earrings of light.
I saw, I hate, you never.
Ashtrays and pillows begin to orbit the room.
Whatever furniture they have   5
rears up on hind legs and howls.

Not even the stove's clock
can catch its breath when they argue.
Its arms windmill, making

the seasons slip a cog.   10
A buckeye tree in the yard goes
green to burnt orange in a matter of minutes.
Their dog turns suddenly old and blind
and cannot read the book of a dead sparrow
held open in its paws.   15

Later, the couple kiss
like guests on a television talk show,
expecting nothing.
Whatever they fought about is a mystery to them now.
The wife heads for the kitchen,   20
sets back the clock, while her husband
demagnetizes the steak knives.
Even their dog remembers its old trick
as it romps in the dark yard.
Play dead, then retrieve, retrieve,   25
the calm rising all around the house
like a blood pressure.

This is a highly visual poem. Underline all the dreamlike details that suggest
the intensity of their argument. What about the future for this couple? What
is suggested at the end about calm "rising . . . like a blood pressure"?

The Paradise of Wings

THEODORE DEPPE

My grandfather called it
the Paradise of Wings, a clearing

hidden in blue hills where thousands
of geese gleaned stubbled corn
beside a tapered lake. His favorite walk —   5
shared with me as a secret — made of that place,
those burnished wings, a sort of gift.

That fall, when flocks funneled above our house,
he'd hoist my sister to his lap
so I could go alone, be his eyes and ears.
I'd wait in a blind of scrub oak, calculate   10
the time to break from hiding, then whirl
my arms until the low sky rose in a wide arc
to settle out of sight behind the ridge.

One day my sister stumbled from the house,   15
panic in her face as she ran to me.
Though Grandfather stopped at the front steps
we ran all the way to the valley
I'd sworn to keep secret.
She made me promise   20
never to leave her alone with him,

told me just enough so that I, too,
feared his hands. Light kept draining
from black water, leaving in its place
an opaque stillness   25
where geese stood about on shelves of rotting ice
and my sister's hate
was the only living thing in paradise.

This poem demonstrates the fact that any subject, no matter how personal, can be handled in poetry. But note, too, that the poem is carefully structured. Compare the tone of the first **stanza** with that of the last one. Which visual details **(images)** account for the differences? Also notice, how there are two entirely different kinds of secrets in this poem. How do they differ?

Desire

PHILIP APPLEMAN

1

The body
tugged like a tide, a pull

stronger than
the attraction of stars.

2

Moons   5
circling their planets,
planets
rounding their suns.

3

Nothing is what
we cannot imagine: 10
all that we know we know
moves in the muscles.

4

Undertow:
I reach for you,   15
oceans away.

It is not easy to write a love poem that doesn't sound **hackneyed**. The first step is to find a fresh and original **metaphor** that will bring originality and sense of authenticity to a well-used subject. Appleman uses the tide right from the start. Notice how it is developed in the second **stanza** (the moon causes the tides) and echoed once again with the sea **images** in the last stanza. The final stanza, by the way, is like a **haiku** in its simplicity, even though it doesn't follow the traditional syllable count. (See pages 204–205 for comparisons.)

Regardless

STEPHEN DUNN

Once, my father took me to the Rockaways
        during a hurricane
to see how the ocean was behaving,

which made my mother furious, whose love
    was correct, protective.
We saw a wooden jetty crumble. We saw water

rise to the boardwalk, felt the wildness
    of its spray
That night there was silence at dinner,

A storm born of cooler, more familiar air.
    My father
always was riding his delightful errors

into trouble. Mother waited for them, alertly,
    the way the oppressed
wait for their historical moment.

Weekdays, after six, I'd point my bicycle
    toward the Fleet Street Inn
to fetch him for dinner. All his friends

were there, high-spirited lonelies, Irish,
    full of laughter.
It was a shame that he was there, a shame

to urge him home. Who was I, then, but a boy
    who had learned to love
the wind, the wind that would go its own way,

regardless. I must have thought damage
    is just what happens.

Three different stanzas refer to storms, but the significance of each differs from the other two. How do they differ, and how do they relate to the concluding use of the word "damage"?

Nuclear Winter

THOMAS MCGRATH

After the first terror
               people
Were more helpful to each other—
As in a blizzard

Much comradeliness, help, even
                              laughter:
The pride of getting through tough times.

Even, months later,
When snow fell in June,
We felt a kind of pride in
                    our
"Unusual weather"
And joked about the wild geese
Migrating south,
Quacking over the 4th of July presidential honkings.
It was, people said,
The way it had been in the Old Days . . .

Until the hunger of the next year.
Then we came to our senses
And began to kill each other.

This is a **narrative poem** in that it tells a story. Like many short stories in fiction, it covers a specific span of time. How long? It also creates a reversal in expectations that gives the work a dramatic jolt. Exactly where does it occur?

The Mapmaker's Daughter

ANITA ENDREZZE

the geography of love is terra infirma

it is a paper boat
navigated by mates
with stars in their eyes

cartographers of the fiery unknown   5

it is the woman's sure hand
at the helm of twilight, the salt
compass of her desire

the map of longing is at the edge
of two distant bodies   10

it is the rain that launches thirst
it is the palm leaf floating on waters
far from shore

the secret passage into the interior
is in my intemperate estuary   15

the sweet and languorous flowering
is in the caliber of your hands

the circular motion of our journeying
is the radius of sky and sea, deep
territories we name
after ourselves   20

This is another love poem. Like "Desire," it uses a series of fresh images. It also uses the sea in many ways. But the construction of this poem is more complex and its style is both more sensual and more dreamlike. Underline each of the nouns that refer to the sea and to boats. Notice how each forms a **metaphor** related to some aspect of love.

As we return to these poems in later chapters, keep in mind that this text is not intended to shape your preferences. That's up to you. Instead, the intent is to help you read a wide range of poems with greater perception and insight. Your ability to create new and effective work on your own depends largely on your understanding of what the **genre** has to offer.

INDEX OF POEMS IN THIS CHAPTER

This alphabetical index of titles is limited to poems printed in this chapter. It is intended as a handy reference for discussion and review. A full index of titles, poets, and authors can be found on page 457.

27 Sources

Where Poems Come From

Many poems spring from what we see and hear in daily life. The poet, however, has to stay alert to what is going on. Unfortunately, it's all too easy to get through the day without examining the world around us. We tend to rush from one project to the next without allowing time for reflection.

When you start writing poetry, make a conscious effort to look closely at the day's events — what you see and hear. You may find it helpful to keep a small notebook with you to jot down impressions and reactions for future development.

Consider the sign that used to mark railroad crossings: STOP, LOOK, and LISTEN. If you live in the city, stop and look at a crowd of faces in the subway. If they remind you of flower petals that have been plastered against a wet, black bough after a storm, jot it down in your notebook. Ezra Pound's poem (on page 194) was not just a verbal snapshot; it was also the connection he made between those faces and a memory of petals on a wet bough. He stopped, looked, and let his mind make a sudden leap, a connection.

It is similar in some ways to a vision Barbara Howes had while standing on the beach. By way of review, here is the first of three stanzas (the entire poem is on page 207):

Serenity of mind poises
Like a gull swinging in air.
At ease, sculptured, held there
For a moment so long-drawn-out all time pauses.

We can be fairly certain that Howes didn't start out planning to write a poem about serenity. Poets don't usually begin by reflecting on an **abstraction**. The stimulus for that poem was almost certainly the sight of a gull poised on an air current. We can't know for sure, of course, but the title, "The Bay at West Falmouth," describes a specific place, not an abstraction.

Fortunately for us, she wasn't the sort to shout out the obvious, "Hey, isn't that pretty!" or to start fumbling for her camera. Instead, she took the time to let that visual **image**, the gull, stimulate her imagination. To her it seemed like a sculpture, and like many sculptures, it seemed to make time pause.

At some point in the writing a further insight came to Howes. That scene, she writes,

> . . . brings peace; as our being open
> to love does . . .

Where did that poem come from? The gull. But it took a poet's imagination to let that vision suggest a sculpture, a pause in time, serenity, and eventually the concept of being "open to love."

This is not to suggest that the poem came to her in final form as she stood at the edge of the bay at West Falmouth, Massachusetts. It's almost never that easy. She probably worked over successive drafts in the weeks that followed. Poems often evolve slowly, occasionally frustratingly, as one searches for the right phrasing. But our concern here is for the moment of conception. The gull for Barbara Howes provided that initial stimulus just as those faces in the Paris subway did for Ezra Pound.

You'll find another good example in Chris Buckley's poem "Intransitive" (page 211). The title, unlike that in Barbara Howes' poem, is abstract, but it is very unlikely that it was the origin. (If you were never introduced to grammatical terms in school, you may have had to look *intransitive* up. It describes a verb that can stand alone without taking an object.)

The poem begins with a recollection of an evening that is

> . . . an adagio
> of rose and grey above autumn trees . . .

and ends after sunset with his seeing

> . . . the first few stars glide out
> overhead and sing, and they were in need
> of nothing more to complete their meaning.

True beauty, he is suggesting, is like an intransitive verb in that it needs nothing more to complete its meaning. It stands alone.

If you review the poem in its entirety, you will see that it contrasts longing (which does need something or someone else to be completed) and acceptance of an especially beautiful scene, but our concern here is for origins. It was not the abstraction recalled from lessons in grammar; it was an evening scene.

Not all poems, of course, spring from a single visual impression, but if you look over the samples in Chapter 26 you will see other examples: a rock pool for Robley Wilson in "On a Maine Beach" (page 208), a white spider sitting on a white flower for Robert Frost in "Design" (page 200), and a cluttered kitchen counter for Maya Angelou in "This Winter Day" (page 207).

Visual impressions rank high among poets, but don't ignore the other senses. Sounds that launch poems may take the form of a fragment of music, an adult crying, or glass breaking. Tactile sensations range from a frosty glass of lemonade to a dentist's drill. Although taste and smells are less often used, occasionally they can provide an intense stimulus. Your first source of poetry, then, is your personal collection of sensory impressions conveniently stored in your memory.

DRAWING ON FRIENDS AND RELATIVES

This second source of poetry may not strike you as clearly. Insights about friends and relatives sometimes creep up on you. But there is plenty to work with when you consider the full range: parents, stepparents, grandparents, siblings, aunts, uncles, teachers, employers, classmates, roommates, spouses, lovers, and even dogs and cats. The relationships you have with these people (and animals) are rarely simple. Often they are charged.

Greeting cards, of course, also deal with many of these categories, but with cartoon-like simplicity. **Sophisticated** poems deal with real or as-if-real people and reveal complex emotions that are often mixed. They probe what is unique in relationships.

Nikki Giovanni's "Balances" (page 214) might seem on first reading to have begun with the abstraction of the title. In the first two of nine irregular **stanzas** she presents the topic and gives a couple of examples:

> in life
> one is always
> balancing

> like we juggle our mothers
> against our fathers

> or one teacher
> against another

That, however, is only a preamble. At the end of the poem we find out what is really on her mind:

> and I've begun
> (as a reaction to a feeling)
> to balance
> the pleasure of loneliness
> against the pain
> of loving you

What started off appearing to be a generalized commentary on how one has to balance relationships turns out to be a reconsideration of a very specific relationship. The poem describes how the speaker has to weigh loneliness against the pain involved in maintaining her love for another person. Although the true concern is withheld until the end of the poem, it was probably the starting point in her mind, the stimulus that started her writing.

Relationships with parents have great potential, but there are risks as well. Unadulterated hostility becomes tedious just as unquestioning love takes on the saccharine sentimentality of greeting card verse even if sincerely felt. Mixed feelings, however, are well worth exploring. Stephen Dunn's "Regardless" (page 220) is just such a blend. The narrator describes his father as one who "always was riding his delightful errors / into trouble," yet as a boy the narrator had "learned to love / the wind, the wind that would go its own way, / regardless . . ."

Changes in attitude or perception lend themselves to poetry because they often provide dramatic impact. Sometimes they produce a real jolt. This is certainly the case in Theodore Deppe's "The Paradise of Wings" (page 218). The first stanza presents what appears to be a warm relationship between a boy and his grandfather. They even share a secret: a hidden clearing where geese come to feed on corn.

In the concluding two stanzas, however, the boy and his sister are shocked into realizing the true nature of their grandfather, and at the end they are left with fear and hate. The poem has its genesis in a terrible shattering of trust, the end of innocence for them both.

Poems like this raise the question of how revealing you should be when basing a poem on someone you know. If you feel that the poem could embarrass or hurt certain readers, consider asking them in advance. You can explain that the apparent speaker in a narrative poem is not necessarily the poet.

But if seeking permission is awkward or impossible, or if you find that the closeness to actual people is intimidating you in the writing process, feel free to disguise some of the physical details. Change locations, events, or even the gender of a particular character. Remember that when writing poetry (or fiction) your first loyalty is to the art form. Your goal is to write the best piece you can. Unlike the journalist, you have no obligation whatever to report accurately the events or physical details that initiated the work. After all, the reason we call these genres "creative" is that they are indeed inventive. Poems, stories, and plays are often generated by personal experience, but they should never be bound by it.

PROBING YOUR TRUE FEELINGS

We think we know what we feel, but we're not always right. Sometimes we confuse what we think we *ought* to feel with our true emotions. In general, leave those socially approved and conventional sentiments to Hallmark cards. That's their specialty. As a poet, exercise the courage to explore your *un*conventional feelings.

As Stephen Dunn points out in another poem, we all have secrets we choose not to reveal. Here, as a reminder, is the opening of his poem "A Secret Life" (page 217):

> Why you need to have one
> is not much more mysterious than
> why you don't say what you think
> at the birth of an ugly baby.

If you keep a private journal (strongly recommended), consider making a list of things you honestly feel but don't tell anyone. If you do so, as Dunn recommends, "late at night," you may understand how such secrets are "like a small fire." They burn "if you get too close," but they may also serve as the genesis of new poems.

EXPLORING AMBIVALENCE

Ambivalence is a crucial element in many poems. It comes from *ambi-*, meaning "both" (as in *ambidextrous*) and *valence*, from the same root as "value." It describes a combining of two quite different emotions — love and hate, fear and desire, courage and cowardice.

Don't confuse this with a change in outlook such as we saw in Theodore Deppe's "The Paradise of Wings" (page 218). With ambivalence the two conflicting emotions or attitudes occur simultaneously.

Feelings of love are often charged with ambivalence. Nikki Giovanni describes it clearly in "Balances" (page 214). At the end of that poem the narrator finds herself caught between "the pleasure of loneliness" and "the pain / of loving you."

Molly Peacock describes a type of ambivalence all of us have felt in "Anger Sweetened" (page 202). The two forces in this case are our desire to be polite and our longing to express exactly what we feel. "What we don't forget," the poem states in the first line, "is what we don't say." The ambivalence we feel about being courteous is common to us all, but it's rarely admitted.

When casting about for a subject that might generate a poem, consider your mixed feelings. And be honest about them! Few student poets make the mistake of attempting love poems that are simple expressions of unalloyed affection. We've heard enough of that in routine song lyrics. But tributes to older people such as grandparents sometimes take on that same simple approach in spite of good intentions. Watch out, too, for the inverse, the expression of unalloyed hostility. Parents are often the target, as are former lovers and suburban life. If you are emotionally unprepared to include some ambivalent feelings, you may be too close to your subject.

Another risk is dealing with widely supported causes. Straightforward campaigns against drugs, street violence, and war are best treated in posters and television spots, not sophisticated poetry. You can, however, make your point with **irony**, a literary form of sarcasm. I will return to this approach in Chapter 34, but you may want to look at various samples in advance. Robley Wilson's "War" (page 230), Dick Allen's "The Narrow Mind" (page 206), and Joseph Bruchac's "Indian Country Again" (page 311) are all excellent examples.

PLAYING WITH LANGUAGE

Although many poems spring from what the poet has seen and felt and from relationships with others, another important source is sheer love of language.

All creative writers pay close attention to how they use words, but poets often take a particular delight in fresh and ingenious phrasing. They assume that their work is going to be read more deliberately than prose and so feel free to push language into new configurations.

E.E. Cummings is a good example. Here once again is "Buffalo Bill's," a poetic tribute to the skill and grace of a great performer from the past:

"Buffalo Bill's"

E.E. CUMMINGS

Buffalo Bill's
defunct
       who used to
       ride a watersmooth-silver
              stallion   5

and break onetwothreefourfive pigeonsjustlikethat
                 Jesus
he was a handsome man
            and what i want to know is
how do you like your blueeyed boy   10
Mister Death

The historical Buffalo Bill was a showman, so it is most appropriate that the poet use some showy tricks himself. He runs words together to create the ripple effect of Buffalo Bill's rapid firing, and Cummings personifies death in a way that is both colloquial in style and serious in theme. What a waste, the poem seems to ask, to have a man of such dazzling ability lost to the stillness of death.

Perhaps it has never occurred to you that you can actually have fun with language. If so, here is an exercise that will start you thinking about language in a nonintellectual way — that is, in a poetic way. Buy a journal, a separate notebook for poetic "sketching," and carefully draw at the top of a fresh page these two shapes:

If each shape had a name, which one would be Kepick and which Oona? Write the name you have selected under each figure and then record these choices: If they are a couple, which is the man? If one is a brand of gasoline and the other a type of oil, which is which?

Suppose one is a melon and the other a lemon. And now listen to them: one is a drum and the other a violin. Too easy? One is a saxophone and the other a trumpet; one is the wind and the other a dog's bark. It is an odd and significant fact that 19 out of 20 people will give identical answers. This is a set of shared associations that is of particular interest to poets.

Thinking of them once again as a couple, make up four nonsense words that are harmonious with Oona and four for Kepick. Now try a few lines of very free and whimsical verse describing Oona and Kepick with your newly invented words used as nouns, verbs, or modifiers. (Surely it would be appropriate if Oona looked feenly in the shane, but how does she feel when Kepick kacks his bip and zabots all the lovely leems?)

There is no end to this. It won't lead directly to sophisticated poetry, but it will help you hear the music in language. The two should not be confused, but poems often have as much to do with sound, rhythm, and overtones as they do with making statements.

AVOIDING PITFALLS

You can think of the following pitfalls as the "seven deadly sins" of poetry, though some find the phrase intimidating. In any case, they are types of poetry that keep showing up in creative writing classes. You'll save hours of futile revision time and will improve the quality of your workshop course if you can stay clear of them.

- *The Impenetrable-Haze Poem.* The conscientious reader struggles from line to line without detecting any direction or coherence. Individual images may seem to make sense, but its segments aren't cohesive. The work as a whole doesn't suggest a theme on which any two people can agree.

    Why is obscurity so common among beginning poets? For some, it's a result of never having learned how to read complex and demanding poetry. Their inability gives them the feeling that if they write carelessly and without purpose, others will be able to make sense of it. A frequent defense: "It means whatever you want it to mean." That's another way of saying that it doesn't mean anything.

    Another cause for obscurity is shyness. The writer is reluctant to reveal genuine feelings or experiences and hides behind a barrier of fuzzy language. As I have noted previously, it takes courage to share what is really important to you. Keep in mind that while complexity is often necessary, obscurity cuts you off from your readers.

- *Truth-in-a-Nutshell.* When a poem tries to define truth, beauty, love, or evil in the abstract, it is apt to sound like a little essay in short lines. It also tends to be boring for lack of a personal element. We're all for truth and beauty and all opposed to evil and injustice, so why remind us once again? Abstractions are always risky, but they can serve if you focus on a very specific truth that your readers haven't yet considered. Stephen Dunn's "A Secret Life" (page 217) is a good example as is Molly Peacock's "Anger Sweetened" (page 202). Beauty, too, has to be presented through a specific example such as the gull in Barbara Howes' "The Bay at West Falmouth" (page 207) or those evening stars in Chris Buckley's "Intransitive" (page 311). In poems like these, it's the central **image** that we respond to and recall after leaving the poem. It implies the abstraction that lies at the heart of each poem.

- *Oh-Poor-Miserable-Me!* Sadly, young poets seem to be most tempted by this misuse of poetry. In some cases it reflects genuine despondency, and those feelings deserve a sensitive response. But a poem that is based on unrelenting self-pity is of more interest to therapists than readers of poetry. Such emotions tend to become repetitious like a song that repeats the same note over and over.

    For some, lamentation can become addictive. Because classmates are often reluctant to be critical, trying to be kind to such a miserable individual, the writer is insulated against negative evaluations. The best approach for the group is to separate the poet from implied speaker with comments such as "we could identify more fully with the narrator if the poem provided some relief or balance." Mature writers know that for a poem to be effective as a literary work it must be presented with some restraint, subtlety, and at least a touch of objectivity. Take a look at Shakespeare's "Sonnet 29" (page 203). The first eight lines are abject misery, but the last six provide a glorious contrast.

• *The Marching-Band Poem.* Every poem should have some type of rhythmical effect, but unvaried **meter** — especially when combined with a blatant **rhyme scheme** — tends to dominate the work. It becomes obtrusive. We're used to a hand-clapping beat and predictable rhyme endings in nursery rhymes, greeting card verse, some ballads, and football cheers, but the subtleties of sophisticated poetry are drowned out by heavy-handed rhythms and rhymes. Later, we will look at specific ways to mute these auditory aspects.

• *Hark, the Antique Language Poem.* Lo, yonder bovine ruminates 'twixt bosky dell and halcyon copse. No, it never gets this bad. But watch out for those dated contractions such as *o'er* and *oft* as substitutes for *over* and *often*. They are particularly tempting when one first tries metered verse. Sometimes they're sprinkled in like chocolate jimmies. Resist the urge. Every age has its own linguistic flavor, and like it or not, you're writing for the 21st century.

• *The Wailing Violin Poem.* Genuine feelings are the stuff of good poetry, but when readers feel that their emotions are being manipulated to evoke tears, they are apt to feel resentment. **Sentimentality** is by nature manipulative. Honest emotions have to spring from genuine feelings.

Elizabeth Holden could have set those violins wailing when she describes a woman of 86 who sees her friends dying in "As the Cold Deepens" (page 201). Instead, she focuses on the image of flies, and we connect that image with the mother. As readers, we sympathize, but we don't feel our emotions being manipulated.

• *The "All Them" Poem.* Most of us resent being included in sweeping generalizations about "all women," "all men," "all students," "all Americans," or "all parents." Every group is comprised of individuals. Poems that refer to any group as if it were made up of clones are offensive at best and prejudicial at worst. The best way to generate a sense of authenticity is to focus on the individual.

Holden's poem is not about elderly women as a class, it is about a particular woman in a particular place facing old age. "The Pardon" by Richard Wilbur (page 213) is not a sweeping statement about how insensitive kids are when dealing with death; it is a narrative about one specific boy dealing with the death of his dog. Wilbur, like Holden, starts with the specific and draws implications from that.

Don't let these warnings inhibit you. If you review the first few lines of the poems in Chapter 26, you will see that your options are almost limitless. Just make sure that the subject matter you are working with is rooted in a personal experience, observation, or insight that is important to you.

SIX WAYS TO JUMP-START A NEW POEM

Don't stare at a fresh sheet of paper, hoping it will give you a topic. Paper doesn't talk. Your new poem has to come out of you. Here are six ways to locate the material that is already within you. It's all there, waiting to be given fresh words.

1. Let other poets get you in the mood. Review about 10 poems in Chapter 26. Ask yourself, "Where might that have come from?" You won't ever know for sure, but just asking the question will stimulate you to look in the same area.

2. If you have been keeping a journal, use it. Look over those scraps of impressions, insights, fantasies, feelings, dreams, and stray lines of verse. If you haven't started one yet, buy a notebook for such musings. Carry it with you; add to it at odd times.

3. Draw on your five senses. List very briefly those objects you saw today that you will remember five years from now (a good exercise for your journal). What is it about them that makes them memorable? Try the same for last summer. Reach back for visual impressions from your childhood. Why have they stuck when thousands of other details slipped through the sieve of memory?

Do the same for sounds. Music may well come to mind first, but don't forget the voice or laugh of a particular person; the sounds of mechanical objects like a car, truck, or motorcycle; or the natural sounds of wind or rain. Describe these with fresh language — no babbling brooks, breathless calms, or howling gales.

Try the same for memorable sensations of touch, taste, and smell. Some may be pleasant, but others will be rancid or bitter. All sensory memories have the potential of generating a poem.

4. Recall some of the most vivid experiences you have had in the past two years. We're shifting here from things seen or heard to episodes that might be developed in narrative form. What makes them vivid? Often the event may be minor, but the emotions it generated are memorable. Keep an eye out for samples of **ambivalence** — opposite reactions existing at the same time.

5. Do the same for the dramatic events of your childhood. Did any of them change your attitude? Did they help you see things in a different light?

6. Now ask yourself some tough questions about your own life. (Remember, no one is listening!) When were you truly frightened? Would what frightened you then frighten you now? Were you ever deeply ashamed? As you look back, was the shame justified? Did you learn anything from it? Have you ever had a moment of elation that turned to disappointment or even depression?

7. Consider your friends and relations. Can you see in any of them contradictions that are worth exploring? Have you ever had to act as a parent to your parent or other older person? What did it feel like? Is there anyone you once hated whom you now understand or perhaps even like? Whose death would really hurt you? Why that person and not others? When dealing with your relationships with others, look closely to see if there is some type of ambivalence worth developing. It may not be as dramatic as love mixed with hatred; it may be a blend of admiration and resentment, respect and disapproval, or pleasure and displeasure.

As soon as you select a topic that might serve as the kernel of a poem, start writing. Get phrases down even before you are sure. Then lines. At this stage, don't worry about the order. Postpone that until later in the process. Lines that come to you early may end up at the end of a developed poem. Phrases you originally put down in a cluster may eventually be separated. Stay loose. Don't be afraid to be, as David Curry says (page 321) "the man / who starts out to write of his grandmother / ends up talking about a leaf . . ." Keep trying different versions. Let the developing poem speak to you as it takes shape.

28 The Impact of Images

• Images defined and contrasted with abstractions (236) • The impact of strong nouns (237) • Images as figures of speech: similes and metaphors (239) • Other figures of speech (241) • The cliché: a dying simile (242) • The image as symbol (244) • Building image clusters (246) • Trust your original vision (247)

Images, as I pointed out earlier, are words that we can respond to with any of the five senses. Usually they are objects we can see, but they can also be sounds, textures, odors, and occasionally even tastes. Images are also referred to as **concrete** nouns, though it is strange to think of the delicate scent of a rose as concrete.

The opposite of an image is an **abstraction**. Abstractions are concepts that the mind must grasp intellectually. *War, peace, love, democracy,* and even the word *abstraction* itself are abstract.

There is nothing reprehensible about abstractions. Civilization (itself an abstraction) depends on them. Mathematics, for example, contains an entire language of abstractions called numbers. We can't see or feel *five*; we can't weigh it or stroke it. But the concept is essential if you are going to build a house or a satellite. Philosophers spend their lives dealing with truth, knowledge, and ethics, all abstractions. Most politicians identify themselves as a Republican or a Democrat and argue about the budget and fiscal responsibility, none of which has been seen until translated into visual representations called cartoons.

Poets also deal with abstractions. In this very volume you have read poems with abstract titles such as "The Pardon," "Balances," "Mystery," and "Desire." Try taking a photograph of any of those! In each case, however, a poet has translated those chilly abstract concepts into sight and sound. Images have impact because we can access their meaning directly, usually in the form of a picture.

In Richard Wilbur's "The Pardon" (page 213), for example, we know intellectually what "pardon" means, but it is the sight of that dead dog that hits us emotionally. Not only do we see it, we smell it and we hear "the flies' intolerable buzz." He uses three types of sense data to thrust that image on us with the same impact that it struck the narrator. In each of these four poems an abstraction has been made vivid with an object we can see.

If you are in doubt about whether a word is abstract or concrete, ask yourself whether it refers to something you can see, hear, taste, smell, or feel. How much does truth weigh? What are the dimensions of death? How big a box do you need to contain happiness?

I have been describing images as the opposite of abstractions, but actually they are points on a continuum. *Serenity*, for example, is an abstraction that, like all true abstractions, cannot be seen or heard. You can't weigh it or put it in a cage. *Bird* is more concrete, but it is still rather general. We know it has feathers and wings, but there is a big difference between a hummingbird and an ostrich. *A gull* is more specific, and "a gull swinging in air,/At ease, sculptured, held there . . ." is a fully developed visual image. We not only see a specific bird, we see it "swinging in air." As you probably remember from Chapter 26, this image is taken from Barbara Howes' poem "The Bay at West Falmouth" (page 207). If you have forgotten how she links that image not only with "the heart's serenity," but also to "being open/to love," review it now so that my analysis won't remain abstract.

Here are some other examples showing the continuum between highly abstract words or concepts and images that a poet might use. In fact, poets *have* used these images in poems you have read just recently. See if you can recall them:

> *Reliability* is an abstraction.
>
> *A workhorse* is one way to make that abstraction visible.
>
> *Ned*, a specific farm horse that has worked for a lifetime until death, is a far more concrete image.
>
> *Chance* is an abstraction.
>
> Seeing a *white spider on a white flower* gives us a visual picture.
>
> Seeing a *white spider on a white flower holding a white moth* is a once-in-a-lifetime chance occurrence that is so unusual as to raise questions about whether there is some design in the natural world.
>
> *Anger* is an abstraction.
>
> *Anger sweetened* gives promise of an image — a teaser of sorts.
>
> But *insects in our stomachs* is a memorably repulsive image.

THE IMPACT OF STRONG NOUNS

As you can see from these examples, a concrete noun has to be specific in order to serve as an effective image. Because poetry relies so heavily on what we see and hear, it is important to select nouns that have impact whenever possible.

In most cases, finding just the right noun means that you won't have to modify it with an adjective. Whenever you do use an adjective, check to make sure that you can't find a more accurate noun, one that doesn't need to be modified. Here is a list of nouns that are modified because they don't exactly describe the object. On the right is a single noun that is more precise and so has greater impact.

a large stream	a river
almost a hurricane	a gale
a small lake	a pond
a loud voice	a shout
extreme fear	terror
excessively thrifty	miserly

There is nothing wrong with most adjectives as such. There are occasions when they provide just the shade of meaning you are trying to express. But think of them as fine-tuning. In many first-draft poems, half of the modifiers can and probably should be removed. Examine each one critically.

There is one modifier that is almost always damaging. *Very* is so over-used in popular magazine articles and advertising that it no longer has meaning. It becomes mere padding. Like underlining and multiple exclamation marks, it merely clutters a line of poetry.

To find just the right noun, you have to be sure about the meaning. We all have words in our passive vocabulary that we understand well enough when we are reading but not well enough to use in speech or writing. Look these up. You may be surprised at the precise meaning.

If you have a computer, seriously consider adding an electronic dictionary. These, unlike spell checkers, provide full definitions without leaving the document you are working on. Since you will want to know about the **overtones** of the words you look up, make sure that the dictionary you select includes derivations. Electronic dictionaries are so much quicker than flipping through the pages of a conventional dictionary that you will find yourself using it far more often.

Whenever you are working on a poem that relies on a particular place, select nouns that will give the reader a sense of being there. We have already noted how Barbara Howes' "The Bay at West Falmouth" (page 207) describes a specific gull, not gulls in general.

In the same way, Stephen Dunn's "Regardless" (page 220) opens with an actual place on a particular day: "the Rockaways/during a hurricane . . ." and describes briefly how the narrator and his father watched "a wooden jetty crumble" and felt "the wetness of its spray." The specific details convince us that this event must have really occurred regardless of whether it did so in reality.

Opening with a specific setting is only one of many approaches, of course. But in these examples the setting is so vivid that one wonders at first whether the work will end up being a purely descriptive poem. None of these initial scenes, however, becomes an end in itself. The descriptive details are all used to present abstract themes.

IMAGES AS FIGURES OF SPEECH

Until now I have been describing images used simply as descriptive details — things seen, heard, felt, smelled, and tasted. Images also serve as the concrete element in almost any **figure of speech**. In fact, some poets and critics use the word *image* exclusively for examples of figurative language.

Figures of speech most commonly take the form of the **simile** and the **metaphor**. These are both comparisons, the simile linking the two elements explicitly with *like* or *as* and the metaphor implying the relationship.

Here are four similes from three different poems you read in Chapter 26. I have already quoted from the first two poems several times without explaining similes or metaphors. This shows how familiar we all are with figurative language. Only as writers do we have to analyze just how both similes and metaphors work and how they are a special type of comparison. The marginal comments are the type you might want to add yourself when studying poems.

1. From Barbara Howes' "The Bay at West Falmouth":

   Serenity of mind poises

   (Like a gull) swinging in air   *simile*

2. From Robley Wilson's "On a Maine Beach":

   ...rocks are (like worn change)   *simile*

3. From Chase Twichell's "Rhymes for Old Age":

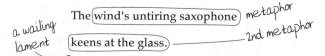

   a wailing lament   The (wind's untiring saxophone)   *metaphor*

   (keens at the glass.) ———— *2nd metaphor*

4. From Robley Wilson's "On a Maine Beach":

   ...Here, when the sea is gone,

   We find (old coins) glowing under the sky   *metaphor*

These examples of similes and metaphors are never simple comparisons. When we compare, for example, a starling with a grackle, we imply that *in most respects* the two objects are similar. But when Barbara Howes describes serenity as being like a gull, she certainly doesn't want us to picture the emotion as having a sharp bill and a raucous cry. Serenity is like a gull *only in certain respects* — in this case the way it seems to float effortlessly in the air. As with most similes, the area of similarity is quite narrow. The impact of the figure of speech depends on how sharply it can make the reader see a new relationship.

A **metaphor** is often described as a simile that doesn't use *like* or *as*, but the difference is much deeper than that. Similes are a special kind of comparison, but they are nonetheless phrased like comparisons. A metaphor, in contrast, is a statement that is literally untrue. We understand its meaning only by implication.

It doesn't make literal sense, for example, when Anita Endrezze begins her poem "The Mapmaker's Daughter" with these two lines:

> the geography of love is terra infirma
> it is a paper boat

This seems to be a commentary on love, but it certainly isn't intended to be read literally. If it's a metaphor, how do we make sense of it?

The best way to analyze how a particular metaphor works is to convert it to a simile. The result may be awkward, but it's a good technique to use with your own work and with published poems. In this case we discover that there are really two related metaphors. The conversion comes out something like this: "A love relationship is *like* being at sea (not on terra firma, solid ground) and is *like* a paper boat."

Notice how compressed the double metaphor in her poem is compared with my awkward translation into similes. No matter how compressed, every simile and metaphor is made up of two elements, the **tenor** and a **vehicle**. These terms were suggested by the critic I.A. Richards and have come into general usage because they are so helpful. The **tenor** is the poet's actual concern (often an abstraction) and the **vehicle** is the image used to represent it. In this example love is the tenor. The vehicle (appropriately in this case) is frail like a paper boat. In addition, that little boat floats on the sea (implied) described as "terra infirma," a made-up antonym for "terra firma."

One important advantage of coming to know and use these terms, **tenor** and **vehicle**, is that they can help you identify and get rid of **mixed metaphors**, those that merely confuse a reader because they have two or more contradictory vehicles. Here is an *invented* example:

> The wind's untiring saxophone
> hammers at the glass

The wind is the tenor here, and first it is described as being *like* the sound of a saxophone. Since *like* is not used, the phrase is a metaphor. The second metaphor is intended to suggest that the wind is also like a hammer pounding at the glass — not quite as effective but usable. Joined together, however, they suggest a bizarre picture of a saxophone being used as a hammer.

Here is the harmonious and effective version we saw in Chase Twichell's "Rhymes for Old Age" (215):

> The wind's untiring saxophone
> keens at the glass.

This version also uses a double metaphor (that is, two vehicles applied to one tenor), but the vehicles are harmonious. A saxophone often produces a wailing sound, and the verb *to keen* means to wail for the dead. The two vehicles work together. In addition, that wail is appropriate to the theme of the poem, a lament for a woman close to death.

OTHER FIGURES OF SPEECH

The term **figurative language** is used primarily to describe similes and metaphors. Most other figures of speech are specialized forms of the metaphor and are of more concern to literary critics than to writers in the process of composition. Three, however, concern us here. They are techniques you may want to use — though sparingly.

Hyperbole is extreme exaggeration used for effect. Not all examples of exaggeration are hyperboles. People exaggerate simply to boast or to get a laugh. Hyperbole, however, is a true figure of speech because we as readers understand that, first, it is not meant to be taken literally and, second, it has an implied meaning. If you look closely at examples of hyperbole, you will see that they can, like metaphors, be converted to similes. Shakespeare, for example, in "Sonnet 3" writes: "Thou doest beguile the world." Obviously, he doesn't mean that she literally charms everyone in the world; it is *as if* she had that power. And in "Sonnet 9" he writes in a darker mood, "The world will wail thee."

More recently, Lucille Clifton in "What the Mirror Said" (page 203) has her narrator look at her reflection and cry, "listen,/you a wonder/you a city / of a woman." This cheerful bit of self-affirmation is not just a casual exaggeration such as we might use in conversation; it is a figure of speech. Converting it to a simile, we end up with something like, "You're so complex and interesting, you're like an entire city."

The **pun** is one of the least appreciated figures of speech. In conversation, it is greeted with groans rather than laughter, but poets from Shakespeare to the present have treated it like a metaphor. Dylan Thomas makes serious use of the pun in a poem that is a lament for a girl killed in a bombing raid of World War II, "A Refusal to Mourn. . .":

> I shall not murder
> The mankind of her going with a grave truth

The word "grave" here has both a literal meaning, "a serious truth," and a figurative use that implies the opposite: the traditional and often empty oration such as those given at the graveside. (Incidentally, the phrase "murder/The mankind" is a hyperbole that could be rephrased as "injure humanity.")

The pun can occasionally be used for serious effect, but it is a risky device. If not handled with great skill, it will spoil the line (or even the poem as a whole) with what appears to be a comic note.

Synecdoche is the third of these helpful terms. It is a figure of speech in which a part is used for the whole. When we say "bread for the starving," we're not just appealing to baking companies. "Bread" represents food in general. Sometimes an individual is used for a group. When we say "the plight of the blue-collar worker," it's understood that we are referring to a whole class of people, not just an individual wearing a blue work shirt.

Poetic use of synecdoche is fresher than those we use in daily speech. Dylan Thomas, for example, uses the phrase "All the sun long" in "Fern Hill" to suggest a summer day.

Figures of speech are important to poetry because they increase the degree of compression. That is, they help suggest more without being wordy. Be careful, though, not to "dress up" a poem by using figures of speech merely for adornment. Sometimes straightforward language is more appropriate.

THE CLICHÉ: A DYING SIMILE

We have all been warned against using clichés since grade school. Yet they remain a temptation — particularly when we are tired or careless. It is important to understand what a cliché is and why it is so damaging to any kind of writing, especially a poem.

In common usage we call any overused phrase a cliché. "Neat as a pin," "clean as a whistle," "strong as an ox," "dead as a doornail," to "know the ropes," and to be "nipped in the bud" are all familiar to us. Notice that these are either similes or metaphors. The cliché, as George Orwell points out in his essay "Politics and the English Language," is actually a dying metaphor — that is, an expression that was once fresh enough to create a clear picture in the reader's mind but has lost its vitality through constant use.

Most clichés are, like the first four in the previous list, similes. The normal function of both metaphors and similes is to clarify an abstract word (*serenity*, for example) by linking it with a concrete one (such as *gull*). But when the same image is used repeatedly, it loses its visual impact. Often, we have forgotten the original image. As Orwell points out, "to toe the line" (literally to place one's toe on the starting line in a race) has strayed so far from the original metaphor that it is now often seen in print as "to *tow* the line."

Some dying metaphors or similes end up being compressed into a single word and a respectable part of the language. For example, we use the word *badger* to mean "harass," oblivious of the fact that the poor badger was originally the victim, not the tormentor. There's no harm in these **dead metaphors** because they have been converted to useful verbs or nouns. What does the damage to poetry are phrases that are both wordy and too familiar to provide a mental picture. They're excess baggage.

There are three different ways of dealing with clichés that appear in an early draft. First, you can work hard to find a fresh simile or metaphor that will allow the reader to see (hear, taste, and so on) the tenor you have in mind. Second, you can drop the figurative language completely and deal with the subject directly. Third, you can twist the cliché around so that it is revitalized in some slightly altered form.

For example, if you discover that you have allowed "blood red" to slide into your verse, you can avoid this ancient cliché with such alternatives as "balloon red," "hot red," or "screaming red," depending on the overtones you want to establish. If none of these will do, go back to just "red."

A good way to improve your skill in dealing with clichés is to apply these techniques to phrases such as "mother nature," "strong as an ox," "wise as an owl," and "where there's smoke, there's fire."

Hackneyed language is a related but broader term. It includes phrases that have simply been overused. They may not be true clichés, but they lack impact because of overuse. Certain subjects tend to generate hackneyed language. Sunsets, for example. The "dying day" is a true cliché, but perfectly respectable words like *golden, resplendent,* and *magnificent* become hackneyed in this context simply from excessive use. It's not the word itself that should be avoided — one cannot make lists; it is the particular combination that is limp from overuse.

In the same way, smiles are too often "radiant," "infectious," or "glowing." Trees, as we have seen, tend to have "arms" and "reach heavenward." The seasons are particularly dangerous: spring is "young" or "youthful," suggesting virginity, vitality, or both; summer is "full blown"; and with autumn some poets slide into a "September Song" with only slight variations of the popular lyrics. Winter is too easily used to suggest sterility and death.

Our judgment of what is hackneyed depends somewhat on the age in which we live. What was fresh and vivid in an earlier period may have become shopworn for us now. "Any port in a storm" was probably fresh in the 18th century when it was first used as a proverb, and "blind as a bat" in the 16th century, but they're tattered from overuse today.

Surprisingly, many hackneyed phrases were stale hundreds of years ago and still won't die. They keep sprouting like tenacious weeds in mass-market poetry. In "Sonnet 130," Shakespeare pokes fun at conventional descriptions of beauty that were stale even in his time in "Sonnet 130":

> My mistress' eyes are nothing like the sun;
> Coral is far more red than her lips' red. . . .
> And in some perfumes is there more delight
> Than in the breath that from my mistress reeks.

His mistress, we hope, realized that the poem was directed not at her but at the hack poets of the day who were content to use phrasing that even then was thoroughly stale. Shakespeare is speaking to us all when he suggests by implication that we must find fresh figures of speech if our work is to have impact.

THE IMAGE AS SYMBOL

A symbol also adds density of meaning to a poem, but the way it functions is the opposite of a figure of speech. As we have seen, a figure of speech introduces an image simply for comparison. A **symbol**, in contrast, uses an image that exists as a part of the poem and informs the reader that it has a greater range of meaning. If that strikes you as confusing in the abstract, consider these examples.

First, here is a simile (in italics) describing an older woman:

> My mother is almost weightless now,
> *Light as some fly* left to die on the window sill.

Here is the same image handled as a metaphor:

> My mother is almost weightless now,
> *a fly* left to die on the window sill.

In both cases, the woman exists in the poem, but the fly is introduced merely to make the comparison.

Now take a look at Elizabeth Holden's use of flies as a symbol in "As the Cold Deepens" (page 201):

> I think of flies
> how they live in a weightless armor
> tough, resistant, like a fingernail.
>
> My mother is almost weightless now

The flies here are the actual insects that the speaker and her mother once swept from the windowsills when they opened their summer house. The narrator recalls those flies and then describes her mother. How do we know that the flies are being used as a symbol? The poet links the two with the word "weightless." The flies are not just a figure of speech; rather, they exist in the poem, and they also amplify some of the characteristics of a frail woman close to death.

We have already seen how Robley Wilson's "On a Maine Beach" (page 208) uses a simile in the very first line. Again, the italics are mine:

> "Look, in these pools how rocks *are like worn change*."

There is no pile of coins in this poem. "Worn change" is introduced figuratively just to help us see a particular aspect of the rocks.

The rock pool itself, however, really exists in the poem. And after a careful reading, we realize that he isn't just describing a pretty aspect of nature. Through a series of hints, he informs us that such rock pools with their cycles of tides take on characteristics similar to our own life cycles. When he describes those snails "spending slow / Round lifetimes half awake," he isn't speaking merely as a naturalist. He has charged this scene with a broader meaning. He is commenting on an aspect of the human condition.

In some poems, the symbolic element may be missed on the first reading. Stephen Dunn's "Regardless" (page 220) is an example. It begins, you remember, with the narrator being taken by his father to watch a hurricane on the coast. In the next to last stanza, the narrator describes himself as

> . . . a boy
>   who had learned to love
> the wind, the wind that would go its own way,
>
> regardless. I must have thought damage
> is just what happens.

The wind in that initial scene seems at first to be simply a detail from his childhood experience, but at the end of the poem we see that "the wind that would go its own way" is a symbol for the father himself. Furthermore, on our second reading, we realize that the damage described in the opening scene is intended as a symbol for the damage caused by the father's heavy drinking. (This is a good example of the fact that a literary poem calls for several readings.)

In distinguishing metaphors from symbols, it helps to recall and use those terms **tenor**, the actual subject, and **vehicle**, the words used to describe that tenor. Ask this simple question, Should I take this vehicle literally? If not (like the "worn change" in the Wilson poem), it is a figure of speech. If the tenor is literally there (like the flies in the Holden poem, the rock pool in the Wilson poem, and the wind in the Dunn poem), ask yourself whether it is serving as a symbol to suggest some broader concern such as mortality in each of those otherwise quite different poems.

At first, this may seem too analytical to be helpful — especially if you are just starting to write poetry. But as you begin to analyze your own work and that of others, these distinctions will be as important and useful to you as the distinction between the major and minor keys is for a musician.

The term **public symbol** refers to symbols that are widely recognized and are almost part of the language. The flag, for example, represents the country, the cross stands for the Christian church, the dove suggests peace, and a shrouded figure holding a scythe is recognized as a symbol of death. These are so common that they can be used in cartoons.

Because public symbols are so overused, they are considered hackneyed. Poets generally avoid them and construct their own **private symbols** instead. Devised for a particular poem, a private or unique symbol has to be introduced in such a way that its meaning is made clear through the context of the poem.

Often the symbolic suggestion in a poem will come relatively late in the writing process. We have no way of knowing, but this may have been the case in Stephen Dunn's symbolic use of the wind in "Regardless."

Important as symbols often are, don't feel that they are essential. Donald Hall's "Names of Horses" (page 216) is a moving tribute to farm horses who served patiently over the years. The poem may remind some readers of generations of workers in a factory or, dare I suggest it, teachers, but there is nothing in the poem to suggest that the horses were intended to be symbols of anything. It's quite sufficient that the poem honor horses as horses. It's a mistake for a reader to force a symbolic suggestion onto a published poem without evidence, just as it is a mistake for a writer to impose a symbol on his or her own work just to make it seem deep.

As you write, examine your subject carefully and determine what it has meant to you. If a symbol comes to mind, let it develop naturally. Revise the poem so that your reader can share the symbolic suggestion. A private symbol that remains a secret is worth nothing, and making readers guess your intent without providing guideposts is a mean-spirited game. On the other hand, you have to be careful not to make it so obvious that the literary intent becomes obtrusive. When symbols are shaped with restraint and subtlety, they will be an organic part of the poem.

BUILDING IMAGE CLUSTERS

Regardless of whether images are used figuratively, symbolically, or simply as enriching details, they are often more effective if presented in clusters. That is, a group of images that have the same source (the sea, a beach, a farm) or are linked visually (a series of circles) gain strength and impact as compared with unrelated images that are used once and then dropped.

When you read a new poem, look for such **image clusters** or groups of related details even before you are entirely clear about the theme.

Philip Appleman's four-stanza poem "Desire" (page 219) is a good example of how images that are related have greater impact than those that have no relationship with each other. In this poem the first stanza focuses on "tide"; the second, on "moons," the cause of tides; and the final stanza highlights "undertow." Although his central concern, *desire*, is identified in the title, it is never mentioned in the body of the poem. He translates that abstraction into details we can see and feel, and those images stand out because of their affinity with each other.

There is an even more complex example of image clusters in "On a Maine Beach" by Robley Wilson, which you first read on page 208. Here is an annotated version showing the connections:

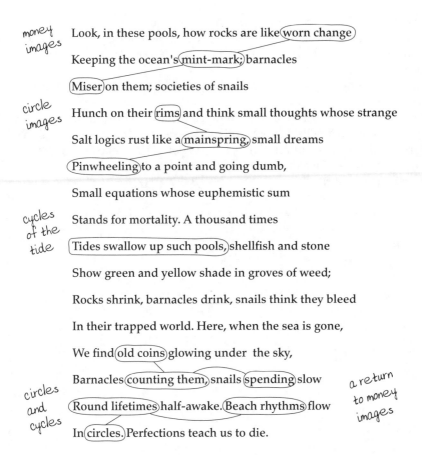

money
images

Look, in these pools, how rocks are like worn change

Keeping the ocean's mint-mark; barnacles

Miser on them; societies of snails

circle
images

Hunch on their rims and think small thoughts whose strange

Salt logics rust like a mainspring, small dreams

Pinwheeling to a point and going dumb,

Small equations whose euphemistic sum

cycles
of the
tide

Stands for mortality. A thousand times

Tides swallow up such pools, shellfish and stone

Show green and yellow shade in groves of weed;

Rocks shrink, barnacles drink, snails think they bleed

In their trapped world. Here, when the sea is gone,

We find old coins glowing under the sky,

Barnacles counting them, snails spending slow

circles
and
cycles

Round lifetimes half-awake. Beach rhythms flow

In circles. Perfections teach us to die.

a return
to money
images

The first pre-image cluster is coins. The second has to do with circles and spirals. As the last line suggests, watching these cycles of living and dying within the rock pool helps us see our own mortality in perspective.

Review this annotated version again and then use it as a model to analyze image clusters in "The Mapmaker's Daughter" by the Native American poet Anita Endrezze (page 222). If you own your own copy of this text, take the time to circle the image clusters. Or you can photocopy the poem and mark the copy. This kind of visual analysis is not only helpful in the process of understanding new work, it will help you adopt the same techniques in your own writing.

TRUST YOUR ORIGINAL VISION

This chapter has presented many ways to use the image. The various techniques will help you develop breadth of meaning and share a variety of emotions in your work. It's a learning process that necessarily involves mastering a number of new terms.

Important as these techniques are, remember that the writing of sophisticated poetry is not a mechanical art. Regardless of how long you revise and try different approaches to your subject, the true heart of your new work lies in your original vision.

A new poem takes shape because strong feelings and insights came to you. Trust these.

Don't be intimidated by all these new concepts. The use of images as metaphors, symbols, image clusters, and all the other techniques covered in this chapter will enhance your initial vision. As you write, keep asking yourself: What were the feelings that launched this work? What were the insights? Honor them as you write.

29 Using the Sound of Language

Poetry was recited aloud long before it was written down to be read from the page. Since the invention of the printing press, we are less dependent on memorization and recitation, but the genre still has its roots in the oral tradition. The growing popularity of poetry readings, both live and recorded, is a good indication of how poetry, far more than prose, continues to appeal to the ear.

All language, of course, relies on sound, but poetry emphasizes that aspect. Essentially, there are three ways to do this. The first is to use words that begin with identical or similar sounds such as *big*, *black bear*. The second is to link sounds within two or more words as in the k*ee*per sl*ee*ps d*ee*ply. The third, rhyme, is an identity of concluding sounds such as in asp*ire* and adm*ire* or anx*iety* and soc*iety*. In addition, some words echo at least faintly the object, sound, or action they describe as in *hiss*, *babble*, and *chickadee*.

When we read for pleasure, we hardly notice these linkages. They may give us only a vague sense that the work sounds melodic. But when we read as writers, that won't do. We have to identify the various techniques by name so we can discuss them accurately and learn how to use them effectively.

The first step is to acquire a basic critical vocabulary. Although it's true that the analysis of poetry in general requires more terms than are needed to examine prose fiction, I have limited the terms used in this text to those that are helpful for writers of poetry.

NONRHYMING DEVICES OF SOUND

Nonrhyming linkages in sound are found in both rhymed and unrhymed poems. Because they are the least technical, they are a good introduction to the element of sound in language.

Significantly, these devices can also be found in prose and oratory. The following passage, for example, is actually prose despite its **lyrical** or musical quality. It comes from Dylan Thomas' "August Bank Holiday" and describes a summer day at the beach not through plot but, in the manner of poetry, through a succession of vivid images. The first paragraph is typical. I have circled some of the linking sounds.

> August Bank Holiday. — A tune on an ice-cream cornet. A
>
> slap of sea and a tickle of sand. A fanfare of sunshades opening.
>
> A wince and whinny of bathers dancing into deceptive water. A
>
> tuck of dresses. A rolling of trousers. A compromise of
>
> paddlers. A sunburn of girls and a lark of boys. A silent
>
> hullabaloo of balloons.

What makes this prose passage sound "poetic"? Primarily, it is all those linkages of sounds — some occurring at the beginning of words and others within words. Notice also how some words themselves echo the action or evoke the object or sensation they describe.

Anyone interested in the sound of poetry should be familiar with the following four nonrhyming techniques. If they are new to you, make an effort to use them in discussions so that they become a part of your active vocabulary.

- **Alliteration** is the repetition of initial sounds (often consonants) in two or more words. Of course they have to be close enough for the reader to sense the linkage. There are three groups of these in the Thomas paragraph:

    *s*lap — *s*ea — *s*and
    *win*ce — *whin*ny (a similarity, not an identity, of sound)
    *d*ancing — *d*eceptive

- **Assonance** is the repetition of similar **vowel** sounds regardless of where they are located in the word. (For those who are unsure about what vowels are and are ashamed to ask, they are the open-mouth sounds *a, e, i, o, u,* and sometimes *y;* all other letters are consonants.) Some good examples in the passage are

    *wi*nce — *whi*nny
    sunb*ur*n — *gir*ls (similarity of sound, not spelling)
    Hullaba*loo* — ball*oo*ns

- **Consonance** is the repetition of consonantal sounds. Whereas *alliteration* is used to describe similarities in initial sounds, *consonance* usually refers to sounds within the words. Often, the two are used in conjunction. There are three sets of consonance in this passage:

> wi*n*ce — whi*nny* (both assonance and consonance here)
> gir*ls* — *l*ark
> si*l*ent — hu*ll*aba*l*oo — ba*ll*oons

- **Onomatopoeia** is often defined as a word that sounds like the object or action it describes, but actually most onomatopoetic words suggest a sound only to those who already know the meaning. We are not dealing with language that mimics life directly; it is usually just an echo. There are three good examples in Thomas' paragraph of poetic prose:

> slap of sea (the sound of a wave on the beach)
> whinny (an echo of a horse's cry)
> hullabaloo (derived from "hullo" and "hello" with an echo of the clearly onomatopoetic "babble")

Such analyses tend to remain abstract and theoretical until one tries the technique in actual composition. Stop now and think of a scene, a friend, or a piece of music that comes to you with the soft, gentle contours you associated with the Oona figure in Chapter 27 (page 231). Now try a paragraph of descriptive prose in which you make use of as many sound devices as possible. Remember that this is prose, so there is no need to worry about rhythm or a rhyme scheme. It might help to circle the linkages in sound. The point of this exercise is merely to help you find and use sound clusters.

Now, by way of contrast, think of a place, a person, or a piece of music that more closely resembles the sharp characteristics of the Kepick figure (page 231). Again, work out one or two prose paragraphs. This exercise is to poetry what preliminary sketches are to a finished painting.

RHYMES, TRUE AND SLANT

True rhyme matches the sound at the ends of words. It can be defined in three short sentences. (1) It is an *identity* of the sound in accented syllables. (2) The identity must begin with the accented **vowel** and *continue to the end*. (3) The sounds preceding the accented vowel must be *unlike* each other.

A distilled definition like this is about as off-putting as reading the rules of chess for the first time. The best approach is to move on to the examples that follow, returning to the three rules only when puzzled.

Here are four sets of true rhymes with the accented sounds in italics:

> c*all*
> t*all*
> enthr*all*
> (*all* is the identical sound; the preceding sounds are c, t, and r)

insp*ire*

adm*ire*

to h*ire*

(*ire* is the identical sound; the preceding sounds are p, m, and h)

h*eater*

m*eet her*

gr*eet her*

Notice that *true rhyme* requires an *identity* in sound. Thus, "*run*" and "*come*" are not true rhymes because of the subtle difference in sound. Nor are "*seen*" and "*cream*." These are called **slant rhymes**, which I will turn to shortly.

Because we are dealing with sound, words with different spelling often rhyme. This is fortunate for those of us writing in English, a language famous for bizarre spelling. "Girl" and "furl" rhyme despite their spelling. The same for "through," "chew," "glue," "flu," "ewe," "PDQ," and "Tyler too." *Oo* sounds in English get the international prize for absurd spelling, but they all rhyme.

Conversely, words with either similar or the same spellings but different pronunciation like "to read" and "having read," do not rhyme. These are known as **eye rhymes**. Look out for words in which the sound that comes before the rhyming sound is also identical. "Night" and "knight" are not true rhymes, for example, because the *n* is the same. Such pairs are technically known as *identities*.

RELATED WORDS	ACCENTED VOWEL SOUND	ACTUAL RELATIONSHIP AND EXPLANATION
1. night/fight	*i*	True rhyme (meets all three requirements)
2. night/knight	*i*	An identity (preceding consonant sounds are identical)
3. ocean/motion	*o*	True rhyme (*cean* and *tion* sound the same); also known as *double* or *feminine rhyme* (two syllables)
4. warring/wearing	*or* and *air*	Consonance or slant rhyme (accented vowel sounds do not match)
5. track to me back to me	*a*	True rhyme (a triple rhyme)
6. dies/remedies	*i* and *em*	Eye rhyme (*dies* is similar only in spelling)
7. When you see us; you will flee us	*e*	Quadruple rhyme — true rhyme (rare and usually appears forced — often comic)

These, then, are the fundamentals of rhyme. Now take a look at the table on page 252. To test yourself, cover all but the left column with your hand and decide which are true rhymes and which are not. Remember to start with the accented **vowel** and sound out the rhyming portion. Trust your ear.

ACHIEVING SUBTLETY IN SOUND

When the sound of language becomes obvious and draws attention to itself, it dominates the entire poem. This is not a problem with nursery rhymes where, as in the case of the Dr. Seuss books, rhyme and rhythm are half the fun. Nor is it a liability with mass-appeal poems such as Kilmer's "Trees" in which, as we have seen, the goal is to soothe with familiar rhythms and well-known truisms. And **occasional verse** — light pieces written for special occasions like anniversaries or birthdays — is frequently written with a pronounced rhyme, often for comic effect. But if you are working with a serious and complex set of themes, obtrusive rhymes can reduce your efforts to a jingle. It's like trying to play a subtle Mozart quartet with an oompah-pah brass band.

The following five ways to mute the impact of rhyme are well worth considering if you find your rhyme scheme is drawing attention to itself:

1. The most frequently used technique is called **enjambment** or run-on lines. An enjambed line is one in which the grammatical construction or the meaning continues into the next line. It is distinguished from **end-stopped lines**, which usually close with a period or semicolon. Rhyme is less noticeable when the reader is drawn without a pause to the next line.

An excellent example of this technique is Maxine Kumin's "Morning Swim," which you read on page 211. This poem is written in rhyming couplets (two-line **stanzas**), a form rarely used today because in unskilled hands the rhyme can easily become monotonous and obtrusive. If you review this poem, however, you will see that 10 of the 12 stanzas are enjambed. Some are fully enjambed, like this one:

> Invaded and invader, I ⌐   No pause here
> ⌐ went overhand on that flat sky.

There is no way you can stop or even pause at the end of that first line. Other lines are partially enjambed, like this couplet:

> that fed the lake that met my sea ‖⌐   slight pause
> ⌐ in which I sang *Abide with Me.*

You could stop at "sea" without being confused, but the sentence does continue into the second line.

Only 2 of the 12 stanzas are truly end-stopped. Here is one:

Fish twitched beneath me, quick and tame.|| *Full pause*

In their green zone they sang my name

As I mentioned, end-stopped lines usually conclude with a period or a semi-colon, but not always. The deciding factor is whether the reader must continue to the next line to make grammatical sense. If you read this poem aloud, you will see how the lines blend, placing those rhymes in the background.

2. A second approach is simply to separate the rhyming lines. If you use a three-line stanza, you can elect to rhyme it *aba, bcb, cdc* or even to leave the middle line unrhymed. A four-line stanza gives you even more choices.

If you take a close look at the rhyme scheme in Anthony Hecht's poem "Lizards and Snakes" (page 212), you will see that it is written as if in four-line stanzas even though the spacing suggests a longer unit. Here are the first two stanzas with a rhyme that occurs on alternate lines, a pattern that can be described as *abab, cdcd,* and so forth.

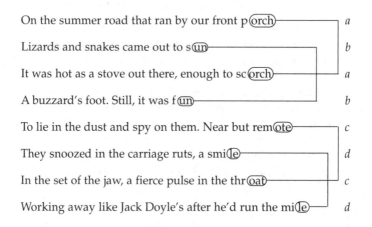

Notice that every rhyme in this stanza is true. In fact, in the entire poem there are only two slant rhymes. (If you look for them, be sure to identify the accented syllable.) Jack Doyle, by the way, was a famous runner whose specialty, the mile, is a convenient rhyme with "smile."

3. A third and much more subtle way to mute the effect of rhyme is to capitalize the beginnings of sentences rather than the beginnings of lines. This is a muting effect many readers fail to spot. Although a majority of metered poems begin each *line* with a capital letter, a few highlight each *sentence* with an initial capitalized letter instead.

It may seem odd that this would have any effect on the impact of the rhyme, but it changes the way we read the work. It emphasizes the sentence structure and downplays the line, encouraging us to read it more like prose. Kumin does this with "Morning Swim" (page 211), as does Molly Peacock in "Anger Sweetened" (page 202).

4. Using an informal or as-if-spoken **tone** also mutes the rhyme. Hecht's "Lizards and Snakes" makes use of this approach. It's as if we were listening to someone recount a childhood experience. The informality is deceptive, of course, because the poem is both rhymed and metered. It is a device often used by Robert Frost in his longer as-if-narrated poems.

5. The fifth way of muting rhyme is by using **slant rhymes**, also known as **off rhymes**. In many cases these are a form of **assonance**, a similarity but not an identity of sound as in *account* and *about*.

Slant rhymes are frequently used in combination with other muting techniques. To hear the difference, read the following two passages aloud. The first is a wooden revision of the second stanza of Richard Wilbur's "The Pardon." Keep in mind that this is *not* how Wilbur wrote it; it is my shameless reworking to make a point:

> I went in close to where the poor dog was.
> I heard the flies' intolerable buzz.
> The air was heavy with honeysuckle-smell.
> It was twined with another whose source I could not tell.

Not only does every line end with a true rhyme, but the rhymes are also emphasized by placing them next to each other in the form of couplets, *aa, bb*. In addition, each line is end-stopped with a period. The rhyme rings out like a gong: *was-buzz / smell-tell*. It's verse like this that gives rhyming couplets a bad name.

Here, then, is how Richard Wilbur really wrote it:

> [I] Went only close enough to where he was
> To sniff the heavy honeysuckle-smell
> Twined with another odour heavier still
> And hear the flies' intolerable buzz.

You can hear the difference even from a casual reading of these two versions, but you have to know what you're looking for to see how the subtlety in Wilbur's version is achieved. The rhyme is there, but *smell* and *still* are slant rhymes. In addition, the scheme is, like the rest of the poem, *abba*. No line in this stanza is a complete sentence ending with a period, so there is no tendency to place a heavy emphasis on the rhyming words.

Wilbur uses slant rhymes sparingly — only three pairs out of 12 in the entire poem — and he distributes them through the poem. If you find that your slant rhymes are bunched toward the end, it probably means that you were sleepy and quit too soon!

Many poets avoid rhyme altogether. Generally, they rely more heavily on images than they do on the sound of language. For example, not only is Donald Hall's "Names of Horses" (page 216) unrhymed, but it also contains very few examples of assonance or consonance. The effect he achieves comes through a succession of highly visual, fresh, and memorable images presented in lines that are so long that they seem to resemble the plodding of the horses he is honoring.

The choice of whether to use rhyme or not will eventually be up to you, but many introductory courses in creative writing require the writing of one or more poems that make use of a regular rhyme scheme using true rhymes in a subtle manner. There is a good reason for this. As in music, painting, and many sports, reading about a technique is not the same as mastering it. Mastery comes by actually doing it. Often repeatedly. Only then do you have a true choice of whether to make further use of it.

SOUND AS MEANING

When working with rhyme, guard against the tendency to treat it as decoration or, worse, as a mechanical game, filling in the appropriate blanks. Sound devices are most effective when they add to the meaning.

It is not possible to do this more than occasionally, but it is a technique worth considering, particularly in the highly important concluding lines. Some of the best examples are found in the final couplet of the English or Elizabethan **sonnet**. We'll take a closer look at that form in Chapter 31, but our concern here is on the way rhymed words can be used to emphasize key concepts or images almost as if they were underlined.

The concluding couplet in Shakespeare's "Sonnet 29" (page 203) is a good example. The narrator has described his mood as truly depressed ("When in disgrace with fortune and men's eyes") until he thinks of his love. Then everything bursts into joy. Here is the concluding couplet with the key images italicized:

> For thy sweet love remembered *such wealth brings,*
> That then I scorn to change my state *with kings.*

Had he attempted to describe his joy with two unrelated images, the conclusion of that poem would have been weakened. Linking "wealth" and "kings" in the rhyming couplet draws those two lines together to highlight his sense of elation.

There is another example of meaning enhanced through rhyme in Maxine Kumin's "Morning Swim" on page 211. In that poem, she links the act of swimming with that of singing a hymn of praise:

and in the rhythm of the swim
I hummed a two-four-time slow hymn

This is more than a casual link of "swim" and "hymn." The rhythmical pattern of four stresses in each line echo the musical "two-four-time" of the hymn the narrator is singing, and the two types of rhythm are joined by the rhyme of the two key words, "swim" and "hymn." Sound and sense are fused.

Nonrhyming sound devices such as **assonance** and **consonance** are less noticeable than rhyme because they are often buried within the line, but they can also be used to link key images. Robley Wilson's "On a Maine Beach" (page 208) has a very loose rhyme scheme with as many slant rhymes as those that are true. But frequently he links key images with assonance. If you look closely at his simile "*ro*cks like w*o*rn change" you will see that visual association is enhanced with the round *o* sounds that I have italicized. They help fuse the **vehicle** ("rocks") and the tenor ("worn change").

If you are tempted to believe that these connections in sound are too subtle to affect the way we as readers respond to a poem, remember how dramatically our associations were altered by mere sound in nonsense words like Kepick and Oona in Chapter 27. Casual readers don't usually notice how the sound of language affects meaning, but perceptive readers can, and poets learn by being perceptive readers.

TRAINING YOUR EAR

It is hard to imagine a musical composer who doesn't spend a lot of time listening to music. Yet, some beginning poets are reluctant to read too much poetry for fear of being influenced. Actually there is no danger of becoming imitative if one reads a wide variety of works. Only by reading — preferably aloud — can one begin to appreciate the ways in which poetry is written for the ear.

So far in this chapter, we have examined a variety of ways in which one can use the sound of language in poetry. But as I have pointed out previously (and will again), passively reading about these techniques is like studying a book on how to play the violin. The learning process doesn't really start until you begin working on your own.

Chapter 35 consists of poems not analyzed in this text. Its purpose is to encourage you to apply what you have learned to look for in poetry. But it is none too soon to begin the process right now, focusing on the sound of poetic language.

Now that you know what to look and listen for in poetry, turn once again to Robley Wilson's "On a Maine Beach" on page 208. True, we have examined that poem from a number of different perspectives, but there is plenty for you to discover on your own.

Begin by reading the entire poem without stopping — preferably aloud. Then go through it critically — that is, analytically — line by line. Mark as many of the rhyme endings and the nonrhyming sound devices as you can find. Now read the poem aloud once again for pleasure. . . . This sequence of reading, analyzing, and then re-reading is a good way to alternate an over-all appreciation of the poem as a whole with close analytical study from the point of view of a fellow poet.

Next, turn to Chase Twichell's "Rhymes for Old Age" on page 215. We haven't worked as much on this poem, so most of the analysis of sound will be up to you. It is similar to the Wilson poem in that it has a rhyme scheme so muted that you may have difficulty sorting it out. The basic pattern for each stanza is *aba cdc*. Look closely and sound out the linked words. You can teach yourself how to identify the sounds in this poem by using the same sequence that you used with the Wilson poem: read for pleasure, read line by line for analysis, and then read nonstop again.

In training your ear to hear the sound of language, be careful not to stress rhyme at the expense of other devices. Alliteration, assonance, conso-nance, and onomatopoeia are equally important.

Another method of training your ear is to listen to recordings of poets reading their own work. Most libraries have collections of audiotapes, video-cassettes, and DVDs. Consider buying tapes or disks for your own personal use. If your local bookstore caters to bestsellers and how-to books, use the Internet. Repeated listening is enormously valuable as well as pleasurable.

Remember, though, that analyzing techniques the way we have done in this chapter requires a close study of the written text. Whenever possible, lis-ten with a copy of the poem in front of you. Make marginal comments and then replay the recording. You will actually hear more as you become in-creasingly familiar with the work.

Finally, write lines in your journal using these various techniques in sound. Don't limit yourself to lines that might develop into finished poems. Let yourself go. To get yourself in the mood, read over John Updike's four-line poem "Winter Ocean" (page 200), which is essentially an exercise in ver-bal sounds.

Experiment with assonance, with alliterative runs, and with varieties of rhyme. Try a few imitations of poets with distinctive styles, such as Anita Endrezze or Richard Wilbur. Sound in poetry is partly a matter of knowing what your options are — technique. But it is also a matter of hearing what you are writing — a sensitivity to the sound of spoken language. Good poetry requires both.

30 Traditional Rhythms

Rhythmical patterns are embedded in every aspect of our lives. We celebrate the passage of each millennium, century, year, and birth date, and our calendars mark the passage of weeks and days in tune with the passages of the sun and moon. Our clocks chime the hours and tick the seconds. Internally, 100 biological clocks keep track of our age, our sleep–wake schedule, the regular functioning of our glands, our breathing, our heartbeat, and our brain waves.

It's no wonder that people in every culture feel the need to echo those cycles with ritual, song, and dance. Childhood chants heard today have been traced back to the 14th century, passed down not by parents or teachers but by older to younger children. They cross lines of class, nationality, and ethnic background.

The rhythms of poetry, then, are not mere adornment. They are not frills to be added for decoration. The rhythms of poetry are echoes of what goes on around us and within us. They echo the rhythms of life.

If you look again at the previous paragraph, you will see how the repetition of key words have created a simple rhythmical pattern: "The rhythms. . . . The rhythms . . . the rhythms," "are not . . . are not . . . " "are echoes . . . " echo . . . " As every evangelical preacher knows, repetition is a basic technique in the establishment of prose rhythms.

Poetry also uses repetition, but because poets control line length, they have many other ways of creating rhythmical patterns. In this respect, poetry is like music. One can sing poems or read song lyrics as if they were poetry. And it seems natural to use the word **verse** to designate both poetry in general and lyrics to be sung. A line of poetry is like a measure in music.

There are two different approaches to creating rhythm in poetry. Although they overlap, it is helpful to examine them separately.

Traditional rhythms, the subject of this chapter, are recurring patterns in the poetic line that have been shared by poets for centuries. Although each poet uses a particular pattern in a slightly different way, part of the pleasure for the reader (and for the poet, too) is the interplay between the familiar beat and the variations developed in a specific work.

Poems using these traditional rhythms are usually organized into **stanzas**, each with a fixed number of lines throughout the poem. With this approach, the rhythm we detect in the first line becomes the model for the entire work. There are many such patterns, some based on stressed words and many more on stressed syllables.

The other approach is **free verse**. With such poems, the rhythms vary from line to line, and if stanzas are used, they frequently vary in length just as paragraphs do in prose. I'll discuss this in Chapter 32.

RHYTHM OF STRESSED WORDS

The simplest traditional rhythm is based on the fact that when we speak, we naturally place greater emphasis on some words than on others. We may not be consciously aware of doing this, but it is a part of how we use the language and is especially important in English. Take, for example, this straightforward sentence:

> I went to town to buy some bread.

Written on the page, it looks like eight one-syllable words of even weight. But imagine how the same sentence might sound to someone who doesn't understand English:

> i-*WENT* t'*TOWN* t'*BUY* s'm*BREAD*

The stressed words have muscled out the unstressed words. No one teaches you to do this; you pick it up by listening to others speaking. It is easy enough for the poet to construct lines in which there are, say, four stressed words — especially in English, which has always relied heavily on stress. This is the system used in *Beowulf*, the Old English epic.

Here is a passage (translated into modern English) in which Beowulf, the hero, pursues a sea monster (metaphorically called the "brine-wolf") to her underwater lair. Read the selection a few times and underline the stressed words:

> Then bore this brine-wolf, when bottom she touched,
> the lord of rings to the lair she haunted,
> whiles vainly he strove, though his valor held,
> weapon to wield against wondrous monster
> that sore beset him; sea-beasts many
> tried with fierce tusks to tear his mail

Poets working in this tradition were concerned primarily with having four stresses in each line. They didn't count the unstressed syllables. Between each pair of stressed words is a pause known as a **caesura**. The beat is so simple and pronounced that one can pound on the table while chanting or singing it — which is probably just what the ancients did in the mead halls more than 1,000 years ago.

Such poems also make frequent use of **alliteration** — similar initial sounds as described in the previous chapter. For this reason, *Beowulf* and many poems of this sort are referred to as **alliterative verse**.

The previous version is a translation of a manuscript that dates from the eighth century, so one might think that its rhythmical system would be of interest only to scholars. But poets are by nature recyclers, making use of whatever techniques they can find. In some respects, rap music draws on that tradition today, whether the musicians have ever read *Beowulf* or not. Boom boxes echo those mead hall rhythms from more than 1,000 years ago.

More deliberately, in the 1970s, the poet and playwright George Keithley wrote a book-length account of the ill-fated Donner party, a group of pioneers most of whom perished trying to cross the Sierra Nevada range in the 1840s. Like *Beowulf*, this is a dramatic story dealing with heroic effort, violence, and death. He adapted the same system of stresses with variations, often using two or three in a line or, as in the following example, two pairs of stressed words. Here is a brief sample from *The Donner Party*, one of the few book-length **narrative poems** to reach a national audience and become a Book of the Month Club selection. I have italicized the stressed words:

> The *tongues* of our *flames licked* at the *dark.*
> In *time,* our *talking floated up* like *smoke*
> and *mingled* with the *chatter* of the *leaves.*
> But the *night* un*nerved* us *even* as we *spoke.*

SYLLABICS: THE COUNTING OF SYLLABLES

Rhythm that relies merely on stressed words in each line lends itself to long narrative poems — especially those with strong echoes of the spoken language. But the weakness of rhythm by stress is monotony. In unskilled hands, it tends to sound like a drinking song. A more sophisticated approach is to count all the syllables in the line rather than just the stressed words.

Syllabic verse establishes a pattern based on the number of syllables in each line. One short but often subtle example of this is the **haiku**. The English version of this ancient Japanese form has just three lines. The first line has five syllables, the second has seven, and the third has five.

The haiku is called a **fixed form** since the rhythmical pattern has been established by tradition. But the form is more than just counting syllables. Unlike most fixed forms, the tradition also includes aspects of the subject matter. Haiku almost always contain images from nature, and they also either state or imply a season. In addition, most suggest a striking similarity or even an apparent identity between two seemingly different objects. Here is a haiku you first read in Chapter 26. Written by the Japanese poet Chora, it makes use of all three characteristics:

> After spring sunset
> Mist rises from the river
> Spreading like a flood.

As you can see, the syllable count in this translation follows the 5-7-5 pattern exactly. The poem also identifies the season, spring, and compares the gentle, harmless movement of spreading mist to that of a potentially devastating flood.

Centuries later, Etheridge Knight, an African American, taught himself to write haiku in prison and composed many that make full use of the same tradition both in structure and in content. Here is one of his haiku that you first read in Chapter 26:

> A bare pecan tree
> slips a pencil shadow down
> a moonlit snow slope.

In this winter scene (the tree is bare), a pecan tree casts a thin shadow down "a moonlit snow slope" just as the poet uses a pencil to catch the scene in verse on a snow-white sheet of paper. Though separated by centuries and dramatically different cultural traditions, these two poets share a fixed form to present a scene with **metaphorical** overtones.

Knight, in commenting on his development as a poet, described his indebtedness to the haiku. He found that the requirements of the form helped him give up abstractions and search instead for simple but striking images. Other examples of his haiku are on page 204.

Another approach to syllabics is to have the same number of syllables in each line. This may not be noticed on first reading, but it gives a subtle sense of structure to the poem.

The most interesting and complex form of syllabics is possible in poems of two or more **stanzas**. The first stanza serves as a pattern for those that follow. Suppose, for example, your first stanza consists of five lines with the following lengths:

> First line: six syllables
> Second line: twelve syllables
> Third line: twelve syllables
> Fourth line: six syllables
> Fifth line: three syllables

This, then, would become the pattern in each of the following stanzas. Since poems written in syllabics aren't rhymed or metered, varied line length can serve as an effective method of creating rhythm.

Keep in mind, however, that the mechanical structure of a poem in syllabics is just that, mechanics, until you link it to the content. In the previous pattern, for example, the relatively short first line might introduce the subject, the longer lines develop it, and the final very short line provides a dramatic summary.

FROM SYLLABICS TO METER

Syllabic poetry has been particularly popular in France, partly because the French language makes less use of stress. In English, for example, we pronounce *animal* with a heavy stress on the first syllable, but the French pronounce *l'animal* with equal weight on each syllable. These natural stresses in English are like a rhythmical system waiting for development. The **alliterative verse** in *Beowulf* and other Old English works of the 12th century and earlier were relatively crude. The next step was to establish identifiable patterns of stressed and unstressed syllables. This became the basis of **meter**.

One of the most helpful introductions to meter is "The Waking" by Theodore Roethke (page 209). Here is the first stanza in which he introduces the notion of entering into life ("I wake") while being aware that he will eventually die ("sleep").

> I wake to sleep and take my waking slow.
> I feel my fate in what I cannot fear.
> I learn by going where I have to go.

Now read the three lines placing exaggerated emphasis on the stressed syllables and whispering those that are not. The first line comes out like this:

> I *WAKE* to *SLEEP* and *TAKE* my *WAK*ing *SLOW*

Notice that we are dealing with syllables here, so "waking" becomes a stressed and unstressed unit. To get the feel of it, write out the next two lines underlining the stressed syllables. The pattern is a perfectly regular series that we can describe as ta-*TUM*, ta-*TUM*, ta-*TUM*. Now with a little revision work (and apologies to Roethke), we can reverse that pattern so that it sounds like *TUM*-ta, *TUM*-ta, *TUM*-ta:

> Waking, sleeping: take it slowly
> (*WAK*ing, *SLEEP*ing: *TAKE* it *SLOW*ly)

If you do the same with the next two lines, you won't have to take my word for it that the mechanical conversion is relatively easy, even if it does do damage to Roethke's original version. What we have done is to start each line with a stressed syllable, making sure that the rest of the line follows the same pattern. All of this, by the way, is something poets can do and prose writers cannot because of the fact that the poet controls the length of the line.

Since it gets cumbersome and a bit silly to talk about how ta-*TUM* differs from *TUM*-ta, it's worth a few moments to learn some standard terminology. I will include here only those terms that are essential for discussing metered poetry. If you don't start using these terms accurately, your discussions will tend to become vague and unhelpful.

First, units of stressed and unstressed syllables are called *feet*. The **foot** we have been describing as "ta-*TUM*" is an **iamb**. The iambic foot is by far the most common in English. One reason for the popularity of the iambic foot is that so many two-syllable words fall naturally into this pattern: ex*cept*, al*low*, dis*rupt*, a*dore*, and the like. In addition, there is a natural tendency for sentences to begin with an unstressed syllable such as *a, the, but, he, she, I*.

There are three other types of feet that are also used as the basis for metered poems, and two that serve as useful **substitutions**, a technique I'll explain shortly.

The **trochee (trochaic foot)** is the reverse pattern we described as *TUM*-ta in the line "*WAK*ing, *SLEEP*ing: *TAKE* it *SLOW*ly." Although trochees can be used as the basic foot for an entire poem, they are more often used as substitutions for an iambic foot in an iambic poem. As we will see, this shift can give a special emphasis to a word or phrase, particularly if it is placed at the beginning of a line. There is a vivid example in Clement Long's poem, "Always the One Who Loves His Father Most" (page 205). The poem is written primarily with iambs, but the title and the identical first and concluding lines all begin with a trochee, "*Al*ways." The effect is like underlining that word.

The **anapest (anapestic foot)**, consists of three syllables — two unstressed followed by one stressed: ta-ta-*TUM*. We see it in words like *interdict* and *re-imburse*, but it is far more common with phrases like *in the air* and *on the deck*. If I take the liberty to do one more revision of the first line of Theodore Roethke's poem in anapests, it might come out like this:

> In a lurch | I awake | but I learn | to relax

This foot tends to create a lively, cheerful beat, as in this anonymous couplet:

> With a swoop | and a glide | the swift | in delight,
>
> Arous|es our en|vy, our long|ing for flight.

Each line here has three anapests and one iamb. Notice how naturally the two iambic substitutions blend in and mute what might have been a singsong effect. Conversely, anapests serve well as substitutions in poems that are basically iambic. The anapest is not used as the basic meter in many poems, but it has real potential for work that is light and **lyrical**.

The **dactyl** is the reverse of the anapest: *TUM*-ta-ta as in "*HEAV*ier," "*FOL*lowing," and "*TALK* to me." It's a weighty foot.

Most metered poems in English use one of these four feet as a basic pattern, and of these more than half are iambic. There are, however, two more feet that are useful when you **scan** a poem — that is, analyze it metrically. You will find yourself also using these two feet as substitutions. The **spondee** consists of two heavy stresses, as in the word "spondee" itself and "heartbreak." The **pyrrhic** is two equally unstressed syllables, as in "in the" or "and the."

The following table will help introduce you to these terms, but if you start using them in discussions you won't need the table for long.

FOOT	ADJECTIVE	STRESS PATTERN	EXAMPLES
iamb	iambic	ta-TUM	except; the deer
trochee	trochaic	TUM-ta	asking; lost it
anapest	anapestic	ta-ta-TUM	understand; in delight
dactyl	dactylic	TUM-ta-ta	heavily; talk to me
spondee	spondaic	TUM-TUM	heartbreak; campsite
pyrrhic	pyrrhic	ta-ta	in the; on a

THE IMPORTANCE OF LINE LENGTH

In most metered poetry, both the basic type of foot and the number of feet in each line are constant throughout the poem. That is, the pattern you see in the first line is the pattern you get in the poem as a whole. This is not a matter of rules, but shifting the meter would be like writing a song that starts out as a waltz and then switches abruptly to a polka.

One of the most popular lengths in English is five feet. This is called **pentameter**, a word that comes from the Greek *penta* for "five" as in *pentagon*. It has been a favorite metrical scheme in English for 400 years. You can see it in Shakespeare's "Sonnet 29" (page 203) and also in several contemporary examples such as "The Waking" by Theodore Roethke (page 209), "Design" by Robert Frost (page 200), and "The Pardon" by Richard Wilbur (page 215). The Roethke poem is the best introduction because it is unusually regular.

The four-footed line, **tetrameter**, is a close second in popularity. **Trimeter**, three feet to a line, is slightly less common, but it is also used widely. Lines that are longer than pentameter and shorter than trimeter are used far less frequently, but for the purpose of clarity, here is a list.

Two feet to each line (rare and usually comic)	*dimeter*
Three feet to each line (fairly common)	*trimeter*
Four feet (sometimes combined with trimeter)	*tetrameter*
Five feet (most common in English)	*pentameter*
Six feet (less used in this century)	*hexameter*
Seven feet (rare)	*heptameter*
Eight feet (a heavy, very rare line)	*octometer*

most common (tetrameter, pentameter, hexameter)

If these terms are new to you, they may seem intimidating at first. But you will find them helpful both when reading metered verse and when composing your own work. The more you use these terms, the quicker they will become part of your active vocabulary.

At this point, it would be helpful to try writing three lines of iambic tetrameter. Take some simple topic, as if you were about to write a haiku, and follow the iambic pattern: ta-*TUM*, ta-*TUM*, and so on. Don't worry about rhyme, and don't feel you have to be profound. This exercise is just to help you feel the rhythm — and to assure you that it is easier than you might think.

Now try shifting your lines so that they are trochaic: *TUM*-ta, *TUM*-ta, and so on. Avoid articles such as *a* and *the* at the beginning of the line since they are unstressed. Once you find a solid first syllable, the rest of the line should follow more easily.

Next, shift the topic to something lighter and try a few lines of anapests: ta-ta-*TUM*. For example, "In a leap and a bound, the gazelle in delight welcomes spring!"

KEEPING METER SUBTLE

Until now, we have been working with **scansion** — the analysis of meter. It is to metrical poetry what grammar is to prose. It is quite true that you probably learned to write prose without knowing much grammar simply by hearing and reading prose sentences most of your life. It is also true that you could write iambic pentameter simply by ear if you had started reading and listening to poetry every day from the time you were three. But you didn't. In some ways, discovering poetry seriously at this late stage is like taking up a new language. But mercifully the transition between learning the mechanics and developing the art is far more rapid.

When you first begin writing metered lines, it is natural to make it as perfect and obvious as possible. You are like a beginning ballroom dancer who still counts out each step. Once you feel at home with the mechanics, try to mute your meter just as you did with rhyme. This doesn't mean being careless; it means studying and adopting the methods of poets you admire.

There are five useful ways of keeping your metrical rhythm from taking over a poem, and often you will find it helpful to use several of them in a single work:

1. One of the most commonly used methods is to make sure that at least some of your words bridge two metrical feet. It is such a simple technique that you may not have noticed it in the poems you have read. Here is a line refashioned from the last stanza of Wilbur's "The Pardon" (page 215). I have rewritten it so that every foot is comprised of two one-syllable words:

But if | my dream | was false | or true

Here, in contrast, is the line as Wilbur wrote it. Notice that three out of the four feet bridge two words and there is an extra unstressed syllable at the end, a fairly common practice:

But wheth | er this | was false | or hon | est dream | ing

There is nothing technically wrong with the first version, but the second avoids the regularity and monotony of a too-blatant metrical line.

2. An equally common method of softening the wooden effect of unvaried meter is called **substitution**. It simply means occasionally substituting a different foot from the one that has been adopted for the poem as a whole.

We have already looked at Richard Wilbur's "The Pardon" (page 215) for examples of how to mute the sound of rhyme. The poem also serves to illustrate how to keep iambic pentameter from becoming monotonous. Here, for instance, is how he uses a trochaic substitution with the phrase "twined with":

To sniff | the heav | ly hon | eysuck | le-smell |
Twined wi th | anoth | er o | dour heav | ier still |

The substitution not only offers variation, but it also emphasizes the metaphor that links the way smells mix and the way vines twist about each other. The substitution, then, is neither arbitrary nor careless. It adds to the emotional impact of the line.

Later in the poem, there is a line that has two substitutions, an anapest and a trochee. I have left it unmarked so that you can **scan** it yourself.

In the carnal sun, clothed in a hymn of flies.

As I have already pointed out, you can give special emphasis to the initial word in a line that is essentially iambic by beginning the line with a trochaic substitution. In "Sonnet 29" (page 203), Shakespeare not only does this, but

he also signals the dramatic shift from his dark mood in the first nine lines
(". . . my self almost despising") to his elation when thinking of his love:

> Haply I think on thee, and then my state,
> Like to the lark at break of day arising

Robley Wilson in "On a Maine Beach" (page 208) also uses iambic pentameter,
but the first four lines start with trochees. It's as if he is grabbing your arm
and saying, "Hey, look at this!"

How many substitutions can a poem absorb and still be called metered?
When *most* of the lines can be scanned as using one type of foot, we call the
poem metered. Even when substitutions are used in almost every line, as in
the Wilson poem, we retain the memory of that iambic beat and assume that
the poem will return to it — as indeed this poem does.

The process is much like listening to a work of jazz in which there are
extensive improvisations. If we are familiar with the original melody, we
retain the memory of it.

With poetry, however, there comes a point when the variations are so
extensive that we can no longer hear the original pattern. In such cases, we
must conclude that the work is unmetered, regardless of what the poet
claims. Effective use of meter, after all, depends on the ear of the informed
reader, not simply on the intention of the poet.

3. A third method of muting meter is **enjambment**, also known as the **run-
on line**. An enjambed line, you remember, is one in which both the grammatical construction and the sense are continued into the next line. It is
opposed to the **end-stopped line**, which is followed by a natural pause —
usually concluded with a period, semicolon, or at least a comma. As I pointed
out in Chapter 29, it is an effective way of softening the impact of rhyme; it
also serves to keep your meter from sounding like a marching band.

Poems vary as to how frequently they use enjambment. Theodore
Roethke's "The Waking" (page 209), for example, is unusual in that only one
line in 19 is truly enjambed. All the rest come to a full stop or, in one case, a
pause with a comma. In Richard Wilbur's "The Pardon" (page 213), however,
all but five lines out of 24 are enjambed, giving the poem a conversational tone.

4. Another way to mute the sound of meter is to avoid a rhyme scheme.
Because a regular rhyme scheme draws attention to the ends of lines, breaking
it up or avoiding it altogether softens the rhythm.

Wilson's "On a Maine Beach" does the former. It contain five pairs of
rhymed words, but they are scattered. The poem doesn't have a regular
rhyme *scheme.*

Some metered poems contain no rhymed endings at all. Unrhymed
iambic pentameter is called **blank verse**. Shakespeare used it frequently, and
so have many contemporary poets.

5. Finally, meter is occasionally muted by altering line length. **Ballads**, for example, often (but not always) alternate iambic tetrameter (lines of four feet) with iambic trimeter. Because ballads are by definition **narrative** poems, they tend to be lengthy, so the reader gets used to the alternating lines.

"Lizards and Snakes" by Anthony Hecht (page 212) is shorter than most ballads, but it does use a variation of ballad meter by alternating iambic pentameter lines with iambic tetrameter.

With shorter poems, there is a risk. Unless the varied line length is visually fairly clear in the first stanza, readers may miss the pattern of line lengths altogether. This can be done by indenting alternate lines.

Stephen Dunn's "Regardless" (page 220) is a somewhat different example of regularly varying line length. It is a loosely metered ballad that develops its own unique pattern of variations. Like Wilson's "On a Maine Beach," there are so many substitutions that one might almost classify it as unmetered. But unlike the Wilson poem, it is written in **stanzas** that are consistently three lines long except for the concluding one. Generally speaking, the first and third lines of each stanza are pentameter and the middle line is trimeter. This pattern is far from consistent, but it visually apparent when you first see the poem on the page. As a result, the meter is so muted that only a close reader will see it.

Keep these five approaches in mind whenever you write metered verse. They will help you maintain a metrical rhythm that is not obtrusive. Only you can tell how pronounced to make your meter and how to mute it, but the more poetry you read the more unconscious those decisions will become.

Review the metered work of such poets as Robert Frost, Theodore Roethke, Richard Wilbur, Anthony Hecht, and Maxine Kumin, all of whom are represented in Chapter 26. If you are drawn to one or two of these poets, take the time to find their collected work in your library. The difference between knowing the mechanics of meter and being able to incorporate it subtly in your own work will depend on how much metered poetry you have read.

31 Stanzas

A Choice of Fixed Forms

In some ways, the stanza is similar to the paragraph in prose. Like the paragraph, the stanza is visually clear on the page, set off with a space before and after. The stanza can also be used to unify a particular thought or feeling.

In **syllabic** and **metered** poetry, however, the stanza serves an additional function not possible in prose. It takes on greater prominence by having a consistent number of lines — usually from two to eight. And if there is a rhyme scheme, the pattern is repeated within this unit. For this reason, a stanza of metered poetry is called a **fixed form**, but it comes in a great variety of sizes and shapes.

In rhyming couplets, for example, each stanza consists of two lines, but the lines can be uniformally long or short. Four-line stanzas give more options in rhyme schemes. The longer the stanza, the greater the variety in the pattern of rhymed and unrhymed lines. In this chapter, we will examine the most popular stanza types and four verse forms that are based on an arrangement of stanzas.

RHYMING COUPLETS: USES AND RISKS

The great asset of rhyming couplets such as we examined in Maxine Kumin's "Morning Swim" (211) is that each pair of lines becomes a tight little unit linked by sound and often by content as well. In the 17th and 18th centuries, poets such as Alexander Pope (1688–1744) and Oliver Goldsmith (1728–1774) used them to deal with subjects we would now handle in prose as essays.

At that time, the couplets were often **end-stopped** (concluded with a comma or a period). Occasionally, they were complete on their own, a two-line poem expressing a pithy saying known as an **epigram**. For example, in warning how a nation can bring on social disaster, Goldsmith wrote:

> Ill fares the land, to hastening ills a prey,
> Where wealth accumulates, and men decay.

The great liability of rhyming couplets, as I pointed out earlier, is monotony. In unskilled hands, the rhythm can become boring and the rhyme obtrusive. As a result, the couplet has fallen on hard times, often reduced to jingles, greeting cards, and **occasional verse**. Even if you are working with a serious, sophisticated topic, your efforts may seem trivial by association with these simple types of verse.

If you are sensitive to these risks, however, the form can lend itself to highly sophisticated contemporary verse. It is particularly effective with **narrative poems** — those that tell a story.

TRIPLETS, RHYMING AND NOT

Triplets (also called **tercets**) provide more variations in rhyme than do couplets. Although rhyming all three lines (described as *aaa*) can become demanding, it's easy to avoid this by keeping the second line unrhymed, *aba, cdc*.

The **terza rima** is a beautiful extension of the triplet and lends itself best to longer poems. The middle line of each triplet is made to rhyme with the first and last lines of the next triplet in this manner:

First stanza	a (b)	a
Second stanza	(b) (c)	b
Third stanza	(c) (d)	c
Fourth stanza	(d) e	d

In this way, each stanza is subtly linked with the next, but the sound linkages blend into the fabric of the poem.

QUATRAINS AND THE BALLAD TRADITION

The four-line stanza, or **quatrain**, is probably the most popular of all **fixed verse forms**. One advantage is that it allows for such a variety of possible rhyme schemes. High on the list is *abab*, unobtrusive yet never fully lost.

A variation of this rhymes the two central lines: *abba*. Richard Wilbur's "The Pardon" (page 213) is a good example, though you will notice that he uses **slant rhymes** in almost every stanza.

Less noticeable (and also less demanding) is *abcb*, which leaves the first and third lines unrhymed.

Perhaps because quatrains are ideal for memorization, the four-line stanza has become the traditional form for **ballads**. The term includes works that are intended to be sung, recited, or read, but what they all have in common is a lively story line and in most cases a four-line stanza.

Ballad meter is one of the few stanza forms in which the lines alternate in length regularly — usually between iambic tetrameter and iambic trimeter. Normally the rhyme scheme is *abcb*. The term *folk ballad* refers most often to those thousands of Scottish and English works in ballad meter that were composed and sung by untrained, often illiterate balladeers from the 14th to the 16th centuries.

The tradition of relatively simple narrative poems dealing with love (often lost or betrayed like our contemporary blues lyrics), war (often laments), and the supernatural is alive today in the form of popular folk songs. In fact, the word *ballad* is still applied equally to poetry and song.

Literary ballads are merely a refinement of this same tradition. "The Rime of the Ancient Mariner," by Samuel Taylor Coleridge, is one of the best known. Although he allowed himself occasional variations in traditional ballad meter, here is a dramatic stanza that contains only one rather inconspicuous substitution:

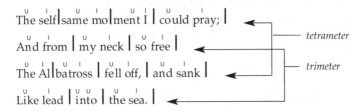

Anthony Hecht's "Lizards and Snakes" (page 212) adapts the ballad form to tell a story that is more complex than it appears on first reading. His stanzas look as if they are eight lines long, but if you draw a line after each fourth line and look at the rhyme scheme, you will see that it is really composed in quatrains like most ballads. He has increased the traditional line length by alternating iambic pentameter with iambic tetrameter. The tetrameter lines are indented. His rhyme scheme is *abab* throughout.

Hecht's variations on the basic ballad form show that there is nothing sacred about literary tradition. But notice that once he establishes his version of the ballad, he stays with it. A poem that begins with a traditional form and then deteriorates toward the end suggests that perhaps the poet was working late at night to meet an early morning deadline.

RHYME ROYAL

If you want to use couplets but fear that they may become monotonous in spite of your best efforts, consider the solution introduced into English by Chaucer. The **rhyme royal** is a seven line stanza in **iambic pentameter** with the following rhyme scheme: ababbcc.

The first three lines are linked with what is essentially a rhyming triplet, aba. Then there are what resemble two rhyming couplets. Don't forget that the first of those two couplets rhymes with the second line of the poem. Schematically, it looks like this:

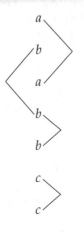

Whether you stop at seven lines or go on repeating the seven-line pattern is up to you. In an age of constant change, it's reassuring to know that something more than 600 years old is as fresh and adaptable today as it was for Chaucer.

SONNETS, ENGLISH AND ITALIAN

Although the ballad lends itself to storytelling, the **sonnet's** precise length is best suited for a single, well-defined theme or set of feelings. Occasionally, sonnets are strung together as a sonnet series, such as *The Golden Gate* by Vikram Seth, but these are rare.

There are two basic types of sonnets, the *English* (also called **Elizabethan**) and the *Italian* (also called **Petrarchan**). They are both 14 lines long, and both are traditionally written in iambic pentameter — five feet to the line. The primary difference between the two is the rhyme scheme.

The English sonnet, made famous by Shakespeare, can be thought of as three quatrains and a final rhyming couplet: *abab, cdcd, efef, gg*. The first eight lines are referred to as the **octave** and the last six as the **sestet**. Often there is a shift in mood or concern at the beginning of the sestet, providing a dramatic contrast. The final rhyming couplet is frequently used to summarize or bring these two contrasting elements into harmony.

Once you read a number of sonnets, you can identify the form in advance just from the basic 14-line shape. Occasionally, English sonnets are printed as an unbroken block, but more often there is a space between the octave and the sestet. This concluding rhyming couplet is another distinguishing characteristic of the English sonnet.

The second basic type, the Italian sonnet, is also based on 14 lines of iambic pentameter, but it is usually arranged as two quatrains and two triplets: *abba, abba, cde, cde.* You can differentiate it from the Elizabethan sonnet immediately by the fact that it has no concluding couplet.

Sonnets are printed in various ways, but here is a schematic representation of the spacing and rhyme scheme often adopted:

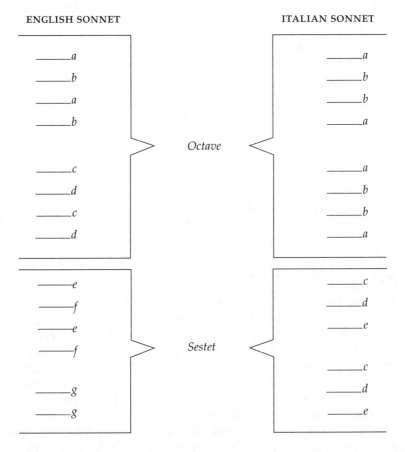

Diagrams are of little use unless applied to specific poems. To benefit from this one, keep one hand on this page and turn back to Shakespeare's "Sonnet 29"

on page 203. If the book is your own copy, you will find it helpful to draw a line between the octave and the sestet and then pencil in the rhyme scheme, *abab* and so forth. Notice that the sestet begins with "Yet in these thoughts" — just a hint of the change in mood. The real shift comes in the next line with the trochaic "Haply."

Now do the same with Robert Frost's sonnet "Design" on page 200. It follows the Italian form faithfully, with one exception: the poem ends with a rhyming couplet as if it were an English sonnet.

THE RONDEAU

There are many poetic forms that British and American poets have adapted from French and Italian models, but I would recommend the **rondeau** for those who are discovering new verse forms. It is relatively brief — usually just one line longer than the sonnet — and it is written in syllabics — with the same number of syllables in each line. It is also a good introduction to the use of a **refrain**.

The most common pattern has three stanzas: a **cinquain** (five lines), a **quatrain** (four lines), and usually a concluding **sestet** (six lines). (Only an engineer would ask why.) There is a **refrain** that appears as the opening of the first line and is repeated at the end of the second and third stanza.

If we designate the refrain as *R*, the rhyme scheme looks like this:

First stanza: *aabba*   (with the refrain opening the first line)
Second stanza: *aabR*   (the refrain as last line)
Third stanza *aabbaR*   (the refrain as last line)

Now turn to James Bertram's tribute to Ernest Hemingway in "Is It Well-Lighted, Papa?" on page 208. Most of his lines have 10 syllables except for the two refrain lines, which have seven. Another fairly common variation is that his third stanza has four rather than five lines. As a result, the poem has 14 lines like a sonnet.

When you try this form, carefully consider your refrain. In Bertram's poem, "Papa" is the nickname for Ernest Hemingway, and the refrain echoes the title of one of Hemingway's better known stories, "A Clean, Well-Lighted Place." Whatever refrain you select should highlight the theme without being too bluntly analytical.

THE PANTOUM

The appeal of the **pantoum** (pronounced panTOOM) is the way in which the stanzas interlock with repeated lines. Originally a Malayan form, it was adopted by both the French and the English. Written in quatrains, the form leaves the choice of meter and total length up to you. The traditional rhyme is *abab*, *bcbc*, *cdcd*. The unique aspect is the way the stanzas interlock through repetition: lines 2 and 4 of each stanza become lines 1 and 3 of the next.

The last stanza of the poem can take one of two patterns: either a couplet comprised of lines 1 and 3 in reverse order (as in the following example) or a concluding quatrain using lines 1 and 3 of the first stanza as lines 4 and 2, respectively. Notice that both approaches reverse the repeated lines in the concluding stanza, ingeniously making the first line of the poem the same as the last.

You have already studied (I hope) "Always the One Who Loves His Father Most" by Clement Long, which appears in its entirety in Chapter 26 on page 205. Here is an annotated version of the first two stanzas and the last stanza:

Always the one who loves his father most,	*a*
the one the father loves the most in turn	*b*
will fight against his father as he must	*a*
Neither knows what he will come to learn.	*b*
The one the father loves the most in turn	*b*
tells the father no and no and no.	*c*
but neither knows what he will come to learn	*b*
nor cares a lot what that could be and so	*c*
....	
will fight against his father, as he must,	*a*
always, the one who loves his father most.	*a*

After studying the pattern here, go back and reread the poem in its entirety on page 205. Notice that this particular pantoum uses unusually regular iambic pentameter and maintains the rhyme scheme with only a few slant rhymes, such as "most" and "must."

As with many verse forms, the mechanics may seem like the main challenge at first. But this stage will soon pass. The next step is to find a topic that lends itself to that particular form. In this particular pantoum, for example, the theme focuses on the changing relationship between fathers and sons that is repeated generation after generation. The repetition of lines in the pantoum lends itself perfectly to the generational cycles the poem is describing.

THE VILLANELLE

The **villanelle** may seem intimidating at first, but if you have tried writing a rondeau or a pantoum, you will find some of the same characteristics — the use of the refrain, in particular. Once you flesh out the mechanical description with the following example, the form will become quite manageable. Far less complex than the rules of chess, a good villanelle can become musical like a melody intensified with repeated phrases.

Before we examine the mechanics of the villanelle, read once again Theodore Roethke's "The Waking" on page 209. We used this poem in earlier chapters to illustrate aspects of meter and rhyme, but you may not have noticed that it is also a villanelle.

In reviewing the poem, note these three aspects: (1) It is comprised of six stanzas, of which the first five are tercets (three lines) and the last is a quatrain (four lines). (2) There are only two rhymes, *a* and *b*. (3) There are two refrains that recur in a regular sequence. Although Roethke has chosen to use unusually regular iambic pentameter lines, other meters are acceptable. Originally, villanelles were written in syllabic lines of equal length.

The following table shows the skeletal form. Don't try to memorize it. Instead, use it as you did with the diagrams of the sonnet and the rondeau. Keep your hand on this page for a guide and see how it is implemented in Roethke's poem. Again, you will understand the pattern best if you mark up the copy of the poem itself — either in your text or on a photocopy.

THE VILLANELLE

(1)	1.	First refrain	*a*
	2.	_____	*b*
	3.	Second refrain	*a*
(2)	4.	_____	*a*
	5.	_____	*b*
	6.	First refrain	*a*
(3)	7.	_____	*a*
	8.	_____	*b*
	9.	Second refrain	*a*
(4)	10.	_____	*a*
	11.	_____	*b*
	12.	First refrain	*a*
(5)	13.	_____	*a*
	14.	_____	*b*
	15.	Second refrain	*a*
(6)	16.	_____	*a*
	17.	_____	*b*
	18.	First refrain	*a*
	19.	Second refrain	*a*

The two refrains of a villanelle are particularly important. Because they are repeated so often, they should be central to the theme. But they should also be used in slightly different ways to avoid repetition.

Roethke's first refrain begins with "I wake to sleep." This is a **paradox** — a statement that on one level is logically absurd, yet on another implies a deeper meaning. In this case, he is describing the fact that we are born only to die eventually. This would be depressing if it weren't for the rest of the refrain, "and take my waking slow." He will make the most of his life.

The second refrain amplifies this with the assertion that he learns "by going where I have to go." He gains experience by doing what must be done.

As for varying the way he uses these refrains, notice how the first four stanzas are simply a statement of belief, but in the fifth stanza the same refrain becomes advice to someone else: "And, lovely, learn by going where to go." Whether he is addressing his love or you the reader is your choice. In either case, the refrain shifts from being an assertion of belief to advice.

If you look carefully at the whole poem, you will notice that Roethke takes certain minor liberties with the form. Some of the rhymes, for example, are slant rhymes, and the one refrain is subtly altered — though without giving up the pentameter. But he is essentially faithful to the form, and if you enjoy this kind of challenge you may want to match his fidelity.

THE APPEAL OF METERED VERSE

Metered verse and its various stanza forms dominated British and American poetry for some 500 years. Although **free verse** (the subject of Chapter 32) rose to ascendancy in the early 1900s, poets such as Robert Frost, Theodore Roethke, and Richard Wilbur continued to work with metrical forms. Since the 1980s, there has been an increased interest in metrics known as the **new formalism**. Although not truly a movement, it has generated fresh and innovative uses of meter.

When one is first introduced to metrical schemes and various stanza forms, they may seem mechanical and limiting. There are new terms to master, just as there are when one begins a new language. But poets who prefer to work metrically don't usually begin by selecting a meter as if it were a mold into which one could pour words. Instead, they are more likely to let a poem begin intuitively and see what kind of line develops. If you have been reading metered poetry, your initial lines may suggest a metrical pattern that seems natural and appropriate for your material.

Once you get beyond the introductory stage in metrics, terms such as iambic pentameter and trochaic trimeter become part of you, a dance step that no longer has to be counted out, a rhythm with infinite varieties. The metrical beat is internal, and the pleasure of writing comes in the interplay between that pattern and your improvisation.

Returning to the parallel with jazz, you will find yourself like a trumpet player alternately straying from the melody and returning to it. Stray too far and too often, and the memory of the melody is lost; stick too close, and you run the risk of monotony. Those who enjoy working with metrical forms find that it adds one more dimension to the genre.

There are two other rewards from writing in meter that its proponents often mention. One is that meeting the requirements of a particular form often encourages them to consider words and phrases that wouldn't have come to mind otherwise. The other is that metrics allows the poet to emphasize a word or phrase by substituting a different foot. We have seen how using the heavy initial beat of a trochaic foot in a basically iambic poem can add emphasis, and how the lilting quality of an anapest can give a lift to a line that is otherwise consistently iambic or trochaic. This provides a delicate control of language.

For others, however, verse forms still seem too restrictive. They would rather devise unique rhythms for each poem in ways we will consider in Chapter 32. But keep in mind that there is no sharp division between the two approaches. Traditional fixed forms can be altered to fit the needs of a particular poem, and even the most intuitive free-verse poem may benefit from techniques we associate with metered verse. The more poetry you read, the more options you will discover.

32 Free Verse

Creating Unique Forms

> • *Free verse: What it rejects and what it retains (280)* • *Freedom from fixed forms: Assets and liabilities (281)* • *Visual patterns: What you see on the page (281)* • *Auditory patterns: what you hear in the reading (285)* • *The poetic line versus the sentence (287)* • *The unmarked border with prose (288)* • *Developing your own rhythms (289)*

As the phrase implies, **free verse** rejects a number of poetic **conventions**. It doesn't use meter or a regular rhyme scheme. There are no limits to line length. When stanzas are used, they tend to be irregular in length. The arrangement of words, phrases, and lines on the page do not conform to any traditional pattern. The pattern is original to that particular poem.

So what's left? Plenty. When you write free verse, you still maintain control of the line just as you do in metered work. This gives you many techniques not shared by writers of prose and even some not shared by writers of metered verse.

Stanzas, for example, can be varied in length or uniform, conspicuous or barely noticeable. As for the sound of language, the writer of free verse may choose either to ignore it or emphasize it through a variety of devices such as **alliteration, assonance, consonance**, repetition, and even scattered rhymes. Most important, free verse has many different ways of creating rhythmic effects.

It would be a mistake, however, to think of free verse as an entirely separate approach. The division between metered and what has come to be called free verse is far from precise. Each nurtures the other. The difference is essentially that metered poetry requires the fresh and ingenious use of fixed forms, whereas free verse, although equally dependent on originality and ingenuity, creates rhythms and auditory patterns that are tailor-made for a particular poem.

The term *free verse* came into vogue around 1900, but it was hardly a radical departure even then. Unmetered poetry without a regular rhyme scheme has had a long and distinguished history. It is rooted in a variety of ancient sources, both written and oral. Examples of what we now call free verse can be found as far back as the Song of Songs, one of the books of the Bible.

FREEDOM FROM FIXED FORMS: ASSETS AND LIABILITIES

When working with free verse, you are at liberty to devise your own visual and auditory patterns — line length, spacing, and linkages in sound. Since there are no regular forms to serve as guidelines, early drafts of new work may be highly intuitive. If you have been working with meter, it may seem as if anything is possible — a heady sensation.

However, you're on your own. It's up to you to create your own rhythms and auditory effects. If you don't pay attention to these aspects, you'll end up writing prose in short lines. Some find that without traditional forms as a base, it is more difficult to determine what is effective and what doesn't work. It's hard to be sure when the poem has reached its full potential.

Although free-verse techniques are not as distinct as those of metered poetry, they can be divided into two closely related categories. The first is **typography**, the arrangement of print on the page. This includes line length, indentations, and extra spaces between words. It also includes the grouping of lines into **stanzas**, usually but not always of varied length.

The other aspect is *auditory*, what you hear when the poem is read. All poetry, of course, appeals to the ear, but free verse relies on somewhat different techniques. Alliteration and assonance, for example, are used far more often than rhyme. And repetition of words and phrases is frequently used to create rhythm and influence the pace of reading.

It's useful to examine these two aspects separately for analysis, but keep in mind that they are closely interrelated. Now that poetry is almost always presented in printed form, the arrangement on the page influences the way we read a poem aloud. We respond to these visual cues both consciously and unconsciously. Conversely, what you as a poet want the poem to sound like when it is presented out loud will affect how you arrange the work on the page. Just as playwrights imagine how their lines will be delivered in a production, poets "hear" a poem as they write.

VISUAL PATTERNS: WHAT YOU SEE ON THE PAGE

Typography, what you see on the page, is especially important in free verse. The length of lines and their indentation are no longer simply cues indicating what fixed form is being used; instead, they can influence the **tone**, the emotional quality of the work, and even the meaning.

Some poets spread their lines out with many different indentations, even leaving extra spaces within the line. Other poets mold their free verse into fairly uniform units that look a lot like metered stanzas. The choice depends partly on the poet's general style and partly on the demands of the individual poem.

Here, for example, is the opening stanza of Thomas McGrath's "Nuclear Winter." The entire poem appears on page 223, but this portion is enough to remind you how he uses a loose typography to highlight certain words and establish a particular mood:

After the first terror
                    people
Were more helpful to each other — As in a blizzard
Much comradeliness, help, even
                              laughter:
The pride of getting through tough times.

As you remember, this is a poem in which the first two of three irregular stanzas are deceptively positive. In the stanza quoted here, the focus is on "people" and "laughter." In the stanza that follows, he indents "our," presumably to stress that same feeling of community. It is not until the final line of the third and final stanza that he hits us with the brutally harsh conclusion.

The lines in this poem are not only irregular; they often end abruptly either with no punctuation where we might expect a comma or with a dash, a colon, or an ellipsis. The three stanzas are so different in length that we hardly notice them. This gives the work a ragged, jerky effect. Why? To prepare us for that brutal conclusion when

    . . . we came to our senses
    And began to kill each other.

This poem is like a 20-line condensation of a doomsday film. The typography is used as a forewarning of the horror to come just as ominous background music often is in films.

Now compare that with Philip Appleman's "Desire" (page 219). To refresh your memory once again, here are the first two of four stanzas:

1

The body
tugged like a tide, a pull
stronger than
the attraction of stars.

2

Moons
circling their planets,
planets
rounding their suns.

Appleman's lines are all relatively short. None are broken or irregular. None contain words flung out to the right margin. As for the stanzas, each has four lines except the last with three. Each stanza is neatly concluded with a period. Numbering them adds even more emphasis. At first glance, one might assume that the poem is metered. The lines do not scan, but in spite of that, the total effect is harmonious and orderly.

The typography of this poem — both the lines and the stanzas — contributes to the poem's central purpose, to turn the abstract concept, desire, into concrete images we can respond to emotionally. Each stanza focuses on a different image, and each image is used as a metaphor.

This regularity of the typography is similar to that of "The Bay at West Falmouth" by Barbara Howes (page 207). Although it does not scan regularly, there are three four-line stanzas that make it resemble quatrains of metered verse. This visual regularity helps emphasize the theme of serenity, a word that is repeated in each stanza.

The scattered typography of McGrath's "Nuclear Winter" can lure less experienced poets into certain pitfalls. Those who are drawn to McGrath's lengthy and fragmented lines should keep in mind that obvious use of typography can be just as obtrusive in a free-verse poem as unvaried use of meter and rhyme can be in traditional work. Because typographical arrangements are so immediately apparent, they have to be used with considerable subtlety. Every writing class has been subjected to some version of this:

> Dark clouds
> 　　　　　brooding
> Cast a spell,
> 　　Chilling the
> 　　　　　　heart
> Omens from the fates:
> 　　　　　　　mortality.

This is too easy, too obvious. The technique is what strikes the reader first. Ideally, typography should enhance the theme and feeling, not take over.

The short-line, short-stanza poem also has its risk. Compression is commendable, but if pushed too far it fades into obscurity. Remember that your work is intended for readers, and you have to give them enough, as Appleman does, to share your feelings.

How do you achieve real freshness and ingenuity in typography? E.E. Cummings' poem "Buffalo Bill's" (page 210) is an example of a highly imaginative and effective use of spacing. Review it now so as to recall the shape of that poem as a whole.

Now take a close look at these three lines:

> and break onetwothreefourfive pigeonsjustlikethat
> 　　　　　　　　　　　　　　　　　　Jesus
> 　　he was a handsome man

Those run-together phrases are a sample of compressed spacing. Cummings actually speeds up your reading with that technique. This may not occur on your first reading, of course, since it takes time to figure out lines that are printed without spaces. But once you are used to the poem, these lines seem to ripple by as if they were moving.

Notice, too, how the word "Jesus" is suspended on the right with space above and below. At first it seems to be an exclamation of admiration about his shooting ability. In prose, it would be followed with an exclamation mark. But as you continue to read, it leaps forward as if tied to "he was a handsome man." Like an optical illusion, it flips back and forth, serving both functions, tricky as Buffalo Bill himself. It would be difficult, if not impossible to match this effect with metered verse.

You may not have noticed that Cummings uses a form of **syllabics** in addition to typography. His run-together phrase "onetwothreefourfive" has exactly the same number of syllables as "pigeonsjustlikethat" — linking the number of his rapid-fire shots and the series of clay pigeons on a skeet range. This is a good example of the fact that when working with the unique rhythms of free verse, you can combine several techniques.

When we analyze poems such as those of McGrath, Appleman, and Cummings, it should become apparent that much of what appeared on first reading to be arbitrary placement is in fact carefully planned to create an effect. But don't expect to find a rational explanation for every typographical element. As with the brush strokes of a painter, many decisions that go into making a poem are intuitive. If it were not for this aspect, typographical rhythms would tend to seem contrived, even forced. This is why it is important to keep working on different versions of the same poem, writing out each and reading them aloud. Trust your ear as much as your mind.

One even more structured form of typography is called **shaped verse**. It molds the shape of the work into the object it is describing. This technique was popular in the 17th century and is well illustrated by Herbert's frequently anthologized "The Altar" and "Easter Wings," as well as by Herrick's "The Pillar of Flame," each of which resembles the object suggested in its title. More recently, contemporaries like Allen Ginsberg have published poems in the shape of atomic clouds and, with the aid of punctuation, rockets.

For unknown reasons, what has for centuries been called *shaped verse* and *pattern poetry* was renamed **concrete poetry** in the early 1960s and hailed as a new technique. It quickly became a fad, often reduced to mere tricks. As a poem begins to rely more and more on its shape, it generally makes less and less use of the sound of language, rhythms, or metaphor. Even the theme becomes simplified. Highly obtrusive visual effects tend to overpower all other aspects. One can, for example, repeat the word *death* all over the page in such a way as to resemble a skull. It takes time and a certain mindless patience to do this, but the result is more like a cartoon than a poem.

If you flip through the poems in Chapter 26 or any standard anthology, you will see that extreme forms of shaped poetry are rare. Used with restraint, however, typography offers a wealth of possibilities.

AUDITORY PATTERNS: WHAT YOU HEAR IN THE READING

Until now, we have been looking at free verse as it appears on the page. Never forget, however, that poetry has its roots in recitation and song. As the printed word became more widely available, oral presentation became less necessary, but the genre still appeals to the ear.

Although free verse does not use regular rhyme schemes, it does occasionally employ scattered internal rhymes. They can be used to add stress or to link related words. More often, free verse employs **alliteration**, the repetition of similar initial sounds. Elizabeth Holden uses it in "As the Cold Deepens" (page 201). Here are the lines in which the speaker describes her aging mother. I have circled the alliterative use of *b* and *h*.

> My mother is almost weightless now
> her flesh shrinks ⓑack toward the ⓑone,
> ⒷBraced in her metal walker
> she ⓗaunts the ⓗalls, prowls
> the margin of ⓗer day . . .

The *b* sounds are in sharp contrast with the sibilance Donald Hall uses in "Names of Horses" (page 216). He is describing the gentle patience of a farm horse with these lines:

> . . . your neck rubbed the window ⓢill
> of the ⓢtall, ⓢmoothing the wood as the ⓢea ⓢmooths glass

An even more noticeable auditory device often associated with free verse is **anaphora** — the repetition of a word or phrase at the beginning of two or more lines or sentences. The effect is often strengthened by using a similar type of sentence, such as a series of questions or pronouncements. This creates what is sometimes called **syntactical rhythms**. It is also frequently employed in speeches and sermons.

Here is a sample of anaphora in poetry combined with syntactical rhythm. It is taken from Walt Whitman's "Passage to India" and refers to that nation then under British control. The anaphoral word is *who* and the syntactical rhythm is created by a series of short questions:

> Ah, who shall soothe these feverish children?
> Who justify these restless explorations?
> Who speak the secret of impassive earth?
> Who bind it to us? what is this separate Nature so
>   unnatural?
> What is this earth to our affections? . . .

In prose, we generally try to avoid redundancies, yet here is a string of them. They seem appropriate in poetry mainly because rhythm is part of the genre and because this particular type of rhythm has long been associated with the oral tradition.

Allen Ginsberg wrote "Howl!" in 1959, 104 years after Whitman first published "Leaves of Grass," and Ginsberg's indebtedness is unmistakable. Here he describes "the best minds of my generation":

> who bared their brains to Heaven under the El
> > and saw Mohammedan angels staggering on
> tenement roofs illuminated,
> who passed through universities with radiant cool
> > eyes hallucinating Arkansas and Blake-light
> tragedy among the scholars of war,
> who were expelled from the academies for
> crazy & publishing obscene odes on the
> windows of the skull,
> > who cowered in unshaven rooms in underwear,
> burning their money in wastebaskets and
> listening to the Terror through the wall, . . .

Ginsberg is clearly influenced by Whitman, but both of them drew on a still earlier source, the Bible. Although the version Whitman knew was in English (the King James translation), and Ginsberg's version was in the original Hebrew, both men were strongly influenced by the rhythmical patterns found there. Compare, for example, the selections quoted previously with this passage from Job 38 : 34–37:

> Canst thou lift up thy voice to the clouds,
> > that abundance of waters may cover thee?
> Canst thou send lightnings, that they may go
> > and say unto thee, Here we are?
> Who hath put wisdom in the inward parts?
> > or who hath given understanding to the heart?
> Who can number the clouds in wisdom?
> > or who can pour out the bottles of heaven?

For full effect, read this passage out loud. Notice that here, like the selections from Whitman and Ginsberg, it is the entire syntactical unit that is repeated to achieve the rhythm. The anaphoral words are cues that signal the repeated form.

If this pattern interests you, you can find many other examples in the Bible. Much of the Book of Job, Genesis, and the Psalms are rich in anaphora and repetitions in sentence structure. Studying these works makes one far more open to the rhythms not only of Whitman and Ginsberg, but also of Lawrence Ferlinghetti, Gregory Corso, John Ashbery, Amiri Baraka, and many other poets writing today.

In the examples we have been considering, anaphora is unmistakable because it is followed by a pronounced similarity of sentence structure. But often it is used alone. Lucille Clifton's poem "What the Mirror Said" (page 203) appears to be light, spontaneous, and conversational. But if you look at it carefully, you will see that in the first half it is structured through three anaphoral words: "listen," "you," and "somebody":

listen,
you a wonder.
you a city
of a woman.
you got a geography
of your own.
listen,
somebody need a map
to understand you.
somebody need directions
to move around you.
listen,
woman,
you not a noplace . . .

This rhythmical use of anaphora is not repeated toward the end of the poem, but Clifton does continue to use the one-word line to create a rhythm as emphatic as thumping one's hand on the table.

All these auditory effects are emphasized in the work of **performance poets**. Sometimes referred to as *standup poets*, they usually present their work orally in public readings. Their verse tends to be highly accessible and entertaining. It appeals to the ear almost as much as singing does.

THE POETIC LINE VERSUS THE SENTENCE

When you read prose, you respond to the punctuation of the sentence even if you can't tell a compound sentence from a compound fracture. You pause at commas, come to a full stop at periods, and take a deep breath at the end of paragraphs.

When you read poetry, you tend to respond the same way to the ends of lines. Sometimes excessively. When schoolchildren recite poetry, they often have to be reminded not to pause at the conclusion of each line. As adults reading to ourselves, we unconsciously pause even when the context suggests that we should keep going.

When you write poetry, you have at your disposal both of these rhythmical devices — sentence structure and line length. Occasionally you will find a poem that emphasizes syntax to the point of ending each line with a period or a comma. Theodore Roethke's villanelle "The Waking" (page 209) is such a poem. Although metered, it is an unusual example of poetry stress-ing sentence structure. Out of 19 lines, all but one are end-stopped, conclud-ing with a period, a comma, or a question mark. The syntactical rhythm — that generated by the sentence structure — matches almost perfectly the line length and, in this case, the meter as well. Such matching, however, is rare — especially in free verse.

In free verse, Philip Appleman's "Desire" (page 219) also stresses the syntax, but as noted previously, the sentences match the stanzas, not the lines. Each of his four stanzas ends with a period. Most poems, however, mute the impact of the sentence by employing enjambment. When a sen-tence runs on into the next line, it is less noticeable.

Some poems avoid all punctuation, relying exclusively on the line for rhythmical effect. This is a technique that lends itself to relatively short poems with short, syntactically simple lines. Haiku, for example, rarely use punctuation.

Nikki Giovanni's "Balances" (page 214) is one of the few longer poems in this volume that uses no punctuation at all. Notice how in these first five lines the lack of punctuation keeps the poem uncluttered. The effect is almost like someone walking step by step along a tightrope.

> in life
> one is always
> balancing
>
> like we juggle our mothers
> against our fathers

The great majority of poems, however, use punctuation along with line length, the two working in subtle harmony or, in some cases, as counterpoint to each other.

THE UNMARKED BORDER WITH PROSE

Between free-verse poetry and prose, there is a misty, unmarked border. There are no signposts and little agreement. Some poets, for example, ignore the deliberate rhythmical systems we have been discussing, preferring in-stead to think in terms of **breath units**. On a literal level, this phrase suggests that a line is broken where the reader of the poem would naturally take a breath when reciting aloud. But different poets seem to have remarkably dif-ferent lung capacities.

In point of fact, lungs have far less to do with poetic composition than does a poet's sense of what is an appropriate rhythm for a particular poem. It was not emphysema that caused Philip Appleman to describe his sense of longing and desire with these concluding lines:

Undertow:
I reach for you,
oceans away.

Nor was it deep-breathing exercises that led Donald Hall to adopt lines like
these in "Names of Horses" (page 216):

For a hundred and fifty years, in the pasture of
    dead horses,
roots of pine trees pushed through the pale curves
    of your ribs,

It seems likely that both poets selected a line length they felt would create
the tone they wanted to achieve.

Somewhere between poetry and prose is a hybrid form called **prose
poetry**. Visually, it resembles a relatively short block of prose writing. Although the poet still controls the length of the lines, few poets vary the length.

The form has its roots in folktales and parables, but most prose poems
published today deal with personal feelings or insights. Such works can be
seen as compressed, highly concentrated samples of **creative nonfiction**.

Many of these works make almost no use of verbal rhythms, sound linkages, and figurative language. In such cases, the primary function of the
form is to assure the reader that the piece should be read deliberately.

In other examples, the work is nudged toward poetry with the use of
imagery and a greater concern for the sound of language. Some draw
heavily on speech rhythms and develop some of the compression we
associate with poetry. Such work might more accurately be described as
poetic prose.

DEVELOPING YOUR OWN RHYTHMS

When you begin composing a new poem, let the first few lines speak to you.
Often they will suggest the kinds of rhythms that are appropriate for that
particular poem. Your emotional involvement with the material, your personal preferences, and the nature of the subject matter will all influence what
develops. And because so many factors are involved, the result will be
unique.

As the poem develops, consider some of the techniques we have examined in this chapter: manipulation of the line on the page, nonrecurrent stanzas, and sound devices like alliteration and anaphora. Although we have
analyzed them separately, they are all interrelated.

Keep in mind that any one of these devices if pushed to an extreme runs
the risk of seeming tricky and obtrusive, dominating the entire poem. Strive to
keep your rhythms subtle. Experiment with a number of different approaches
and trust your feelings.

With this in mind, here is an exercise that will help you explore your free-verse options. First, read the following five passages. Ignore the fact that they are taken from a poem you will read in Chapter 35. In fact, don't even look at the poem yet. Focus on the images in isolation and how they affect you:

1. But this evening as I took the footpath back up the long hill to the house . . .
2. Doubtless, I have as much now as then.
3. I gave in to longing then, and liked it.
4. When I was six or seven . . .
5. . . . that old desire to float to where the clouds turn red.

Now select two out of the five that touched you in some personal way. It may be a specific memory or perhaps only a feeling. Write a short free-verse poem in which you use one of the passages you chose somewhere in the poem. It can appear anywhere, but it must be word for word.

Then write another poem that includes your second choice word for word. See if you can establish a different mood and use different free-verse techniques.

These are just exercises — the type one might include in one's journal. But they will help you probe your own feelings and develop them in the fluid form of free verse.

Another helpful exercise is to take a descriptive prose passage from an article about nature or travel. This time, don't limit yourself to the wording of the original. Find your own language to add freshness and intensity to the passage and then, as previously, devise two different rhythmical approaches.

In addition to exercises like these in your journal, spend some time each day examining the rhythms of published poetry. Because most poetry contains rhythmical patterns of some sort, every anthology and literary quarterly can serve as a source for study. By combining practice work in your journal and extensive, careful reading, you will soon find a way to express your own concerns in increasingly effective free verse.

33 A Sense of Order

Organization is something we associate with factual writing. Making outlines and being logical seems far removed from creative writing. We like to think of poetry as being free as a butterfly. Remember, though, that butterflies can migrate thousands of miles, successfully navigating with hidden techniques in spite of all their twists and turns. The organization of thoughts and feelings in poetry can be just as hidden and just as important.

There is no need to be overly concerned with organization when you begin writing a new poem. It's a good idea to stay flexible in your early drafts, letting the ideas and images take shape freely.

After you have completed one or two drafts, however, stop and take a close, analytical look at what holds your poem together. Why have you placed a particular line before another? Just what kind of organization did you have in mind? If your poem has lost its sense of direction, it will probably lose your reader's rapt attention as well.

There are many different ways of organizing the content of a poem. This chapter will deal with five of the most useful. Obviously, not all of your work will require structure like this. The longer the poem, the greater the need. Examining these frequently used strategies closely will give you the option of adopting one of them or devising a system of your own.

CONTRASTS AND COMPARISONS

Developing contrasts and comparisons is one of the most frequently used method of organizing a poem. In some cases the contrast may be directly stated, but in others it may be so subtle that it remains almost subliminal.

Philip Appleman's "Coast to Coast" (page 210) is a clear and straightforward example. Three of his five stanzas describe the pleasures of driving across the country; the remaining two (opening and closing) stanzas are a lament for what is lost when we fly.

These two alternatives are dramatized with very precise images. For drivers before the construction of the superhighways, there was plenty to see from "graves or gardens" to "the flash of finches and the scud of crows." ("Scud," by the way, is an interesting word choice worth looking up.)

In contrast, jet travel renders us "blind to milkweed, riverbanks . . . ," and in the last stanza "blind again" in an "air-conditioned heaven." Every line in the poem contributes to that contrast.

Because comparisons, as opposed to contrasts, link similar elements, you might think they would have less impact. But often they can be used effectively. Some of the best examples are seen in haiku, which by tradition contain some kind of literal or metaphorical comparison. Because these poems are so short, the comparison often dominates the entire work. Etheridge Knight draws on this tradition in his haiku on page 204, comparing convicts at the end of a workday with lizards in this brief but haunting picture:

> Eastern guard tower
> glints in sunset; convicts rest
> like lizards on rocks.

The comparison is enhanced by the fact that the convicts are being looked down on by guards in the tower just as we humans look down on lizards.

For a longer example of a comparison poem, review Barbara Howes' "The Bay at West Falmouth" (page 207). It starts off, you remember, with a simile in the first two of 12 lines, and this comparison dominates the whole poem. It is a good example of what is called a **controlling image**. Controlling (or dominant) images are usually metaphors, but in this case it is a simile:

> Serenity of mind poises
> Like a gull swinging in air,

Everything in this poem depends on and amplifies the initial comparison between a sense of serenity and a gull poised in flight.

SHIFTS IN MOOD

Poems based on some fundamental shift in mood or attitude are closely related to those with contrasts. They focus, however, on inner perceptions and feelings rather than on external objects and events. One of the more famous of these is Shakespeare's "Sonnet 29," often referred to by its opening phrase, "When in Disgrace with Fortune" (page 203).

The entire **octave** — the first eight lines — is downbeat. The speaker describes feeling like an outcast; he is one who has cursed his fate, envying others. But in the **sestet**, just about at the point where we think he is indulging in excessive self-pity, the poem shifts with the word "yet."

> Yet in these thoughts my self almost despising,
> Haply I think on thee, and then my state,

> Like to the lark at break of day arising
> From sullen earth, sings hymns at heaven's gate,

The poem is a good example of how Elizabethan sonnets frequently adopt a new tone at the beginning of the sestet. What concerns us here, though, is the fact that while the organization of the poem is based in part on the traditional division of the sonnet, what we notice first is the dramatic shift in mood. In fact, even readers entirely unfamiliar with the structure of a sonnet will respond to that shift in the narrator's emotions.

The organization of Dorothy Barresi's "Mystery" (page 218) is also based on a shift in emotions, but the tone is entirely different. She uses bizarre exaggeration, an extended **hyperbole**, to create a dreamlike satire. Arguments between the couple erupt abruptly, dominating the entire house in such a nightmare fashion that the poem becomes grotesquely comic:

> Ashtrays and pillows begin to orbit the room
> Whatever furniture they have
> rears up on hind legs and howls.

But later in an astonishing reversal of mood:

> . . . the couple kiss,
> Like guests on a television talk show,
> expecting nothing.
> Whatever they fought about is a mystery to them now.

Whereas Barresi deals satirically with what we take to be a repeated cycle, some contrast poems focus seriously on a single dramatic or even traumatic event. Theodore Deppe's "The Paradise of Wings" (page 218) is dark, clearly a turning point in the relationship between two young people and their grandfather. First, the bond between the grandson and his grandfather is revealed through their sharing of a special place:

> My grandfather called it
> the Paradise of Wings, a clearing
> hidden in blue hills where thousands
> of geese gleaned stubbled corn
> beside a tapered lake. His favorite walk —
> shared with me as a secret — . . .

But later, after his sister "stumbles from the house / panic in her face," they both come to fear the grandfather. As for that secret spot, it has become utterly transformed for them:

> . . . my sister's hate
> was the only living thing in paradise.

In the fiction section of this text, I described how important it is in short stories to establish **tension** either through conflict or other means. Tension is not absolutely essential in poetry, but as you can see from these examples it can generate a sense of vitality, even drama. One of the best ways to create a form of tension in a poem is to introduce a prominent shift in attitude.

OPINIONS AND ARGUMENTS

Opinions and argument differ mainly in intensity. There are an infinite number of degrees between the two, and any of them can be used to establish a sense of order in a poem.

Stephen Dunn's "A Secret Life" (page 217) is essentially an opinion. Like many successful opinion poems, it runs counter to generally held convictions. He is countering the widely held notion that we should be completely open about our feelings.

His unorthodox view is expressed directly in the title, "A Secret Life" and the opening four lines:

> Why you need to have one
> is not much more mysterious than
> why you don't say what you think
> at the birth of an ugly baby.

There it is: an overt statement of his theme. And he sticks with it through 27 lines.

A counter opinion about honesty is presented by Molly Peacock in "Anger Sweetened" (page 202). Her opening line is "What we don't forget is what we don't say." The poem goes on to describe memories of what we should have said as like "grasshoppers covered / by coagulating chocolate" that we must eventually eat, playing on the cliché "eat your words."

The great risk of organizing a poem on the basis of an argument or an opinion is that too often the theme is essentially a **truism**, a widely held belief like the assertions that there shouldn't be so many poor people in a rich nation, that we shouldn't be cutting down the rain forests, and that battered women need protection. These are all good causes, but they won't be helped with verse. Nor will they develop into sophisticated poetry.

Poems organized around safe topics are unsuccessful mainly because they do not say anything new. They do not provide energy regardless of how carefully they have been written.

The opinion poems by Stephen Dunn and Molly Peacock succeed in spite of the bluntly thematic opening partly because they are unorthodox views and the themes they express are quirky. In addition, they are both witty. We are assured from the opening lines that we are not dealing with heavy-handed editorials.

David Curry's poem "To Those Who are Programming Computers to Produce Poetry" (page 321) is also an opinion, but it is presented with the intensity of an argument. Borrowing from a debating technique, the narrator addresses his opponent directly both in the title and in the opening line: "Do you really understand . . . ?" He then goes on to describe the imprecise, unpredictable nature of the creative process.

His indignation with computer geeks mounts in the concluding stanzas:

> Poems are *written* you robot fools,
> out of spinnings and crossings
> too complex for your machine.
> They come on like the days, flawed and
> beautiful and of this world.

How do you handle a subject that makes you angry? If you feel that strongly about a subject, your first inclination may be to plunge directly into your subject. Occasionally, that works. There is a risk, however, that your reader will see the argument coming and react negatively even before finishing. Consider using that old football ploy, the end run. This evasive tactic can help disguise your intent, at least at first.

Thomas McGrath does this with "Nuclear Winter" (page 223). His title suggests that the poem will focus on a social issue, but the opening is deceptively positive:

> After the first terror
> > people
> Were more helpful to each other —
> As in a blizzard

As you remember, he lulls the reader through most of the poem. It is only in the last three lines that he drops the metaphorical bomb:

> Then we came to our senses
> And began to kill each other.

His anger at the continued stockpiling of nuclear weapons is constant; it is only the *tone* that takes the final and dramatic shift. More about this in Chapter 34.

An entirely different way to handle strong feelings is to filter them through a metaphor. In the previous chapter, we examined how Dick Allen does this in "The Narrow Mind" (page 206). The **controlling image**, you remember, is a metaphor using a frog living in "a small backwater." The image (the **vehicle**) is laughably absurd, but the poet's anger is not. The attack on narrow-minded people (the **tenor**) is presented entirely through implication.

At first reading, it may seem odd that a poem that so clearly attacks those with a narrow mind would end with such a gentle, almost whimsical tone. His concluding advice, you remember, is that we must

> . . . row around it or overwhelm it
> With goodness and mercy and bribes.

Remember, though, that this poem attacks those with a narrow, prejudicial mind. Had it ended on a harsh note, recommending, say, that all such creatures be driven away, the poem would end up being narrow-minded itself.

If you are tempted to start a poem calling for world peace or a defense of the beleaguered ozone layer and whales, I would urge you to re-read these three opinion-based poems. And don't shy away from wit and irony. No matter what tone you use, remember that if it isn't more artful than prose in short lines, it isn't really a poem.

POETIC NARRATIVES

A **narrative** is a story, a sequence of events. Although long and complex stories are, with some notable exceptions, written in prose as novels, story telling is a natural and popular organizing principle in poetry.

Narrative poems use many of the techniques we are used to in fiction. They tell a story, and like most stories they have a **plot** that is often begun with rising action and concluded with a climax. They almost always have a central figure, the **protagonist**, or in first-person poems, the **narrator**.

Traditionally, the folk **ballad**, and more recently the literary ballad, were the dominant forms of narrative poetry. Often they dealt with tragedy — death in combat, drownings at sea, or exile. That tradition is alive and well in the form of American popular folk ballads such as "Casey Jones" and in blues lyrics. There is no sharp line between narrative poetry intended to be read on the page, recited, or sung.

Anthony Hecht's "Lizards and Snakes" (page 212) is a highly condensed contemporary ballad. As I pointed out in Chapter 31, Hecht adapted the literary ballad by using a slightly longer line and by running his quatrains together to form eight-line stanzas. What concerns us here, however, is the way the story line is used as a basic method of organization. The narrator, speaking in the first person, explains the background, and then describes the events and the outcome. It is a relatively simple story, actually no more than an **anecdote** that begins with playful humor and ends on a more serious note.

The reference to "carriage ruts" places the event back when belief in a literal devil was more common. The implied theme suggests that what seems funny at one stage in your life changes as you grow up. But it isn't the theme that hangs the story together; it is the story line that provides the structure.

The narrative line in "Lizards and Snakes" is blatant. In other poems, however, plot is so underplayed that you hardly think of the work as telling a story. Still, the mere hint of a sequence of actions can provide an organizational structure.

"The Pardon" by Richard Wilbur (page 213) is a good example. It's a more sophisticated poem than "Lizards and Snakes," so you may want to review it now to refresh your memory. The poem also begins in the first person with a narrator who recalls a childhood experience. In this case, a boy of 10, finds the body of his dog. The story line continues through to the burial. Then it jumps forward to when he has a nightmare about the experience. On waking, he begs "death's pardon." The poem has a complex theme about denial of death, guilt, and the hope of redemption, and these concerns dominate the poem. The organization, however, is relatively simple and straightforward.

The story line in Maxine Kumin's "Morning Swim" (page 211) is even simpler. The narrator simply goes swimming in the early morning and has a spiritual experience. That's barely a plot in fictional terms, but it is enough to unify the poem. It's a good reminder that a narrative sequence can be slight and still provide an effective structure for a poem.

THE CONTROLLING IMAGE

A **controlling image** is one that shapes an entire poem, giving it a sense of order. It is also referred to as a *dominant image,* which is a more descriptive phrase.

In most cases, the controlling image takes the form of a metaphor, but it can also be a simile or even a direct statement. To be a true controlling image, however, it must be one that influences the whole poem, not just a portion.

"The Mapmaker's Daughter" by Anita Endrezze (page 222) is a classic example of a poem organized throughout by a controlling image. The subject of the poem is love. This is a risky choice because of all the Hallmark verses and popular song lyrics that clutter our lives. Indeed, some may feel that Endrezze skirts dangerously close to the sentimental in this poem. But her dreamlike, sensual treatment is fresh. Review it now before I provide a guided tour.

Endrezze identifies the subject or **tenor** of the poem, love, in the first two lines:

> the geography of love is terra infirma.
> it is a paper boat

At the very outset, the subject is presented as something we can see, a boat. After that, she is careful not to use the word "love" again. It is too **abstract** and badly overused.

The boat becomes a controlling image. We learn about the two "mates," the sea "far from shore," the woman at the helm, armed with "the map of longing," and the "secret passages" they will explore. The voyage is misty, dreamlike, and occasionally erotic, but we are able to navigate our way, led by the "compass of her desire." Her "map of longing" is, returning to the subject at hand, part of that intricate controlling metaphor.

Dick Allen uses a far darker controlling metaphor in "The Narrow Mind" (206). Like Andrezze, he identifies the subject (the **tenor**) at the outset — in the title itself. The vehicle is a frog, but this is no Kermit. It "feeds on what's been whispered to it / In secret meetings at dusk . . . " It believes in omens like the flight of birds. It insists on not being contradicted. The reader is warned: "The brighter you are, the more likely it will greet you / With suspicion . . ."

Although this creature is clearly odious, the narrator is careful at the end of this poem not to be narrow-mindedly hostile. If we can't get it to move away, we are urged to "overwhelm it / With goodness and mercy and bribes."

The great advantage of using a controlling image in the form of a metaphor is that in doing so you establish a clear structure, an unmistakable sense of order. The risk, however, is that it is difficult to sustain a single metaphor for long without it beginning to seem contrived. Make sure that the central metaphor is, as with these two poems, fresh and complex enough to provide a variety of insights. A few flashes of sly wit will also help keep such a poem from becoming pompous.

Incidentally, poems relying on a controlling metaphor are close to what is known as the **riddle poem**. Such poems do not identify the tenor at all, forcing the reader to guess what the subject is. The whole poem becomes a riddle.

Riddle poems go back to the time of *Beowulf*, were particularly popular in the Middle Ages, and are still being written. In its classic form, the last line asks the question, "Who am I?" On its simple level, the riddle poem is just a game and entertaining for those who like literary games, but occasionally it is developed with serious complexity.

THE PASSAGE OF TIME

The passage of time can also be used to establish a sense of order. A common pattern is to draw on the way our attitudes change between childhood and adulthood. Both "Lizards and Snakes" and "The Pardon" do this in ways we have already discussed.

There is an almost subliminal use of time as an organizing principle in Elizabeth Holden's "As the Cold Deepens (201)." As you remember, the narrator is helping her 86-year-old mother open their summer house, but you may not remember how subtly the poem is structured with references to time.

The fact that they are opening their summer house informs us in the first stanza that this is spring. The fifth stanza begins with "At noon . . . " And the final stanza begins with, "It is hard to hold the light" and ends with "The glass is cold." In a literal sense, the whole poem can be seen as the memory of a single day, but metaphorically it suggests the stages of life: youth (spring), midlife (noon), and finally death with that chilling last line.

Of all the poems you have read in this text, the most complex use of time as an organizational device is seen in Donald Hall's "Names of Horses" (page 216). Turn to it now and review it carefully. See if you can sort out three different time cycles woven together in that poem.

The first of these sequences is based on seasons of the year. It starts out "All winter" and moves in the second stanza to "April," turns to summer with "noon's heat," and finally to the autumn with "one October" in the fifth stanza. This use of seasons is clear and fairly common as a device.

The second sequence is longer and based on the stages of a single horse's life. The opening four stanzas focus on the mature years when the horse can do heavy work; the fifth stanza starts when he is "old and lame" and is taken out to be shot; and the seventh stanza deals with the horse after death, when the roots of trees "pushed through the pale curves of your ribs."

The third cycle is the longest and most subtle. Far lengthier than the four seasons of a single year, longer even than the story of one horse's life and death, it is the succession of horses moving through the same cycle "generation on generation." In a sense, this is similar to the view of an elderly teacher describing the passage of class after class over the years.

This poem combines three different cycles of time to produce a single, unified effect. The process is similar to the way a single, sustained note played on a cello is actually comprised of high, medium, and low frequencies working together to produce what we hear as one note with rich overtones. This is what we mean when we say that a poem has **resonance**.

34 Varieties of Tone

"I really want that."

This looks like a clear, unambiguous statement. How could we mistake its meaning? Easily. In fact, we can't even respond until we identify the speaker and the tone of voice. Here are three different situations, each implying a different tone. Notice how the meaning changes, even though the words do not:

1. An armed man in a darkened parking lot says this, pointing to your car keys.
2. A teenager says this about a celebrity's elegant estate shown on television.
3. A woman says this with a sarcastic sneer about an unexpected tax bill.

The literal statement, the **denotation**, is the same in each case. But the implied meaning, the **connotation**, in each is entirely different. The first is a threat. It would be a big mistake to laugh. The second is a joke. It would be a mistake to lecture the kid about the cost of real estate. And the third means exactly the opposite of the literal statement. She hardly expects you to ask, "You *like* paying taxes?" Clearly, tone in everyday speech is not just an adornment to language; it's often an essential part of the meaning.

Tone is equally important in poetry, but instead of being revealed by seeing a speaker and hearing his or her voice, it's communicated entirely by cues within the work. In most cases, you can't discuss the meaning of a poem without determining the tone.

When we refer to the tone of a poem, we use such words as *reflective, loving, comic, satiric,* and *ironic.* Remember, though, that in poetry there are as many different shadings of tone as there are in the spoken language. Like the names of colors, the terms we use are convenient segments of a spectrum.

Here are some of the many different tones used in the poems you read in Chapter 26. If your memory of a particular work has faded, take the time to review it. Keep in mind that some poems use more than one tone.

REFLECTIVE TONES

Such poems tend to be thoughtful and contemplative. They are almost never argumentative or comic. The poet is sharing an observation and some insights as if saying, "Hey, look at this."

We have already examined several different aspects of Robley Wilson's "On a Maine Beach" (208), but consider it now in terms of tone. Wilson does not take a stand or propose an argument; he merely invites the reader to examine the details of the scene and consider its implications.

Many reflective poems focus on some aspect of nature. Wilson's poem is similar in this respect to Robert Frost's "Design" (200). Frost, you remember, describes seeing a white spider on a white flower holding a white moth. He concludes with an observation, but it is expressed in speculative terms, not as an intense argument.

Reflective poems can be melancholy when dealing with those who are ill or who face other misfortunes. Such a poem is referred to as an **elegy** when it honors someone who has died, but the tone is also used for those close to death. Elizabeth Holden's memories of her mother in "As the Cold Deepens" (page 201) uses that tone, even though her subject is not yet bedridden. Chase Twichell's description of a woman close to death in "Rhymes for Old Age" (page 215) is a poignant tribute.

James Bertram's poem addressed to Ernest Hemingway, "Is It Well-Lighted, Papa?" (page 208) is a true elegy. It is both reflective and somber — yet with touches of quiet humor as well.

Although these three poems share a melancholy or somber tone, they differ subtly in how close they are to their subject. This aspect is called **distance**. When the subject matter is treated with detachment or objectivity, the poem is said to have greater distance than those that seem more subjective and personal. Twichell, for example, is careful to stay clear of sentimentality by using starkly clinical details. She maintains greater distance between her narrator and the woman in bed by not naming the patient or identifying her relationship with the speaker:

> The form in the bed
> is a soul diminished
> to a fledgling

The poem is no less compassionate than the others, but it is less intimate. Holden, in contrast, reduces the distance and makes the poem more personal by identifying the subject:

> My mother is almost weightless now,
> Her flesh shrinks back toward bone

Bertram reduces the distance still further by shifting from the third person to direct address:

> Is it well-lighted, Papa - this place
> where you have gone . . . ?

Although "Papa" was also a nickname for Hemingway, the poet's repeated use of that name in the refrain suggests something close to a son's affection for his father.

In this connection, I have a word of caution: melancholy poems indulging in self-pity are unfortunately common in student work. Although most such poems are sincere, some may be motivated by a hope that dwelling on personal misery will protect the poet from harsh criticism. How can readers come down hard on someone raised by abusive alcoholics? The answer is simple: a critique of a poem is not a critique of the poet. A poem should be evaluated as a work of art.

LOVING TONES

A love poem can be beautiful, genuine, and moving, but it's a high-risk challenge. As I pointed out in Chapter 33, it is difficult to express love without echoing greeting-card verse and song lyrics. To remind yourself that love can be described convincingly with freshness and sincerity, review Philip Appleman's "Desire" (page 219), Anita Endrezze's "The Mapmaker's Daughter." (page 222), and Shakespeare's "Sonnet 29" (page 203). Dramatically different as they are, they each give the impression of referring to a real person (although without proof, remember) and expressing genuine feelings. Appearance of sincerity, however, never justifies a poem that lacks fresh expression. Each of these poems is energized by highly original and striking images.

THE WIDE RANGE OF HUMOR

A wry tone bridges the serious and the comic. It evokes a smile, if not a laugh. Introducing even mild humor provides a kind of objectivity, a distancing that can serve as an antidote to self-pity.

Theodore Roethke in "The Waking" (page 209) is a good example. He is talking about the brutal fact that we are all mortal. If he had started with "We're born without hope, doomed to die," most of us would quickly move on to another poem before getting to the second stanza. The statement is sadly true, but the tone is that of a whiner. Instead, Roethke begins with "I wake to sleep, and take my waking slow." The metaphor of "sleep" refers to death, but the tone is light, almost whimsical, and his determination to make the most of life while it lasts provides a wry acceptance of our mortality. In the final stanza, he is even more aware of what is to come:

This shaking keeps me steady. I should know.
What falls away is always. And is near.

But even recognizing the eternal quality of death ("What falls away is always") and his advancing age ("And is near"), he maintains his light, wry tone and ends with the assurance that he will learn and grow until the very end (which, incidentally, he did).

Humor is too often avoided by beginning poets for fear of not being taken seriously. There is an unfortunate confusion in the English language between *serious* as a dark, furrow-browed emotion and *serious* meaning complex or insightful. Roethke's wry approach to death should reassure you that it is quite possible to express serious themes with some degree of humor.

Humor also allows a poet to turn what some might think of as a liability into an affirmation. Lucille Clifton's "What the Mirror Said" (page 203) does just this. The speaker looks in the mirror and glories in her size:

you a wonder,
you a city
of a woman.

She is so complex that someone would have to have a map to understand her. We smile. It's a comic use of **hyperbole**, an exaggeration used for effect. Notice, however, that we smile *with* the speaker, not at her. It is not a ridiculing poem; it is affirming.

As in Roethke's poem, Clifton's humor doesn't obscure the underlying suggestions. By implication, the poem jabs at the contemporary notion of beauty. This is clearly a woman's statement.

Incidentally, there is a longer and equally exuberant example of humor from an African American woman's point of view in Chapter 35, but because those poems are intended for you to practice your critical skills without me standing at your shoulder, I will not comment on it further except to identify the title, "We" on page 313.

For another example of how a comic tone can be used to describe a serious subject, review Dorothy Barresi's poem "Mystery" (page 218). Her subject is marital discord. She makes us wonder whether a marriage can survive. Yet, her tone is truly comic.

She starts with a pun in the second line, comparing the initial accusations flung by husband and wife at each other as "little earrings" — both hard little gems and shouts that make the ears ring. Soon "Ashtrays and pillows begin to orbit the room" and the furniture "rears up on hind legs and howls." We smile at the exaggeration, another example of *hyperbole*, which in this case is almost on the level of a cartoon. At the end of the poem, the battle has ended and peace returns. But take a second look at the last two lines:

> the calm rising all around the house
> like a blood pressure.

"Rising . . . like a blood pressure"? That's no happy and contented calm. It's an armed truce that is ominously building toward another outbreak of hostilities. The tone is comic on the surface, but the marriage trembles and erupts like a volcanic hot spot.

SATIRE: ATTACK BY RIDICULE

Satire criticizes or ridicules through some form of exaggeration. In mild satire, the exaggeration may be only a matter of selecting some characteristics and neglecting others. The tone may be a gentle kidding. At the other extreme, satire may be wildly exaggerated and the tone vitriolic.

Satire on television and in magazines such as *Mad* and *National Lampoon* tends to be relatively simple. Like cartoons, it is designed as one-shot entertainment. Satire in sophisticated poetry, on the other hand, usually has more intricacies and nuances. It probes the subject more deeply. It draws us back for repeated readings.

We have already seen how Dick Allen's "The Narrow Mind" (page 206) ridicules the type of person described in the title through a **controlling image**. The self-satisfied and unthinking frog in the swamp is a bizarre and in many ways laughable metaphor, but behind the humor is a type of person we all detest. More specifically, the **vehicle** (the frog) is comic, but the **tenor** (a narrow-minded person) is despicable.

The tone of Carole Oles' "The Gift" (page 202) is even more scathing. She is attacking the way in which some women are raised to become nothing more than property for a husband. Like Dick Allen, Oles has selected a subject that has been handled in countless articles and books. A head-on attack might not be fresh enough to have impact. So she turns instead to **satire**.

Oles does not reveal her satiric tone at the opening. In fact, the first few lines may seem almost sweet:

> Thinking she was the gift
> they began to package it early.

But within a few lines we realize that their gift is not *for* the girl, it *is* the girl! Referring to this poor female as *it* gives you an idea of how she is being raised as a product. (Notice that Dick Allen also used *it* to describe the subject of his poem.) After they have straightened her teeth and curled her hair and taught her to speak in honeyed tones, she is given to a man who puts her on exhibit as a trophy. Her ultimate function is to provide him with a son. She is nothing more than the property of her husband.

This vehement satire is presented in the form of a **parable**. The parable is one of the oldest literary forms and is found frequently in the work of the Greek author Aesop and in the Bible. The traditional fable is a short **allegorical** story in verse or prose designed to instruct. Oles' highly contemporary and dreamlike use of this form is most appropriate. The tone is charged with indignation and rage, but like most parables the poem's aim is to instruct.

If you plan to work with a social issue you feel strongly about, think carefully before you plunge into a direct attack. It may be that you can hold your reader and create a more memorable impression through some type of satire.

THREE TYPES OF IRONY

Both serious and comic poems can and often do make use of **irony**. All three forms of irony are based on a reversal of some sort. **Verbal irony** (also called **conscious irony**) is our primary concern here. On its simplest level, it takes the form of sarcasm that we use conversationally when we say the opposite of what is obviously true. When we respond to a hurricane with the statement, "Great day for a picnic," no one doubts our sanity because we are used to this kind of irony in everyday speech.

In poetry, however, irony is usually subtler and may not be at all sarcastic. It is often achieved by bringing together elements we normally consider incongruous. There are several examples in these lines from Richard Wilbur's "The Pardon" (page 213). The scene, you will remember, is the one in which the **persona** dreams he sees the ghost of his dog. In this passage certain words are in sharp and *ironic* contrast with other words in the same line. It is ironic to have a hymn associated with a "carnal sun" and a swarm of flies. It is equally ironic to think of death as "breeding." And there is a grim irony in those "lively eyes" of a dog that died some time ago.

There is another sample of irony in Chase Twichell's "Rhymes for Old Age" (page 215) that you may have spotted in earlier readings of that poem. She describes the process of dying this way:

> One slips into it undressed,
> as into first love . . .

When an ironic contrast is phrased in a way that makes it sound like a complete contradiction, it is called a **paradox**. John Donne, for example, in his sonnet "Death Be Not Proud," ends with these lines:

> One short sleep past, we wake eternally,
> And death shall be no more; Death, thou shalt die.

On a literal level, it is illogical to say that death shall die, but metaphorically it makes sense as a description of eternal life.

Irony like these examples is called *verbal* because it is formed with words, not from events in life. It is a kind of word play. It is also called *conscious* irony because the writer is intentionally linking the incongruous items.

There are two other uses of the word irony that, though less often found in poetry, should be mentioned here to avoid confusion. **Cosmic irony** refers to occurrences in daily life. Since it is often on a smaller scale than "cosmic" would imply, think of it as *irony of events*. The reversal occurs when the outcome is radically different from what one would normally expect. Consider, for example, the Olympic swimmer who drowns in the bathtub, the fire chief who becomes an arsonist, or the drought-stricken farmers who finally receive rain only to be flooded.

There is an example of cosmic irony in Clement Long's poem, "Always the One Who Loves His Father Most" (page 205). The central theme of this work is the ironic assertion that "the one who loves his father most . . . will fight against his father as he must."

The third type is **dramatic irony**, in which characters in a play speak lines that the audience knows have an entirely different significance. In the Greek play *Oedipus Rex*, for example, a messenger says, "I bring good news" and the well-read audience shudders, knowing that disaster is at hand. More about that in the drama section of this volume.

YOU AND YOUR PERSONA

When we discuss a poem, we never know for sure whether the speaker in the poem represents the poet or an imagined character. We have no biographical assurance that Robert Frost actually saw a white spider on a white flower holding a white moth. He may have made it up or heard about someone else's experience. And we have no knowledge as to whether Richard Wilbur actually had a dog as a child. Perhaps he preferred cats. These details are biographical gossip. It doesn't concern us here.

What does concern us is the implied character who has had these experiences. Occasionally, we may say "Frost questions . . ." or "Wilbur feels that . . . ," but in most cases it is better to refer to "the **persona**," "the speaker," or "the narrator."

It is true that the current trend for confessional poetry has tended to blur the distinction between the actual writers and their personas. But assuming that poets are always writing about themselves can lead you to false assumptions. And, worse, not using the phrase "the persona . . ." in discussions can lead to that highly unfortunate and counterproductive notion that criticizing the poem is criticizing the poet as a person. It's important not to confuse the poet and the poem.

As a writer, you have a choice. You can create the illusion of writing about your own experience, drawing on your own life, or you can filter your material through a character distinctly unlike yourself. This is a matter of establishing **distance**.

Oddly, whether you use the first person, *I*, or the third person does not make a major difference in tone. Robley Wilson does not use *I* in "On a Maine Beach," nor does Chase Twichell in her description of an unnamed patient in "Rhymes for Old Age." But both *seem* more personal than Anthony Hecht's "Lizards and Snakes," which, although told in the first person, has the sense of a fabricated tale.

There is one way to establish a tone that is unmistakably not the voice of the poet. It is called a **dramatic monologue**. Such poems are written in the first person as if being addressed to a silent listener by a narrator. Since the narrator reveals some of his or her own character in the telling, the approach has some of the flavor of a monologue in a play. Frequently, the persona expresses attitudes unmistakably contrary to what we assume the poet would feel, as in the frequently anthologized poem by Robert Browning, "My Last Duchess" (the Duke is a snob and a murderer) and T.S. Eliot's "The Lovesong of J. Alfred Prufrock" (Prufrock is a self-justifying loser). The approach was more popular in the 19th century than today, but it has interesting possibilities.

EXAMINING YOUR TRUE FEELINGS

Tone is not usually your first concern when you begin a new poem. In fact, you may not even be sure what your attitude toward your subject will be when you start. You can be drawn toward an occurrence, an experience, a relationship, or a setting, without knowing why. It may take one or two drafts before you realize that what attracts you to the material is a sense of love or perhaps anger or a feeling of nostalgia. The very act of translating experience or feelings into lines of verse occasionally opens up veins of emotions you hadn't expected — some stratum of love for someone you thought you hated, a hidden fear of a situation you thought you enjoyed, or anxiety in an area where you thought you were secure.

At some point in the revision process, you should stop and ask this crucial question: Is this what I *really* feel? Does the poem, for example, merely echo conventional sentiments (mothers and nature are wonderful; war and poverty are terrible), or does it honestly explore the complexity of what you feel?

More subtly, have you been softening the implications of your poem through psychic modesty? That is, have you been reluctant to reveal your private feelings? If so, the poem will probably lack a sense of power and authenticity.

Surprisingly, this reluctance to reveal personal feelings or experiences is the primary cause of obscurity. Hiding one's true feeling behind an impenetrable fog is an understandable but unfortunate weakness in many poems.

When the theme or a central image has two or more possible meanings, the result is **ambiguity**. *Intentional* ambiguity can be used effectively to suggest that two or more meanings are equally true or that they combine to suggest a third, broader conclusion. *Unintentional* ambiguity, on the other hand, places a barrier between the poem and the reader. When this happens, ask yourself whether you are hiding your true feelings behind a smoke screen.

Expressing your inner feelings and revealing uncomfortable experiences often take considerable courage. If you are still uneasy about dealing with those personal details, consider presenting the material through an invented character, a persona. This may provide some sense of objectivity while still being true to the subject matter.

Modesty isn't always the problem. Exaggerating personal agony or a painful experience can sometimes result in **sentimentality**. Intentional sentimentality is a form of dishonesty because it cheapens genuine feelings. It is contaminated with details selected to stimulate the tear ducts. It's a trick rather than a sharing of true emotions.

But what about *unintentional* sentimentality? That is far more common. Occasionally, you may honestly believe that you are the most miserable, most misunderstood person on Earth or, on a happier note, that your grandmother really is unbelievably perfect. Remember, though, that if the poem *sounds* sentimental to others, it *is* sentimental. Perhaps a wry, slightly distanced tone would help provide perspective and hold your readers.

In the same way, if you overdramatize a conflict or protest, going beyond your real feelings, your poem may lose some of its dramatic impact and may come across as **melodramatic**. When readers believe that emotions such as indignation or rage have been inflated just to attract attention, the poem will lose credibility. Consider some form of irony. Take another look at Dick Allen's "The Narrow Mind" (page 206) or Carole Oles' "The Gift" (page 202).

When you are finally satisfied, let others read the poem. Resist the temptation to explain what you had hoped would come through. This is your time to learn from them. At some point in the discussion, ask them directly to describe the tone. If they are vague, urge them to be specific. Listen carefully.

After the discussion, go back to work again. Decide which of their comments justify further effort. Your revision process will not be complete until you have established just the right tone.

35 Poems for Self-Study

A creative writing textbook has certain advantages over even the most conscientious instructor: it will, if you want, travel with you over the years; it's not limited to office hours; and you can ask it for advice at three in the morning. But this book has one significant drawback: it can't make sure that you are actively applying what you have read.

As I explained in the Preface, textbooks in history, chemistry, or anatomy have an easier goal. They are designed primarily to inform. If you read and recall the contents, you will get an A. These are what I described as *content texts*. Textbooks in creative writing, in contrast, deal not only with facts, but also with a process. *Process texts* require a different approach. I am repeating this here because the distinction is crucially important and prefaces are often read hastily.

Chapter 26 introduced you to a group of poems, most of which were used in later chapters as examples of poetic techniques. If you merely recalled the terminology, you weren't making full use of the text. To focus on the *process* of writing poetry, you must apply these techniques to your own work and to published work not discussed here.

Most of the following poems have not been used to illustrate poetic techniques in this text. With considerable restraint, I have refrained from commenting on all but one. They are for you to read and analyze. You can do this on your own or discuss them in class, but in either case the process will be active, not passive.

As with any collection of poems, some will appeal to you more than others. Personal preferences vary. But this is not a popularity contest. Instead, use these poems to exercise your own critical abilities.

CRITICAL QUESTIONS

The following questions are intended to help you read poems analytically. Don't use them as a check list, but keep them handy as suggestions of what to look for. If you are discussing poems in a class or group, these questions should help eliminate the dead silence that often follows the reading of a new work:

What aspects make this work a poem rather
     than a short sample of prose?
Which images have impact?
Are any images used as figures of speech?
Are there symbolic suggestions?
What kinds of rhythms are developed?
How is line length used?
What about the sound of language: assonance?
     consonance? rhyme? anaphora?
Are there stanzas? If so, how are they used?
How are thoughts and feelings organized?
How would you describe the tone?
Are the techniques used in this poem
     similar to any other poem in this
     collection or in Chapter 26?

At the end of this chapter, there is an index of poems similar to the one in Chapter 26. If you put a bookmark on the first page of this index, it will be easy to compare poems.

The complete index of titles of work in all three genres, along with names of poets, authors, and dramatists, appears on page 457. Finally, all literary terms used in this text appear in the Glossary-Index at the end of this book.

Grandmother

PAULA GUN ALLEN

Out of her own body she pushed
silver thread, light, air
and carried it carefully on the dark, flying
where nothing moved.

Out of her body she extruded
shining wire, life, and wove the light
on the void

From beyond time,
beyond oak trees and bright clear water flow,
she was given the work of weaving the strands
of her body, her pain, her vision
into creation, and the gift of having created,
to disappear.

After her,
the women and the men weave blankets into tales of life,
memories of light and ladders,
infinity-eyes, and rain.
After her I sit on my laddered rain-bearing rug
and mend the tear with string.

Indian Country Again

JOSEPH BRUCHAC

It is time for soldiers to remember
the cemeteries of suicide angels,
carved heads tucked like robins
beneath their left wings.

Old men as grave
as perched birds of prey
have bowed wise heads
that have grown gray
not so much from age
as from the falling decades
of battlefield dust.

They've reassured us we can trust
only what they have told to us.
They've learned a new way
to write words on the wind.

They know the Evil One's hiding place.
They've brought Custer's bugle
from its sacred case.

Let us make the distant desert ours.
Great bouquets of smoke will billow up.
Black roses will hide the falling stars.

Let us sound the charge
against brown-skinned men.
It is time to ride headlong
into Indian Country again.

Intransitive

CHRISTOPHER BUCKLEY

Evening is that old tune I never tire of
especially when, as now, it is an adagio

of rose and grey above the autumn trees
and the turning leaves are nothing more
than brown and dead across the lawns.

When I was six or seven and climbed
the eucalyptus, or the pines,
I was in love, and wondering
at the underlay of music and everything
equally unattainable in the light —
I gave in to longing then, and liked it.

Doubtless, I have as much now as then —
and there is nothing less in an on-shore breeze
riffling the agapanthus and blue hibiscus,
or in the little salt on the air
lifting my lungs to breathe
as simple as that old desire to float
to where clouds turn red and dim,
to where the past dies out of us, and sleeps.

But this evening as I took the footpath
back up the long hill to the house,
I noticed the first few stars glide out
overhead and sing, and they were in need
of nothing more to complete their meaning.

for Deb & Edith Wylder

Burning the Letters

ANDREA HOLANDER BUDY

This was before they were married,
before she understood what he had done
to her heart, before she understood
that she had let him. His words meant something

before she understood what he had done.
He stood beside her at the stainless steel sink.
She let his words mean something —
their thick current, the blame she'd accepted.

He stood beside her at the sink
and lit the first page, turned it to flame.
Its thick current, the bruise she'd expected,
passed through her. The words she'd written

lit the first page and turned it to flame.
The stack was nine inches thick, copies
of the words she'd written
for other men — words to herself, really.

The stack was thick with copious
marks on paper her heart had made
for other men, words from her, real
words he wanted to end.

The marks her heart had made
he wanted turned to ash, page by page.
He wanted them to end like this:
black on white, blue light, orange flame,

page after violent page turned to ash
until there was nothing at all, not one page,
black or white. Blue flame, orange light —
what had defined her no longer saved.

Then there was nothing at all, not even rage.
Her heart stood vacant before him —
it neither defined nor saved her.
This was before they were married.

We

JANEYA K. HISLE

We women,
We sisters
    you and me.
We be rollin' our necks with our hands on our hips.
We be braidin' our hair.
We be paintin' our lips.
We be peekin' our windows 'cause we just *gotta* see.
But whatever We be . . . We be beautifully.

We women,
We sisters
    you and me.

We pure gold: We make good Mamas.
And we bold: We bring the drama.
We give a lot.
We play a lot.

We pray a lot cause men stray a lot.
We infiltrate: desegregate.
We complicate.
We instigate.
We always runnin' late
    for a date
        but we so great
           we know they'll wait.

We women,
We sisters
  you and me.

We love.
We love our mothers.
We love our brothers.
We love each other.
And We strong: We be copin'
And We slick: We be scopin'
And no one knows shoes like We.
And no one knows blues like We.

'Cause We earth, moon and stars.
We give birth.
We fix cars.
We cook meals.
We close deals.
We wear pants with high heels.

We got life, love and Spirit in all that We do.
We women,
We sisters
    me and you.

Dog Bite

APRIL LINDNER

The worst for him was his friend turned wolf,
and the blood that splattered as he ran. The worst
for us: the hospital, his upper lip tugged back
to show the gash — the flesh halved deeply,
cleanly — while I hold him for the needle
that rubs pain out. He submits
to the quick stitch, the thread black
against pink skin, calm now he sees

the doctor can be trusted, his voice
soothing, his face clean shaven,
the clues that signal kindness to a child.
He's worried, though, about his pet
who *didn't mean it, Mom*. His voice is flat.
He knows the months he's tried to woo this dog
were over when it leapt for his throat
and caught his mouth. The scars, at least,
will be invisible. At home, he'll sleep
big boy between his parents, till he's sure
no beast will tear into his dreams. And we
will want him there, our bodies makeshift walls.
We who led the stranger to our home,
fixed him a bowl, taught him to sleep
under our blankets, we who taught our son
to rub the muzzle that sheathes the teeth.

Going Bananas

RITA MARIA MARTINEZ

My father rises each morning
to the fourteen varieties of banana trees
he's cultivated with unrivaled
care, each tree casting shade across our lawn,
each racimo an offering my father hacks
with his machete, a small cruelty
he performs like a doctor circumcising
a newborn, though I like to think
he is unburdening these trees,
casting weight off the tired trunks
of his Aromatic; his Honduran Goldfinger
and its hybrids (Fhia-3 and Fhia-18);
his twenty-two-foot tall Saba,
tallest banana tree in the world;
his Apple Sugar, a.k.a. Mansano;
his plátano Enano: Dwarf Cavendish,
sweet midgets sacrificed
to the blender for smoothies;
his Jamaican Red, his Cuban Red;
his Misi Luki; his Mysore; his 3640;
his Gran Nain; and my favorite, Orinoco —
plátano Burro he hauls into the house
with the pride of a hunter.

When he enters the kitchen wearing
his sweat-stained *Going Bananas* T-shirt
my mother stares at the shoot
dangling from his hands
like a third arm and smiles,
though I know she's thinking
of resin that'll cling to the cutting board
and her fingers, but he submits los plátanos
like a boy bringing a drawing
to be exhibited on the refrigerator door,
so she strips, slices, mashes, fries
until they're crunchy, sweet and salted,
tostones, mini-sunflowers humbly
acquiescing beside the breaded steak
on my father's ivory dinner plate.

What Lips My Lips Have Kissed

EDNA ST. VINCENT MILLAY

What lips my lips have kissed, and where, and why,
I have forgotten, and what arms have lain
Under my head till morning; but the rain
Is full of ghosts tonight, that tap and sigh
Upon the glass and listen for reply;
And in my heart there stirs a quiet pain
For unremembered lads that not again
Will turn to me at midnight with a cry.

Thus in the winter stands the lonely tree,
Nor knows what birds have vanished one by one,
Yet knows its boughs more silent than before:
I cannot say what loves have come and gone;
I only know that summer sang in me
A little while, that in me sings no more.

Love Song for Chloe

DAVID YOUNG

I guess your beauty doesn't
bother you, you wear it easy
and walk across the driveway
so casual and right it makes
my heart weigh twenty pounds

as I back out and wave
thinking She's my summer
peaches, corn, long moondawn dusks
watermelons chilling in a tub
of ice and water: mirrored there
the great midsummer sky
rolling with clouds and treetops
and down by the lake
the wild canaries
swinging on the horse mint
all morning long.

The Light Comes Brighter

THEODORE ROETHKE

The light comes brighter from the east; the caw
Of restive crows is sharper on the ear,
A walker at the river's edge may hear
A cannon crack announce an early thaw.

The sun cuts deep into the heavy drift,
Though still the guarded snow is winter-sealed,
At bridgeheads buckled ice begins to shift,
The river overflows the level field.

Once more the trees assume familiar shapes,
As branches lose last vestiges of snow,
The water stored in narrow pools escapes
In rivulets; the cold roots stir below.

Soon field and wood will wear an April look,
The frost be gone, for green is breaking now;
The ovenbird will match the vocal brook,
The young fruit swell upon the pear-tree bough.

And soon a branch, part of a hidden scene,
The leafy mind, that long was tightly furled,
Will turn its private substance into green,
And young shoots spread upon our inner world.

Lot's Wives

PIREENI SUNDARALINGHAM

We stood,
as women before us have stood,

looking back at our burning cities,
watching the smoke
rise from our empty homes.

It was quiet then. And cold.

We heard their cries, the caged birds
clawing at their perches, our daughters
naked in the hungry mob.

Such death. The smell of justice
drifting on the burnt wind.

We saw it all,
saw the fire fall like rain,

saw our tears
track stiff, white veins
down our bodies,

saw the brine crawl
from salt-cracked skin.

Now, turning in the restless night,
we dream we stand there still,
alone on the hill's black belly.

We, the forgotten,
whose names were swallowed by God.

Autobiography of an Immigrant

JENNIVER TSENG

My birthplace is incidental.
Never forget your Mother Country.

Our town was nowhere, nothing but dirt.
Our village was known for its temples and ponds.

The way my mother ran the house was backwards.
You don't taste fish like that here.

I don't remember what my father said.
We memorized everything our father said.

Chinese don't marry for love.
My father and mother loved each other very much.

Chinese families are unified; nothing can break them.
I haven't talked to my sister since I was twelve.

I spoke every language fluently; I was at the top of my class.
My English is terrible, I forget my Chinese.

Chinese children obey their parents' orders.
I ran away from home.

Your daddy is a very cautious person.
I left my country at night; I hid from the government.

The sea voyage took three weeks.
I walked on the water.

There was nothing special about my journey.
Our ship was lost at sea.

The barrels, filled with oranges, overflowed
After days of rain. The oranges spilled

Across the dark deck, a few fell in
To the black water. It was a catastrophe.

Our hunger, such as you can't imagine.

Solo

CHASE TWICHELL

Nothing to watch but the snow,
the muted road slowly unbending.
I've always been alone, and that knowledge

has been like a sheet of cold glass
between me and the world,

though it meant I could
lose myself in lonely beauties,
for example the tiny

darting fish in the headlights,
their almost wordlike scribbling.

Now that's all changed.
Now I want something altogether different.
I want to be a flake of frozen cloud,

a minnow of light that can swim
silver-bodied into the questions,

the shadowy currents
of all I long to know.
That darkness without shores.

That's what I want to be. One fish
in the numberless fish of the snow.

War

ROBLEY WILSON

Sometimes I have wanted to go to war.
The stories are always good — Thermopylae
Was good, the Gallic campaigns were as good
As you could get against barbarians,
The Crusades were outright inspirational.

Everyone ought to go off to a war
Before he is too old to have the good
Of it. The people we call pacifist
Forget (or never learned) the power of it,
The sense of godliness killing provides.

Who would not want to be an angel, high
Over the enemy's cities with wings
Broad as the foreshadow of death? What boy
Cannot recall from his pitiless dreams
That carnage laid about him in his bed

Of adults and girls? War is for the young
And keeps them young; war is to make a man
Immortal; war is to subvert boredom
And all the dull authority of states.
Who favors war knows what liberty is.

Think about us. War would spare us the vice
Of guilt, the curse of inadequate love,
The remorse of aimlessness. War transforms;
It is a place to start from, props up pride,
Writes history. Out of war, art makes itself.

Sometimes I have wanted to go to war,
To turn flame in anyone's heart. Old names
Dazzle me: Alexander, Genghis Khan,
Caesar, Napoleon — will any man
Shrink from riding such fame to his grave?

Are you the one gone soft now over peace?
Nonsense. Woman has always profited
From men at war. Since time began, if you
Camp-followed any conqueror, you too
Could count a hundred lovers on the sand.

Maiden Voyages

JUDY KRONENFELD

on the radio, Bach's
Brandenburg, my first
sophisticated music, spilling
like tinkling crystal from city
windows as I lay in my high
bed–promising
a life of wonder . . .

my daughter come and gone
in the old swaying
boat of a car, after her first sight
of her grandmother, broken
in body, turning
and turning over
the rich fields
of ancient memory

Time like a great steamer
gliding through the straits
into open sea
though no streamers
on its bow

just the dark ship,
the furling wake
of the waters, merging into
the dusk ahead

To Those Who Are Programming
Computers to Produce Poetry

DAVID CURRY

Do you really understand that the man
who starts out to write of his grandmother
ends up talking about a leaf, or vice-

versa? How will you bank synapses, joy
and grief, the stuff of the heart
that precedes and will happen after

its century? What is the button
for a true eye, seeing, socketed
in a head whose mind comes down

from fish and kindergarten?
Poems are *written,* you robot fools,
out of spinnings and crossings

too complex for your machine.
They come on like the days,
flawed and beautiful and of this world.

The Afterlife

MAURYA SIMON

Like a hover-craft heavily straining against
Gravity, rising above choppy waves and spray,
Tipping this way and that as it struggles to level
Itself on spumes of startled air, so my soul

Floats upward from the swirl of sheets,
From the fumes of sleep-drenched flesh,
And rises mightily to poise and right itself
Above the dream-fray of my earthly body.

Its passenger, in thought-balloons, cries:
"Stop! I'm dizzy, I'm afraid," but it sails on
And upward toward the ceiling, light-hearted,
A defiant dirigible, unstartled and sublime —

My soul meanders through the room, then glides
Unbidden through the walls into the carousel
Of night, joining vast tides of turning lights.
How easy it is to say good-bye now to what

Once was firm and dear, to that word *forever,*
To the slumbering, land-locked urges I wore
Like negligees, to green webs and arctic silence.
There's no progress here, no weather to defy,

No nature, nor gods or devils, no history, no
Science: only the *yes* to a wealth of nothingness,
To golden storehouses of unknowing, and (perhaps)
To something large and looming, calling me back.

INDEX OF POEMS IN THIS CHAPTER

This index of titles is limited to poems printed in this chapter.

In addition, a full index of all titles from all three genres together with names of poets, authors, and playwrights can be found on page 457. For literary terms, turn to the Glossary-Index at the end of the book

36 Troubleshooting Guide: Poetry

Topics For Quick Review

This alphabetical list focuses on recurring problem areas in the writing of poetry. It is similar to the troubleshooting guides at the ends of the fiction and drama sections.

The primary function of this guide is to assist you as you revise new work. If you believe that a poem you are working on is deficient in a particular way, look up the trouble area here. This list is your quickest way to locate where the topic is discussed in the text.

In addition, some instructors of creative writing classes use it to supplement their written comments on a particular poem. Rather than taking the time to explain a poetic technique that was covered in the text or in class, they can simply ask you to review certain pages.

For a more complete and detailed listing of terms and concepts in all three genres, use the Glossary-Index at the end of this text. It lists alphabetically the literary terms mentioned in this text along with brief definitions.

Subject areas to consider:

Aging: "As the Cold Deepens" (page 201); "Rhymes for Old Age" (page 215)

Nature: "On a Maine Beach" (page 208); "Design" (page 200)

Black identity: "We" (page 313); "What the Mirror Said" (page 203)

Animals: "Names of Horses" (page 216); "The Pardon" (page 213); "Dog Bite" (page 314)

Death: "Is It Well-Lighted, Papa?" (page 208); "The Pardon" (page 213); "The After-life" (322)

Status of women: "The Gift" (page 202); "What the Mirror Said" (page 203); "We" (page 213); "Burning the Letters" (page 312)

Childhood: "The Pardon" (page 213); "Lizards and Snakes" (page 212); "The Paradise of Wings" (page 213)

Love: "The Mapmaker . . ." (page 222); "Desire" (page 219); "Balances"(page 214); "Sonnet 29" (page 203)

Generations: "Grandmother" (page 310); "Always the One . . ." (page 205); "Maiden Voyages" (page 321)

Storms: "Winter Ocean" (page 200); "Regardless" (page 220)

War: "A Nuclear Winter" (page 223); "War" (320)

PART III

The Writing of Drama

....

37 Drama

A Live Performance

> • *The appeal of a live performance (328)* • *The six distinctive aspects of drama: dramatic impact, visual appeal, auditory aspects, physical production, continuous action, a spectator art (329)* • *Getting started: selecting a concept, primary characters, a plot outline (331)*

Those who have written short stories are at an advantage when turning to drama. There are many similarities between the two genres. Both depend heavily on **plot**. Both reveal **character** through action and **dialogue**. Both are presented with a distinctive **tone** and are unified with some kind of **theme**. Experience with either genre improves one's skill in the other.

There is, however, one fundamental difference that sets drama apart as a unique genre: a play is a live performance. It is a physical presentation in which actors (the term now includes both genders) perform and speak their lines for an audience.

Although most of us have read more plays than we have seen performances, it is important to remember that a script is only a portion of what goes into a finished dramatic work. It is a skeleton. The written script provides the lines to be spoken and brief notes about the action, but ultimately the play itself is a cooperative effort shared by actors, a director, set designers, stage crews, lighting crews, and many others. A good playwright keeps this in mind. In this respect, writing a play is significantly different from working alone on a poem or a work of fiction.

The physical aspect of a theatrical performance is drama's greatest asset and explains why it is still flourishing today despite competition with film and television. Ever since the first "talking movie," critics have predicted the end of **legitimate theater** — live performance on a stage. But not even the competition of television and DVD has stopped the opening of new theaters. Most major and many middle-size cities have resident companies, and these are augmented with university theaters offering both student and professional productions.

Legitimate theater continues to be popular in part *because* of television, not in spite of it. The cost of mass-audience television programs requires that they appeal to the widest possible audience. Sponsors demand it. As a result, there is a certain uniformity in sitcom and action-drama scripts. Plots, characters, and themes are frequently reduced to the simplest level and repeated with ritualistic regularity. Those who prefer subtlety and originality remain hungry for legitimate theater.

Every **genre** has its special attributes — qualities that distinguish it fundamentally from other forms of writing. It is a mistake to think of a play as fiction acted out on the stage, as a poem performed, or as a low-budget version of film. It is none of these things. Before you begin writing your first play script, consider carefully the true assets of this genre.

THE SIX DISTINCTIVE ASPECTS OF DRAMA

There are six characteristics of drama that distinguish it from the other genres. You will be able to find plays that do not contain all six, just as you can find some poems that make little use of rhythm and some stories without dialogue. But these are rare. Most playwrights value all six characteristics as the prime assets of the genre.

- First, **drama** is by definition a *dramatic art*. That is, it generally has an emotional impact or force. In the case of comedy, we call it vitality. This is not just a tradition; it is a necessity in an art form that requires an audience to give its undivided attention for two-and-a-half to three hours.

This impact is often established early in a play with a **dramatic question** that seizes the attention of the audience long before the **theme** becomes evident. Dramatic questions are usually blunt and simple: Is this stranger a threat? Who are they waiting for? Why do these characters hate each other?

Often these initial questions develop into specific conflicts and generate **tension**. Although the need for tension is not as strong in very short plays and in comedies, it remains a common characteristic in all drama.

Irony and satire often add to the dramatic impact of a play, just as they can in fiction. This is particularly true in comedy. Still another device is the use of surprise. Unusual or unexpected developments are effective in holding the attention of an audience.

Dramatic impact, however, is difficult to sustain. If maintained relentlessly, the audience will become numb. For this reason, most full-length plays work up to a series of dramatic peaks, allowing the emotions of the audience to relax in between.

This system of rising and falling action does not follow any prescribed pattern and is often intuitive on the part of the playwright, just as it is in the writing of short stories. But the need for such structure tends to make drama

330 Drama: A Live Performance

more sharply divided into scenes and acts — divisions that help control the dramatic impact.

- Second, drama is a *visual art*. Plays thrive on action. The way characters move about and interact physically is often as important as the lines. This concern for the visual extends beyond the characters. The set itself can be an important part of the production. Sophisticated lighting boards can convert the set from a somber tone to a vibrant factor instantly. The quest for visual impact has led some playwrights to experiment with mixed media by adding projected images.

- Third, drama is an *auditory art*. It appeals to the ear. Except for brief stage directions, every word in the script is **dialogue** and is intended to be spoken out loud. Even thoughts. The sound of those lines becomes very important. In some respects, this element brings some playwrights closer to poets than to writers of fiction. Repetition, for example, is a technique found in both drama and poetry. For this reason, playwrights often read their lines out loud or have others read them, listening to the composition rather than studying it on the page.

This special attention to the sound of language applies as much to plays that are realistic as it does to those that are dreamlike. Not only are the sounds important, silence can be used dramatically. Sometimes it has as much dramatic impact as a shout.

- Fourth, drama is a *physically produced art*. This is sometimes difficult to remember for those who have been writing fiction. Since sets have to be constructed with wood and nails, there is not the freedom to shift from scene to scene the way one can in a short story or film. Scriptwriters must keep in mind what kinds of demands they are placing on set designers and stage crews.

This requirement may seem like a limitation at first, but there are compensating assets. Playwrights have an intense, almost personal contact with their audiences that is entirely different from the detached connection fiction writers have with their readers. Also, the constraints of the stage often stimulate the imagination. For many playwrights, these aspects outweigh any disadvantage.

- Fifth, drama is a *continuous art*. It's nonstop. Members of the audience, unlike readers of fiction or poetry, watch a performance from beginning to end at one sitting. They can't linger on a sage observation or a moving episode. They can't turn back a page or review an earlier scene.

As you become involved in play writing, you will find that the flow of drama is an aspect you can use. There is a momentum to a play that you can control. With practice, you can make one portion of a scene seem to move rapidly and another more slowly. Fiction writers can't maintain quite this kind of control over their material.

- Finally, and closely connected, drama is a *spectator art*. Even more than with spectator sports, audience reaction is important. In contrast, most poets are relatively far removed from the readers of their work. Except for **performance poets**, few revise a work because of a critical review or poor public response. Some novelists will revise on the basis of comments from trusted friends, but once the book is in print, the revision process almost always ends.

Not so with plays. Playwrights often revise when their work is in rehearsal, after the opening-night reviews, and even later. They frequently base their revisions on audience reaction — those awful moments when it laughs at the wrong moment or squirms with boredom.

This does not mean that dramatists are slaves to the reactions of audiences and critics. In most cases, playwrights have a basic conception of the work that remains unalterable. But there is a direct and dynamic relationship between playwrights and their audiences. For many, this is one of the real pleasures in writing for the legitimate stage.

GETTING STARTED

Poems frequently begin with an image; stories are usually launched with a character in an ongoing situation. Plays more often begin with what is called a **concept**.

A dramatic concept includes a basic situation, some type of conflict or struggle, and an outcome, all in capsule form. A clear, useful concept can be expressed in two or three complete sentences. You can, of course, start a play as tentatively as you might begin a story, hoping to shape and develop the plot as you work through the first draft. But such an approach is generally not as successful in play writing because so much depends on the whole dramatic structure.

Plays, like stories, often evolve from personal experience, but the need to create a dramatic situation with conflict or struggle between two or more people often requires transformations of the original episode right from the start. Although there are many fine exceptions, plays are less likely to be based directly on a single personal experience than are stories.

As you cast about for a concept that has dramatic potential, recall stories you have heard about your family and accounts told to you about people you don't know. Remember that basic transformations may help even at this early stage. Consider any event as long as the characters and situation are familiar enough for you to make a revised version credible.

If you keep a literary journal, jot down a number of possible concepts. If one seems to take shape in your mind, devise fictitious names and give a brief description of what occurs. Next, write a sample of dialogue. Try to "hear" your characters interacting. See if you can create a little scene that at least roughly contributes to the concept you have in mind. Read the lines out loud. Imagine actors (male or female) saying those lines. Close your eyes and visualize the scene.

If you have done all this and you believe that the concept has potential, begin to block out the action. That is, develop an outline in which each brief sequence of events is described in a telegraphic phrase or sentence. Such an outline might start this way:

1. Morning: Tammy and Max are in a frenzied attempt to clean up the apartment, urging each other to hurry.
2. Doorbell rings. Mrs. Colton (young landlady) enters. Looks around, disapproving. Tammy and Max apologize for remaining mess.
3. Tammy leaves. She must go to work. Exits.
4. Mrs. Colton launches a tirade against Tammy. Her attitude toward Max, however, is distinctly friendly. Max continues to pick up the place, defending Tammy as best he can.

This is a basic triangle. Is it enough for your original concept? Or should you add the landlady's husband? Let your imagination run.

Since this outline is for your own benefit, adopt whatever form seems natural to you. Most playwrights, however, find notes on plot and characters helpful at this stage because drama, much more than fiction, is constructed in specific **scenes**.

Even if you are writing a one-act play with a single **set** — a good pattern to start with — you will want to think in terms of scenes. I will have more to say about this in the chapter on plot (Chapter 39), but from a playwright's point of view a scene is not a major subdivision of an act written into the script. It is a far shorter unit created simply by a character entering or leaving the stage. The little outline presented here, for example, contains four such scenes.

Some short plays have been written without these subtle yet important divisions, but they are rare. *Hello Out There*, which is presented in Chapter 38, uses eight such scenes. After your initial reading, review the script and mark these divisions. You will see how they provide structure for the play.

As for the form of the script, follow the pattern used by the plays included in this volume. At first it may seem monotonous to repeat the name of each speaker, but it is the customary practice, one that actors depend on in rehearsal. If you are working with a computer (almost universal now), you may want to program the name of each major character as a macro so that it will appear on the left margin with a simple two-stroke command.

Stage directions are written in italics. Italics in manuscript are still indicated by underlining, even though your computer is capable of producing special type. Underlining is a traditional signal to the printer. Place directions in parentheses when they are short. It is helpful to list the names of your characters after the title, arranging them in order of appearance.

There are four complete plays in this section. The first two are serious, **realistic**, and highly dramatic. The third is dreamlike, initially comic, but serious in theme. The third is a **farcical, satiric fantasy**, although it also has a serious theme. These four short works are markedly different in **tone** and treatment, and are a good indication of the enormous latitude you have in developing a play.

To get started, begin with a good concept — not just an idea, but a situation with potential conflict between two or more characters. Describe it in two or three complete sentences. Then develop your characters, fleshing them out with notes about their backgrounds and personalities. These notes are for your own benefit. (Rarely do playwrights describe more than basic physical characteristics in the script.) Next, block out the action by outlining a plot scene by scene.

As you write, keep in mind that your script is more than something to be read silently on the page. Visualize what is going on, scene by scene. Where are your actors sitting or standing? Have you given them enough to do? Read their lines out loud. Imagine the impact of each scene on your audience. Even if you have never worked with drama, remember that your script is the first step in the creation of what you hope will be a live performance before a live audience.

38 Hello Out There

for George Bernard Shaw

A Play

by William Saroyan

Characters

A YOUNG MAN
A GIRL
A MAN
TWO OTHER MEN
A WOMAN

Scene

There is a fellow in a small-town prison cell, tapping slowly on the floor with a spoon. After tapping a minute, as if he were trying to telegraph words, he gets up and begins walking around the cell. At last he stops, stands at the center of the cell, and doesn't move for a long time. He feels his head, as if it were wounded. Then he looks around. Then he calls out dramatically, kidding the world.

YOUNG MAN: Hello — out there! (*Pause.*) Hello — out there! Hello — out there! (*Long pause.*) Nobody out there. (*Still more dramatically, but more comically, too.*) Hello — out there! Hello — out there!

A GIRL'S VOICE is heard, very sweet and soft.

THE VOICE: Hello.
YOUNG MAN: Hello — out there.
THE VOICE: Hello.
YOUNG MAN: Is that you, Katey?
THE VOICE: No — this here is Emily.
YOUNG MAN: Who? (*Swiftly.*) Hello out there.
THE VOICE: Emily.

YOUNG MAN: Emily who? I don't know anybody named Emily. Are you that girl I met at Sam's in Salinas about three years ago?

THE VOICE: No — I'm the girl who cooks here. I'm the cook. I've never been in Salinas. I don't even know where it is.

YOUNG MAN: Hello out there. You say you cook here?

THE VOICE: Yes.

YOUNG MAN: Well, why don't you study up and learn to cook? How come I don't get no jello or anything good?

THE VOICE: I just cook what they tell me to. (*Pause.*) You lonesome?

YOUNG MAN: Lonesome as a coyote. Hear me hollering? Hello out there!

THE VOICE: Who you hollering to?

YOUNG MAN: Well — nobody, I guess. I been trying to think of somebody to write a letter to, but I can't think of anybody.

THE VOICE: What about Katey?

YOUNG MAN: I don't know anybody named Katey.

THE VOICE: Then why did you say, Is that you Katey?

YOUNG MAN: Katey's a good name. I always did like a name like Katey. I never *knew* anybody named Katey, though.

THE VOICE: *I* did.

YOUNG MAN: Yeah? What was she like? Tall girl, or little one?

THE VOICE: Kind of medium.

YOUNG MAN: Hello out there. What sort of a looking girl are *you?*

THE VOICE: Oh, I don't know.

YOUNG MAN: Didn't anybody ever tell you? Didn't anybody ever talk to you that way?

THE VOICE: What way?

YOUNG MAN: You know. Didn't they?

THE VOICE: No, they didn't.

YOUNG MAN: Ah, the fools — they should have. I can tell from your voice you're O.K.

THE VOICE: Maybe I am and maybe I ain't.

YOUNG MAN: I never missed yet.

THE VOICE: Yeah, I know. That's why you're in jail.

YOUNG MAN: The whole thing was a mistake.

THE VOICE: They claim it was rape.

YOUNG MAN: No — it wasn't.

THE VOICE: That's what they claim it was.

YOUNG MAN: They're a lot of fools.

THE VOICE: Well, you sure are in trouble. Are you scared?

YOUNG MAN: Scared to death. (*Suddenly.*) Hello out there!

THE VOICE: What do you keep saying that for all the time?

YOUNG MAN: I'm lonesome. I'm as lonesome as a coyote. (*A long one.*) Hello — out there!

THE GIRL appears, over to one side. She is a plain girl in plain clothes.

THE GIRL: I'm kind of lonesome, too.

YOUNG MAN (*turning and looking at her*): Hey — No fooling? Are you?

THE GIRL: Yeah — I'm almost as lonesome as a coyote myself.

YOUNG MAN: Who *you* lonesome for?

THE GIRL: I don't know.

YOUNG MAN: It's the same with me. The minute they put you in a place like this you remember all the girls you ever knew, and all the girls you didn't get to know, and it sure gets lonesome.

THE GIRL: I bet it does.

YOUNG MAN: Ah, it's awful. (*Pause.*) You're a pretty kid, you know that?

THE GIRL: You're just talking.

YOUNG MAN: No, I'm not just talking — you *are* pretty. Any fool could see that. You're just about the prettiest kid in the whole world.

THE GIRL: I'm not — and you know it.

YOUNG MAN: No — you are. I never saw anyone prettier in all my born days, in all my travels. I knew Texas would bring me luck.

THE GIRL: Luck? You're in jail, aren't you? You've got a whole gang of people all worked up, haven't you?

YOUNG MAN: Ah, that's nothing. I'll get out of this.

THE GIRL: Maybe.

YOUNG MAN: No, I'll be all right — *now*.

THE GIRL: What do you mean — now?

YOUNG MAN: I mean after seeing you. I got something now. You know for a while there I didn't care one way or another. Tired. (*Pause.*) Tired of trying for the best all the time and never getting it. (*Suddenly.*) Hello out there!

THE GIRL: Who you calling now?

YOUNG MAN: You.

THE GIRL: Why, I'm right here.

YOUNG MAN: I know. (*Calling.*) Hello out there!

THE GIRL: Hello.

YOUNG MAN: Ah, you're sweet. (*Pause.*) I'm going to marry *you*. I'm going away with *you*. I'm going to take you to San Francisco or some place like that. I *am*, now. I'm going to win myself some real money, too. I'm going to study 'em real careful and pick myself some winners, and we're going to have a lot of money.

THE GIRL: Yeah?

YOUNG MAN: Yeah. Tell me your name and all that stuff.

THE GIRL: Emily.

YOUNG MAN: I know that. What's the rest of it? Where were you born? Come on, tell me the whole thing.

THE GIRL: Emily Smith.

YOUNG MAN: Honest to God?

THE GIRL: Honest. That's my name — Emily Smith.

YOUNG MAN: Ah, you're the sweetest girl in the whole world.

THE GIRL: Why?

YOUNG MAN: I don't know why, but you are, that's all. Where were you born?

THE GIRL: Matador, Texas.

YOUNG MAN: Where's that?

THE GIRL: Right here.

YOUNG MAN: Is this Matador, Texas?

THE GIRL: Yeah, it's Matador. They brought you here from Wheeling.

YOUNG MAN: Is that where I was — Wheeling?

THE GIRL: Didn't you even know what town you were in?

YOUNG MAN: All towns are alike. You don't go up and ask somebody what town you're in. It doesn't make any difference. How far away is Wheeling?

THE GIRL: Sixteen or seventeen miles. Didn't you know they moved you?

YOUNG MAN: How could I know, when I was out — cold? Somebody hit me over the head with a lead pipe or something. What'd they hit me for?

THE GIRL: Rape — that's what they *said.*

YOUNG MAN: Ah, that's a lie. (*Amazed, almost to himself.*) She wanted me to give her money.

THE GIRL: Money?

YOUNG MAN: Yeah, if I'd have known she was a woman like that — well, by God, I'd have gone on down the street and stretched out in a park somewhere and gone to sleep.

THE GIRL: Is that what she wanted — money?

YOUNG MAN: Yeah. A fellow like me hopping freights all over the country, trying to break his bad luck, going from one poor little town to another, trying to get in on something good somewhere, and she asks for money. I thought she was lonesome. She *said* she was.

THE GIRL: Maybe she was.

YOUNG MAN: She was *something.*

THE GIRL: I guess I'd never see you, if it didn't happen, though.

YOUNG MAN: Oh, I don't know — maybe I'd just mosey along this way and see you in this town somewhere. I'd recognize you, too.

THE GIRL: Recognize me?

YOUNG MAN: Sure, I'd recognize you the minute I laid eyes on you.

THE GIRL: Well, who would I be?

YOUNG MAN: Mine, that's who.

THE GIRL: Honest?

YOUNG MAN: Honest to God.

THE GIRL: You just say that because you're in jail.

YOUNG MAN: No, I mean it. You just pack up and wait for me. We'll high-roll the hell out of here to Frisco.

THE GIRL: You're just lonesome.

YOUNG MAN: I been lonesome all my life — there's no cure for that — but you and me — we can have a lot of fun hanging around together. You'll bring me luck. I know it.

THE GIRL: What are you looking for luck for all the time?

YOUNG MAN: I'm a gambler. I don't work. I've *got* to have luck, or I'm a bum. I haven't had any decent luck in years. Two whole years now — one place to another. Bad luck all the time. That's why I got in trouble back there in Wheeling too. That was no accident. That was my bad luck following me around. So here I am, with my head half busted. I guess it was her old man that did it.

THE GIRL: You mean her father?

YOUNG MAN: No, her husband. If I had an old lady like that, I'd throw her out.

THE GIRL: Do you think you'll have better luck, if I go with you?

YOUNG MAN: It's a cinch. I'm a good handicapper. All I need is somebody good like you with me. It's no good always walking around in the streets for anything that might be there at the time. You got to have somebody staying with you all the time — through winters when it's cold, and springtime when it's pretty, and summertime when it's nice and hot and you can go swimming — through *all* the times — rain and snow and all the different kinds of weather a man's got to go through before he dies. You got to have somebody who's right. Somebody who knows you, from away back. You got to have somebody who even knows you're wrong but likes you just the same. I know I'm wrong, but I just don't want anything the hard way, working like a dog, or the *easy* way, working like a dog — working's the hard way and the easy way both. All I got to do is beat the price, always — and then, I don't feel lousy and don't hate anybody. If you go along with me, I'll be the finest guy anybody ever saw. I won't be wrong any more. You know when you get enough of that money, you *can't* be wrong any more — you're right because the money says so. I'll have a lot of money and you'll be just about the prettiest, most wonderful kid in the whole world. I'll be proud walking around Frisco with you on my arm and people turning around to look at us.

THE GIRL: Do you think they will?

YOUNG MAN: Sure they will. When I get back in some decent clothes, and you're on my arm — well, Katey, they'll turn around and look, and they'll see something, too.

THE GIRL: Katey?

YOUNG MAN: Yeah — that's your name from now on. You're the first girl I ever called Katey. I've been saving it for you O.K.?

THE GIRL: O.K.

YOUNG MAN: How long have I been here?

THE GIRL: Since last night. You didn't wake up until late this morning, though.

YOUNG MAN: What time is it now? About nine?

THE GIRL: About ten.

YOUNG MAN: Have you got the key to this lousy cell?

THE GIRL: No. They don't let me fool with any keys.

YOUNG MAN: Well, can you get it?

THE GIRL: No.

YOUNG MAN: Can you *try?*

THE GIRL: They wouldn't let me get near any keys. I cook for this jail, when they've got somebody in it. I clean up and things like that.

YOUNG MAN: Well, I want to get out of here. Don't you know the guy that runs this joint?

THE GIRL: I know him, but he wouldn't let you out. They were talking of taking you to another jail in another town.

YOUNG MAN: Yeah? Why?

THE GIRL: Because they're afraid.

YOUNG MAN: What are they afraid of?

THE GIRL: They're afraid these people from Wheeling will come over in the middle of the night and break in.

YOUNG MAN: Yeah? What do they want to do that for?

THE GIRL: Don't *you* know what they want to do it for?

YOUNG MAN: Yeah, I know all right.

THE GIRL: Are you scared?

YOUNG MAN: Sure I'm scared. Nothing scares a man more than ignorance. You can argue with people who ain't fools, but you can't argue with fools — they just go to work and do what they're set on doing. Get me out of here.

THE GIRL: How?

YOUNG MAN: Well, go get the guy with the key, and let me talk to him.

THE GIRL: He's gone home. Everybody's gone home.

YOUNG MAN: You mean I'm in this little jail all alone?

THE GIRL: Well — yeah — except me.

YOUNG MAN: Well, what's the big idea — doesn't anybody stay here all the time?

THE GIRL: No, they go home every night. I clean up and then I go, too. I hung around tonight.

YOUNG MAN: What made you do that?

THE GIRL: I wanted to talk to you.

YOUNG MAN: Honest? What did you want to talk about?

THE GIRL: Oh, I don't know. I took care of you last night. You were talking in your sleep. You liked me, too. I didn't think you'd like me when you woke up, though.

YOUNG MAN: Yeah? Why not?

THE GIRL: I don't know.

YOUNG MAN: Yeah? Well, you're wonderful, see?

THE GIRL: Nobody ever talked to me that way. All the fellows in town — (*Pause.*)

YOUNG MAN: What about 'em? (*Pause.*) Well, what about 'em? Come on — tell me.

THE GIRL: They laugh at me.

YOUNG MAN: Laugh at *you?* They're fools. What do they know about anything? You go get your things and come back here. I'll take you with me to Frisco. How old are you?

THE GIRL: Oh, I'm of age.

YOUNG MAN: How old are you? — Don't lie to me! Sixteen?

THE GIRL: I'm seventeen.

YOUNG MAN: Well, bring your father and mother. We'll get married before we go.

THE GIRL: They wouldn't let me go.

YOUNG MAN: Why not?

THE GIRL: I don't know, but they wouldn't. I know they wouldn't.

YOUNG MAN: You go tell your father not to be a fool, see? What is he, a farmer?

THE GIRL: No — nothing. He gets a little relief from the government because he's supposed to be hurt or something — his side hurts, he says. I don't know what it is.

YOUNG MAN: Ah, he's a liar. Well, I'm taking you with me, see?

THE GIRL: He takes the money I earn, too.

YOUNG MAN: He's got no right to do that.

THE GIRL: I know it, but he does it.

YOUNG MAN (*almost to himself*): This world stinks. You shouldn't have been born in this town, anyway, and you shouldn't have had a man like that for a father, either.

THE GIRL: Sometimes I feel sorry for him.

YOUNG MAN: Never mind feeling sorry for him. (*Pointing a finger.*) I'm going to talk to your father some day. I've got a few things to tell that guy.

THE GIRL: I know you have.

YOUNG MAN (*suddenly*): Hello — out there! See if you can get that fellow with the keys to come down and let me out.

THE GIRL: Oh, I couldn't.

YOUNG MAN: Why not?

THE GIRL: I'm nobody here — they give me fifty cents every day I work.

YOUNG MAN: How much?

THE GIRL: Fifty cents.

YOUNG MAN (*to the world*): You see? They ought to pay money to *look* at you. To breathe the *air* you breathe. I don't know. Sometimes I figure it never is going to make sense. Hello — out there! I'm scared. You try to get me out of here. I'm scared them fools are going to come here from Wheeling and go crazy, thinking they're heroes. Get me out of here, Katey.

THE GIRL: I don't know what to do. Maybe I could break the door down.

YOUNG MAN: No, you couldn't do that. Is there a hammer out there or anything?

THE GIRL: Only a broom. Maybe they've locked the broom up, too.

YOUNG MAN: Go see if you can find anything.

THE GIRL: All right. (*She goes.*)

YOUNG MAN: Hello — out there! Hello — out there! (*Pause.*) Hello — out there! Hello — out there! (*Pause.*) Putting me in jail. (*With contempt.*) Rape! Rape? *They* rape everything good that was ever born. His side hurts. They laugh at her. Fifty cents a day. Little punk people. Hurting the only good thing that ever came their way. (*Suddenly.*) Hello — out there!

THE GIRL (*returning*): There isn't a thing out there. They've locked everything up for the night.

YOUNG MAN: Any cigarettes?

THE GIRL: Everything's locked up — all the drawers of the desk, all the closet doors — everything.

YOUNG MAN: I ought to have a cigarette.

THE GIRL: I could get you a package maybe, somewhere. I guess the drug store's open. It's about a mile.

YOUNG MAN: A mile? I don't want to be alone that long.

THE GIRL: I could run all the way, and all the way back.

YOUNG MAN: You're the sweetest girl that ever lived.

THE GIRL: What kind do you want?

YOUNG MAN: Oh, any kind — Chesterfields or Camels or Lucky Strikes — any kind at all.

THE GIRL: I'll go get a package. (*She turns to go.*)

YOUNG MAN: What about the money?

THE GIRL: I've got some money. I've got a quarter I been saving. I'll run all the way. (*She is about to go.*)

YOUNG MAN: Come here.

THE GIRL (*going to him*): What?

YOUNG MAN: Give me your hand. (*He takes her hand and looks at it, smiling. He lifts it and kisses it.*) I'm scared to death.

THE GIRL: I am, too.

YOUNG MAN: I'm not lying — I don't care what happens to me, but I'm scared nobody will ever come out here to this Godforsaken broken-down town and find you. I'm scared you'll get used to it and not mind. I'm scared you'll never get to Frisco and have 'em all turning around to look at you. Listen — go get me a gun, because if they come, I'll kill 'em! They don't understand. Get me a gun!

THE GIRL: I could get my father's gun. I know where he hides it.

YOUNG MAN: Go get it. Never mind the cigarettes. Run all the way. (*Pause, smiling but seriously.*) Hello, Katey.

THE GIRL: Hello. What's *your* name?

YOUNG MAN: Photo-Finish is what they *call* me. My races are always photo-finish races. You don't know what that means, but it means they're very close. So close the only way they can tell which horse wins is to look at a photograph after the race is over. Well, every race I bet turns out to be a photo-finish race, and my horse never wins. It's my bad luck, all the time. That's why they call me Photo-Finish. Say it before you go.

THE GIRL: Photo-Finish.

YOUNG MAN: Come here. (THE GIRL *moves close and he kisses her.*) Now, hurry. Run all the way.

THE GIRL: I'll run. (THE GIRL *turns and runs. The* YOUNG MAN *stands at the center of the cell a long time.* THE GIRL *comes running back in. Almost crying.*) I'm afraid. I'm afraid I won't see you again. If I come back and you're not here, I —

YOUNG MAN: Hello — out there!

THE GIRL: It's so lonely in this town. Nothing here but the lonesome wind all the time, lifting the dirt and blowing out to the prairie. I'll stay *here.* I won't *let* them *take* you away.

YOUNG MAN: Listen, Katey. Do what I tell you. Go get that gun and come back. Maybe they won't come tonight. Maybe they won't come at all. I'll hide the gun. When they let me out you can take it back and put it where you found it. And then we'll go away. But if they come, I'll kill 'em! Now, hurry —

THE GIRL: All right. (*Pause.*) I want to tell you something.

YOUNG MAN: O.K.

THE GIRL (*very softly*): If you're not here when I come back, well, I'll have the gun and I'll know what to do with it.

YOUNG MAN: You know how to handle a gun?

THE GIRL: I know how.

YOUNG MAN: Don't be a fool. (*Takes off his shoe, brings out some currency.*) Don't be a fool, see? Here's some money. Eighty dollars. Take it and go to Frisco. Look around and find somebody. Find somebody alive and halfway human, see? Promise me — if I'm not here when you come back, just throw the gun away and get the hell to Frisco. Look around and find somebody.

THE GIRL: I don't *want* to find anybody.

YOUNG MAN (*swiftly, desperately*): Listen, if I'm not here when you come back, how do you know I haven't gotten away? Now, do what I tell you. I'll meet you in Frisco. I've got a couple of dollars in my other shoe. I'll see you in San Francisco.

THE GIRL (*with wonder*): San Francisco?

YOUNG MAN: That's right — San Francisco. That's where you and me belong.

THE GIRL: I've always wanted to go to *some* place like San Francisco — but how could I go alone?

YOUNG MAN: Well, you're not alone any more, see?

THE GIRL: Tell me a little what it's like.

YOUNG MAN (*very swiftly, almost impatiently at first, but gradually slower and with remembrance, smiling, and* THE GIRL *moving closer to him as he speaks*): Well, it's on the Pacific to begin with — ocean water all around. Cool fog and seagulls. Ships from all over the world. It's got seven hills. The little streets go up and down, around and all over. Every night the foghorns bawl. But they won't be bawling for you and me.

THE GIRL: What else?

YOUNG MAN: That's about all, I guess.

THE GIRL: Are people different in San Francisco?

YOUNG MAN: People are the same everywhere. They're different only when they love somebody. That's the only thing that makes 'em different. More people in Frisco love somebody, that's all.

THE GIRL: Nobody anywhere loves anybody as much as I love you.

YOUNG MAN (*shouting, as if to the world*): You see? Hearing you say that, a man could die and still be ahead of the game. Now, hurry. And don't forget, if I'm not here when you come back, get the hell to San Francisco where you'll have a chance. Do you hear me?

THE GIRL *stands a moment looking at him, then backs away, turns and runs. The* YOUNG MAN *stares after her, troubled and smiling. Then he turns away from the image of her and walks about like a lion in a cage. After a while he sits down suddenly and buries his head in his hands. From a distance the sound of several automobiles approaching is heard. He listens a moment, then ignores the implications of the sound, whatever they may be. Several automobile doors are slammed. He ignores this also. A wooden door is opened with a key and closed, and footsteps are heard in a hall. Walking easily, almost casually and yet arrogantly, a* MAN *comes in.*

YOUNG MAN (*jumps up suddenly and shouts at* THE MAN, *almost scaring him*): What the hell kind of jailkeeper are you, anyway? Why don't you attend to your business? You get paid for it, don't you? Now, get me out of here.

THE MAN: But I'm not the jailkeeper.

YOUNG MAN: Yeah? Well, who are you, then?

THE MAN: I'm the husband.

YOUNG MAN: What husband you talking about?

THE MAN: You know what husband.

YOUNG MAN: Hey! (*Pause, looking at* THE MAN.) Are you the guy that hit me over the head last night?

THE MAN: I am.

YOUNG MAN (*with righteous indignation*): What do you mean going around hitting people over the head?

THE MAN: Oh, I don't know. What do you *mean* going around — the way you do?

YOUNG MAN (*rubbing his head*): You hurt my head. You got no right to hit anybody over the head.

THE MAN (*suddenly angry, shouting*): Answer my question! What do you mean?

YOUNG MAN: Listen, you — don't be hollering at me just because I'm locked up.

THE MAN (*with contempt, slowly*): You're a dog!

YOUNG MAN: Yeah, well let me tell you something. You *think* you're the husband. You're the husband of nothing. (*Slowly.*) What's more, your wife — if you want to call her that — is a tramp. Why don't you throw her out in the street where she belongs?

THE MAN (*draws a pistol*): Shut up!

YOUNG MAN: Yeah? Go ahead, shoot — (*Softly.*) and spoil the fun. What'll your pals think? They'll be disappointed, won't they. What's the fun hanging a man who's already dead? (THE MAN *puts the gun away*). That's right, because now you can have some fun yourself, telling me what you're going to do. That's what you came here for, isn't it? Well, you don't need to tell me. I *know* what you're going to do. I've read the papers and I know. They have fun. A mob of 'em fall on one man and beat him, don't they? They tear off his clothes and kick him, don't they? And women and little children stand around watching, don't they? Well, before you go on *this* picnic, I'm going to tell you a few things. Not that that's going to send you home with your pals — the other heroes. No. You've been outraged. A stranger has come to town and violated your women. Your pure, innocent, virtuous women. You fellows have got to set this thing right. You're men, not mice. You're homemakers, and you beat your children. (*Suddenly.*) Listen, you — I didn't know she was your wife. I didn't know she was anybody's wife.

THE MAN: You're a liar!

YOUNG MAN: Sometimes — when it'll do somebody some good — but not this time. Do you want to hear about it? (THE MAN *doesn't answer.*) All right I'll tell you. I met her at a lunch counter. She came in and sat next to me. There was plenty of room, but she sat next to me. Somebody had put a nickel in the phonograph and a fellow was singing *New San Antonio Rose*. Well, she got to talking about the song. I thought she was talking to the waiter, but *he* didn't answer her, so after a while *I* answered her. That's how I met her. I didn't think anything of it. We left the place together and started walking. The first thing I knew she said, This is where I live.

THE MAN: You're a dirty liar!

YOUNG MAN: Do you want to hear it? Or not? (THE MAN *does not answer.*) O.K. She asked me to come in. Maybe she had something in mind, maybe she didn't. Didn't make any difference to me, one way or the other. If she was lonely, all right. If not, all right.

THE MAN: You're telling a lot of dirty lies!

YOUNG MAN: I'm telling the truth. Maybe your wife's out there with your pals. Well, call her in. I got nothing against her, or you — or any of you. Call her in, and ask her a few questions. Are you in love with her? (THE MAN *doesn't answer.*) Well, that's too bad.

THE MAN: What do you mean, too bad?

YOUNG MAN: I mean this may not be the first time something like this has happened.

THE MAN (*swiftly*): Shut up!

YOUNG MAN: Oh, you know it. You've always known it. You're afraid of your pals, that's all. She asked me for money. That's all she wanted. I wouldn't be here now if I had given her the money.

THE MAN (*slowly*): How much did she ask for?

YOUNG MAN: I didn't ask her how much. I told her I'd made a mistake. She said she would make trouble if I didn't give her money. Well, I don't like bargaining, and I don't like being threatened, either. I told her to get the hell away from me. The next thing I knew she'd run out of the house and was hollering. (*Pause.*) Now, why don't you go out there and tell 'em they took me to another jail — go home and pack up and leave her. You're a pretty good guy, you're just afraid of your pals.

THE MAN *draws his gun again. He is very frightened. He moves a step toward the* YOUNG MAN, *then fires three times. The* YOUNG MAN *falls to his knees.* THE MAN *turns and runs, horrified.*

YOUNG MAN: Hello — out there! (*He is bent forward.*)

THE GIRL *comes running in, and halts suddenly, looking at him.*

THE GIRL: There were some people in the street, men and women and kids — so I came in through the back, through a window. I couldn't find the gun. I looked all over but I couldn't find it. What's the matter?

YOUNG MAN: Nothing — nothing. Everything's all right. Listen. Listen, Kid. Get the hell out of here. Go out the same way you came in and run — run like hell — run all night. Get to another town and get on a train. Do you hear me?

THE GIRL: What's happened?

YOUNG MAN: Get away — just get away from here. Take any train that's going — you can get to Frisco later.

THE GIRL (*almost sobbing*): I don't want to go any place without you.

YOUNG MAN: I can't go. Something's happened. (*He looks at her.*) But I'll be with you always — God damn it. Always!

He falls forward. THE GIRL *stands near him, then begins to sob softly, walking away. She stands over to one side, stops sobbing, and stares out. The excitement of the mob outside increases.* THE MAN, *with two of his pals, comes running in.* THE GIRL *watches, unseen.*

THE MAN: Here's the son of a bitch!
ANOTHER MAN: O.K. Open the cell, Harry.

The THIRD MAN *goes to the cell door, unlocks it, and swings it open. A* WOMAN *comes running in.*

THE WOMAN: Where is he? I want to see him. Is he dead? (*Looking down at him, as the* MEN *pick him up.*) There he is. (*Pause.*) Yeah, that's him.

Her husband looks at her with contempt, then at the dead man.
THE MAN (*trying to laugh*): All right — let's get it over with.
THIRD MAN: Right you are, George. Give me a hand, Harry.

They lift the body.

THE GIRL (*suddenly, fiercely*): Put him down!
THE MAN: What's this?
SECOND MAN: What are you doing here? Why aren't you out in the street?
THE GIRL: Put him down and go away.

She runs toward the MEN.
THE WOMAN *grabs her.*

THE WOMAN: Here — where do you think *you're* going?
THE GIRL: Let me go. You've no right to take him away.
THE WOMAN: Well, listen to her, will you? (*She slaps* THE GIRL *and pushes her to the floor.*) Listen to the little slut, will you?

They all go, carrying the YOUNG MAN's *body.* THE GIRL *gets up slowly, no longer sobbing. She looks around at everything, then looks straight out, and whispers.*

THE GIRL: Hello — out — there! Hello — out there!
CURTAIN

39 The Dramatic Plot

• The importance of concept (347) • The scene as the basic unit of drama (348) • Providing dramatic questions (351) • Controlling the pace through rising and falling action (353) • Using subplots (354)

A good dramatic plot starts with a good concept. As I explained in Chapter 37, a **concept** is a very brief description that includes a basic situation, some type of conflict or struggle, and an outcome.

A concept is not the same as a theme. **Themes**, which we will examine in Chapter 48, are the abstract ideas implied by a play. They are the portion of a play that comments on the human condition. Because thematic statements are abstract, they don't include a description of what occurs or even the names of characters.

The *concept*, on the other hand, is a compressed plot statement, from one to three complete sentences, about what happens to whom. There is nothing intellectual about a concept. Think of it as a quick sales pitch.

Crass as concept statements may seem, they are important because they keep you on track. Many concept statements are too vague to be helpful. Here are some concepts for launching new plays that are distinctly un-promising, and ways they could be improved:

- "It's a play about jealousy."
  Too general. Who is jealous of whom? Why? And what is the outcome? A better version: "Because Estelle could never forget her unfaithful father, she couldn't trust her husband until she confronted her past."

- "War is hell."
  This is a **truism** that has been repeated so often it no longer has impact. To become meaningful, it would have to contain some notion of the plot and the primary characters. Here is one possibility: "For years the family revered the memory of Frank, who had been killed in the Vietnam War, but only belatedly did they realize how seriously his younger brother had been psychologically damaged in the same war."

- "A college student's first summer job."
  Yawn! We need specifics and some assurance that this is going to be a fresh treatment of a frequently used situation. For example: "Kathleen is

delighted to be hired as a mechanic at an auto repair shop but faces a moral dilemma when she discovers that her new friends are reconditioning stolen cars."

These revised concepts briefly describe who is involved (the primary characters) and what happens to them. They don't, of course, do justice to the complexities and insights that good plays provide, but composing such statements is a good way to test whether you have a situation that is dramatic enough to keep your audience in the theater. The concept is the starting point, whereas the theme, the intellectual component of a play, often takes shape in the writing and is highlighted in subsequent drafts.

We can be fairly certain, for example, that the starting point of William Saroyan's *Hello Out There* was not an abstract theme about dangers of hypocrisy in society and the fundamental need for individuals to make genuine contact with one another. Plays, like stories, rarely spring from abstract principles. It's more likely that he began with a vision of a well-meaning drifter held in a small-town jail on a false rape charge and a young woman trapped in the same town, a prisoner in a different way. These two join forces, trying to break free, only to be overwhelmed in the end. A concept like this describes specific people in a particular dramatic situation and an outcome. Once you have a clear, interesting concept, you are ready to block out a plot.

THE SCENE AS THE BASIC UNIT OF DRAMA

As I explained earlier, the word *scene* is often used to describe subdivisions of acts in longer plays. They may be written into the program notes and often indicate a lapse of time or a change of setting. In some cases, they replace acts altogether.

For dramatists and actors, however, the word *scene* also refers to each unit of action that begins with an entrance or an exit and ends with the next shift of characters on the stage. To avoid confusion, think of these as *secondary scenes*. They are the essential and basic units of action for the playwright, the actors, and the director. Occasionally, a secondary scene may have a dramatic unity in itself. That is, it may build to a **climax** and then be punctuated by the departure of one or more characters. For greater impact, it may conclude with an **exit line**, a memorable, startling, or dramatically revealing statement.

More often, the unity is subtler. It establishes the almost unnoticed rise and fall of action that distinguishes the play that is "dramatic" from one that seems "flat" or "dull."

Hello Out There is an excellent example of careful scene construction. It is a one-act play presented in one primary scene. There is one stage set and one apparently uninterrupted flow of action. But from a playwright's point of view, the work is divided into eight secondary scenes. Each is marked by an exit or entrance, and each has an influence on the rise and fall of dramatic impact.

Here are the scenes listed in an outline form that some playwrights find helpful when planning a new play. The word *girl* is used rather than the more contemporary *young woman* simply to conform with Saroyan's script.

1. Man alone on stage; talks to girl offstage
2. Girl enters; they get to know each other
3. Girl exits; man gives a brief monologue
4. Girl returns; they make a pact
5. Girl exits; husband enters, argues, shoots
6. Husband exits, girl returns
7. Husband and pals return, drag body out
8. Girl alone on stage; repeats the refrain

This sparse outline demonstrates how many separate units will be involved, but it doesn't indicate which are major scenes and which are minor, which are highly dramatic and which merely develop relationships. Each secondary scene deserves a closer look.

Although the opening scene has only one actor on the stage, it is far from static. Notice that the man is not musing philosophically to himself or addressing the audience. His first lines call out for contact with someone else, and then almost at once he is interacting with the young woman even before she is on stage. This is no prologue. Psychologically, the play begins as soon as these two characters are in voice contact.

Incidentally, this same technique of opening a play with a central character alone on the stage is also employed in the next play you will read, *Reckoning* by Tony Padilla (page 356). Look for it.

The second scene in *Hello Out There* begins when the young woman actually appears. If we read the script on the page hastily as if it were fiction, her entrance might not seem significant. But when we read analytically as a playwright would, we picture the scene, imagining the action from the audience's point of view. In production, her arrival on stage is the psychological start of a new scene.

This second scene is the longest in the play. Saroyan has to fill in a lot of background and, in addition, draw these two strangers together convincingly. It would have been possible to have Emily on stage from the start, but postponing her entrance helps emphasize the loneliness of the central character, a loneliness he shares with all the primary characters. It also keeps the lengthy second scene from becoming even longer.

The third scene is brief. She goes out to look for tools, and he is left on the stage alone. But the scene is important because it allows him to lash out vehemently against what he sees as injustice. The fact that he is alone on the stage indicates to the audience that he is speaking his inner convictions, his true feelings expressed out loud. Were it not for this little scene, we might suspect that he was cynically lying to the girl simply to save himself.

The fourth scene is one in which Emily and Photo-Finish make the pact to meet in San Francisco. Notice that their relationship has grown with surprising speed. In fiction, one might be tempted to spread out the action over the course of a day or more, but in plays the dramatic development tends to be compressed.

Emily leaves, ending the fourth scene, and there is only a moment of sound effects before a new character suddenly appears on the stage. The tension mounts as we learn that this is the angered husband. An argument pushes the dramatic impact to new levels, and the husband draws his gun. The scene culminates with three shots.

This is the **climax** of the play. A climax is rarely the final scene of a full-length **tragedy**. It is the major turning point that initiates the falling action (see **plot**). As short as *Hello Out There* is, it adopts many of the characteristics of a traditional tragedy.

In the sixth scene, the husband has fled and Emily returns. The dying **hero** and heroine are alone on the stage. If this were an opera, this is where the final duet might be sung. As realistic drama, it is a brief, terse, and yet tender moment.

But a problem arises here. How is the playwright going to maintain dramatic interest in the brief yet important section that follows the death of the protagonist? Once again, a new secondary scene is prepared for — the seventh.

First, the audience hears activity building offstage. Saroyan is careful to include this in his stage directions: "The excitement of the mob outside increases." Mob? It is only four characters — the husband, two friends, and then the wife. But they burst on the stage and have the dramatic impact of a mob.

Emily demands that they put the body down — in what we can assume is the first dramatically assertive act of her life. She is slapped and pushed to the floor.

The last of these secondary scenes is so brief that it consists of only one line. But to understand just how powerful the device is, imagine the girl delivering that last line with the other characters still on stage, struggling to drag the body off. Emily would be literally upstaged. Her line would be a mere continuation of the preceding dialogue. Having her alone on the stage, probably with a single beam of light on her, isolates the final words. Her plight — now matching that of Photo-Finish at the beginning of the play — becomes the focal point.

When one first reads a play like this, it is easy to assume that it is one continual flow of action. True, many of these scenes could be combined by eliminating all exits and entrances up to the point of the husband's arrival. But that long, unbroken scene would lose much of its energy. It might well seem to drag. Exits and entrances in this play provide the basic organizational structure with which the dramatic impact is heightened and lowered and then heightened again in regular succession, holding the audience from beginning to end.

At the other extreme, too many very short scenes can make the play seem choppy and insubstantial. Because most of us have seen more films than plays, it is easy to be influenced by the rapid pace of cinema scenes. The camera not only can blend extremely brief units of action into an apparently smooth flow, it can also shift setting without a break. Changing the set on the stage, however, is time consuming and tends to shatter the illusion of reality. For this reason, many full-length plays and almost all one-act plays maintain a single set. There is a tendency, also, to use plots that cover a single time span. Although there are excellent exceptions, skipping a year or more lends itself better to longer plays.

In judging the length of your secondary scenes, keep imagining the effect on your audience. Too many very short scenes reduce the chance to develop character and relationships; lengthy scenes (especially those that lack physical action) may create monotony and slow the pace. You can make these decisions more easily if you have a chance to hear your script read aloud or, best of all, to see it in production.

PROVIDING DRAMATIC QUESTIONS

How are you going to hold your audience in their seats? When you write fiction, this is less of a problem. A story or novel can be read in installments. But when you produce a play, you are asking an audience to give it their uninterrupted attention. They can't even take a bathroom break.

Because of this, most plays are energized with a series of **dramatic questions**. These are like lures to hold the interest of the audience. They are similar to those in fiction (Where are we going? What will this stranger be like?), but they are far more important.

Looking at the full range of drama from Sophocles to our own decade, there are certain dramatic questions that recur frequently. This recurrence does not make the plays redundant; one hardly notices the similarity. But their widespread use does suggest just how valuable dramatic questions are.

1. *Will he come?* Shakespeare charged the first act of *Hamlet* with this question, applying it to the ghost. More recently, it has been broadened to cover the full length of plays. Clifford Odets' *Waiting for Lefty*, written in the 1930s, Samuel Beckett's *Waiting for Godot*, and Harold Pinter's *The Dumb Waiter* all rely heavily on anticipation of a character who never appears. And to some degree, the question is a factor in *Hello Out There* as soon as the threat of a lynching is raised.

2. *Who did it?* This is, of course, the literary version of "Whodunit?" We find it running the full length of drama from Sophocles' *Oedipus Rex* to Tennessee Williams' *Suddenly Last Summer*. The trial scenes in Herman Work's *The Caine Mutiny Court-Martial* and, in a loose sense, Robert Anderson's *Tea and Sympathy* and Arthur Miller's *The Crucible* are simply variations of this question. In some cases, the audience knows who is guilty; the dramatic question arises in an attempt on the part of the *characters* to find out. It is a highly variable device, although the trial scene has become overused.

3. *Will he or she succeed?* This is by far the most used of all dramatic questions. It has been applied to noble and evil characters alike. The answer is rarely a simple "yes" or "no" since the audience has visualized these alternatives from the start. More often, the conclusion is qualified: the protagonist wins in some significant way but at a price or, conversely, loses the struggle but gains in a way not previously anticipated by the audience.

In Saroyan's play, Photo-Finish faces overwhelming odds and loses his life, but Emily, although still trapped, achieves for the first time a moment of assertiveness.

4. *Will he or she discover what we know?* The classic example is Sophocles' play *Oedipus Rex*, in which the attention of the audience is held by a character gradually discovering terrible truths about himself. It is also a factor in Shakespeare's *Othello*. And it has been adapted in plays of psychological self-discovery such as Arthur Miller's *Death of a Salesman*.

5. *Will a compromise be found?* This question has held audiences in such varied plays as Sophocles' *Antigone* (the answer is "no") and John Galsworthy's *Strife* (the answer is "yes" but with terrible consequences for both sides). Both plays, by the way, carefully avoid the temptation to pit blameless individuals or groups against opponents who are totally evil. Such plays end up being **melodramas** no matter how well-intentioned.

6. *Will this episode end in violence?* This question is frequently used in contemporary drama. In fact, it is one of the final questions in *Hello Out There*. Even though almost every indication points to a tragic ending, we keep hoping otherwise until the shots are fired. There is high drama in violence, but relying on it excessively drags the work down to the level of the least imaginative television thriller.

7. *What's happening?* This is the question most frequently asked of plays in the **absurdist** tradition. These works plunge the audience into a confusing, often inexplicable environment. Playwrights like Pinter, Beckett, Ionesco, and occasionally Albee use ambiguity as a dramatic question.

This is, however, a risky device for the novice. Like free verse, it seems easy at first but can all too easily slide into meaninglessness. It requires genuine wit or intellectual ingenuity to keep the play alive. In short, a dull play is not improved by being made an obscurely dull play.

The opening dramatic question is often referred to as the **hook**. It arouses interest from the start. But most plays move from one dramatic question to the next so that the audience is kept wondering about immediate problems, as well as about what the ultimate resolution will be. *Hello Out There* is a good example of how the playwright can create a new question just as an old one has been resolved.

The opening scene poses the question, "What is happening?" We begin to receive answers from Emily, but we are now concerned with "Will they succeed?" When it appears that they won't, we wonder "Will there be violence?"

Playwrights, of course, don't start with such questions; they start by shaping a plot. Early in the revision process, however, they examine just how successfully the play will hold the audience. If a scene seems to drag, the fault may be due to a lack of action or excessive length, but more often it simply needs a better dramatic question.

CONTROLLING THE PACE

Pace is all important in a play. Scenes that seem slow continue to be revised well into production. Although one rarely hears about a play in which the pace is too rapid, it is possible to race too quickly through scenes that should unfold character or clarify aspects of the plot. And too much dramatic voltage at the beginning of a play can create a slump later on. Or, worse, it can numb an audience into indifference. All these problems call for work on pacing.

Traditional terms are helpful if we remember that they apply mainly to the plots of traditional plays. **Rising action**, for example, accurately describes the mounting complications with which many plays from all historical periods are begun. In full-length dramas, problems may be compounded with **subplots** involving secondary characters acting as **foils** to highlight or set off the major characters. The **climax** is not the very end but the turning point at which the protagonist's fortunes begin to fail. From there on, we have **falling action**, which in tragedies results in a **catastrophe** or **denouement** — often the death of the hero.

Sound old-fashioned? True, Aristotle described drama in those terms. True, they apply to Greek and Elizabethan tragedies. But they also apply to many modern works by such playwrights as Eugene O'Neill, Arthur Miller, and Tennessee Williams. In condensed form, they can also be seen in William Saroyan's *Hello Out There*.

The rising action involves the young man meeting an ally and planning an escape. There is an element of desperate hope there. The climax occurs when the enraged husband returns. From there on it is falling action through to the death of the protagonist. Although the play is brief and in one act, the plot structure is similar to that of a traditional three-act play or a Shakespearean tragedy of five acts.

This plot pattern continues to be popular not because playwrights who use it are imitative but because it is good theater. It lends itself to a variety of situations and it holds audiences.

There are, in addition, other effective ways to handle the pacing of a dramatic plot. One focuses on characterization and is sometimes referred to as the *onion approach*: a series of scenes exposes the inner life of a character or a couple like peeling the layers of an onion. Eugene O'Neill's *The Iceman Cometh* reveals a single character this way; Edward Albee's *Who's Afraid of Virginia Woolf?* exposes the illusions of a couple with equal intensity.

Another type of loose structure is sometimes called the *Grand Hotel* pattern. The title refers to a film based on a novel by Vicki Baum. This approach weaves together many different stories and is sometimes used in plays. Arthur Miller's relatively short *A Memory of Two Mondays*, for example, deals with the men who work in the shipping room of an auto-parts warehouse. It is concerned almost equally with all the characters.

The pace in loosely structured plays like this is controlled not by the rise and fall of a protagonist, but by a series of dramatic questions arising from the problems faced by a number of different characters.

With **satiric** works, which I will examine in more detail in Chapter 47, pace can also be controlled by posing and then answering dramatic questions. In addition, one can increase the level of exaggeration. Many such plays intentionally start on a low key. This avoids the risk of establishing a pace in the opening that you can't sustain. When you read the two satiric plays included later in this volume, notice how each begins with a deceptively mild opening scene.

Clearly, there are no rigid rules about how to construct a good plot. Whether you are writing a serious play or a comedy, you are free to draw on certain traditional patterns or experiment with new approaches. This is not to say, however, that anything will work. You must maintain forward movement in some way. If you don't create dramatic questions and don't make use of rising and falling action, you will have to find some other method of keeping your production alive. If you ignore pacing and let your play go slack, your audience will quickly lose interest.

USING SUBPLOTS

A **subplot** is a sequence of actions involving secondary characters that runs parallel to the main plot. It is rarely used in short plays because of the time required to introduce secondary characters in any detail, but as soon as you start working with a longer play, the technique is well worth considering. In most cases, a subplot either echoes the main plot or provides a contrast. If, for example, the main plot deals with a couple's serious marital conflict, the subplot might introduce another couple with similar but less serious problems. Or the subplot might contrast the challenges faced by a woman as single parent with those faced by a man in similar circumstances.

Often the subplot is lighter than the primary plot, thereby establishing a tonal contrast. It can even provide comic relief, a technique of easing tension that I will discuss in more detail in Chapter 47.

When the characters in a subplot face problems, they are usually resolved before the conclusion of the main plot so as not to interfere. The only exception to this is the "Grand Hotel pattern," in which there are many equally important plots. These are not, however, true subplots since there is no central and dominant story line.

After you have written several short plays, you will want to expand your horizons with a full-length work. Much will depend on how much drama you have read and seen in production. Earlier in this chapter, I referred to many well-known plays. If you are serious about play writing, you will want to read as many of these as you can. They will give you a good sense of how to plot a longer work, including those with subplots.

Plot is also important in fiction and even in some narrative poems, but it is central in most plays. Although extended monologues are often presented dramatically as stage productions, they are not true dramas. Often they depend more on sophisticated wit and verbal ingenuity than they do on a dramatic story line and the interrelationship between characters. The long history of drama is dominated by visual activity and the lure of an unfolding plot.

A dramatic plot gives you as a dramatist an opportunity to seize and hold the attention of an audience with a sustained intensity rarely given to the writer of fiction. This direct and charged contact between artist and viewer is one of the special rewards for the playwright.

40 Reckoning

A Play

by Tony Padilla

Characters

JOE: A corporate giant who finds himself on the brink of mental illness due in part to his submersion into his work. He is in his early forties and in good physical condition.

MARY: An intelligent, self-made woman of ambiguous motives. She is the same age as Joe.

Time & Place

The near-future.

A large bright room. There are two large, comfortable chairs sitting SC[1] next to each other with identical side tables next to them. A large painting dominates the US[2] wall.

When the lights come up Joe is sitting on one of the chairs. He is obviously uncomfortable and finds it difficult to sit still. He stands and walks around a bit before sitting back down. Mary enters.

MARY: Hello Joe, are you comfortable? Can I get you anything?

JOE: Water would be nice.

MARY: I'll be right back.

    She exits and after a few moments returns with a tray holding two glasses and a large bottle of water. She puts the tray on the table furthest from Joe, pours water into one of the glasses and hands it to him.

JOE: Thanks.

MARY: [*After a beat[3]*] I'm glad you're here Joe. I know you wouldn't be here if you hadn't done some research. What did you find out?

---

[1] Stage center

[2] Up stage (rear of stage)

[3] A quick pause

JOE: Just enough to know you're worth looking into.

MARY: We're more than *worth looking into*. We both know the pain you're in. You need us, you need to be here. . . .

JOE: That decision is *mine* isn't it?

MARY: Of course. [*Beat*] Did you know that all our clients are men?

JOE: Interesting. All of them? I have no problem with that. I prefer the company of men.

MARY: The drive that fuels the success you and our other clients enjoy creates this selection. And since you're here you have faced the fact that things *have to change* for you. You should feel good about that.

JOE: I don't feel good about anything yet. Just tell me what you've done for other people and what you plan to do for *me*.

MARY: Sure. Then you can tell me about yourself and I'll determine whether we'll accept you as a client . . . or not.

JOE: [*Beat*] I'm sorry I didn't mean to sound like. . . .

MARY: You don't have to apologize. I welcome your honesty. If we accept you, we accept you as you are. [*Beat*] We have a forty-years-old gentleman who's had no physical contact with anyone for five years. He can't stand to be looked at. He becomes hysterical, hyperventilates, and passes out.

JOE: So what does he want to change?

MARY: Everything! He came to us because he wanted to feel the way he felt when he first told his wife he loved her . . . the way he felt when his first child was born. He wanted to feel the optimism of youth again. Do you remember those feelings?

JOE: No. [*Beat*] Feelings are overrated. I can never deal with people crying and pouring out their hearts to me. It makes me very uncomfortable. Actions speak louder than tears any day.

MARY: You don't believe that . . . that's why you're here. We constantly deal with men who need to be driven to tears. In their case tears are a badge of honor.

JOE: So what do you do for these men? How did you treat them?

MARY: In one instance the first thing we did was give a man a plant he was responsible for keeping alive . . . a bigger job than it sounds. We built from there. Soon he'll be taking his family to Italy and adding a greenhouse to his property.

JOE: And does he still have a successful business?

MARY: He has a successful *empire*! [*Beat*] You're not alone Joe.

JOE: [*Beat*] No?

MARY: Men have always found themselves embracing what they do and detaching themselves from what they feel and how they express it.

JOE: What exactly would I have to do?

MARY: [*Slight pause*] I can't tell you exactly what your treatment programs will be. Why don't you tell me what it was like for you growing up?

JOE: What's the matter? Didn't you find out enough in your research? [*Beat*] Don't expect me to get sexual.

MARY: What you tell me is up to you.

JOE: [*Defensively*] Of course it is. [*He regrets having said that but says nothing about it. He stands and walks around but never goes too close near her.*] I was an only child. Mom had looks, Dad had money. I never saw them argue . . . but I never saw them kiss either. How much of this is really important?

MARY: I'll conclude that when you're done. What type of kid were you in school?

JOE: I was the smart type. [*Beat*] I always looked to the future. I have no use for the past. I try to forget it. Unless you hurt me . . . then I don't forget. [*Beat*] I didn't spend a lot of time with girls in high school . . . probably one of the reasons I graduated a year early.

MARY: That must've made your parents proud.

JOE: I was only doing what I was supposed to do. I don't think you should get praise for that.

MARY: Then how does one get praise from you?

JOE: By going above and beyond what you're supposed to do!

MARY: That's a lot to ask.

JOE: If you can't do that, you're just ordinary. [*Beat*] I didn't date much in college either. I think every girl I met in college was just looking for a husband.

MARY: That's funny . . . most college girls think the boys they meet can't seem to let go of Mommy.

JOE: I made good friends in college . . . all of them men. [*Laughs*] We all had a genius I.Q.

MARY: All our clients have a genius I.Q. I do too.

JOE: So I guess in here I wouldn't stand out . . . just another schmuck trying to regain some . . . social skills?

MARY: Humanity.

JOE: Humanity? That's a little strong isn't?

MARY: I meant the humanity that you need to get in touch with yourself.

JOE: What about drugs? Do you comatose men into happy bliss so they can take Italian vacations and build greenhouses?

MARY: They could do that on their own without coming here. [*Beat*] So you managed to leave college without a wife. Then what?

JOE: Leaving college without a wife was a bigger accomplishment than you might think. After school I started a company. I dedicated my life to it . . . then. A few years went by, and all of a sudden I found myself with a wife and kids, and my friends becoming incredibly boring.

MARY: So you found yourself married *all of a sudden*?

JOE: Yes, doesn't every man? *All of a sudden* was just a figure of speech.

MARY: I don't believe there is such a thing as *just a figure of speech*.

JOE: A few of us friends grew up together, grew rich together, then grew apart. Today I wouldn't walk across the street to see any of them. They're all idiots, traitors.

MARY: [*Slowly, deliberately*] Including Emilio Vega?

JOE: [*Surprised*] What do you know about Emilio Vega?

MARY: I know he was important to you . . . that everybody but you thought his death was an accident. [*Beat*] Like you, too much was not enough for him. He had alienated everyone he had ever met. Nobody cared about him at the time when he needed it . . . so he *decided* to die.

JOE: Yeah, well, he died rich and powerful.

MARY: And alone and miserable. He decided to die because he couldn't stand the agony of perpetual exclusion.

JOE: You know what they say, *life's a bitch and then you die.*

MARY: [*Beat*] Do you think Emilio's death scared you into coming here?

JOE: I'm sure it had some effect on me. He was the first man I ever loved and admired.

MARY: And now he's dead. Do you feel guilty, do you think his life was irrelevant?

JOE: No, I don't.

MARY: What do you have left to accomplish? You're known world wide, rich, feared, respected.

JOE: Are *you* ready to die?

MARY: No, I have a few . . . issues . . . to deal with before I'm ready.

JOE: Obviously I have a few *issues* of my own. [*Beat*] Excuse me I need to use the bathroom.

MARY: [*Pointing*] Second door on the right.
   He exits.
   She loses her composure, becomes visibly upset. She sits and gets up a few times. It appears as if she's going to throw up, but doesn't. She pours herself some water, drinks then walks around taking deep breaths. When he enters she shows no sign of being upset.

JOE: [*Entering*] If you're going to treat me, I should know what kind of woman you are . . . beyond the *credentials* I mean.

MARY: That's fair enough. Why don't you tell me what you know first and I'll fill in the blanks . . .

JOE: To *you* of course. [*Paces around but keeps his distance from her*] You had an average, middle class up-bringing . . . always had a date but never a steady boyfriend . . . no cheerleading . . . you were more the library type. [*Beat*] You haven't mentioned that we went to the same college at the same time. I don't remember you.

MARY: I remember you.

JOE: I was memorable. You don't seem to like men very much. I mean you like men, but you don't *like* men . . .

MARY: What else have you found out?

JOE: You were brilliant. You put yourself through school. Your parents were killed by a drunk driver, and you made sure the drunk paid for it. You withdrew from society, got a second degree. You have few friends, no husband, no steady boyfriend.

MARY: I think you have more information than you need. Does your family know about your plans to join us here?

JOE: [*Matter-of-factly*] I haven't told them anything. This is *my* business. They wouldn't care anyway.

MARY: Of course they would.

JOE: No they wouldn't. I don't want them running my life. Living with a family is no different than running a company. They suck all the energy out of a man. They kill your passion. . .

MARY: Do you consider yourself a *passionate* man?

JOE: We probably don't think of passion in the same way.

MARY: Probably not, but I thought one of the reasons you were here was to get in touch with certain passions . . . that would get you close to your family again.

JOE: Yeah, well, it's just not going to happen. [*Beat*] Is there any reason why I should remember you?

MARY: Many reasons, but that's not where we want to go right now.

JOE: Why not? It could be interesting.

MARY: [*Perhaps a bit too sternly*] Not to me! [*Softer*] I'm not the same person you knew . . .

JOE: I'm sure you're not. Are you sure I knew you?

MARY: I'd bet my life on it.

JOE: Then it must be true. Come on, why should I remember you?

MARY: [*After a pause, matter-of-factly*] Because you told me you loved me . . . because you asked me to marry you.

JOE: [*Shocked*] What? I don't think so! You got me confused with someone else. The only woman I ever proposed to is my wife.

MARY: [*Calmly, without anger*] You proposed to Olivia Kent, do you remember her? She was beautiful, sophisticated, rich. You were a sophomore, she was a junior. You proposed but she didn't accept. After Olivia it was my turn. I thought you were right out of a romance novel. You told me you loved me and I believed you. We had a few wonderful months . . . then you disappeared. You dropped out of sight . . . out of school, out of town and completely out of my life. Not a phone call, not a note . . . nothing . . . ever!

JOE: Olivia Kent wanted to marry me. I rejected her! I didn't want to be controlled by her father. Is this why I'm here because I hurt you twenty years ago? People hurt each other everyday, get over it . . . or is this part of your selection process?

MARY: You should face the effect you've had . . .

JOE: What I have to face is that all of a sudden you've made this more complicated for me.

MARY: You need to come to terms with the way you've related to people in. . . .

JOE: I come to terms with things as they happen, I don't wait a generation. Some things you forget out of self-defense.

MARY: Do you believe the past can come back to haunt you?

JOE: No, I don't spend time thinking about shit like that.

MARY: You've never made a mistake? Never backed the wrong guy? Never abused your power or neglected responsibility? How does anyone get to be where you are and stay clean?

JOE: *You don't!* But the past coming back to haunt me is not something I worry about.

MARY: The past is fluid, it leaks into your present when you least expect it. When it does there is a reckoning to be done. We'll design a program to help you.

JOE: How will you do that if everyone I know, including you, would rather see me disappear?

MARY: We have to find a way.

JOE: Look, whether we had a relationship or not, I can't remember, so I can't *feel anything* about it.

MARY: That's a very convenient justification. Sooner or later you'll have to face up to yourself.

JOE: In a perfect world people might do the right thing. In the real world, we make deals, contracts, money, accept casualties, forget unpleasant memories, and avoid responsibility. Once in a while it all catches up to you. It caught up to Emilio Vega.

MARY: [*Pause. Calmly*] Will you please take your clothes off down to your shorts?

JOE: [*Laughs, caught by surprise*] What? This is how you'll determine if I'm worthy of joining your little asylum? A little kinky isn't it?

MARY: I need to know to what extent you're willing to go to get the most out of your treatments. Every man we've treated has gone through a similar exercise.

JOE: [*Begins to undress down to his t-shirt and shorts. He enjoys his words as he speaks*] My life is proof of how far I'm willing to go to get what I want. How is parading my naked body in front of you anything but a stupid attempt at humiliating me? [*Laughs, walks up to her*] Do you want me to take off my shorts? I'm proud of my body.

MARY: [*Steps away from him with a bemused laugh*] I'm well aware of that. Down to the shorts will be just fine.

JOE: I bet you would be a different woman if you had met the right man.

MARY: I met you.

JOE: Yeah, but I was never the right man for anybody.

MARY: You don't believe that. When you got married you were happy.

JOE: You're right. For about three years everything was perfect.

MARY: What do you think happened?

JOE: I'm not sure but success demanded more than I expected. It fed on itself and spoiled everything.

MARY: A lot of people mistake success for fulfillment.

JOE: [*Indignantly*] What does a woman like you know about fulfillment? You are going to teach *me* how to love again? [*With laughter in his voice*] Based on what, intuition? books you've read?

MARY: You don't know as much about me as you think you do. I have enough experience to help you.

JOE: Why can't you just admit that this is all really personal? It's all about your feelings, your revenge. [*Starts getting dressed and becomes agitated*] Come on, let's get this over with. Let me hear your *professional* rejection so I can go away with the gratification that it wasn't your *personal* opinion. I think your rejection will be a lot better than a trip to Italy. And I hate watering plants. Have you considered that I might be the victim?

MARY: Of what? Of over-indulgence? Of self-importance? No. I haven't.

JOE: [*With some anger*] Maybe you should! I am here because I don't know where else to go or what else to do. It's called desperation!

MARY: I can help.

JOE: How can you help a man who betrayed you, broke your heart and vanished from your life without a word?

MARY: I healed. I got over you.

JOE: Just like that?

WRY: No, not *just like that.*

JOE: So what now? I come to you looking for help; you reject me and that makes us even?

MARY: No, we will never be even. It took time but I managed to convince myself that what you did really had nothing to do with me.

JOE: Did you think I would just come out and admit I was an asshole and beg you to forgive me?

MARY: It was a mistake to talk about our past.

JOE: Bullshit! If I hadn't said anything, *you* would have. You've carried this a long time. You couldn't pass up the chance to see my reaction. I'm just not sure what you really want from me.

MARY: [*Pause. She's cool, emotionally detached*] I think I have all the information we need from you.

JOE: [*Sternly*] Are you sure? So what's it going to be, am I in or am I out?

MARY: That's not how it works . . .

JOE: *You* make the policies. Make an exception for an old lover. Just tell me . . . am I in or am I out?

MARY: [*Pause*] It's not that simple.

JOE: Why not?

MARY: It just isn't! [*Pause*] We'll look over your file and I'll let you know as soon as I can. [*After a beat she exits*]

JOE: [*Calling after her*] You can't just walk out on me. You stupid woman, did you think I was going to marry you, start having kids when I had a brilliant life ahead of me? I had ambitions beyond your imagination, dreams beyond your comprehension, [*Softly as if in a trance*] I'm no Emilio Vega . . . I'm what this country's all about . . . look at me, I've always been the future. [*Beat. On the verge of tears in a fetal position he calls out to her*] Come back here. You have to help me . . . you have to help me . . . you have to help me . . . you have to help me. . . . [*He keeps repeating it as his voice and the lights fade out*]

41 Conflict

Generating Emotional Impact

> • *Generating emotional impact through conflict (364)* • *Person against person (364)* • *Triangular conflicts (366)* • *Melodrama: When conflict dominates theme and characterization (367)* • *Inner conflicts and how to reveal them (368)* • *Comic conflicts (370)* • *Creating a network of conflicts (370)*

Almost all plays over the course of the past 2,500 years are conflict driven. That is, conflict is the prime energizing force. This is not just a matter of tradition. It is a natural response to the fact that plays are intended to be produced before a live audience. They require uninterrupted attention.

When we say that a work is "dramatic" or "powerful," we are implying that conflict of some type has been used convincingly. Dramatic questions, described on page 351, arouse curiosity; conflict arouses rapt attention. To achieve this, conflicts have greater emotional power and tend to run through the length of a drama. In serious drama, they may evoke fear, excitement, anger, or commitment. They pump adrenaline. In comedy, they evoke laughter. Conflict comes in many forms, some more subtle than others.

PERSON AGAINST PERSON

Most plays pit a **protagonist** against an **antagonist** in one way or another. (The word *hero* is often avoided because it implies greatness. *Protagonist* is both morally neutral and gender neutral.) The antagonist is usually an individual, but in addition he or she often suggests a particular attitude or some aspect of society. Occasionally the antagonist takes the form of a group such as a gang.

In *Hello Out There* the antagonist appears at first to be the husband. After all, he pulls the trigger. But he is responding to his buddies, so they too are a part of the opposing force, as is the wife. She has clearly lied about what really happened to save her own reputation. All this deceit in the name of "honor."

On a broader level, these characters suggest a brutal and reprehensible aspect of our society. This **symbolic** aspect of the conflict gives Saroyan an opportunity to comment on society as a whole. And he unmistakably takes sides.

One of the themes of the play is presented when Photo-Finish learns how the townspeople treat Emily and how they are accusing him of rape. "Rape? *They* rape everything good that was ever born." When there is still hope of escape, she asks, "Are people different in San Francisco?" He replies:

> People are the same everywhere. They're different only when they love somebody. More people in Frisco love somebody, that's all.

While the vigilantes act as if the wife is an innocent victim, the play suggests that Emily and Photo-Finish are the true victims.

The conflict in Tony Padilla's play "Reckoning" is less blatant. At first, Joe and Mary seem to be simply sparring. He is sounding her out as to what counseling might do for him, and she makes it clear that he, like many of their clients, needs assistance in spite of being financially successful.

The first real blow is landed when she reveals that she knows about the death of Emilio Vega. Joe admits that Vega was "the first man I ever loved and admired." He died, Joe adds, "rich and powerful."

She points out that he died "alone and miserable." Furthermore, she suggests that Vega's death may have "scared" Joe into coming there to seek help.

The conflict between the two of them is intensified once again when she reveals that when she and Joe were attending the same college they had an affair and he proposed to her:

> You told me you loved me and I believed you. We had a few wonderful months . . . then you disappeared . . . not a phone call, not a note . . . nothing . . . ever!

Wham! The conflict is dramatized with the revelation of a deep personal grievance that has lasted for years.

He struggles to defend himself, pointing out that "People hurt each other everyday, get over it," but she keeps pressing him to deal with the implications of his past actions. She describes this with a poignant metaphor:

> The past is fluid. It leaks into your present when you least expect it. When it does, there is a reckoning to be done.

At the end of the play, she leaves him alone on the stage, echoing the way he left her years before. His final cries for help are unanswered, just as hers must have been.

In a sense, this is a revenge play. But who has won? As she points out, ". . . we will never be even." As often happens in life, the consequences of thoughtless cruelty hurt all who are involved.

Both this play and *Hello Out There* are rooted in conflict between individuals, and both plays are equally concerned with attitudes found widely in our society. For Saroyan, the antagonists are modeled on those narrow-minded bullies who are willing to lie and even kill those who are weaker; for Padilla, the antagonist is the self-centered chauvinist for whom material success is the highest value.

Plays that deal passionately with social, moral, or racial issues often adopt a political stance. I will have more to say about socially conscious drama and themes of protest in Chapter 48. What concerns us here is the way in which conflict between specific individuals is often used as a **vehicle** to reveal disturbing aspects of our society.

TRIANGULAR CONFLICTS

Three-way conflicts have certain advantages over those limited to two opponents. Triangles add more than just an additional character. They compound the possibilities of character development.

The first pattern that comes to mind is the love triangle, the relationship of two individuals threatened by a third. Such a conflict often generates jealousy and rage. This pattern has a venerable history. Stories of a wife's betrayal by a husband who has fallen in love with another woman have been told and retold from Euripides' tragedy, *Medea,* around 440 B.C., to Robinson Jeffers' modern verse play with the same name. The same pattern of betrayal and revenge is repeated endlessly in contemporary play and film scripts on both serious and comic levels.

If you plan to use a love triangle as the basis of conflict in a one-act play, you will have to work hard to achieve originality. The sexy baby-sitter or an obliging secretary are **stereotypes**, too familiar for use. But triangles do continue to exist in life, and in some cases the unique circumstances of an actual case will suggest a fresh dramatic situation.

Triangles don't necessarily have to involve love relationships. Three individuals vying for a job, a promotion, or an award become a triangle. Two parents and a child often become a triangle in conflict. Two senior workers who find themselves having to take orders from a newly promoted younger associate can be an explosive triangle.

The third member of a triangle doesn't even have to be a person. In contemporary dramas, both husbands and wives have been seduced by professional commitments that become the third member of a triangle. A married person's involvement with a political cause or a religious faith can also have the impact of an infidelity.

Watch out, once again, for versions that have been overdone. The marriage that is threatened by a husband's preoccupation with his business can, if not done in a fresh manner, become as hackneyed in drama as in fiction. Padilla's *Reckoning* touches on that, but so much more is going on thematically that the bare bones of the business-versus-love pattern don't dominate.

Merely reversing the sexes doesn't add much if the characters are still cardboard. And there should be a moratorium on drama plots based on painters and writers who wreck their marriages for the sake of art. But even setting these aside, there are enough triangulations left to serve future dramatists for the foreseeable future.

MELODRAMA: WHEN CONFLICT DOMINATES THEME AND CHARACTERIZATION

Anyone who has watched television dramas or action-thriller films has been bombarded by **melodrama**. Such work is usually based on a simple struggle between good and evil. The loyalty of the audience is fixed from start to finish. It's our team versus theirs, our country versus theirs, law enforcers against lawbreakers, good people (or loyal dogs) against aggressors. Seeing this pattern so often in television dramas and popular film can be numbing. We wait for the concluding car chase, shoot-out, or blockbusting explosion as if it were a sports event.

There is nothing wrong with nonsadistic melodrama as popular entertainment. It is to sophisticated drama what a superhero comic strip is to literary fiction. Even Abraham Lincoln enjoyed a good melodrama as a way to forget the burden of his office, just as many intelligent people today find pleasure in a James Bond film. But if you want to write a play that offers more than escape, you will want to guard against melodrama.

Melodrama destroys subtlety in two different ways. First, it has the power to simplify the **theme** of a play to the level of an adventure story. Second, it tends to turn the characters into stereotypes — mere **stock characters** with no depth or complexity. Melodrama turns conflict into an end in itself.

There are many ways to generate compelling drama without having it spill over into melodrama. *Hello Out There* is a good example. If Saroyan had only been interested in creating a thriller, he probably would have focused on the vigilante gang, introducing them from the start and dropping all those references to loneliness. The theme would be reduced to a simple matter of life versus death.

It's unlikely that a melodrama like this would bother to develop a parallel between being a prisoner in a cell and being trapped in a small, mean-spirited community. Nor would it take the time to show how violence is often motivated by attempts to "save face."

Characterization would be reduced to a simple level as well. Photo-Finish would undoubtedly be made blameless and heroic. We would no longer see his weaknesses — his perilous lifestyle, his habit of taking risks, or his reliance on luck for survival.

As for Emily, she might cry and scream a lot to rouse the emotions, but we would not get to know her as a person or understand the life she leads in that oppressive little town.

The husband would also be simplified so as to become pure evil, the kind of villain we love to hate. We would no longer see him as a weak man who is unsure about his wife and intimidated by his pals.

Tony Padilla is equally careful to keep a potentially melodramatic plot from blotting out the subtlety of themes and characterization in *Reckoning*. It might have been tempting to make Joe a stereotypical male chauvinistic pig who never wavers from his egotistical drive for success and who eventually blows his brains out. As such, it would follow the pattern of many forgettable plays and television dramas.

Instead, Padilla makes sure that we see Joe's many sides as he vacillates from arrogance ("I was memorable") to briefly humble (". . . I was never the right man for anybody . . ."), to self-pity ("Have you ever considered that *I* might be the victim?") to desperation (". . . you have to help me . . . you have to help me . . .").

And Mary is no paragon of sympathy and compassion. She abandons him in the end just as she was abandoned by him years before.

The shorter the play, the more likely it is that a violent conflict between central characters will overpower both the theme and characterization. Novice playwrights are sometimes tempted to push conflict to the point of murder or suicide simply to keep a lackluster script lively. Before you go to this extreme, make sure that your characters and themes are strong enough to prevent them from being overpowered by the action.

Fortunately, you have the ability as playwright to adjust the level of conflict almost as easily as you turn the volume up or down on a radio. And you can do this without changing the structure of the play. Murder can be moderated to a fight, and a fight downgraded to a verbal attack. Suicide can be downsized to poignant expressions of despair, as it is in *Reckoning*.

INNER CONFLICTS AND HOW TO REVEAL THEM

Presenting inner conflicts is one of the best ways to achieve subtlety in characterization. The very phrases with which we describe such indecision suggest dramatic tension: a character is "of two minds," "struggling with himself," or even "at war with herself." Such individuals are torn between love and fear, courage and timidity, or anger and affection. Or they may be attracted to two different people, two opposing ethical positions, or two sexual identities. Inner conflict is part of the human condition.

But how is one to reveal what goes on in the mind of a character in a genre that depends almost entirely on dialogue and actions? If you have been writing fiction, your first inclination may be to consider **monologues**. After all, Shakespeare used them. The soliloquies of Hamlet and Lady Macbeth are among the most quoted dramatic lines in the language. But remember that those monologues were embedded in five-act plays. If we hadn't heard those famous passages so often and studied them so carefully out of context, they would blend into the work as a whole. In addition, Elizabethan drama accepted the convention of major characters expressing their inner conflicts eloquently in **blank verse**. Most contemporary, realistic plays are intended to reflect more closely the behavior and speech of daily life. Inner debate expressed through a monologue often seems artificial.

When monologues are used in realistic drama today, they are usually brief. Saroyan's first scene begins with a short monologue, and he repeats the device by having Photo-Finish alone on the stage in the abbreviated third scene. This second monologue is particularly important because it is the only hard evidence the audience has that Photo-Finish really is fond of Emily and is not just using her for escape. Although Emily's two-sentence monologue at the very end of the play takes only a moment, it effectively reveals her inner lament.

During the 1960s and 1970s, there was a certain vogue for long monologues among playwrights in the **absurdist** school. Their plays were often dreamlike, philosophical, and talky. The best of them maintained interest through flashes of insight and wit, but the approach was short lived. It takes remarkable skill on the part of both the playwright and the actor to hold the attention of an audience with thoughts alone. Most amateur attempts fail.

A far more effective way to reveal inner conflict is to provide your protagonist with a *confidant*, a personal friend who is not quite central to the action. If you are working with two couples, the wives or the husbands can sometimes express inner conflict when talking with each other, revealing private feelings that they are reluctant to share with their partners. In longer plays, the confidant may be a **foil**, a minor character who mainly serves to set off a primary character by contrast. The foil is often a relatively comic character in an otherwise serious play.

Another approach is to use action. People often reveal their inner conflicts unconsciously through their behavior. It is not difficult to have your characters do the same. There is a small example in *Hello Out There* that, although easily missed, represents a well-used device. Emily is torn between the desire to do whatever Photo-Finish asks and her fear of leaving him for a minute. When he asks her to go and look for cigarettes, she does leave, but almost at once she comes running back. Alternating behavior like this can also be used in more significant scenes. A character starts to do one thing, then abruptly does another. Often no lines are needed to spell out the inner conflict.

Padilla uses significant action twice. On your first reading of the script, you may have missed their importance, but in production they are unmistakable. The first is at the very opening of the play. Joe, alone on the stage, is described as being "obviously uncomfortable and finds it difficult to sit still." Soon, he "stands and walks around a bit before sitting back down." Our very first impression of him, then, is far from the self-assured and successful man he tries to portray.

Midway through the play, Mary also has a moment alone on the stage. As soon as he leaves "She loses her composure, becomes visibly upset. . . . It appears as if she is going to throw up . . ." No dialogue is needed. She is clearly torn between her role as a calm and objective psychological counselor and her actual feelings of anguished fury.

Sometimes inner conflict takes the form of indecision; in other cases it is true **ambivalence**, two opposing desires that exist simultaneously. In either case, it is an excellent way to humanize a character and make him or her credible.

It is also an effective way to avoid melodrama. Melodramatic heroes such as James Bond are never torn with indecision or ambivalence. Uncertainty is a far more human characteristic.

Although conflict is an enormously important aspect of most plays, it's not usually where one starts when planning a new work. The concept is too abstract. Plays are almost always about people, so focus on specific people and their relationship with each other. Try to describe what they are dealing with in the form of a **concept**. Once you have that in place, you will be able to see where the major conflicts lie and start revising the script to make the best use of them.

COMIC CONFLICTS

All types of conflict lend themselves to comedy. The most common is antagonism between individuals: husbands and wives, brothers and sisters, or individuals and a stranger. Triangles multiply the possibilities, just as they do in serious drama.

The intensity of conflict in comedies ranges from gentle satire, as in the play you will be reading in Chapter 42, to extreme exaggeration known as farce and slapstick, comedy pushed to its absurd ultimate as in *Valley Forgery*, which is in Chapter 46.

If you have the feeling that the first draft of a comedy you are writing lacks vitality, look closely at the lines of conflict. It may be that they could be exaggerated for comic effect.

CREATING A NETWORK OF CONFLICTS

Until now, we have been examining various types of conflict as if they were separate and distinct. A well-developed drama, however, contains a network of conflicts that reinforce each other.

On first reading, Tony Padilla's *Reckoning* may seem to be almost exclusively a conflict between a woman and a man who has treated her badly. But if that were the only theme, the play would simply be reiterating a familiar **truism**. The fact is that Joe's decision to seek counseling must have been made long before he is reminded of his prior relations with Mary years ago.

His own statements about himself reveal that he has been struggling with conflicts for years, most of them inner struggles. There is, for one, his image of himself as strong and self-sufficient countered by his desperate need for help. In addition, there is his life-long conviction that financial success is all that counts countered by his realization that "success demanded more than I expected. It fed on itself and spoiled everything."

Mary, too, is dealing with intense inner conflict. Her effort to appear perfectly in control is, as we have already seen, countered by a suppressed set of angry uncertainties.

Hello Out There provides an even more complex network of conflicts. Many of them are revealed through dialogue and action. Primarily, of course, it is a struggle between Photo-Finish and his antagonist, the outraged husband. In a simple melodrama, that conflict would stand alone as the prime and perhaps only concern of the work. Saroyan has made sure, however, that it is only one of many interrelated conflicts.

When the play opens, no antagonist is in sight (similar in this regard to *Reckoning*). The first major conflict to be introduced is this solitary prisoner pitted against those who have jailed him. The enemy is "them," a vague notion of forces outside the jail. This conflict of man against society is highlighted when we learn that the name of the town is Matador. If the town is the bullfighter, he is the bull in the pen, waiting for the deadly sport to begin.

Next, we learn that Emily is also pitted against this town. Her life is not threatened, but her spirit is. She is not just lonesome, she is alienated. The men in town, she reports, laugh at her. Her father takes what little money she earns. She is willing to take great risks to escape.

Their conflict with this oppressive town is soon overshadowed by the direct confrontation between Photo-Finish and the husband. But the man is not acting alone. The town remains an antagonist, the "matador," right through to the end of the play.

Although the husband is the enemy, he has his own conflicts. First, it is clear that he and his wife are antagonists. He actually puts his gun away when Photo-Finish starts revealing the truth. The man keeps calling Photo–Finish a liar, but he continues to listen. And when he is asked whether he is in love with his wife, he doesn't answer. Pathetically, when he is told that his wife asked for money, he responds with, "How much did she ask for?" Clearly, this is a tormented relationship.

We see even more conflicts when it is revealed that this husband is being driven by pressures from his wife and friends. As Photo-Finish puts it, "You're a pretty good guy, you're just afraid of your pals." Saroyan has him repeat this line for emphasis. As with so many acts of violence, the perpetrator is motivated in part by fear of his own peer group. This doesn't excuse his actions, but it does humanize him. When you look closely at what drives these characters, it is clear that this play is far from the simple television plot of man against the mob. The tragic killing is a result of a network of conflicts. In the end, Emily is also a victim and in conflict with the town, although now she has money and a new assertiveness.

At first, it may seem almost impossible to generate so many different conflicts in the limited time frame of a relatively short one-act play. But if your characters are well developed in your mind, you will see that none of them is purely good or purely bad. They are all driven by different and conflicting forces and needs. Once you understand this, identifying and dramatizing a variety of conflicts will become a natural part of the revision process through successive drafts.

The play that follows as the next chapter is different from both *Hello Out There* and *Reckoning* in many respects. First, it is **nonrealistic**. It creates its own world. Second, it is much shorter. Third, although it explores serious insights about the creative process, it is essentially a comedy. Read it through once for pleasure; then read it again for analysis. Ask yourself what the play is suggesting about the relationship between writers and the individuals they use as models to create a literary work.

In addition, examine the different conflicts that run though this play. Even though the work is short and comic, these conflicts are what gives the play its sense of dramatic energy.

42 Coulda, Woulda, Shoulda

A Play

by Glenn Alterman

Characters

CY
YETTA
MARTY

Scene

A small, simply decorated kitchen. It is about 11:30 A.M. Yetta is seated at the kitchen table finishing her coffee. Cy is rushing around, getting dressed.

CY: You're kidding? He said that?

YETTA: That's what he said.

CY: When?

YETTA: This morning when I gave him his bath.

CY: What a kid.

YETTA: Could you bust?

CY (*looking around*): Where's my belt?

YETTA: On the chair. (*He gets it, puts it on.*) Stood up in the tub, put his hand on my shoulder and said, "Ma, I want to be a rabbi."

CY: A rabbi? You're kidding? Every morning it's something else.

YETTA: At first, first, I thought he said "a rabbit."

CY (*stops for a moment*): What?

YETTA: Yeah, thought he said "I want to be a rabbit, Ma." Almost dropped the sponge I laughed so hard. I mean can you imagine? But then he looked at me, seemed so serious. You know those eyes of his. Said it again, loud and clear, black and white. Looked like a little Moses in the tub waiting for the waters to part. (*Slowly, very strong.*) "Ma, I want to be a rabbi. A rabbi, you understand?" I stopped, smiled, what could I. . . ? Said, "Sure, okay honey, if that's what you want." Washed the soap off, towel-dried him, baby powder, kissed him on the head and gave him a big hug. Well he gave me a look, got upset, started to cry.

CY: Cry? Why?

YETTA: I don't know. I asked him, wouldn't answer. Looked at me like I was the worst mother in the world. Like I'd just stabbed him in the heart or something. Ran to his room, slammed the door, locked it shut. Wouldn't let me in. Couldn't get him out. Been in there all morning.

CY: All morning?

YETTA: All morning long!

CY: You're kidding? Where's my shoes?

YETTA: By the sink. (*He gets the shoes, starts putting them on.*) I've been sitting here, waiting for you to get up. We've got a problem, Cy.

CY: I'll say, our son — Marty! I'm taking that lock off his door first thing when I get home tonight. Enough of this shit!

YETTA: What are you talking about? You've got to go talk to him.

CY: Me? About what? I didn't have no fight with him.

YETTA: What fight? Who fought? A misunderstanding, that's all.

CY: I don't got time for this now. He'll come out when he's good and ready. And stop giving him so many baths for Christ's sake!

YETTA: Talk to him.

CY: Didn't you hear me?

YETTA: He's your son!

CY: I'm late. I'll talk to my son — later.

YETTA: When, at four in the morning when you get home?

CY (*grabbing his coat, starting to go*): Whenever!

YETTA (*blocking the door*): The drunks of the world can wait!

CY: Hey, the drunks of the world put food on this table and don't you forget it. You should thank God we got that bar. (*Then, looking through his coat pocket.*) Where's my keys?

YETTA (*ignoring him, looking toward the bedroom, calling sweetly*): Marty, come on out. Daddy's leaving for work, come say good bye.

CY (*looking around*): Where the hell's. . . ?

YETTA (*sweetly, calling to the bedroom*): Marty.

CY: Where the hell are they?

YETTA: On the bureau, where you left them!

CY (*as he storms off, calling to the bedroom*): Marty, come on out. I don't got all day. (*Yetta looks anxiously toward the bedroom. Loud banging.*) Martin get out of there! You hear me? Out!

(*It's quiet for a moment. Then returning, carrying the keys, under his breath*):

He doesn't want to come out.

YETTA: So you're just gonna leave?

CY: What do you want me to do, break the door down?

YETTA (*turning away, upset*): Go 'head, go. GO!

CY (*He starts to leave, but then returning, upset*): Why's it always gotta be this way? Huh, why? Why do I got to leave here almost every day with you crying and me with a knot in my stomach? Why, huh, I'm asking you?

YETTA (*tensely, looking straight at him*): I am not crying!

CY: Can't I leave here just once, JUST ONCE YETTA, a pleasant goodbye, kiss on the cheek? Why's it always got to be Marty's been bad, or Marty's. . . ? Always something!

YETTA (*furiously*): The drunks of the world are waiting. Go ahead, go!

MARTY (*from the bedroom, yelling*): Stop it! Stop it already, both of you!

(*A light change. They both turn toward the bedroom. A door slams. Marty enters. He's in his forties, wearing large children's pajamas, a pair of glasses and a black hat. He's carrying a pen and pad.*)

YETTA: What? What's wrong?

MARTY: I can't concentrate! This constant arguing, bickering back and forth!

YETTA: You don't have to yell.

MARTY: Why, did anybody ever just talk here?

CY: Told you he'd come out when he was good and ready.

YETTA: Marty, take your hat off in the house.

MARTY: Ma, I'm trying to finish this scene, please!

YETTA: So what's stopping you? We were just . . .

MARTY: Please, I've got a whole play ahead of me.

YETTA (*very cool*): Sorry, Mister Playwright.

MARTY: Alright, let's just go back a bit. You were standing here, Ma, I'm still in the bedroom, and he's about to leave.

YETTA: But you're here now, just say goodbye. What's the big. . . ?

MARTY: Ma, please, don't tell me how to write my play. I'm still a kid in this scene. There's a scene later on when he leaves us that's the big goodbye scene.

YETTA: He leaves us?

MARTY: Yeah, but it's not for years. There's still five scenes before . . .

YETTA: What happens then?

MARTY: Ma!

YETTA: What? After he leaves, what happens then? Tell me.

MARTY: You divorce. He runs around; starts drinking, becomes a drunk. Finally, burnt out, broke, he has to move back in with his mother, gets diabetes, loses both his legs. There's a big father-son hospital scene. And then when I leave, he dies.

CY: I die? Alone?

MARTY: Yeah, but it's not till late in the second act.

YETTA: What happens to me?

MARTY: You . . . never remarry, Ma. End up bitter, alone, miserable in Miami.

YETTA: That's it?

CY: This is a comedy?

YETTA: Was that all true? Is that what really happens?

MARTY: It's a play, Ma, make-believe.

CY: So you made all that up, right? It's not really. . . ?

MARTY: Let's see, where were we? Ma, you were just about to cry. Dad . . .

YETTA: Does he really leave us?

MARTY: How do I know? I'm not God.

CY: Of course not Yetta! I'd never leave, I swear!

MARTY: You liar! You leave when I'm eleven years old.

CY: But you just said. . . !

MARTY: I make it up as I go along.

CY: What are you tryin' to pull here, huh?

MARTY: Nothing.

CY: Got to start trouble again, don't you?

MARTY: What?

CY: Some things never change!

MARTY: What are you talking about?

CY: You, Mister Playwright! It's just like when you were a kid, little mister in-between.

YETTA: Why are you blaming him?

CY: How she cooed and pampered you — her little Lord Fauntleroy.

MARTY: I hated . . . That's why I always ran to my room. Dad, you've got it all wrong!

CY: Yeah, wrong, right! You sucked up all her. . . ! Nothing left for me. No room left at the inn!

MARTY (*throwing his pad and pen down*): That's bullshit!

YETTA: What's going on here?

MARTY: You were too busy fooling around with all your girlfriends! Never home with us. Couldn't wait to. . . !

YETTA: What's all this blame? Blaming!

CY: Only reason I fooled around was because your mother wouldn't. . . !

YETTA: The play, Marty! Your play! WHAT THE HELL'S GOING ON HERE?

(*Marty and Cy look at her. It's quiet in the room for a moment, then*)

MARTY: Nothing, Ma, nothing. This is part of the play. A dramatic moment. Dad and me were rehearsing the big father-son confrontation scene, top of the second act.

YETTA: So much anger, hostility? Can't you fix it? Make it funny?

MARTY: Ma, this isn't "It's a Wonderful life." You can't always make things better. Now let's see, where were we?

CY (*putting his arm around Marty's shoulders*): Marty, you gotta change that ending. Please, me dying all alone like that, it's just too sad.

MARTY: Everybody's a critic.

CY: Please?! Couldn't you just. . . ?

MARTY (*walking away from him*): I'm sorry, I can't.

YETTA: You've made me the villain here, you realize that?

MARTY: No I didn't.

YETTA: Couldn't you just . . .

MARTY: Coulda-woulda-shoulda! What happened, happens. It all stays in the play!

CY (*upset, starting to leave, going toward the bedroom*): Well then it happens without me!

MARTY: Dad, you don't leave yet! We've still got . . .

CY (*as he leaves*): No? Just watch me! (*He leaves, goes to the bedroom, slams the door.*)

MARTY (*calling to him*): Dad, that's my room! (*Marty turns to Yetta. She looks at him for a moment, then starts to leave.*)

MARTY: Where are you going?

YETTA: I'm sorry, Marty.

MARTY: But Ma, you don't leave.

YETTA: No? You still haven't finished the play yet, remember? And what happens, happens. (*She leaves, goes to Marty's bedroom.*)

MARTY (*calling to her*): Ma. Ma!

(*We hear the bedroom door slam and lock. A light change. Marty slowly looks around the kitchen. He picks up the pen and pad off the floor, writes something.*)

"Marty slowly looks around the kitchen. He picks up the pen and pad off the floor, writes something."

(*He sits down, takes his hat off and puts it on the table.*)

"He sits down, takes his hat off and puts it on the table."

(*Suddenly he turns toward his bedroom.*)

"Suddenly he turns toward his bedroom and calls out . . ."

(*Just as Marty opens his mouth . . .*

Blackout)

CURTAIN

43 The Nonrealistic Play

Hello Out There and *Reckoning* are essentially **realistic** plays. They create an illusion that reflects and conforms with the world about us. Events may be surprising, but they are believable. They avoid the **deus ex machina**, the improbable event used to solve a problem. The passage of time is chronological. The plot in some realistic plays may skip ahead a week or a year, but the jump is made clear. There is no imprecise blurring of past and present or of different centuries. Realistic settings are clearly defined (a living room, a jail cell, a forest), borrowed from the world as we know it. Characters are mortal and limited in the same way as we are. They may behave in bizarre ways, but they can't fly like birds or turn into frogs.

The term *realism* also applies to a period in literary history, but I will use the term in its nonhistorical, purely descriptive sense. Realistic plays mimic life.

Nonrealistic drama, on the other hand, is an illusion that in some ways resembles a dream. Such plays often *seem* real just as dreams usually do, but the plot may be an illogical sequence of events in which time is distorted or ignored, characters may behave in ways that lack motivation, and the setting may be strange or a satiric exaggeration.

Nonrealistic drama is a broad term that covers a variety of approaches, all of which depart from what we think of as the natural order. It includes **fantasies**, dream plays, and cartoonish **satires**. Like **free verse**, these plays don't abandon all form; they merely replace the familiar **conventions** of realism with new rules designed for that particular play.

At first glance, realistic and nonrealistic drama appear to be entirely different. Actually they have much in common and frequently borrow techniques from each other. I will begin with their differences, but keep in mind that there is no sharp line between them.

DISTORTIONS OF TIME

Realistic drama keeps track of time. If there is a gap, it is often printed in the program notes: "Next week," the audience is told, or "A year later." Or the shift may simply be made clear from the dialogue. Nonrealistic plays tend to ignore or twist time.

Samuel Beckett's *Waiting for Godot* has become a prototype for **theater-of-the-absurd** plays and illustrates the way time can be ignored. There is nothing in the script that indicates a historical period. You can think of it as a contemporary or a medieval drama — take your pick. And while there are references to times of the day, there is also a sense that this has been going on forever. The play is like a long and rather hazy dream with no distinct beginning or end. This indifference to both historical time and clock time is common in nonrealistic plays.

Another approach to time is to warp it. Time warps are popular in science fiction, but they are often given some kind of rational explanation. In nonrealistic drama, time frequently slides forward or backward without explanation.

Time in *Coulda, Woulda, Shoulda* is particularly inventive. As the play opens, we see a young married couple with a child of about four or five. The familiar kitchen setting and the two parents seem to suggest that this is going to be a realistic play. Our assumption, however, is shattered when Marty the son enters. The stage directions tell us that he is "in his forties, wearing large children's pajamas, a pair of glasses and a black hat. He's carrying a pen and pad."

What's going on? In one sense, time has leaped forward 35 years. Marty has grown up. You could show this in a realistic play by starting a new scene without the parents or with them grown old, thereby accounting for the passage of time "logically." But in this play the parents remain just as they were, and Marty appears as an adult — a blend of the 40-year-old playwright and the child he was, still in his pajamas.

Later he confirms this fusing of time periods by saying, "I'm still a kid in this scene." On one level he is referring to the script he, Marty, is writing in which the character based on himself is still a child; but in another sense the line refers to the scene in the play we are watching. He is *both* the 40-year-old playwright and the child in the same scene.

Is this logical? Not literally. But think for a moment what it would be like to be writing a play that includes a character based on yourself at four or five. As you write, aren't you both the playwright and the child? The distortion of time then becomes a **metaphor**: the situation is *like* being a writer and a child at the same moment.

Alterman doesn't stop there with his time tricks. Marty as playwright begins to tell his parents what will happen to them in the future. His father will become a drunk, go broke, get diabetes, and lose both his legs. As for his mother, she will end up "bitter, alone, miserable in Miami."

Is the playwright, Glenn Alterman, saying that this is what will really happen to the parents, or is Marty, the playwright in the play, making this up? We laugh partly because it smacks of **therapy writing**, the psychological revenge that tempts all writers with a grudge. But to Cy this is no joke.

The distortion of time becomes a commentary on the illusion of theater in this exchange:

> YETTA: Was that all true? Is that what really happens?
> MARTY: It's a play, Ma, make-believe.

She has believed his story enough to be alarmed at the future that seems to be in store for her and her husband. We smile at how quickly she has been taken in by something that is "only a play." But what about us in the audience? Aren't we accepting the illusion that these people on the stage are going through a real crisis?

Toward the end of the play, there is one more time shift. Marty's father leaves and then his mother. But notice that they don't go outside. Instead, they go into Marty's room and slam the door. Where are they really? They are in the playwright's mind. The bedroom, after all, is the room for memory and for dreams.

If you look closely at what this play does with time, you will see that there are three scenes. The first, with the parents alone, is unmistakably the past. It is Marty's childhood presented realistically. The second is a dreamlike blend with the parents as they once were and the son grown, an "unrealistic" mix of two periods. We accept the absurdity of it just as we accept similar distortions in dreams. The final scene begins as soon as both parents are offstage. Marty, alone, is writing a play about Marty the playwright. And what will happen when he calls out to them after the last line of the play? We can't say for sure, but isn't it logical that the three of them will go through this again? Anyone who has written about people who were once close to them will remember how frequently these confrontations occur.

The distortion of time in this play occurs within the life of the protagonist. We can call this type *biographical time warps*. Another way to bend time is to slide historical periods together, creating *historical time warps*. Characters from history can appear in contemporary time periods; characters from the present can slide back. When those shifts are made in fairly simple drama and films designed for mass audiences, they are usually introduced with a so-called scientific explanation involving some kind of time machine. The concept was not entirely new even when H.G. Wells popularized it in *The Time Machine* in 1895, and it has been repeated in plays, films, and novels regularly ever since. When historical time warps are used in more sophisticated contemporary works, however, the half-hearted attempt to provide an as-if scientific mechanical explanation is usually dropped. The result is looser, more dreamlike. You will be reading an example of this, *Valley Forgery*, in Chapter 46.

I have focused on time because it is one of the most visible distortions in many (although not all) nonrealistic dramas. In a broader sense, however, it constitutes a different approach to plot itself. The realistic plot seems logical because it conforms to our daily lives. The nonrealistic plot seems logical and "real" because it echoes our dreams. After all, our dreams have the power to evoke pleasure, fear, laughter, and tears. The same is true of drama.

DISTORTIONS OF CHARACTER

Characters in realistic drama, as in realistic fiction, are a mix of consistency and variation. The variations are what give a character individuality, but they have to be explained at some point. If a normally kind father strikes his child apparently without cause, the audience expects to find out what drove him to it before the play ends.

Characterization in nonrealistic drama may be confusing in literal terms, but usually there is a symbolic explanation. Marty in *Coulda* is a good example. In the central portion of the play, he is both a child in pajamas and an adult "in his 40s." His parents treat him as a child ("Marty, take your hat off in the house") and also as an adult playwright ("Sorry, Mister Playwright"). He also has a third role, that of a seer or oracle who can literally see into the future. His mother asks, "After he leaves, what happens then?" And when Cy learns what is in store for him, he says, "I die? Alone?" They're not talking about a play being written, they've come to believe that this is their future.

So in a single character we have a child, an adult playwright, and an oracle of future events. Alterman the playwright is doing in dramatic terms what Pablo Picasso did in art when he drew figures portraying simultaneously both frontal and profile views. There is a logic there, but it is a symbolic logic, not a literal representation.

The parents are also treated symbolically, although with less distortion. In the opening scene, they appear to be highly realistic. They are fond and concerned parents. The father's growing irascibility in no way violates what we would expect in a realistic play. But as soon as their son appears as a grown man, they are seen in a different light. They become credulous individuals, prepared to believe that their son can see into the future. At the end of the play, they serve a different function. By entering Marty's room, they become mere memories rather than flesh-and-blood characters. The implication is that they may be recalled by Marty as playwright at any time.

Coulda is an inventive mix of realistic and nonrealistic elements. In other plays, we are in a nonrealistic dream world from start to finish. In a bitter and brutal play called *The Lesson* by Eugene Ionesco, a raving professor berates his young students in a manner that by realistic standards we would classify as child abuse. Eventually he kills them for no apparent reason. If we made the mistake of viewing this play as an attempt at realism, we would find it an appalling act of violence without credible motivation. The arbitrary nature of the killing would lead us to judge the play to be a failure. "That's just not believable," we would say.

But the playwright is not concerned with psychological motivation or even characterization. His theme has to do with the nature of authority and the abuses of absolute power. He has, in effect, drawn a savage cartoon to illustrate his point. Cartoons have the power to argue, even shock, but they deal with ideas, not people as people.

When characters in nonrealistic plays are satiric representations of abstractions like the professor in *The Lesson,* they are usually "flat." They don't have much or any background. They seem to spring fully formed from nowhere. But this doesn't mean that such characters are more easily created. You must make sure that the audience understands your intent. If you are too obvious, the play may turn into a simple skit, but if you are not clear enough, the audience will be too baffled to applaud.

When historical figures are used in nonrealistic plays (as they are in *Valley Forgery* which appears in Chapter 46), characterization is often comically different or even the opposite from the generally accepted view of that individual. It's easy enough to do this in an adolescent way just to get laughs — as simple and forgettable as drawing a mustache on a photo of the Mona Lisa. But when it is done with skillful wit (as it is in *Valley Forgery*), distortion of historical or public figures can create memorable satire.

For a highly successful full-length play using this approach, look up *Picasso at the Lapin Agile* by the comedian Steve Martin. In this play, Picasso the artist meets and argues with Einstein and Lenin. Far more than slapstick, it maintains a comic tone while suggesting true insights.

DREAMSCAPE SETTINGS

Many nonrealistic plays call for realistic sets. *Coulda* takes place in a realistic kitchen. But in some plays the set itself is nonrealistic. The distortions are often symbolic. Elmer Rice's *The Adding Machine* deals with a protagonist who is a cipher in a highly mechanical and stratified society in which his associates go by numbers rather than names. Appropriately, he is named Mr. Zero. His apartment is covered with numbers — on the walls, on the furniture, and even on the lampshades. The set amplifies the symbolic imagination that dominates the play.

Sometimes a dreamlike set is so striking and so fanciful that it remains in the memory long after the characters have been forgotten. The set in Ionesco's play *The Chairs,* for example, is the interior of a castle in the middle of the sea. The semicircular room is sparse but has a total of ten doors — all of which are used. The script calls for the realistic sound of boats moving through the water as guests arrive, but we have no idea where they are coming from. The audience does not ask itself where this might be; it accepts this dreamlike setting just as it accepts the time warps in *Coulda.*

RISKS IN THE NONREALISTIC APPROACH

Because there are no clear guidelines in nonrealistic drama, it is easy to start with an unpromising concept. Here are three approaches that are likely to get you off to a bad start.

The first is the too-familiar **allegory**. No matter what you do with characters who resemble Adam and Eve, they will still resemble all the cartoons we have seen over the years. The same applies to Christ-like figures no matter how sincere your intent. And the last-couple-on-earth plot is as tired in drama as it is in fiction. You're in trouble if the audience's reaction at the very outset is, "Oh, not again."

Another type to guard against is the humorless sermon. It seems to be a particularly great temptation in nonrealistic plays because they often are what is known as thesis driven rather than character driven. That is, nonrealistic plays are often dominated by an idea rather than rooted in character. For this very reason, the thesis stands out blatantly. Your message may reflect your deepest convictions, but you're not going to win converts by having a character shout, "Don't you realize that violence generates more violence?" or "The trouble with you rich slobs is . . ." or "Under the skin we're all the same." A good rule to follow is: Don't have your protagonist state the theme of the play directly. Let him or her reveal it through action or some indirect reference. It doesn't matter how noble your convictions may be, sermons are not good drama.

This doesn't mean that your plays should be bland. Nor should they be without convictions. Look at how Saroyan slides in his strongly held beliefs. It does mean that you have to present your case obliquely. Have your characters talk about specifics, not broad moral statements.

Another approach is to use comic lines. When Marty the protagonist in *Coulda* tells his parents that his mother will "end up bitter, alone, miserable in Miami," his father says "This is a comedy?" It's a laugh line, but in an almost subliminal way it also contributes to the theme. It asks a larger question: Just what is comedy? Where is the division between comedy and serious drama? In this case, Marty, the would-be playwright in the play, is writing what seems like a melodramatic and humorless script, but the playwright Alterman is a witty writer with a flare for comedy. We laugh at aspects of the play we are watching, but hidden just below the surface is a serious exploration of how difficult it is to write a play based on people who still have a strong emotional hold on you. That valuable insight sneaks up on you after the curtain drops.

The third and most serious danger for beginning playwrights will sound familiar to those who have already read the warnings in the fiction section. It is the hopelessly obscure nonrealistic play. If your audience can't see any coherent pattern, they will simply walk out. You can't depend on novelty value alone. And you can't draw on the emotional appeal of characterization the way realistic drama often does because your approach is necessarily idea oriented. Make sure that the ideas you are working with hold together and suggest insights that are logical and compelling. Martin Esslin puts it this way in *The Theatre of the Absurd:*

> Mere combinations of incongruities produce mere banality. Anyone attempting to work in this medium simply by writing down what comes into his mind will find that the supposed flights of spontaneous invention have never left the ground, that they consist of incoherent fragments of reality that have not been transposed into a valid imaginative whole.[4]

As often as this wise warning is repeated, obscure and confused plays continue to be the bane of drama workshops. When they get into production, they are an agony to watch. Some are unintelligible because the playwright has not read his or her script from the audience's point of view. Private references known only to the playwright, personal visions from waking or sleeping dreams, and symbols too elusive to be grasped even after a careful reading all contribute to the unintentionally obscure play.

Worse, some plays are knowingly obscure. The motive may be a misguided notion that sounding deep will win a following. Or it may be a simple disdain for the audience. It should (but doesn't) go without saying that drama is one of the most public arts. It involves not only the writer but producers, directors, actors, and, ultimately, audiences. It should never be treated as a private indulgence.

LEARNING FROM NONREALISTIC PLAYS

When one first approaches nonrealistic drama, it sometimes seems like literary anarchy without limits or traditions. Actually it has a significant history from which one can learn a lot. Although the focus of this text is on the process of writing, not literary history, a brief introduction to the two major schools of nonrealistic drama will be helpful for any writer. Studying what has been done in the past is one of the best ways to discover new directions for your own work.

The first of these two schools is **expressionism**. This movement, closely associated with painting but also including fiction and poetry, began around 1900 and continued through the 1920s. Early examples in drama are seen in the plays of the Swedish playwright August Strindberg. Plays such as *The Dance of Death* and *The Dream Play* are readily available in translation and provide vivid contrasts to realistic drama. Strindberg's plots were often dreamlike, his characters primarily symbolic rather than realistic, and his tone often dark and pessimistic.

---

[4] *The Theatre of the Absurd,* Martin Esslin, Penguin Books.

Another excellent example of early expressionism is the work of the Czech dramatist Karel Capek. His nightmarish vision of the future, *R.U.R.*, is an early sample of science fiction complete with robots who revolt against their masters. More thematically comprehensible than many of Strindberg's dense works, *R.U.R.* has a strong and clear element of social protest. This contemporary-sounding play was written in 1920. It has often been imitated.

For a good example of American expressionism, I would recommend Elmer Rice's *The Adding Machine*, a play I described previously with regard to the highly symbolic and dreamlike set. Costumes, set, action, and dialogue are all distorted as they are in dreams, but also as in dreams there is an internal consistency that allows us to make sense of it all. We know what it means to be treated like a number, and most of us have occasionally been made to feel like a zero. What we see and hear in this play is distorted, but what we feel is sadly familiar and real.

In the 1950s and 1960s, there was a new surge of interest in nonrealistic drama. This movement became known as **theater of the absurd**. Many of the playwrights shared the existential notion that life is absurd in the sense of being without ultimate meaning. Oddly, few of them recognized the other important aspect of existential thought — that we create meaning and values through our actions. As a result, absurdist plays tend to be pessimistic and often cynical.

This school is best represented by the works of Eugene Ionesco, whose plays *The Lesson* and *The Chairs* I have already described. Other such playwrights include Samuel Beckett, Harold Pinter, and occasionally Edward Albee.

MAKING CHOICES

As I have pointed out, there are very real risks in the nonrealistic approach. In spite of these dangers, however, there are also distinct assets. It is a particularly tempting approach if your theme is more important to you than are your characters. You can cut through to the heart of your statement in a bold and imaginative manner without having to create credible characters or to construct a plausible plot. You are working with a medium that, like the political cartoon and the poster, lends itself to strong statements. As for form, you can let your imagination take flight. Like free verse, nonrealistic drama offers freedoms and also the obligation to find new and effective structures.

You may already have a strong preference for one approach over the other. Many playwrights do. But in deciding which basic route to take, keep an open mind. Consider the special nature of your projected play. If you are deeply concerned with the complexities of character, it may be best to work in a realistic manner. If, however, the concept you have in mind is charged with a strong idea or has come to you in a satiric vein, you may want to consider the freedom of the nonrealistic play. Your final decision will be based partly on the type of drama you enjoy and partly on the nature of the work at hand.

44 Dramatic Characterization

• The playwright's dependence on dialogue and action (386) • Using dialogue to reveal character (386) • Action that reveals feelings (388) • Creating depth of character (389) • Characters in flux: "Character change" and shifts in audience perception (391) • When and why to use minor characters (392)

Creating complex and convincing characters in a play presents a special challenge: the playwright is almost wholly dependent on dialogue and action. Fiction writers can quote a character's thoughts naturally and frequently without slowing the action, and occasionally they can comment directly on a character through exposition. Not so for playwrights.

Although it's possible to enter the mind of characters through monologues, the technique is rarely used today because of the way it interrupts the action. As I have already pointed out, monologues are relatively common in Elizabethan drama, but using the technique in contemporary work often seems like an unrealistic intrusion.

As for exposition, the playwright must resort to something like a chorus. Although a few writers like Arthur Miller and Thornton Wilder have done this, having an outside observer not only slows the action, it also breaks the audience's sense of entering into the play, an illusion that has become an important part of contemporary drama.

As a result, on the rare occasions when a character's inner thoughts are presented directly, it is through a very brief monologue or a revealing bit of action when that character is alone on the stage. This way it seems as if the character is thinking aloud.

With some interesting exceptions, then, contemporary dramatists develop their characters through what they say and what they do. Although these two aspects are necessarily interlocked, it helps to look at each separately.

USING DIALOGUE TO REVEAL CHARACTER

When we first meet people, we listen to what they say and how they say it. We have the feeling that we are getting to know them. Singles bars thrive on this illusion. But first impressions are notoriously inaccurate. Sometimes it takes months or even years to get an accurate picture. In a play, it has to happen in a single performance.

For many seeing *Hello Out There* for the first time, the first impression of Photo-Finish is negative. He is in jail and accused of rape. Even if the charges are exaggerated, he seems untrustworthy. And when he turns his gambler's charm on a naive girl, we suspect that he may be lying to save his own skin.

Because of this, Saroyan faces a true playwriting challenge. How can he induce an audience to look favorably and sympathetically at a small-time gambler and drifter who has been jailed for rape?

Saroyan begins by giving Photo-Finish lines that are hesitant, nonthreatening, and appealing. They focus on loneliness and reach out for sympathy and companionship. Furthermore, all that repetition has comic overtones. For much of the audience, his sad and bewildered tone is enough to create trust. This alone is a demonstration of how rapidly a good playwright can influence the audience's judgment about character from the very start.

In spite of this, however, some of the audience will have lingering doubts about his actual feelings toward Emily. He is, after all, a gambler, a drifter, in a life-and-death situation, and Emily is no beauty. Does he really feel love for her? Or does he see her as the last chance for escape?

Saroyan clears up any lingering doubts by providing Photo-Finish with that brief monologue in which he describes his true feelings. When Photo-Finish says to himself that she is "the only good thing that ever came their way," we are hearing his honest feelings.

Notice, incidentally, the speed with which these two characters meet and fall in love — a risky pace in life and even a bit rushed for fiction. But a play is neither life nor fiction. Audiences are used to seeing slightly stylized and compressed plots. By the time the play rushes to its climax, the audience has come to accept the two principal characters as tragic victims.

The two characters in Padilla's *Reckoning* are revealed at a more gradual pace. This is due in part to the fact that they are more complex and more fully drawn. Joe appears at first to be insufferably arrogant and egotistical — almost a **stereotype** of the hard-driving businessman. Bit by bit, however, his apparent self-assurance is eroded by what he says. Gradually we learn that he is unsure of himself and in serious need of help. This is not revealed in some long, uninterrupted confession like those that frequently appear at the end of murder mysteries. Instead, his dialogue gives him away in a series of brief, inadvertent admissions. He admits that he may have been jolted by the death of his old friend Emilio, that he sometimes neglected responsibility in his rise to power, and that he had come to seek help out of "desperation." His final collapse is a dramatic conclusion, but it has been prepared for.

In contrast, for the first third of the play Mary seems to be no more than a **foil**, a secondary character whose main purpose is to expose Joe's true character. Gradually, however, we learn that she knows far more than she originally revealed. Furthermore, she appears to have a plan. Although she is also unsure of herself, she is far from an objective counselor. In fact, she is charged with anger and resentment. We come to realize that the play is as much about her as it is about him. In the end, she is in control of the situation and he is in despair.

Although *Coulda, Woulda, Shoulda* is a comic play, much shorter, and nonrealistic, it also uses dialogue to reveal both the outer appearance of characters and something of the inner life as well. Although all three characters are revealed in some detail (rare in so short a play), the treatment of the father, Cy, is a particularly helpful example.

When we first see him, he is hurrying to get to work as the owner of a bar. He makes it clear through dialogue that he doesn't want to spend time talking with his son who has locked himself in his room. "I don't got time for this now," he says. "He'll come out when he's good and ready."

Our first impression of Cy is negative: he seems like a stereotype of the work-oriented father. Soon, however, we are shown a softer side. When he hears how his son has portrayed him in the play he is writing, Cy reveals his inner insecurity and his fears about death:

> Marty, you gotta change that ending. Please, me dying all alone like that, it's just too sad.

This is a comic shift, but it does more than simply produce laughter. It reveals through dialogue the father's sadly vulnerable side.

ACTION THAT REVEALS FEELINGS

The visual aspect of drama is so important that the next chapter is devoted to it. But it is worth considering here the specific ways action can be used to reveal character.

As I pointed out in the chapter on conflict, Emily's infatuation with Photo-Finish in *Hello Out There* is vividly revealed in a short scene that has no dialogue at all. Although she wants to do whatever Photo-Finish asks, she is also terrified of leaving him for a minute. When he asks her to go and look for cigarettes, she leaves but almost at once comes running back. That exit and reentrance dramatizes her **ambivalence**, the presence of two opposing emotions.

Later Photo-Finish reveals the depth of his feelings for her by giving her his last $80 to escape her own imprisonment in that town and get to San Francisco on her own. It's a minor action, but it provides one more assurance that his love for her is genuine.

The opening of *Coulda, Woulda, Shoulda* makes dramatic use of action. While his wife tries to talk with him, Cy is in constant motion looking for his shoes, his belt, and then his car keys. His wife has to point out where he left them. This man who appeared at first to be macho and dominant is revealed through action to be dependent on his wife for the simple mechanics of getting dressed.

Padilla also uses action at the very outset of *Reckoning* to show Joe's nervous anxiety even before we know where he is or the nature of the interview to come. This brief scene with him alone on the stage will help remind the audience in later scenes that he is not a one-dimensional egotist. The technique is somewhat similar to the one used by Saroyan in *Hello Out There*, although the characters are quite different.

Later, you remember, Padilla uses the same technique with Mary. In her brief scene when she is alone on stage, she reveals her anguish through her actions.

CREATING DEPTH OF CHARACTER

The central characters in serious, realistic dramas are usually presented in some depth. Ideally, the audience ends with the feeling that they have come to know the character fairly well. Achieving this effect in a short one-act play requires careful planning, but it can be done. Look at how much Saroyan manages to reveal about Photo-Finish in only a few minutes of playing time:

- He is lonely but not a whiner.
- He has a whimsical sense of humor, yet can be serious about practical matters of survival.
- He is not educated, but he has insights about human character such as why some people are kind and others heartless.
- He exhibits a merry quality in the way he treats Emily, yet he is a realist about his chances of survival.

Notice how many of these characteristics are contrasts. Credible contrasts like these make the difference between one-dimensional characters often found in **melodramas** and convincing characters who are shown with some degree of depth.

The key to creating a convincing character is to balance consistency with variation. Photo-Finish is consistently outraged at how the town has treated Emily and has trapped him. And he is consistently concerned for Emily's future. But he is not presented as the a perfect hero or as an absolute villain. He is both a small-time hustler who has been living precariously on the fringes of the racetrack world and also someone who can see the good qualities in a young woman like Emily and can even appreciate the conflicts that motivate the outraged husband.

The same applies to Emily. On the one hand, she is consistently a gentle, naive, small-town girl. Yet, on the other hand, she is capable of great loyalty, and at the end of the play she is elevated in stature with her concluding cry, "Hello out there!" We take her seriously.

Coulda, Woulda, Shoulda is half the length of *Hello Out There* and essentially a comedy, but even that play contains more depth of characterization than one would expect. We have a brief glimpse of Marty as a solemn child who wants to become a rabbi. This gives us an insight into what makes him such a serious and dedicated playwright as an adult. We see how close he has been to his mother (although he denies it) and how he resents his father's infidelities. Marty the character is clearly not a mere echo of Alterman the playwright. We know this by the fact that Marty the character is writing what appears to be a heavy-handed and humorless melodrama, while the play we are reading (or watching) is a comedy packed with satirical details.

The father, too, has surprising complexity considering the brevity of the play. As I pointed out earlier, he appears at first to be a workaholic whose only concern is his job. But later we learn that much of his time has been with other women, a charge he doesn't deny. Furthermore, his rather harsh self-assurance in the opening scene turns to fear of "dying all alone like that."

The contrasts that make the father in that play more complex than in most extremely short plays are multiplied tenfold in Padilla's *Reckoning*. As we have seen, while a portion of him is arrogant, sexist, vain, and blindly insensitive to others, he is also childishly insecure, lonely, and fearful about the future. Which is the real Joe? Both.

His concluding lines are worth a close look. Even in his desperation he tries to hang on to old delusions. "I had . . . dreams beyond your comprehension" he says as if that justified his behavior. In addition, he says "I'm what this country's all about." This is not only a last note of bravado, it is also a hint that the play is more than a psychological study. It is, like *Hello Out There*, a commentary on a darker side of our society.

Turning now to your own work, one of the best ways to combine both consistency and some measure of contrast is to write out a character sketch for each of your major characters. Put down more than you will ever need: what their childhood was like, whether they have sisters or brothers, where they went to school, what they are good at, and what their weaknesses are. Determine some aspects that suggest consistency ("gentle temperament; almost never loses her temper") and some contrasting trait ("can't stand messy people or a disorderly house"). These notes are not to be included in your script, and you may not use more than a small portion of the points directly, but you will come to know your principle characters as people rather than just types.

If you have trouble writing more than a few sentences, try basing your description on a friend or member of your family. But be inventive. Don't lock yourself into the personality of that particular individual. Make a point of transforming some aspects so you will begin to deal with a newly formed stage character. Alter a basic element such as age, gender, or appearance so you don't lose friends or, worse, become inhibited out of respect for the person who served as model.

Keep in mind that the process of creating a dramatic character is almost never pure invention; he or she is a transformation of people you know or have met. The goal is to create new and interesting characters who are generally consistent and yet also reveal certain contrasting traits.

CHARACTERS IN FLUX

Drama by definition cannot be static. Like dance, it is always in motion. This aspect applies not only to plot, but also to the primary characters. Major characters in realistic drama almost always go through some type of significant development, for good or for bad. They are not the same at the end of the play as they were at the beginning. Photo-Finish in *Hello Out There*, for example, takes on a tragic maturity as he faces death; Joe in *Reckoning* moves in the opposite direction, revealing himself as a pathetic and desperate failure.

This aspect of serious drama is often referred to as *character change*, but the term is a bit misleading. Characters in plays rarely go through a fundamental personality change any more than people do in life. Only in comedies do villains finally see the light, go through a complete character transformation, and undo the damage they have done. Still, there's no harm in using the term *character change* as long as we make it clear that what we mean is in most cases a shift in the character's attitude.

Such shifts in attitude can be highly dramatic. In plays, as in life, characters can be shaped by events and end up stricken with remorse, given new hope, shattered by a crisis, or strengthened by it. Friendships form between unlikely pairs, and "ideal" couples become alienated. Quite often a naive character is suddenly made aware of some harsh aspect of life; occasionally a sophisticated character is taught how to appreciate some simple truth. The impact of these shifts is similar to the jolt we feel when an apparently trustworthy character turns out to be dishonest or one we had assumed was incompetent has actually been in control. These are all the stuff of powerful drama.

Where does one find characters who have gone through such a shift in outlook? Start with your own life. Even if you feel that your development has been uneventful, it has in fact moved in stages, each one introduced by some fresh view of yourself or the world about you. Always keep in mind that you can transform a relatively mild personal experience into an event that generates dramatic impact. Play writing is, after all, a creative art, and playwrights are drawn to exaggeration.

In addition, consider what you have heard about other members of your family, present and past. Almost every family has stories with dramatic potential. Don't be shy. Imaginative transformations can disguise anything. Also look for "cold material" — reports you have read in the newspaper or history texts, stories about strangers. If you take this route, consider grafting the events onto someone you have known. This linkage will help make your characterization more convincing.

The further you get from your own life and experience, the greater the danger that you will begin to borrow from something you have seen on television or in a movie. Sometimes this happens entirely unconsciously. As I have pointed out previously, the dark recesses of our memories contain throngs of stock characters from half-remembered fiction and film. If you let them sneak into your play, they will seem like uninvited guests, no more convincing than mannequins. You are on safer ground when you develop characters who are at least partially linked to people you know.

A different way to achieve that all-important sense of change and discovery is to reverse the process: allow the character to remain the same but provide information that will dramatically shift the audience's perception of him or her. Oddly, this approach can generate just as much impact.

This approach is found more often in comedy. It is, for example, the technique used in *Coulda, Woulda, Shoulda*. Before the son, Marty, appears on the stage, we assume we are about to meet a child. The jolt comes when we see Marty "in his forties . . . wearing large children's pajamas." It's still Marty, but at a different period of his life. Our view of him has changed. (There is an echo here of what grandparents perceive when looking at their grandchildren. They simultaneously "see" them at different stages of their lives.)

This method of shifting the audience's view can also be used in serious dramas. On its simplest level, it is seen regularly in murder mystery scripts in which the least-likely suspect turns out to be the actual killer.

Some playwrights have used the same technique with greater ingenuity and subtlety in full-length plays. One of the best-known examples is a central device in *The Country Girl* by Clifford Odets. It concerns the efforts of an older actor to make a comeback. For much of the play, the audience is convinced that he is doing his best to cope with a difficult wife. But it turns out that he is an alcoholic and she has been heroically trying to cover for him. The characters have not changed, but our perception of them at the end of that play is dramatically reversed.

There are all kinds of deceits that can be created in this manner and then exposed dramatically. Some are the result of conscious scheming, as in the Odets play, but others develop from self-deception. If you are working with this type of reversal, drop small hints along the way so that when the correct view is revealed the audience will have that special sense of, "Oh, I should have seen it."

WHEN AND WHY TO USE MINOR CHARACTERS

E.M. Forster's distinction between "**round**" and "flat" characters in fiction applies just as well to drama. "Flat" characters are like cardboard cutouts, and they rarely change or develop. Normally we don't learn about their background or what they are like.

In spite of this, they can be essential elements of a play. When they provide a single and important function, they can become a **catalyst** — necessary elements for the advancement of plot or for the development of a major character without themselves changing.

The two men who accompany the husband in *Hello Out There*, for example, are "flat" yet extremely important. Their presence just outside the jail room drives the husband to the point of murder. They are essential elements, but as individuals they are faceless, even interchangeable, and utterly consistent.

In comedies most or all of the characters are flat. There are, however, different degrees of character development. *Coulda, Woulda, Shoulda* is a comedy, but as we have seen the play provides some depth to the two parents, especially the father. The closer a play comes to **slapstick**, broad and boisterous comedy written mainly for laughs, the flatter the characters will be. As you will see, the satiric characters in *Valley Forgery* (Chapter 46) are essentially flat. Their function is to present ideas in a comic fashion through a what-if fantasy.

There is a tendency to become careless with minor characters, creating them to perform trivial tasks that are not truly essential — delivering pizza or mail. From a practical point of view, production costs place a premium on plays with a minimum number of actors. In addition, there is an aesthetic factor. Plays have more power when a lot is suggested by a few carefully developed characters rather than being cluttered by needless minor characters.

Characterization in a realistic play is a continuing concern at every stage of writing. It takes time and many revisions to make major characters both vivid and credible. You have to consider both consistency and variation. Realistic drama is, among other things, the illusion of getting to know total strangers surprisingly well in a very short period of time.

45 Visual Impact

Writers can use the stage in many different ways. They can read their poetry or fiction, present monologues, or read their play scripts. But only if their performance has a lively visual component, something to look at, do we call it drama.

This visual aspect, what Aristotle called the **spectacle**, includes a variety of elements: the physical **set**, the lighting, the costumes, and, most important, the action of actors. The playwright's job is not merely to create lines for actors to speak; he or she must also create a lively visual environment.

This chapter has one urgent message that I will repeat several times in different ways: when you write any type of play script, it is essential to maintain a mental picture of what your stage looks like scene by scene, moment by moment. In short, remember that a play is to be seen, not just heard.

THE IMPACT OF THE FAMILIAR: THE REALISTIC SET

The term **set** includes everything the audience sees, except the actors themselves. Although each set designer will approach a play differently, playwrights usually specify at least briefly the locale and how the stage should look. Generally speaking, sets fall into one of three loosely defined types: realistic, symbolic, or bare.

The **realistic set** is so common today that we tend to think of it as the traditional approach. Actually it is a fairly recent development — less than 200 years out of the 2,500-year-old tradition of Western drama. Truly realistic details on the stage had to wait until the introduction of electric lights. When Ibsen's plays were first produced in England in the late nineteenth century, audiences gasped with amazement at the sight of a perfectly reproduced living room scene complete with real books in bookcases, portraits on the walls, and doors that opened and shut. Soon the stage directions for plays began to reflect this new realism by including the most minute descriptions, even to the title of a book left "carelessly" on a coffee table.

Audiences no longer respond with that kind of naive wonder, of course. Film and television have made realism commonplace. But when a realistic set is constructed with skill and imagination, it can still create enormous impact. Even today, highly effective sets presented on traditional stages are occasionally greeted with applause even before the first character appears. The audience is applauding the illusion of the familiar.

How much detail should a script include? There is no standard policy, but most are brief. One reason is that there is such a variety of stages today that playwrights can no longer be sure of just how their work will be presented.

The traditional stage has what is known as a **proscenium arch**, which forms a picture frame for the action and uses a curtain to open and close separate acts. But many stages now do not have an arch or a single picture effect because they are open on three sides. This design, called a **thrust stage**, allows more of the audience to sit close to the action. In such theaters, the lowering of a curtain is replaced by a dimming of the lights.

Theater in the round, or **arena theater**, extends this concept further by having the audience encircle the playing area as it does in a circus tent. The playwright's description of the set in the script should be flexible enough to allow set designers to adapt to a wide variety of stages.

In *Hello Out There*, for example, Saroyan merely states that this is to be "a small-town prison cell." On a traditional stage, this might be handled realistically with walls and barred windows. But on a stage that is surrounded on all sides by the audience, the cell might be suggested by no more than a few bars suspended in dreamlike fashion. A good deal can be left to the imagination of the audience, even in a realistic play.

DISTORTIONS THAT ENHANCE REALISM

A realistic stage set always requires imagination. In fact, it is the distortions of reality that stimulate the imagination. A living room on the stage, for example, has no fourth wall. The audience imagines itself in that room even though in a literal sense we are looking at a half-dismantled house.

In a play called *Period of Adjustment* by Tennessee Williams, the focal object is a television set. But what the audience saw in the Broadway production was the back of the set. The set was meticulously realistic, yet from a literal point of view the audience was impossibly wedged between the back of the television set and an invisible wall.

In other plays, the audience finds itself behind fireplaces. Oddly, even the least imaginative theatergoers accept this kind of distortion and imagine themselves being in the room with the characters.

The significance of this illusion for playwrights is that one can use a high degree of distortion to achieve a realistic effect. This is particularly helpful in

The Collection, showing emphasis on the modern apartment, with the other areas dark.

The Collection, showing emphasis on the telephone booth, which is, in the play, some distance from either home.

Set design for Harold Printer's *The Collection* by William Ritman. Illustrations by Richard Tuttle. Reprinted by permission of William Ritman and Richard Tuttle.

The Collection, showing emphasis on the ornate apartment, with the other areas dark.

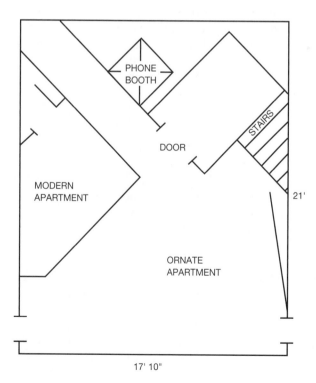

The Collection: a diagram of the stage, showing the technique of representing three entirely different scenes simply by shifts in lighting. Note how the unusual angles add both variety and depth, even on a small stage.

plays that include both indoor and outdoor scenes. A yard may be separated from the interior of, say, a kitchen by a low board; a door may be used to suggest the division between two areas without adjoining walls. The same applies to the second story of a house suggested only by a flight of stairs. If the actors treat these divisions as real, the audience will perceive them in the same way.

An ingenious use of realistic design is seen in William Ritman's set for Harold Pinter's *The Collection*. Working closely with the director and the playwright, Ritman managed to present the illusion of three entirely separate yet realistic settings on the relatively small stage of the Cherry Lane Theatre in New York. It has been duplicated on larger stages since then. As the action shifts from one area to the next, the lights on the other two are dimmed. The illustrations (drawn by Richard Tuttle) appear on pages 396 and 397. Turn to them now and notice how the illusion of one's location shifts simply with a change in lighting.

The great advantage of a set like this is that the playwright does not have to stop the action for a change of set. As I have mentioned, dropping the curtain or even dimming the lights breaks the illusion and returns the audience to the theater itself. If in addition you ask a stage crew to scurry about in the dark and change a set, that break becomes even lengthier and more distracting. A set divided into different playing areas allows a playwright to maintain a steady flow of action.

A word of warning, however. If you, like most people, have watched more television dramas and films than plays, you may unwittingly suggest an impossibly complex set. Remember that whatever you call for in the script will have to be built with wood and held together with nails. Short one-act plays normally call for a single, very simple set.

THE SYMBOLIC SET

No matter how many distortions are used in a realistic set, the goal is to place the audience in an environment that is similar to the world in which we live. The goal of the **symbolic set** is in some ways just the opposite: it takes the audience out of this world. As in dreams, the surroundings may generate familiar emotions — anxiety, fear, confusion, or even childlike pleasure — but they don't resemble a familiar place.

Also like dreams, the symbolic set "makes sense" on a symbolic rather than a literal level. The undefined but dreary landscape of *Waiting for Godot* by Samuel Beckett, for example, does not bring to mind any specific place on Earth, but it does seem to echo the dreary and uncertain lives of the characters who try without much success to make sense of life itself.

Other symbolic sets may be far more specific in detail. In Chapter 43, I pointed out how precise Ionesco is in describing the reception room of the castle in the middle of the sea in *The Chairs*, but you won't find that island in any atlas. Ionesco, like Elmer Rice, uses the set to suggest pictorially certain aspects of the human condition.

Some symbolic sets give delight through deception. The set of William Carlos Williams' play *Many Loves* is actually a series of tricks. As the audience enters the theater, the curtain is already raised, and stagehands and electricians are still at work preparing the stage. One is on a ladder repairing a hanging lamp; another vacuums the floor. Members of the audience tend to check their watches and mumble about sloppy amateur productions. Only gradually do they realize — usually one at a time — that the play has already begun. The members of the stage crew are in fact the characters. Then actors begin rehearsing a play, and the audience gradually becomes absorbed in that "reality."

Just as the play within a play appears to be a major concern, a director jumps up from the first row and objects. And so does the playwright — not Williams but the author of the play-within-a-play. Our attention turns to the relationship between these two men. The "many loves" of the title are as unstable as the audience's perception of the true setting of this play.

Nonrealistic plays like *Coulda, Woulda, Shoulda* can be presented with realistic settings, and essentially realistic plays like Arthur Miller's *After the Fall* (based partly on Marilyn Monroe) can employ dreamlike shifts that are themselves highly symbolic. The choice is yours as to whether you want a stage set that suggests an as-if-real place or one that is designed to mimic a mood or suggest a theme in a dreamlike fashion.

THE BARE STAGE

This third approach, the *bare stage* (see **set**), can be used in either realistic or nonrealistic plays. Thornton Wilder's *Our Town* is one of the most famous examples of an almost bare-stage play. The script calls for a few folding chairs, two stepladders, and a plank, which in certain scenes is laid between the ladders. The play is realistic and serious in tone, and leaving the stage almost bare in no way reduces the illusion of reality.

When *Our Town* was first produced in 1938, presenting a major production without an elaborate set was considered innovative. Yet, no one was confused. Like many daring experiments in theater, it was based on an old tradition. Elizabethan audiences had to use their imaginations to visualize the rapid succession of scenes in Shakespearean plays. If this approach interests you, examine closely how Shakespeare ingeniously identifies the setting at the beginning of each new scene.

If you are writing a longer play and plan to call for such a set, be sure that you indicate through the dialogue and stage directions where the characters are and what the audience is being asked to imagine.

Here are some suggestions for making the best use of your set no matter what type:

- Don't assume that because your play is nonrealistic the set should be. And conversely, if your play is realistic, don't feel bound to call for an elaborately realistic set. Select a stage set that will be the most effective for your particular play.
- Consider ways in which the set can have an impact right from the start. Think twice before you call for the too-familiar sitcom living room — couch centered, two upholstered chairs on either side, front door to the left, kitchen door to the right, and stairs. We've been there too often.
- Be practical. Remember that some stages are small, budgets are tight, and there are limits to what one can build. Don't make impossible demands.
- Be brief. Let set designers adapt your basic description to the type of stage and budget they are working with. (Notice now brief the descriptions of the set are in the four plays included in this volume.)
- Above all, use the set. Keep it in mind as you write, and give your characters a chance to move about in the space you have provided.

LIGHTING FOR EFFECT

Lighting is the newest of all dramatic techniques. The Greeks depended on the sun, as did the Elizabethans. And from the time of the first enclosed theaters in the late sixteenth century until 1914, lighting consisted of a glare of footlights designed simply to illuminate actors.

In 1914, the first spotlights were hung on the balcony rail of Wallack's Theater in New York. That was a radical improvement. But the progress made since the mid-1960s with modern lighting boards is a quantum leap forward for drama. Although some playwrights leave lighting cues entirely to the director, others see lighting as an integral part of the whole effect and write basic instructions into the script.

The most obvious use of lighting is to suggest the time of day. It is a simple matter to have the lights rise in the early morning or slowly dim as the sun sets. If the fading light also echoes an increasingly somber mood of the scene, the lighting will be even more effective.

On a more subtle level, lights are used to reflect the tone of the scene, whether inside or out. Quiet, low-key, or intimate scenes are enhanced with lowered lights; and conversely, scenes that are lively or dramatic can be charged with brighter lights. Techniques like these can be effective with any type of drama, but they are more frequently associated with nonrealistic plays.

In addition to influencing the overall tone of a scene, lights can be used to highlight a particular portion of the set while leaving other areas dark. As you can see from the illustrations of the three-part setting for *The Collection*, lighting effectively directs the audience's attention from one portion of the stage to another. Selective lighting actually has the power to change the set.

In Arthur Miller's *After the Fall*, a play that gives the illusion of a sequence of memories, lighting becomes essential to achieve the effect. Miller states in the script that his characters must "appear and disappear instanta-neously, as in the mind; but it is not necessary that they walk off the stage." This is normally achieved through a complex series of lighting shifts. The technique is well worth considering if you have many scenes. It allows you to create virtual sets without the distracting break in illusion caused by con-ventional scene shifts.

Lighting can also place a special emphasis on a character or highlight a key speech the way music occasionally does in film. Although Saroyan doesn't provide light cues in *Hello Out There*, it would be dramatic to isolate Emily at the very end with a single overhead spot in an otherwise darkened stage.

COSTUMES: REALISTIC AND SYMBOLIC

Like the lighting, the costumes are a visual effect that in some cases is left to the costume designer. In other cases, descriptions are written into the stage directions. In realistic plays with a contemporary setting, there is usually no mention of costumes in the script. Plays set in an earlier historical period may call for some description, although the director has the option of using contemporary dress. Nonrealistic plays, however, may make special use of costume to achieve symbolic significance. In such cases, playwrights some-times become very specific.

The script for Alterman's *Coulda, Woulda, Shoulda* initially makes no mention of costume, so most directors would use what would be natural for a bar owner and his wife. But the costume of Marty, the son, is precisely described in the script. His entrance is a dramatic turning point. It is the moment when an apparently realistic play suddenly becomes nonrealistic. How is this change achieved? First, with a simple but significant stage direction: "A light change." This signals that something important will hap-pen. Second, the door opens and, as you remember, the audience is jolted by the sight of an adult Marty "wearing large children's pajamas, a pair of glasses, and a black hat."

It is essential that the playwright be precise in the description of costume here, and it is equally essential that a director follow those directions. The fact that the character who has been described as a child is now standing there as a man "in his forties" is startling, but that alone doesn't communi-cate the symbol the playwright has in mind. Marty is not just a child grown up, he is simultaneously an adult playwright (he is carrying a pen and pad) and a child in his pajamas.

Why the black hat? Remember that as a little boy he had announced that he wanted to become a rabbi. He did not become a rabbi, but he wears the black hat that is frequently worn by rabbis, and in the tradition of prophets he seems to have the power to predict the future. In fact, he has to remind his mother. "I'm not God." But as any playwright knows, creating a good play is the next best thing.

It is the use of costume, then, that helps blend the adult character named Marty with the child described in the opening scene.

CHARACTERS IN MOTION

A play is not a radio drama. This may seem obvious, yet in a short-play contest I recently judged, more than half the entries consisted of two motionless characters talking. Whether serious or witty, they could have been delivered by two actors reading the script while sitting on stools.

The movement of characters on the stage is a crucial visual component. It is almost as important as the lines they speak. This physical activity can be used in many ways, but the most fundamental one is to divide one secondary scene from the next.

As I described in Chapter 39 on plot, most plays are divided into a number of secondary scenes. Those units are begun and ended by entrances and exits. On this basic level, then, the activity of the actors unobtrusively reveals just how the play is organized.

Hello Out There is a model of how entrances and exits can be used to create a sequence of scenes that become the skeletal framework of the play. To review that structure of eight scenes, see page 349.

Remember, too, how important Marty's entrance is in *Coulda, Woulda, Shoulda*. It transforms an apparently realistic play into an ingeniously innovative drama. Equally important, the scene toward the end of the play begins when first one parent and then the other leaves the stage. Significantly, they enter Marty's bedroom, leaving Marty to go on writing the very play we are watching. How could all that be achieved without entrances and exits?

Although the opening and closing scenes in *Reckoning* that show Joe alone on the stage and the one that does the same with Mary are all brief, they are charged with meaningful action. The characters reveal their anxiety and tension almost entirely through their actions. Without moving characters off stage and back again, none of these important scenes would be possible.

The degree and type of action within longer scenes can be used to determine the pacing of a play. As in fiction, a scene in which there is a lot of talk and not much action may be necessary to fill in background or develop character, but there is not much forward motion. A lively scene with plenty of action moves the play forward again. Such shifts determine what can be described as the rhythm of the play.

Most plays — serious or comic — begin by defining the situation, developing that situation, and then rushing forward with fast scenes to a climax and a conclusion. The flow or rhythm of a play can't be left to chance.

Up to a point, a good director can enliven a static scene by adding **stage business**, minor activity such as crossing the room, opening a window, or pacing up and down. But there are limits to this. And occasionally you may find that you have made matters even more difficult for the director by specifying that your characters sit while they talk.

In Chapter 44, I pointed out how action in the opening scene of *Coulda, Woulda, Shoulda* helps reveal two apparently contradictory aspects of the father. This opening scene deserves a close review because it clearly illustrates how a potentially talky and slow-moving scene can be energized with an apparently trivial sequence of activities.

The two parents, you remember, are discussing their young son. It is exactly the kind of scene that can easily drag. To maintain vitality the playwright has kept the father, Cy, in constant action. Stage directions in the script call for him to be "rushing around, getting dressed." Toward the end of that scene, he grabs his coat and starts to leave. His wife physically blocks the door, insisting that he talk with his son. As she continues to call to Marty, Cy discovers he doesn't have his car keys. Just before Marty's entrance, Cy finds the keys. All this activity is going on while the dialogue is filling us in on their relationship with each other and with their son.

Imagine that opening as it would be if the couple were sitting on the couch without moving. Not even an inventive director could have devised enough casual **stage business** to maintain vitality.

Notice, by the way, the brevity of the stage directions. Unlike exposition in fiction, they never explain motivation such as "In his haste to get to work . . ." or "Anxious to avoid dealing with his son . . ." Alterman's parenthetical stage directions are so terse that the casual reader might easily miss them. But no actor or director would. They provide the action that makes the difference between a static scene and one that has dramatic energy.

How does all this apply to your own work? Start by examining how action is specified in a number of plays. Try to analyze its function. We all have a tendency to read play scripts as if they were fiction. But if you hope to develop your ability as a playwright, you should analyze dramatic techniques — especially the use of action.

Next, analyze your own first draft scene by scene. Consider the emotional impact of each scene. If two characters are getting to know each other (such as in the early scenes in *Hello Out there*), you can afford to move slowly — for a while at least. But when a lot is going on (as in the climatic scenes of that play), action may outweigh dialogue, making it a fast scene.

Many playwrights take the time to outline their plays scene by scene right from the start. This is a particularly helpful technique if you are new to the genre. It can save a great deal of rewriting later.

If it appears from your outline that an individual scene will go on too long, the solution may be to revitalize it by adding more action; or it may be enough to cut unnecessary lines. In more severe cases, consider breaking the scene into two by adding an entrance or exit. It is far easier to do this in the outline than to revise a completed draft.

If you are having trouble generating significant action, write a description of each scene without quoting any of the dialogue. If you find yourself summarizing certain scenes with bland statements like "They sit at the kitchen table and blame each other for the state of their marriage," you may have some serious rewriting to do.

WRITING FROM THE 10TH ROW CENTER

When you write fiction, you tend to enter the scene and imagine it through the eyes of a chosen character. To a large degree, you are within the work. Writing drama is different partly because there is no single point of view and also because you are writing for a live audience. As a result, when you work on a script a good portion of you remains outside the action. You are seeing and hearing each scene as if you were in the best seat of the house — the 10th row center.

If you have been writing fiction and are turning to drama for the first time, it may take a while to maintain this objectivity. It's important, though, because a play script is not an end in itself. It is a description of what, with hard work and luck, will become a performance. With this in mind, the scriptwriter must also be a spectator.

Out there in the 10th row looking at your own work, you will never confuse the script and the play. Although scripts don't micromanage details about the set, the lighting, and costuming, they have to provide opportunities for set designers, directors, and actors.

As for pacing, remember that scripts can be read silently at five times the speed of a play in performance. The reader can skim over dreary, static scenes and get to the good parts. Not so with the audience of a production. They are trapped in their seats. One way for you as writer to share that experience is to read the entire play out loud. That way you will remain a spectator in the 10th row. If some scenes are tedious, you too will have to endure them. You will find out what it is like to squirm in your seat and check the theater for exit signs.

You are not, however, a passive spectator. The other part of you is a playwright in control. It is up to you to judge whether a character has been long-winded or if everyone on stage has been glued to the floor like so many talking mannequins. It is up to you as playwright to determine when another character should come in with some fresh insight. It's up to you to devise ways of using the set or lighting. When you revise with an acute awareness of what the audience is seeing and hearing, you are not just writing a script, you are shaping a play designed for performance.

The play that follows in Chapter 46 is *Valley Forgery* written by Patricia Montley. It is, like many of her published and produced works, a **satire**. Like all satires, it uses exaggeration to ridicule attitudes, institutions, and, in this case, historical figures.

While simple satiric skits are often written just for laughs, sophisticated satire like this play usually imply some strong convictions as well. *Valley Forgery* is no exception. The social and political views are woven into both the plot and the dialogue.

Read it once for pleasure. Relax and enjoy it. Then go though it again, analyze it scene by scene, character by character. What made you laugh and why? What public policies and attitudes are being ridiculed? What ideals are reflected? Remember that if you are serious about play writing you can learn as much from a satiric comedy as from a tragedy.

46 Valley Forgery

A Play

by Patricia Montley

The action takes place on the banks of the Delaware River in 1776.

Characters

MARTHA WASHINGTON, 40 TO 45 — A BORN LEADER WITHOUT PRETENTIONS; SHREWD, WARM, NATURAL

FANNY HOWE, 55 TO 65 — LIVELY, CLEVER, RHETORICAL

MARIE ANTOINETTE, 20 TO 30 — SHORT, DARK, PLUMP, PASSIONATE, OUTLANDISHLY ROMANTIC, FIERY

Setting

Martha's boat, Down Right. Fanny's boat, with Fanny asleep in it, Down Left. At Center a hibachi with seat-logs Left and Right of it and a higher seat-log Up of it. At Up Left Center, a tall rock.

AT RISE

Lights up on MARTHA, Down Right, posing in boat like Washington in "Washington Crossing the Delaware." FANNY, unseen by MARTHA, is asleep in boat Down Left. MARTHA holds pose, surveying the river until she spots land. She "paddles" Up, gets out of boat, takes duffle bag out, drags boat to shore and turns it upside down.

MARTHA: 'Deed I don't know what's got into that man. He's daft as a demented moose to be holing up in this Pennsylvania ice rink when he could be home in Virginny roasting chestnuts and singing carols. For a man who calls himself the Father of His Country, he sure is lacking in family spirit. Well, that's men for you — full of inconsistencies. Take this joker of a ferryman who didn't want me to make this dangerous trip up the Delaware and then rented me a boat with a leak. (*Takes long underwear from duffle bag.*) Now these long johns are soaked. I'll hang them on that rock over there. (*Crosses Up Left to rock and spreads out underwear with bottoms draped down front of rock.*) Drat it all! They'll be stiff as an icicle shortly. Oh well — nothing like stiff drawers to keep a soldier in shape. (*Spots campfire.*) What's this? The remains of a campfire. (*Sees knapsack on Up log-seat.*) Look here — a knapsack — with the initials "M.A." (*Searches knapsack.*) Hmm . . . cheese . . . French cheese. And a bottle of wine . . . Chateau Versailles, 1769 . . . empty. (*Drops knapsack. Letter falls out, unnoticed. MARTHA crosses Down of fire and stoops to get warm, her back to audience. FANNY wakes up and stretches. Her first speech is not heard by MARTHA.*)

FANNY: Sure and it's damp as a baby's diaper out here and me poor ailing back is breaking with the stiffness. Christmas in Killarney was never at all like this. Faith — would you look here now! I've drifted all the way into shore. (*Gets out at Down Left of boat.*) O, Blessed St. Patrick, let it be the shores of Philadelphia, for I've no desire to be rowing any farther this night. (*Spots MARTHA.*) But what's this I'm seeing? Why it's another traveler. I've a mind to be getting directions from that one. (*Crosses Right.*) Ah — begging your pardon, Miss, but would you be —

MARTHA: (*Jumping up.*) Who are you?!

FANNY: Me name is Fanny Howe and I'm looking for Philadelphia.

MARTHA: Well, you're not far off. It's a few miles that way. But come and get warmed up a bit.

FANNY: (*Crosses Right.*) Thanks then. I'm near to freezing.

MARTHA: Have you got family in Philly, Fanny?

FANNY: I have, indeed. And I'm just coming to remind him of it.

MARTHA: Remind who?

FANNY: Me family: Major General William Howe of His Majesty's fiftieth regiment. I'm the general's long-suffering wife.

MARTHA: How do you do. I'm Martha Washington of Mount Vernon, Virginia. (*They shake hands.*)

FANNY: (*Sits on Left log-seat.*) Is your husband also in Philadelphia then?

MARTHA: (*Crosses Right to duffle bag.*) No, I'm afraid the town's not big enough for both our husbands. And since yours won the last battle, he's got the city for the winter. (*Takes bag of marshmallows from duffle bag and starts back Left with them.*) My George is up the road a piece at Valley Forge, freezing and starving himself like a sadistic little Spartan — (*She pops a marshmallow in her mouth,*) —just because he's too embarrassed about losing to come home for Christmas. (*Sits on Right log-seat.*)

FANNY: Well, I'm sure he could go to California for all Sir William cares. I know me husband, and I'm telling you, Martha, once himself is cozied into some posh winter quarters, he's not about to go out in the snow to be fighting any battles. It's a summer soldier, he is.

MARTHA: (*Roasting a marshmallow.*) Tell me, Fanny, how did a decent Irish woman like you ever get tied up with a limey soldier like Howe?

FANNY: (*Stands*) Well, the British is a bad lot — and I don't blame you for wanting to be rid of the whole crowd of them. (*Crosses Down Left.*) But

Sir William cut a fine figure in his bright red coat and flashing saber when he come to be stationed in Ireland in '63. Oh, the man was a picture. He'd a slew of medals on his chest and a string of stories on his tongue that'd charm the sense out of any innocent Irish lass — (*Reaches into her boat for tea kettle and two mugs.*) — especially one as had nothing more exciting to look forward to than minding bar in her father's public house for the rest of her life. (*Crosses back Right to fire.*) Anyways to cut it short — for to tell the truth, I'm bored talking about it — Sir William got to thinking there'd be no end to his stay in Ireland. So himself decided to get married. Little did the bride suspect that after the honeymoon, she's still be tending bar while her soldier-husband went gallivanting around the colonial countryside courting trouble.

MARTHA: Yes, and trouble's not all he's courting, so I hear.

FANNY: Don't I know it! Rumor has a way of traveling, you know. And now it's after making trans-Atlantic flights.

MARTHA: You know, Fanny, you've got a natural way with words. Did you ever think of submitting this story to *Redbook Magazine?*

FANNY: Oh, to be sure. I've already got a whole pile of rejection slips — from *Ladies Home Journal* and *Good Housekeeping* and all the rest of them. (*She takes out rejection slips from pocket.*) They're all telling me the story won't sell on account of its being too common.

MARTHA: Yes, I guess there's truth in that. Ah — I think you dropped one there.

FANNY: Where?

MARTHA: There by the knapsack.

FANNY: (*Picking up a piece of paper that had earlier fallen from the knapsack.*) This bit of paper? No, this one's not mine. It seems to be a page from some sort of military manual. (*Reads*) "Regulations for the Order and Discipline of the Troops of the United States." (*Marie Antoinette enters Up Left, unnoticed by others.*)

MARIE: Mon Dieu! I am discovered! (*Crosses Right to rock and hides behind it.*)

MARTHA: Let me see. (*Takes paper from FANNY and crosses Down Right.*) Hmm . . . look here, there's something handwritten on the back. It's a letter . . . from the looks of it, a love letter. Some of it's in French.

FANNY: And is it signed then?

MARTHA: Yes. "Yours till Niagara falls, Joseph L." And it's addressed to "M.A."

FANNY: M.A.? Do you know anyone with those initals?

MARTHA: No. And I don't think I'd want to. This turkey sounds really freaky.

MARIE: Freaky! (*Reveals herself, crosses Center.*) You Anglo-Saxons are all bumpkins! (*FANNY jumps up and she and MARTHA look at each other.*)

MARTHA: Who's that? (*Together*)

FANNY: Who's that?

MARIA: C'est moi, of course!

MARTHA: Mademoiselle, this must be your campsite. My name is Martha Washington and this is Fanny Howe.

FANNY: Fanny Conolly Howe.

MARIE: I am pleased to make your acquaintances, Mesdames. My name is Marie . . . eh . . . Marie Adrienne Lafayette.

MARTHA: (*Putting letter in pocket.*) Ah — Madame Lafayette! How happy I am to meet you at last. I'm very fond of your husband, you know.

MARIE: Is that right?

MARTHA: (*Crossing Up.*) Oh, yes. He's been to dinner at Mount Vernon many times. A charming young man, your Joseph.

MARIE: Oui — tres charmant! Do you by any chance know where he is?

MARTHA: Why of course — he's at Valley Forge with George.

MARIE: Yes, of course, but —

MARTHA: Ah, I see — you don't know the way there. Well, my dear, I'm going that way myself — to take George some thermal undies for Christmas. We can go together.

MARIE: Magnifique! (*To FANNY,*) And you also, Madame?

FANNY: (*Cool. Giving MARIE the once-over.*) No, not I. *My* marital obligations take me to more comfortable quarters.

MARTHA: My husband will be so pleased to see you again.

MARIE: (*Nervous*) Again?

MARTHA: (*Crossing Center towards MARIE.*) Why yes. The last time he returned from Paris, he spoke of nothing but the lovely time he had with you and Monsieur Lafayette at your country chateau.

MARIE: He did?

MARTHA: (*Stalking Left behind MARIE.*) Yes, he went on and on about your grand stature.

MARIE: Well, the journey has taken a lot out of me.

MARTHA: (*Crossing back to Right of MARIE.*) And your gorgeous blonde hair —

MARIE: I am afraid it is a little dirty now.

MARTHA: And your sparkling blue eyes.

MARIE: They change the color with the light.

MARTHA: Yes, I am sure General Washington will be delighted to see you — whoever you are, my mysterious Madame Imposter! (*Takes MARIE's arm threateningly.*)

MARIE: You are making a big mistake.

MARTHA: It's you who have made the mistake. Now perhaps you will tell us who you really are!

FANNY: (*Finally recognizing her.*) Faith and begorra! She don't have to!

MARTHA: What? (*Together*)

MARIE: Quoi?

FANNY: Sure and there's not a living soul in the whole of Europe that don't know the flippant face of the vixen of Versailles. (*Grabs MARIE's other arm.*) This is the sovereign strumpet herself — Marie Antoinette!

MARIE: (*Breaks away and jumps up on Up log.*) Oui! Marie Antoinette! The grand and glorious Queen of France! Vive la reine! And now, Mesdames, if you value your impudent little lives, you will grovel at the feet of the mighty monarch of France, and she may — because of her noble and generous nature — deign to spare your insignificant selves.

FANNY: (*Crosses Down Left and sits on edge of boat.*) Would you listen to the airs of this one!

MARTHA: Madame, this is the United States of America! There'll be no groveling here!

MARIE: No groveling? Very well then — just kiss my hand. Go ahead — baisez la main de la reine. (*Steps down to level with MARTHA.*) Well? Baisez — baisez!

MARTHA: There'll be no baisaying of hands either. How can you indulge in such undemocratic deportment while less than twenty miles off, our American boys are starving — with not even horsemeat to eat?

MARIE: Then . . . let them eat steak! What do I care for starving Yankees?

MARTHA: You shall see, Madame — your audacity will not go unpunished. In America, even queens must come to justice!

MARIE: The justice for the queens! What a ridiculous ideal What are you going to do, hein?

MARTHA: Well, since you're so hot to join Monsieur Lafayette, we will go to Valley Forge, where you will be forced to acknowledge your scandalous behavior.

MARIE: Scandalous behavior! Ha! You Americans are such naive idealists.

FANNY: Do you mean to be suggesting that it's a decent sort of queenly behavior to be making cuckolds of kings?

MARIE: My Louis, a cuckold? That is a good one! (*Pushes MARTHA aside and crosses Down Right.*) Mesdames, you are both from backward, underdeveloped nations and so your innocence must be excused. But in France we live in an age of sexual freedom called The Enlightenment. My Louis and I — we are a totally liberated couple. In the French court, we are the leaders of the Let Set — I let him do what he wants; he lets me do what I want. Versailles is a veritable palace of sexual delights: mate-swapping, group orgies, the latest crazes in S and M, touchy-feely, and sundry other kinky perversions. Our policy there is: among two or more consenting adults of any sex or species, nothing is a no-no. (*Sits on boat Down Right.*)

MARTHA: Be that as it may, our policy here is that there are many no-no's — among them impersonation and adultery.

MARIE: "Adultery!" How medieval!

FANNY: (*Crosses Right to MARIE.*) Medieval, is it? Well then, it must be deserving of a medieval punishment. What do you say to that, you Loose Lassie, you!? (*Shakes her by the ear.*)

MARIE: I say there will be no punishment at all. You have no proof that your accusations are true.

MARTHA: (*Takes out letter and waves it.*) No proof, eh? What about this?

MARIE: Mon Dieu! I forgot about the letter!

MARTHA: (*Crossing Down to MARIE.*) The letter found on the ground beside your knapsack.

FANNY: Aye — and in the presence of a witness.

MARIE: How incriminating!

MARTHA: How indecent!

FANNY: What does it say?

MARTHA: You asked for it. (*Reads with heavy American accent.*) "Ma chere petite bonne aime Marie Antoinette, how I —"

MARIE: (*Stands and snatches letter from MARTHA.*) Give it to me! Such passionate words must be read avec une grande sensibilite! Americans have no sense of these things. (*Reads, crossing to Center.*) "Ma chere petite bonne aimee Marie Antoinette. How I miss the sight of your little poodle face, with its dreamy doe eyes, its tiny wet-kitten nose, its pouting little monkey mouth —"

FANNY: By the sound of it so far, the lad's a frustrated veterinarian.

MARIE: (*Crossing Left.*) "I am desperate for the taste of your bon-bon kisses. I am mad with lust to touch the tips of your fingers, the tips of your toes, the tips of your ear lobes, and . . . other assorted tips."

FANNY: Thank God for generalizations!

MARIE: "But to get to the heart of the matter —"

FANNY: Oh, no!

MARIE: "We are to be garrisoned here at Valley Forge for the winter."

FANNY: Whew!

MARIE: "This nincompoop Washington is afraid to march on Hairy Howe, the Don Juan of the Delaware —"

FANNY: (*Collapses onto boat at Down Right.*) Oh, me poor heart!

MARIE: "And even more afraid to march home to his wife, the Termagant of the Potomac."

MARTHA: Think of the dinners I wasted on that one!

MARIE: (*Crossing to Up of fire.*) "So here we are. The nights are cold. Unless I have the passionate pants of my hot-blooded little poodle to keep me warm, I shall perish. You must save me from this fate. You must come to me, my Little Cream Puff, or my game with life is lost. I adore you, I love you, I long for you, I live for you, etcetera, etcetera." Signed: "Yours till Niagara falls — Joseph L." So! Now you have seen the flame of the true passion — and will never see it again. (*Tosses letter into fire.*)

MARTHA: (*Crosses Left, retrieves letter.*) Oh, no you don't, my Little Cream Puff! You won't get off the hook that easily!

MARIE: (*Crosses to Right log-seat and kneels on it.*) Oh, Madame, you must not show this letter to your nincompoop husband. He will take the stripes off my Joseph's shoulder and put them on his back. Please — I beg of you! I will do anything — anything!

FANNY: Would you be up for signing a peace treaty?

MARIE: (*Standing*) Quoi? (*Together*)

MARTHA: What?

FANNY: Would you be willing to forge King Louis' name on a treaty of peace with Britain?

MARTHA: What are you up to, Fanny?

FANNY: (*Stands*) Are you after thinking this Lafayette is the only lad who's writing such blarney to his mistress? Why, they'll all be wooing their wenches if this war's to be dragging on forever, I'm telling you, it's got to be stopped — war means the breaking down of the nuclear family!

MARTHA: (*Sits on Left log-seat.*) And do you really think we can get away with forging a peace treaty?

FANNY: Why not I ask you? It's your two countries fighting against mine, ain't it? Well now, if we all three sign our husbands' names on a treaty of peace, what's to keep the fighting going on?

MARTHA: Well, I'm game. (*To MARIE.*) How about you, Toots?

MARIE: (*Sits on Right log-seat.*) I will do anything to get the letter back.

FANNY: All right, then. (*Sits on Down Right boat and takes out pencil and rejection slip. Writes on the back of this.*) Let's be getting on with the terms of agreement. So now . . . All that the limeys care about is trade and waterways and the like. So you give us the right to be cruising up and down the Mississippi River as much as we please.

MARTHA: Fine, fine.

FANNY: What do you want?

MARTHA: (*Crosses Left to boat and picks up map hanging over side of it.*) Well, the only thing Yankee men give a hoot about is land. They're all real-estate crazy. So you give us . . . Oh, I don't know . . . how about all the land as far west as the Missouri?

MARIE: No, no, you may not have the French Quarter. We must keep the Louisiana.

MARTHA: No sweat. Make it as far west as the Mississippi.

FANNY: Just as you say then. (*Writes*)

MARTHA: And as far south as the thirtieth parallel.

FANNY: (*Writing*) Thir . . . ti . . . eth parall —

MARTHA: No, wait. A round number will sound too logical. It might give us away. Should be something the men would come up with — something arbitrary. Make it the thirty-first parallel.

FANNY: (*Erases and writes.*) Thirty-first parallel.

MARTHA: And to the north, make the border . . . the Hudson Bay. (*Tosses map into boat.*)

MARIE: (*Stand.*) No. No. You must not give Canada to the Americans. It would mean the corruption of their language.

MARTHA: (*Crosses to Left Log-seat and sits.*) Oh, very well then. Keep Canada.

FANNY: (*Crosses to Right Log-seat and sits.*) I've got it all down now — a fine settlement. So then — (*Offers it to Martha.*) — here it is for the signing.

MARTHA: (*Takes paper and pencil, starts to sign, hesitates.*) You know, there's something . . . incomplete about this.

FANNY: Well, sure and it's understood that the fourth boundary be the great ocean itself.

MARTHA: I don't mean that.

MARIE: Mais qu'est-ce que c'est?

MARTHA: (*Stands, crosses Left.*) I mean here we are — for the first time in history — three women drawing up an important document that will have a great effect on the future of our world . . .

FANNY: Aye — so?

MARTHA: So I think we should take advantage of the opportunity and give ourselves a few rights.

FANNY: Rights for women?

MARIE: It is tres radical!

MARTHA: (*Crosses Up to rock.*) Yes, I have it now! We'll draw up an act giving ourselves rights the same as the men! The Equal Rights Act we'll call it. (*Writes on treaty, using top of rock to rest on.*) E-qual . . . Rights . . . Act. We'll make this ERA a part of the treaty.

FANNY: What sort of rights are you thinking of?

MARTHA: (*Crossing Down.*) Oh, you know — property rights, suffrage, educational opportunites, equal pay for equal work — the whole bit.

MARIE: Ha! What a joke! I assure you, Mesdames, it will never happen in France. Equality means the end of romance. And France will never abandon the romance for the reason!

MARTHA: What about the British Empire?

FANNY: Not a chance will it have there. The British Empire is built on the principle of Divine Right: the men think they're divine, even though the women know we're right.

MARTHA: Well, this is the United States of America! Land of opportunity for all! Cradle of Democracy! Fount of Freedom! Lover of Liberty —

MARIE: Oui, oui, so what?

MARTHA: So I think the ERA will have a chance here. I tell you in this country it will happen!

MARIE: When?

MARTHA: When?

FANNY: Aye — when?

MARTHA: Well, maybe not tomorrow.

MARIE: Ha!

MARTHA: But someday.

FANNY: Someday?

MARTHA: Someday soon.

MARIE: How soon?

MARTHA: Well, maybe a hundred years. Two hundred at the outside.

MARIE: Deux cents ans! Mon Dieu!

FANNY: Blessed St. Patrick! You won't be around in another two hundred years, woman! Who's to see to this ERA business?

MARTHA: (*Crosses Down.*) I am not the Mother of my Country for nothing. My daughters will see to it. Or my daughters' daughters. Or my daughters' daughters' daughters. Or my —

MARIE: C'est bon, c'est bon. But how will they find out about it?

MARTHA: I'll pass this document on to them.

FANNY: That'll be a bit dangerous, won't it though? I mean supposing it falls into the "wrong hands?" Why then it'll be woe to the lass as was harboring it.

MARIE: She has a point there, no?

MARTHA: Yes, I guess you're right. But I refuse to just let it go to the winds.

MARIE: Ah — then let it go to the waters.

MARTHA: What?

FANNY: I know what the lass means. You want to be putting that paper into some sort of bottle and tossing it into the Delaware — to be discovered by posterity.

MARTHA: Well, the idea's got possibilities.

MARIE: Un moment! (*Crosses Up Center.*) I have an empty wine bottle in my knapsack.

MARTHA: (*Crossing Down Center.*) That way it won't have far to go to reach some enterprising American Congresswoman.

MARIE: Congresswoman! Ha! (*Crosses to Down Left of MARTHA.*)

FANNY: (*Crosses to Down Right of MARTHA.*) Let her be, lass. In a country of dreamers, the crazy woman is queen.

MARIE: Voilá la bottle, Madame Washington.

MARTHA: (*Holding document.*) And voilá the hope of America! (*MARTHA rolls up paper and stuffs it into bottle, while reciting. MARIE and FANNY strike appropriate poses at the end of each phrase, as music fades in.*) We the Founding Mothers of these United States, in order to form a perfect union, establish justice, provide for the common defense against domestic tragedy, promote the general welfare of both sexes, and secure the blessings of liberty to our daughters, do ordain and establish that — (*FANNY and MARIE go down on one knee.*) — equality of rights under the law shall not be denied or abridged on account of sex. (*She tosses bottle into audience.*)

MARIE: Liberté!

FANNY: Equality!

ALL: Sorority!

THE END

47 The Voices of Comedy

It may seem odd to analyze comedy. We think of it as springing from an intuitive ability. Although it is true that a sense of humor can't be taught, almost no one is totally humorless. You don't have to be an accomplished comedian to capture a comic experience, exaggerate it, and turn it into a dramatic scene or an entire play.

It helps, though, if you know what you are doing. As with any art, one learns from the successes and failures of others. Some approaches will muddy an excellent concept; others will bring out the best. Matters of timing and tone can spell the difference between success and failure. Inserting a farcical scene, for example, into a play that is otherwise built around a gently humorous development of character can do real damage. A blockbuster opening may seem great in an early draft, but it's the wrong tactic if the play runs down from there on. You can avoid a lot of rewriting if you determine what type of comedy is appropriate for your particular play before you even outline the plot.

TONAL CHOICES: HUMOR AND WIT

Although there is no sharp line between humor and wit, and both are often found in the same work, they do refer to significantly different approaches. *Humor* tends to be gentle and supportive. It shares with an audience foibles that we have experienced or are familiar with, such as the awkwardness of young people in love, the tensions associated with rituals like a job interview or a wedding, or the anxieties, frustrations, and misunderstandings that parents face dealing with children and the reverse. We tend to smile or laugh *with* such characters, not *at* them.

Humor is often based on incongruities: the priest at a beer party, the gang member at an art opening, a man married to a woman half his age, or the reverse. Some of these situations have been overused in the endless stream of situation comedies for television, but fresh events occur in our daily lives and can be developed with greater insight than one usually finds on the tube.

Wit, on the other hand, tends to be sharper than humor. It is often based less on the human condition than on verbal tricks: jokes, puns, and plays on words. It often appears in the dialogue of characters who are clever, even snide. But wit can be used to ridicule characters who are serious or pompous. When wit is used to criticize characters, attitudes, or institutions through exaggeration, we call it **satire**, a form of comedy I will turn to shortly.

Wit can get nasty. Members of the audience remain outside the characters or institutions being ridiculed and laugh *at* them rather than *with* them. If you can imagine a graph that measures emotional response, humor would be shown by a gently undulating line while wit would produce spikes.

Gentle humor is the dominant tone at the beginning of *Coulda, Woulda, Shoulda*. When the mother reports that their son had announced solemnly that he wanted to become a rabbi and she thought he said *rabbit*, the audience smiles. The tone there is warm.

The tone becomes somewhat sharper, however, when the father's macho comments on how they should discipline their son are contrasted with his utter dependence on her to find his belt, his shoes, and even his car keys.

The son, Marty, is satirized still more sharply when he announces what will become of the characters in his plays that are based on his parents. The father, you remember, becomes a drunk, loses both legs, and dies alone. The mother ends up "bitter, alone, miserable in Miami." Nothing sweet and gentle there. It's a harsh yet comic picture of therapy writing at its worst — work that is more concerned with expressing hostility than with literary merit.

The wit and satire in this play is not limited to one-line retorts like those that often dominate situation comedies. Generally speaking, it is based on character and inconsistent attitudes. We learn about the father's infidelities, making him seem tough and thoughtless, but at the same time we see how shaken he is on hearing that in Marty's play he will die alone and unloved.

"This is a comedy?" the father cries out, incapable of separating himself from his son's script. The wit is partially based on his inability to differentiate creative work and what is real and also on his assumption that comedy should be consistently funny. His wife puts this even more directly: "So much anger, hostility?" she asks. "Can't you fix it? Make it funny?"

Her pathetic cry is one that is shared by many theatergoers over the years. Unwittingly she has touched on an important aspect of comedy. It often is a mix of the darkest aspects of life (reflected in Marty's dysfunctional family and the depressing melodrama he is writing) and comic turns that make us laugh.

SATIRE: FROM SUBTLE TO FARCICAL

Satire ridicules by comic exaggeration. Those two elements, ridicule and exaggeration, are fundamental in all satires. Good satire defines its target carefully, aiming not just for laughs (although that's an important element) but for critical insight. The tone of the criticism can vary enormously, running from the mildest sort of friendly spoof to the most vitriolic attack. Hostile satire can become so savage that it is hardly recognizable as comedy, but if the playwright's intention is to evoke laughter, the work is still satire.

Because of this comic element, one often misses the fact that every satire is also to some degree a moral statement. Even the silliest satiric skits on television attacks people (usually public figures), types (particularly the pompous and hypocritical), or institutions (the bigger the better). Because stage plays have the advantage of being aimed at smaller, more selective audiences, satires tend to be more sophisticated. Often they are more challenging and provocative. And there are fewer taboos. It is no accident that totalitarian regimes maintain tight control of theaters and playwrights. Satire can be an effective weapon against injustice and oppression.

As we have seen, all three characters in *Coulda, Woulda, Shoulda* are being satirized. Marty is ridiculed as an egotistical writer who allows his hostile feelings to dominate the play he is writing (which itself is a satire of melodramatic scripts). The father, as we have seen, is portrayed as a hypocritical mix of toughness and fearful insecurity, and the mother is one of those who confuses life and creative work. One of the reasons why we laugh is that we see these characters as exaggerations of familiar types — and possibly aspects of ourselves. The tone of the satire is critical but far from savage. It is softened with some degree of compassion — especially for the mother.

The comedy in *Valley Forgery* has been pushed to the level of farce. We call it that because of the degree of exaggeration: the characters are almost cartoons, and the situation is wildly implausible. It is not, however, slapstick, the least subtle form of comedy designed simply for laughs — on the level of *The Three Stooges*. *Valley Forgery* has serious themes that one would never find in slapstick.

The satire in this play ridicules not only personality types, but also political and social institutions to a greater degree than the other three plays.

Of the three characters, Martha Washington is the most stable. She is described initially as "a born leader," and she is the one with specific plans. If it weren't for her, the plot might lose all sense of direction.

Still, she is far from the historical figure portrayed for school kids. In her very first lines she ridicules her husband as one who "sure is lacking in family spirit." Her language is direct and informal. In addressing the wife of General Howe, commander in chief of the British forces, she echoes the phrasing of Hollywood Westerns: "I'm afraid the town's not big enough for both our husbands."

Of the three, Marie Antoinette, wife of Louis XVI and queen of France is the most exaggerated as a flighty, amoral coquette. Fanny Howe describes herself as a former Irish bartender who married to escape Ireland. For all her blithe cynicism about her marriage, she is the one who suggests that the three women forge a peace treaty to put an end to the war.

In some respects, each character is a **stereotype**. But in a comedy, this is perfectly acceptable — especially when presented with a sense of delight and, in this case, even admiration. After all, they end up opposing war and launching a long-range campaign to establish equal rights for all.

The satire of national types and the comic clash of personalities are so prominent that one almost misses the attack on a variety of institutions and political leaders. Both opposing generals, George Washington and General Howe are viewed as primarily concerned with securing or holding warm quarters for the winter. They also get low rating as husbands. The exaggerated description of French morality becomes comic in its excess.

IRONY: REVERSALS OF THE EXPECTED

There are several types of **irony**, but they are all based on a reversal of expectation. The most common form, *verbal irony*, is limited to speech. The speaker knowingly says something that is the opposite or clearly different from the intended meaning like a golfer saying "great shot" when his opening drive veers into the woods. It is similar to sarcasm but it's not necessarily critical.

In the opening scene of *Valley Forgery*, Martha Washington discovers that her husband's long underwear are soaked and will freeze in the winter air. She responds with wry irony: "Oh well — nothing like stiff drawers to keep a soldier in shape." Later Marie Antoinette reads a portion of the letter her lover has written describing her as a "poodle face" with "doe eyes" and "wet kitten nose." Fanny responds by saying "the lad's a frustrated veterinarian."

Dramatic irony is much less used — even in plays — but it can be highly effective. It describes a statement made by a character who has no idea how wrong or inaccurate the pronouncement really is. For example, a play about Abraham Lincoln's childhood might have a teacher say of the young Lincoln, "He'll never amount to anything."

A third and much more common type of irony has to do with events, not spoken words. Called *cosmic irony* or *irony of fate*, it describes occurrences that are dramatically different from the expected. It would apply, for example, to the head of an Auto Safety Department dying in a car crash.

Cosmic irony in drama is often simply implied and so tends to be less obvious than verbal irony. We may easily miss it on first reading. It is, for example, ironic in *Coulda, Woulda, Shoulda* that a young playwright who practically plays god in the ruthless manipulation of his dramatic characters is himself a terrible writer.

On a happier note, there is a comic irony with serious underlying implications at the end of *Valley Forgery*. These three women who are rewriting the U.S. Constitution are based on historical figures who didn't even have the right to vote.

PACING: MAINTAINING THE FLOW

In Chapter 39, I stressed the importance of establishing for your own benefit a **concept** that briefly describes the situation and the characters of a play you plan to write. This is just as important in writing comedy. It will map out your course without limiting the direction the play may take as you write.

Most successful comedies plunge into an ongoing situation that gives the audience a sense of what is happening and also establishes the **tone** — whether it will be light humor, biting satire, or something in between.

In a short, light skit it may be enough to expand on the original concept with a series of comic turns such as is often done on *"Saturday Night Live."* But the longer and more sophisticated your comedy, the more you will have to pay attention to sustaining the forward motion of the plot. This means creating a series of **dramatic questions** of the sort I described in Chapter 39 (see page 351).

Although the two comedies you have read are quite different, they both make full use of dramatic questions to keep the plot rolling and hold the interest of the audience. *Coulda, Woulda, Shoulda*, you remember, opens with an amusing report by the mother about what their son had said. The tone grows a bit sharper as they begin to argue about child discipline. That scene is kept alive partly from the argument and partly from all the activity as the father looks for his shoes, his coat, and his car keys. This scene last just three minutes of playing time. Any longer and it might have become repetitious.

Marty's appearance as an adult thrusts the plot forward by posing a major dramatic question: What is going on? We then learn about Marty's hostility toward both parents and his literary revenge through the play he is writing. This scene is concluded with still another jolt: his father has in fact been unfaithful for years.

The final dramatic question is a twist that no theatergoer could have anticipated: Why are the parents leaving through Marty's bedroom door? The answer is that they are his invented characters, vivid yet insubstantial. The climax of the play is not a physical confrontation but a sudden realization on the part of the audience. We now see the parents as part of a **metaphor** about the creative process.

This play is extremely short and a bit bizarre in concept, but it is far more complex than a simple skit. It is constructed with a series of new discoveries that, in addition to making the most of the theme, maintain a forward motion in much the same way as is used in most full-length comedies.

Pacing is even more important in *Valley Forgery* because of its length. The longer a comedy, the greater the risk of having a slow or repetitious section stall the forward motion of the plot. To avoid that, the playwright has made extensive use of dramatic questions. Here is a list of them:

- Fanny appears on stage. Who is she?
- They discover a love letter. Who wrote it?
- They discover a woman who introduces herself as Marie. Who is she really?
- Fanny recognizes Marie as Marie Antoinette, queen of France. What's *she* doing here?
- The letter turns out to be from Marie's lover. Who is he?
- The three women discuss forging a peace treaty. Can they alter history?
- Their ambition grows to include an equal rights proclamation. Again, can they succeed?

The final question is left to history as the women place the revised U.S. Constitution in a bottle to be discovered by future generations. What might have been an aimless skit designed just for laughs has been structured as carefully as a serious drama like *Hello Out There*.

Why bother? We can assume that this play was not written to be a simple bit of entertainment. There are serious issues being suggested, which I will turn to in Chapter 48 on dramatic **themes**.

COMIC RELIEF IN SERIOUS WORK

To this point, we have been treating comedy as if it were totally distinct from serious drama. Actually, the two are frequently blended.

One of the most common weaknesses in student-written plays is a failure to use **comic relief** in plays that are weighed down with unrelieved drama. The result is like bread made without yeast. The play Marty is trying to write in *Coulda, Woulda, Shoulda* appears to be just such a work.

Most of us were introduced to the technique of comic relief when we first read a Shakespearean tragedy or his history plays. Shakespeare had a talent for judging just how much the audience could take and how to relieve the pressure with some kind of wit or satire. His clowns (as in *King Lear*) specialize in wit: jokes, puns, and clever phrasing. They often comment on the more serious aspects of the play in ironic terms. In the history plays such as *Henry IV: Parts I and II* and more briefly in *Henry V*, he employs satire of character in the form of Sir John Falstaff, a loudmouthed liar and reveler who becomes engaging and memorable because of his wit.

Contemporary dramas frequently contain a brief sample of comic relief even when the play is fundamentally serious. You may recall *Hello Out There* as unrelieved tragedy, but Photo-Finish as a character is given a whimsical sense of humor that bubbles unexpectedly until the crisis looms toward the end of the play. The constant repetition of "Hello out there" in the first two scenes usually receives gentle laughter in production. His calling her Katey and later saying that it is a name "I've been saving for you" is not a laugh line, but it provides a light touch in an otherwise dark play. The same is true of his description of San Francisco as different because "More people in

Frisco love someone, that's all." Without these lighter touches, the drama would have run the risk of becoming a **melodrama**.

In longer contemporary plays comic relief often takes a form that Shakespeare found effective: adding a witty minor character who can comment on the action or even kid the protagonist without being centrally involved. In a variation of that, the comic figure is developed as a **foil**, a secondary character who sets off the protagonist by a contrast in attitude. In the plays you have read, the lightweight Marie in *Valley Forgery* comes close to being a foil to the shrewd and competent Martha Washington.

PITFALLS TO AVOID

Comedies are such fun to read and to watch that we forget they require just as much work as serious drama. No checklist is going to guard against all the potential problems, but there are four areas that cause many student plays (and even a few produced plays) to fail. Consider them carefully.

• **Poor pacing.** This heads the list. It is natural enough to let a first draft pour out as the ideas occur, but then it is time to take a close look at how successfully the forward motion of the play is sustained.

If you feel that this may be a problem, review carefully the sequence of dramatic questions in the two comedies you have read. If your play is very short (less than five minutes playing time), a lively initial concept may hold the audience without further work. But if it is any longer, the need for dramatic questions increases.

• **Fragmentation.** Sometimes writing a satire becomes such fun that one forgets what is supposed to hold the play together. Stop and ask yourself just what the target is. You have no problem if the **themes** are closely related as they are in each of the comedies you have read. (More about themes in Chapter 48.) But if you kept veering off onto unrelated topics as you wrote, you may have to do some serious trimming.

A lack of **plot** may also leave the play fragmented. Review the plots of *Coulda, Woulda, Shoulda* and *Valley Forgery* to see how comedy and even farce use plot to provide structure.

• **Imitation.** No form of contemporary writing in any genre is more subject to being imitative than comic drama. As I have pointed out, television writers pump an endless stream of popular comic dramas into the American consciousness 365 days a year. These half-remembered fragments are deeply embedded, so it's all too easy to let them slide into your work inadvertently.

Remind yourself that television is forever imitating last year's sitcoms shamelessly. Professional scriptwriters know they are not working for the ages; like managers of fast-food chains, they are meeting a commercial demand. But when we write for the stage, we hope to create something a little more enduring. With this in mind, be sure that both your characters and your plot are original.

• **Slapstick** occurs when the effort to generate laughs dominates both plot and thematic content. The term comes from vaudeville and refers to the stick designed to make a loud "whack!" when actors hit each other.

There's nothing wrong with slapstick, but as we have seen it is possible to write comic drama with satiric wit and themes of substance.

• **Visually static comedy** is the final pitfall. In Chapter 45, I emphasized how much any drama depends on action. The need is even greater in a comedy.

Standup comics can be highly entertaining, but what they do is not drama. Plays rely on plot, and dramatizing a plot requires action.

The best way to avoid a static script is to read your script while focusing on what your characters are doing. Make sure that their actions keep each scene visually active.

DEVELOPING A COMIC SENSE

If you are interested in writing comedy, you need to engage in two essential activities: read as many comic plays as you have time for, and see as many as you can afford. Never mind what century; you can learn from the few surviving samples of Greek comedies just as you can from the Elizabethan period and from contemporary works.

One advantage to reading plays is that you can finish one in a single setting. The more you read, the better. Granted, Elizabethan English slows you down, but start with a play you have read before and you will see how much more rewarding the second experience is. To find contemporary dramas, turn to Appendix B in the back of this book and follow through by spending time in the nearest library.

Naturally, you will find some works that strike you as unsuccessful. Be careful not to shrug them off. Often you can learn from the weakness of a play if you take the time to analyze exactly what you would have done differently.

Attending actual performances, professional or amateur, will give you an even richer understanding of what goes into successful comedies. Whenever possible, read the script in advance and then attend a performance while the work is still fresh in your mind. Remember that you are not concerned primarily with entertainment; you are in a learning mode. Compare your response to the script with your experience seeing the play in performance. If you remain critically alert, you will get a sense of what aspects of comedy work well on stage.

48 Dramatic Themes

The **theme** in drama is the portion of the work that comments on the human condition. It is similar to a theme in fiction except that in plays it is frequently presented in bolder and more vivid ways — that is, more dramatically.

Be careful not to confuse theme with plot. **Plot** is what happens. A plot outline includes the names of characters and a brief description of the action. Theme, in contrast, deals with abstract ideas, not events. It is a description of the concerns and insights suggested by the play.

The *plot* of Shakespeare's *Hamlet*, for example, might be described in highly condensed form: "A Danish prince named Hamlet has been urged by the ghost of his murdered father to avenge the father's death, but Hamlet delays taking action and eventually is killed along with his mother and his stepfather."

The *theme*, on the other hand, might be described this way: "The agonizing conflict between our instinct for vengeance and our ethical code of civilized restraint can lead an individual to inaction and disaster." Notice that the thematic statement does not name a particular character or identify exactly what happened. It focuses on the idea behind the play, not the events or characters.

A play can have more than one theme, but to be precise each should be described in a complete sentence. Referring to the theme of *Hamlet* simply as "revenge" or "indecision" is too vague to be helpful. Taking the time to describe in complete sentences one or two themes in an early draft of your own work often helps clarify your intent. If you find it impossible to do so, it may mean that what you have is more of a **skit** than a play.

As in fiction, what appears at first to be a single theme is often made up of a number of different but closely related concerns. The longer and more intricate a play, the more thematic suggestions it may contain. But as we will see, even short plays can contain a variety of related concerns. For this reason, the phrase **central concern** is in some ways more accurate than *theme*. I will use the two terms synonymously, as I did in the fiction section.

Themes do not generally provide answers to the questions a play raises. *Hamlet* doesn't instruct you on how to deal with unruly stepfathers, and *Hello Out There* is hardly good advice on how to earn a living at the racetrack or how to handle a lynch mob. Themes explore, they do not preach.

A **thesis** play, in contrast, presents a strong argument — usually social or political — directly. I will return to that approach later in this chapter.

The four plays in this volume are quite different in treatment: two tragedies, a comedy, and a farce. Yet each has a cluster of related themes. The plays are helpful models for your own work because they manage to suggest a lot in a very short space.

As we examine them, however, keep in mind that the complexity of thematic suggestion that you see in a published play is not usually what came to the playwright in the first draft. Themes often develop slowly as the writer moves through successive drafts.

DEVELOPING THEMES IN TRAGEDIES

Hello Out There is remembered by theatergoers mainly for its dramatic impact, but if it had nothing more to offer than that, it would be a melodrama. The terror of an individual facing a lynch mob has been repeated frequently in film and television dramas. What keeps Saroyan's play from becoming a simple thriller is partly the characterization; but to an even greater extent it is due to the complexity of themes. For all the tension and eventual violence, the play provides important insights about the human condition.

Saroyan has woven several themes together. Your selection of which one you believe is *the* theme depends on which aspects of the play you found the most compelling. This is not to say that the play means whatever you want it to mean. Specific themes are clearly and intentionally stressed. Which one seems the most important, however, will vary with each individual.

Here are three thematic statements, each of which is suggested in the play through dialogue and action:

1. The world is full of genuinely lonely people whose efforts to make contact with others are frustrated at every turn.
2. Being poor and young in a small, mean-spirited town is very much like being a prisoner in a jail.
3. If you depend heavily on luck to survive, the time may come when the odds run against you.

This is not an exhaustive list; probably you could add to it. But as a start the list does represent a core, and we can support each one not just with conjecture but with hard evidence from the play.

I put the one about lonely people first because Saroyan places such heavy emphasis on it. His main technique is repetition. "Hello out there" is clearly the cry of a lonely person. It is not only used in the title, but it also appears as the opening and closing lines. In between, it is repeated twenty-five times! Saroyan also repeats the word "lonesome" twelve times, six of them just before and just after Emily appears for the first time.

How does Saroyan get away with so much redundancy? In a factual essay, these repetitions would be considered serious errors in style. But a play is not an essay. A dramatic performance, remember, is a continuous art form in that it flows by the audience nonstop. Repeating a line of dialogue in a fast-moving play is an effective way of highlighting an important phrase and stressing the fact that it has thematic significance. Repetition like this is like a refrain in a poem or a repeated chorus in a ballad. It is a reminder of how drama often borrows from the techniques of poetry.

Photo-Finish is not the only character who is lonely and reaching out for contact with someone else. Emily is equally isolated. She repeats the word "lonesome" five times. She tells Photo-Finish that the men in town laugh at her, and her father takes what little she earns. She has hung around the jail just to be able to talk with this new prisoner. She describes her feelings directly:

> It's so lonely in this town. Nothing here but the lonesome wind all the time, lifting the dirt and blowing out to the prairie.

Even the woman who has accused Photo-Finish of rape is given the benefit of the doubt. She is pictured as a sad and lonely woman alienated from her husband.

As in many tragedies, there is a moment when it seems as if this yearning for companionship will be fulfilled by Photo-Finish and Emily, but then his luck runs out and she ends up being as lonely and isolated as he had been at the beginning of the play.

The second thematic statement shifts the emphasis to the parallel between Emily's life trapped in an isolated prairie town and someone held in jail. Those who have identified with her might see this as a primary theme. Clearly it is *a* theme even if it isn't the dominant one. The fact that the playwright has so carefully placed her in exactly the same position as Photo-Finish was at the beginning of the play and has given her the very same lines is ample evidence that this was one of his concerns.

The third thematic statement, the one suggesting that those who depend fully on luck will eventually fail, is supported partly through the action of the play as well as from the young man's nickname. In explaining it to Emily, he tells her that he has earned that reputation because the horses he bets on always lose by a nose. The fact that he is a gambler stresses the theme of luck, and his bad track record adds an ominous note.

As a writer you have to be careful about significant names like Photo-Finish. If your choice is too obviously significant, you undermine the sense of realism. If Saroyan had named his protagonist *Hy Risk,* it would seem obvious and contrived. But *Photo-Finish* is explained as a nickname and so seems plausible — although hardly subtle.

As you may have noticed, Saroyan also uses names of towns to highlight certain thematic aspects. The town where the protagonist is about to meet his death like a bull in the arena is called "Matador." And the town from which the freewheeling, irresponsible men come is "Wheeling." Saroyan makes sure that the audience does not miss these names by repeating each one twice — a recognition of the fact that in drama significant details have to be repeated if they are to be remembered.

The various themes or concerns in *Hello Out There* are presented fairly directly, and if you work with the script closely they may seem too obvious. But remember that the audience cannot dwell on technique. If they notice symbolic details like the name "Matador," they will do so almost subliminally. It's possible to find names that are thematically suggestive without being so obvious that they seem contrived. Many people have read or seen Arthur Miller's *Death of a Salesman* without noticing that the protagonist, a man who is low in the social order, is appropriately named Willy Loman.

The themes in Tony Padilla's *Reckoning* are not highlighted to the same degree. Because there is so much emphasis on Joe, it might be tempting to settle on a thematic statement that is limited to his problems. We might propose something like this: "Those who focus their entire lives on acquiring power and wealth may end up desperate for love and companionship."

This statement is certainly true of one aspect, but it misses the fact that the play deals with two people. Mary may have fewer lines, but she is far from being a minor character. She is a vital part of the play. Her situation should be reflected in the thematic statement. This might be closer: "Those who focus their entire lives on acquiring power and wealth not only risk a serious emotional crisis, they do terrible damage to those who have been close to them as well."

Or we could make more use of the play's title and Mary's statement about one's past. Consider this: "When thoughtless and cruel actions of the past catch up with you, you may face a final reckoning."

The precise wording of a play's theme will vary according to what aspect one sees as the most significant. Whatever the wording, however, it should reflect the core of what the play is suggesting. When examining a play of your own, make sure that the theme you have in mind will be evident to your audience even though different viewers may phrase it differently.

SLIDING THEMES INTO COMEDY

In spite of serious themes, *Coulda, Woulda, Shoulda* is a comedy because the complications that arise early in the play are more or less resolved at the end. There is no catastrophe (see **plot**) as there is in most tragedies. Also, there are many details that are satiric and just plain funny.

But *Coulda, Woulda, Shoulda* was not written merely to produce laughter. It is a play that, unlike most sitcoms, has themes worth examining and intricacies that call for a second look. In short, it has **resonance**.

Again, there is no one "correct" statement of the theme, but here are four that are clearly supported by evidence from the script:

1. Writing a play may seem like playing God, but a play is still only an illusion of reality.
2. Writing a play about one's parents can become a vehicle for expressing old resentments.
3. Nonwriters often misunderstand the way writers distort and refashion memories to meet the needs of a literary work.
4. Writing a play sometimes requires a writer to invent both a past and a future for his or her characters.

The first statement focuses on what we mean by *creative* writing. There is indeed something godlike in creating people and places on the stage. Indeed, Quakers until fairly recently felt that the writing of both fiction and drama was too presumptuous to be encouraged in school. But as *Coulda, Woulda, Shoulda* clearly demonstrates, the process is far from divine creation. "I'm not God," Marty assures his mother, although she still believes that he can change the future through his writing.

The second — the emotional difficulties encountered when one is writing about parents — is one that will be recognized by anyone who has tried to do so. There is something sadly comic about Marty's harsh dramatic treatment of his parents. He pictures his father getting a divorce, turning to drink, getting diabetes, losing his legs, and then dying. What a revenge! As for his mother, she ends up "bitter, alone, miserable in Miami." That takes care of her!

The theme suggested here is that it is all too easy to take out one's hostilities on individuals — especially parents — when writing drama. We see this through the kind of dark melodrama Marty is writing.

The third thematic suggestion focuses on the fact that many theatergoers (and readers of fiction as well) misunderstand the creative process. They often assume that what they see happen on stage is what actually occurred in the playwright's life. The parents in this play are a comic extension of that misapprehension. They assume that their son is not only reporting the past as it occurred, but that he is also controlling the future. "It's a play, Ma, make-believe," Marty tells her, but she doesn't accept that and neither does her husband.

The fourth thematic statement focuses on a playwright's concern for time. In the act of writing, one must look back to childhood — often to unpleasant episodes — and into the future. What might become of these characters? Where will they end up? It is all invention, but it should be convincing.

In addition to these major concerns, there is a secondary thematic suggestion that adds depth to the characterization. The play touches on the fact that although some, like Cy, believe that their first loyalty is to earning a living even at the expense of being a caring, considerate parent, others, like Marty, are willing to risk financial insecurity to express themselves through art. This theme is not developed at length, but it provides a dramatic tension between father and son in this play.

These are all serious concerns, but rather than being thrust at the reader through repetition of key words and phrases as are the themes in *Hello Out There*, they are slid in almost unnoticed midst the laughter. The moment when Marty enters is a perfect example. The audience, having expected to see the child, is jolted at seeing a man in his forties in kids' pajamas. The first reaction is to laugh. For many, the thematic aspect won't come until later in the play or even after the performance. It takes a moment to realize that we are looking at both the writer as he is (the adult man with his pen and pad) and the child that is within him.

Comedies can have just as many serious themes as tragedies, but they tend to be presented less directly, woven into the laughter.

POLITICAL THEMES IN FARCE

We have already seen how the first two-thirds of *Valley Forgery* is spent satirizing personal conflicts between these three women and the countries they represent. In the last third, however, the playwright turns to political and social issues not raised in the other three plays. Intentionally or not, the audience has been lulled with gentle satire before receiving some serious assertions.

The first has to do with the war with Great Britain. Fanny, wife of the British general, proposes that the three women forge their husbands' names on a peace treaty. The implication is that if women had been politically in control there would have been no War of Independence. This country would have evolved as a nation without bloodshed as did Canada. It's a comic moment, but it's also a challenging and controversial assertion. Thanks to the farcical tone, the playwright has slid it into the play without launching an argument.

This theme is soon expanded to the point where the three women conspire to rewrite the U.S. Constitution with the revised opening, "We the Founding Mothers of these United States." Revolutionary? Sure. But these intensely political themes are encased in a farcical play as ingeniously as their proclamation is slid into the wine bottle. At some point in the future we may be asking, "Was she kidding?"

THE THESIS PLAY: SOCIAL AND POLITICAL ISSUES UP FRONT

As we have seen, **themes** are special concerns. They are intellectual aspects often implied rather than stated directly. A **thesis**, in contrast, is a strong personal conviction that in most cases is stated bluntly. Theses often present an argument based on social, political, or religious beliefs.

Drama has a long history of thesis plays. Medieval miracle plays were often written to intensify religious belief. During the depression years of the 1930s, vehement political protests were made through plays. Corporations like Coca-Cola commissioned and produced plays for employees designed to strengthen their feelings of loyalty, and political activists in the 1960s and 1970s put on plays opposing the Vietnam War.

Today, **black theater** is a dynamic force in socially concerned drama. Some plays develop themes of black identity, sharing the black experience with the whole society. Others present a specific thesis — a demand for political or social change or a call for reform.

The development of black theater is relatively recent. With a few rare exceptions, theater was a white art form until well into the 1960s. Black playwrights like Langston Hughes, Ossie Davis, and Lorraine Hansberry are known to most for one successful play each, but few white theatergoers can name the others they wrote. Langston Hughes alone turned out more than 20 plays; but black playwrights, as well as black directors and actors, have been deprived of audiences and of the training that comes from regular production. This backlog of artistic frustration amplifies a deep sense of social injustice, producing themes of bitter denunciation.

The harshest of these are written consciously and directly to a white audience. Plays like *The Toilet* by Amiri Baraka (LeRoi Jones) are intentionally designed to shock white, middle-class theatergoers.

Other protest plays reach out to white audiences with similar but less strident appeals for social action. In Charles Gordone's *No Place to Be Somebody*, for example, the plot of the play is stopped twice for lengthy monologues delivered like prose poems from the center of the stage. One of these is formally titled "There's More to Being Black Than Meets the Eye." The other is a verse narrative of what it is like for a black to try living like a white suburbanite, suffering the scorn of both urban blacks and white neighbors.

In a different approach, some plays address themselves to black audiences. The seven plays selected originally by the Free Southern Theater group for their pilot program are good examples: *Purlie Victorious* by Ossie Davis and *Do You Want to Be Free?* by Langston Hughes, among others. Another important play of the period is Martin Duberman's *In White America*. August Wilson has also achieved wide critical acclaim.

Women have also had a significant impact on drama since the mid-1990s. As with black drama, plays by women vary from those that explore the woman's experience to those that make strong social or political statements.

One of the more innovative playwrights is Ursule Molinaro, whose works vary from brief, nonrealistic plays in the absurdist tradition to full-length works. Her work and others by women have been collected in an anthology called *The New Women's Theater,* edited by Honor Moore. For a retrospective collection that gives historical perspective, I recommend *Plays By and About Women,* edited by Victoria Sullivan and James Hatch.

If you are committed to a social or political issue and hope to present it in the form of a thesis play, remember that there is a risk that it may end up being read and seen mainly by those who already agree with you. This is commonly called "preaching to the faithful."

One solution is to insert one's convictions into a farce the way Patricia Montley does in *Valley Forgery* and many of her other comedies.

FINDING YOUR OWN THEMES

When you start planning a new play, you will probably focus on the plot and the characters. Plays, like stories, usually begin when the writer imagines two or more characters facing some type of challenge or conflict. But before you start outlining that plot, see if you can describe the theme in a single, complete sentence. If there are a number of themes (as there are in the plays you have read here), use a complete sentence for each.

Take a close look at these thematic sentences. If they do not reflect your genuine feelings, the play will probably not ring true. Conventional concerns, or **truisms**, are often early warning signs that you have settled for **hackneyed** situations and **stock characters**. Plays that have vitality, whether they are serious or comic, usually have themes that are strongly felt by the dramatist.

Don't limit yourself to social or political convictions. Look at *Coulda, Woulda, Shoulda.* There is not even a hint of political concerns there. Instead, it explores the nature of the creative process and our attitudes toward drama specifically. These are important concerns, but they are not major public issues.

Where should you look to find themes that are important to you? For starters, consider your own roots. You probably have dealt with conflicts or tensions and certain successes and defeats associated with them. If your own life has been relatively secure, what about your parents' lives?

Even if you feel that your life has been essentially uneventful, it hasn't been entirely smooth. No one's is. Seek out those situations that made you mad, frustrated, or challenged, and transform them until they are large enough and significant enough for the stage.

Finding good thematic material for a play is similar to the process in fiction. But there are these three differences: First, you need a situation or an incident that dramatizes genuine conflict. Fiction also thrives on conflict, but it can be relatively subtle. Drama calls for a confrontation with real impact. Look at the three plays you have read. Each is driven by a fundamental conflict.

Remember that you need a theme that can be handled on a physical stage in a limited period of time. Never mind dramatizing *War and Peace*. Focus your theme on one manageable incident. If your concern is racial justice, for example, let one specific situation stand for the general problem. If the events you have in mind include several different settings or one that occurred over a span of several years, see if you can transform them into a plot that can be handled with a single set and a single time period. Unity of place and time are far more important in drama than they are in fiction, especially if your play is short.

Finally, consider ways to reiterate your theme. Remember how these thematic repetitions in *Hello Out There* seemed so blatant when examined on the page? They blend together in an actual performance just the way brush strokes in a Rembrandt portrait merge when viewed from a proper distance.

This chapter mentions a number of plays you probably have not read. If you take the time to track some of these down in your library or on the Internet and read them analytically, you will learn firsthand how different playwrights handle a great variety of themes. Background like this will help you find themes that reflect your own experience regardless of whether you are working with tragedy, comedy, or farce.

49 Troubleshooting Guide: Drama

Topics for Quick Review

This alphabetical list of topics is limited to drama. It is similar to the guides at the ends of the nonfiction/fiction and poetry sections. Each guide focuses on frequently recurring problem areas.

This troubleshooting guide can be used in two different ways. First, it can assist you as you revise. If you believe that a play you are working on is lacking in a particular way, see if the problem area is listed here. This list is a quick way to locate where the topic is discussed in the text.

Second, this guide can also be used by instructors in creative writing classes to supplement their written comments on a particular play script. Rather than taking the time to explain some aspect of drama, they can simply ask you to review certain pages.

For a more complete and detailed listing of terms and concepts in all three genres, use the Glossary-Index at the end of this text. It alphabetically lists all the literary terms mentioned in this text, along with brief definitions and page references.

A

SUBMITTING WORK FOR PUBLICATION

> • *Deciding when to submit your work (435)* • *Preparing and sending your manuscript (436)* • *Computers: advice for the uninitiated (438)* • *Submitting stories and poems (439)* • *Submitting book-length works (440)* • *Literary agents (442)* • *Placing a play (442)* • *A balanced approach to publication (443)*

Some novice writers submit material long before there is any chance of publication; an equal number are reluctant to submit even though they are ready. The sad fact is that even writers who have taken creative writing courses often know little about the aspects of marketing.

First, let's clear away a number of myths about publishing. One hears, for example, that nothing is published without "pull," that neither fiction nor drama can succeed without sex and violence, that poetry must be obscure to gain critical approval, that agents are unreliable, that book publishers are only interested in the bottom line, and that you have to live in New York to publish a play. Even more fanciful is the notion that if a piece of writing is really good it will be published without serious effort on the part of the writer.

Publication is no more fair than life itself. There will always be good works that are not accepted and incompetent material that is. But be assured that if talent, practice, and a practical system of submission are combined, one can alter the odds in one's favor.

There are two tests that will help you decide whether you are ready to submit material. First, you should have written in that particular genre for some time. When you read that a story is an author's first publication, it doesn't mean that he or she is a novice. In most cases, he or she has been writing for years. So-called "first novels" have usually been preceded by considerable practice in short stories and quite frequently by one or two unpublished novels as well.

The second test is whether you have been a regular reader. I have repeatedly stressed the need to read carefully and regularly in the genre of your choice. Writers who do not spend twice as much time reading as they do writing are at an enormous disadvantage. They risk settling into a rut, repeating themselves in style and content. Successful writers and poets are almost always perpetual students. Through reading they are not only discovering new approaches for their own work, they are getting to know individual magazines and book publishers.

If you have been writing for some time and have been an active, conscientious reader, you may be ready for the long and sometimes frustrating process of submitting material.

Preparing and Sending Your Manuscript

Your manuscript should be printed or typed on standard white paper — not glossy, not tinted, not super quality. The preferred computer font is 12 point. It prints 10 characters per inch (*cpi*). If in doubt, check with a ruler. Avoid 10 point, which is smaller. Remember that the larger the point number, the larger the type.

For short stories and nonfiction works, everything but your name and address should be double spaced. Poetry can be single spaced. If a long poem has to be continued to a second or more pages, type "cont." at the bottom right corners. There is no need to do this on fiction manuscripts, but be sure to number your pages in the upper right corner.

Resist the strong temptation to use fancy type, italics, gothic, script, or little smiling faces. These suggest that you are an eager amateur. With all manuscript submissions, underline the material that is to be printed in italics. (Don't use italic font unless you have been asked to submit a CD.) Don't vary your type size because editors like to estimate the word count if you haven't provided it.

Don't use a separate title page on any work being submitted to a magazine. Instead, place your name and address on the left side of the first page about two inches down from the top. Type "Fiction," "Nonfiction," or "A Poem" on the right. On prose work, add the word count directly below that. It used to be a common to provide your social security number there, but the proliferation of scam artists has discouraged this. There's always time to supply it if the work is accepted for publication.

The title is centered, usually in capital letters, about one third of the way down the page. Remember that your name and address are single spaced and all fiction is double spaced. Here is how it looks:

```
Woody B. Grate                          Fiction
205 Main St.                            5,280 wds.
Middletown, IL 62666



                        LOOKING FORWARD
```

The story begins two double-spaces below the title. Remember to indent the first line of each new paragraph three or five spaces.

The pages (after the first) should be numbered in Arabic numerals along with your last name in the upper right corner: Smith 2, Smith 3, and so on. It is surprising (and irritating for editors) how many writers forget to do this. Any computer can do it for you without fail.

Don't place a story in a folder or binder and do not staple it. A simple paper clip will do unless you are otherwise instructed. Novels are normally sent loose in a box (although some contests prefer big elastic bands).

Cover letters are not necessary with poetry or fiction unless you have something specific to say. If the editor has added a kind word to a previous rejection slip or has actually written a letter, be sure to remind him or her. In any case, be brief and factual. Defending or even explaining one's work is a sure sign of an author's amateur status.

If all this seems rather restrictive, remember that freshness and original-ity belong in what you write, not the packaging.

Who should you send it to? If you don't know anyone on the staff, merely send the manuscript to the fiction or poetry editor at the address given in the magazine or in a directory. But if you have met or corresponded with an editor or even a junior reader, send it to him or her.

Be sure to read the current issue. Sending a manuscript to a dead or oth-erwise departed editor is not a promising start.

For mailing, the envelope should be large enough so the manuscript does not need to be folded. If you buy 9 1/2″ × 12 1/2″ envelopes for sending, you can include a 9″ × 12″ self-addressed, stamped envelope (SASE) for its return. If this is too complicated, merely fold the second 9″ × 12″ envelope so it can be placed inside the first with the manuscript. In either case, be sure that your address and proper postage are on it. Failure to do so not only ir-ritates the editor, but also increases your chances of never seeing it again.

Poems and stories are sent first class. Novels are wrapped or boxed and sent in padded mailers. "Media mail" (book rate) is slightly cheaper, but it is slow and sometimes unreliable. First or Priority Mail is preferred. United Parcel Service rates vary by zone and may be cheaper in some cases, but some contests forbid its use for unknown reasons.

In the case of novel manuscripts, collections of stories, and collections of poems, title pages are always used. The title is placed about three inches from the top and below that your name, address, phone number, and e-mail address, all centered.

When submitting any work, long or short, to a contest, it is essential to send for guidelines or to download them from the Internet. They will tell you whether the manuscript is to be submitted "blind" or not. "Blind" sub-missions guard against favoritism by requiring two title pages. The first is complete as described previously, and a second one is limited to the title alone. Your name should not appear anywhere after that first title page.

In awaiting a reply from a regular submission, allow about two months for poetry and three for short stories. A novel manuscript and contest submissions usually linger for a half-year or more. The waiting period for all work grows longer every year, and infuriatingly the number of submissions that receive no response at all is increasing. In spite of this, resist the temptation to inquire about work sent until at least twice the expected time has passed.

Keeping records is extremely important. It is impossible to remember what went out when and to which magazine if you don't keep a submissions list or notebook. In addition, it is invaluable to record not only which editors had a kind word or two, but which magazines sent specifically worded rejection slips.

Rejection slips have a hierarchy. The lowest level is merely a printed statement saying that they appreciated receiving the manuscript but were unable to use it. As a half-step up, some magazines have a more encouraging but still anonymous slip saying something like "this was of particular interest to us" or "we hope to see more of your work." Take these seriously. Next on the scale is the penned comment on the bottom of the slip like "good dialogue" or "try us again."

All of these are irritatingly brief, but they are worth recording. Be careful, however, not to inundate a magazine with weekly submissions. An editor who has commented on one poem is not going to be impressed with a flood of inferior work. Treat such individuals as potential allies who deserve only your best efforts.

The highest point on this rejection scale is the *letter*. Even if brief, this is close to acceptance. If they suggest specific revisions that seem appropriate, revise and resubmit promptly. If they don't, send your next really good piece. These are two situations in which you should definitely include a short cover letter.

Computers: Advice for the Uninitiated

If you already work with a computer, skip this section. But if you are among the dwindling few who still type, read this carefully. It could save you hours of work both in the composition of new work and in the preparation of the manuscript.

Should you get a computer? If you spend four or more hours per week writing prose or poetry and can afford the investment, you are foolish not to buy one. In most undergraduate writing classes today, almost no one uses a typewriter.

A computer will not create a good writer any more than a new car will produce a good driver. But it will certainly aid in your process of development. It will reduce the routine task of retyping successive drafts, allowing you to focus on the creative aspect of writing. You can move blocks of fiction or lines of poetry almost instantly, and you can compare one version with an earlier one with the click of two keys. Best of all, what you see is always a neat, clear draft. You can read it at a steady pace, judging the flow accurately.

There are, however, three disadvantages that no salesperson or computer magazine will warn you about. First, your typing accuracy will deteriorate. Corrections are so easy that you become permanently careless. The spell check feature will lull you into false confidence. It is no substitute for proofreading because it is useless when it comes to spotting fifth-grade errors like confusing *its* and *it's* or *to, two,* and *too.*

Second, your computer *will* die with no warning at some point. It will plunge all your unsaved work into oblivion. I stress *will*, not *when*. In addition, even a three-second break in electrical power will delete your most recent and unsaved work. Your only safeguard is to make backup copies on CDs or diskettes and to update them at least daily. Having lived through two disasters, I save my work every hour.

Finally, you will bore all your noncomputing friends. Conversationally, computers are even more addictive than baseball.

What kind to buy? That's a big topic, but here are some basic guidelines:

- Talk with friends about their computer experiences. Often they will tell you more than you really want to hear.
- If your primary need is writing, don't spend extra money for capabilities required by business firms, chemical laboratories, and computer-game freaks. Encyclopedias that talk are valuable only for the blind.
- If it is your first purchase, stick to major brands that offer a full-year guarantee, and make sure it is in writing. Unlike automobiles, computers are just as likely to have major breakdowns in the first year as in the third.
- Beware the lure of the Web! Yes, it has some educational value when used with specific goals in mind. But for some people, surfing becomes a black hole, sucking up all available free time. Serious writers must be on guard against all types of addiction.

Submitting Stories and Poems

Poets should select a group of three or four carefully revised poems to be submitted as a packet. Writers of fiction limit each submission to one story. Once the choice is made, send the work out repeatedly. A single rejection means absolutely nothing. A manuscript is not "dead" until it has been turned down by at least 10 or 15 magazines.

The best approach is to send the work out on the very day it is returned. Otherwise you are apt to lose courage. As a practical matter, just as many manuscripts are accepted after six or eight rejections as after only one. This is largely due to the fact that so many nonliterary factors go into selecting a work for publication. They include the number and kind of manuscripts on hand, the balance of a particular issue, and the personal preferences of the first reader.

The process of submitting poems and stories to magazines one at a time is so tediously slow that you may be tempted to double submit. Sending the same manuscript to different publishers at the same time may seem like a good shortcut.

Generally speaking, however, this is risky. Editors are overworked, and for them to accept a work, allot space for it in the next issue, and then hear at the last moment that the story has been accepted elsewhere is infuriating. The literary world is smaller than you might think, and writers who get a reputation for secretly double submitting may find their work disappearing without being read.

The good news is that a small but increasing number of literary quarterlies have specifically stated in directories "multiple submissions accepted." If you take advantage of this, be sure to notify them at once if your work is accepted by another publication.

Don't submit "blind" — that is, to magazines you haven't read. Directories such as those listed in Appendix B can be helpful, but they won't tell you enough to make a judgment as to whether a particular magazine is your kind of publication. "Blind submissions" not only waste your time and money, but they are also a terrible burden for the editors, who frequently work for little or no salary.

As I have suggested in earlier chapters, the place to start studying publications is your nearest library. Pick out the literary quarterlies. Because there will be a confusing array of magazines, you may want to use the list of literary journals in Appendix B as a guide. Pick out several magazines, read them, and see if any print work like yours. Take notes on these: how many poems and how many stories or nonfiction works they print, the name of the poetry or fiction editor, and the address. Directories (including the one in Appendix B) cannot be perfectly current.

Submitting Book-Length Works

If you are planning to circulate a book-length manuscript, the approach is different. If yours is a mainstream novel — aimed at a broad audience — you should search for a literary agent, a topic I will turn to shortly. But if your manuscript is innovative or experimental or is a collection of stories or poems, you are on your own. Look over your shelves and list the publishers who handle work that is somewhat similar to yours. Then do the same in a bookstore. Next, look up the addresses of the publishers in *The International Directory of Little Magazines & Small Presses*. Major presses are listed in *Literary Market Place* (known as *LMP*). Make a list of those that seem to be printing your kind of work.

At this point, you will save a great deal of time, postage, and frustration if you compose a query letter.

Query letters should be no longer than one page. Simply describe the work in positive (but not glowing) terms and attach this to a bibliography. You can include a couple of sample poems, a story, or a chapter, but this is not necessary unless your list of previous publications is very scant.

Because these query packets are not actual submissions, you can send out many as you want. Although the body of this form letter will be the same, be sure to address each one to a specific individual, not "Dear Editor."

Most of your queries will bring you negative responses, some scribbled on the letter you so carefully composed, and a surprising number won't be answered at all. But don't get discouraged. Every rejection has saved you the expense of mailing the entire manuscript as well as months of waiting. Remind yourself that small presses are only able to publish a few titles a year; eventually your query letters will catch one editor on the very month that he or she is ready to consider new submissions.

Once you have found one or two publishers willing to read your book-length manuscript, submit to each one in turn until you have been rejected by at least 13 or 14 publishers. This will take about three years — time enough for you to complete the next novel or collection.

Circulating novels and book-length collections of short works raises three questions that are asked at every writers' conference:

• First, what about *vanity presses*? A vanity press is a for-profit publishing firm that charges the author for all publication costs. Distribution is largely or entirely up to the author. Many such organizations are perfectly honest, but some make promises about distribution and sales potential that are fanciful. Since all the costs and their profit margin will be paid by you, be sure to read their proposed contract very carefully.

Cooperative presses are quite different. They are generally nonprofit and run by individuals who love books and are willing to live a marginal economic life to work with them. Such presses are used less for novels, but they are a growing outlet for collections of poems and stories. The author still has to pay, but because no one is making a profit, the investment is liable to be less. It is a shared venture.

• Second, is it ethical and honorable to make use of a personal contact at a publishing house? Yes and yes. We're not talking about high-finance profits here; we're trying to find someone who can help bring a literary work to a small reading public. Friendships can help.

Even if your acquaintance is only a volunteer, submit through him or her. Using such a connection won't get a bad manuscript published, but it may get your work to someone sympathetic. And if your work is finally rejected, you are apt to receive a lengthier comment if your reader has at least a slight personal connection with you.

- Third, should we believe those tantalizing reports about agents submitting a novel manuscript to a group of publishers at the same time? Yes, they're called "brokered offerings," and they usually involve astronomical royalty figures. Unfortunately, such events are limited to writers who have already published several highly successful best sellers.

Literary Agents

Literary agents are not for everyone. If you write short fiction, poems, or plays, agents probably can't help you. Placing material in literary quarterlies is an honor well worth struggling for, but agents are business people who live on 15 percent of their clients' royalties. Unlike writers, they can't afford to work for love alone.

However, if you have completed a mainstream novel or if you have a group of 10 or more stories most of which have been published in magazines, an agent could be of great help.

Most reputable agents limit their charges to a flat 15 percent commission on all material sold through them and make no other charges whatever, regardless of how much postage or time they spend. For that, they negotiate a good contract, explain the fine print, and take care of renewals. If they accept you as a client, they expect to handle all your work.

A few agencies are now requiring a "reading fee" for unpublished writers. For this they will decide whether to take you on as a client. Don't confuse this with a "criticism fee," for which you will receive a critical report. Watch out for those who charge "overhead" — additional fees. Although these fees may become standard practice, the basic 15 percent contract is still widely used.

If you are unpublished, it will be difficult but not impossible to find an agent. Some writers try to place their first book and then secure an agent to handle the contract when it is offered by a publisher. Others send query letters to many different agents (addresses in *LMP* and *Novel & Short Story Writer's Manual*) describing the completed manuscript they want to place. It is perfectly acceptable to send out many query letters at the same time. Be sure to ask them to recommend another agent if they cannot take on your work themselves. Occasionally they will recommend a younger, hungrier agent who is looking for new clients.

Placing a Play

Marketing a play requires a somewhat different approach. There are four basic techniques that can be adopted separately or together:

- *Enter play contests.* The best listings are in the *Dramatists Sourcebook* (Theater Communications Group, 355 Lexington Ave., New York, NY 10017). This annual is fully revised each August. In addition, consider *Poets and Writers Magazine* (201 W. 54th St., New York, NY 10019).

- *Submit to theaters.* Again, use the *Dramatists Sourcebook.* Another listing appears in *Writer's Market* (Writer's Digest Books), but it is much shorter. Each theater has special needs, requirements, and deadlines, so read the fine print carefully.

- *Work with a theater group.* Any theater experience will be useful. In addition, you will meet people who will guide you. Even as a volunteer you will benefit.

- *Submit to publishers of plays.* The two major publishers are Baker's Plays and Samuel French (their addresses are in Appendix B). They accept many new plays (mostly mainstream) each year. If you are offered a contract, consider the terms carefully.

There is probably no other branch of the arts more committed to personal contact than drama. "Networking" is the polite word; more bluntly, "pull." If you know a producer, director, actor, or even a stagehand, write to him or her.

This emphasis on contacts is not necessarily a matter of commercial corruption. The fact is that although book publishers come to know potential writers through little magazines (which they read with professional care), producers have no such resource. They may be completely unaware of a playwright whose work has appeared in small theaters in another state. This situation will continue until there are more little magazines willing to specialize in original play scripts and more low-budget stage companies in the smaller cities. Meanwhile, playwrights must struggle with the particularly difficult task of getting known through networking.

A Balanced Approach to Submission

Writers of fiction, poetry, and drama owe it to themselves to adopt a realistic attitude toward publication. It is naive to assume that marketing your work is crass and demeaning. Publishers have no way of discovering you if you make no effort to circulate your work. On the other hand, a mania to publish at all costs can be damaging to the creative process. It often leads to imitative and conventional work and to feelings of hostility toward editors and publishers.

To avoid these most unrewarding extremes, begin with an honest evaluation of your own work. Then follow through with a planned, long-range program of submissions. There are, of course, writers who achieve wide recognition very suddenly; but this is rare and not always a blessing. Ideally, creative work is a way of life, and the effort to publish is an important though not a central portion of that life.

B
RESOURCES FOR WRITERS

General Reference Books

The following six reference books are annuals of particular interest to writers of fiction and poetry. They can be found in most libraries or ordered on the Internet. For more details, simply go to Google and type in the title.

A specialized directory and information book for dramatists is described in the drama section of this appendix.

• *The International Directory of Little Magazines & Small Presses,* Dustbooks. By far the most inclusive listing of little magazines, quarterlies, literary journals, and small presses. It devotes a paragraph to each magazine, describing what it publishes and listing names of editors, payment scale, and the like. Includes helpful cross-listings by subject, genre, and region. It does not list large-circulation magazines or major publishers. No "how-to" articles. Strongly recommended.

• *The Directory of Poetry Publishers,* Dustbooks. An in-depth poetry supplement to the previous publication. Provides information on more than 2,000 book and magazine publishers of poetry.

• *Literary Market Place,* R.R. Information Today Co. *LMP* does not list magazines, but it remains the most authoritative (and most expensive) annual listing of mainstream book publishers, literary agents, writers' conferences, and addresses of those in publishing. Entirely factual. No articles on how to write or market your material. It costs more than $300 (in paperback!), but most libraries have it. Small presses are listed on www.literarymarket-place.com.

- *Novel & Short Story Writer's Market*, Writer's Digest Books. A representative listing of literary magazines (mercifully separated from "romance markets" and the like), as well as literary agents and conferences. Devotes a helpful paragraph on each item. Less complete than *The International Directory* from Dustbooks (listed previously) but far cheaper. Recommended as a valuable source for fiction writers in spite of lightweight "how-to" articles and commercial listings.

[Note: Don't confuse this with *Writer's Market* (not listed here), also from Writer's Digest Books, a directory with a broader scope including poetry magazines and outlets for plays. Not recommended because of its emphasis on consumer magazines (aviation, sports, travel) and trade magazines (pest control, podiatry management).]

- *Poet's Market*, Writer's Digest Books. Less complete than *The Directory of Poetry Publishers* from Dustbooks but useful for poetry writers in spite of many commercial listings.

Informative Magazines

These magazines provide information and advice for writers, poets, and, to a lesser degree, dramatists. They do not generally publish fiction or poetry. Consult library copies or the Internet (through Google) for current subscription rates.

- *The Writer's Chronicle*, AWP, MSN 1E3, George Mason University, Fairfax, VA 22030-4444. Published by Associated Writing Programs; tabloid format; six times a year. Essays, articles, and information on grants, awards, and the annual AWP conference. Circulation 13,000.
- *Poets and Writers Magazine*, 72 Spring St., New York, NY 10012. This nonprofit publication is a must for anyone who writes poetry or fiction. Published six times a year. Articles deal with problems faced by all literary writers: how to find time to write when teaching, how to arrange readings, publishing translations, and dealing with small presses. Also the best source of contest and grant application deadlines, dates of conferences and readings, and winners of awards. Circulation: 58,000. Strongly recommended.
- *Publishers Weekly*, 360 Park Ave. So., New York, NY 10010. Of primary interest to those in the business end of publishing. Covers which books are about to be released, who is doing what in the field, author profiles, and future trends.
- *Writer's Digest* (www.writersdigest.com). Fiction and verse outlets, articles on writing and upcoming conferences. The focus is heavily on mass markets — gothic novels, confessionals, and greeting card verse.

Large-Circulation Magazines: Fiction and Poetry

Sadly, the number of large-circulation magazines publishing even a few quality stories and poems regularly have dwindled steadily since the mid-1980s. Now that *The Atlantic* has abandoned fiction, there are only three left. Beginners without agents are not encouraged to submit, but everyone interested in contemporary fiction and poetry (and social issues) will benefit from subscribing to at least one.

- *Esquire.* Some fiction. Stories tend to be vivid and dramatic. Emphasis is on articles, some trendy and some serious. Published twice a month.
- *Harper's.* A monthly. Some fiction. Mostly articles, features, and reviews.
- *The New Yorker.* For decades, a major source of literary fiction and highly influential journalism. A weekly except for one double issue. Normally one story each week; more in the annual fiction issue. Also thoughtful reviews of fiction and the arts. Of the three, this is by far the most valuable for writers of fiction and poetry.

Little Magazines: Poetry and Fiction

These magazines, also known as *literary journals* and *quarterlies* (although they may appear from one to six times a year), publish fiction, poetry, articles, and reviews in varying proportions. The slow demise of large-circulation literary magazines is compensated for by the proliferation of little magazines.

The following list, a small sampling of the literally hundreds of good literary journals being published today, has been selected especially for writers of fiction and poetry. They should all be available in your public or university library. (If not, urge your librarian to add the missing titles.) Be sure to read at least one or two copies before deciding whether to subscribe or submit. If you plan to submit, use Google to download their specific guidelines. Most do not read in the summer months.

Collectively, these periodicals offer a valuable picture of what is being written today. If you take creative writing seriously, subscribe to at least two. Subscription rates are usually less than one entirely forgettable evening at a restaurant.

- *Agni,* Boston University, 236 Bay State Rd., Boston, MA 02215. (www.agnimagazine.org) Fiction, poetry, and excerpts from novels; two issues a year. Submit September 1 to May 1 only.
- *American Poetry Review,* 1721 Walnut St., Philadelphia, PA 19103. Mostly poetry and articles about poetry; some fiction, art, and interviews. Six times a year in tabloid form; circulation 17,000, far higher than most little magazines.
- *Beloit Fiction Journal,* Box 11, Beloit College, Beloit, WI 53511. Fiction only. Accepts short shorts. One issue a year.

- *Beloit Poetry Journal*, P.O. Box 151, Farmington, ME 04938. All poetry; a quarterly established in 1950. (Not connected with the fiction journal listed previously.)
- *The Black Warrior Review*, P.O. Box 862936, Tuscaloosa, AL 35486-0027. A balance of fiction, poetry, art, interviews, and reviews; two issues a year.
- *Field*, 50 N. Professor St., Oberlin College, Oberlin, OH 44074. Devoted to poetry (including long poems) and essays on poetry. Two issues a year.
- *The Georgia Review*, Gilbert Hall, The University of Georgia, Athens, GA 30602-9009 (www.uga.edu/garev). A balance of fiction, poetry, interviews, criticism, and reviews. Highly competitive.
- *The Gettysburg Review*, Gettysburg College, Gettysburg, PA 17325-1491. Fiction, poetry, articles, and satire.
- *Glimmer Train*, 1211 NW Glisan St., Suite 207, Portland, OR 97209-3054. Fiction and an occasional interview. A quarterly. Send SASE for submission guidelines or download from www.glimmertrain.com.
- *Indiana Review*, Ballantine Hall 465, Indiana University, Bloomington, IN 47405-7103. Fiction (6–8 stories), poetry (30+), and essays. Three issues a year.
- *The Missouri Review*, 1507 Hillcrest Hall, University of Missouri, Columbia, MO 65211. Fiction, poetry, articles, interviews, and reviews. Three issues a year.
- *New England Review*, Middlebury College, Middlebury, VT 05753. Fiction, poetry, articles, longer poems, and parts of novels.
- *The North American Review*, University of Northern Iowa, Cedar Falls, IA 50614-0516. Mostly fiction. No postmodern work. Nonfiction and some poetry. Published five times a year. Founded in 1815, it is the nation's oldest quarterly yet thoroughly contemporary.
- *Paris Review*, 62 White St., New York, NY 10013. Fiction primarily; also poetry and articles; famous for its interviews with authors and poets. Circulation: 10,000. Allow a shocking eight months for a decision.
- *Ploughshares*, Emerson College, 120 Boylston St., Boston, MA 02116-4624. Fiction and poetry primarily; revolving editorship; three issues a year (one devoted to fiction). Submit August 1 to March 31 only.
- *Poetry*, 60 West Walton St., Chicago, IL 60610. Poetry and reviews. Twelve issues a year. Informally known as "Poetry Chicago."
- *Poetry East*, Department of English, 802 W. Belden, DePaul University, Chicago, IL 60614. Mainly poetry; also fiction, articles, interviews, and criticism. Some issues limited to a particular topic.
- *Poetry Miscellany*, English Department, UT, Chattanooga, TN 37403. Mostly poetry with some essays, interviews, and translations. An impressive list of contributors.
- *Prairie Schooner*, 201 Andrews Hall, P.O. Box 880334, Lincoln, NE 68588-0334. Fiction, poetry, articles, and interviews. Founded 1927.
- *Sewanee Review*, University of the South, 735 University Ave., Sewanee, TN 37383-1000. Articles, fiction, and poetry, in about that order. Submit September 1 to May 31 only.
- *StoryQuarterly*, 431 Sheridan Rd., Kenilworth, IL 60043-1220. An all-story annual anthology. Recent issues contained more than 40 titles each. Used in many

creative writing courses. Next reading period October 2006 to March 2007. Details on www.storyquarterly.com.

- *TriQuarterly*, 629 Noyes St., Evanston, IL 60208-4302. Fiction, poetry, and criticism. Tends to be innovative or experimental. Read first; then write for submission guidelines.
- *The Virginia Quarterly Review*, One West Range, Charlottesville, VA 22904-4223 (www.virginia.edu/vqr). Several stories in each issue. Also poetry, articles, and reviews, in about that order. Highly competitive. Established in 1925.

Poetry Anthologies

Anthologies contain the works of many different writers. The following will introduce you to a wide variety of contemporary poets. *Collections*, in contrast, are limited to the work of one author or poet. Use anthologies to browse and explore. Get to know those whose work you enjoy. Then consider collections of those writers you particularly admire. You can order them through your local (preferably independent) bookstore or through the Internet at www.barnesandnoble.com or www.amazon.com. If a title is out of print, check those two for used copies or try www.bookgarden.com.

Collections are often available (with no shipping charges) at poetry readings as well. Owning your own copy will allow you to study the poet's work at leisure.

- *The Best American Poetry*, Simon & Schuster. An annual with different editors each year. An excellent survey of current work.
- *Beyond the Frontier: African American Poetry for the 21st Century*, E. Ethelbert Miller, ed., Black Classic Press. A substantial collection of contemporary poetry by African Americans.
- *Contemporary American Poetry*, A. Poulin Jr., and Michael Waters, eds., Houghton Mifflin. This extensive paperback collection offers a good variety of poets. Women and black poets are well represented. It is frequently adopted for college courses.
- *The Extraordinary Tide: New Poetry by American Women*, Susan Aizenberg, ed., Columbia University Press. Poetry by established and emerging women poets.
- *The Harvard Book of Contemporary American Poetry*, Helen Vendler, ed., Belknap Press. Work by 35 modern American poets with biographical information. Not available in paperback.
- *No More Masks! An Anthology of Twentieth-Century American Women Poets*, Florence Howe, ed., Perennial. 104 poets over a span of 75 years.
- *Poems for the Millennium*, Rothenberg & Joris, University of California Press. Highly experimental and innovative poetry from the modern and postmodern schools. No metered or rhymed poetry.
- *Strong Measures: Contemporary American Poetry in Traditional Forms*, Dacey and Jauss, eds., Longman. A 492-page paperback devoted to poetry in a great variety of metrical forms. No free verse. Includes a useful appendix with helpful definitions

of metrical terms. At the opposite end of the spectrum from *Poems for the Millennium* (listed previously).

- *The Vintage Book of Contemporary American Poetry*, J.D. McClatchy, ed., Vintage. Each poet is represented by several poems, a valuable policy.

Poets Writing About Their Craft

By far the best way to learn from poets is to read their own poetry first. After you have done that, it is often helpful to read what they have written in prose about their craft. Here is a brief sampling:

- *Letters to a Young Poet*, Rainer Maria Rilke, W.W. Norton. A true classic.
- *On the Poet and His Craft: Selected Prose of Theodore Roethke*, Ralph J. Mills, ed., University of Washington Press. Out of print but still available on the Web.
- *Poetry and the Age*, Randall Jarrell, University Press of Florida.
- *The Triggering Town: Lectures and Essays on Poetry and Writing*, Richard Hugo, W.W. Norton.
- *Twentieth Century Pleasures: Prose on Poetry*, Robert Hass, Ecco.

Listening to Poetry

There are two ways to hear poets read their own work. First, attend poetry readings. Most colleges and universities offer poetry readings that are open to the public. So do many libraries. Coffeehouses often have "open mike" evenings in which anyone may read. Poets also read at writers' conferences (listings in *LMP*, ads in *Poets and Writers*).

The second approach is through recordings. Most libraries have good audio- and videocassette collections. Compact discs and tapes may also be ordered through good music stores or the Internet. Recordings allow you to locate and then follow a printed version of each poem. You can also repeat a poem or a stanza as many times as you want.

Fiction Anthologies

There are two widely read annual anthologies of short stories published in magazines during the previous year. Although no two editors will agree on the "best" stories published in any year, these volumes provide a fine overview of good contemporary fiction:

- *The Best American Short Stories*, Houghton Mifflin. This volume has been published annually since 1915. Edited for 36 years by Martha Foley, the collection is still referred to informally as "the Foley collection." The editorship is now changed each year.

- *The O. Henry Prize Stories*, Anchor. Better known as "The O. Henry collection," this is another view of the best fiction published during the previous year. An excellent companion work to *The Best American Short Stories*.

In addition to these two annuals, there are many short story anthologies of recent work designed mainly for college use. They offer a broader yet still contemporary selection:

- *The Graywolf Annual: Short Stories, Graywolf Press*. This (1984) and other anthologies (. . . *by Men* and . . . *by Women*) are out of print, but used copies are available on the Web.
- *Look Who's Talking*, Bruce Weber, ed., Simon & Schuster. An inexpensive collection of American stories from the 1930s to the present, many with a strong sense of voice. Out of print, but used copies still available on the Web at last report.
- *The Norton Anthology of Contemporary Fiction*, R.V. Cassill and Joyce Carol Oates, eds., W.W. Norton. A solid collection of fairly recent fiction.
- *The Scribner Anthology of Contemporary Short Fiction*, Michael Martone and Lex Williford, eds., Touchstone. Fifty American stories since 1970 with emphasis on the 1980s and 1990s.
- *Sudden Fiction*, Robert Shapard and James Thomas, eds., Gibbs Smith. All stories under 2,000 words. Uneven quality, but some excellent.
- *You've Got to Read This*, Ron Hansen, ed., Harper Perennial. A variety of stories, mostly 20th century, each with an introduction.

As with poetry anthologies, these volumes will introduce you to a variety of work. When you find an author you admire, see if he or she has published a collection of stories. In many cases, you can find such volumes in your local library. If you want to order your own copy, do so through your local book store or the Internet.

A number of university presses publish collections of short stories by a single author in paperback. Among these are The Johns Hopkins University Press, the University of Pittsburgh Press, and the University of Tennessee Press, among others. Access these through Google for a list of their short story collections and prices.

Outside the university, small publishers like The Permanent Press (4170 Noyac Rd., Sag Harbor, NY 11963) and Sarabande Books (2234 Dundee Rd., Suite 200, Louisville, KY 40205) publish new fiction and will provide you with catalogues. Write them or use the Web.

Books About the Craft of Fiction

As in the case of poetry, there is no substitute for reading extensively in the genre itself, but as a supplement here are four works on fiction writing that will be useful:

- *The Art of Fiction: Notes on Craft for Young Writers*, John Gardner, Vintage. Sound advice.
- *Becoming a Writer*, Dorothea Brande, Jeremy P. Tarchen. Classic advice regarding attitude and commitment, not specific technique.
- *Writing Down the Bones: Freeing the Writer Within*, Natalie Goldberg, Shambhala (distributed by Random House). Recommended mainly for the hesitant and the inhibited.
- *Writing Fiction: A Guide to Narrative Craft*, Janet Burroway, Longman.

Books for Playwrights

- *Best American Short Plays*, Applause Theater and Cinema Books. This annual has been published for more than half a century. Back issues can be found in many libraries.
- *Dramatists Sourcebook*, Theatre Communications Group, 520 8th Ave., 24th floor, New York, NY 10018-4156. This annual is fully revised each August. Contains a wealth of current information including submission policies of many theaters, contests, and the like. Recommended as an essential source for any playwright.
- *One Act: 11 Short Plays of the Modern Theatre*, Samuel Moon, ed., Grove Press. A good variety of 20th-century short plays including some innovative work, but none more recent than the 1970s.
- *Take 10: New 10-Minute Plays*, Eric Lane and Nina Shengold, eds., Vintage. Thirty-two short plays. Great variety.
- *Twenty-Four Favorite One-Act Plays*, Van H. Catmell and Bennett Cerf, eds., Doubleday. A paperback collection containing a variety of fairly traditional plays from the past 100 years.

Publishers of Play Scripts

This list includes publishers who buy, print, and sell play scripts or simply publish scripts. Most include both one-act and full-length works. Those that deal largely with schools and regional companies prefer traditional work. Check *Dramatists Sourcebook* for Web sites and e-mail addresses.

- *Baker's Plays*, P.O. Box 699222, Quincy, MA 02269. In business since 1845, Baker's Plays offers not only a great many rather light comedies and mysteries for younger audiences, but also a number of serious dramas that have had Broadway success. These scripts are relatively inexpensive to buy and offer a good way to study plays not found in drama anthologies. They accept unsolicited manuscripts (that is, those not sent through agents).
- *Confrontation*, Martin Tucker, ed., English Department, C.W. Post College of Long Island University, Brookville, NY 11548. Publishes one-act plays for "literate audiences."

- *Contemporary Drama Service*, Meriwether Publishing Ltd., 885 Elkton Dr., Colorado Springs, CO 80907. Arthur Zapel, ed. Publishes 50 to 60 plays a year, many short, most are positive. Query with synopsis.
- *The Dramatic Publishing Co.*, P.O. 311 Washington St., Woodstock, IL 60098. Established in 1885, this company prints from 40 to 60 titles a year.
- *Poems & Plays*, Gaylord Brewer, ed., English Department, Middle Tennessee State University, Murfreesboro, TN 37132. Publishes one-act and short plays and poetry. An annual. Accepts scripts October 1 to December 31 only.
- *Prism International*, Creative Writing Program, University of British Columbia, Buch. E462-1866 Main Mall, Vancouver, BC, V6T 1Z1, Canada. Publishes one-act plays and excerpts from full-length plays up to 40 pages.
- *Samuel French, Inc*, 45 W. 25th St., New York, NY 10010. The oldest (1830) drama publishing house in this country, Samuel French has branches in England and Canada and publishes about 50 titles a year.

Although there are relatively few periodicals that publish plays, there are more than 100 theaters that read new scripts for possible production. They are listed in *Dramatists Sourcebook* (best list) and *Writer's Market* (less complete), both previously described.

Remember, finally, that if your interest is in playwriting, it is essential that you see as many productions as you can. Whenever possible, combine your study of the script with seeing the work performed. Each approach will provide insights that the other cannot.

A Final Note

If you are in college, it will seem as if you have no time to do anything but complete your assignments. And if you are out of college, you may find yourself being swept along with the demands of daily life. We all like to believe that we "have no time." But the fact is that the allocation of time is fundamentally a matter of personal choice. Consciously or unconsciously, we set priorities. Serious writers allocate time not only to write, but also to expand their abilities and vision through these resources.

CREDITS

Allen, Dick, "The Narrow Mind" from ODE TO THE COLD WAR: POEMS NEW AND SELECTED. Copyright © 1997 by Dick Allen. Reprinted with the permission of Sarabande Books, Inc. (www.sarabandebooks.org).

Allen, Paula Gunn, "Grandmother" from LIFE IS A FATAL DISEASE. Albuquerque: West End Press, 1997. Reprinted by permission of the author.

Alterman, Glenn, "Coulda, Woulda, Shoulda." Copyright © 1996 by Glenn Alterman. Reprinted with permission of the playwright.

Angelou, Maya, "This Winter Day" from OH PRAY MY WINGS ARE GONNA FIT ME WELL by Maya Angelou. Copyright © 1975 by Maya Angelou. Used by permission of Random House, Inc.

Appleman, Philip, "Coast to Coast" from NEW AND SELECTED POEMS, 1956–1996 (University of Arkansas Press, 1996) and "Desire" from LET THERE BE LIGHT (HarperCollins) by Philip Appleman. Copyright © by Philip Appleman. Reprinted by permission of the author.

Barresi, Dorothy, "Mystery" from ALL OF THE ABOVE by Dorothy Barresi. Copyright © 1991 by Dorothy Barresi. Reprinted by permission of Beacon Press, Boston.

Beilenson, Peter (trans.), "After Spring" (Chora) and "Even with Insects" (Issa) from CHERRY BLOSSOMS, JAPANESE HAIKU, SERIES III, translated by Peter Beilenson. Copyright © 1960 by Peter Pauper Press. Reprinted by permission of the publisher.

Bertram, James, "Is It Well-Lighted, Papa?" is reprinted by kind permission of the author.

Bruchac, Joseph E., III, "Indian Country Again" from NORTH AMERICAN REVIEW, March–April 2003, p. 32. Reprinted by permission of the author.

Buckley, Christopher, "Intransitive" from DUST LIGHT, LEAVES. Vanderbilt University Press, 1986. Copyright © Christopher Buckley, 1986. Reprinted by permission of the author.

Budy, Andrea Hollander, "Burning the Letters" from THE OTHER LIFE, Ashland, Oregon: Story Line Press, 2001. Copyright © 2001 by Andrea Hollander Budy. Reprinted with the permission of the author.

Clifton, Lucille, "What the Mirror Said" by Lucille Clifton. First appeared in AMERICAN RAG. Now appears in **good woman: poems and a memoir 1969–1980,** published by BOA Editions, Ltd. Copyright © 1978 by Lucille Clifton. Reprinted by permission of Curtis Brown, Ltd.

Cummings, E. E., "Buffalo Bill's." Copyright 1923, 1951, © 1991 by the Trustees for the E. E. Cummings Trust. Copyright © 1976 by George James Firmage, from COMPLETE POEMS: 1904–1962 by E. E. Cummings, edited by George J. Firmage. Used by permission of Liveright Publishing Corporation.

Curry, David, "To Those Who Are Programming Computers to Produce Poetry." Copyright © 1979 by David Curry. Originally appeared in CONTENDING TO BE THE DREAM, published by the New Rivers Press, 1979. Reprinted by permission of the author.

Daniels, Jim Ray, "Minding the Store." Originally appeared in THE NORTH AMERICAN RE-VIEW, January/February, 2000. Copyright © 2000 by Jim Ray Daniels. Reprinted by permission of the author.

Daviss, Jackson Jodie, "Gotta Dance" first appeared in the Summer 1992 edition of STORY. Reprinted by permission of the author.

INDEX OF AUTHORS
AND TITLES

GLOSSARY-INDEX

This section lists alphabetically all literary terms used in this text as well as a few others. For handy and concise lists of problem areas in each genre, see the troubleshooting guides that are placed as a final chapter at the end of each section. In addition, an Index of Authors and Titles appears on page 457.

This Glossary-Index can be used both for a review of literary terms and as an index. The definitions are limited to the aspects discussed in the text. Numbers refer to pages. The abbreviation ff. indicates that the discussion continues on the following page(s). Words in capital letters indicate a cross-reference either in the same form or in a closely related form. For example, METERED may be found under Meter, RHYMING under Rhyme.

Abstraction, 155, 236ff. A word or phrase that refers to a concept or state of being. It is at the opposite end of the scale from *concrete* words (see IMAGE), which refers to objects we can see and touch. *Peace* is an abstraction; *dove* is a concrete word.

Absurdist, 369. See THEATER OF THE ABSURD.

Adjective, 237ff. A word that modifies (describes) a noun. Similar to *adverb*, a word that modifies a verb. Often, finding just the right noun eliminates the need for any modification.

Adverb. A word that modifies (describes) a verb. Often, finding just the right verb eliminates the need for any modification.

Allegory, 147, 383. A work of FICTION, VERSE, or DRAMA in which characters, setting, and other details form an all-inclusive SYMBOLIC system. *Pilgrim's Progress* and George Orwell's *Animal Farm* are good examples.

Alliteration, 250, 285. See SOUND DEVICES.

Alliterative verse, 261. A RHYTHMICAL system based on a regular pattern of stressed syllables in each line without regard to the unstressed syllables. It usually employs a CAESURA, a pause, in the middle of most lines. So-called because it traditionally makes regular use of *alliteration* (see SOUND DEVICES). Example: *Beowulf*.

Allusion. A reference, usually brief, to a familiar person or thing, often a detail from literature.

Ambiguity, 307. A THEME or IMAGE in literature that has two or more possible meanings. *Intentional ambiguity* can be used effectively to expand thematic suggestion or increase RESONANCE by suggesting that two or more meanings are equally true or that they combine to suggest a third, broader conclusion. *Unintentional ambiguity* is a weakness usually resulting in confusion of intent or damaging obscurity.

Ambivalence, 24, 26, 229ff. Conflicting or contrasting emotions that are held at the same time. It may be expressed by a writer or a character directly or implied through a character's behavior. Lack of ambivalence sometimes results in SIMPLE WRITING.

Anapestic foot, 264. See METER.

Anaphora, 285ff. Repetition of a word or phrase at the beginning of two or more lines, sentences, or clauses. It is a common RHYTHMICAL technique in FREE VERSE and is also found in some PROSE, especially oratory.

Anecdote, 33, 44, 296. A clever, sometimes humorous account often told in conversation rather than written. Anecdotal FICTION tends to be SIMPLE and short, depending more on a twist of events (PLOT) than on CHARACTERIZATION.

Antagonist, 364. A character who opposes the PROTAGONIST in a NARRATIVE work.

Archaic diction, 233. Words that are primarily associated with an earlier period and are no longer in general use.

Arena stage, 395. See STAGE DESIGNS.

Assonance, 250, 257. See SOUND DEVICES.

Author's intrusion, 62ff, 136. Any passage in FICTION written from the author's point of view (see MEANS OF PERCEPTION).

Automatic writing, 45. See STREAM OF CONSCIOUSNESS.

Ballad, 269, 271. A NARRATIVE POEM often (but not always) written in *ballad meter*: quatrains (four-line STANZAS) of alternating iambic tetrameter and trimeter (see LINE) with a RHYME SCHEME of *abcb*. *Folk ballads* are often intended to be sung and are relatively SIMPLE. *Literary ballads* are, generally, a SOPHISTICATED use of the old form.

Ballad meter, 269, 272. See BALLAD.

Base time, 87. The primary time period in a work of fiction or a play from which a flash-forward departs. See PLOT.

Black theater, 429ff. Plays written by African Americans. Although playwrights like Langston Hughes and Ossie Davis wrote many works in the 1930s and 1940s, the term often refers to those who have come into prominence since the 1960s, such as Amiri Baraka, Paul Carter Harrison, Lonne Elder III, Adrienne Kennedy, and August Wilson.

Black verse. VERSE written by African Americans such as Lucy Smith, David Henderson, Rita Dove, Lucille Clifton (page 203), Maya Angelou (page 207), Gwendolyn Brooks, Nikki Giovanni (page 214), Eitheridge knight (204), and emerging poets like Janeya Histle (page 313).

Blank verse, 268. Unrhyming iambic pentameter (see VERSE and METER).

Breath units, 288. A system of RHYTHM in FREE VERSE allegedly based on the natural rhythm of breathing.

Caesura, 261. A pause or complete break in the RHYTHM of a LINE of VERSE, frequently occurring in the middle. Particularly noticeable in Old English ALLITERATIVE VERSE (also see SOUND DEVICES) such as *Beowulf*. Also found in METERED VERSE.

Catalyst, 393. A seemingly minor event or line of dialogue in fiction or drama that nonetheless reveals some aspect of the THEME or advances the plot in some significant way. Sometimes a minor ("flat") CHARACTER unwittingly serves as catalyst.

Catastrophe, 353. The final disaster (often death) for the protagonist in a TRAGEDY. Also called the *denouement* (see PLOT.)

Central concern, 162ff. See THEME.

Characterization, 36, 132ff., 386ff. The technique of creating a fictional character in FICTION or DRAMA. Basic elements: consistency, complexity, and individuality. SIMPLE characterization stresses consistency at the expense of complexity and often results in a STOCK CHARACTER or a *stereotype,* a form of SIMPLE WRITING. Fully developed characters are called "round," and those that are not are called "flat."

Chronology, 84. See PLOT.

Cinquain, 275. A five-line STANZA.

Cliché, 247ff. A METAPHOR or simile that has become so familiar from overuse that the vehicle (see METAPHOR AND SIMILE) no longer contributes any meaning whatever to the tenor. It provides neither the vividness of a fresh metaphor nor the strength of a single, unmodified word. "Good as gold" and "crystal clear" are clichés. The word is also used informally to describe overused but nonmetaphorical expressions such as "tried and true" and "each and every." See HACKNEYED LANGUAGE.

Climax, 350. The turning point in a tragedy in which the fortunes of the PROTAGONIST begin to decline. See PLOT.

Closure, 141. The reader's sense that a story, novel, or poem has come to a natural or appropriate end. Lack of closure results in the reader's confusion or, in fiction, disbelief.

Comedy, 415ff. DRAMA or FICTION that is light in TONE and ends happily. Comedy usually employs humor, wit, and occasionally SATIRE. *Comic relief* is a comic interlude in an otherwise serious work intended to lighten the TONE. *Farce* is comedy in which CHARACTERIZATION and PLOT are highly exaggerated for comic effect. *Slapstick* is an extremely SIMPLE skit designed only for laughs.

Comic relief, 420ff. COMEDY used briefly in a serious play to lighten the TONE.

Commercial fiction, 39. FICTION that is relatively SIMPLE and conforms to certain CONVENTIONS of PLOT and CHARACTER, usually for the sake of wide popularity. Short story forms include the "pulps" (confessionals and romance periodicals) and the "slicks." Novel types include "gothic," "romance," and "action thrillers" designed primarily for a mass market.

Conceit. A relatively elaborate or fanciful metaphor. The term is used both in a descriptive sense (as in the conceits of John Donne) or in a negative sense implying artificial complexity.

Concept, 331, 347ff. A one-paragraph, factual description of the basic plot and characters in a play or film script. Not to be confused with THEME, which describes in abstract terms the ideas suggested by the work, the portion that comments on the human condition.

Concrete poetry, 284. A trendy and needless synonym for SHAPED POETRY.

Concrete words, 156, 236. See ABSTRACTION.

Conflict, 102ff. See TENSION.

Connotation, 300. An unstated suggestion implied by a word, phrase, passage, or other element in a LITERARY work. The term ranges from the emotional overtones or implications of a word or phrase to the symbolic significance of a character, setting, or sequence of actions. Contrasted with *denotation,* the literal meaning.

Conscious irony, 305ff. See IRONY.

Consonance, 250. See SOUND DEVICES.

Consonant, 250, 251ff. See VOWEL.

Controlling image, 297ff. An IMAGE used repeatedly throughout the length of a poem that determines the nature or form of that work. Also known as a *controlling metaphor* or *controlling simile* of the work. It is often but not always a SYMBOL.

Convention, 124ff. Any pattern or device in LITERATURE that is repeated in different works by a number of different writers. It is a broad term that includes basic aspects like PLOT, DIALOGUE, dramatic SCENES, and the FIXED FORMS of POETRY like the SONNET and BALLAD. It also refers to recurring patterns in subject matter, both subtle and HACKNEYED. The term includes everything that is not unique in a work of LITERATURE.

Cooperative press, 141. See VANITY PRESS.

Cosmic irony, 120. IRONY based on a reversal of expected events, not words. Same as *irony of fate*. See IRONY.

Couplet, 270. A poetic STANZA with two lines. See STANZA.

Creative nonfiction, 1ff. Factual PROSE in which there is some degree of personal involvement on the part of the writer and a heightened concern for language. It includes reminiscence, travel, nonacademic history, and informal biography. It is more personal and imaginative than journalism and formal essays and is distinguished from FICTION primarily because it is faithful to actual events, places, and people. Also called *literary nonfiction*.

Creative writing, 1ff. The writing of poetry (see VERSE), FICTION, DRAMA, and CREATIVE NONFICTION. Although all forms of writing require some degree of creativity, *creative writing* (also called *imaginative writing*) implies a high commitment to artistic merit, drawing on LITERARY techniques including STYLE, as opposed to more utilitarian *factual writing* such as analysis, description, and argumentation. Consequently *creative writing* is used to describe college courses in the writing of POETRY, FICTION, DRAMA, and CREATIVE NONFICTION and excludes courses in expository writing, assertive writing, journalism, and (usually) COMMERCIAL WRITING.

Crisis. Generally used as a synonym for CLIMAX and so avoided in this text to avoid confusion.

Dactylic foot, 265, See METER.

Dead metaphor, 242. A METAPHOR (or simile) that has entered the language as a word without its former visual association. Unlike a CLICHÉ, it has lost its overused metaphorical roots and become an independent word, acceptable in general usage. Examples: a *current* of electricity, a *cliffhanger* election, *slapstick* comedy, a *seedy* hotel, a *deadline*.

Denotation, 192, 300. See CONNOTATION.

Denouement, 353. See its synonym, CATASTROPHE, and also PLOT.

Density, 174ff., 194ff. The degree of compression in a poem, play, or work of fiction. High density means that a lot is implied about character and/or THEME. The PACE may necessarily be slower. Low density reveals less but usually increases the pace.

Deus ex machina, 378. The use of an unexpected and improbable event to solve a problem in drama or fiction. Literally "a god out of a machine," it is an unconvincing turn of events. Occasionally used for comic effect.

Dialect, 125. DIALOGUE that echoes a regional or ethnic speech pattern. Often it is achieved by word choice and word order rather than the obtrusive use of phonetic spelling.

Dialogue, 37, 123ff, 133ff. Any word, phrase, or passage that quotes a character's speech directly. In FICTION it normally appears in quotation marks. *Monologue* describes relatively lengthy and uninterrupted speeches. *Soliloquies* are monologues spoken in plays. *Interior monologues* are directly quoted thoughts in fiction or poetry, usually written without quotation marks. *Indirect dialogue* in FICTION (also called *indirect discourse*) echoes the phrasing of dialogue without actually quoting.

Dialogue tag, 125. The phrase that identifies the speaker in fiction such as "he said" or "she said." In contemporary fiction, the repeated use of "said" is preferred to finding alternatives such as "responded," "complained," "cried out," or "expostulated."

Diction, 172ff. The choice of words in any piece of writing. Diction is a significant factor in determining STYLE.

Dimeter, 266. A LINE of VERSE with two feet. Relatively rare. (See METER).

Distance, 136, 301. The aspect of TONE that suggests how close an author (or narrator) appears to be to his or her fictional material. Highly autobiographical and apparently personal work gives the illusion of having little distance. TRANSFORMING the PROTAGONIST or the SETTING or adding an IRONIC or humorous TONE increases the distance.

Double rhyme, 252. See RHYME.

Drama, 328ff. A NARRATIVE acted by performers on a stage. Drama is generally dramatic (has emotional impact), visual (is intended to be seen), and auditory (is intended to be heard). In contrast to the written script, drama is presented physically on a stage, moves continuously in production, and is designed for spectators, not readers. A *script* is the written text itself, including the dialogue and brief notations on the action.

Dramatic conflict, 364ff. See TENSION.

Dramatic irony, 379, 418. IRONY in which a character unwittingly reveals something that the audience and, in some cases, other characters realize is important.

Dramatic monologue, 307. A poem (see VERSE) that is presented in the first person as if it were speech or thoughts of a particular character or PERSONA. The speaker often unwittingly reveals aspects of his or her character or attitudes.

Dramatic question, 105ff, 351ff. The series of emotional questions in a play or work of FICTION that serve to hold the attention of an audience or readers. They arouse curiosity or generate SUSPENSE. An initial dramatic question is called a *hook*. When dramatic questions are stressed at the expense of THEME or CHARACTERIZATION, the result is usually MELODRAMA.

Elegy, 301. A poem written in a mournful TONE, especially one that is a lament for the dead. The adjective is *elegiac* (pronounced el-i-JI-uk).

Elizabethan sonnet, 273ff. See SONNET.

End-stopped line, 253, 268. See ENJAMBMENT.

Enjambment, 253, 268. LINES in VERSE in which the grammatical construction, the meaning, or both are continued from the end of one line to the next. It is often used to mute the rhythmical effect of METER and/or RHYME. It is contrasted with end-stopped LINES, which are usually terminated with a period or a semicolon.

Epic poem, 188. A long NARRATIVE POEM that deals with mythic, legendary, or historical events and is often FOCUSED on a HERO as in *The Iliad* and *Beowulf*. *Epic* is now used loosely to describe lengthy novels and films dealing with historical events.

Epigram, 271. A brief and pithy saying in VERSE. It may appear as a portion of a longer poem (especially as a couplet) or as a short poem in itself. For example, Goldsmith's warning:

> Ill fares the land, to hastening ills a prey,
>
> Where wealth accumulates, and men decay.

Epiphany, 89. A moment of awakening or discovery on the part of a FICTIONAL character, the reader, or both. Originally suggested by James Joyce, this term is generally limited to FICTION.

Exit line, 348. In drama, a comic or strikingly dramatic line of DIALOGUE used to conclude a SCENE.

Exposition, 38, 136, 176. Factual writing as in an essay or report. In fiction, it refers to passages that give background information or commentary directly, not through action or dialogue. It is one of the five NARRATIVE MODES.

Expressionism, 384. See REALISTIC DRAMA.

Eye rhyme, 252. See RHYME.

Fable, 147. A short tale usually dealing with animals and illustrating a moral. Aesop's fables are among the best known. When the fable form is extended so all the characters form an overall symbolic system, the result is an ALLEGORY such as George Orwell's *Animal Farm*.

Factual writing, 1ff. See CREATIVE WRITING.

Falling action, 353. See PLOT.

Falling meter. See METER.

Fantasy, 148. Highly imaginative fiction based on a self-contained imaginary world.

Farce, 417. COMEDY in which CHARACTERIZATION and PLOT are exaggerated for comic effect. Often SATIRIC as in *Valley Forgery*.

Feminine rhyme, 252. See RHYME.

Fiction, 1ff, 38. A NARRATIVE (characters doing something) in PROSE in which the author's primary commitment is to an artistic creation that may or may not draw on actual events, places, or people. It is differentiated from CREATIVE NONFICTION in which the writer is committed to a true account of events. (See CREATIVE WRITING.) It may be SIMPLE as with most COMMERCIAL WRITING or SOPHISTICATED. Fiction is also loosely subdivided by length (see page 41): *short-short stories* (usually 3–6 typed, double-spaced pages); *short stories* (most often 7–25 pages); *novellas* (about 50–150 pages); *novels* (usually longer than 200 pages).

Figurative language, 156ff. See IMAGE.

Figure of speech 239. See IMAGE.

First-person narration, 64ff. See PERSON.

Fixed forms, 270ff. Traditional VERSE forms that follow certain CONVENTIONS in METER, RHYME scheme, or syllabics (see RHYTHM). Examples: the BALLAD, SONNET, and HAIKU.

Flashback, 86, 177. A SCENE in fiction or drama that occurs previous to the primary PLOT period known as BASE TIME.

Flash-forward, 88. The reverse of a FLASHBACK. See PLOT.

Flat character, 132, 392. See CHARACTERIZATION.

Focus, 51, 65ff. In fiction the character who is the primary concern of the story or novel. He or she is also referred to as the PROTAGONIST. In first-person fiction the focus is usually but not always on the narrator.

Foil, 369. A secondary character in FICTION or DRAMA who sets off a primary character by contrast in attitude, appearance, or other ways. Not to be confused with the ANTAGONIST, who is an opponent of the PROTAGONIST.

Foot, 264ff. See METER.

Forewarning, 105. The technique in FICTION or drama of preparing the reader or audience for a shift in TONE or for some turn of PLOT. Informally referred to as a *pre-echo.*

Formula, 36, 41. Popular CONVENTIONS that characterize SIMPLE FICTION and DRAMA. These conventions are usually patterns of PLOT combined with STOCK CHARACTERS. Sample: The-sincere-brunette who competes with the-scheming-blonde for the attentions of the-rising-young-executive who at first is "blind to the truth" but who finally "sees the light."

Frame story, 88. See PLOT.

Free-form rhythms, 280. An informal synonym for FREE VERSE.

Free verse, 280ff. VERSE that is written without METER, relying instead on RHYTHMICAL patterns derived from TYPOGRAPHY, syntactical elements, repetition of words and phrases, syllabics (see RHYTHM), or so-called breath units (see RHYTHM). Free verse contains no regular RHYME, depending instead on SOUND DEVICES such as assonance, consonance, and alliteration.

Genre, 27, 320. Any of several types of imaginative writing. In common usage, genres refer to FICTION, CREATIVE (LITERARY) NONFICTION, POETRY, and DRAMA. Confusingly, subdivisions of popular fiction such as "mysteries," "Westerns," and "science fiction" are referred to as *genre writing.*

Gimmick, 43, 142. A colloquial term describing an attention-getting twist of PLOT or odd aspect of CHARACTER. Generally used in a pejorative sense to describe a contrived and often unconvincing device.

Hackneyed language, 31, 243. A broad term that includes CLICHÉS as well as non-metaphorical phrases and words that have been weakened by overuse such as "tried and true." Such language is often found in SIMPLE WRITING.

Haiku, 205, 261. Originally a Japanese VERSE form. In English it is usually written as a three-line poem containing five syllables in the first LINE, seven in the second, and five in the third. Traditionally, the haiku draws on some aspect of nature and either states or implies a particular season.

Heptameter, 266. A LINE of VERSE with 7 feet (see METER).

Hero, 364. The central male character in a work of fiction, drama, or narrative poetry. Increasingly, PROTAGONIST is preferred as being gender neutral and free from the implication of greatness.

Heroic couplet, 270ff. Rhyming couplets (see LINE) in iambic pentameter (see METER).

Hexameter, 266. A LINE of VERSE with six feet (see METER).

Hook, 352. See DRAMATIC QUESTION.

Hyperbole, 241, 303. A figure of speech (see IMAGE) employing extreme exaggeration not to be taken literally, often in the form of a simile or METAPHOR. Example: "you a wonder/ you a city / of a woman."

Iambic foot, 264. The most popular type of METER in English: (ta-*TUM*).

Identity, 252. See RHYME.

Image, 189ff, 836ff. An item that can be perceived by one of the five senses. The most common are visual details. Images (especially visual ones) are called *concrete words* as opposed to those that are ABSTRACT. When several closely related images are used near each other, they are called an *image cluster* (page 246). Images may be used literally, as a SYMBOL, or in a figure of speech (see METAPHOR AND SIMILE). A figure of speech (also called *figurative language*) uses an image in a stated or implied comparison. Other figures of speech include similes, PUNS, HYPERBOLE, and SYNECDOCHE.

Image cluster, 246ff. See IMAGE.

Imaginative writing. Same as CREATIVE WRITING.

In medias res. Literally, "in the middle of things." It refers to a work of FICTION that begins abruptly in the middle of an ongoing plot.

Indirect discourse, 126ff. See DIALOGUE.

Interior monologue, 127. See DIALOGUE.

Internal rhyme. See RHYME.

Irony, 179ff., 305ff, 418ff. A reversal of meaning or events. There are three types: (1) *Verbal* or *conscious* irony, in which the author or a character makes a statement that he or she knows is the opposite of the intended meaning (like saying, "Great day for a sail" during a hurricane). It is similar to sarcasm. (2) *Dramatic irony* in which a character makes a statement that is unknowingly the opposite from what readers or the audience knows will occur. (3) *Cosmic irony* or *irony of fate* in which an event is surprisingly or dramatically different from reasonable expectations (like the firefighter who dies from smoking in bed).

Italian sonnet, 273. See SONNET.

Journal, 146. An informal notebook for recording personal reactions to works recently read, ideas for future work, fragments, and reflections on the pleasures and frustrations of life.

Legitimate theater, 328. Plays performed by actors on a stage as contrasted with cinema, television DRAMA, and the like.

Level of usage, 173. The degree of formality or informality in PROSE or VERSE. It ranges from formal word choice and grammatical construction to colloquial phrasing and slang.

Line, 188ff, 265ff. A unit of VERSE that when printed usually appears without being broken, the length of which is determined by the poet alone. The inclusion of the line as part of the art form rather than merely a printer's concern is one of the fundamental distinctions between VERSE and PROSE. In METERED VERSE, lines usually contain the same number of *feet* (see METER); in *sprung rhythm* and *alliterative* VERSE, lines are linked by having the same number of stressed syllables; and in FREE VERSE, the length of lines is more of a visual concern (see TYPOGRAPHY). The following terms describe most line lengths in metered verse: (1) monometer (one foot), (2) dimeter (two feet), (3) trimeter (three feet), (4) tetrameter (four feet), (5) pentameter (five feet), (6) hexameter (six feet), (7) heptameter (seven feet), and (8) octometer (eight feet). Trimeter, tetrameter, and pentameter are the most frequently used.

Literary nonfiction, 1ff.

Literature, 1ff. PROSE or VERSE in which style, suggestion, and implication are developed with some degree of conscious care. Literary writing is differentiated from purely factual and utilitarian writing such as reports, news items, and scientific articles, as well as from personal writing such as diaries, letters, and journals. In this text, the term SOPHISTICATED WRITING is often used as a synonym for *literary writing* to avoid implying a value judgment.

Local color, 111. See REGIONALISM.

Lyric, 250. A relatively short poem expressing a strongly felt personal emotion. Thus, poems of love, deep feeling, observation, and contemplation are *lyrics* in contrast with BALLADS and other types of NARRATIVE POETRY. *Lyrical* is often used loosely to describe poetry that sounds musical because of its SOUND DEVICES and RHYTHM. *Lyric* is derived from a Greek term for VERSE to be accompanied by a lyre.

Means of perception, 60ff. The character through whose eyes a piece of FICTION appears to be presented. This character is also the one whose thoughts are revealed directly. The term is synonymous with *point of view* and *viewpoint*. It is generally limited to a single character in short fiction.

Melodrama, 33, 42, 43, 367. SIMPLE WRITING (usually DRAMA or FICTION) that is dominated by SUSPENSE and exaggerated forms of dramatic TENSION. It usually makes use of STOCK CHARACTERS. SOPHISTICATED LITERATURE also uses conflict but keeps it from dominating the THEME or CHARACTERIZATION.

Metafiction, 149. FICTION in which the theme deals with the act of writing itself. It is generally less concerned with realism and CHARACTERIZATION than with commentary on the genre. John Barth's story "Lost in the Funhouse" is a classic and entertaining example.

Metamorphosis, 48. Same as TRANSFORMATION.

Metaphor and Simile, 156ff, 240ff. A *simile* is a figure of speech (see IMAGE) in which one item (usually an abstraction) is compared with another (usually a concrete noun) that is different in all but a few significant respects. The comparison (a type of *analogy*) uses *like* or *as*. Thus, "She fought like a lion" suggests courage but not the use of claws and teeth. The item being described (the woman) is called the *tenor* (see VEHICLE AND TENOR) and the item introduced merely for comparison (the lion) is the *vehicle*. A *metaphor* implies rather than states a similar comparison without using *like* or *as* — "She was a lion when fighting for civil rights." A *controlling image* (or controlling simile) is a figure of speech that dominates a poem. It may or may not also be a SYMBOL.

Meter, 263ff. See table on page 265. A system of STRESSED and unstressed syllables that creates RHYTHM in certain types of verse. The CONVENTIONALIZED units of stressed and unstressed syllables are known as *feet*. Metered verse normally contains the same number of feet in each LINE and basically the same type of foot throughout the poem. The effect is usually muted by occasionally substituting other types of feet. If the pattern ends on a stressed syllable, it is called *rising meter*; if the pattern ends on an unstressed syllable, it is called *falling meter*.

Mixed metaphor, 240. A METAPHOR that is internally confusing or illogical because the two vehicles (see METAPHOR AND SIMILE) are contradictory. Example: "The bitter taste of rejection rang in his ears."

Modes, 37ff, 175. See NARRATIVE MODES.

Monologue, 307. See DIALOGUE.

Monometer. A LINE of VERSE with one foot. Rare (see LINE).

Narrative, 1, 213, 296ff. Any work that tells a story; that is, characters doing something. It can take the form of FICTION, CREATIVE NONFICTION, DRAMA, and NARRATIVE POETRY.

Narrative modes, 37ff, 175. The five methods by which FICTION can be presented: DIALOGUE, thoughts, action, description, and EXPOSITION. Most fiction is comprised of all five in varying proportions. Unusual emphasis on any one affects the STYLE.

Narrative poetry, 213, 296. VERSE that tells a story. It may take the form of the BALLAD, the EPIC, or a tale in verse such as Hecht's "Lizards and Snakes" (page 212).

Narrator, 60, 296. A character in fiction or a NARRATIVE POEM who appears to be telling the story. He or she may be clearly identified as in first-person writing (see MEANS OF PERCEPTION) or implied as in most third-person writing. A narrator is often but not always the PROTAGONIST.

Neutral style. See STYLE.

New formalism, 278. A poetic movement (begun in the 1980s and 1990s) reflecting a renewed interest in metrical forms and, often, innovative use of such forms. Also called *neoformalism.*

Nonrealistic drama, 378. See REALISTIC DRAMA.

Nonrecurrent stanzas, 281ff. STANZAS of unequal length often used in FREE VERSE. They serve some of the same functions as paragraphs in PROSE.

Novel, 39. A work of FICTION usually more than 200 double-spaced pages (see FICTION).

Novella, 39. A work of FICTION usually around 50 to 150 double-spaced pages (see FICTION).

Occasion. In poetry the event or situation that appears to have initiated the narrator's concern. Not all poems have an occasion stated or implied, but some make it clear as in Robert Frost's "Design" (page 200) and Richard Wilbur's "The Pardon" (page 213).

Occasional verse, 195. VERSE written for a particular occasion such as an anniversary, birthday, death, or dedication. Many are literarily simple and comic, but others are serious.

Octave, 273. An eight-lined STANZA in METERED VERSE. Also, the first eight lines of a SONNET.

Octometer, 266. A LINE of VERSE with 8 feet (see METER).

Ode. A LYRIC poem, usually metered and serious, commemorating or honoring a person, place, or event.

Off rhyme, 255. See RHYME.

Omniscient point of view, 63. The MEANS OF PERCEPTION in which the author enters the minds of all major characters. *Limited omniscience* restricts the means of perception to a limited number of characters. Most short FICTION and many novels limit the means of perception to a single character.

Onomatopoeia, 251. A similarity between the sound of a word and the object or action it describes. See SOUND DEVICES.

Orientation. The sense in FICTION, DRAMA, or NARRATIVE POETRY of being somewhere specific. A more general term than SETTING, it includes awareness of geography (real or invented), historical period, season, and time.

Overtone, 172. See CONNOTATION.

Overwriting, 174. FICTION or VERSE that is overblown, excessive in phrasing, or overly modified. It strikes the reader as artificial or affected. Informally called *purple prose.* It is the opposite of a sparse or economical STYLE.

Oxymoron. An apparent contradiction presented either as a figure of speech (see IMAGE), as in Roethke's "I wake to sleep," or as a simple phrase, such as "a silent scream" or "cruel kindness."

Pace, 90ff., 129, 353ff., 419. The reader's sense that a story or play either moves rapidly or drags. This is determined by the RATE OF REVELATION and the STYLE.

Pantoum, 275ff. A VERSE form in quatrains. The type of meter and length is up to the poet. The traditional rhyme is abab, bcbc, cdcd. The stanzas interlock through repetition: lines 2 and 4 of each stanza become lines 1 and 3 of the next. The last stanza of the poem can take one of two patterns: a couplet comprised of lines 1 and 3 in reverse order or a concluding quatrain using lines 1 and 3 of the first stanza as lines 4 and 2, respectively. Example: "Always the One Who Loves His Father Most" by Clement Long (page 205).

Parable, 289. A short, usually ALLEGORICAL story used to illustrate some moral lesson or religious principle.

Paradox, 305. A statement that on one level is logically absurd, yet on another level implies a reasonable assertion. Example from Heller's *Catch-22:* "The Texan turned out to be good-natured, generous, and likable. In three days no one could stand him."

Parody, Paraphrase, 126ff. A satiric (see SATIRE) imitation of a work of FICTION, VERSE, or DRAMA, or of a writer's style designed to ridicule the original.

Passive voice,. Grammatical construction in which the subject is hidden: "Mistakes were made" as opposed to the active construction, "I made a mistake." Use of passive construction tends to weaken one's STYLE.

Pathos. Work that evokes feelings of sympathy or pity. Unsuccessful, excessive, or insincere pathos produces *bathos*.

Pentameter, 265. A LINE of VERSE with five feet. The most commonly used line length in English. (See METER.)

Person, 64ff. Any of several methods of presenting fiction: (1) First person ("I") gives the illusion of a story being told directly by a NARRATOR either in an inconspicuous STYLE or "as-if-told." (2) Third person ("he" or "she") is equally popular. (3) The "you" form implies that the reader is being addressed directly. Rarely used. (4) The "they" form is used least of all. *Person* is *how* a story is presented; the MEANS OF PERCEPTION is *who* appears to present it.

Performance poet, 287.

Persona, 306ff. The narrator, implied or identified, in a work of fiction or a poem. It distinguishes the fictional character from the author or the poet.

Personification. Attributing human characteristics to inanimate objects, as in "the enraged sea."

Petrarchan sonnet, 273. See SONNET.

Plot, 86ff. The sequence of events in FICTION, DRAMA, or NARRATIVE POETRY. It may be chronological, or it may be nonchronological in any of four ways: By *flashback* (inserting an earlier scene), by *multiple flashbacks*, by a *flash-forward* (rare), or by using a *frame* (beginning and ending with the same scene). *Base time* is the primary plot time period. A *subplot* is a secondary plot that echoes or amplifies the main plot or provides *comic relief* (see COMEDY). In traditional tragedies the increasing complications are called *rising action*, the turning point is the *climax*, followed by *falling action*, which in turn leads to the final *catastrophe* (also called the *denouement)*, often the death or symbolic death of the PROTAGONIST.

Poetic, 250, 289. In addition to being an adjective for *poetry* (see VERSE), this term is used to describe what is informally called *poetic prose:* fiction or drama that makes special use of RHYTHM, SOUND DEVICES, figurative language (see IMAGE), SYMBOL, and compression of meaning and implication.

Poetry, 187ff. See VERSE.

Point of view, 60ff. See MEANS OF PERCEPTION.

Postmodern fiction, 149: A fairly recent stylistic approach that emphasizes ingenuity of language itself and often focuses on writing as writing. It makes little or, in some cases, no use of plot and traditional characterization. Reader interest is often (but not always) sustained with wit and verbal inventiveness.

Premise fiction, 147. FICTION based on a single identifiable distortion of the world as we know it.

Private symbols, 245. See SYMBOL.

Proscenium arch, 395. See STAGE DESIGNS.

Prose, 187. Writing in which the length of the LINES is not determined by the writer and so is not part of the art form. As a result, sentences, not lines, are the basic organizing unit. Prose also tends to be less concerned with RHYTHM, SOUND DEVICES, and compression of statement than is VERSE.

Prose poetry, 289. A hybrid literary form in which the writer maintains control over line length, as in VERSE, but generally ignores other poetic devices such as a regular RHYTHMICAL SYSTEM, SOUND DEVICES, and figurative language (see IMAGE).

Prose rhythm, 259. RHYTHM in PROSE writing achieved through SYNTAX (sentence length and type), paragraph length, and most often by ANAPHORA, repetition of words or phrases particularly at the beginning of a series of sentences.

Prosody. The construction of a poem (see VERSE) including SCANSION (metrical scheme), stanzaic patterns (see STANZA), DICTION, phrasing, and the like. Don't confuse this with PROSE.

Protagonist, 364ff. The main character in a work of FICTION, a play, or a NARRATIVE POEM. This character is often opposed by an *antagonist*. The term is broader than *hero*, which is gender specific and suggests greatness. Protagonists who are base or ignoble are sometimes referred to as *antiheroes*.

Public symbols, 245. See SYMBOL.

Pun, 241. The humorous use of a word with two different meanings or two words spelled or pronounced the same with different meanings. Enjoyed by many from Shakespeare to Dylan Thomas but scorned by others.

Purple prose, 174. A colloquial synonym for OVERWRITING.

Pyrrhic foot, 265. See METER.

Quatrain, 271. A poetic STANZA with four lines.

Rate of revelation, 90. In FICTION or DRAMA, the rate at which new information or insights regarding CHARACTER, THEME, or PLOT are given to the reader or audience. It is one of the primary factors that determine PACE of such work.

Realism, 32, 378. FICTION and DRAMA in which characters, events, and settings resemble those in everyday life. In fiction this is contrasted with *fantasy, science fiction*, ALLEGORICAL fiction, and most METAFICTION and POSTMODERN work. A more precise term, *verisimilitude*, describes the *illusion* of reality. Thus, Kafka's dreamlike scenes "seem real" (have verisimilitude) without being conventionally realistic.

Realistic drama, 378. DRAMA in which, like realistic fiction, characters, events, and settings resemble those in everyday life. Costume, set, and PLOT conform to what we see in daily life. This is opposed to *nonrealistic drama*, which creates its own world in somewhat the same manner as a dream. *Expressionism* is sometimes used as a synonym for nonrealistic drama, but more strictly it refers to a dramatic school culminating in the 1920s and 1930s with the works of O'Neill, Rice, and others.

Refrain, 275. A phrase, LINE, or STANZA that is repeated periodically in a poem.

Regionalism, 111. FICTION and VERSE that draw on the customs, traditions, attitudes, and occasionally the DICTION of a particular geographic region. It is a more contemporary term than *local color* writing, a term that is tainted by certain 19th-century authors who adopted the patronizing TONE of an outsider.

Resonance, 81, 299. The aspect of TONE in SOPHISTICATED WRITING created by the use of suggestive details such as SYMBOLS, figurative language (see IMAGE), and other layers of meaning. It is a complexity of suggestion not found in SIMPLE WRITING. Resonance adds to the DENSITY of a work.

Rhyme, 267ff. Two or more words in poetry (see VERSE) in which the final syllables are identical or similar. In *true rhyme* the matching sounds are identical from the accented VOWEL to the end of the word, and the sound preceding the accented vowels in each word must be unlike. (If the sounds preceding the accented vowel in each word are the same, the pair is known as an *identity*, not a rhyme.) In *slant rhyme* and *off-rhyme* the matching vowel sounds are similar but not precisely the same. *Double rhyme*, also called *feminine rhyme*, is a two-syllable rhyme as in "running" and "sunning." In an *eye rhyme* (also called *sight rhyme*), the concluding syllables look alike but sound different (like *have* and *grave*). *Internal rhyme* links two or more rhyming words within the same line.

Rhyme royal, 273. A seven-line STANZA in iambic pentameter (see LINE) with a RHYME SCHEME of ababbcc.

Rhyme scheme, 270. A recurring pattern of RHYMED endings repeated regularly in each STANZA of METERED VERSE.

Rhythm, 291. A systematic variation in the flow of sound. Traditional rhythms include established patterns such as METER, ALLITERATIVE VERSE, and syllabic patterns (see SYLLABIC VERSE). FREE VERSE creates unique rhythmical systems for each poem by means of LINE length, TYPOGRAPHY, ANAPHORA, and the like. PROSE rhythms are achieved by repeating key words or phrases (ANAPHORA) and SYNTACTICAL patterns.

Riddle poem, 298. A poem that poses a riddle. It may provide the answer in the last line or leave that for the reader to guess.

Rising action, 263. See PLOT.

Rising meter. See METER.

Rondeau 275.

Round character, 132, 392. A fully developed character in fiction or drama. Opposite of a *flat character* usually designed to serve some minor function. (See CHARACTERIZATION.)

Run-on line, 253. Same as ENJAMBMENT.

SASE, 438. "Self-addressed stamped envelope," which should accompany any submission you want to be returned.

Satire, 180ff., 304ff., 416ff. A form of wit in which an exaggerated and comic view of characters, places, or institutions is used for the purpose of criticism or ridicule. At least some measure of exaggeration (if only through a biased selection of details) is necessary for satire to be effective.

Scansion, 266. The analysis of METER in metered VERSE, identifying the various feet (see METER) and the type of LINE used.

Scene, 85ff., 348ff. In DRAMA, (1) a formal subdivision of an *act* marked in the script and indicated to the audience by lowering the curtain or dimming the lights (designated in this text as *primary scenes*), or (2) a more subtle subdivision of the PLOT suggested by the exit or the entrance of a character (*secondary scenes*). In FICTION, the scene is a less precise unit of action marked either by a shift in the number of characters or a shift in time or place.

Script, 328. The written text of a play (see DRAMA) including the dialogue and brief notations on the action. The script is not to be confused with a performance.

Sentimentality, 233, 308. A form of SIMPLE WRITING that is dominated by a blunt appeal to the emotions of pity and love. It does so at the expense of subtlety and literary sophistication. (See SOPHISTICATED WRITING.)

Septet, 273. A seven-line STANZA in METERED VERSE. It is the stanza form used in RHYME ROYAL.

Sestet, 273. A six-line STANZA in METERED VERSE. Also the last six lines of the SONNET.

Set, 394ff. In DRAMA, everything the audience sees except the actors themselves. Three basic types: (1) realistic (the illusion of an actual place or places as in *The Collection* shown on pages 396 and 397, (2) symbolic (adopting dreamlike distortions), and (3) the bare stage.

Setting, 36, 107. In FICTION and DRAMA, the geographical area in which a PLOT takes place. More generally, the time of day, the season, and the social environment as well. In DRAMA, the setting is usually specified briefly at the beginning of the script.

Shaped poetry, 284. VERSE in which TYPOGRAPHY is employed in an extreme fashion to make the lines, words, and word fragments suggest a shape or picture that becomes of greater importance than RHYTHM or sound. Occasionally called *concrete poetry*.

Short-short story, 38. A work of FICTION usually around three to six double-spaced pages.

Short story, 38. A work of FICTION usually around seven to 25 double-spaced pages. See FICTION.

Simile, 156ff. See METAPHOR AND SIMILE.

Simple writing, 34ff., 192ff. Writing in which the THEME is blatant or a TRUISM, the STYLE is limited to a single effect and/or the TONE is limited to a single emotion. It includes the adventure and horror story (MELODRAMA), many love stories, most greeting card verse (SENTIMENTALITY), most patriotic VERSE and politically partisan FICTION and DRAMA (propaganda), and that which is single-mindedly sexual or sadistic (pornography). It also includes work that is so personal or so obscure that it remains unintelligible even to conscientious readers. Antonyms for *simple* are SOPHISTICATED and LITERARY.

Slant rhyme, 255. See RHYME.

Slapstick, 393, 422. An extremely SIMPLE play or skit designed only for laughs. See COMEDY.

Sonnet, 273. A METERED and RHYMED poem of 14 LINES usually in iambic pentameter (see LINE). The Italian or Petrarchan sonnet is often rhymed *abba, abba; cde, cde*. The first eight lines are known as the OCTAVE and the last six as the SESTET. The Elizabethan sonnet (see Shakespeare's "Sonnet 29," page 203) is often thought of as three quatrains and a final rhyming couplet: *abab, cdcd, efef gg*.

Sophisticated writing, 34ff, 192ff. Writing in which the THEME is fresh and insightful, the STYLE makes rich use of the techniques available, and the TONE provides some measure of RESONANCE. An objective, value-free synonym for LITERARY WRITING, it is the opposite of SIMPLE WRITING. Not to be confused with the popular use of *sophisticated* as worldly.

Sound devices, 249ff. The technique of linking two or more words by *alliteration* (similar initial sounds), *assonance* (similar vowel sounds), *consonance* (similar consonantal sounds), *onomatopoeia* (similarity between the sound of the word and the object or action it describes), or RHYME. In addition, *sound clusters* link groups of words with related vowel sounds that are too disparate to be called true samples of assonance.

Spondaic foot, 265. See METER.

Stage business, 402. Minor action or facial expressions on the part of an actor, often not included in the script.

Stage designs, 395. (1) The *conventional stage* has a raised playing area that is located behind a *proscenium arch* from which a curtain is lowered between acts and SCENES. It resembles a picture frame. (2) A *thrust stage* has no arch and no single picture effect because it extends into the audience and is open on three sides. The curtain is replaced by a dimming of the lights. (3) *Theater in the round* or *arena theater* extends this concept further by having the audience encircle the playing area as it does in a circus tent.

Stanza, 270. In METERED poetry a regularly recurring group of lines usually separated by spaces and unified by LINE length, metrical system, and often by a RHYME scheme. Common forms include the *couplet* (two lines), *tercet* or *triplet* (three lines), quatrain (four lines), *cinquain* (five lines), SESTET (six lines), *septet* (seven lines), and OCTAVE (eight lines). The term is occasionally applied to irregular units in FREE VERSE, which are used more like paragraphs in PROSE.

Stereotype, 164, 366. See STOCK CHARACTER.

Stock character, 37, 430. Characters in FICTION or DRAMA that are SIMPLE and also conform to one of a number of types that have appeared over such a long period and in so many different works that they are familiar to readers and audiences. Their DIALOGUE is often HACKNEYED. Minor characters are often stock types, but when major characters appear so, the work as a whole may be SIMPLE as opposed to SOPHISTICATED. Also known as *stereotypes* or *"flat"* as opposed to *"round"* characters.

Stock situation. A situation in FICTION or DRAMA that is too familiar to have freshness or impact.

Story, 38. See FICTION.

Stream of consciousness, 45, 148. FICTION appearing to resemble a character's thoughts quoted directly without exposition. Although wandering and disjointed, such passages are designed to reveal character. This is in sharp contrast with *automatic writing,* in which the writer's goal is not CHARACTERIZATION (or even FICTION), but random self-expression.

Stress, 260, 263. In metered VERSE, the relative force or emphasis placed on a particular syllable. In "awake," for example, the second syllable is stressed. (See METER.)

Style, 148, 170ff. The manner in which a work is written. It is determined by a writer's choices, both conscious and unconscious, regarding DICTION (the type of words used), SYNTAX (the type of sentences), NARRATIVE MODE (relative importance of DIALOGUE, thoughts, action, description, and EXPO-SITION), and PACE (the reader's sense of forward movement). It is closely connected with TONE. *Neutral* or *inconspicuous* style is that in which no one technique is noticeable.

Subplot, 354. See PLOT.

Substitution, 267. The technique in METERED VERSE of occasionally replacing a foot (see METER) that has become the standard in a particular poem with some other type of foot. Example: Using a trochee for emphasis in a poem that is generally iambic.

Suspense, 90. A heightened form of curiosity that creates excitement and a sense of drama. In moderation, it provides effective TENSION. When it dominates the work, the result is MELODRAMA.

Syllabic verse, 261ff. A system of RHYTHM in poetry based on the number of syllables in each line. In HAIKU the three lines have five, seven, and five syllables, respectively. In syllabic poems of more than one STANZA the pattern established in the first stanza is repeated in all the rest.

Symbol, 244ff, 158, 398. Any detail such as an object, action, or state in a work of literature that has a range of meaning beyond and usually larger than itself. *Public symbols* are those that are recognized by the public at large — the flag, the cross, Uncle Sam, Father Time. *Private* (or *unique*) symbols are those devised by individual writers for a particular work. Usually the *vehicle* (see VEHICLE AND TENOR) is introduced directly as a detail in the story or poem and the *tenor* is implied indirectly. This is in contrast with FIGURES OF SPEECH, such as similes and METAPHORS, in which the vehicle is introduced merely to serve as a comparison and has no other function.

Synecdoche, 242. A FIGURE OF SPEECH in which a part is used for the whole. "Many hands," for example, suggests many people; "bread for the poor" suggests food generally.

Syntactical rhythm, 285. See RHYTHM.

Syntax, 173. Sentence structure; the arrangement of words in the sentence. It is sometimes used to create RHYTHM in FREE VERSE and less often in PROSE. (See PROSE RHYTHM.)

Tag, 125. See DIALOGUE TAG.

Tenor, 157. See VEHICLE AND TENOR.

Tense, 177. The various forms a verb can take. The past tense ("She ran to the window") is traditional in fiction, but the present tense ("She runs to the window") is increasingly popular. The past perfect ("She had run to the window shortly before the explosion") is often used briefly to introduce a flashback (see PLOT).

Tension, 101ff. A force and a counterforce within a work of LITERATURE. In FICTION, DRAMA, and NARRATIVE POETRY, it can be created through conflict between a character and another character, a group, an aspect of nature, or an inner struggle. It can also be generated when the writer withholds information to arouse the reader's curiosity or a sense of suspense. In VERSE, tension is more often generated by a contrast or conflict in THEME, TONE, or both. Tension provides a sense of vitality in a work.

Tercet, 271. Same as triplet. A poetic STANZA with three lines. See STANZA.

Terza rima, 271. A traditional VERSE form consisting of iambic pentameter tercets (see STANZA) in which each stanza is linked to the next through an interlocking rhyme scheme of *aba, bcb, cdc,* and so on.

Tetrameter, 265. A LINE of VERSE with four feet. This and PENTAMETER are the two most common line lengths in English. (See METER.)

Theater of the absurd, 385. A somewhat loosely defined dramatic "school" in the *expressionistic* (see REALISTIC DRAMA) tradition beginning in the 1950s. Shared convictions: that life is "absurd" in the sense of lacking ultimate meaning and that the intellect cannot determine truth. Shared techniques: the use of nonrealistic situations, SATIRE, and a tendency to develop a static quality rather than a DRAMATIC PLOT. Examples include works by Ionesco, Beckett, Pinter, and some by Albee, Genet, and Adamov.

Theater in the round, 395. See STAGE DESIGNS.

Theme, 37, 362ff., 423ff,. The portion of a LITERARY work that comments on the human condition. It is the primary statement, suggestion, or implication of the work. The term is used interchangeably with *central concern*. It does not have the moral implications of *message* or the didactic element of *thesis*. A thesis states or clearly implies a particular conviction or recommends a specific course of action. A *theme* is phrased in abstract terms in contrast with a *concept* that describes plot and characters.

Therapy writing, 33. CREATIVE WRITING motivated more by the need to express the writer's personal emotional problems than the desire to create a literary work of merit.

Thesis, 429ff. See THEME.

Third-person narration, 65. See PERSON.

Thrust stage, 395. See STAGE DESIGNS.

Tone, 30ff., 177ff., 300ff. The emotional quality of a LITERARY work itself and of the author's implicit attitude toward the work as well. Some critics prefer to separate the two aspects of this definition, but most writers tend to think of them as two forms of the same quality. Tone is described with adjectives like "exciting," "sad," merry," "eerie," or "depressing," as well as with terms like "satiric," "sardonic," "ironic," and "dramatic."

Tragedy, 353, 424. DRAMA that is generally serious in TONE and focuses on a PROTAGONIST who in most cases faces a climax and an eventual downfall, often but not always death.

Transformation, 48ff., 79ff. Radical alteration of an experience or of an early outline of a story or play in order to create a fresh LITERARY work. (Also called *metamorphosis*.) It often precedes the first draft and so is far more basic than *revision*. The process can be either conscious or unconscious. Its function is to clarify existing patterns, to break up patterns that appear to be too neat or contrived, or to help a writer regain control over an experience that is still too personal to develop in LITERARY form.

Trimeter, 265. A LINE of VERSE with three feet (see METER.)

Triplet, 271. Same as *tercet*. A poetic STANZA with three lines. (See STANZA.)

Trochaic foot, 264. See METER.

True rhyme, 257. See RHYME.

Truism, 194, 347. A statement that reiterates a well-known truth; a platitude.

Typography, 281ff. The technique in VERSE (and particularly FREE VERSE) of arranging words, phrases, and lines on the printed page to create a RHYTHMICAL effect. When used to an extreme degree to create a picture, it is called SHAPED POETRY.

Unique rhythm, 284. See RHYTHM.

Vanity press, 441. A commercial publisher that charges the author part or, more often, all of the printing costs. *Cooperative presses*, in contrast, are usually nonprofit and share the expense with the author or poet. Regular commercial publishers assume all costs themselves and pay the author an advance and a percentage (generally between 10 and 15 percent) of the sales.

Vehicle and tenor, 157ff. The two components of a metaphor or simile: The *vehicle* is an IMAGE, usually a concrete object, that is introduced for the sole purpose of objectifying an abstract concept. The *tenor* is the subject, usually an implied abstraction. Example: She was a tiger in debate. In a symbol the vehicle is an actual part of the work (like Alcatraz in the story "Escapes") and the tenor is implied (being trapped in an unrewarding lifestyle).

Verbal irony, 179, 305. See IRONY.

Verisimilitude, 107. See REALISM.

Verse, 193. LITERARY writing that, in contrast with PROSE, uses line length as an aspect of the art form and is typically concerned with SOUND, RHYTHM, and compression of language. Although *verse* is often used as a general synonym for *poetry*, many prefer to limit the word *poetry* to SOPHISTICATED verse.

Viewpoint, 60ff. See MEANS OF PERCEPTION.

Villanelle, 277ff. A French verse form of 19 lines in iambic pentameter (see LINE) divided into five tercets (see STANZA) and a final four-line STANZA. The poem has only two rhymes. They are arranged in this pattern: *aba aba aba aba aba abaa.* Line 1 is a REFRAIN that is repeated entirely as lines 6, 12, and 18, and line 3 is repeated to form lines 9, 15, and 19. One of the challenges of this form (other than the mechanics) is to give subtly different meanings to the repeated lines. An example: "The Waking" by Theodore Roethke, page 209.

Visual rhythm, 281. See TYPOGRAPHY.

Voice, 170. Sometimes used as a broad and unneeded synonym for style. More accurately, it describes styles that are pronounced, especially those presented through a first-person narrator. The voice often contributes to CHARACTERIZATION, as in "Gotta Dance" (page 166). Voice can also refer to the author's attitude toward his or her work as in a *serious, flippant,* or *satiric* voice.

Vowels, 250. Those letters that are sounded with the lips open and without obstruction or constriction in the flow of air: *a, e, i, o, u,* and sometimes *y.* All the rest are *consonants,* letters in which the flow of air is restricted with the lips or tongue. An important distinction in the analysis of RHYME.